The Oxford Dictionary of

Literary
Quotations

The Oxford Dictionary of

Literary Quotations

edited by **Peter Kemp**

OXFORD
UNIVERSITY PRESS

OXFORD
UNIVERSITY PRESS

Great Clarendon Street, Oxford OX2 6DP

Oxford University Press is a department of the University of Oxford.
It furthers the University's objective of excellence in research, scholarship,
and education by publishing worldwide in

Oxford New York

Auckland Bangkok Buenos Aires Cape Town Chennai
Dar es Salaam Delhi Hong Kong Istanbul Karachi Kolkata
Kuala Lumpur Madrid Melbourne Mexico City Mumbai Nairobi
São Paulo Shanghai Singapore Taipei Tokyo Toronto

Oxford is a registered trade mark of Oxford University Press
in the UK and in certain other countries

Published in the United States
by Oxford University Press Inc., New York

British Library Cataloguing in Publication Data
Data available

Library of Congress Cataloging in Publication Data
Data available
ISBN 0-19-866281-5

10 9 8 7 6 5 4 3 2 1

Designed by Jane Stevenson
Typeset in Photina and Argo
by Inter-active Sciences Ltd
Printed in Great Britain
by Biddles Ltd
King's Lynn, Norfolk

Contents

Project Team

Managing Editor	Elizabeth Knowles
Associate Editor	Susan Ratcliffe
Library Research	Ralph Bates
Reading Programme	Jean Harker Verity Mason Helen Rappaport
Proof-reading	Carolyn Garwes Penny Trumble

Preface to Second Edition

No dictionary of literary quotations could hope to be the last word on the subject. So the opportunity of returning to this book in order to revise, refresh and enlarge it has been a welcome one. By reorganizing the format and sifting out material that seemed dated or repetitive, it has been possible to add almost nine hundred new quotations about writers and writing.

As might be expected, some of these reflect developments in the literary world over the last few years. The arrival of phenomena such as Harry Potter is registered, as is the departure of some familiar figures (defending the killing-off of his Inspector Morse, Colin Dexter declared, 'I have contributed quite enough to the "crime scene", since I am reliably informed that I am responsible for 81 body-bags in and around Oxford, including three Heads of Colleges'). Ted Hughes's observations about his 1997 versions of tales from Ovid's *Metamorphoses* ('the seeds of European literature') tellingly testify to the persisting connections between recent writers and their distant predecessors.

Bringing things up to date hasn't been the only satisfaction in preparing this new edition. Fascinating quotations have turned up from remote eras. Fearsome penalties invoked against remiss users of a clay-tablet library in ancient Assyria make our present system of fines look absurdly lenient: the gods are called upon to punish anyone 'who breaks this tablet or puts it in water or rubs it until you cannot recognize it' with 'a curse which cannot be relieved, terrible and merciless, as long as he lives, may they let his name, his seed, be carried off from the land, may they put his flesh in a dog's mouth!' At the opposite extreme to this ferocious state of affairs, from the Egypt of Ramses II (1279–1213 BC) comes an inscription soothingly describing a library as a 'Clinic for the Soul'.

Expanded geographically as well as historically, this edition brings in additional findings from areas such as North America and Australia, as well as further quotations from non-anglophone sources. Portugal's great nineteenth-century novelist, Eça de Queiroz, comments with amused irony on the English taste for romantic novels, which are sold 'much like tea and tobacco' and 'read in much the same way as a cigar is smoked or a cup of tea is drunk'. In a chilling couple of sentences, Adolf Hitler reveals, 'Without my imprisonment, *Mein Kampf* would never have been written. That period gave me the chance of deepening various notions for which I then had only an instinctive feeling.'

Hitler's remark is to be found among the quotations grouped under Solitude, one of a number of new themes incorporated into this book. Others include Collaboration, Interruption, Illustration, Omission, Graffiti, and those ultimate literary pronouncements, Epitaphs. Where its predecessor was divided into two parts—The Writer's World and Writers and their Works—this edition dovetails them into a single alphabetical sequence of topics and authors. The re-design should, it is intended, make reference easier and quicker, while still encouraging browsing.

This anthology owes much to the knowledge and generosity of friends, whom I wish to thank for their assistance. Besides continuing contributions from some who helped with the earlier volume, I am indebted for useful material to Andrew Holgate, Caroline Gascoigne, John Dugdale, and Terence Blacker. John Gross offered numerous invaluable suggestions and Mark Lawson alerted me to sources of quotations that have enriched the book. I should also like to express my gratitude to Oxford University Press for giving me the chance to prepare this new edition of the dictionary, and to Susan Ratcliffe, in particular, for the unfailing expertise and shrewdness she has brought to every stage of the production of the final text.

As before, the compiling of *The Oxford Dictionary of Literary Quotations* has been both pleasurable and thought-provoking. That readers should also find it so is the book's aim.

PETER KEMP

December 2002

Introduction

Fossils, mantras, jokes, boasts, grumbles, aphorisms, outbursts, insights, insults, epigrams, epitaphs: literary quotations can be many things. What they have in common is a shared concern with a phenomenon unique to our species—the ability to provoke thought, stir emotion, excite the imagination, and give different kinds of pleasure by means of words.

This book brings together more than 4,000 observations about this activity by outstanding practitioners of it and a host of other commentators. Chronologically, the quotations extend from Ancient Egypt to the present-day world of the Internet and multiculturalism via Belshazzar's Feast, Periclean Athens, Imperial Rome, early Christian monasteries, a medieval Japanese court, a twelfth-century Persian library, the Mermaid Tavern in Elizabethan England, eighteenth-century coffee houses, Victorian publishers' offices, and numerous other literary enclaves. Remarks about the life of letters are to be found ranging from A (the captain of twenty-four lead soldiers in an old French conundrum about print) to Z (a 'whoreson . . . unnecessary letter', according to Kent in *King Lear*). Authors comment on all aspects of their craft from inspiration to last words (a particularly resonant term in this context).

One theme that looms with especial insistence is the motivation for writing. What possesses people to devote time and energy—sometimes the bulk of their lives—to making marks on paper (or papyrus or parchment) that they hope will make marks on other people's minds and sensibilities? Answers vary widely. For some authors, literature, which temporarily endows life with shape and significance, constitutes a substitute for things actuality lacks: a kind of aesthetic comfort blanket. Others, such as Muriel Spark, see their books ('glimpses that seem like a microcosm of reality') as reflections of a deity's larger-scale devices and designs. Amusedly mocking the notion of art as 'uplift', Julian Barnes puts in a good word for it as a survival-mechanism: 'Art is not a *brassière*. At least, not in the English sense. But do not forget that *brassière* is the French for life-jacket'. There are writers who consider it their vocation to jolt readers into viewing the familiar world afresh, writers who offer escapist retreat from the world, writers whose aim is to change the world.

Many authors acknowledge a craving for attention. Others unabashedly admit to being in the business for the money—a motive voiced with brisk frankness by Frances Hodgson Burnett when she submitted her first story to a magazine in the 1860s: 'My object is remuneration.' D. H. Lawrence's miner father may have gasped with outraged amazement at his son's earnings from his novel, *The White Peacock*, 'Fifty pounds! An' tha's niver done a day's hard work in thy life.' But, elsewhere, authors regularly chafe about the inadequacy of their increments. According to Samuel Johnson, 'No man but a blockhead ever wrote except for money.' Despite this, writers are actuated by all kinds of incentives: indignation (Juvenal), rancour (D. H. Lawrence: 'I like to write when I feel spiteful; it's like having a good sneeze'), loneliness (Henry James), fun (Robert Burns), boredom (Graham Greene), nosiness (Margaret Atwood). These miscellaneous motives typify the diversity of authors' reactions to most aspects of their profession. Notably, just one theme unites them in near-unanimity: the iniquity of publishers. Harold Macmillan's demurral, 'Publishers should not have the Garter', proves the least of reservations on this subject. The Canadian novelist Robertson Davies attempts a case for the defence: 'Very harsh things have been said about publishers, but there can be nothing but good in the heart of a man who regales an author with figgy pudding.' Eliza Acton's *Modern Cookery* (1845), however, gives a more traditional view of a publisher's desserts. Her recipe, 'Poor Author's Pudding', is a meagre mix of not much more than milk and bread; 'The Publisher's Pudding'—baked in a '*thickly* buttered basin' covered with 'a sheet of buttered writing paper'—drips with cream, egg yolks, almonds, nutmeg, cherries, 'best Muscatel raisins', and 'best cognac'.

The impulsion to write is something numerous writers compare to a painful involuntary seizure: the Muse as malady. Metaphors of illness and dementia are rife. For Juvenal, in the Rome of the Emperor Domitian, writing is an 'incurable disease'. Almost two millennia later, George Orwell likens literary composition to 'a long bout of some painful illness'. As usual, voices can be heard putting the opposite case. With characteristic paradox, G. K. Chesterton maintains that making things up is a prophylactic against losing a grip on reality: while the rigidly logical go mad, the imaginative stay sane. In an image of wonderfully vivid virulence, Ibsen suggests that writing constitutes a therapeutic purge:

> I kept a scorpion in an empty beer bottle on my table. Now and then the animal was sick; then I used to throw it a piece of soft fruit, which it hurled itself on with fury and into which it poured out its poison; then it became healthy again.
>
> Is there not something similar in us poets? The laws of Nature hold for the intellectual field as well.

Some authors—most famously, Flaubert—speak of literature as a kind of *cordon sanitaire*: the Ivory Tower as a gated community amid the unruly wasteland of life. 'The only way not to be unhappy', Flaubert asserts, 'is to shut yourself up in Art.' His bulletins from his writing-desk hardly bear this out, though. 'Stylistic abscesses' and sentences that 'keep itching without coming to a head' plague him. When not irritated by this authorial eczema, he is afflicted by even more alarming symptoms. As he describes a military assault on Carthage in his historical novel, *Salammbô*, muscular aches and pains rack his arms. As he pens the scene in which Emma Bovary dies from arsenic-poisoning, he vomits his dinner into his chamber-pot.

Though usually less drastic than this, the strains of composition are generally agreed to be severe. 'What a heavy thing is a pen!' Zola groans. Plying his, Balzac likens himself to a galley-slave. Other authors compare themselves to an ox heaving a plough (Martial), a bricklayer (H. L. Mencken), a carpenter (William Golding), and an old woman sprawled on the hearth trying to blow a few pitiful sticks of firewood into a blaze (Samuel Richardson). For Joseph Conrad, completing *Nostromo* is as stressful as sailing round Cape Horn in the face of terrible winter storms. Edna Ferber regards writing as 'a combination of ditch-digging, mountain-climbing, treadmill and childbirth'. For Patrick White, it's equivalent to self-evisceration.

The long line of tribulations by which authors are bedevilled begins with writer's block. Veteran battlers against this such as Conrad or George Gissing feelingly testify to its tortures. Paul Scott alludes with a shudder to the 'implacable, blank sheet of white paper'. For Graham Greene, agonizing over 'the dreaded essential opening sentences', even that blank sheet of paper isn't empty of tormenting suggestion: the term 'foolscap' takes on cruelly mocking implications; the ruled lines start to resemble prison bars. To overcome writer's block, authors favour differing remedies. Zola informs Edmond de Goncourt that he finds a bout of copulation handy for dislodging it. H. G. Wells concurs. Dreams can kick-start Greene's imagination. Erskine Caldwell recommends penning limericks as a warm-up exercise. More widely, drink and drugs are much advocated, and much relished, as stimulants. 'No verse can give pleasure for long, nor last, that is written by drinkers of water', Horace affirmed in the last century BC. Throughout twenty succeeding centuries, authors have agreed, and held up their chosen inspirational tipple: Canary wine (Ben Jonson), brandy (Samuel Johnson), whisky (Burns), claret (Keats), gin-and-water (Byron). Opium is advocated (by De Quincey and Baudelaire) as a turner of 'the keys of Paradise'. W. H. Auden experiments with LSD. Barbara Pym thinks there's something to be said for Camp coffee essence.

Pym is perhaps the most poignant contributor to another category of authorial woes: rejection. 'The letter I wrote to *The Author* about not getting published was never published', she informs Philip Larkin, a fellow rueful connoisseur of literary chagrins (which continue to take new forms: in his 2nd January entry in his 1997 journal, Alan Bennett reports with glum glee, 'Sent a complimentary (sic) copy of Waterstone's Literary Diary which records the birthdays of various contemporary figures. Here is Dennis Potter on 17 May, Michael Frayn on 8 September, Edna O'Brien on 15 December, so naturally I turn to my own birthday. May 9 is blank except for the note: first British Launderette is opened on Queensway, London 1949'). Some manuscripts never make it into print for other reasons—among them, accidental incineration. Isaac Newton's dog reportedly knocks over a candle and sets fire to 'the almost finished labours of some years'. John Stuart Mill's housemaid burns the first version of Carlyle's *The French Revolution*. Conrad achieves an acme of lucklessness when an oil-lamp explodes on his study table and destroys in a blaze the much-toiled-over manuscript of his story, 'The End of the Tether'.

More sinister than the chance singeing of scripts is the deliberate burning of books. Ideological arson is a menace authors have always had to be conscious of, as has its grim companion, ideological homicide. George Bernard Shaw's chilly quip, 'Assassination is the extreme form of censorship', takes on contemporary configurations with the fatwa levelled at Salman Rushdie—declaring that he and his publishers are '*madhur el dam* (those whose blood must be shed)'—and the hanging of the writer, Ken Saro-Wiwa, in Nigeria.

Less lethal modes of censorship—from prudish bowdlerization to political correctness—still constitute an impediment of which authors are uncomfortably aware. Trying to express himself under the constraints of Tsarist Russia, Chekhov feels as though there's a bone stuck in his throat. Editorial interference with texts, such as the 'damned cutting and slashing' that Byron berates John Murray for perpetrating on his work, irks others. A vexation that can occur after manuscripts achieve publication is the risible misprint: Henry James finds that a scene he admired as full of 'idle vistas and melancholy nooks' becomes populated by 'idle sisters and melancholy monks'.

Apprehension at the idea of being written about often agitates those who write. It's an anxiety that peers nervously in three directions. First, there's edginess about reviewers and critics, figures who—from Grub Street hacks to jargon-clad deconstructionists—get a predictably bad press here. Newspapers and the publicity-machine are another bugbear (while authors before the rise of interviews, 'profiles', and PR wistfully covet renown, some of their modern counterparts shrink from celebrity—'a mask that eats into the face', John Updike observes with typically elegant sageness). Even posthumously, authors wincingly recognize, they can be brought to book by biography. Over the last three centuries, this can be seen swelling into an increasing source of dread: 'one of the new terrors of death' (John Arbuthnot), 'exhumation' and 'Cannibalism' (Rudyard Kipling). Gladstone may have deplored J. W. Cross's *Life of George Eliot* as ' a Reticence, in three volumes', but reticence is something likely subjects of literary biography usually can't say enough in favour of.

The formidable array of harassments authors document themselves as enduring leaves you curious to discover what compensations for all this are on offer. One considerable reward, it emerges, is the sense of having—in some way and for some time at least—thwarted extinction. 'I shall not altogether die', Horace tells us across a span of 2,000 years. A quotation surviving from Pharaonic Egypt has a scribe, more than three millennia ago, expressing his faith that 'The scroll is better than the carved stone' for durability. Horace considers his poetry 'a monument more lasting than bronze'. Showing the long shelf-life of that image, Shakespeare trusts his own verses will outlive marble and gilded monuments. In a more ambivalent but still celebratory metaphor, Longfellow speaks of leaving 'footprints on the sands of time'.

Closer-to-hand gratifications are available too, of course. Whether Graham Greene's *Brighton Rock* will prove more lasting than bronze remains to be seen, but, in the meantime, its author notes in a letter, 'a new shade for knickers and nightdresses' from Peter Jones department store has been named after it. The fillip of seeing people enjoying your work is savoured by Martial in the first century AD:

> All Rome is mad about my book:
> It's praised, they hum the lines, shops stock it,
> It peeps from every hand and pocket.

Nearly two thousand years later, J. M. Barrie appealingly confesses to the Critics' Circle in London, 'For several days after my first book was published I carried it about in my pocket, and took surreptitious peeps at it to make sure that the ink had not faded.' Enthusiasm for the book as object and concept—'the greatest interactive medium of all time', in the recent words of the head of Penguin Books—glows through authors' comments across the centuries.

Some writers plume themselves on the power of the pen (a potency that alluringly glints even from Saint Augustine's malediction on poetry as 'devil's wine'). In his scathing lines on the Soviet invasion of Czechoslovakia in August 1968, Auden simultaneously proclaims and exemplifies articulacy's telling strengths:

But one prize is beyond his reach,
The Ogre cannot master Speech.
About a subjugated plain,
Among its desperate and slain,
The Ogre stalks with hands on hips,
While drivel gushes from his lips.

It's nicely in accord with this that Czechoslovakia's President after the country regained independence should be a playwright, Vàclav Havel.

As well as the outer world, the inner one has its distinctive satisfactions for authors. A taking motif—especially evident in the nineteenth century—is a writer's enthralled involvement with his or her characters. Jane Austen declares her affection for Elizabeth Bennet and her belief that no one tolerable could dislike her. There are haunting glimpses of what it feels like, on finishing a novel, to see your creations now fading away. In his preface to *David Copperfield*, Charles Dickens registers a novelist's pangs of regret at the spectacle of 'a crowd of the creatures of his brain . . . going from him for ever'. Conrad, completing *Almayer's Folly* on 24th April 1894, watches as, after the final scratch of his pen, the 'band of phantoms' he has co-existed with for several years 'dissolve' and 'are made pallid and indistinct by the sunlight of this brilliant and sombre day'.

Literature, Zola stresses, is 'a human secretion'. One of the fascinations in collecting quotations about it lies in the reminders this brings of the extraordinarily diverse personalities that have exuded this imaginative by-product, and the remarkably changing circumstances under which they have done so. The urge to produce literature persists but the tools of the writer's trade alter. Papyrus and parchment are replaced by paper. Quills give way to print. Henry James can be observed 'trying to make use of an accursed "fountain" pen' and, later, apologizing voluminously for recourse to the 'typewriting machine'. Under Seamus Heaney's gaze, 'the dead-pan cloudiness of a word processor' takes on oracular promise.

Another authorial accessory—a dictionary—is described by one writer here as 'a frozen pantomime'. A dictionary of literary quotations is, among other things, a frozen cavalcade. Open it anywhere and vignettes of literary life in different eras flicker into view: a Roman poet near the Forum passing a bookshop whose doorposts are plastered with advertisements; a medieval scribe noting down the affinities between his mental processes and the concentration-and-pounce of his mousing cat; Lady Murasaki, at the Japanese court around 1000 AD, casting a caustic eye over a rival's accomplishments ('She thought herself so clever and littered her writings with Chinese characters . . .'); Shakespeare commenting on the scenic deficiencies of the Globe; Edward Gibbon receiving inspiration for his *Decline and Fall of the Roman Empire* as he sits 'musing amidst the ruins of the Capitol, while the barefoot friars were singing vespers in the Temple of Jupiter' on the fifteenth of October 1764; Jane Austen joking as to whether the copyright of *Sense and Sensibility* 'should ever be of any value'; a Victorian magazine editor warning an author, 'You have left your hero and heroine tied up in a cavern under the Thames for a week, and they are not married'; Arnold Bennett, at dinner chez H. G. Wells, fretting at Shaw's garrulity and longing to have a verbal 'scrap' with Virginia Woolf; Philip Larkin almost meeting a fatal accident as he listens to the Immortality Ode on his car radio while speeding down the M1; the adapter of

Middlemarch for television grousing that his task was 'like getting an elephant into a suitcase'.

While this dictionary's miscellany of quotations exhibits the variety and individuality of literary achievement, it also displays the multiple filaments— allusion, homage, sequels, parodies, quotations, titles borrowed from others' lines—that weave authors together into a web of imaginative interconnectedness. Genres can be seen evolving, mutating, and splitting apart into new forms. Christopher Frayling remarks on the way four classic horror stories—*Frankenstein*, *Dracula*, *The Hound of the Baskervilles*, and *Dr Jekyll and Mr Hyde*—have spawned swarming progeny in twentieth-century popular culture. Other boom-areas within that culture—best-sellers, romantic fiction, crime writing—also give rise to clusters of comment, including tribute from more recognizedly 'literary' fellow-authors. Arnold Bennett deplores the prejudice of assuming that the work of a writer who enjoys 'immense circulation . . . merits only indifference and disdain'. Robert Graves applauds Agatha Christie's detective novels, in 1944, as first-rate specimens of 'the most characteristic pleasure-writing of this epoch'. The most consequential development throughout recent centuries of writing makes itself eloquently heard too. Despite misogynist bigotry—male strictures such as Voltaire's claim, 'the composition of tragedy requires *testicles*', and Hawthorne's recommendation that the faces of female authors should be 'deeply scarified with an oyster shell'— women growingly establish literature as every bit as much their province as men's.

Irrepressibly expansive and exploratory, literature, for Margaret Atwood, is 'a revelation of the full range of our human response to the world'. Fullness is something a work on the scale of this volume would be foolhardy to lay claim to, but its selection of soundings from over 3,000 years of writing does aim to give a sense of the range of human response to literature. Throughout the putting-together of this dictionary, one quotation included in it nagged uncomfortably: the author of Ecclesiastes's sigh that 'Of making many books there is no end'. Hammond Innes's disclosure that he has felt impelled to plant trees to replace 'some of the timber used up by my books' gave pause too.

Ultimately, the justification for this venture must be that it hopes to cast light— both for the hunter of references and the interested browser—on a phenomenon without which human existence would be inconceivably poorer. 'If writing did not exist, what terrible depressions we should suffer from', wrote Sei Shōnagon, an attendant at the imperial Japanese court a thousand years ago. This book is for all who agree with her—and who are intrigued by the patterns and diversities the forms and practices of literature have taken over the centuries.

Inevitably, in a work that conforms to Dr Johnson's directive—

> He used to say that no man read long together with a folio on his table: —Books, said he, that you may carry to the fire, and hold readily in your hand, are the most useful after all

—pressures of selectivity have been tight. The Tools of the Trade section, for instance, could have been extended almost indefinitely to incorporate all the idiosyncratic paraphernalia writers have relied on, and should perhaps have included some literary furniture—such as that of Balzac who, Arnold Bennett admiringly noted, 'literally wore out four chairs'. Also inevitably, some quotations—several cited in this introduction—turned up too late for inclusion in the body of the text.

Credit for the text, whose basis came from the files of the Oxford University Press, is very much due to the editorial staff and researchers of the OUP's Dictionary Department: their knowledge, scholarship, and keen expertise have been exemplary. In addition, a large debt of gratitude is owed to the generosity and acumen of friends who have supplied choice quotations. Particular thanks must go to A. S. Byatt, David Grylls, Rhoda Koenig, Laurence Lerner, and Ruth Rendell, all of whom have added considerably to the scope and quality of this book.

PETER KEMP

January 1997

How to Use the Dictionary

The Oxford Dictionary of Literary Quotations is organized by themes, ordered alphabetically from **Accolade and Admiration**, **Adaptation**, and **Joseph Addison** to **Writer's Block**, **Writing**, and **W. B. Yeats**. The themes cover both aspects of literary life and individual writers. Theme titles range from broad general categories such as **Art**, **Death**, and **Morality**, to more specific categories such as **Characters**, **Description**, **The Power of the Pen**, **Punctuation**, **Tools of the Trade**, and **Words**. Literary genres have their own themes, from **Ballads** through **Horror and the Gothic** to **Science Fiction** and **Travel Writing**. Themes on the subject of an individual author such as **John Milton** or **Agatha Christie** appear in the alphabetical sequence according to the last name of the author, and the headings consist of the authors' names and dates.

Related topics may be covered by a single theme. Where helpful, this is made explicit in the title, as in **Grammar and Usage**, **Humour and Comedy**, and **Newspapers and Magazines**. A cross-reference from the second element of the pair appears in its appropriate place in the alphabetic sequence both in the main text and in the **List of Themes**, so that '**Mystery** see **Crime and Mystery**' follows **Movements and Trends** and precedes **Names**. Where themes are closely related, 'see also' references are given immediately following the theme title. The heading **Fame** is thus followed by the direction 'see also **Reputation and Achievement**', and **Humour and Comedy** by 'see also **Irony, Wit and Satire**'.

Quotations are arranged in chronological order. Where possible, quotations are precisely dated, as by the composition date of a letter or diary, or the publication of a book published in the author's lifetime, or by external circumstances, as a contemporary comment on a specific event. When the date is uncertain or unknown, and the quotation cannot be related to a particular event, the author's date of death has been used to date the quotation.

Contextual information regarded as essential to a full appreciation of the quotation precedes the text in an italicized note; information seen as providing useful amplification follows in an italicized note.

Each quotation is accompanied by the name of the author to whom it is attributed; dates of birth and death (where known) are also given. In general, the authors' names are given in the form by which they are best known, so that we have H. G. Wells (rather than Herbert George Wells) and Rebecca West (rather than Cicily Isabel Fairfield). Bibliographical information as to the source from which the quotation is taken follows the author's name; titles and dates of publication are given, but full finding references are not. Where a quotation cannot be traced to a citable source, 'attributed' is used to indicate that the attribution is generally accepted, but that a specific reference has not been traced.

Cross-references are made within themes and to specific items within other themes. In each case the reference is to the page number followed by the unique quotation number on the page. So **45:2** indicates the second quotation on page 45.

Authors who have their own thematic entries are typographically distinguished by the use of bold (of **Balzac,** by **Chaucer**) in context or source notes.

Indexes

There is an author index for tracing quotations by named authors (and collections with authorial status, such as **The Bible**), and a keyword index for tracing individual quotations. Brief biographical information is given in the author index. In the keyword index, both the keywords and the entries following each keyword, including those in foreign languages, are in strict alphabetical order. Singular and plural nouns (with their possessive forms) are grouped separately.

References are to the page number, followed by the unique quotation number on the page, as **53:2**.

List of Themes

A

Accolade and Admiration
Achievement *see* Reputation and Achievement
Adaptation
Joseph Addison
Age
Agents
Anna Akhmatova
Allusion *see* Quotation and Allusion
Kingsley Amis
Martin Amis
Matthew Arnold
Art
W. H. Auden
Audience
Jane Austen
Autobiography

B

Francis Bacon
Bad Writing *see* Good and Bad Writing
Ballads
Honoré de Balzac
J. M. Barrie
Charles Baudelaire
Samuel Beckett
Max Beerbohm
Beginning
Hilaire Belloc
Alan Bennett
Arnold Bennett
Best-sellers
John Betjeman
The Bible
Biography
William Blake
Books
Borrowed Titles
Borrowing Books
James Boswell

Bertolt Brecht
Brevity
Anne Brontë
Charlotte Brontë
Emily Brontë
Rupert Brooke
Thomas Browne
Elizabeth Barrett Browning
Robert Browning
John Bunyan
Edmund Burke
Fanny Burney
Robert Burns
Lord Byron

C

Thomas Carlyle
Lewis Carroll
Catullus
Censorship
Cervantes
Raymond Chandler
Characters
Thomas Chatterton
Geoffrey Chaucer
Anton Chekhov
G. K. Chesterton
Children's Literature
Choice of Words
Agatha Christie
Closing Lines
Samuel Taylor Coleridge
Colette
Collaboration
Comedy *see* Humour and Comedy
Conversation *see* Dialogue and Conversation
Ivy Compton-Burnett
William Congreve
Cyril Connolly
Joseph Conrad
James Fenimore Cooper

Pierre Corneille
Noel Coward
Abraham Cowley
Creativity *see* Inspiration and Creativity
Crime and Mystery
Criticism
Critics

D

Dante Alighieri
Death
Dedications
Description
Dialogue and Conversation
Diaries
Charles Dickens
Emily Dickinson
Dictionaries
John Donne
Fedor Dostoevsky
Drama
Drink and Drugs
John Dryden

E

Earning a Living
Editors and Editing
Effort
George Eliot
T. S. Eliot
Ralph Waldo Emerson
Ending
Epitaphs
Erotic Writing and Pornography
Essays

F

Fables and Fairy Stories
Fame
Family and Friends
Fantasy

Accolade and Admiration see also Reputation and Achievement, Rivalry

1 How far thou didst our Lyly outshine,
Or sporting Kyd, or Marlowe's mighty line.

Ben Jonson c.1573–1637: 'To the Memory of My Beloved, the Author, Mr William Shakespeare' (1623)

2 The praise of ancient authors proceeds not from the reverence of the dead, but from the competition, and mutual envy of the living.

Thomas Hobbes 1588–1679: *Leviathan* (1651) 'A Review and Conclusion'

3 The reciprocal civility of authors is one of the most risible scenes in the farce of life.

Samuel Johnson 1709–84: preface to *Christian Morals* (1756)

4 Biographers, translators, editors,—all, in short, who employ themselves in illustrating the lives or the writings of others, are peculiarly exposed to the *Lues Boswellianae*, or disease of admiration.

Lord Macaulay 1800–59: in *Edinburgh Review* January 1834

5 It is not until the pack has yelled itself hoarse that the level voice of justice is heard in praise.

Max Beerbohm 1872–1956: letter, May 1894

6 You reduce me to mere gelatinous grovel.

Henry James 1843–1916: letter to H. G. Wells, 20 November 1899

7 I live for your agglomerated lucubrations.

Henry James 1843–1916: letter to H. G. Wells, 18 November 1902

8 People ask you for criticism, but they only want praise.

W. Somerset Maugham 1874–1965: *Of Human Bondage* (1915)

9 You have *fixed* my life—however short. You did not light me: I was always a mad comet; but you have fixed me. I spun round you as a satellite for a month, but I shall swing out soon, a dark star in the orbit where you will blaze.

Wilfred Owen 1893–1918: letter to Siegfried Sassoon, 5 November 1917

10 The worst tragedy for a poet is to be admired through being misunderstood.

Jean Cocteau 1889–1963: *Le Rappel à l'ordre* (1926) 'Le Coq et l'Arlequin' p. 20

11 My literary success puzzled and embarrassed my old friends far more than it impressed them, and in my own family it created a kind of constraint which increased with the years. None of my relations ever spoke to me of my books, either to praise or blame—they simply ignored them.

Edith Wharton 1862–1937: *A Backward Glance* (1934)

12 Every genius needs praise.

Gertrude Stein 1874–1946: Edmund White *The Burning Library* (1994)

13 I have always been an admirer, I regard the gift of admiration as indispensible if one is to amount to something; I don't know where I would be without it.

Thomas Mann 1875–1955: letter, 1950; Marcel Reich-Ranicki *Thomas Mann and His Family* (1987)

14 With each book you write you should lose the admirers you gained with the previous one.

André Gide 1869–1951: Edmund White *The Burning Library* (1994)

15 It would be nice if sometimes the kind things I say were considered worthy of quotation. It isn't difficult, you know, to be witty or amusing when one has something to say that is destructive, but damned hard to be clever and quotable when you are singing someone's praises.

Noël Coward 1899–1973: William Marchant *The Pleasure of His Company* (1981)

1 [The middle-aged novelist] is more afraid to read his
favourable critics than his unfavourable, for with terrible
patience they unroll before his eyes the unchanging
pattern of the carpet.

Graham Greene 1904–91: *Ways of
Escape* (1980); see **177:3**

Achievement see **Reputation and Achievement**

Adaptation see also **Screenwriting**

2 All things considered, I prefer cinema to stage. The movie
is just a silly stunt for silly people—but the theatre is more
compromising since it is capable of falsifying the very soul
of one's work both on the imaginative and on the
intellectual side.
   on adaptations

Joseph Conrad 1857–1924: letter,
18–23 August 1920

3 It is the work of a staff of 'writers' to distinguish this
quality, separate it and obliterate it.
   *on Hollywood's treatment of a book with something
   remarkable about it*

Evelyn Waugh 1903–66: in *Daily
Telegraph* 30 April 1947

4 Book—what they make a movie out of for television.

Leonard Louis Levinson 1904– :
Laurence J. Peter (ed.) *Quotations for
our Time* (1977)

5 The work was like peeling an onion. The outer skin came
off with difficulty . . . but in no time you'd be down to its
innards, tears streaming from your eyes as more and more
beautiful reductions became possible.
   on adapting books for serial reading

Edward Blishen 1920– : *Donkey
Work* (1983)

6 The less it resembled my book, the better I felt.
   on the film of his novel, The Witches of Eastwick

John Updike 1932– : letter to his
agent, 10 July 1987

7 My play wasn't written for this box. My play was written
for small men locked in a big space.
   on the televising of Waiting for Godot

Samuel Beckett 1906–89: James
Knowlson *Damned to Fame* (1996)

8 I had a great deal of say . . . but the producer didn't have a
great deal of listen.
   on the adaptation for television of The Hitch-Hiker's Guide
   to the Galaxy

Douglas Adams 1952–2001: Stan
Nicholls (ed.) *Wordsmiths of Wonder*
(1993)

9 Andrew Davies said adapting *Middlemarch* was like getting
an elephant into a suitcase; Jane Austen is much easier. In
Pride and Prejudice the plot works like a Swiss clock.
   a producer's view on adapting for television

Sue Birtwistle 1945– : in *Guardian*
13 October 1995

10 All the adaptations I saw before were with people in stiff
suits standing up very straight making polite conversation
through pursed lips in drawing rooms. But I felt the story
is more about young men and women in the prime of their
lives with lots of hormones pounding around.
   on Pride and Prejudice

Andrew Davies 1936– : at Banff
Television Festival, 1999

on Warren Clarke's portrayal of Hill's Superintendent Dalziel:
11 REGINALD HILL: For the sake of my art you should be seven
   stones heavier.
   WARREN CLARKE: For the sake of my heart, I shouldn't.

Reginald Hill 1936– : in *Mail on
Sunday* 30 July 2000

1 The illustrated adult classic is now a rarity. It has given way to the television costume drama, which is an even more powerful image, sometimes best avoided if you feel passionately about the book.

Shirley Hughes 1927– : *A Life Drawing* (2002)

2 People were grumpy about having had to get up so early, and some of the extras were moaning about their costumes . . . It suddenly hit me that something I had done way back there was responsible for all these people being upset at eight in the morning . . . It was like the responsibility of having a business.

Zadie Smith 1975– : in *Observer* 25 August 2002

Joseph Addison 1672–1719
English poet, dramatist, and essayist; co-founder of *The Spectator*

3 Whoever wishes to attain an English style, familiar but not coarse, and elegant but not ostentatious, must give his days and nights to the volumes of Addison.

Samuel Johnson 1709–84: *Lives of the English Poets* (1779–81) 'Addison'

4 The style of Mr Addison is adorned by the female graces of elegance and mildness.

Edward Gibbon 1737–94: *Memoirs of My Life* (1796)

5 Undoubtedly it is due to Addison that prose is now prosaic—the medium which makes it possible for people of ordinary intelligence to communicate their ideas to the world.

Virginia Woolf 1882–1941: *The Common Reader* (1925)

Age

6 *Quand vous serez bien vieille, au soir, à la chandelle,*
Assise auprès du feu, dévidant et filant,
Direz, chantant mes vers, en vous émerveillant,
Ronsard me célébrait du temps que j'étais belle.

When you are very old, and sit in the candlelight at evening spinning by the fire, you will say, as you murmur my verses, a wonder in your eyes, 'Ronsard sang of me in the days when I was fair.'

Pierre de Ronsard 1524–85: *Sonnets pour Hélène* (1578)

7   But years hath done this wrong,
To make me write too much, and live too long.

Samuel Daniel 1563–1619: *Philotas* (1605) 'To the Prince'; dedication

8 Amidst the mortifying circumstances attendant upon growing old, it is something to have seen the *School for Scandal* in its glory.

Charles Lamb 1775–1834: *Elia* (1823)

9 I am past thirty, and three parts iced over.

Matthew Arnold 1822–88: letter, to Arthur Hugh Clough, 12 February 1853

10 When you are old and grey and full of sleep,
And nodding by the fire, take down this book
And slowly read and dream of the soft look
Your eyes had once, and of their shadows deep.

W. B. Yeats 1865–1939: 'When You Are Old' (1893)

11 I've been dissecting for forty years. Let me dream a little in my waning days.
    to Octave Mirabeau, on his review of Zola's final novel Fécondité

Émile Zola 1840–1902: letter, 29 November 1899

1 Byron!—he would be all forgotten today if he had lived to be a florid old gentleman with iron-grey whiskers, writing very long, very able letters to *The Times* about the Repeal of the Corn Laws.

Max Beerbohm 1872–1956: *Zuleika Dobson* (1911)

2 You think it horrible that lust and rage
Should dance attention upon my old age;
They were not such a plague when I was young;
What else have I to spur me into song?

W. B. Yeats 1865–1939: 'The Spur' (1939)

3 Old age is a tangle of Disappointment, Despair, Doubt, Dereliction, Drooping, Debt, and Damnable Deficiency and everything else that begins with a D.

Hilaire Belloc 1870–1953: letter, 24 April 1940

4 Oh yes, between 50 and 60 I think I shall write out some very singular books if I live.

Virginia Woolf 1882–1941: attributed

a final letter to a young correspondent:
5 Dear Elise,
Seek younger friends; I am extinct.

George Bernard Shaw 1856–1950: letter, 1949

6 With sixty staring me in the face, I have developed inflammation of the sentence structure and a definite hardening of the paragraphs.

James Thurber 1894–1961: in *New York Post* 30 June 1955

7 Each year brings new problems of Form and Content, new foes to tug with: at Twenty I tried to
vex my elders, past Sixty it's the young whom
I hope to bother.

W. H. Auden 1907–73: 'Shorts I' (1969)

8 A writer's old age can be very strange. Sometimes it's like his books: Evelyn Waugh, who made such fun of Apthorpe's 'thunder-box', died in the w.c. Zola, like the miners in *Germinal*, was suffocated by charcoal fumes.

Graham Greene 1904–91: Marie-Françoise Allain *The Other Man, Conversations with Graham Greene* (1983)

9 I am getting progressively less fond of poems about old age as I near the Pearly Gates.

Philip Larkin 1922–85: letter, 30 January 1984

10 The age of an author is of no consequence; if they are any good, they were born old and wise.

Robertson Davies 1913–95: speech in honour of Mavis Gallant, Toronto, 14 October 1993

11 You reach an age when every sentence you write bumps into one you wrote thirty years ago.

John Updike 1932– : in *Writers on Writing: Collected Essays from The New York Times* (2001)

12 They say your intelligence blunts with age, but the reverse has happened to me. I think more imaginatively because I have such an enormous amount to draw on, 50 years of thinking and living. I am like my garden, my brain has been mulched and manured, things have grown and I am more complicated.

Jonathan Miller 1934– : in *The Times* 13 November 2001

Agents

13 The author's agent fosters in authors the greed for an immediate money return . . . at the cost of all dignity and repose.

William Heinemann 1863–1920: in *The Author* c.1890; George Greenfield *Scribblers for Bread* (1989)

1 Mrs Morland very wittily defined an agent as someone whom you pay to make bad blood between yourself and your publisher.

Angela Thirkell 1890–1961: *Pomfret Towers* (1938)

2 Talking of agents, when I opened the morning paper one morning last week I saw that it had finally happened: somebody shot one. It was probably for the wrong reasons, but at least it was a step in the right direction.

Raymond Chandler 1888–1959: letter to Charles Morton, 17 December 1951; see **232:8**

3 [The kind of insight which] turns many a bitter young man into a jaundiced literary critic, had the opposite effect on Peters. He gave up his job as a critic and became a catalyst.
of the literary agent A. D. Peters (1892–1973)

Arthur Koestler 1905–83: in *Dictionary of National Biography* (1917–)

4 Agents have not changed much since I first became dependent upon them. To be dependent on an agent is like entrusting your most precious future to your mother-in-law or your bookmaker.

John Osborne 1929–94: *Almost a Gentleman* (1991)

Anna Akhmatova 1889–1966
Russian poet

5 She was the stern and overbearing abbess of a convent in which the rules were strict to a fault and all sins had to be atoned for.

Nadezhda Mandelstam 1899–1980: *Hope Abandoned* (1974)

6 The gloomy tones of hopelessness before death, mystic experiences intermingled with eroticism—this is the spiritual world of Akhmatova, a leftover from the old aristocratic culture which has sunk once and for all into the oblivion of 'the good old days of Catherine'. Half nun, half harlot, or rather a harlot-nun whose sin is mixed with prayer.

Andrei Zhdanov 1896–1948: Roberta Reeder *Anna Akhmatova: Poet and Prophet* (1995)

Allusion see Quotation and Allusion

Kingsley Amis 1922–95 see also **100:3**, **257:8**
English novelist and poet

7 *Lucky Jim* is a remarkable novel. It has been greatly praised and widely read, but I have not noticed that any of the reviewers have remarked on its ominous significance. I am told that today rather more than 60 per cent of the men who go to the universities go on a Government grant. This is a new class that has entered upon the scene . . . They are scum.

W. Somerset Maugham 1874–1965: in *Sunday Times* 25 December 1955

8 When it comes down to it, Lucky Jim is Just William, bigger and bespectacled, literate and funny, but scarcely grown-up. What Christine is to the one, a bag of bulls' eyes is to the other.

Simon Gray 1936– : in *The Times* 3 February 1966

9 That's Kingsley Amis, and there's no known cure.
on spotting him looking disgruntled at a party

Robert Graves 1895–1985: attributed

Martin Amis 1949–
English novelist

1 A kind of male turkeycocking which is extremely bad for the industry.
on Martin Amis's demands for a large advance on a new book

2 If I was reviewing Martin under a pseudonym, I would say he works too hard and it shows.

3 Each of his sentences bears its manufacturer's logo.

A. S. Byatt 1936– : in *Sunday Times* 8 January 1995

Kingsley Amis 1922–95: in *Guardian* 26 August 1995

Adam Mars-Jones 1954– : in *Waterstone's Quarterly Guide* Spring/Summer 1996; attributed

Matthew Arnold 1822–88
English poet and essayist

4 I met Matthew Arnold and had a few words with him. He is not as handsome as his photographs—or as his poetry.

5 Arnold is a dandy Isaiah, a poet without passion, whose verse, written in a surplice, is for freshmen and for gentle maidens who will be wooed to the arms of these future rectors.

6 Arnold is a poet to whom one readily returns. It is a pleasure, certainly after associating with the riff-raff of the early part of the century, to be in the company of a man *qui sait se conduire*.

7 A recognizably Celtic temperament—gaiety on top . . . profoundly melancholy, sceptical and pessimistic, underneath.

Henry James 1843–1916: letter to Charles Eliot Norton, 31 March 1873

George Meredith 1828–1909: in *Fortnightly Review* July 1909

T. S. Eliot 1888–1965: 'The Use of Poetry and the Use of Criticism' (1933)

A. L. Rowse 1903–97: *Matthew Arnold: Poet and Prophet* (1976)

Art

8 Life is short, the art long.
often quoted 'Ars longa, vita brevis' after Seneca De Brevitate Vitae, *and translated 'That lyf so short, the craft so long to lerne' by* **Chaucer**

9 In art the best is good enough.

10 The only time a human being is free is when he or she makes a work of art.

11 The excellence of every art is its intensity, capable of making all disagreeables evaporate, from their being in close relationship with beauty and truth.

12 The arts babblative and scribblative.

Hippocrates c.460–357 BC: *Aphorisms*; see also **153:5**

Johann Wolfgang von Goethe 1749–1832: *Italienische Reise* (1816–17) 3 March 1787

Friedrich von Schiller 1759–1805: Edmund White *The Burning Library* (1994)

John Keats 1795–1821: letter to George and Thomas Keats, 21 December 1817

Robert Southey 1774–1843: *Colloquies on the Progress and Prospects of Society* (1829)

1 No, imbeciles! No! Fools and cretins that you are, a book will not make a plate of soup; a novel is not a pair of boots; a sonnet is not a syringe; a drama is not a railway; they are not these forms of civilization which have made humanity march on the road to progress.

Théophile Gautier 1811–72: *Mademoiselle de Maupin* (1835); see **236:9**

2 The only way not to be unhappy is to shut yourself up in Art and count all the rest as nothing.

Gustave Flaubert 1821–80: letter, 13 May 1845

3 If art does not enlarge men's sympathies, it does nothing morally.

George Eliot 1819–80: letter to Charles Bray, 5 July 1859

4 Art requires, about all things, a suppression of one's self.

Henry James 1843–1916: 'Mr Walt Whitman' (1865)

5 Art is a human product, a human secretion; it is our body that sweats the beauty of our works.

Émile Zola 1840–1902: 'Le Moment artistique' (1868)

6 Art and the summer lightning of individual happiness: these are the only real goods we have.

Alexander Herzen 1812–70: *Collected Works* vol. 16

7 It appears to me that no one can ever have made a seriously artistic attempt without becoming conscious of an immense increase—a kind of revelation of freedom. One perceives . . . that the province of art is all life, all feeling, all observation, all vision—it is all experience.

Henry James 1843–1916: 'The Art of Fiction' (1888)

8 All art is immoral.

Oscar Wilde 1854–1900: *Intentions* (1891) 'The Critic as Artist'

9 Art finds her own perfection within, and not outside of herself. She is not to be judged by any external standard of resemblance. She is a veil, rather than a mirror.

Oscar Wilde 1854–1900: *Intentions* (1891) 'The Decay of Lying'

10 To evoke in oneself a feeling one has once experienced and having evoked it in oneself then by means of movements, lines, colours, sounds, or forms expressed in words, so to transmit that feeling—this is the activity of art.

Art is a human activity consisting in this, that one man consciously by means of certain external signs, hands on to others feelings he has lived through, and that others are infected by these feelings and also experience them.

Leo Tolstoy 1828–1910: *What is Art?* (1898)

11 Art must be parochial in the beginning to become cosmopolitan in the end.

George Moore 1852–1933: *Hail and Farewell: Ave* (1911)

12 Art and Religion are, then, two roads by which men escape from circumstance to ecstasy. Between aesthetic and religious rapture there is a family alliance. Art and Religion are means to similar states of mind.

Clive Bell 1881–1964: *Art* (1914)

13 It is art that *makes* life, makes interest . . . and I know of no substitute whatever for the force and beauty of its process.

Henry James 1843–1916: letter to H. G. Wells, 10 July 1915

14 Art exists that one may recover the sensation of life; it exists to make one feel things, to make the stone *stony*. The purpose of art is to impart the sensation of things as they are perceived and not as they are known. The technique of art is to make objects '*unfamiliar*', to make forms difficult, to increase the difficulty and length of perception because the process of perception is an aesthetic end in itself and must be prolonged. *Art is a way of experiencing the artfullness of an object; the object is not important.*

Victor Shklovsky 1893–1984: 'Art as Technique' (1917)

1 The rhetorician would deceive his neighbours,
The sentimentalist himself; while art
Is but a vision of reality.

W. B. Yeats 1865–1939: 'Ego Dominus Tuus' (1917)

2 Art is vice. You don't marry it legitimately, you rape it.

Edgar Degas 1834–1917: Paul Lafond *Degas* (1918)

3 The lower one's vitality, the more sensitive one is to great art.

Max Beerbohm 1872–1956: *Seven Men* (1919)

4 Art is significant deformity.

Roger Fry 1866–1934: Virginia Woolf *Roger Fry* (1940)

5 Art is not life and cannot be
A midwife to society.

W. H. Auden 1907–73: *New Year Letter* (1941)

6 Art is not Magic, i.e., a means by which the artist communicates or arouses his feelings in others, but a mirror in which they may become conscious of what their own feelings really are: its proper effect, in fact, is disenchanting.

W. H. Auden 1907–73: 'The Poet of the Encirclement' (1943)

7 Art is the imposing of a pattern on experience, and our aesthetic enjoyment is recognition of the pattern.

Alfred North Whitehead 1861–1947: *Dialogues* (1954) 10 June 1943

8 *L'art est un anti-destin.*
Art is a revolt against fate.

André Malraux 1901–76: *Les Voix du silence* (1951)

9 Art is born of humiliation.

W. H. Auden 1907–73: Stephen Spender *World Within World* (1951)

10 Art is parasitic on life, just as criticism is parasitic on art.

Kenneth Tynan 1927–80: in *Observer* 6 July 1958

11 The final purpose of art is to intensify, even, if necessary, to exacerbate, the moral consciousness of people.

Norman Mailer 1923– : in *Western Review* Winter 1959

12 An artist must be a reactionary. He has to stand out against the tenor of the age and not go flopping along.

Evelyn Waugh 1903–66: George Plimpton (ed.) *Writers at Work* 3rd series (1967)

13 *Beauty plus pity*—that is the closest we can get to a definition of art.
    on **Kafka**'s Metamorphosis

Vladimir Nabokov 1899–1977: *Lectures on Literature* (1980)

14 Do not imagine that Art is something which is designed to give gentle uplift and self-confidence. Art is not a *brassière*. At least, not in the English sense. But do not forget that *brassière* is the French for life-jacket.

Julian Barnes 1946– : *Flaubert's Parrot* (1984)

15 A revelation of the full range of our human response to the world—that is, what it means to be human on earth.

Margaret Atwood 1939– : in an interview, December 1986; Earl G. Ingersoll (ed.) *Margaret Atwood: Conversations* (1990)

16 Art comes out of art; it begins with imitation, often in the form of parody.

Alan Bennett 1934– : *Writing Home* (1994)

W. H. Auden 1907–73
English poet

1 I sometimes think of his poetry as a great war, admire intensely the mature, religious, and logical fighter, and deprecate the boy bushranger.

Dylan Thomas 1914–53: in *New Verse* November 1937

2 The high-water mark, so to speak, of Socialist literature is W. H. Auden, a sort of gutless Kipling.

George Orwell 1903–50: *The Road to Wigan Pier* (1937)

3 Soon we will have to smooth him out to see who it is.

Igor Stravinsky 1882–1971: diary, 15 August 1951

4 English Auden was a superb, magnetic, wide-angled poet . . . American Auden, on the other hand, was a walking readers' digest: names—Rilke, Kierkegaard, Goethe, James—clung to him like Coney Island confetti.

Philip Larkin 1922–85: in *New Statesman* 5 October 1973

5 My face looks like a wedding cake left out in the rain.

W. H. Auden 1907–73: Humphrey Carpenter *W. H. Auden* (1981)

6 People sometimes divide others into those you laugh at and those you laugh with. The young Auden was someone you could laugh-at-with.

Stephen Spender 1909–95: *W. H. Auden* (1973)

7 Auden killed his own poetry by going to America where, having sacrificed the capacity to make art out of life, he tried to make art out of art instead.

Philip Larkin 1922–85: *Required Writing* (1983)

8 Behind it all, the tow-haired moled impassive face weathers slowly to that last incredible relief map, webbed with a thousand ironies.

Philip Larkin 1922–85: in *Observer* 11 September 1983

9 He didn't love God, just fancied him.

Anonymous: unattributed comment; John Mortimer *In Character* (1983)

10 Auden of the last years, when he had begun to resemble in his own person an ample, flopping, ambulatory volume of the *OED* in carpet slippers.

Seamus Heaney 1939– : in *London Review of Books* 4 June 1987

Audience

11 *Pro captu lectoris habent sua fata libelli.*
The reader's fancy makes the fate of books.

Terentianus Maurus fl. late 2nd cent. AD: *De Syllabis et Metris*

12 Authors have established it as a kind of rule, that a man ought to be dull sometimes; as the most severe reader makes allowances for many rests and nodding places in a voluminous writer.

Joseph Addison 1672–1719: *The Spectator* 23 July 1711

13 'Till authors hear at length, one gen'ral cry,
Tickle and entertain us, or we die.
The loud demand from year to year the same,
Beggars invention and makes fancy lame.

William Cowper 1731–1800: 'Retirement' (1782)

14 A book is a mirror: if an ape looks into it, an apostle is hardly likely to look out.

Georg Christoph Lichtenberg 1742–99: *Aphorisms*

15 The book . . . requires to be read in the clear, brown, twilight atmosphere in which it was written; if opened in the sunshine, it is apt to look exceedingly like a volume of blank pages.

Nathaniel Hawthorne 1804–64: preface to *Twice-Told Tales* (1851)

1 —*Hypocrite lecteur,—mon semblable,—mon frère!*
Hypocritical reader, my fellow-man, my brother!

Charles Baudelaire 1821–67: 'Au Lecteur' (1855)

2 Do not fire too much over the heads of your readers.

Anthony Trollope 1815–82: letter to George Eliot, 1862

3 Every book is, in an intimate sense, a circular letter to the friends of him who writes it. They alone take his meaning; they find private messages, assurances of love, and expressions of gratitude, dropped at every corner. The public is but a generous patron who defrays the postage.

Robert Louis Stevenson 1850–94: dedicatory letter to *Travels with a Donkey* (1879)

4 Camerado, this is no book,
Who touches this touches a man,
(Is it night? Are we here together alone?)
It is I you hold and who holds you.
I spring from the pages into your arms—decease calls me forth.

Walt Whitman 1819–92: 'So Long!' (1881)

5 It is perhaps hardly too much to say that the future of English fiction may rest with this Unknown Public—a reading public of three millions which lies right out of the pale of true literary civilization—which is now waiting to be taught the difference between a good book and a bad.

Wilkie Collins 1824–89: Q. D. Leavis *Fiction and the Reading Public* (1932)

6 What kind of talent is required to please this mighty public? That was my first question, and was soon amended with the words, 'if any'.

Robert Louis Stevenson 1850–94: *Essays Literary and Critical* (1923) 'Popular Authors'

7 One writes only half the book; the other half is with the reader.

Joseph Conrad 1857–1924: letter to Cunninghame Graham, 1897

8 I should so much have loved to be popular!

Henry James 1843–1916: Alfred Sutro *Celebrities and Simple Souls* (1933)

9 Writing in English is the most ingenious torture ever devised for sins committed in previous lives. The English reading public explains the reason why.

James Joyce 1882–1941: letter, 5 September 1918

10 An author ought to write for the youth of his own generation, the critics of the next, and the schoolmasters of ever afterward.

F. Scott Fitzgerald 1896–1940: letter, April 1920

11 The whole duty of a writer is to please and satisfy himself, and the true writer always plays to an audience of one.

William Strunk 1869–1946 and **E. B. White** 1899–1985: *The Elements of Style* (1959 ed.)

12 When a man writes a letter to himself, it is a pity to post it to somebody else. Perhaps the same is true of a book.

D. H. Lawrence 1885–1930: *Aaron's Rod* (1922)

13 Better to write for yourself and have no public, than to write for the public and have no self.

Cyril Connolly 1903–74: in *New Statesman* 25 February 1933

14 The great poet, in writing himself, writes his time.

T. S. Eliot 1888–1965: *Selected Essays* (1934) 'Shakespeare and the Stoicism of Seneca'

15 That ideal reader suffering from an ideal insomnia.
his target audience

James Joyce 1882–1941: *Finnegans Wake* (1939)

16 The play was consumed in wholesome fashion by large masses in places of public resort; the novel was self-administered in private.

Flann O'Brien 1911–66: *At Swim-Two-Birds* (1939)

1 The demand that I make of my reader is that he should devote his whole LIFE to reading my works.

James Joyce 1882–1941: Richard Ellmann *James Joyce* (1982)

2 The best of the communications an author has to make is to his own generation, and he is wise to let the generation that succeeds his choose its own exponent.
on the falling off of a writer's powers in old age

W. Somerset Maugham 1874–1965: *A Writer's Notebook* (1949) written in 1944

3 I have momentarily become an object of curiosity to Americans and I find that they believe that my friendship and confidence are included in the price of the book.
in response to the large amount of correspondence he received following publication of Brideshead Revisited

Evelyn Waugh 1903–66: in *Life* 8 April 1946

4 It is no easy trick to keep your characters and your story operating on a level which is understandable to the semi-literate public and at the same time give them some intellectual and artistic overtones which that public does not seek or demand or in effect recognize, but which somehow subconsciously it accepts and likes.

Raymond Chandler 1888–1959: letter to Bernice Baumgarten, 16 April 1951

5 Let us invent a character, a nice respectable, middle-class, middle-aged, maiden lady, with time on her hands and the money to help her pass it. She enjoys pictures, books, music, and the theatre and though to none of these arts (or rather, for consistency's sake, to none of these three arts and the one craft) does she bring much knowledge or discernment, at least, as she is apt to tell her cronies, 'does know what she likes'. Let us call her Aunt Edna . . . Aunt Edna is universal, and to those who may feel that all the problems of the modern theatre might be solved by her liquidation, let me add that I have no doubt at all that she is also immortal.

Terence Rattigan 1911–77: *Collected Plays* (1953) vol. 2, preface

6 A work of art has no importance whatever to society. It is only important to the individual, and only the individual reader is important to me.

Vladimir Nabokov 1899–1977: *Strong Opinions* (1973)

7 The ideal reader of my novels is a lapsed Catholic and a failed musician, short-sighted, colour-blind, auditorily biased, who has read the books that I have read. He should also be about my age.

Anthony Burgess 1917–93: George Plimpton (ed.) *Writers at Work* 4th Series (1977)

8 Once I've finished a novel IT, not I, is telling its story, and one hopes that it will—like some space-probe—go on beaming its message, its light, for some time.

Susan Hill 1942– : interview, *Bookshelf* BBC Radio 4, 30 April 1982

9 The Ideal Reader is the reader who reads what you write according to the text, just what's on the page, is conscious of everything that you are doing in a literary way, responds on an emotional level at the right places, laughs at the jokes, doesn't mistake irony for straight comment, gets the puns . . . [and] who reads the book on the first read-through to see what happens.

Margaret Atwood 1939– : in an interview, November 1983; Earl G. Ingersoll (ed.) *Margaret Atwood: Conversations* (1990)

10 Novelists who write for a public are, in my opinion, no good; they've discovered who their readers are and, in submitting to their judgement, they're dishing things up like short-order cooks.

Graham Greene 1904–91: Marie-Françoise Allain *The Other Man, Conversations with Graham Greene* (1983)

1 It's the job of the novelist to provide the information through which the book is read. You can't really expect the reader to bring anything other than their interest.

Salman Rushdie 1947– : interview in *Independent* 10 September 1988

2 I occasionally have an anti-Roth reader in mind. I think, 'How he is going to hate this!' That can be just the encouragement I need.

Philip Roth 1933– : George Plimpton (ed.) *The Writer's Chapbook* (1989)

3 The world may be full of fourth-rate writers but it's also full of fourth-rate readers.

Stan Barstow 1928– : in *Daily Mail* 15 August 1989

4 The literary masterpieces of the twentieth century were for the most part the work of novelists who had no large public in mind. The novels of Proust and Joyce were written in a cultural twilight and were not intended to be read under the blaze and dazzle of popularity.

Saul Bellow 1915– : in *Writers on Writing: Collected Essays from The New York Times* (2001)

5 How to be a friend to a reader so the reader won't stop reading, how to be a good date on a blind date with a total stranger.

Kurt Vonnegut Jr. 1922– : in *Writers on Writing: Collected Essays from The New York Times* (2001)

Jane Austen 1775–1817 see also **2:9**, **66:1**, **245:3**
English novelist

6 I think I may boast myself to be, with all possible vanity, the most unlearned and uninformed female who ever dared to be an authoress.

Jane Austen 1775–1817: letter, 11 December 1815

7 Till 'Pride and Prejudice' showed what a precious gem was hidden in that unbending case, she was no more regarded in society than a poker or a fire-screen, or any other thin upright piece of wood or iron that fills its corner in peace and quietness. The case is very different now: she is still a poker—but a poker of whom everyone is afraid.

Mary Russell Mitford 1787–1855: letter, 1815

8 What should I do with your strong, manly, spirited sketches, full of variety and glow?—How could I possibly join them on to the little bit (two inches wide) of ivory on which I work with so fine a brush, as produces little effect after much labour?

Jane Austen 1775–1817: letter to J. Edward Austen, 16 December 1816

9 The Big Bow-Wow strain I can do myself like any now going; but the exquisite touch, which renders ordinary commonplace things and characters interesting, from the truth of the description and the sentiment, is denied to me.

Sir Walter Scott 1771–1832: W. E. K. Anderson (ed.) *Journals of Sir Walter Scott* (1972) 14 March 1826

10 Miss Austen being, as you say, without 'sentiment', without *poetry*, maybe *is* sensible, real (more *real* than *true*), but she cannot be great.

Charlotte Brontë 1816–55: letter to George Henry Lewes, 18 January 1848

11 When I take up one of Jane Austen's books . . . I feel like a barkeeper entering the kingdom of heaven. I know what his sensation would be and his private comments. He would not find the place to his taste, and he would probably say so.

Mark Twain 1835–1910: Q. D. Leavis *Fiction and the Reading Public* (1932)

12 You could not shock her more than she shocks me;
Beside her Joyce seems innocent as grass,
It makes me most uncomfortable to see
An English spinster of the middle class
Describe the amorous effects of 'brass',

W. H. Auden 1907–73: *Letter to Lord Byron* (1936)

JANE AUSTEN · **AUTOBIOGRAPHY** 13

Reveal so frankly and with such sobriety
The economic basis of society.

1 Regulated hatred.

D. W. Harding 1906– : title of an article on the novels of Jane Austen, in *Scrutiny* March 1940

2 Her novels are the Maxims of La Rochefoucauld set in motion.

Giuseppe di Lampedusa 1896–1957: *The Sirens and Selected Writings* (translated by David Gilmour, 1995)

Autobiography see also Biography

3 I am commencing an undertaking, hitherto without precedent, and which will never find an imitator. I desire to set before my fellows the likeness of a man in all the truth of nature, and that man myself.
 Myself alone! I know the feeling of my heart, and I know men. I am not made like any of those I have seen; I venture to believe that I am not made like any of those in existence.

Jean-Jacques Rousseau 1712–78: *Confessions* (1782)

refusing an offer to write his memoirs:
4 I should be trading on the blood of my men.

Robert E. Lee 1807–70: attributed, perhaps apocryphal

disclaiming any intention of recording his inner (or even family) life:
5 No man ever did so truly, and no man ever will.

Anthony Trollope 1815–82: *Autobiography* (1883)

6 If you do not want to explore an egoism you should not read autobiography.

H. G. Wells 1866–1946: *Experiment in Autobiography* (1934)

7 Reformers are always finally neglected, while the memoirs of the frivolous will always eagerly be read.

Henry 'Chips' Channon 1897–1958: diary, 7 July 1936

8 Autobiographies ought to begin with Chapter Two.

Ellery Sedgwick 1872–1962: *The Happy Profession* (1948)

9 Every autobiography . . . becomes an absorbing work of fiction, with something of the charm of a cryptogram.

H. L. Mencken 1880–1956: *Minority Report* (1956)

10 He made the books and he died.
 his own 'sum and history of my life'

William Faulkner 1897–1962: letter to Malcolm Cowley, 11 February 1949

11 Every autobiography is concerned with two characters, a Don Quixote, the Ego, and a Sancho Panza, the Self.

W. H. Auden 1907–73: *The Dyer's Hand* (1962)

12 Only when one has lost all curiosity about the future has one reached the age to write an autobiography.

Evelyn Waugh 1903–66: *A Little Learning* (1964)

13 My problem is that I am not frightfully interested in anything, except myself. And of all forms of fiction autobiography is the most gratuitous.

Tom Stoppard 1937– : *Lord Malquist and Mr Moon* (1966)

14 An autobiography is an obituary in serial form with the last instalment missing.

Quentin Crisp 1908–99: *The Naked Civil Servant* (1968)

15 Because I am too imaginative.
 on being asked why she had refused to write an autobiography

Sylvia Townsend Warner 1893–1978: Claire Harman (ed.) *Diaries of Sylvia Townsend Warner* (1994)

1 I have no guarantee of what is written here but memory, a known cheat.

Lucy M. Boston 1892–1990: *Perverse and Foolish: a Memoir of Childhood and Youth* (1979)

2 I regard that [autobiography] as the height of egotism.

Roald Dahl 1916–90: on 16 May 1983; Jeremy Treglown *Roald Dahl* (1994)

3 Interviews are an art form in themselves. As such, they're fictional and arranged. The illusion that what you're getting is the straight truth from the writer and accurate in every detail is false.

Margaret Atwood 1939– : in an interview, December 1986; Earl G. Ingersoll (ed.) *Margaret Atwood: Conversations* (1990)

4 Autobiographies tell more lies than all but the most self-indulgent fiction.

A. S. Byatt 1936– : *Sugar* (1988)

5 To ask an author who hopes to be a serious writer if his work is autobiographical is like asking a spider where he buys his thread. The spider gets his thread right out of his own guts, and that is where the autor gets his writing, and in that profound sense everything he writes is autobiographical.

Robertson Davies 1913–95: speech, Ontario Science Centre, Toronto, 26 November 1989

6 There's no such thing as autobiography. There's only art and lies.

Jeanette Winterson 1959– : in *Guardian* 5 July 1994

7 Once I read autobiography as what the writer thought about her or his life. Now I think, ' That is what they thought *at that time*.' An interim report—that is what an autobiography is.

Doris Lessing 1919– : 'Writing Autobiography'; in David Fuller and Patricia Waugh (eds.) *The Arts and Sciences of Criticism* (1999)

8 In a way, an autobiography seems to me like a household book of accounts—what has been acquired, to what purpose has it been put, was too much paid for it and did it teach you anything?

Elizabeth Jane Howard 1923– : *Slipstream: a Memoir* (2002)

Francis Bacon 1561–1626
English lawyer, courtier, philosopher, and essayist

9 The fear of every man that heard him was, lest he should make an end.

Ben Jonson c.1573–1637: *Timber, or Discoveries made upon Men and Matter* (1641) 'Dominus Verulamius'

10 He was no striped frieze; he was shot silk.

Lytton Strachey 1880–1932: *Elizabeth and Essex* (1928)

Bad Writing see Good and Bad Writing

Ballads

11 Certainly I must confess mine own barbarousness, I never heard the old song of Percy and Douglas, that I found not my heart moved more than with a trumpet.

Philip Sidney 1554–86: *The Defence of Poetry* (1595)

12 Light be the turf on the breast of the heaven-inspired poet who composed this glorious fragment!
on hearing an old man singing the original of 'Auld Lang Syne'

Robert Burns 1759–96: letter to Mrs Dunlop, 7 December 1788

1 The farmer's daughter hath soft brown hair;
   (*Butter and eggs and a pound of cheese*)
   And I met with a ballad, I can't say where,
   Which wholly consisted of lines like these.

C. S. Calverley 1831–84: 'Ballad' (1872)

2 The true ballads touch a depth and breadth of life, a
   seriousness and summary finality, that belongs to the
   species rather than to individuals, and which shuts
   instantly against the author who separates himself, by
   name or by rôle or by motive, from the general dumb
   chorus of human evidence.

Ted Hughes 1930–98: in *Guardian* 14 May 1965

3 The steel and bite of the ballads, so remorseless and yet so
   lyrical, entered my literary bloodstream, never to depart.

Muriel Spark 1918– : *Curriculum Vitae* (1992)

Honoré de Balzac 1799–1850
French novelist

4 If I'm not a genius, I'm done for.

Honoré de Balzac 1799–1850: letter to his sister Laure, 1819

5 Between you and me, I am not deep, but I am very wide,
   and it takes time to walk around me.

Honoré de Balzac 1799–1850: letter to Countess Maffei, 1837

6 What a man Balzac would have been if he had known
   how to write!

Gustave Flaubert 1821–80: letter, 1852

7 What a man! . . . He crushes the entire century.

Émile Zola 1840–1902: letter, 1867

8 Hair in disorder, eyes lost in a dream, a genius who, in his
   little room, is able to reconstruct bit by bit the entire
   structure of his society and to expose life in all its
   tumultuousness for his contemporaries and for all
   generations to come.

Auguste Rodin 1840–1917: in *L'Art et les artistes* February 1900

9 The Russians make us debate some point of view peculiar
   to the author, Flaubert etherealizes all with his conviction
   that life is no better than a smell of cooking through a
   grating. But Balzac leaves us when the book is closed amid
   the crowd that fills the boxes and the galleries of grand
   opera.

W. B. Yeats 1865–1939: 'Louis Lambert' (July, 1934)

10 Balzac observed all the things that Marx did not.

Régis Debray 1940– : *Teachers, Writers, Celebrities* (1981) 'Balzac, or Zoology Today'

J. M. Barrie 1860–1937
Scottish writer and dramatist

11 A little child whom the Gods have whispered to.

Mrs Patrick Campbell 1865–1940: letter to G. B. Shaw, January 1913

12 The cheerful clatter of Sir James Barrie's cans as he went
   round with the milk of human kindness.

Philip Guedalla 1889–1944: *Supers and Supermen* (1920) 'Some Critics'

Charles Baudelaire 1821–67
French poet and critic

1 You are as unyielding as marble and as penetrating as an English fog.

Gustave Flaubert 1821–80: letter to Baudelaire, 13 July 1857

2 Baudelaire is the first seer, king of poets, *a true God.*

Arthur Rimbaud 1854–91: letter, 15 May 1871

3 The only downright repulsive face of a poet that I am yet acquainted with is that of Baudelaire.

George Gissing 1857–1903: *Commonplace Book* (1962)

Samuel Beckett 1906–89 see also **154:14**
Irish dramatist, novelist, and poet

4 A play in which nothing happens, twice.
    reviewing Waiting for Godot *in* Irish Times, *1954*

Vivian Mercier 1919–89: *Beckett/ Beckett* (1977)

5 A special virtue attaches to plays which remind the drama of how much it can do without and still exist. By all the known criteria, Samuel Beckett's 'Waiting for Godot' is a dramatic vacuum. Pity the critic who sees a chink in its armour, for it is all chink.

Kenneth Tynan 1927–80: *Curtains* (1961) 'Waiting for Godot'

6 I couldn't have done it otherwise, gone on I mean. I could not have gone on through the awful wretched mess of life without having left a stain upon the silence.

Samuel Beckett 1906–89: Deirdre Bair *Samuel Beckett* (1978)

7 The bleakness I admire; but there are superior bleaknesses, frankly.

Anita Brookner 1928– : in *Independent* June 2002

Max Beerbohm 1872–1956
English critic, essayist, and caricaturist

8 The younger generation is knocking at the door, and as I open it there steps spritely in the incomparable Max.
    on handing over the theatre review column to Max Beerbohm

George Bernard Shaw 1856–1950: in *Saturday Review* 21 May 1898 'Valedictory'

9 Tell me, when you are alone with Max, does he take off his face and reveal his mask?

Oscar Wilde 1854–1900: W. H. Auden *Forewords and Afterwords* (1973)

10 He has the most remarkable and seductive genius—and I should say about the smallest in the world.

Lytton Strachey 1880–1932: letter to Clive Bell, 4 December 1917

Beginning see also Ending

11 *Semper ad eventum festinat et in medias res*
    Non secus ac notas auditorem rapit.

He always hurries to the main event and whisks his audience into the middle of things as though they knew already.

Horace 65–8 BC: *Ars Poetica*; see **17:7**

12 The last thing one knows in constructing a work is what to put first.

Blaise Pascal 1623–62: *Pensées* (1670)

1 The futility of all prefaces I long ago realized; for the more a writer strives to make his views clear, the more confusion he creates.

Johann Wolfgang von Goethe 1749-1832: *Poetry and Truth* (1814)

2 My way is to begin with the beginning.

Lord Byron 1788-1824: *Don Juan* (1819-24) canto 1, st. 7

3 I am finding it very hard to get my novel started. I suffer from stylistic abscesses; and sentences keep itching without coming to a head.
    on beginning Madame Bovary

Gustave Flaubert 1821-80: letter, 23 October 1851; see **108:3**

4 I began and read the first number of *Bleak House*. It opens with exaggerated and verbose description. London fog is disagreeable even in description, and on the whole the first number does not promise much.

Henry Crabb Robinson 1775-1867: diary, 19 March 1852

5 Beginnings are always troublesome . . . Even Macaulay's few pages of introduction to his 'Introduction' in the English History are the worst bit of writing in the book.

George Eliot 1819-80: letter to Sara Hennell, 15 August 1859

6 'Where shall I begin, please your Majesty?' he asked. 'Begin at the beginning,' the King said, gravely, 'and go on till you come to the end: then stop.'

Lewis Carroll 1832-98: *Alice's Adventures in Wonderland* (1865)

7 Perhaps the method of rushing at once 'in medias res' is, of all the ways of beginning a story . . . the least objectionable. The reader is made to think the gold lies so near the surface that he will be required to take very little trouble in digging for it.

Anthony Trollope 1815-82: *The Duke's Children* (1880); see **16:11**

8 There is no difficulty in beginning; the trouble is to leave off!

Henry James 1843-1916: in 1891; Leon Edel (ed.) *The Diary of Alice James* (1965)

9 In these days of rush and hurry, a novelist works at a disadvantage. He must leap into the middle of his tale with as little delay as he would employ in boarding a moving tramcar. He must get off the mark with the smooth swiftness of a jack-rabbit surprised while lunching. Otherwise, people throw him aside and go out to picture palaces.

P. G. Wodehouse 1881-1975: *A Damsel in Distress* (1919)

10 I find it only too easy to write opening chapters—and at the moment the story is not unfolding. I squandered so much on the original 'Hobbit' (which was not meant to have a sequel) that it is difficult to find anything new in that world.
    of the genesis of The Lord of the Rings

J. R. R. Tolkien 1892-1973: letter to Stanley Unwin, February 1938; Humphrey Carpenter *J. R. R. Tolkien* (1977)

11 The beginning of a book holds more apprehensions for the novelist than the ending. After living with a book for a year or two, he has come to terms with his unconsciousness—the end will be imposed. But if a book is started in the wrong way, it may never be finished.

Graham Greene 1904-91: *In Search of a Character* (1961)

12 The dreaded essential opening sentences.

Graham Greene 1904-91: *In Search of a Character* (1961)

13 The long uphill struggle in playwriting is getting to the top of page one.

Tom Stoppard 1937- : letter to Anthony Smith, January 1964

14 A good beginning means a good book.

John Braine 1922-86: *Writing a Novel* (1974)

1 Such a sentence makes you hear the sound of books slapping shut all over the library.
   of the opening sentence of Ivanhoe

Joan Aiken 1924– : *The Way to Write for Children* (1982)

2 I . . . have an entire cemetery of abandoned books, or rather, of fragments.

Graham Greene 1904–91: Marie-Françoise Allain *The Other Man, Conversations with Graham Greene* (1983)

3 One of the most difficult things is the first paragraph. I have spent many months on a first paragraph and once I get it, the rest comes out very easily. In the first paragraph you solve most of the problems with your book. The theme is defined, the style, the tone.

Gabriel García Márquez 1928– : George Plimpton (ed.) *The Writer's Chapbook* (1989)

4 If you read twenty or thirty pages by a writer, and want to continue, you are in his sea and swimming in that sea. He can write quite badly after that. Because by that time, you're in his sea, and you're moving forward.

Brian Moore 1921–99: Rosemary Hartill *Writers Revealed* (1989)

Hilaire Belloc 1870–1953
British poet, essayist, historian, novelist

5 Wells and I, contemplating the Chesterbelloc, recognize at once a very amusing pantomime elephant, the front legs being that very exceptional and un-English individual Hilaire Belloc, and the hind legs that extravagant freak of French nature, G. K. Chesterton.

George Bernard Shaw 1856–1950: in *New Age* 15 February 1908

6 He was a provocative, aggressive, contrary old man, enunciating his theories in clipped tones as though they were papal encyclicals.

James Lees-Milne 1908–97: *Holy Dread: Diaries 1982–1984* (2001) 12 May 1983

Alan Bennett 1934–
English dramatist and diarist

7 There was a time when I thought my only connection with the literary world would be that I had once delivered meat to T. S. Eliot's mother-in-law.

Alan Bennett 1934– : *Writing Home* (1994)

8 He is both glum and funny, a mixture the English always find endearing.

John Carey 1934– : in *Sunday Times* 9 October 1994

9 Winsome, lose some.
   cancelling an interview with the Independent *after the paper described him as winsome*

Alan Bennett 1934– : in *Daily Telegraph* 18 March 1995 'They Said It'

Arnold Bennett 1867–1931
English novelist

10 I'd like to write an essay on [Arnold] Bennett—sort of pig in clover.

D. H. Lawrence 1885–1930: letter to Aldous Huxley, 27 March 1928

1 It was perhaps a part of his competent autonomy that Bennett was so remarkably free from the normal infantilism of the human male. He was not so dependent upon women for his comfort and self-respect as most of us are; he was not very deeply interested in them from that point of view. And he had not that capacity for illusion about them which is proper to our sex. The women in his books are for the most part good hard Staffordshire ware, capable, sisterly persons with a tang to their tongues.

H. G. Wells 1866–1946: *Experiment in Autobiography* (1934)

2 Arnold Bennett knew his eggs. Whatever his interest in good writing, he never showed the public anything but AVARICE. Consequently they adored him.

Ezra Pound 1885–1972: letter to Laurence Pollinger, May 1937

Best-sellers see also **Popular Fiction**

3 All Rome is mad about my book:
It's praised, they hum the lines, shops stock it,
It peeps from every hand and pocket.

Martial AD c.40–c.104: *Epigrammata* tr. James Michie

4 Kansas City's literary tone is improving. The six best sellers here last week were 'Fools of Nature' [etc.].
OED's *earliest citation for the term 'best-seller'*

Anonymous: in *Kansas Times & Star* 25 April 1889

5 I attribute my good fortune to the simple fact that I have always tried to write straight from my own heart to the hearts of others.
on the success of her first novel, The Romance of Two Worlds, *in 1886*

Marie Corelli 1855–1924: Jerome K. Jerome (ed.) *My First Book* (1894)

6 If *Hamlet* and *Oedipus* were published now, they wouldn't sell more than 100 copies, unless they were pushed.

D. H. Lawrence 1885–1930: letter to Edward Garnett, 1913

7 Nearly all bookish people are snobs, and especially the more enlightened among them. They are apt to assume that if a writer has immense circulation, if he is enjoyed by plain persons, and if he can fill several theatres at once, he cannot possibly be worth reading and merits only indifference and disdain.

Arnold Bennett 1867–1931: in *Evening Standard* 19 July 1928

8 A best-seller is the gilded tomb of a mediocre talent.

Logan Pearsall Smith 1865–1946: *Afterthoughts* (1931)

9 Even the most critical reader who brings only an ironical appreciation of their work cannot avoid noticing a certain power, the secret of their success with the majority. Bad writing, false sentiment, sheer silliness, and a preposterous narrative are all carried along by the magnificent vitality of their author.

Q. D. Leavis 1906–81: *Fiction and the Reading Public* (1932)

10 The principle of procrastinated rape is said to be the ruling one in all the great best-sellers.

V. S. Pritchett 1900–97: *The Living Novel* (1946) 'Clarissa'

11 I am delighted that you liked *Brideshead*. I was pleased with it at the time but I have been greatly shaken by its popularity in U.S.A.

Evelyn Waugh 1903–66: letter, 2 February 1946

12 A best-seller was a book which somehow sold well simply because it was selling well.

Daniel J. Boorstin 1914– : *Images* (1961)

13 Only a person with a Best-Seller mind can write Best-Sellers.

Aldous Huxley 1894–1963: attributed

1 Best-sellers are about murder, money, revenge, ambition, and sex, sex, sex. So are literary novels. But best-selling authors give you more per page.

Ken Follett 1949– : Barry Turner *The Writer's Companion* (1996)

2 I was tired of writing a lot of serious stuff that didn't pay the bills. I wanted to create a best-seller.
of writing The Godfather

Mario Puzo 1920–99: in *Daily Telegraph* 19 October 1996

3 Simply at the level of cash takings, Parnassus will not see his like again. For the larger part of an extremely long career . . . the author of *In Memoriam* and *Idylls of the King* was a regular, and spectacular, best-seller, outstripping most fiction writers of his day.
on **Tennyson**

Ian Hamilton 1938– : *The Trouble with Money and Other Essays* (1998)

John Betjeman 1906–84 see also 65:8
English poet

4 I came to the conclusion that a man who could give such pleasure with his pen couldn't be much of a secret agent. I may well be wrong.
view of the IRA army council's head of civilian intelligence on John Betjeman's role as a press attaché in wartime Dublin

Diarmuid Brennan: report, c.1941; in *Guardian* 22 April 2000

5 Leica-sharp in detail.

Philip Larkin 1922–85: *Required Writing* (1983)

6 Betjeman's cachet is by now that of a cherished public monument. It would be only mildly surprising to hear that he had been acquired by the National Trust.

John Carey 1934– : in *Sunday Times* 9 January 1983

7 No one else has his breadth of poetic reception. Betjeman picks it all up: the decay of surviving nineteenth-century institutions, the decline of the Church, the altered countryside and ways of living, subtopia and socialism, and all the tiny vivid little manifestations of sadness and snobbery and silliness, and with his simple loving enthusiasm transmutes it to poetry. He is a subtle poet, but not a sophisticated one.

Philip Larkin 1922–85: *Further Requirements* (2001)

The Bible

8 Hooly writ is the scripture of puples, for it is maad, that alle puplis schulden knowe it.

St Jerome c.AD 342–420: attributed, in J. Forshall and F. Madden (eds.) *The Holy Bible . . . in the Earliest English Versions* (1850) vol. 1 'The Prologue' [probably by John Purvey, c.1353–c.1428]

9 The devil can cite Scripture for his purpose.

William Shakespeare 1564–1616: *The Merchant of Venice* (1596–8)

10 I walk many times into the pleasant fields of the Holy Scriptures, where I pluck up the goodly green herbs of sentences, eat them by reading, chew them up musing, and lay them up at length in the seat of memory . . . so I may the less perceive the bitterness of this miserable life.

Elizabeth I 1533–1603: Adam Fox (ed) *A Book of Devotions* (1970)

1 The pencil of the Holy Ghost hath laboured more in describing the afflictions of Job than the felicities of Solomon.

Francis Bacon 1561–1626: *Essays* (1625) 'Of Adversity'

2 You cannot name any example in any heathen author but I will better it in Scripture.

James I 1566–1625: Thomas Overbury 'Crumms Fal'n From King James's Table'

3 Blessed Lord, who hast caused all holy Scriptures to be written for our learning; Grant that we may in such wise hear them, read, mark, learn, and inwardly digest them, that by patience, and comfort of thy holy Word, we may embrace, and ever hold fast the blessed hope of everlasting life.

The Book of Common Prayer 1662: *Collects*; collect for the second Sunday in Advent

4 I have not for these things fished in other men's waters; my Bible and my Concordance are my only library in my writing.

John Bunyan 1628–88: 'Solomon's Temple Spiritualized' (1688); preface

*Samuel **Johnson** noticed that **Collins**'s only literary possession was a testament:*
5 I have but one book, but that is the best.

William Collins 1721–59: in *Dictionary of National Biography*

6 There is a book, who runs may read,
Which heavenly truth imparts.

John Keble 1792–1866: *The Christian Year* (1827) 'Septuagesima'; see **226:8**

7 The English Bible, a book which, if everything else in our language should perish, would alone suffice to show the whole extent of its beauty and power.

Lord Macaulay 1800–59: T. F. Ellis (ed.) *Miscellaneous Writings of Lord Macaulay* (1860) 'John Dryden' (1828)

8 There's a great text in Galatians,
Once you trip on it, entails
Twenty-nine distinct damnations,
One sure, if another fails.

Robert Browning 1812–89: 'Soliloquy of the Spanish Cloister' (1842)

9 He [the translator] will find one English book and one only, where, as in the *Iliad* itself, perfect plainness of speech is allied with perfect nobleness; and that book is the Bible.

Matthew Arnold 1822–88: *On Translating Homer* (1861)

10 Never forget, gentlemen, never forget that this is *not* the Bible. This, gentlemen, is only a *translation* of the Bible.
to a meeting of his diocesan clergy, as he held up a copy of the 'Authorized Version'

Richard Whately 1787–1863: H. Solly *These Eighty Years* (1893)

11 We have used the Bible as if it was a constable's handbook—an opium-dose for keeping beasts of burden patient while they are being overloaded.

Charles Kingsley 1819–75: *Letters to the Chartists*

12 LORD ILLINGWORTH: The Book of Life begins with a man and a woman in a garden.
MRS ALLONBY: It ends with Revelations.

Oscar Wilde 1854–1900: *A Woman of No Importance* (1893)

13 The New Testament, and to a very large extent the Old, *is* the soul of man. You cannot criticize it. It criticizes you.

John Jay Chapman 1862–1933: letter, 26 March 1898

of reading the Bible daily with his mother:
14 The one essential part of all my education.

John Ruskin 1819–1900: in *Dictionary of National Biography*

15 An apology for the Devil: It must be remembered that we have only heard one side of the case. God has written all the books.

Samuel Butler 1835–1902: *Notebooks* (1912)

1 I read the book of Job last night. I don't think God comes well out of it.

Virginia Woolf 1882–1941: letter to Lady Robert Cecil, 12 November 1922

2 Those who talk of the Bible as a 'monument of English prose' are merely admiring it as a monument over the grave of Christianity.

T. S. Eliot 1888–1965: *Religion and Literature* (1935)

3 By the way, do you ever read the Bible? I suppose not very often, but I had occasion to the other night and believe me it is a lesson in how not to write for the movies. The worst kind of overwriting. Whole chapters that you could have said in one paragraph. And the dialogue!

Raymond Chandler 1888–1959: letter to Edgar Carter, 28 March 1947

4 The number one book of the ages was written by a committee, and it was called the Bible.

Louis B. Mayer 1885–1957: attributed

5 I know of no book which has been a source of brutality and sadistic conduct, both public and private, that can compare with the Bible.

Reginald Paget 1908–90: in *Observer* 28 June 1964

6 It's just called 'The Bible' now. We dropped the word 'Holy' to give it a more mass-market appeal.
   a publisher's view

Judith Young 1940– : attributed, 1989

Biography see also Autobiography

7 Many brave men lived before Agamemnon's time; but they are all, unmourned and unknown, covered by the long night, because they lack their sacred poet.

Horace 65–8 BC: *Odes*

8 Our Grubstreet biographers watch for the death of a great man, like so many undertakers, on purpose to make a penny of him.

Joseph Addison 1672–1719: *Freeholder* (1715–6)

9 Curll (who is one of the new terrors of Death) has been writing letters to everybody for memoirs of his life.

John Arbuthnot 1667–1735: letter to Jonathan Swift, 13 January 1733; see **23:3, 23:11**

10 There has rarely passed a life of which a judicious and faithful narrative would not be useful.

Samuel Johnson 1709–84: 'Dignity and Uses of Biography' (1750)

11 Nobody can write the life of a man, but those who have eat and drunk and lived in social intercourse with him.

Samuel Johnson 1709–84: James Boswell *Life of Samuel Johnson* (1791) 31 March 1772

12 If a man is to write *A Panegyric* he may keep vices out of sight; but if he professes to write *A Life*, he must represent it as it really was.

Samuel Johnson 1709–84: James Boswell *Life of Samuel Johnson* (1791) 1777

13 A funeral oration rather than a history.
   of Thomas Sprat's Life of Cowley *(1668)*

Samuel Johnson 1709–84: in *Dictionary of National Biography*

14 It is a task, not unworthy of a genius, to arrange these minute notices of human nature, and of human learning.
   of anecdotes

Isaac D'Israeli 1766–1848: *A Dissertation on Anecdotes* (1793)

15 Many of the greatest men that ever lived have written biography. Boswell was one of the smallest men that ever lived, and he has beaten them all.

Lord Macaulay 1800–59: in *Edinburgh Review* 1831

16 Lives of great men all remind us
   We can make our lives sublime,
   And, departing, leave behind us
   Footprints on the sands of time.

Henry Wadsworth Longfellow 1807–82: 'A Psalm of Life' (1838)

1 A well-written Life is almost as rare as a well-spent one.

Thomas Carlyle 1795–1881: *Critical and Miscellaneous Essays* (1838) 'Jean Paul Friedrich Richter'

2 There is no life of a man, faithfully recorded, but is a heroic poem of its sort, rhymed or unrhymed.

Thomas Carlyle 1795–1881: *Critical and Miscellaneous Essays* (1838) 'Sir Walter Scott'

3 Then there is my noble and biographical friend who has added a new terror to death.
   on Lord Campbell's Lives of the Lord Chancellors being written without the consent of heirs or executors

Charles Wetherell 1770–1846: Lord St Leonards *Misrepresentations in Campbell's Lives of Lyndhurst and Brougham* (1869); also attributed to Lord Lyndhurst (1772–1863); see **22:9, 306:2**

4 No quailing, Mrs Gaskell! no drawing back!
   apropos her undertaking to write the life of Charlotte **Brontë**

Patrick Brontë 1777–1861: letter from Mrs Gaskell to Ellen Nussey, 24 July 1855

5 I never *did* write a biography, and I don't exactly know how to set about it; you see I have to be accurate and keep to facts; a most difficult thing for a writer of fiction.
   while writing her Life of Charlotte Brontë

Elizabeth Gaskell 1810–65: letter to Harriet Anderson, 15 March 1856

6 Mind, no biography!
   injunction to his daughters

William Makepeace Thackeray 1811–63: John Sutherland *Is Heathcliff a Murderer?* (1996)

7 I think you are quite right to look over your old letters and papers and decide for yourself what should be burned. Burning is the most reverential destination one can give to relics which will not interest any one after we are gone. I hate the thought that what we have looked at with eyes full of living memory should be tossed about and made lumber of, or (if it be writing) read with hard curiosity.

George Eliot 1819–80: letter to Cara Bray, November 1880

8 Biographers are generally a disease of English literature.

George Eliot 1819–80: Michael Holroyd 'How I Fell into Biography' (1988)

9 Every great man nowadays has his disciples, and it is always Judas who writes the biography.

Oscar Wilde 1854–1900: *Intentions* (1891) 'The Critic as Artist'

10 It is not a Life at all. It is a Reticence, in three volumes.
   on J. W. Cross's Life of George Eliot

W. E. Gladstone 1809–98: E. F. Benson *As We Were* (1930)

11 It occurred to him that, in a world governed by the law of mortality, men might be handsomely entertained on one another's remains . . . He had learned the wisdom of the grave-digger in *Hamlet*, and knew that there are many rotten corpses nowadays, that will scarce hold the laying in. So he seized on them before they were cold, and commemorated them in batches . . . His books commanded a large sale, and modern biography was established.
   on the bookseller and publisher Edmund Curll (*1675–1747*)

Walter Raleigh 1861–1922: *Six Essays on Johnson* (1910); see **22:9**

12 My sole wish is to frustrate as utterly as possible the post-mortem exploiter . . . I have long thought of launching, by a provision in my will, a curse not less explicit than Shakespeare's own on any such as try to move my bones.

Henry James 1843–1916: letter, 7 April 1914; see **91:8**

on hearing that Arthur Benson was to write the life of Rossetti:

1 No, no, no, it won't do. *Dear* Arthur, we know just what he can, so beautifully, do, but no, oh no, this is to have the story of a purple man written by a white, or at the most, a pale green man.

Henry James 1843–1916: George Lyttelton, letter to Rupert Hart-Davis, 28 February 1957

2 Those two fat volumes, with which it is our custom to commemorate the dead—who does not know them, with their ill-digested masses of material, their slipshod style, their tone of tedious panegyric, their lamentable lack of selection, of detachment, of design? They are as familiar as the *cortège* of the undertaker, and wear the same air of slow, funereal barbarism.

Lytton Strachey 1880–1932: *Eminent Victorians* (1918) preface

3 Discretion is not the better part of biography.

Lytton Strachey 1880–1932: Michael Holroyd *Lytton Strachey* vol. 1 (1967)

4 How far we are going to read a poet when we can read about a poet is a problem to lay before biographers.

Virginia Woolf 1882–1941: *The Common Reader* (2nd series, 1932)

5 A biography should be a dissection and demonstration of how a particular human being was made and worked.

H. G. Wells 1866–1946: *Experiment in Autobiography* (1934)

6 A shilling life will give you all the facts.

W. H. Auden 1907–73: 'A Shilling Life' (1936)

7 If I have given you delight
By aught that I have done,
Let me lie quiet in that night
Which shall be yours anon:

And for the little, little span
The dead are borne in mind,
Seek not to question other than
The books I leave behind.

Rudyard Kipling 1865–1936: 'The Appeal' (1940)

8 The 'Higher Cannibalism' in biography . . . The exhumation of scarcely cold notorieties, defenceless females for choice, and tricking them out with sprightly inferences and 'sex' deductions to suit the mood of the market.

Rudyard Kipling 1865–1936: *Something of Myself* (1937)

9 Anyone turning biographer commits himself to lies, to concealment, to hypocrisy, to flattery, and even to hiding his own lack of understanding, for biographical truth is not to be had, and even if it were it couldn't be used.
in a letter to Arnold Zweig who had suggested being his biographer

Sigmund Freud 1856–1939: Paul Roazen *Freud and his Followers* (1971)

10 There never was a good biography of a good novelist. There couldn't be. He is too many people, if he's any good.

F. Scott Fitzgerald 1896–1940: Edmund Wilson (ed.) *The Crack-Up* (1945)

11 Almost any biographer, if he respects facts, can give us much more than another fact to add to our collection. He can give us the creative fact; the fertile fact; the fact that suggests and engenders.

Virginia Woolf 1882–1941: *The Death of the Moth* (1942) 'The Art of Biography'

12 And kept his heart a secret to the end
From all the picklocks of biographers.
of Robert E. Lee

Stephen Vincent Benét 1898–1943: *John Brown's Body* (1928)

13 Just how difficult it is to write biography can be reckoned by anybody who sits down and considers just how many people know the truth about his or her love affairs.

Rebecca West 1892–1983: in *Vogue* 1 November 1952

1 Biography is in some ways the most brutish of all the arts. It shifts about uncomfortably in the strangely uncertain middle ground between deliberate assassination and helpless boot-licking.

Dennis Potter 1935–94: in *The Times* 24 February 1968

2 At least the plain truth of documents is on my side. That, and only that, is what I would ask of my biographer— plain facts.

Vladimir Nabokov 1899–1977: *Strong Opinions* (1973)

3 The past exudes legend: one can't make pure clay of time's mud. There is no life that can be recaptured wholly; as it was. Which is to say that all biography is ultimately fiction.

Bernard Malamud 1914–86: *Dubin's Lives* (1979)

4 What novelist, given the choice, wouldn't prefer you to reread one of his novels rather than read his biography?

Julian Barnes 1946– : *Flaubert's Parrot* (1984)

5 Poets' real biographies are like those of birds . . . Their real data are in the way they sound. A poet's biography is in his vowels and sibilants, in his metres, rhymes and metaphors.

Joseph Brodsky 1940–96: *Less Than One* (1986)

6 A writer's life stands in relation to his work as a house does to a garden, related but distinct. It is the business of critical biography to make the two overlap—to bring some of the furniture out to the garden, as it were, and spread flowers all over the house.

Mavis Gallant 1922– : *Paris Notebooks: Essays and Reviews* (1986)

7 I read biographies backwards, beginning with the death. If that takes my fancy I go through the rest. Childhood seldom interests me at all.

Alan Bennett 1934– : *Writing Home* (1994)

8 It's an excellent life of somebody else. But I've really lived inside myself, and she can't get in there.
on a biography of himself

Robertson Davies 1913–95: interview, in *The Times* 4 April 1995

9 A burglar at the subject's keyhole, shamelessly marketing voyeuristic delights.
on biographers

Janet Malcolm: in *London Review of Books* 19 October 1995

10 The shadow in the garden.
said to be Saul Bellow's description of his biographer James Atlas

Anonymous: in *New Yorker* 26 June 1995; see **26:2**

11 Biographies are likely to be either acts of worship or acts of destruction. And the best ones have elements of both.

Humphrey Carpenter 1946– : in conversation with Lyndall Gordon; John Batchelor (ed.) *The Art of Literary Biography* (1995)

12 Biographers know nothing about the intimate sex lives of their own wives, but they think they know all about Stendhal's or Faulkner's.

Milan Kundera 1929– : *Testaments Betrayed* (1995)

13 The problem with biographies of writers is that the early parts of their lives are very interesting—what's laid out is all the material they're eventually going to use—but after a certain point the most significant thing a writer does is—write books. All the interest is in the work.

David Malouf 1934– : in *Daily Telegraph* 7 September 1996

14 I have done my best to die before this book is published. It now seems possible that I may not succeed . . . I shall try to keep my sense of humour and the perspective of eternity.
to his biographer, Humphrey Carpenter, shortly before publication

Robert Runcie 1921–99: postscript to the biography; in *The Times* 7 September 1996

1 Biography is the mesh through which our real life escapes.

Tom Stoppard 1937– : *The Invention of Love* (1997)

2 [The arrival of biographers] casts the shadow of the tombstone across one's life.

Saul Bellow 1915– : in *Times Literary Supplement* 12 December 1997; see **25:10**

3 Both biographers and tabloid newspapers dig into people's secret lives. It's a bit like the difference between archaeology and tomb-robbing. They are both doing the same thing, but with different motives. The tomb robber takes for monetary gain, but the archaeologist is interested in every detail of the life and what we can learn from it.

Kathleen Jones 1922– : in *Independent* 8 May 1999

William Blake 1757–1827
English poet

4 There is no doubt that this poor man was mad, but there is something in the madness of this man which interests me more than the sanity of Lord Byron and Walter Scott.

William Wordsworth 1770–1850: Henry Crabb Robinson *Reminiscences*

5 Blake saw a treefull of angels at Peckham Rye,
And his hands could lay hold on the tiger's terrible heart.
Blake knew how deep is Hell, and Heaven how high,
And could build the universe from one tiny part.

William Rose Benét 1886–1950: 'Mad Blake' (1918)

6 Or that William Blake
Who beat upon the wall
Till truth obeyed his call.

W. B. Yeats 1865–1939: 'An Acre of Grass' (c.1938)

Books see also Illustrations, Reading

7 A large book is like great evil.
  proverbially contracted 'Great book, great evil'

Callimachus c.305–c.240 BC: fragment 465

8 *Cui dono lepidum novum libellum*
Arido modo pumice expolitum?

To whom shall I give my nice new little book polished dry with pumice?

Catullus c.84–c.54 BC: *Carmina* no. 1

9 You want to take my poems wherever you go,
As companions, say, on a trip to some distant land?
Buy this. It's packed tight into parchment pages, so,
Leave your rolls at home, for this takes just one hand!
  on the codex

Martial AD c.40–c.104: written AD85/86; Lionel Casson *Libraries in the Ancient World* (2001)

10 Homer on parchment pages!
The *Iliad* and all the adventures
Of Ulysses, foe of Priam's kingdom!
All locked within a piece of skin
Folded into several little sheets!

Martial AD c.40–c.104: *Epigrammata* tr. W. C. A. Ker

11 The reading of good books is like a conversation with the best men of past centuries—in fact like a prepared conversation, in which they reveal only the best of their thoughts.

René Descartes 1596–1650: *Le Discours de la méthode* (1637)

12 An empty book is like an infant's soul, in which anything may be written. It is capable of all things, but containeth nothing.

Thomas Traherne c.1637–74: *Centuries of Meditations*

1 Their books of stature small they took in hand,
Which with pellucid horn securèd are,
To save from finger wet the letter fair.

William Shenstone 1714–63: *The Schoolmistress* (1742)

2 I hate books; they only teach us to talk about things we know nothing about.

Jean-Jacques Rousseau 1712–78: *Émile* (1762)

3 He used to say, that no man read long together with a folio on his table:—Books, said he, that you may carry to the fire, and hold readily in your hand, are the most useful after all.

Samuel Johnson 1709–84: John Hawkins *Works of Samuel Johnson* (1787) vol. 11

4 A book reads the better which is our own, and has been so long known to us, that we know the topography of its blots, and dog's ears, and can trace the dirt in it to having read it at tea with buttered muffins.

Charles Lamb 1775–1834: *Last Essays of Elia* (1833)

5 Books think for me.

Charles Lamb 1775–1834: *Last Essays of Elia* (1833) 'Detached Thoughts on Books and Reading'

6 A good book is the best of friends, the same to-day and for ever.

Martin Tupper 1810–89: *Proverbial Philosophy* Series I (1838) 'Of Reading'

7 A good book is the purest essence of a human soul.

Thomas Carlyle 1795–1881: speech in support of the London Library, 24 June 1840

8 No furniture so charming as books.

Sydney Smith 1771–1845: Lady Holland *Memoir* (1855); see **27:15**

9 Books are made not like children but like pyramids . . . and they're just as useless! and they stay in the desert! . . . Jackals piss at their foot and the bourgeois climb up on them.

Gustave Flaubert 1821–80: letter to Ernest Feydeau, November/December 1857

10 All books are divisible into two classes, the books of the hour, and the books of all time.

John Ruskin 1819–1900: *Sesame and Lilies* (1865)

11 There is no Frigate like a Book
To take us Lands away
Nor any Coursers like a Page
Of prancing Poetry.

Emily Dickinson 1830–86: *Complete Poems* (1955) 'A Book (2)'

12 Child! do not throw this book about;
Refrain from the unholy pleasure
Of cutting all the pictures out!
Preserve it as your chiefest treasure.

Hilaire Belloc 1870–1953: *A Bad Child's Book of Beasts* (1896) dedication

13 Authors are actors, books are theatres.

Wallace Stevens 1879–1955: *Opus Posthumous* (1957)

14 It is a mistake to think that books have come to stay. The human race did without them for thousands of years and may decide to do without them again.

E. M. Forster 1879–1970: attributed

15 Books do furnish a room.

Anthony Powell 1905–2000: title of novel (1971); see **27:8**

16 Books are . . . funny little portable pieces of thought.

Susan Sontag 1933– : in *Time*, 1978

17 It's certainly difficult to think of a better symbol of civilization.

Philip Larkin 1922–85: *Required Writing* (1983)

1 After all, human beings come and go, while books remain forever.

Amos Oz 1939– : in *New Yorker* 25 December 1995 'Chekhov in Hebrew'

2 The book is the greatest interactive medium of all time. You can underline it, write in the margins, fold down a page, skip ahead. And you can take it anywhere.
on taking over as head of Penguin Books

Michael Lynton: in *Daily Telegraph* 19 August 1996

3 Some pages have browned to a pale toast colour with the years, but others have remained a fresh, almost chalky white; there are thin, fragile pages, and others that feel downy, almost velvety to the touch. Pepys was a fine calligrapher when he made time to write slowly, as he did for his Diary, and his pages are as beautiful as pieces of embroidery, with their neatly spaced symbols, the curly, the crotchety and the angular, interspersed with longhand for names, places and any other words that took his fancy.
on the manuscript of Pepys's Diary

Claire Tomalin 1933– : *Samuel Pepys: The Unequalled Self* (2002)

4 You can't tell a book by its cover.

Anonymous: proverb

5 A book is like a garden carried in the pocket.

Anonymous: Chinese proverb

Borrowed Titles

6 Antic hay (1923).

Aldous Huxley 1894–1963

My men, like satyrs grazing on the lawns,
Shall with their goat feet dance an antic hay.

Christopher Marlowe 1564–93: *Edward II* (1593)

7 Arms and the man (1898).

George Bernard Shaw 1856–1950

Arma virumque cano, Troiae qui primus ab oris
Italiam fato profugus Laviniaque venit
Litora, multum ille et terris iactatus et alto
Vi superum, saevae memorem Iunonis ob iram.
I sing of arms and the man who first from the shores of Troy came destined an exile to Italy and the Lavinian beaches, a man much buffeted on land and on the deep by force of the gods because of fierce Juno's never-forgetting anger.

Virgil 70–19 BC: *Aeneid*

8 Blithe spirit (1942).

Noël Coward 1899–1973

Hail to thee, blithe Spirit!
Bird thou never wert,
That from Heaven, or near it,
Pourest thy full heart.

Percy Bysshe Shelley 1792–1822: 'To a Skylark' (1819)

9 Blue remembered hills (1984).

Dennis Potter 1935–94

What are those blue remembered hills,
What spires, what farms are those?

A. E. Housman 1859–1936: *A Shropshire Lad* (1896)

10 Brave new world (1932).

Aldous Huxley 1894–1963

How beauteous mankind is! O brave new world,
That has such people in't.

William Shakespeare 1564–1616: *The Tempest* (1611)

11 Cakes and ale (1930)

W. Somerset Maugham 1874–1965

Dost thou think, because thou art virtuous, there shall be no more cakes and ale? — **William Shakespeare** 1564–1616: *Twelfth Night* (1601)

1 Darkness visible (1979). — **William Golding** 1911–93

No light, but rather darkness visible
Served only to discover sights of woe. — **John Milton** 1608–74: *Paradise Lost* (1667)

2 The darling buds of May (1958). — **H. E. Bates** 1905–74

Rough winds do shake the darling buds of May,
And summer's lease hath all too short a date. — **William Shakespeare** 1564–1616: sonnet 18

3 Devices and desires (1989). — **P. D. James** 1920–

We have followed too much the devices and desires of our own hearts. — **The Book of Common Prayer** 1662: *Morning Prayer* General Confession

4 Far from the madding crowd (1874). — **Thomas Hardy** 1840–1928

Far from the madding crowd's ignoble strife,
Their sober wishes never learned to stray. — **Thomas Gray** 1716–71: *Elegy Written in a Country Churchyard* (1751)

5 For whom the bell tolls (1940). — **Ernest Hemingway** 1899–1961

Any man's death diminishes me, because I am involved in Mankind; And therefore never send to know for whom the bell tolls; it tolls for thee. — **John Donne** 1572–1631: *Devotions upon Emergent Occasions* (1624)

6 The golden bough (1890–1915). — **James George Frazer** 1854–1941

A mighty tree, that bears a golden bough. — **Virgil** 70–19 BC: *Aeneid* bk. 6; William Pitt's 1743 translation

7 Gone with the wind (1936). — **Margaret Mitchell** 1900–49

I have forgot much, Cynara! gone with the wind. — **Ernest Dowson** 1867–1900: 'Non Sum Qualis Eram' (1896)

8 The grapes of wrath (1939). — **John Steinbeck** 1902–68

He is trampling out the vintage where the grapes of wrath are stored. — **Julia Ward Howe** 1819–1910: 'Battle Hymn of the Republic' (1862)

9 The heart is a lonely hunter (1940). — **Carson McCullers** 1917–67

My heart is a lonely hunter that hunts on a lonely hill. — **Fiona McLeod** 1855–1905: 'The Lonely Hunter' (1896)

10 His dark materials (title of trilogy beginning with *Northern Lights*, 1995). — **Philip Pullman** 1946–

Unless the almighty maker them ordain
His dark materials to create more worlds. — **John Milton** 1608–74: *Paradise Lost* (1667)

11 Remembrance of things past (1913-27, translation by C. K. Scott-Moncrieff and S. Hudson of *À la recherche du temps perdu*). — **Marcel Proust** 1871–1922

When to the sessions of sweet silent thought
I summon up remembrance of things past. — **William Shakespeare** 1564–1616 sonnet 30

12 The seven pillars of wisdom (1926). — **T. E. Lawrence** 1888–1935

Wisdom hath builded her house, she hath hewn out her seven pillars. — **Bible**: Proverbs

1 The sound and the fury (1929).

> It is a tale
> Told by an idiot, full of sound and fury,
> Signifying nothing.

William Faulkner 1897–1962

William Shakespeare 1564–1616: *Macbeth* (1606)

2 Tender is the night (1934).

> Already with thee! tender is the night.

F. Scott Fitzgerald 1896–1940

John Keats 1795–1821: 'Ode to a Nightingale' (1820)

3 Where angels fear to tread (1905).

> For fools rush in where angels fear to tread.

E. M. Forster 1879–1970

Alexander Pope 1688–1744: *An Essay on Criticism* (1711)

Borrowing Books see also Libraries

4 Your *borrowers of books*—those mutilators of collections, spoilers of the symmetry of shelves, and creators of odd volumes.

Charles Lamb 1775–1834: *Essays of Elia* (1823) 'The Two Races of Men'

5 Please return this book; I find that though many of my friends are poor arithmeticians, they are nearly all good bookkeepers.

Sir Walter Scott 1771–1832: attributed, perhaps apocryphal

6 Never lend books, for no one ever returns them; the only books I have in my library are those that other people have lent me.

Anatole France 1844–1924: *La Vie littéraire* (1888)

7 What a bad sign it is to get the *Oxford Book of Victorian Verse* out of the library.

Barbara Pym 1913–80: diary, 1933

8 Yes, the collection of a lifetime and I guard it well. I never lend! Only fools lend books. All the books on this shelf once belonged to fools.

Anonymous: 'a man [who] is proudly displaying his library to an envious visitor', quoted by Bertrand Russell to C. Williams-Ellis *Architect Errant* (1971)

James Boswell 1740–95
Scottish lawyer; biographer of Samuel Johnson

9 Were you to die, it would be a limb lopped off.

Samuel Johnson 1709–84: A. N. Wilson *Penfriends from Porlock* (1988); attributed

10 It is the story of a mountebank and his zany.
> *of Boswell's* Tour of the Hebrides

Horace Walpole 1717–97: letter to Hon. Henry Conway, 6 October 1785

11 He was always labouring at notoriety, and, having failed in attracting it in his own person, he hooked his little bark to them whom he thought most likely to leave harbour, and so shone with reflected light, like the rat that eat the malt that lay in the house that Jack built.

Sir Walter Scott 1771–1832: letter, 30 January 1829

12 The Life of Johnson is assuredly a great, a very great work. Homer is not more decidedly the first of heroic poets, Shakespeare is not more decidedly the first of dramatists, Demosthenes is not more decidedly the first of orators, than Boswell is the first of biographers.

Lord Macaulay 1800–59: *Essays Contributed to the Edinburgh Review* (1843) vol. 1 'Samuel Johnson'

Bertolt Brecht 1898–1956
German dramatist and poet

1 No bitterness could put out that cigar
Or stop the stubborn twisting of its smoke.
Confronted with the facts, he saw the joke.
The moral of the play? 'That's how things are.'

John Willett 1917– : 'Sonnet in memory of Brecht' (1956)

2 I don't regard Brecht as a man of iron-grey purpose and intellect, I think he is a theatrical whore of the first quality.

Peter Hall 1930– : attributed, 1962

3 Personally, I would rather have written Winnie the Pooh than the collected works of Brecht.

Tom Stoppard 1937– : attributed, 1972

Brevity

4 It is a foolish thing to make a long prologue, and to be short in the story itself.

Bible: II Maccabees

5 I strive to be brief, and I become obscure.

Horace 65–8 BC: *Ars Poetica*

6 Ek gret effect men write in place lite;
Th' entente is al, and nat the lettres space.

Geoffrey Chaucer c.1343–1400: *Troilus and Criseyde*

7 Words are like leaves; and where they most abound,
Much fruit of sense beneath is rarely found.

Alexander Pope 1688–1744: *An Essay on Criticism* (1711)

8 In all pointed sentences, some degree of accuracy must be sacrificed to conciseness.

Samuel Johnson 1709–84: 'The Bravery of the English Common Soldier' in *The British Magazine* January 1760

9 Was there ever yet anything written by mere man that was wished longer by its readers, excepting *Don Quixote*, *Robinson Crusoe*, and the *Pilgrim's Progress*?

Samuel Johnson 1709–84: Hester Lynch Piozzi *Anecdotes of . . . Johnson* (1786)

10 Another damned, thick, square book! Always scribble, scribble, scribble! Eh! Mr Gibbon?

William Henry, 1st Duke of Gloucester 1743–1805: Henry Best *Personal and Literary Memorials* (1829); also attributed to the Duke of Cumberland and King George III; D. M. Low *Edward Gibbon* (1937)

Laman Blanchard, a young poet, had submitted some verses entitled 'Orient Pearls at Random Strung' to Household Words:
11 Dear Blanchard, too much string—Yours. C.D.

Charles Dickens 1812–70: Frederick Locker-Lampson *My Confidences* (1896)

12 If there is anywhere a thing said in two sentences that could have been as clearly and as engagingly said in one, then it's amateur work.

Robert Louis Stevenson 1850–94: letter to William Archer, February 1888

13 Brevity is the sister of talent.

Anton Chekhov 1860–1904: letter to Alexander Chekhov, 11 April 1889; L. S. Friedland (ed.) *Anton Chekhov: Letters on the Short Story . . .* (1964)

14 I summed up all systems in a phrase, and all existence in an epigram.

Oscar Wilde 1854–1900: letter, from Reading Prison, to Lord Alfred Douglas, January–March 1897

1 The covers of this book are too far apart.

Ambrose Bierce 1842–c.1914: attributed

explaining why he wrote opinions while standing:
2 Nothing conduces to brevity like a caving in of the knees.

Oliver Wendell Holmes Jr. 1841–1935: Catherine Drinker Bowen *Yankee from Olympus* (1944); attributed

3 I have never believed that arithmetic is important for the appreciation of literature. I have been criticized for writing too concisely, but I find that Babel's style is even more concise than mine . . . It shows what can be done. Even when you've got all the water out of them, you can still clot the curds a little more.

Ernest Hemingway 1899–1961: remark made to Ilya Ehrenburg and quoted by him in a speech on Isaac Babel, Moscow, 11 November 1964

4 Long books, when read, are usually overpraised, because the reader wishes to convince others and himself that he has not wasted his time.

E. M. Forster 1879–1970: note from commonplace book, in O. Stallybrass (ed.) *Aspects of the Novel and Related Writings* (1974)

5 Windbags can be right. Aphorists can be wrong. It is a tough world.

James Fenton 1949– : in *The Times* 21 February 1985

6 A book should be like a play. You do not return to a play every night for a week and you should not have to do so with a book.
on his novels' brevity

Georges Simenon 1903–89: Patrick Marnham *The Man Who Wasn't Maigret* (1992)

Anne Brontë 1820–49
English novelist

7 The books and poems that she wrote serve as a matter of comparison by which to test the greatness of her two sisters. She is the measure of their genius—like them, but not with them.

Mrs Humphry Ward 1851–1920: preface to the Haworth edition of the Brontë's works (1924)

8 A sort of literary Cinderella.

George Moore 1852–1933: *Conversations in Ebury Street* (1924)

Charlotte Brontë 1816–55
English novelist

9 Here at Haworth . . . one day resembles another—and all have heavy lifeless physiognomies . . . I shall soon be 30—and I have done nothing yet . . . I feel as if we were all buried here—.

Charlotte Brontë 1816–55: letter to Ellen Nussey, 24 March 1845

10 Charlotte has been writing a book, and it is much better than likely.
to his daughters Anne and Emily, on first reading Jane Eyre; *in a letter of August 1850, Mrs Gaskell gives the wording as* 'Charlotte has been writing a book—and I think it is a better one than I expected'

Patrick Brontë 1777–1861: Elizabeth Gaskell *The Life of Charlotte Brontë* (1857)

1 [I have] lost (or won if you like) a whole day in reading it
. . . It is a fine book though—the man and woman capital
. . . The plot of the story is one with which I am familiar.
Some of the love passages made me cry—to the
astonishment of John who came in with the coals . . . It is
a woman's writing, but whose? . . . Give my respects and
thanks to the author.
on reading Jane Eyre *for the first time*

William Makepeace Thackeray
1811–63: letter to W. S. Williams, 23
October 1847

2 She showed that abysses may exist inside a governess and
eternities inside a manufacturer.

G. K. Chesterton 1874–1936: *Twelve
Types* (1902)

3 She does not attempt to solve the problems of human life;
she is even unaware that such problems exist; all her
force, and it is the more tremendous for being constricted,
goes into the assertion 'I love, I hate, I suffer'.

Virginia Woolf 1882–1941: *The
Common Reader* (1925)

Emily Brontë 1818–48
English novelist and poet

4 It is rustic all through. It is moorish, and wild, and knotty
as a root of heath.
on the setting of Emily Brontë's Wuthering Heights

Charlotte Brontë 1816–55: preface
to the 1850 edition

5 Indeed, I have never seen her parallel in anything,
stronger than a man, simpler than a child, her nature
stood alone.

Charlotte Brontë 1816–55: preface
to Emily Brontë *Wuthering Heights*
(1850 ed.)

6   She—
(How shall I sing her?)—whose soul
Knew no fellow for might,
Passion, vehemence, grief,
Daring, since Byron died.

Matthew Arnold 1822–88:
'Haworth Churchyard' (1855)

Rupert Brooke 1887–1915
English poet

7 A young Apollo, golden-haired,
Stands dreaming on the verge of strife,
Magnificently unprepared
For the long littleness of life.

Frances Cornford 1886–1960:
'Youth' (1910)

8 *The Morning Post*, which has always hitherto disapproved
of him, is now loud in his praises because he has
conformed to their stupid axiom of literary criticism that
the only stuff of poetry is violent physical experience, by
dying on active service.
having seen the notice of Brooke's death in The Morning
Post

Charles Sorley 1895–1915: letter,
April 1915

9 He energized the Garden-Suburb ethos with a certain
original talent and the vigour of a prolonged adolescence.
His verse exhibits . . . something that is rather like Keats's
vulgarity with a Public School accent.

F. R. Leavis 1895–1978: *New Bearings
in English Poetry* (1932)

Thomas Browne 1605–82
English author and physician

1 Sir Thomas Browne seemed to be of opinion that the only business of life was to think, and that the proper object of speculation was, by darkening knowledge, to breed more speculation, and 'find no end in wandering mazes lost'.

William Hazlitt 1778–1830: 'Character of Sir T. Brown as a Writer' (1820)

2 Who would not be curious to see the lineaments of a man who, having himself been twice married, wished that mankind were propagated like trees!

Charles Lamb 1775–1834: quoted by William Hazlitt, in *New Monthly Magazine* January 1826

3 His immense egotism has paved the way for all psychological novelists, autobiographers, confession-mongers, and dealers in the curious shades of our private life. He it was who first turned from the contacts of man with man, to their lonely life within.

Virginia Woolf 1882–1941: *The Common Reader* (1925)

Elizabeth Barrett Browning 1806–61
English poet; wife of Robert **Browning**

4 Mrs Browning's death is rather a relief to me, I must say: no more Aurora Leighs, thank God! A woman of real genius, I know; but what is the upshot of it all? She and her sex had better mind the kitchen and their children; and perhaps the poor: except in such things as little novels, they only devote themselves to what men do much better, leaving that which men do worse or not at all.

Edward Fitzgerald 1809–83: letter to W. H. Thompson, 15 July 1861; see **34:6**

5 The simple truth is that she was the poet, and I the clever person by comparison.

Robert Browning 1812–89: letter to Isa Blagden, 19 August 1871

6 Ay, dead! and were yourself alive, good Fitz,
How to return your thanks would pass my wits.
Kicking you seems the common lot of curs—
While more appropriate greeting lends you grace:
Surely to spit there glorifies your face—
Spitting from lips once sanctified by Hers.
   rejoinder to Edward Fitzgerald, who had 'thanked God my wife was dead'

Robert Browning 1812–89: in *Athenaeum* 13 July 1889; see **34:4**

7 With her profuse feathery curls half hiding her small face, and her large, soft, pleading eyes, she always reminded me of a King Charles spaniel. Something unutterably pathetic looked out of those soft dog like eyes, and I could fancy that when her beloved dog 'Flush' was young and handsome there might have been a likeness.

Eliza Ogilvy 1822–1912: *Recollections of Mrs Browning* (1893)

Robert Browning 1812–89 see also **308:8**, **178:3**
English poet; husband of Elizabeth Barrett **Browning**

8 I always held that Mr Browning was a master in clenched passion . . . concentrated passion . . . burning through the metallic fissures of language.

Elizabeth Barrett Browning 1806–61: letter to Mary Russell Mitford, 14 February 1843

1 A great gossip and a very 'sympathetic' easy creature.

Henry James 1843–1916: letter, 31 January 1877

2 One of my latest sensations was going one day to Lady Airlie's to hear Browning read his own poems—with the comfort of finding that, at least, if you don't understand them, he himself apparently understands them even less. He read them as if he hated them and would like to bite them to pieces.

Henry James 1843–1916: letter, 26 July 1880

3 When it was written, God and Robert Browning knew what it meant; now only God knows.
   of Sordello

Robert Browning 1812–89: attributed

4 The mental quality which I felt most in him was celerity, or (if I may coin the word) immediateness.

William Michael Rossetti 1829–1919: 'Portraits of Robert Browning' in *The Magazine of Art* 1890

5 Meredith's a prose Browning, and so is Browning.

Oscar Wilde 1854–1900: *Intentions* (1891) 'The Critic as Artist'

6 Chaos, illumined by flashes of lightning.
   on Robert Browning's 'style'

Oscar Wilde 1854–1900: Ada Leverson *Letters to the Sphinx* (1930)

7 The mere act of writing seemed to have a peculiar effect on him, for I have known him to be obscure even in a telegram.

Sidney Colvin 1845–1927: *Memories and Notes of Persons and Places 1852–1912* (1921)

John Bunyan 1628–88
English writer and Nonconformist preacher

8 'Pilgrim's Progress', about a man that left his family it didn't say why . . . The statements was interesting, but tough.

Mark Twain 1835–1910: *The Adventures of Huckleberry Finn* (1884)

9 A tinker out of Bedford,
   A vagrant oft in quod,
   A private under Fairfax,
   A minister of God . . .
   A pedlar from a hovel,
   The lowest of the low—
   The Father of the Novel,
   Salvation's first Defoe . . .

Rudyard Kipling 1865–1936: 'The Holy War' (1917)

10 Just as Oliver Cromwell aimed to bring about the kingdom of God on earth and founded the British Empire, so Bunyan wanted the millennium and got the novel.

Christopher Hill 1912– : *A Turbulent, Seditious, and Factious People: John Bunyan and his Church, 1628–1688* (1988)

Edmund Burke 1729–97
Irish-born Whig politician and man of letters

11 If a man were to go by chance at the same time with Burke under a shed, to shun a shower, he would say— 'this is an extraordinary man.'

Samuel Johnson 1709–84: James Boswell *Life of Samuel Johnson* (1791) 15 May 1784

1 [Edmund Burke] is not affected by the reality of distress touching his heart, but by the showy resemblance of it striking his imagination. He pities the plumage, but forgets the dying bird.
on Burke's Reflections on the Revolution in France

Thomas Paine 1737–1809: *The Rights of Man* (1791)

2 As he rose like a rocket, he fell like the stick.
on Burke's losing the debate on the French Revolution to Charles James Fox, in the House of Commons

Thomas Paine 1737–1809: *Letter to the Addressers on the late Proclamation* (1792)

3 From the first time I cast my eyes on anything of Burke's . . . I said to myself, 'This is true eloquence: this is a man pouring out his mind on paper.' All other styles seemed to me pedantic and impertinent . . . I conceived too that he might be wrong in his main argument, and yet deliver fifty truths in arriving at a false conclusion.

William Hazlitt 1778–1830: 'On Reading Old Books' (1826)

Fanny Burney 1752–1840 see also 323:7
English novelist

4 'Richardson would have been really *afraid* of her;—there is merit in *Evelina* which he could not have borne.—No it would not have done!' . . . (Then, shaking his head at me, he exclaimed) 'O, you little *Character-monger*, you!'

Samuel Johnson 1709–84: Fanny Burney, letter to her sister Susan, September 1778

5 All those whom we have been accustomed to revere as intellectual patriarchs seemed children when compared to her; for Burke sat up all night to read her writings, and Johnson had pronounced her superior to Fielding.

Lord Macaulay 1800–59: in *Edinburgh Review* January 1843

Robert Burns 1759–96
Scottish poet

6 The Poetic Genius of my Country found me as the prophetic bard Elijah did Elisha—at the plough; and threw her inspiring mantle over me.

Robert Burns 1759–96: *Poems* 1787 (2nd ed.); dedication

7 What an antithetical mind!—tenderness, roughness— delicacy, coarseness—sentiment, sensuality—soaring and grovelling, dirt and deity—all mixed up in that one compound of inspired clay!

Lord Byron 1788–1824: diary, 13 December 1813

8 I would have taken the poet, had I not known what he was, for a very sagacious country farmer of the old Scotch school.

Sir Walter Scott 1771–1832: J. G. Lockhart *Life of Robert Burns* (1828)

9 A Burns is infinitely better educated than a Byron.

Thomas Carlyle 1795–1881: *Notebooks* 2 November 1831

10 The Confession of Augsburg, the Declaration of Independence, the French Rights of Man, and the 'Marseillaise', are not more weighty documents in the history of freedom than the songs of Burns.

Ralph Waldo Emerson 1803–82: speech, 25 January 1859

11 He is a myth evolved by the popular imagination, a communal poetic creation, a Protean figure: we can all shape him to our likeness, for the myth is endlessly adaptable.

Edwin Muir 1887–1959: 'The Burns Myth' (1947)

Lord Byron 1788–1824 see also 4:1
English poet

1 Mad, bad, and dangerous to know.
   after their first meeting at a ball in March 1812

Lady Caroline Lamb 1785–1828: diary, 1812; Elizabeth Jenkins *Lady Caroline Lamb* (1932)

2 If I could envy any man for successful ill nature I should envy Lord Byron for his skill in satirical nomenclature.

Sydney Smith 1771–1845: letter to Lady Holland, March 1818

3 You speak of Lord Byron and me—there is this great difference between us. He describes what he sees—I describe what I imagine. Mine is the hardest task.

John Keats 1795–1821: letter, 17–27 September 1819

4 The world is rid of Lord Byron, but the deadly slime of his touch still remains.

John Constable 1776–1837: letter, May 1824

5 If they had said that the sun or the moon had gone out of the heavens, it could not have struck me with the idea of a more awful and dreary blank in creation than the words: 'Byron is dead!'

Jane Welsh Carlyle 1801–66: letter, 20 May 1824

6 Whatever he does, he must do in a more decided and daring manner than any one else; he lounges with extravagance, and yawns so as to alarm the reader!

William Hazlitt 1778–1830: *The Spirit of the Age* (1825)

7 Lord Byron makes man after his own image, woman after his own heart; the one is a capricious tyrant, the other a yielding slave.

William Hazlitt 1778–1830: *The Spirit of the Age* (1825)

8 Our Lord Byron—the fascinating—faulty—childish— philosophical being—daring the world—docile to a private circle—impetuous and indolent—gloomy and yet more gay than any other.

Mary Shelley 1797–1851: letter, 19 January 1830

9 It still saddens me that Lord Byron, who showed such impatience with the fickle public, wasn't aware of how well the Germans can understand him and how highly they esteem him. With us the moral and political tittle-tattle of the day falls away, leaving the man and the talent standing alone in all their brilliance.

Johann Wolfgang von Goethe 1749–1832: letter to John Murray, 29 March 1831

10 I never heard a single expression of fondness for him fall from the lips of any of those who knew him well.

Lord Macaulay 1800–59: letter, 7 June 1831

11 Lord Byron is great only as a poet; as soon as he reflects, he is a child.

Johann Wolfgang von Goethe 1749–1832: Johann Peter Eckermann *Conversations with Goethe* (1836–48)

12 From the poetry of Lord Byron they drew a system of ethics, compounded of misanthropy and voluptuousness, a system in which the two great commandments were, to hate your neighbour, and to love your neighbour's wife.

Lord Macaulay 1800–59: *Essays Contributed to the Edinburgh Review* (1843) 'Moore's *Life of Lord Byron*'

13 What helps it now, that Byron bore,
   With haughty scorn which mocked the smart,
   Through Europe to the Aetolian shore
   The pageant of his bleeding heart?
   That thousands counted every groan,
   And Europe made his woe her own?

Matthew Arnold 1822–88: 'Stanzas from the Grande Chartreuse' (1855)

1 In a room at the end of the garden to this house was a magnificent rocking-horse, which a friend had given my little boy; and Lord Byron, with a childish glee becoming a poet, would ride upon it. Ah! why did he ever ride his Pegasus to less advantage?

Leigh Hunt 1784–1859: *Autobiography* (rev. ed., 1860)

2 Always looking at himself in mirrors to make sure he was sufficiently outrageous.

Enoch Powell 1912–98: in *Sunday Times* 8 May 1988

Thomas Carlyle 1795–1881
Scottish historian and political philosopher

3 As soon as that man's tongue stops, that woman's begins!
of Jane and Thomas Carlyle at one of Samuel Rogers's breakfast parties

Samuel Rogers 1763–1855: Francis Espinasse *Literary Recollections and Sketches* (1893)

4 Carlyle is a poet to whom nature has denied the faculty of verse.

Alfred, Lord Tennyson 1809–92: letter to W. E. Gladstone, c.1870

5 Rugged, mountainous, volcanic, he was himself more a French revolution than any of his volumes.

Walt Whitman 1819–92: *Specimen Days* 10 February 1881

6 I never much liked Carlyle. He seemed to me to be 'carrying coals to Newcastle', as our proverb says; preaching earnestness to a nation which had plenty of it by nature, but was less abundantly supplied with several other useful things.

Matthew Arnold 1822–88: letter, 25 March 1881

7 It was very good of God to let Carlyle and Mrs Carlyle marry one another and so make only two people miserable instead of four.

Samuel Butler 1835–1902: letter, 21 November 1884

8 Carlyle was so poisonous it's a wonder his mind didn't infect his bloodstream.

John Carey 1934– : in *Sunday Times* 1983

Lewis Carroll 1832–98
English writer and logician

9 He was as fond of me as he could be of anyone over the age of ten.

Ellen Terry 1847–1928: Derek Hudson *Lewis Carroll* (1954)

10 On the afternoon of 4 July 1862, in the Long Vacation, a minute expedition set out from Oxford up the river to Godstow. It returned laden with a treasure compared with which that of the *Golden Hind* was but dross.

Walter de la Mare 1873–1956: *Lewis Carroll* (1932)

Catullus c.84–c.54 BC
Roman poet

11 *Gratias tibi maximas Catullus*
Agit pessimus omnium poeta,
Tanto pessimus omnium poeta,
Quanto tu optimus omnium's patronum.
Catullus gives you warmest thanks,
And he the worst of poets ranks;

Catullus c.84–c.54 BC: *Carmina* no. 49, tr. William Marris

As much the worst of bards confessed,
As you of advocates the best.
letter of thanks to Cicero

1 There beneath the Roman ruin where the purple flowers
  grow,
Came that 'Ave atque Vale' of the Poet's hopeless woe,
Tenderest of Roman poets nineteen-hundred years ago,
'Frater Ave atque Vale'—as we wander'd to and fro
Gazing at the Lydian laughter of the Garda Lake below
Sweet Catullus's all-but-island, olive-silvery Sirmio!

Alfred, Lord Tennyson 1809–92:
Tiresias (1885) 'Frater Ave atque Vale'

Censorship

2 He who breaks this tablet or puts it in water or rubs it
until you cannot recognize it [and] cannot make it be
understood, may Ashur, Sin, Shamash, Adad and Ishtar,
Bel, Nergal, Ishtar of Nineveh, Ishtar of Arbela, Ishtar of
Bit Kidmurri, the gods of heaven and earth and the gods of
Assyria, may all these curse him with a curse which
cannot be relieved, terrible and merciless, as long as he
lives, may they let his name, his seed, be carried off from
the land, may they put his flesh in a dog's mouth!

Anonymous: inscription on clay
tablet found in ruins of royal palace
at Ashur, Assyria, 7th–3rd century BC;
Lionel Casson *Libraries in the Ancient
World* (2001)

3 Tell it not in Gath, publish it not in the streets of Askelon;
lest the daughters of the Philistines rejoice.

Bible: II Samuel

4   'Pictoribus atque poetis
Quidlibet audendi semper fuit aequa potestas.'
Scimus, et hanc veniam petimusque damusque vicissim.

'Painters and poets alike have always had licence to dare
anything.' We know that, and we both claim and permit
others this indulgence.

Horace 65–8 BC: *Ars Poetica*

5 I beg you, read my verses with the same
Face as you watch Latinus on the stage
Or Thymele the dancer. Harmless wit
You may, as Censor, reasonably permit:
My life is strict, however lax my page.

Martial AD c.40–c.104: *Epigrammata*
tr. James Michie

6 As good almost kill a man as kill a good book: who kills a
man kills a reasonable creature, God's image; but he who
destroys a good book, kills reason itself, kills the image of
God, as it were in the eye.

John Milton 1608–74: *Areopagitica*
(1644)

7 If we think to regulate printing, thereby to rectify
manners, we must regulate all recreations and pastimes,
all that is delightful to man . . . And who shall silence all
the airs and madrigals, that whisper softness in chambers?

John Milton 1608–74: *Areopagitica*
(1644)

8 I disapprove of what you say, but I will defend to the death
your right to say it.
*his attitude towards Helvétius following the burning of the
latter's* De l'esprit *in 1759*

Voltaire 1694–1778: attributed to
Voltaire, the words are in fact S. G.
Tallentyre's summary; *The Friends of
Voltaire* (1907)

9 The jaws of power are always opened to devour, and her
arm is always stretched out, if possible, to destroy the
freedom of thinking, speaking, and writing.

John Adams 1735–1826: *A
Dissertation on the Canon and the
Feudal Law* (1765)

1 No government ought to be without censors: and where the press is free, no one ever will.

Thomas Jefferson 1743–1826: letter to George Washington, 9 September 1792

2 Wherever books will be burned, men also, in the end, are burned.

Heinrich Heine 1797–1856: *Almansor* (1823)

3 Neither Bowdler's, Chambers's, Brandram's, nor Cundell's 'Boudoir' Shakespeare, seems to me to meet the want: they are not sufficiently 'expurgated'. Bowdler's is the most extraordinary of all: looking through it, I am filled with a deep sense of wonder, considering what he has left in, that he should have cut *anything* out.

Lewis Carroll 1832–98: preface to *Sylvie and Bruno* (1889); see **93:2**

4 It takes away any desire you have to express yourself freely; whenever you write, you get a feeling there's a bone stuck in your throat.
   on Russian censorship

Anton Chekhov 1860–1904: letter, 19 January 1895

5 Imagine the future historian writing in wonderment of the absurd reticence with which our novelists treat sexual subjects, and comparing this with their licence to describe in detail the most hideous of murders.

George Gissing 1857–1903: *Commonplace Book* (1962)

6 Assassination is the extreme form of censorship.

George Bernard Shaw 1856–1950: *The Showing-Up of Blanco Posnet* (1911)

7 Writers often achieve a power of concentration which political liberty or literary anarchy would have allowed them to escape, when they are constrained by the tyranny of a monarch or of a poetic, by the strictness of prosodic rules or of the official religion.

Marcel Proust 1871–1922: *Guermantes Way* (1921)

8 I think you can leave the arts, superior or inferior, to the general conscience of mankind.
   on the censorship of films

W. B. Yeats 1865–1939: speech in the Irish Senate, 1923

9 If we can't stamp out literature in the country, we can at least stop its being brought in from outside.
   a Customs officer's view

Evelyn Waugh 1903–66: *Vile Bodies* (1930)

10 *All* fiction . . . is censored in the interests of the ruling class.

George Orwell 1903–50: in *Horizon* March 1940

11 Wherever there is an enforced orthodoxy—or even two orthodoxies, as often happens—good writing stops.

George Orwell 1903–50: 'The Prevention of Literature' (1946)

12 It's red hot, mate. I hate to think of this sort of book getting into the wrong hands. As soon as I've finished this, I shall recommend they ban it.
   words spoken by Tony Hancock

Ray Galton 1929– and **Alan Simpson** 1930– : 'The Missing Page', *Hancock's Half Hour* (BBC) 26 February 1960

13 Freedom of the press is guaranteed only to those who own one.

A. J. Liebling 1904–63: 'The Wayward Press: Do you belong in Journalism?' (1960)

14 If decade after decade the truth cannot be told, each person's mind begins to roam irretrievably. One's fellow countrymen become harder to understand than Martians.

Alexander Solzhenitsyn 1918– : *Cancer Ward* (1968)

15 I'm all in favour of free expression provided it's kept rigidly under control.

Alan Bennett 1934– : *Forty Years On* (1969)

1 Woe to that nation whose literature is cut short by the intrusion of force. This is not merely interference with freedom of the press but the sealing up of a nation's heart, the excision of its memory.

Alexander Solzhenitsyn 1918– : in *Time* 25 February 1974

2 I dislike censorship. Like an appendix it is useless when inert and dangerous when active.

Maurice Edelman 1911–75: attributed, 1982

3 Censorship, like charity, should begin at home, but, unlike charity, it should end there.

Clare Booth Luce 1903–87: attributed, 1982

4 A censor is a man who knows more than he thinks you ought to.

Laurence J. Peter 1919– : attributed, 1982

5 I suppose that writers should, in a way, feel flattered by the censorship laws. They show a primitive fear and dread at the fearful magic of print.

John Mortimer 1923– : *Clinging to the Wreckage* (1982)

6 I would like to inform all the intrepid Muslims in the world that the author of the book entitled *The Satanic Verses*, which has been compiled, printed and published in opposition to Islam, the Prophet and the Qur'an, as well as those publishers who were aware of its contents, have been declared *madhur el dam* [those whose blood must be shed]. I call on all zealous Muslims to execute them quickly, wherever they find them, so that no-one will dare to insult Islam again. Whoever is killed in this path will be regarded as a martyr.
  *fatwa against Salman **Rushdie***

Ruhollah Khomeini 1900–89: issued 14 February 1989; Malise Ruthven *A Satanic Affair* (1990); see **41:7, 229:1**

7 The Khomeini cry for the execution of Rushdie is an infantile cry. From the beginning of time we have seen that. To murder the thinker does not murder the thought.

Arnold Wesker 1932– : in *Weekend Guardian* 3 June 1989; see **41:6**

8 What is freedom of expression? Without the freedom to offend, it ceases to exist.

Salman Rushdie 1947– : in *Weekend Guardian* 10 February 1990

9 It's very, very easy not to be offended by a book. You just have to shut it.

Salman Rushdie 1947– : in *Daily Telegraph* 8 October 1994 'They Said It'

10 I believe that political correctness can be a form of linguistic fascism, and it sends shivers down the spine of my generation who went to war against fascism.

P. D. James 1920– : in *Paris Review* 1995

Cervantes 1547–1616
Spanish novelist

11 Cervantes on his galley sets the sword back in the sheath
(*Don John of Austria rides homeward with a wreath.*)
And he sees across a weary land a straggling road in
    Spain,
Up which a lean and foolish knight forever rides in vain,
And he smiles, but not as Sultans smile, and settles back
    the blade . . .

G. K. Chesterton 1874–1936: 'Lepanto' (1915)

12 He has ridden for three hundred and fifty years through the jungles and tundras of human thought—and he has gained in vitality and stature. We do not laugh at him any longer. His blazon is pity, his banner is beauty. He stands

Vladimir Nabokov 1899–1977: Fredson Bowers (ed.) *Lectures on Don Quixote* (1983)

for everything that is gentle, forlorn, pure, unselfish, and
gallant.

1 If there is one novel you should read before you die, it is
Don Quixote.
   announcing the result of a poll of 100 famous authors for
   '*the most meaningful book of all time*'

Ben Okri 1959– : speech, Nobel
Institute, 7 May 2002

Raymond Chandler 1888–1959
American writer of detective fiction

2 If my books had been any worse, I should not have been
invited to Hollywood, and if they had been any better, I
should not have come.

Raymond Chandler 1888–1959:
letter to Charles W. Morton, 12
December 1945

3 Having just read the admirable profile of Hemingway in
the *New Yorker* I realize that I am much too clean to be a
genius, much too sober to be a champ, and far, far too
clumsy with a shotgun to live the good life.

Raymond Chandler 1888–1959:
Philip Durham *Down These Mean
Streets a Man Must Go* (1963)

Characters

4 I must confess that I think her as delightful a creature as
ever appeared in print, and how I shall be able to tolerate
those who do not like *her* at least I do not know.
   of '*Elizabeth Bennet*'

Jane Austen 1775–1817: letter, 29
January 1813

5 I am going to take a heroine whom no-one but myself will
much like.
   on starting Emma

Jane Austen 1775–1817: J. E. Austen-
Leigh *A Memoir of Jane Austen* (1926
ed.)

6 Shakespeare's characters are men; Ben Jonson's are more
like machines, governed by mere routine, or by the
convenience of the poet, whose property they are.

William Hazlitt 1778–1830: *Lectures
on the English Comic Writers* (1818)

7 The effect of reading this work is like an increase of
kindred. You find yourself all of a sudden introduced into
the midst of a large family . . . people whose real existence
and personal identity you can no more dispute than your
own senses, for you see and hear all that they do or say.
   on Richardson's Sir Charles Grandison

William Hazlitt 1778–1830: *Lectures
on the English Comic Writers* (1818)

8 I draw from life—but I always pulp my acquaintance
before serving them up. You would never recognize a pig
in a sausage.

Frances Trollope 1780–1863:
remark, c.1848; S. Baring-Gould *Early
Reminiscences 1834-1864* (1923)

9 You are not to suppose any of the characters in *Shirley*
intended as literal portraits . . . We only suffer reality to
suggest, never to *dictate*.

Charlotte Brontë 1816–55: letter to
Ellen Nussey, 16 November 1849

10 My poor Bovary, without a doubt, is suffering and weeping
at this very hour in twenty villages in France.

Gustave Flaubert 1821–80: letter, 14
August 1853

11 If she had been faultless, she could not have been the
heroine of this story; for I think some wise man of old
remarked, that the perfect women were those who left no
histories behind them.

Mary Elizabeth Braddon 1837–1915:
Aurora Floyd (1863)

1 It was with many misgivings that I killed my old friend Mrs Proudie. I could not, I think, have done it, but for a resolution taken and declared under circumstances of great momentary pressure.

Anthony Trollope 1815–82: *Autobiography* (1883)

2 I have lived with my characters, and thence has come whatever success I have attained.

Anthony Trollope 1815–82: *Autobiography* (1883)

3 It is not improbabilities of incident but improbabilities of character that matter.

Thomas Hardy 1840–1928: *The Mayor of Casterbridge* (1886)

4 We can only vary our characters by altering the age, the sex, the social position, and all the circumstances of life, of that *ego* which nature has in fact enclosed in an insurmountable barrier of organs of sense. Skill consists in not betraying this *ego* to the reader, under the various masks which we employ to cover it.

Guy de Maupassant 1850–93: preface to *Pierre et Jean* (1887)

5 What is character but the determination of incident? What is incident but the illustration of character?

Henry James 1843–1916: 'The Art of Fiction' (1888)

6 My souls (or characters) are conglomerates, made up of past and present stages of civilization, scraps of humanity, torn-off pieces of Sunday clothing turned into rags—all patched together as is the human soul itself.

Johan August Strindberg 1849–1912: preface to *Miss Julie* (1888)

7 When you think of Tolstoy's Anna Karenina, all Turgenev's gentlewomen with their seductive shoulders vanish into thin air.

Anton Chekhov 1860–1904: letter, 24 February 1893

8 In every first novel the hero is the author as Christ or Faust.

Oscar Wilde 1854–1900: attributed

9 Six characters in search of an author.

Luigi Pirandello 1867–1936: title of play (1921)

10 When the characters are alive, really alive before their author, the latter merely follows them in the words and actions which they in fact suggest to him.

Luigi Pirandello 1867–1936: *Six Characters in Search of an Author* (1921)

11 We may divide [fictional] characters into flat and round . . . The test of a round character is whether it is capable of surprising in a convincing way. If it never surprises, it is flat. If it does not convince, it is flat pretending to be round.

E. M. Forster 1879–1970: *Aspects of the Novel* (1927)

12 When writing a novel a writer should create living people; people not characters. A *character* is a caricature.

Ernest Hemingway 1899–1961: *Death in the Afternoon* (1932)

13 I have just got a letter asking me why I don't give Bloom a rest. The writer of it wants more Stephen. But Stephen no longer interests me to the same extent. He has a shape that can't be changed.

James Joyce 1882–1941: Frank Budgen *James Joyce and the Making of Ulysses* (1934)

14 True writers encounter their characters only *after* they've created them.

Elias Canetti 1905–94: *The Human Province* (1973) notebook 1946

15 People in life hardly seem definite enough to appear in print.

Ivy Compton-Burnett 1884–1969: attributed in *Times Literary Supplement* 29 May 1982

16 But really, the way we writers knock our characters about! There ought to be a society to protect them. We have them bound, gagged, raped, tortured, shipwrecked and murdered . . . I myself have stood by while my own characters were subjected to the most ridiculous

Michael Frayn 1933– : *Constructions* (1974)

humiliations. They're our herd of swine. We cast out all our devils into them, and then ritually destroy them.

1 Each writer is born with a repertory company in his head. Shakespeare has perhaps twenty players, and Tennessee Williams has about five, and Samuel Beckett one—and maybe a clone of that one. I have ten or so, and that's a lot. As you get older, you become more skilful at casting them.

Gore Vidal 1925– : in *Times Herald* (Dallas) 18 June 1978

2 I have to watch my characters crossing the room, lighting a cigarette. I have to see everything they do, even if I don't write it down. So my eyes get tired.

Graham Greene 1904–91: interview with John Mortimer in *Sunday Times* 16 March 1980

3 The main characters in a novel must necessarily have some kinship to the author, they come out of his body as a child comes from the womb, then the umbilical cord is cut.

Graham Greene 1904–91: *Ways of Escape* (1980)

4 She moves out of our minds as easily as she moves out of Harrods.
of Virginia Woolf's 'Mrs Dalloway'

Graham Greene 1904–91: Marie-Françoise Allain *The Other Man, Conversations with Graham Greene* (1983)

5 Show me a character totally without anxieties and I will show you a boring book.

Margaret Atwood 1939– : Geoff Hancock *Canadian Writers at Work* (1986) 'Tightrope-Walking over Niagara Falls'

6 All characters in this story are imaginary and no reference is intended to any living person. Readers who think that they can identify the creations of the author's fancy among their own acquaintance are paying the author an extravagant compliment, which he acknowledges with gratitude.
disclaimer at the beginning of the novel

Robertson Davies 1913–95: *Tempest-Tost* (1986)

7 I sometimes lose interest in the characters and get much more interested in the trees and animals.

Toni Morrison 1931– : George Plimpton (ed.) *The Writer's Chapbook* (1989)

8 I always think of my novels as being the lives of the characters.

Patrick White 1912–90: *Patrick White Speaks* (1990)

9 I'm not too keen on characters taking over; they do as they are damn well told.

Iain Banks 1954– : Stan Nicholls (ed.) *Wordsmiths of Wonder* (1993)

10 I don't go round looking for material from my life that will make a novel, nor do I turn people whom I know into characters. Once I have invented characters I see things through their eyes.

Graham Swift 1949– : Clare Boylan (ed.) *The Agony and the Ego* (1993); attributed

11 Once a character has gelled it's an unmistakable sensation, like an engine starting up within one's body. From then onwards one is driven by this other person, seeing things through their eyes, shuffling round the shops as a 57-year-old man and practically feeling one has grown a beard.

Deborah Moggach 1948– : Clare Boylan (ed.) *The Agony and the Ego* (1993)

12 Inventing really evil people is great fun. It is difficult to make a good person attractive and not boring.

Mary Wesley 1912–2002: attributed, 1995

13 A lot of people have written saying that I have let them down, I've been so cruel. Well, I loved him too.
on killing off Inspector Morse

Colin Dexter 1930– : in *Observer* 16 July 2000

1 I suppose the first realistically flawed actors on the narrative stage were in the Bible. There is precious little perfection of character in the Old Testament.

Rosellen Brown : in *Writers on Writing: Collected Essays from The New York Times* (2001)

2 There's the phenomenon well known to writers whose characters, given their head, take off and do or say things the writer did not foresee. The writing has a Ouija board will of its own.

Diane Johnson 1934– : in *Writers on Writing: Collected Essays from The New York Times* (2001)

3 There were no innocent blondes in crime fiction.
on writing for the crime magazines

Ed McBain 1926– : in *Writers on Writing: Collected Essays from The New York Times* (2001)

4 Often I feel when I'm writing certain characters and their traits that I have already seen them on TV. In sitcoms or whatever.

Zadie Smith 1975– : in *Observer* 25 August 2002

Thomas Chatterton 1752–70
English poet, fabricator of the Rowley poems by a supposed 15th-century monk

5 He was an instance that a complete genius and a complete rogue can be formed before a man is of age.

Horace Walpole 1717–97: letter to William Mason, 24 July 1778

6 I thought of Chatterton, the marvellous boy,
The sleepless soul that perished in its pride.

William Wordsworth 1770–1850: 'Resolution and Independence' (1807)

Geoffrey Chaucer c.1343–1400
English poet

7 The worshipful father and first founder and embellisher of ornate eloquence in our English, I mean Master Geoffrey Chaucer.

William Caxton c.1421–91: Caxton's edition (c.1478) of Chaucer's translation of Boethius *De Consolacione Philosophie*

8 Dan Chaucer, well of English undefiled,
On Fame's eternal beadroll worthy to be filed.

Edmund Spenser c.1552–99: *The Faerie Queen* (1596)

9 'Tis sufficient to say, according to the proverb, that here is God's plenty.

John Dryden 1631–1700: *Fables Ancient and Modern* (1700)

10 Of all English writers Chaucer is the clearest. He is as precise and slick as a Frenchman.

James Joyce 1882–1941: Frank Budgen *James Joyce and the Making of Ulysses* (1934)

Anton Chekhov 1860–1904 see also 309:4
Russian dramatist and short-story writer

11 My country house is full of people, they never leave me alone; if only they would go away I could be a good writer.
written towards the end of his life

Anton Chekhov 1860–1904: attributed

12 You know I can't stand Shakespeare's plays, but yours are even worse.
remark to Chekhov, after seeing Uncle Vanya

Leo Tolstoy 1828–1910: P. P. Gnedich *Kniga Zhizni Vospominaniya* (1929)

1 All Russians are brutal, except Chekhov. People dislike his plays as they are all about nothing. *I* like them very much.
in conversation with fellow-novelist Elizabeth Taylor

Ivy Compton-Burnett 1884–1969: A. N. Wilson *Penfriends from Porlock* (1988)

2 Chekhov must have been the sanest person in 19th-century Europe. He was sanity raised to the power of genius.

John Carey 1934– : in *Sunday Times* 1987

G. K. Chesterton 1874–1936 see also **18:5**, **92:7**
English essayist, novelist, and poet

3 Chesterton is like a vile scum on a pond . . . all his slop—it is really modern Catholicism to a great extent, the *never* taking a hedge straight, the mumbo-jumbo of superstition dodging behind clumsy fun and paradox . . . I believe he creates a milieu in which art is impossible.

Ezra Pound 1885–1972: letter to John Quinn, 21 August 1917

4 Chesterton's resolute conviviality is about as genial as an *auto da fé* of teetotallers.

George Bernard Shaw 1856–1950: *Pen Portraits and Reviews* (1932)

5 My real judgement of my own work is that I have spoilt a number of jolly good ideas in my time.

G. K. Chesterton 1874–1936: *Autobiography* (1936)

6 Chesterton had a body like a slag heap, but a mind like the dawn sky. He saw the world new, as if he'd just landed from another planet.

John Carey 1934– : in *Sunday Times* 1978

Children's Literature

7 What toys, the daily reading of such a book, may work in the will of a young gentleman, or a young maid . . . wise men can judge, and honest men do pity.
of Malory's Le Morte D'Arthur *as unsuitable reading for the young*

Roger Ascham 1515–68: *The Schoolmaster* (1570)

8 As an actor does his part,
So the nurses get by heart
Namby-pamby's little rhymes,
Little jingle, little chimes.

Henry Carey c.1687–1743: 'Namby-Pamby' (1725)

9 Too rigid precepts
often fail,
Where short amusing
tales prevail.
The author doubtless
aims aright
Who joins instruction
with delight.

Thomas Boreman fl. 1730–34: in *Oxford Companion to Children's Literature*

10 Babies do not want to hear about babies; they like to be told of giants and castles, and of somewhat which can stretch and stimulate their little minds.

Samuel Johnson 1709–84: Hester Lynch Piozzi *Anecdotes of . . . Johnson* (1786)

11 Remember always that the parents buy the books, and that the children never read them.

Samuel Johnson 1709–84: Hester Lynch Piozzi *Anecdotes of . . . Johnson* (1786)

12 It is children that read children's books (when they are read); but it is parents that choose them.

William Godwin 1756–1836: letter to Charles Lamb, 10 March 1808

1 Never in all my early childhood, did anyone address to me the affecting preamble, 'Once upon a time!' I was told about missionaries, but never about pirates; I was familiar with humming-birds, but I had never heard of fairies.

Edmund Gosse 1849–1928: *Father and Son* (1907)

2 No one can write a book which children will like, unless he write it for himself first.

A. A. Milne 1882–1956: *Once on a Time* (ed. 2, 1925) preface

3 Young people are gluttons for detail and have an acute sense of what is fit and proper in that respect.

John Buchan 1875–1940: *The Novel and the Fairy Tale* (1931)

4 Since the tales had to be read by children, before people realized that they were meant for grown-ups . . . I worked the material in three or four overlaid tints and textures, which might or might not reveal themselves according to the shifting light of sex, youth, and experience. It was like working lacquer and mother o' pearl, a natural combination, into the same scheme as niello and grisaille, and trying not to let the joins show.

Rudyard Kipling 1865–1936: *Something of Myself* (1937)

5 It is worth noting a rather curious fact, and that is that the school story is a thing peculiar to England. So far as I know, there are extremely few school stories in foreign languages.

George Orwell 1903–50: 'Boys' Weeklies' (1939)

6 What do we ever get nowadays from reading to equal the excitement and the revelation in those first fourteen years?

Graham Greene 1904–91: *The Lost Childhood* (1951)

7 Children prefer incident to character; if character is to be drawn, it must be done broadly, in tar or whitewash.

A. A. Milne 1882–1956: *Once on a Time* (1965 ed.); introduction

8 It may be better for them to read some things, especially fairy-stories, that are beyond their measure rather than short of it. Their books like their clothes should allow for growth, and their books at any rate should encourage it.

J. R. R. Tolkien 1892–1973: *Tree and Leaf* (1964) 'On Fairy-Stories'

9 Publishers and authors seem to think that the smaller the child, the larger the book must be—for what reason, since their arms are short and their eyesight usually at its best, it is hard to imagine.

Penelope Mortimer 1918– : 'Thoughts Concerning Children's Books' (1966)

10 Revolts may come, revolts may go, but brats go on forever. And I would like to do a perfectly stunning brat book!

Arthur Ransome 1884–1967: A. N. Wilson *Penfriends from Porlock* (1988)

11 Political history is far too criminal and pathological to be a fit subject of study of the young. Children should acquire their heroes and villains from fiction.

W. H. Auden 1907–73: attributed

12 Teenagers are natural pessimists (and who should blame them?) . . . The teenage novel has a duty to portray the successive tidal waves of feeling that wash over adolescents.

Joan Aiken 1924– : *The Way to Write for Children* (1982)

13 Victorian children's stories are full of children who cannot read anywhere except in a deeply embrasured window seat.

Robertson Davies 1913–95: lecture, Yale, 20 February 1990

14 [Many] authors of juvenile classics . . . have had the ability to look at the world from below and note its less respectable aspects, just as little children playing on the floor can see the chewing gum stuck to the underside of polished mahogany tables and the hems of silk dresses held up with safety pins.

Alison Lurie 1926– : *Don't Tell The Grown-Ups* (1990)

1 Children's literature is a strange phenomenon. It is something that virtually all of us come across; it involves millions of pounds changing hands and yet very few adults take it seriously.

Michael Rosen 1946– : introduction to Michael Rosen and Jill Burridge *Treasure Islands 2* (1993)

2 An idea will come to me as a concentrated short burst, comparable to poems as opposed to prose. Then it seems right for a children's book. Sometimes, it's because the matter of which I'm writing is too deep or too metaphysical for adults.

Russell Hoban 1925– : Michael Rosen and Jill Burridge *Treasure Islands 2* (1993)

3 You know how it is in the kids' book world; it's just bunny eat bunny.

Anonymous: unattributed comment; Julia Vitullo-Martin and J. Robert Moskin (eds.) *The Executive's Book of Quotations* (1994)

4 One does not write *for* children. One writes so that children can understand. Which means writing as clearly, vividly and truthfully as possible. Adults might put up with occasional lapses; children are far less tolerant.

Leon Garfield 1921–96: in his obituary, *Daily Telegraph* 4 June 1996

5 When you are writing for children, the story is more important than you are. You can't be self-conscious, you just have to get out of the way.

Philip Pullman 1946– : interview in *Bookseller* 9 August 1996

6 The powerful attraction, of course, was the compelling combination of words and pictures in boxes strung out across the page. Text written in speech balloons is inexplicably easy to read.
   on children's comics

Shirley Hughes 1927– : *A Life Drawing* (2002)

7 In these more anxious times when children are more closely guarded we are severely limited as to plots. Publishers' fear of depicting anything in the least dangerous has reached a point where stories for the young child tend to be somewhat bland. A stark contrast to young adult fiction which seems to be pushing limits in the opposite direction.

Shirley Hughes 1927– : *A Life Drawing* (2002)

Choice of Words see also Style

8 A word fitly spoken is like apples of gold in pictures of silver.

Bible: Proverbs

9 You will have written exceptionally well if, by skilful arrangement of your words, you have made an ordinary one seem original.

Horace 65–8 BC: *Ars Poetica*

10 I have revered always not crude verbosity, but holy simplicity.

St Jerome c.AD 342–420: letter 'Ad Pammachium'

11 A loose, plain, rude writer . . . I call a spade a spade.

Robert Burton 1577–1640: *The Anatomy of Melancholy* (1621–51)

12 His words . . . like so many nimble and airy servitors trip about him at command.

John Milton 1608–74: *An Apology for Smectymnuus* (1642)

13 A thing well said will be wit in all languages.

John Dryden 1631–1700: *An Essay of Dramatic Poesy* (1668)

14 True ease in writing comes from art, not chance,
   As those move easiest who have learned to dance.
   'Tis not enough no harshness gives offence,
   The sound must seem an echo to the sense.

Alexander Pope 1688–1744: *An Essay on Criticism* (1711)

1 Apt Alliteration's artful aid.

Charles Churchill 1731–64: *The Prophecy of Famine* (1763)

2 Don't, Sir, accustom yourself to use big words for little matters. It would *not* be *terrible*, though I *were* to be detained some time here.
   when Boswell said it would be 'terrible' if Johnson should not be able to return speedily from Harwich

Samuel Johnson 1709–84: James Boswell *Life of Samuel Johnson* (1791) 6 August 1763

3 Dialect words—those terrible marks of the beast to the truly genteel.

Thomas Hardy 1840–1928: *The Mayor of Casterbridge* (1886)

4 How often misused words generate misleading thoughts.

Herbert Spencer 1820–1903: *Principles of Ethics* (1879)

5 His life was that of a pearl-diver, breathless in the thick element while he groped for the priceless word, and condemned to plunge again and again. He passed it in reconstructing sentences, exterminating repetitions, calculating and comparing cadences, harmonious *chutes de phrases*, and beating about the bush to deal death to the abominable assonance.
   *of **Flaubert***

Henry James 1843–1916: 'Gustave Flaubert' (1893)

6 I knew exactly what I had got to say, put the words firmly in their places like so many stitches, hemmed the edges of chapters round with what seemed to me the graceful flourishes, touched them finally with my cunningest points of colour, and read the work to papa and mamma at breakfast next morning, as a girl shows her sampler.

John Ruskin 1819–1900: in *Dictionary of National Biography* (1917–)

7 An average English word is four letters and a half. By hard, honest labour I've dug all the large words out of my vocabulary and shaved them down till the average is three and a half letters . . . I never write metropolis for seven cents because I can get the same money for city. I never write policeman, because I can get the same money for *Cop*.

Mark Twain 1835–1910: *Mark Twain's Speeches* (1923)

8 The minute a phrase becomes current it becomes an apology for not thinking accurately to the end of the sentence.

Oliver Wendell Holmes Jr. 1841–1935: letter to Harold Laski, 2 July 1917

9 I could not write the words Mr Joyce uses: my prudish hands would refuse to form the letters.

George Bernard Shaw 1856–1950: *Table Talk of G. B. S.* (1925)

10 And it is that word 'hummy', my darlings, that marks the first place in 'The House at Pooh Corner' at which Tonstant Weader fwowed up.

Dorothy Parker 1893–1967: review as 'Constant Reader' in *New Yorker* 20 October 1928

11 All my life I have nearly always known *what* to write, but since I tried to get it all on twelve pages, since I have restricted myself in this way, I have had to pick and choose words that are, first, significant; second, simple; and third, beautiful.

Isaac Babel 1894–1940: interview, Union of Soviet Writers, 28 September 1937

12 Trying to learn to use words, and every attempt
   Is a wholly new start, and a different kind of failure
   Because one has only learnt to get the better of words

T. S. Eliot 1888–1965: *East Coker* (1940); see **329:15**

For the thing one no longer has to say, or the way in
  which
One is no longer disposed to say it.

1 Words are chameleons, which reflect the colour of their
environment.

Learned Hand 1872–1961: in
*Commissioner v. National Carbide
Corp.* (1948)

2 We must use words as they are used or stand aside from
life.

Ivy Compton-Burnett 1884–1969:
Mother and Son (1955)

3 The phrase . . . a clutch of words that gives you a clutch at
the heart.
  when asked about the basic point to all fine writing

Robert Frost 1874–1963: interview in
1960; E. Connery Latham (ed.)
Interviews with Robert Frost (1967)

4 They're perfect sentences. Very direct sentences, smooth
rivers, clear water over granite, no sinkholes.
  *of **Hemingway**'s* A Farewell to Arms

Joan Didion 1934– : George
Plimpton (ed.) *The Writer's Chapbook*
(1989)

Agatha Christie 1890–1976
English writer of detective fiction

5 Agatha's best work is, like P. G. Wodehouse and Noel
Coward's best work, the most characteristic pleasure-
writing of this epoch and will appear one day in all decent
literary histories. As *writing* it is not distinguished, but as
story it is superb.

Robert Graves 1895–1985: letter, 16
July 1944

6 I'm a sausage machine, a perfect sausage machine.

Agatha Christie 1890–1976: G. C.
Ramsey *Agatha Christie* (1972)

7 She shows us the ace of spades face up. Then she turns it
over, but we still know where it is, so how has it been
transformed into the five of diamonds?

Julian Symons 1912–94: *Bloody
Murder* (1972)

Closing Lines see also Opening Lines

8 *L'amor che muove il sole e l'altre stelle.*
  The love that moves the sun and the other stars.

Dante Alighieri 1265–1321: *Divina
Commedia* 'Paradiso'

9 The world was all before them, where to choose
Their place of rest, and Providence their guide:
They hand in hand, with wandering steps and slow,
Through Eden took their solitary way.

John Milton 1608–74: *Paradise Lost*
(1667)

10 And so I betake myself to that course, which is almost as
much as to see myself go into my grave—for which, and
all the discomforts that will accompany my being blind,
the good God prepare me!

Samuel Pepys 1633–1703: *Diary* 31
May 1669

11 Silent, upon a peak in Darien.

John Keats 1795–1821: 'On First
Looking into Chapman's Homer'
(1817); see **126:1**

12 I lingered round them, under that benign sky: watched the
moths fluttering among the heath and hare-bells; listened
to the soft wind breathing through the grass; and
wondered how any one could ever imagine unquiet
slumbers for the sleepers in that quiet earth.

Emily Brontë 1818–48: *Wuthering
Heights* (1847)

13 Come, children, let us shut up the box and the puppets, for
our play is played out.

William Makepeace Thackeray
1811–63: *Vanity Fair* (1847–8)

1 And they lived happily ever after.
   traditional ending to a fairy story

Anonymous: recorded (with slight variations) from the 1850s

2 And the new sun rose bringing the new year.

Alfred, Lord Tennyson 1809–92: *Idylls of the King* 'The Passing of Arthur' (1869)

3 'Justice' was done, and the President of the Immortals (in Aeschylean phrase) had ended his sport with Tess.

Thomas Hardy 1840–1928: *Tess of the D'Urbervilles* (1891)

4 After all, tomorrow is another day.

Margaret Mitchell 1900–49: *Gone with the Wind* (1936)

5 The creatures outside looked from pig to man, and from man to pig, and from pig to man again, but already it was impossible to say which was which.

George Orwell 1903–50: *Animal Farm* (1945)

6 So that, in the end, there was no end.

Patrick White 1912–90: *The Tree of Man* (1955)

7 Overhead, without any fuss, the stars were going out.

Arthur C. Clarke 1917– : 'The Nine Billion Names of God' (1967)

8 The stars are indispensable.

Philip Roth 1933– : *I Married a Communist* (1998)

9 Let this give man hope.

Ted Hughes 1930–98: *Alcestis/ Euripides* (1999)

10 And so I set these things down before the onset of the first of a thousand small physical degradations as, in a still-distant suburb, Death strides whistling towards me.

Barry Humphries 1934– : *My Life As Me* (2002)

Samuel Taylor Coleridge 1772–1834
English poet, critic, and philosopher

11 Cultivate simplicity, Coleridge.

Charles Lamb 1775–1834: letter to Coleridge, 8 November 1796

12 Coleridge dined with us. He brought his ballad [*The Ancient Mariner*] finished. A beautiful evening, very starry, the horned moon.

Dorothy Wordsworth 1771–1855: 'Alfoxden Journal' 23 March 1798

13 An Archangel a little damaged.

Charles Lamb 1775–1834: letter to Wordsworth, 26 April 1816

14 Coleridge, for instance, would let go by a fine isolated verisimilitude caught from the penetralium of mystery, from being incapable of remaining content with half knowledge.

John Keats 1795–1821: letter to George and Thomas Keats, 21 December 1817

15 He talked on for ever; and you wished him to talk on for ever.

William Hazlitt 1778–1830: *Lectures on the English Poets* (1818)

16 You will see Coleridge—he who sits obscure . . .
A cloud-encircled meteor of the air,
A hooded eagle among blinking owls.

Percy Bysshe Shelley 1792–1822: 'Letter to Maria Gisborne' (1820)

17 And Coleridge, too, has lately taken wing,
But, like a hawk encumbered with his hood,
Explaining metaphysics to the nation—
I wish he would explain his explanation.

Lord Byron 1788–1824: *Don Juan* (1819–24)

1 The owner of a mind which keeps open house, and entertains all comers.

William Hazlitt 1778–1830: *The Spirit of the Age* (1825)

2 His forehead was prodigious—a great piece of placid marble; and his fine eyes, in which all the activity of his mind seemed to concentrate, moved under it with a sprightly ease, as if it was pastime to them to carry all that thought.

Leigh Hunt 1784–1859: *Autobiography* (1850)

3 Amputated kind of completeness.
  of Coleridge's fragmentary 'The Ballad of the Dark Ladie'

Ted Hughes 1930–98: *A Choice of Coleridge's Verse* (ed. Hughes, 1996)

Colette 1873–1954
French novelist

4 Colette wrote of vegetables as if they were love objects and of sex as if it were an especially delightful department of gardening.

Brigid Brophy 1929–95: Anne Stibbs (ed.) *Like a Fish Needs a Bicycle* (1992)

Collaboration

5 I thought that working with him would keep under the particular devil that spoils my work for me as quick as I turn it out.
  on collaborating with Ford Madox Ford; see **52:7**

Joseph Conrad 1857–1924: 18 October 1898

6 Two men wrote a lexicon, Liddell and Scott;
  Some parts were clever, but some parts were not.
  Hear, all ye learned, and read me this riddle,
  How the wrong part wrote Scott, and the right part wrote Liddell.
  of Henry Liddell (1811–98) and Robert Scott (1811–87) co-authors of the Greek Lexicon *(1843), Liddell being in the habit of ascribing to his co-author usages which he criticised in his pupils, and which they said that they had culled from the* Lexicon

Edward Waterfield: L. E. Tanner *Westminster School: A History* (1934)

7 For hours after I had gone to bed the voices would reach me through the floor. Sometimes the tones would appear to mingle in pleasant accord, their ideas flowing easily, amused laughs and chuckles. At others sounds of wordy strife and disagreement penetrated to my ears, and raised voices came distinctly into my room. Then F. M. H., who was a very tall man, would relieve his feelings by thumping the oaken beam that crossed the ceiling below and my small son would stir in his sleep and mutter sleepily: 'Mama, dear, moo-cows down there.'
  on Conrad's collaboration with Ford Madox Ford; see **52:5**

Jessie Conrad: *Joseph Conrad and his Circle* (1935)

8 'Who wrote that song?'
  'Rodgers and Hammerstein. If you can imagine it taking *two* men to write one song.'
  of 'Some Enchanted Evening' (1949)

Cole Porter 1891–1964: G. Eells *The Life that Late He Led* (1967)

1 Our work was done conversationally. One or the other—
not infrequently both simultaneously—would state a
proposition. This would be argued, combated perhaps,
approved or modified; it would be written down by the
(wholly fortuitous) holder of the pen, would be scratched
out, scribbled in again.
  on writing with Martin Ross

Edith Œ Somerville 1858–1949:
William Trevor *Excursions in the Real
World* (1993); see **53:4**

2 It's nice to have company when you come face to face
with a blank page.

George S. Kaufman 1889–1961:
Howard Teichmann *George S.
Kaufman: an Intimate Portrait* (1973)

3 It has always seemed to me as unnatural for two people to
write a book together as for three people to have a baby.

Evelyn Waugh 1903–66: letter, 30
July 1962

4 Two women—one writer.
  of Edith Somerville and Martin Ross; see **53:1**

William Trevor 1928– : *Excursions in
the Real World* (1993)

Comedy see **Humour and Comedy**

Conversation see **Dialogue and Conversation**

Ivy Compton-Burnett 1884–1969
English novelist

5 There's not much to say. I haven't been at all deedy.
  on being asked about herself

Ivy Compton-Burnett 1884–1969:
in *The Times* 30 August 1969

6 She saw life in the relentless terms of a Greek tragedy, its
cruelties, ironies—above all its passions—played out
against a background of triviality and ennui.

Anthony Powell 1905–2000: in
Spectator 6 September 1969

William Congreve 1670–1729
English dramatist

7 Every sentence is replete with sense and satire, conveyed
in the most polished and pointed terms. Every page
presents a shower of brilliant conceits, is a tissue of
epigrams in prose, is a new triumph of wit, a new
conquest over dullness. The fire of artful raillery is
nowhere else so well kept up.

William Hazlitt 1778–1830: *Lectures
on the English Comic Writers* (1818)

8 William Congreve is the only sophisticated playwright
England has produced; and like Shaw, Sheridan and
Wilde, his nearest rivals, he was brought up in Ireland.

Kenneth Tynan 1927–80: *Curtains*
(1961) 'The Way of the World'

Cyril Connolly 1903–74
English writer

9 He gave pleasure a bad name.

E. M. Forster 1879–1970: Noel
Annan *Our Age* (1990)

Joseph Conrad 1857–1924
Polish-born English novelist

1 A Polish nobleman, cased in British tar!
self-description

Joseph Conrad 1857–1924: letter, 22 May 1890

2 For me, writing—*the only possible writing*—is just simply the conversion of nervous force into phrases.

Joseph Conrad 1857–1924: letter, October 1903

3 You knock about in the wide waters of expression like the raciest and boldest of privateers.

Henry James 1843–1916: letter to Conrad, 1 November 1906

4 No one has known—for intellectual use—the things you know, and you have, as the artist of the whole matter, an authority that no one has approached.

Henry James 1843–1916: to Joseph Conrad, 1 November 1906

5 The secret casket of his genius contains a vapour rather than a jewel.
reviewing Conrad's Notes on Life and Letters (*1921*)

E. M. Forster 1879–1970: Cedric Watts *Joseph Conrad* (1994)

6 What is Conrad but the wreck of Stevenson floating about on the slip-slop of Henry James?

George Moore 1852–1933: letter from G. W. Lyttelton, 8 March 1956

7 Conrad spent a day finding the *mot juste*; then killed it.

Ford Madox Ford 1873–1939: Robert Lowell *Notebook 1967–68* (1969)

8 Joseph Conrad's *Heart of Darkness* prophetically inaugurated the twentieth century.

Thomas Mann 1875–1955: attributed

9 He thought of civilized and morally tolerable human life as a dangerous walk on a thin crust of barely cooled lava that might break and let the unwary sink into fiery depths.

Bertrand Russell 1872–1970: Norman Sherry *Conrad and his World* (1972)

10 He seems to write books about the sea, the Malay archipelago and the Congo, but he is really writing about the desperate, convoluted, hopeless heart of man.

Anthony Burgess 1917–93: in *Observer* 6 May 1979

James Fenimore Cooper 1789–1851
American writer

11 *Deerslayer* is just simply a literary *delirium tremens*.

Mark Twain 1835–1910: 'Fenimore Cooper's Literary Offences' (1895)

Pierre Corneille 1606–84
French dramatist

12 Corneille is to Shakespeare . . . as a clipped hedge is to a forest.

Samuel Johnson 1709–84: Hester Lynch Piozzi *Anecdotes of . . . Johnson* (1786)

13 To my mind, the style of Racine has aged much more than the style of Corneille. Corneille is wrinkled, Racine has withered. Corneille remains magnificent, venerable, and powerful. Corneille has aged like an old man, Racine like an old woman.

Victor Hugo 1802–85: *Tas de pierres* (1942)

Noël Coward 1899–1973
English dramatist, actor, and composer

1 Baring his teeth as if unveiling a grotesque memorial, and cooing like a baritone dove, he displays his two weapons— wit and sentimentality.

Kenneth Tynan 1927–80: 'A Tribute to Mr Coward' (1953)

2 There are only two great playwrights in Britain today, Terence Rattigan and myself.

Noël Coward 1899–1973: attributed, 1964

Abraham Cowley 1618–67 see also **246:4**
English poet

3 He more had pleased us, had he pleased us less.

Joseph Addison 1672–1719: *An Account of the Greatest English Poets* (1694)

4 Who now reads Cowley? if he pleases yet, His moral pleases, not his pointed wit.

Alexander Pope 1688–1744: *Imitations of Horace* (1737)

5 When Homer spoke, the great tradition Of verse commanded, taught and led; With Milton it began to nod, And Cowley was its *Ichabod*.

A. D. Hope 1907–2000: 'Conversation with Calliope' (1972)

Creativity see Inspiration and Creativity

Crime and Mystery

6 Detection is, or ought to be, an exact science, and should be treated in the same cold and unemotional manner. You have attempted to tinge it with romanticism, which produces much the same effect as if you worked a love-story or an elopement into the fifth proposition of Euclid.

Arthur Conan Doyle 1859–1930: *The Sign of Four* (1890)

7 Why bother yourself about the cataract of drivel for which Conan Doyle is responsible? I am sure he never imagined that such a heap of rubbish would fall on my devoted head in consequence of his stories.
   Bell was the inspiration for Sherlock Holmes

Joseph Bell 1837–1911: *Joseph Bell: an Appreciation by an Old Friend* (1913)

8 Death seems to provide the minds of the Anglo-Saxon race with a greater fund of amusement that any other single subject.

Dorothy L. Sayers 1893–1957: introduction to *The Third Omnibus of Crime* (1935)

9 I generally thought of a character or two, and then of a set of incidents, and the question was how my people would behave. They had the knack of just squeezing out of unpleasant places and of bringing their doings to a rousing climax.

John Buchan 1875–1940: *Memory-Hold-the-Door* (1940)

10 Down these mean streets a man must go who is not himself mean, who is neither tarnished nor afraid.

Raymond Chandler 1888–1959: in *Atlantic Monthly* December 1944 'The Simple Art of Murder'

1 Hammett took murder out of the Venetian vase and dropped it into the alley.

Raymond Chandler 1888–1959: in *Atlantic Monthly* December 1944 'The Simple Art of Murder'

2 It seems to have been taken for granted, quite wrongly, that because murder novels are easy reading they are also light reading. They are no easier reading than Hamlet, Lear or Macbeth. They border on tragic and never quite become tragic. Their form imposes a certain clarity of outline which is only found in the most accomplished 'straight' novels.

Raymond Chandler 1888–1959: letter to James Sandoe, 17 October 1948

3 Detective stories—the modern fairy tales.

Graham Greene 1904–91: 'Journey into Success' (1952)

4 In the melodrama of the brutal thriller we come as close as it is normally possible for art to come to the pure self-righteousness of the lynching mobs.

Northrop Frye 1912–91: *The Anatomy of Criticism* (1957)

5 Sapper, Buchan, Dornford Yates, practitioners in that school of Snobbery with Violence that runs like a thread of good-class tweed through twentieth-century literature.

Alan Bennett 1934– : *Forty Years On* (1969)

6 The setting for the crime stories by what we might call the Mayhem Parva school would be a cross between a village and a commuters' dormitory in the South of England, self-contained and largely self-sufficient. It would have a well-attended church, an inn with reasonable accommodation for itinerant detective-inspectors, a village institute, library and shops—including a chemist's where weed killer and hair dye might conveniently be bought.

Colin Watson 1920–83: *Snobbery with Violence* (1971)

7 What the detective story is about is not murder but the restoration of order.

P. D. James 1920– : in *Face* December 1986

8 A genre which has traditionally been bedevilled by rules, regulations, and rituals reminiscent of a third-rate Masonic cult.

Michael Dibdin 1947– : preface to *The Picador Book of Crime Fiction* (1993)

9 It is, it ought to be, it must be a morality.
the views of 'Ellis Peters' on writing a thriller

Edith Pargeter 1913–95: in *Daily Telegraph* 16 October 1995; obituary

10 I had an interest in death from an early age. It fascinated me. When I heard 'Humpty Dumpty sat on a wall,' I thought, 'Did he fall or was he pushed?'

P. D. James 1920– : in *Paris Review* 1995

11 With Agatha Christie ingenuity of plot was paramount— no one looked for subtlety of characterization, motivation, good writing. It was rather like a literary card trick. Today we've moved closer to the mainstream novel, but nevertheless we need plot.

P. D. James 1920– : in *Paris Review* 1995

12 Murder itself is not interesting. It is the impetus to murder, the passions and terrors which bring it to pass and the varieties of feelings surrounding the act that make a sordid or revolting event compulsive fascination. Even the most ardent readers of detective fiction are not much preoccupied with whether a Colt Magnum revolver or a Bowie knife was used to dispatch the victim. The perpetrator's purpose, the 'why', is what impels them to read on.

Ruth Rendell 1930– : introduction to *The Reason Why: An Anthology of the Murderous Mind* (1995)

1 All over England, it seemed to me, bodies were being discovered by housemaids in libraries. Village poison pens were tirelessly at work. There was murder in Mayfair, on trains, in airships, in Palm Court lounges, between the acts. Golfers stumbled over corpses on fairways. Chief Constables awoke to them in their gardens. We had nothing like it in West Cork.
on reading detective stories as a child

William Trevor 1928– : acceptance speech on winning the David Cohen Award, 1999

2 I got a suffocating grey impression of armaments catalogues and code nerds and excessively factual dialogue disclosing how every double-cross has another behind it and all roads lead to a vast distrust.
on Cold War thrillers

John Updike 1932– : *More Matter* (1999)

3 When I'm asked why I write crime fiction, I always answer that I enjoy playing games.

Minette Walters 1949– : Barry Turner (ed.) *The Writer's Handbook 2000* (1999)

4 It seemed to me quite poignant that this genre should have flourished as a kind of therapeutic reaction to the horrors of the Great War.
on Golden Age crime fiction of the 1920s and 1930s

Kazuo Ishiguro 1954– : in *Independent* 1 April 2000

5 A Private Eye was Superman wearing a fedora.

Ed McBain 1926– : in *Writers on Writing: Collected Essays from The New York Times* (2001)

6 For me, Private Eye stories were the easiest of the lot. All you had to do was talk out of the side of your mouth and get in trouble with the cops.

Ed McBain 1926– : in *Writers on Writing: Collected Essays from The New York Times* (2001)

7 The mystery whose power as a storytelling form persisted despite its long-term residence in the low-rent precincts of critical esteem.

Scott Turow 1949– : in *Writers on Writing: Collected Essays from The New York Times* (2001)

8 I have contributed quite enough to the 'crime scene', since I am reliably informed that I have been responsible for 81 body-bags in and around Oxford, including three Heads of Colleges.

Colin Dexter 1930– : 'Why I had to kill off Morse' in *Daily Telegraph* 2002

Criticism see also Critics, Reviews, Scholarship

9 Tear him for his bad verses, tear him for his bad verses.

William Shakespeare 1564–1616: *Julius Caesar* (1599)

10 To judge of poets is only the faculty of poets; and not of all poets, but the best.

Ben Jonson c.1573–1637: *Timber, or Discoveries made upon Men and Matter* (1641)

11 One should look long and carefully at oneself before one considers judging others.

Molière 1622–73: *Le Misanthrope* (1666)

12   He hears
On all sides, from innumerable tongues
A dismal universal hiss, the sound
Of public scorn.

John Milton 1608–74: *Paradise Lost* (1667)

13 The pleasure of criticism destroys (more literally, removes) in us that of being moved by beautiful things.

Jean de la Bruyère 1645–96: *Les Caractères ou les moeurs de ce siècle* (1688)

1 Yet let not each gay turn thy rapture move,
For fools admire, but men of sense approve.

Alexander Pope 1688–1744: *An Essay on Criticism* (1711)

2 A true critic ought to dwell rather upon excellencies than imperfections, to discover the concealed beauties of a writer, and communicate to the world such things as are worth their observation.

Joseph Addison 1672–1719: *The Spectator* 2 February 1712

3 Criticism is a study by which men grow important and formidable at very small expense.

Samuel Johnson 1709–84: in *The Idler* 9 June 1759

4 You *may* abuse a tragedy, though you cannot write one. You may scold a carpenter who has made you a bad table, though you cannot make a table. It is not your trade to make tables.

Samuel Johnson 1709–84: James Boswell *Life of Samuel Johnson* (1791) 25 June 1763

5 Of all the cants which are canted in this canting world,— though the cant of hypocrites may be the worst,—the cant of criticism is the most tormenting!

Laurence Sterne 1713–68: *Tristram Shandy* (1759–67)

6 If it is abuse,—why one is always sure to hear of it from one damned goodnatured friend or another!

Richard Brinsley Sheridan 1751–1816: *The Critic* (1779)

7 In the character of his Elegy I rejoice to concur with the common reader; for by the common sense of readers uncorrupted with literary prejudices . . . must be finally decided all claim to poetical honours.

Samuel Johnson 1709–84: *Lives of the English Poets* (1779–81) 'Gray'

8 The ultimate end of criticism is much more to establish the principles of writing, than to furnish *rules* how to pass judgement on what has been written by others; if indeed it were possible that the two could be separated.

Samuel Taylor Coleridge 1772–1834: *Biographia Literaria* (1817)

9 An author nowadays no longer hangs dangling on the frown of a lord, or the smile of a lady of quality . . . but throws himself boldly, making a lover's leap of it, into the broad lap of public opinion, on which he falls like a feather-bed; and which, like the great bed of Ware, is wide enough to hold us all very comfortably!

William Hazlitt 1778–1830: *Lectures on the English Comic Writers* (1818)

10 Praise or blame has but a momentary effect on the man whose love of beauty in the abstract makes him a severe critic of his own Works. My own domestic criticism has given me pain without comparison beyond that Blackwood or the [Edinburgh] Quarterly could possibly inflict.

John Keats 1795–1821: letter to J. A. Hessey, 8 October 1818; see **248:6**

11 Criticism makes its appearance like Ate: it pursues authors, but limpingly.

Johann Wolfgang von Goethe 1749–1832: *Sayings in Prose*

12 Never, after I had taken critical pen in hand, did I pass the thoroughly delightful evenings at the playhouse which I had done when I went only to laugh or be moved.
on becoming a theatre critic

Leigh Hunt 1784–1859: *Autobiography* (rev. ed., 1860)

13 I am bound by my own definition of criticism: *a disinterested endeavour to learn and propagate the best that is known and thought in the world.*

Matthew Arnold 1822–88: *Essays in Criticism* First Series (1865) 'The Function of Criticism at the Present Time'

14 We must grant the artist his subject, his idea, his *donnée*: our criticism is applied only to what he makes of it.

Henry James 1843–1916: 'The Art of Fiction' (1888)

1 Criticism is not only medicinally salutary: it has positive popular attractions in its cruelty, its gladiatorship, and the gratification given to envy by its attacks on the great, and to enthusiasm by its praises.

George Bernard Shaw 1856–1950: preface to *Plays Unpleasant* (1898)

2 Works of art are of an infinite solitariness, and nothing is less likely to bring us near to them than criticism. Only love can apprehend and hold them, and can be just towards them.

Rainer Maria Rilke 1875–1926: *Briefe an einen jungen Dichter* (1929) 23 April 1903

3 I always find French criticism of English work very instructive, disconcerting, and tonic.

Arnold Bennett 1867–1931: diary, 25 October 1903

4 I will try to account for the degree of my aesthetic emotion. That, I conceive, is the function of the critic.

Clive Bell 1881–1964: *Art* (1914)

5 You don't expect me to know what to say about a play when I don't know who the author is, do you?

George Bernard Shaw 1856–1950: *Fanny's First Play* (1914)

6 The European view of a poet is not of much importance unless the poet writes in Esperanto.

A. E. Housman 1859–1936: in *Cambridge Review* 1915

7 Never trust the artist. Trust the tale. The proper function of a critic is to save the tale from the artist who created it.

D. H. Lawrence 1885–1930: *Studies in Classic American Literature* (1923)

8 Parodies and caricatures are the most penetrating of criticisms.

Aldous Huxley 1894–1963: *Point Counter Point* (1928)

9 How many children had Lady Macbeth?
 satirizing the style of criticism represented by A. C. Bradley's 'detective interest' in plot and emphasis on 'character'

L. C. Knights 1906–97: title of essay (1933); see **60:11**

10 There's only one kind of critic I do resent . . . The kind that affects to believe that I am writing with my tongue in my cheek.

James Joyce 1882–1941: Frank Budgen *James Joyce and the Making of Ulysses* (1934)

11 An author of talent is his own best critic—the ability to criticize his own work is inseparably bound up with his talent: it *is* his talent.

Graham Greene 1904–91: 'Some Notes on Somerset Maugham' (1935–8)

12 I was never, in the true sense, a critic; never an enlightening judge of excellence. I knew what was good, but I was apt to be puzzled as to the constituents of its goodness, and was a foggy eulogist. Badness is easy game, and to badness I always turned with relief. Badness is auspicious to the shower-off. Its only drawback is that it isn't worth writing about.

Max Beerbohm 1872–1956: letter, c.1942

13 Think before you speak is criticism's motto; speak before you think creation's.

E. M. Forster 1879–1970: *Two Cheers for Democracy* (1951)

14 Drama criticism is essentially a fallible verbal reflexion of how a particular entertainment struck a unique mind on one special evening . . . The last thing a critic ought to be concerned with is the people who read him first. He should write for posterity.

Kenneth Tynan 1927–80: unpublished note for speech at Foyles lunch, 21 November 1952; Kathleen Tynan *The Life of Kenneth Tynan* (1987)

15 Poetry is what is lost in translation. It is also what is lost in interpretation.

Robert Frost 1874–1963: Louis Untermeyer *Robert Frost* (1964)

16 Interpretation is not (as some people assume) an absolute value, a gesture of mind situated in some timeless realm of capabilities. Interpretation must be evaluated . . . Like the fumes of the automobile and of heavy industry which befoul the urban atmosphere, the effusion of interpretation

Susan Sontag 1933– : in *Evergreen Review* December 1964

of art today poisons our sensibilities. In a culture whose already classic dilemma is the hypertrophy of the intellect at the expense of energy and sensual capability, interpretation is the revenge of the intellect upon art.

1 The work of criticism is rooted in the unconscious of the critic just as the poem is rooted in the unconscious of the poet.

Randall Jarrell 1914–65: *A Sad Heart at the Supermarket* (1965)

2 Drama criticism . . . [is] a self-knowing account of the way in which one's consciousness has been modified during an evening in the theatre.

Kenneth Tynan 1927–80: *Tynan Right and Left* (1967)

3 The important thing is that you make sure that neither the favourable nor the unfavourable critics move into your head and take part in the composition of your next work.

Thornton Wilder 1897–1975: George Plimpton (ed.) *The Writer's Chapbook* (1989)

4 Like thinking about the technique of skiing when you're half-way down a hill.
   on writing about her own writing

Margaret Atwood 1939– : in an interview, February 1976; Earl G. Ingersoll (ed.) *Margaret Atwood: Conversations* (1990)

5 Writing criticism is to writing fiction and poetry as hugging the shore is to sailing in the open sea.

John Updike 1932– : foreword to *Hugging the Shore* (1983)

6 Analyzing Giraudoux is like plucking a hummingbird and sorting out the feathers for colour and size.

Mavis Gallant 1922– : *Paris Notebooks: Essays and Reviews* (1986)

7 I enjoyed your article, but I preferred my own.

Umberto Eco 1932– : speaking to Jeremy Treglown, editor of the *TLS*, c.1982–4; Derwent May *Critical Times: The History of the Times Literary Supplement* (2001)

8 No critical display is more offensive than that which praises one author by damning another, as though critical judgement were a seesaw on which one reputation cannot rise unless another is lowered.

Carolyn G. Heilbrun 1926– : *Hamlet's Mother and Other Women* (1990) 'Virginia Woolf and James Joyce'

9 Criticism cannot help being magisterial, but the court in which the magistrate presides is a court of love.

A. D. Hope 1907–2000: Kevin Hart *A. D. Hope* (1992)

10 Criticism is a life without risk.

John Lahr 1941– : *Light Fantastic* (1996)

11 Personally I have always thought 'how many children had Lady Macbeth?' a perfectly good question. I am also curious about how old Hamlet is, what subjects he studied at the University of Wittenberg, and what grades he got for his studies there.

John Sutherland 1938– : introduction to *Is Heathcliff a Murderer?* (1996); see **59:9**

Critics

12 Critics are like brushers of noblemen's clothes.

Henry Wotton 1568–1639: Francis Bacon *Apophthegms New and Old* (1625)

13 They who write ill, and they who ne'er durst write,
   Turn critics out of mere revenge and spite.

John Dryden 1631–1700: *The Conquest of Granada* (1670)

14 You who scribble, yet hate all who write . . .
   And with faint praises one another damn.
   of drama critics

William Wycherley c.1640–1716: *The Plain Dealer* (1677)

1 Some have at first for wits, then poets passed,
Turned critics next, and proved plain fools at last.

Alexander Pope 1688–1744: *An Essay on Criticism* (1711)

2 He whom nature has made weak, and idleness keeps ignorant, may yet support his vanity by the name of a critic.

Samuel Johnson 1709–84: in *The Idler* no. 61 9 June 1759

3 Every good poet includes a critic; the reverse will not hold.

William Shenstone 1714–63: *Works . . .* (1764) 'On Writing and Books'

4 He gets at the substance of a book directly; he tears out the heart of it.
   *of Samuel **Johnson***

Mary Knowles 1733–1807: James Boswell *Life of Samuel Johnson* (1791) 15 April 1778

5 He wreathed the rod of criticism with roses.
   of Pierre Bayle

Isaac D'Israeli 1766–1848: *Curiosities of Literature* (9th ed., 1834)

6 To characterize Hamlet as a thorough-going weakling, Shakespeare allows him to appear, in his conversation with the players, as a good theatre critic.

Heinrich Heine 1797–1856: *The Romantic School* (1836)

7 There spoke up a brisk little somebody,
Critic and whippersnapper, in a rage
To set things right.

Robert Browning 1812–89: *Balaustion's Adventure* (1871)

8 What is important, then, is not that the critic should possess a correct abstract definition of beauty for the intellect but a certain kind of temperament, the power of being deeply moved by the presence of beautiful objects.

Walter Pater 1839–94: *Studies in the History of the Renaissance* (1873) 'Preface'

9 The good critic is he who relates the adventures of his soul in the midst of masterpieces.

Anatole France 1844–1924: *La Vie littéraire* (1888)

10 The lot of critics is to be remembered by what they failed to understand.

George Moore 1852–1933: *Impressions and Opinions* (1891) 'Balzac'

11 A louse in the locks of literature.
   of the critic John Churton Collins (1848–1908)

Alfred, Lord Tennyson 1809–92: Evan Charteris *Life and Letters of Sir Edmund Gosse* (1931)

12 After all, one knows one's weak points so well, that it's rather bewildering to have the critics overlook them and invent others.

Edith Wharton 1862–1937: letter, 19 November 1909

13 The critic's symbol should be the tumble-bug; he deposits his egg in someone else's dung otherwise he could not hatch it.

Mark Twain 1835–1910: *Mark Twain's Notebook* (1935)

14 The principal thrill of reading Saintsbury is the sensation of looking down on literature as with the comparative eye of God.
   of the critic G. E. B. Saintsbury

Edmund Wilson 1895–1972: in *New Republic* 8 February 1933; see **61:15**

15 For 18 years he *started the day* by reading a French novel (in preparation for his history of them) an act so unnatural to man as to amount almost to genius.
   of the critic G. E. B. Saintsbury

Stephen Potter 1900–69: *The Muse in Chains* (1937); see **61:14**

16 Remember, a statue has never been set up in honour of a critic!

Jean Sibelius 1865–1957: Bengt de Törne *Sibelius: A Close-Up* (1937)

17 The great critics, of whom there are piteously few, build a home for truth.

Raymond Chandler 1888–1959: letter to Frederick Lewis Allen, 7 May 1948

1 A dramatic critic is a man who leaves no turn unstoned.

George Bernard Shaw 1856–1950: in *New York Times* 5th November 1950

2 A critic is a bundle of biases held loosely together by a sense of taste.

Whitney Balliett 1926– : *Dinosaurs in the Morning* (1962)

3 Critics are like eunuchs in a harem; they know how it's done, they've seen it done every day, but they're unable to do it themselves.

Brendan Behan 1923–64: attributed

4 A critic is a man who knows the way but can't drive the car.

Kenneth Tynan 1927–80: in *New York Times Magazine* 9 January 1966

5 No degree of dullness can safeguard a work against the determination of critics to find it fascinating.

Harold Rosenberg 1906–78: *Discovering the Present* (1973)

6 A sneer of critics.
  his collective noun

Peter Nichols 1927– : diary, 6 February 1974

7 The gifted student does not need help—except only in one particular: He needs to have it confirmed that literature is by writers and not by critics, that critics should be thrown out of the window and the young one should (as his instinct tells him) go ahead and try his own talent and strength.

Christina Stead 1902–83: letter to Michael Costigan, June 1977

8 There is, perhaps, no more dangerous man in the world than the man with the sensibilities of an artist but without creative talent. With luck such men make wonderful theatrical impresarios and interior decorators, or else they become mass murderers or critics.

Barry Humphries 1934– : *More Please* (1992)

9 Asking a playwright how he felt about critics was like asking a lamppost how it felt about dogs.

Christopher Hampton 1946– : in *The Times* 4 April 1995; see **144:12**

Dante Alighieri 1265–1321
Italian poet

10 He stood bewildered, not appalled, on that dark shore which separates the ancient and the modern world . . . He is power, passion, self-will personified.

William Hazlitt 1778–1830: *Lectures on the English Poets* (1818) 'On Poetry in General'

11 Dante, who loved well because he hated,
Hated wickedness that hinders loving.

Robert Browning 1812–89: 'One Word More' (1855)

12 Neither the world, nor the theologians, not even Charles Williams had told me the one great obvious, glowing fact about Dante Alighieri of Florence—that he was simply the most incomparable story-teller who ever set pen to paper.

Dorothy L. Sayers 1893–1957: *Further Papers on Dante* (1957) ' . . . And Telling You a Story'

Death see also Last Words

13 *Non omnis moriar.*
  I shall not altogether die.

Horace 65–8 BC: *Odes*

14 Rigidly classical, you save
Your praise for poets in the grave.
Forgive me, it's not worth my while
Dying to earn your critical smile.

Martial AD c.40–c.104: *Epigrammata* tr. James Michie

1 With one foot already in the stirrup.
   apprehending his own, imminent death

Cervantes 1547–1616: *Los Trabajos de Persiles y Sigismunda* (1617)

2 When one man dies, one chapter is not torn out of the book, but translated into a better language.

John Donne 1572–1631: *Devotions upon Emergent Occasions* (1624)

3 Any man's death diminishes me, because I am involved in Mankind; And therefore never send to know for whom the bell tolls; it tolls for thee.

John Donne 1572–1631: *Devotions upon Emergent Occasions* (1624)

4 Men fear death as children fear to go in the dark; and as that natural fear in children is increased with tales, so is the other.

Francis Bacon 1561–1626: *Essays* (1625) 'Of Death'

5 Death is still working like a mole,
   And digs my grave at each remove.

George Herbert 1593–1633: 'Grace' (1633)

6 Can storied urn or animated bust
   Back to its mansion call the fleeting breath?

Thomas Gray 1716–71: *Elegy Written in a Country Churchyard* (1751)

7 It matters not how a man dies, but how he lives. The act of dying is not of importance, it lasts so short a time.

Samuel Johnson 1709–84: James Boswell *Life of Samuel Johnson* (1791) 26 October 1769

8 I am dying as fast as my enemies, if I have any, could wish, and as easily and cheerfully as my best friends could desire.
   in his last illness, to his doctor

David Hume 1711–76: William Smellie *Literary and Characteristical Lives* (1800)

9 When I asked if there was anything she wanted, her answer was that she wanted nothing but death.
   of her sister Jane's last illness

Cassandra Austen 1772–1845: letter to Fanny Knight, May 1817

10 When I have fears that I may cease to be
   Before my pen has gleaned my teeming brain.

John Keats 1795–1821: 'When I have fears that I may cease to be' (written 1818)

11 Darkling I listen; and, for many a time
   I have been half in love with easeful Death,
   Called him soft names in many a musèd rhyme,
   To take into the air my quiet breath;
   Now more than ever seems it rich to die,
   To cease upon the midnight with no pain.

John Keats 1795–1821: 'Ode to a Nightingale' (1820)

12 I know the colour of that blood;—it is arterial blood;—I cannot be deceived in that colour; that drop of blood is my death-warrant—I must die.
   on coughing up blood and recognizing the fatal symptom of tuberculosis

John Keats 1795–1821: to his friend Charles Armitage Brown; Hyder E. Rollins (ed.) *The Keats Circle* (ed. 2, 1965)

13 I shall soon be laid in the quiet grave—thank God for the quiet grave—O! I can feel the cold earth upon me—the daisies growing over me—O for this quiet—it will be my first.

John Keats 1795–1821: letter from Joseph Severn to John Taylor, 6 March 1821

14 Death cancels everything but truth; and strips a man of everything but genius and virtue. It is a sort of natural canonization.

William Hazlitt 1778–1830: *The Spirit of the Age* (1825) 'Lord Byron'

15 The last breath he drew in he wished might be through a pipe and exhaled in a pun.

Charles Lamb 1775–1834: William Charles Macready diary, 9 January 1834

1 With the dead there is no rivalry. In the dead there is no change. Plato is never sullen. Cervantes is never petulant. Demosthenes never comes unseasonably. Dante never stays too long. No difference of political opinion can alienate Cicero. No heresy can excite the horror of Bossuet.

Lord Macaulay 1800–59: *Essays Contributed to the Edinburgh Review* (1843) 'Lord Bacon'

2 Unless one is a moron, one always dies unsure of one's own value and that of one's works. Virgil himself, as he lay dying, wanted the Aeneid burned.

Gustave Flaubert 1821–80: letter, 19 September 1852

3 Fear death?—to feel the fog in my throat,
The mist in my face.

Robert Browning 1812–89: 'Prospice' (1864)

4 Don't worry, you'll survive. No one dies in the middle of Act Five.

Henrik Ibsen 1828–1906: *Peer Gynt* (1867)

5 For though from out our bourne of time and place
The flood may bear me far,
I hope to see my pilot face to face
When I have crossed the bar.

Alfred, Lord Tennyson 1809–92: 'Crossing the Bar' (1889)

6 So here it is at last, the distinguished thing!
on experiencing his first stroke

Henry James 1843–1916: Edith Wharton *A Backward Glance* (1934)

7 Webster was much possessed by death
And saw the skull beneath the skin;
And breastless creatures underground
Leaned backward with a lipless grin.

T. S. Eliot 1888–1965: 'Whispers of Immortality' (1919)

8 The dead don't die. They look on and help.

D. H. Lawrence 1885–1930: letter to J. Middleton Murry, 2 February 1923

9 A man's dying is more the survivors' affair than his own.

Thomas Mann 1875–1955: *The Magic Mountain* (1924)

10 To die will be an awfully big adventure.

J. M. Barrie 1860–1937: *Peter Pan* (1928)

11 Too late for fruit, too soon for flowers.
recovering from an illness during which his life had been in danger

Walter de la Mare 1873–1956: John Bailey diary, 3 April 1928

12 And what the dead had no speech for, when living,
They can tell you, being dead: the communication
Of the dead is tongued with fire beyond the language of the living.

T. S. Eliot 1888–1965: *Four Quartets* 'Little Gidding' (1942)

13 I want to go on living even after death!

Anne Frank 1929–45: diary, 4 April 1944

14 Do not go gentle into that good night,
Old age should burn and rave at close of day;
Rage, rage against the dying of the light.

Dylan Thomas 1914–53: 'Do Not Go Gentle into that Good Night' (1952)

15 The only thing that really saddens me over my demise is that I shall not be here to read the nonsense that will be written about me . . . There will be lists of apocryphal jokes I never made and gleeful misquotations of words I never said. *What* a pity I shan't be here to enjoy them!

Noël Coward 1899–1973: diary, 19 March 1955

16 Who wields a poem huger than the grave?

e. e. cummings 1894–1962: 'but if a living dance upon dead minds'; *selected poems 1923–1958*

17 Fear of death is too much of a screaming close-up to allow the poetic faculty to function properly, but demands expression by reason of its very frightfulness.

Philip Larkin 1922–85: in *Listen* Spring 1959

1 Life is a great surprise. I do not see why death should not
be an even greater one.

Vladimir Nabokov 1899–1977: *Pale Fire* (1962)

2 Dying,
Is an art, like everything else.

Sylvia Plath 1932–63: 'Lady Lazarus' (1963)

3 If there wasn't death, I think you couldn't go on.

Stevie Smith 1902–71: in *Observer* 9 November 1969

4 Death is nothing if one can approach it as such. I was just
a tiny night-light, suffocated in its own wax, and on the
point of expiring.

E. M. Forster 1879–1970: Philip Gardner (ed.) *E. M. Forster: Commonplace Book* (1985)

5 Death has got something to be said for it:
There's no need to get out of bed for it;
Wherever you may be,
They bring it to you, free.

Kingsley Amis 1922–95: 'Delivery Guaranteed' (1979)

6 Death is a displaced name for a linguistic predicament.

Paul de Man 1919–83: David Lehman *Signs of the Times* (1991)

7 Death is the great Maecenas, Death is the great angel of
writing. You must write because you are not going to live
any more.

Carlos Fuentes 1928– : in *Writers at Work* (6th series, 1984)

8 So the last date slides into the bracket,
that will appear in all future anthologies—
And in quiet Cornwall and in London's ghastly racket
We are now Betjemanless.

Gavin Ewart 1916–95: 'In Memoriam, Sir John Betjeman (1906–84)' (1985)

9 Most deaths in novels are there for a reason, so that the
death will point up the meaning of the whole story . . . I
wanted to say that death isn't like that. It just happens,
not necessarily to the person who deserves to be dead.
commenting on the death of a character in her novel Still
Life

A. S. Byatt 1936– : in an interview, April 1988; George Greenfield *Scribblers for Bread* (1989)

10 My only regret is to die four pages too soon—if I can
finish, then I'm quite happy to go.

Dennis Potter 1935–94: interview with Melvyn Bragg on Channel 4, March 1994, in *Seeing the Blossom* (1994)

Dedications

11 Go, litel bok, go, litel myn tragedye,
Ther God thi makere yet, er that he dye,
So sende myght to make in som comedye!
But litel bok, no makyng thow n'envie,
But subgit be to alle poesye;
And kis the steppes, where as thow seest pace
Virgile, Ovide, Omer, Lucan, and Stace.

Geoffrey Chaucer c.1343–1400: *Troilus and Criseyde*

12 If the first heir of my invention prove deformed, I shall be
sorry it had so noble a godfather.

William Shakespeare 1564–1616: *Venus and Adonis* (1593) dedication

13 What I have done is yours; what I have to do is yours;
being part in all I have, devoted yours.

William Shakespeare 1564–1616: *The Rape of Lucrece* (1594)

14 To the onlie begetter of these insuing sonnets, Mr. W. H.

William Shakespeare 1564–1616: *Sonnets* (1609) dedication (also attributed to Thomas Thorpe, the publisher)

1 Perhaps when you again appear in print you may choose to dedicate your volumes to Prince Leopold: any historical romance, illustrative of the history of the august House of Coburg, would just now be very interesting.

James Stanier Clarke c.1765–1834: letter to Jane Austen, 27 March 1816; see **122:1**

2   Look with favour
Upon the chapters in your hand . . .
The mind's reflections coldly noted,
The bitter insights of the heart.

Alexander Pushkin 1799–1837: *Eugene Onegin* (1833) 'Dedication' (translated by Babette Deutsch)

3 A dedication, for me, is a serious thing. It is an offering of my thoughts given in affection and esteem.

Joseph Conrad 1857–1924: letter, 29 August 1896

4 To live is to battle with trolls in the vaults of heart and brain. To write: that is to sit in judgement over one's self.
    dedicatory lines which Ibsen said he once inscribed in a copy of one of his books

Henrik Ibsen 1828–1906: letter, 16 June 1890

5 To my daughter Leonora without whose never-failing sympathy and encouragement this book would have been finished in half the time.

P. G. Wodehouse 1881–1975: dedication to *The Heart of a Goof* (1926)

6 One can find Evelyn's biography in the dedications to his books, each displaying a further step in his social progress.
    a 'cruel contemporary' on Evelyn **Waugh**

Anonymous: in *Time* 12 July 1948

7 She was the beat of my heart for thirty years. She was the music heard faintly on the edge of sound. It was my great and now useless regret that I never wrote anything really worth her attention, no book that I could dedicate to her. I planned it. I thought of it, but I never wrote it. Perhaps I couldn't have written it.
    after the death of his wife

Raymond Chandler 1888–1959: letter to Leonard Russell, 29 December 1954

8 I'd be delighted to accept the dedication of *The Contenders*, but Heaven knows when I'll be able to return it—Sunday writers like myself do about a book a decade, and the queue is already in existence.

Philip Larkin 1922–85: letter to John Wain, 15 January 1957

Description

9 The business of a poet, said Imlac, is to examine, not the individual, but the species; to remark general properties and appearances: he does not number the streaks of the tulip, or describe the different shades in the verdure of the forest.

Samuel Johnson 1709–84: *Rasselas* (1759)

10 Damn description, it is always disgusting.

Lord Byron 1788–1824: letter, 6 August 1809

11 I at one time used to think some parts of *Sir Charles Grandison* rather trifling and tedious, especially the long description of Miss Harriet Byron's wedding-clothes, till I was told of two young ladies who had severally copied out the whole of that very description for their own private gratification. After that I could not blame the author.

William Hazlitt 1778–1830: *Lectures on the English Comic Writers* (1818)

12 Description is always a bore, both to the describer and to the describee.

Benjamin Disraeli 1804–81: letter, 1830; *Home Letters* (1885)

1 Such epithets, like pepper,
  Give zest to what you write;
  And if you strew them sparely,
  They whet the appetite:
  But if you lay them on too thick,
  You spoil the matter quite!

Lewis Carroll 1832–98:
'Phantasmagoria' (1876)

2 Merely corroborative detail, intended to give artistic
  verisimilitude to an otherwise bald and unconvincing
  narrative.

W. S. Gilbert 1836–1911: *The Mikado*
(1885)

3 No human being ever spoke of scenery for above two
  minutes at a time, which makes me suspect we hear too
  much of it in literature.

Robert Louis Stevenson 1850–94:
Memories and Portraits (1887)

4 You must describe your women in such a way that the
  reader feels your tie is off and your waistcoat open.
  Women and nature both. Let yourself go.

Anton Chekhov 1860–1904: letter,
20 October 1888

5 My attitude towards adjectives is the story of my life. If
  ever I write my autobiography, I'll call it *The Story of an
  Adjective*. In my youth I thought that the sumptuous must
  be conveyed by sumptuous means. But I was wrong. It
  turned out that one must very often proceed by opposites.

Isaac Babel 1894–1940: interview,
Union of Soviet Writers, 28
September 1937

6 It is easier to describe the threshold of divine revelation
  than the working of a pair of scissors.

C. S. Lewis 1898–1963: attributed;
perhaps summarizing a passage in
Studies in Words (1960)

7 Our language lacks words to express this offence, the
  demolition of a man.
    of a year spent in Auschwitz

Primo Levi 1919–87: *If This is a Man*
(1958)

8 I don't know if you care for descriptions? I don't.
    to the novelist Elizabeth Taylor

Ivy Compton-Burnett 1884–1969:
Hilary Spurling *Secrets of a Woman's
Heart: the Later Life of Ivy Compton-
Burnett* (1984)

9 When I describe a scene, I capture it with the moving eye
  of the cine-camera rather than with the photographer's
  eye—which leaves it frozen.

Graham Greene 1904–91: Marie-
Françoise Allain *The Other Man,
Conversations with Graham Greene*
(1983)

10 I am interested in detail. I enjoy decoration. By
   accumulating this mass of detail you throw light on things
   in a longer sense.

Patrick White 1912–90: *Patrick
White Speaks* (1990)

11 Details fascinate me. I love to pile up details. They create
   an atmosphere.

Muriel Spark 1918– : *Curriculum
Vitae* (1992)

Dialogue and Conversation see also Speech

12   Give 'em words;
   Pour oil into their ears, and send them hence.

Ben Jonson *c.*1573–1637: *Volpone*
(1606)

13 Language most shows a man: Speak, that I may see thee.
   It springs out of the most retired and inmost parts of us,
   and is the image of the parent of it, the mind. No glass
   renders a man's form or likeness so true as his speech.

Ben Jonson *c.*1573–1637: *Timber, or
Discoveries made upon Men and
Matter* (1641)

1 A transition from an author's books to his conversation, is too often like an entrance into a large city, after a distant prospect. Remotely, we see nothing but spires of temples, and turrets of palaces, and imagine it the residence of splendour, grandeur, and magnificence; but when we have passed the gates, we find it perplexed with narrow passages, disgraced with despicable cottages, embarrassed with obstructions, and clouded with smoke.

Samuel Johnson 1709-84: in *The Rambler* 5 May 1784

2 'My idea of good company, Mr Elliot, is the company of clever, well-informed people, who have a great deal of conversation; that is what I call good company.' 'You are mistaken,' said he gently, 'that is not good company, that is the best.'

Jane Austen 1775-1817: *Persuasion* (1818)

3 They tell me I say ill-natured things. I have a weak voice; if I did not say ill-natured things, no one would hear what I said.

Samuel Rogers 1763-1855: Henry Taylor *Autobiography* (1885) vol. 1

4 One shouldn't talk when one is tired. One Hamletizes, and it seems a lie.

D. H. Lawrence 1885-1930: *Women in Love* (1921)

5 Shaw talked practically the whole time, which is the same thing as saying he talked a damn sight too much . . . I really wanted to have a scrap with Virginia Woolf, but got no chance.
    of a dinner party at H. G. **Wells***'s*

Arnold Bennett 1867-1931: diary, 4 November 1926

6 As soon as the dialogue begins, I become merely a recording instrument, and my hand never hesitates because my mind has not to choose, but only to set down what these stupid or intelligent, lethargic or passionate, people say to each other in a language, and with arguments, that appear to be all their own.

Edith Wharton 1862-1937: *A Backward Glance* (1934)

7 In conversation I am bedevilled; in written expression an angel will visit.

Janet Frame 1924- : note to Frank Sargeson, 1955

8 Flocking together is the last thing writers should do—it's different with painters; they have to go to each other's studios to look at the work. But I don't think writers have any particular conversation. Particularly nowadays when they talk about publishers and grants.

Mavis Gallant 1922- : in 1987; Janice Kulyk Keefer *Reading Mavis Gallant* (1989)

9 The Watergate tapes are the most famous and extensive transcripts of real-life speech ever published. When they were released, Americans were shocked, though not all for the same reason. Some people—a very small number— were surprised that Nixon had taken part in a conspiracy to obstruct justice. A few were surprised that the leader of the free world cussed like a stevedore. But one thing that surprised everyone was what ordinary conversation looks like when it is written down verbatim.

Steven Pinker 1954- : *The Language Instinct* (1994)

10 Obvious Rule No. 36. Good dialogue creates its own inbuilt pace and variety.

Alan Ayckbourn 1939- : *The Crafty Art of Playmaking* (2002)

Diaries

1 And so I betake myself to that course, which is almost as much as to see myself go into my grave.
on being forced by failing eyesight to give up keeping his diary

Samuel Pepys 1633–1703: diary, 31 May 1669; see **50:10**

2 What though his head be empty, provided his commonplace book be full.

Jonathan Swift 1667–1745: *A Tale of a Tub* (1704)

3 A page of my Journal is like a cake of portable soup. A little may be diffused into a considerable portion.

James Boswell 1740–95: *Journal of a Tour to the Hebrides* (1785) 13 September 1773

4 As a lady adjusts her dress before a mirror, a man adjusts his character by looking at his journal.

James Boswell 1740–95: *Life of Samuel Johnson* (1791)

5 That remarkable attitude preserved by him throughout his diary . . . that unflinching—I had almost said, that unintelligent—sincerity which makes it a miracle among human books.

Robert Louis Stevenson 1850–94: 'Samuel Pepys' in *Cornhill Magazine* July 1881

6 I never travel without my diary. One should always have something sensational to read in the train.

Oscar Wilde 1854–1900: *The Importance of Being Earnest* (1895)

7 What sort of diary should I like mine to be? . . . I should like it to resemble some deep old desk, or capacious hold-all, in which one flings a mass of odds and ends without looking them through.

Virginia Woolf 1882–1941: diary, 20 April 1919

8 One need not write in a diary what one is to remember for ever.

Sylvia Townsend Warner 1893–1978: diary, 22 October 1930

9 A diary is an assassin's cloak which we wear when we stab a comrade in the back with a pen.

William Soutar 1848–1943: diary, 27 April 1934

10 A diary is like drink; we tend to indulge in it over often: it becomes a habit that would seduce us to say more than we ought to say.

William Soutar 1848–1943: diary, 27 April 1934

11 What is more dull than a discreet diary? One might just as well have a discreet soul.

Henry 'Chips' Channon 1897–1958: diary, 26 July 1935

12 I always say, keep a diary and some day it'll keep you.

Mae West 1892–1980: *Every Day's a Holiday* (1937 film)

13 Here, gossip achieves the epigrammatic significance of poetry. To keep such a diary is to render a real service to the future.
of the Goncourt Brothers' Journals

Christopher Isherwood 1904–86: diary, 5 July 1940

14 In Gide's *Journal* I have just read again how he does not wish to write its pages slowly as he would the pages of a novel. He wants to train himself to rapid writing in it. It is just what I have always felt about this journal of mine. Don't ponder, don't grope—just plunge something down.

Denton Welch 1915–48: diary, 1948

15 After the writer's death, reading his journal is like receiving a long letter.
after reading **Kafka**'s *diary*

Jean Cocteau 1889–1963: diary, 7 June 1953

16 The moment a man sets his thoughts down on paper, however secretly, he is in a sense writing for publication.

Raymond Chandler 1888–1959: working notes on the Julia Wallace murder case; in *Raymond Chandler Speaking* (1962)

1 To write a diary every day is like returning to one's own vomit.

Enoch Powell 1912–98: interview in *Sunday Times* 6 November 1977

2 I am a great believer in diaries, if only in the sense that bar exercises are good for ballet dancers: it's often through personal diaries . . . that the novelist discovers his true bent—that he can narrate real events and distort them to please himself, describe character, observe other beings, hypothesize, invent.

John Fowles 1932– : George Plimpton (ed.) *The Writer's Chapbook* (1989)

3 I have decided to keep a full journal, in the hope that my life will perhaps seem more interesting when it is written down.

Sue Townsend 1946– : *Adrian Mole: The Wilderness Years* (1993)

Charles Dickens 1812–70 see also **102:2, 102:3, 297:11**
English novelist

4 The soul of Hogarth has migrated into the body of Dickens.

Sydney Smith 1771–1845: letter, 1837

5 There is no contemporary English writer whose works are read so generally through the whole house, who can give pleasure to the servants as well as to the mistress, to the children as well as to the master.

Walter Bagehot 1826–77: in *National Review* 7 October 1858 'Charles Dickens'

6 He describes London like a special correspondent for posterity.

Walter Bagehot 1826–77: in *National Review* 7 October 1858 'Charles Dickens'

7 The greatest of superficial novelists . . . It were, in our opinion, an offence against humanity to place Mr Dickens among the greatest novelists.

Henry James 1843–1916: 'Our Mutual Friend' (1865)

8 A splendid muse of fiction hath Charles Dickens,
But now and then just as the interest thickens
He stilts his pathos, and the reader sickens.

Augustus De Morgan 1806–71: Henry Crabb Robinson's diary, 17 March 1865

9 He had a large loving mind and the strongest sympathy with the poorer classes. He felt sure a better feeling, and much greater union of classes, would take place in time. And I pray earnestly it may.

Queen Victoria 1819–1901: diary, 11 June 1870

10 Heartlessness masked by a style overflowing with feeling.
of Dickens's novels

Franz Kafka 1883–1924: diary

11 Of all the Victorian novelists, he was probably the most antagonistic to the Victorian age itself.

Edmund Wilson 1895–1972: *The Wound and the Bow* (1941) 'The Two Scrooges'

12 My own experience in reading Dickens . . . is to be bounced between violent admiration and violent distaste almost every couple of paragraphs, and this is too uncomfortable a condition to be much alleviated by an inward recital of one's duty not to be fastidious, to gulp the stuff down in gobbets like a man.

Kingsley Amis 1922–95: *What Became of Jane Austen?* (1970)

13 It does not matter that Dickens' world is not lifelike; it is alive.

Lord David Cecil 1902–86: *Early Victorian Novelists* (1978)

Emily Dickinson 1830–86
American poet

1 Sappho would speak, I think, quite openly,
And Mrs Browning guard a careful silence,
But Emily would set doors ajar and slam them
And love you for your speed of observation.

Amy Lowell 1874–1925: 'The Sisters' (1925)

2 You who desired so much—in vain to ask—
Yet fed your hunger like an endless task,
Dared dignify the labour, bless the quest—
Achieved that stillness ultimately best,
Being, of all, least sought for: Emily, hear!

Hart Crane 1899–1932: 'To Emily Dickinson' (1927)

Dictionaries

3 *Lexicographer*. A writer of dictionaries, a harmless drudge.

Samuel Johnson 1709–84: *A Dictionary of the English Language* (1755)

4 *Dull*. To make dictionaries is dull work.
   8th definition of 'dull'

Samuel Johnson 1709–84: *A Dictionary of the English Language* (1755)

5 But these were the dreams of a poet doomed at last to wake a lexicographer.

Samuel Johnson 1709–84: *A Dictionary of the English Language* (1755)

6 Every quotation contributes something to the stability or enlargement of the language.
   on citations of usage in a dictionary

Samuel Johnson 1709–84: *A Dictionary of the English Language* (1755)

7 All dictionaries are made from dictionaries.

Voltaire 1694–1778: *Philosophical Dictionary* (1764)

8 Dictionaries are like watches, the worst is better than none, and the best cannot be expected to go quite true.

Samuel Johnson 1709–84: letter to Francesco Sastres, 21 August 1784

9 At painful times, when composition is impossible and reading is not *enough*, grammars and dictionaries are excellent for *distraction*.

Elizabeth Barrett Browning 1806–61: letter to Mary Russell Mitford, April 1839

10 When I feel inclined to read poetry I take down my Dictionary. The poetry of words is quite as beautiful as that of sentences. The author may arrange the gems effectively, but their shape and lustre have been given by the attrition of ages.

Oliver Wendell Holmes 1809–94: *The Autocrat of the Breakfast Table* (1858)

11 Neither is a dictionary a bad book to read. There is no cant in it, no excess of explanation, and it is full of suggestion, the raw material of possible poems and histories.

Ralph Waldo Emerson 1803–82: *The Conduct of Life* (1860)

12 What a comfort a Dictionary is!

Lewis Carroll 1832–98: *Sylvie and Bruno Concluded* (1893)

13 Here's a book full of words; one can choose as he fancies,
As a painter his tint, as a workman his tool;
Just think! all the poems and plays and romances
Were drawn out of this, like the fish from the pool.

Oliver Wendell Holmes 1809–94: 'A Familiar Letter'

1 I am not a literary man . . . I am a man of science, and I
am interested in that branch of Anthropology which deals
with the history of human speech.
   account of himself by the first Editor of the Oxford English
   Dictionary

James A. H. Murray 1837–1915:
lecture to the Ashmolean History
Society, Oxford; K. M. E. Murray
Caught in the Web of Words (1977)

of the work-room of the New English Dictionary *in the Old
Ashmolean, Oxford:*
2 That great dusty workshop, that brownest of brown
studies.

J. R. R. Tolkien 1892–1973: *c.*1919;
Humphrey Carpenter *J. R. R. Tolkien*
(1977)

3 Once or twice recently I have looked up a word in the
dictionary for fear of being again accused of coining, and
have found it there right enough—only to read on and
find that the sole authority quoted is myself in a half-
forgotten novel.
   in conversation with Robert Graves

Thomas Hardy 1840–1928: Robert
Graves *Goodbye to All That* (1929)

4 Useful as daylight, firm as stone,
Wet as a fish, dry as a bone,
Heavy as lead, light as a breeze—
Frank Wilstach's book of similes.

Franklin P. Adams 1881–1960: 'Lines
on Reading Frank J. Wilstach's *A
Dictionary of Similes*'; in *The New York
World c.*1922–30

5 O precious codex, volume, tome,
Book, writing, compilation, work
Attend the while I pen a pome,
A jest, a jape, a quip, a quirk.

Franklin P. Adams 1881–1960: 'To a
Thesaurus'; in *The New York World
c.*1922–30

6 I've been in *Who's Who*, and I know what's what, but it'll
be the first time I ever made the dictionary.
   on having an inflatable life jacket named after her

Mae West 1892–1980: letter to the
RAF, early 1940s; Fergus Cashin *Mae
West* (1981)

7 Actually if a writer needs a dictionary he should not write.
He should have read the dictionary at least three times
from beginning to end.

Ernest Hemingway 1899–1961:
letter to Bernard Berenson, 20 March
1953

8 The greatest masterpiece in literature is only a dictionary
out of order.

Jean Cocteau 1889–1963: attributed

9 [The] collective unconscious of the race is the OED.

James Merrill 1926– : in *American
Poetry Review* September/October
1979 'On James Merrill'

10 Big dictionaries are nothing but storerooms with
infrequently visited and dusty corners.

Richard W. Bailey 1939– : *Images of
English* (1991)

11 How he loved that dictionary . . . When it was near by and
he was praising it ('This, this is the one'), he would
sometimes pat and even stroke the squat black book, as if
it were one of his cats.
   of his father's Concise Oxford Dictionary

Martin Amis 1949– : in *Independent*
4 June 2000

12 She wrote her early poems very slowly, thesaurus open on
her knee . . . chewing her lips, putting a thick dark ring of
ink around each word that stirred her on the page of the
thesaurus.
   on Sylvia **Plath**

Ted Hughes 1930–98: Seamus
Heaney *Finders Keepers* (2002)

John Donne 1572–1631
English poet and divine

1 Donne, for not keeping of accent, deserved hanging.

Ben Jonson c.1573–1637: in *Conversations with William Drummond of Hawthornden* (written 1619) no. 3

2 Dr Donne's verses are like the peace of God; they pass all understanding.

James I 1566–1625: remark recorded by Archdeacon Plume (1630–1704)

3 The Muses' garden with pedantic weeds
O'erspread, was purged by thee; the lazy seeds
Of servile imitation thrown away,
And fresh invention planted.

Thomas Carew c.1595–1640: 'An Elegy upon the Death of Dr John Donne' (1640)

4 But God, who is able to prevail, wrestled with him, as the Angel did with Jacob, and marked him; marked him for his own.

Izaak Walton 1593–1683: *Life of Donne* (1670 ed.)

5 With Donne, whose muse on dromedary trots,
Wreathe iron pokers into true-love knots.

Samuel Taylor Coleridge 1772–1834: 'On Donne's Poetry' (1818)

6 Tennyson and Browning are poets, and they think; but they do not feel their thought as immediately as the odour of a rose. A thought to Donne was an experience; it modified his sensibility.

T. S. Eliot 1888–1965: 'The Metaphysical Poets' (1921)

Fedor Dostoevsky 1821–81
Russian novelist

7 It seems to me that he has never loved, that he has only imagined that he has loved, that there has been no real love on his part. I even think that he is incapable of love; he is too much occupied with other thoughts and ideas to become strongly attached to anyone earthly.
    a wife's view

Anna Dostoevsky 1846–1918: in 1887; *Dostoevsky Portrayed by His Wife* (1926)

8 The humour of Dostoevsky is the humour of a bar-loafer who ties a kettle to a dog's tail.

W. Somerset Maugham 1874–1965: *A Writer's Notebook* (1949) written in 1917

9 No matter how much of a shabby animal you may be, you can learn from Dostoevsky and Chekhov etc., how to have the most tender, unique, and coruscating soul on earth.

D. H. Lawrence 1885–1930: 'Preface to Mastro-don Gesualdo' (1923)

10 The grimacing, haunted creature . . . fierce mouthings from prehistoric ages.

Joseph Conrad 1857–1924: Cedric Watts *Joseph Conrad: Writers and their Work* (1994)

11 The novels of Dostoevsky are seething whirlpools, gyrating sandstorms, waterspouts which hiss and boil and suck us in. They are composed purely and wholly of the stuff of the soul. Against our wills we are drawn in, whirled round, blinded and suffocated, and at the same time filled with a giddy rapture.

Virginia Woolf 1882–1941: *The Common Reader* (1925) 'The Russian Point of View'

Drama

1 Let a play have five acts, neither more nor less.
Horace 65–8 BC: *Ars Poetica*

2 For what's a play without a woman in it?
Thomas Kyd 1558–94: *The Spanish Tragedy* (1592)

3   Can this cockpit hold
The vasty fields of France? or may we cram
Within this wooden O the very casques
That did affright the air at Agincourt?
William Shakespeare 1564–1616: *Henry V* (1599)

4   The play's the thing
Wherein I'll catch the conscience of the king.
William Shakespeare 1564–1616: *Hamlet* (1601)

5 Then to the well-trod stage anon,
If Jonson's learnèd sock be on,
Or sweetest Shakespeare fancy's child,
Warble his native wood-notes wild.
John Milton 1608–74: 'L'Allegro' (1645)

6 I saw Hamlet Prince of Denmark played, but now the old play began to disgust this refined age.
John Evelyn 1620–1706: diary, 26 November 1661

7 *Qu'en un lieu, qu'en un jour, un seul fait accompli
Tienne jusqu'à la fin le théâtre rempli.*
Let a single completed action, all in one place, all in one day, keep the theatre packed to the end of your play.
Nicolas Boileau 1636–1711: *L'Art poétique* (1674)

8 To wake the soul by tender strokes of art,
To raise the genius, and to mend the heart;
To make mankind, in conscious virtue bold,
Live o'er each scene, and be what they behold:
For this the Tragic Muse first trod the stage.
Alexander Pope 1688–1744: Prologue to Addison's *Cato* (1713)

9 There still remains, to mortify a wit,
The many-headed monster of the pit.
Alexander Pope 1688–1744: *Imitations of Horace* (1737)

10 O Lord, Sir—when a heroine goes mad she always goes into white satin.
Richard Brinsley Sheridan 1751–1816: *The Critic* (1779)

11 I consider it injurious for a dramatic work to be first made available to the public by a stage performance . . . [because it] can never be understood and judged in isolation as a piece of literature. Judgement will always include both the piece and its performance.
Henrik Ibsen 1828–1906: letter, 1872

12 The play was a great success, but the audience was a total failure.
after the first performance of Lady Windermere's Fan
Oscar Wilde 1854–1900: Peter Hay *Theatrical Anecdotes* (1987)

13 What the American public always wants is a tragedy with a happy ending.
explaining to Edith **Wharton** *why* The House of Mirth, *her first play, wouldn't run on Broadway*
William Dean Howells 1837–1920: in October 1906; R. W. B. Lewis *Edith Wharton* (1975)

14 The ever-importunate murmur, 'Dramatize it, dramatize it!'
Henry James 1843–1916: *The Altar of the Dead* (1909 ed.) preface

15   My curse on plays
That have to be set up in fifty ways,
On the day's war with every knave and dolt,
Theatre business, management of men.
W. B. Yeats 1865–1939: 'The Fascination of What's Difficult' (1910)

16 I regard the theatre as the greatest of all art forms, the most immediate way in which a human being can share with another the sense of what it is to be a human being.
Thornton Wilder 1897–1975: in *Paris Review* 1956

1 Theatre's a vulgar form by definition. Hundreds of spectators coughing like seals, some bellowing with laughter, others wondering out loud why they've come, all seriously affecting one another's enjoyment, these are the conditions under which even the most austere text is acted.

Peter Nichols 1927– : diary, 15 March 1970

2 I've never much enjoyed going to plays . . . The unreality of painted people standing on a platform saying things they've said to each other for months is more than I can overlook.

John Updike 1932– : George Plimpton (ed.) *Writers at Work* 4th Series (1977)

3 Drama is life with the dull bits left out.

Alfred Hitchcock 1899–1980: attributed

4 Do you know what the most difficult aspect of playwriting is? I'll tell you. It's dealing with the money people.

Tennessee Williams 1911–83: in *Paris Review* 1981

5 [Tennessee] Williams recognized that great theatre begins with great talkers, and that great talkers obey two rules: they never sound like anyone else and they never say anything directly.

Edmund White 1940– : in *New Republic* 13 May 1985

6 Theatre is a recreation. It can be much more, but unless it's recreation, I don't see the point of it.

Tom Stoppard 1937– : in *Village Voice* 4 April 1995

7 A play, I think, ought to make sense to commonsense people. Drama is akin to other inventions of man in that it ought to help us to know more, and not merely to spend our feelings.
   of The Crucible

Arthur Miller 1915– : attributed, 1996

8 I think if I've contributed anything to the sum of modern playwriting it has been to encourage comedy and drama to exist together as they used to in days of old.

Alan Ayckbourn 1939– : *The Crafty Art of Playmaking* (2002)

Drink and Drugs

9 No verse can give pleasure for long, nor last, that is written by drinkers of water.

Horace 65–8 BC: *Epistles*

10 When the wine is in, the wit is out.

Thomas Becon 1512–67: *Catechism* (1560)

11 But that which most doth take my Muse and me
Is a pure cup of rich Canary wine,
Which is the Mermaid's now, but shall be mine.

Ben Jonson c.1573–1637: 'Inviting a Friend to Supper' (1616); see **76:4**

12   What things have we seen,
Done at the Mermaid! heard words that have been
So nimble, and so full of subtil flame,
As if that every one from whence they came,
Had meant to put his whole wit in a jest,
And had resolved to live a fool, the rest
Of his dull life.

Francis Beaumont 1584–1616: 'Letter to Ben Jonson'; see **76:4**

13 I have left off wine and writing; for I really think that a man must be a bold writer who trusts to wit without it.

John Gay 1685–1732: letter to Dean Swift; *Life and Letters* (1921)

14 Let schoolmasters puzzle their brain,
With grammar, and nonsense, and learning,
Good liquor, I stoutly maintain,
Gives genius a better discerning.

Oliver Goldsmith 1728–74: *She Stoops to Conquer* (1773)

1 Claret is the liquor for boys; port, for men; but he who aspires to be a hero (smiling) must drink brandy.

Samuel Johnson 1709–84: James Boswell *Life of Samuel Johnson* (1791) 7 April 1779

2 Freedom and Whisky gang thegither!

Robert Burns 1759–96: 'The Author's Earnest Cry and Prayer' (1786)

3 A man may surely be allowed to take a glass of wine by his own fireside.
   on being encountered drinking a glass of wine in the street, while watching his theatre, the Drury Lane, burn down

Richard Brinsley Sheridan 1751–1816: T. Moore *Life of Sheridan* (1825)

4 Souls of poets dead and gone,
   What Elysium have ye known,
   Happy field or mossy cavern,
   Choicer than the Mermaid Tavern?
   Have ye tippled drink more fine
   Than mine host's Canary wine?

John Keats 1795–1821: 'Lines on the Mermaid Tavern' (1820); see **75:11**, **75:12**

5 Away! away! for I will fly to thee,
   Not charioted by Bacchus and his pards,
   But on the viewless wings of Poesy.

John Keats 1795–1821: 'Ode to a Nightingale' (1820)

6 O, for a draught of vintage! that hath been
   Cooled a long age in the deep-delvèd earth,
   Tasting of Flora and the country green,
   Dance, and Provençal song, and sunburnt mirth!

John Keats 1795–1821: 'Ode to a Nightingale' (1820)

7 Gin-and-water is the source of all my inspiration.

Lord Byron 1788–1824: *Conversations* (1824)

8 Thou hast the keys of Paradise, oh just, subtle, and mighty opium!

Thomas De Quincey 1785–1859: *Confessions of an English Opium Eater* (1822, ed. 1856)

9 *L'Opium agrandit ce qui n'a pas de bornes,*
   Allonge l'illimité,
   Approfondit le temps, creuse la volupté,
   Et de plaisirs noirs et mornes
   Remplit l'âme au-delà de sa capacité.

Charles Baudelaire 1821–67: 'Le Poison' (1857)

   Opium magnifies things that have no limits, prolongs the boundless, makes Time more profound, deepens voluptuousness, and fills the soul to overflowing with dark and gloomy pleasures.

10 To tell the story of Coleridge without the opium is to tell the story of Hamlet without mentioning the ghost.

Leslie Stephen 1832–1904: *Hours in a Library* (1874–9)

11 And malt does more than Milton can
   To justify God's ways to man.
   Ale, man, ale's the stuff to drink
   For fellows whom it hurts to think.

A. E. Housman 1859–1936: *A Shropshire Lad* (1896); see **245:1**

12 Whisky and beer for fools; absinthe for poets.

Ernest Dowson 1867–1900: Phil Baker *The Dedalus Book of Absinthe* (2001)

13 A pipe for the hour of work; a cigarette for the hour of conception; a cigar for the hour of vacuity.

George Gissing 1857–1903: *Commonplace Book* (1962)

14 After all, most struggling poets drink Camp coffee instead of nectar and find it just as inspiring and much cheaper.

Barbara Pym 1913–80: 'Young Men in Fancy Dress' (written c.1930); Hazel Holt *A Lot to Ask* (1990)

1 If you ever get that depressed unable-to-concentrate feeling, try taking Benzedrine Tablets, but not too many.

W. H. Auden 1907–73: letter, April 1940

2 Drink heightens feeling. When I drink, it heightens my emotions and I put it in a story.

F. Scott Fitzgerald 1896–1940: Andrew Turnbull *Scott Fitzgerald* (1962)

3 A man you don't like who drinks as much as you do. *definition of an alcoholic*

Dylan Thomas 1914–53: Constantine Fitzgibbon *Life of Dylan Thomas* (1965)

4 Very few writers can write on alcohol but I am one of the exceptions. I don't miss alcohol physically at all, but I do miss it mentally and spiritually.

Raymond Chandler 1888–1959: letter to Roger Machell, 14 October 1958

5 A man shouldn't fool with booze until he's fifty; then he's a damn fool if he doesn't.

William Faulkner 1897–1962: James M. Webb and A. Wigfall Green *William Faulkner of Oxford* (1965)

6 It's hard to say why writing verse, Should terminate in drink or worse.

A. P. Herbert 1890–1971: 'Lines for a Worldly Person'

7 LSD? Nothing much happened, but I did get the distinct impression that some birds were trying to communicate with me.

W. H. Auden 1907–73: George Plimpton (ed.) *The Writer's Chapbook* (1989)

8 *The Confidential Agent* . . . was completed in six weeks under the influence of benzedrine.

Graham Greene 1904–91: Marie-Françoise Allain *The Other Man, Conversations with Graham Greene* (1983)

9 Really, I can't imagine the drug scene. My generation are drinkers and smokers; I wouldn't stick a needle into myself for a hatful of golden guineas.

Philip Larkin 1922–85: letter, 15 September 1985

10 No other human being, no woman, no poem or music, book or painting, can replace alcohol in its power to give man the illusion of real creation.

Marguerite Duras 1914–96: *Practicalities* (1987, tr. 1990)

11 One simply pulls the cork out of the bottle, waits three minutes, and two thousand or more years of Scottish craftsmanship does the rest.

J. G. Ballard 1930– : George Plimpton (ed.) *The Writer's Chapbook* (1989)

12 It was a stupidity and a weakness. I've not touched it for years, but it's in your vocabulary. If something bad happens in your life, it's always there in the background, waiting for you to trip up. *on taking drugs*

Irvine Welsh 1957– : in *Guardian* 25 July 1998

John Dryden 1631–1700 see also 91:10, 134:2
English poet, critic, and dramatist

13 Ev'n copious Dryden, wanted, or forgot, The last and greatest art, the art to blot.

Alexander Pope 1688–1744: *Imitations of Horace* (1737)

14 Remember Dryden, and be blind to all his faults.

Thomas Gray 1716–71: letter to James Beattie, 2 October 1765

15 'You forget glorious John,' said Mordaunt. 'Ay, glorious you may well call him.'

Sir Walter Scott 1771–1832: *The Pirate* (1821)

1 His mind was of a slovenly character,—fond of splendour, but indifferent to neatness. Hence most of his writings exhibit the sluttish magnificence of a Russian noble, all vermin diamonds, dirty linen and inestimable sables.

Lord Macaulay 1800–59: in *Edinburgh Review* January 1828 'John Dryden'

2 Dryden's genius was of that sort which catches fire by its own motion: his chariot-wheels got hot by driving fast.

Samuel Taylor Coleridge 1772–1834: *Table Talk* (1836)

3 He is the most masculine of our poets; his style and rhythms lay the strongest stress of all our literature on the naked thew and sinew of the English language.

Gerard Manley Hopkins 1844–89: letter to Robert Bridges, 6 November 1887

4 If Dryden's plays had been as good as their prefaces he would have been a dramatist indeed.

Harley Granville-Barker 1877–1946: *On Dramatic Method* (1931)

5 There *Dryden* sits with modest smile,
The master of the middle style.

W. H. Auden 1907–73: *New Year Letter* (1941)

Earning a Living see also **Money**

6 Barefaced poverty drove me to writing verses.

Horace 65–8 BC: *Epistles*

7 Poor starving bard, how small thy gains!

Jonathan Swift 1667–1745: 'On Poetry' (1733)

8 *Patron.* Commonly a wretch who supports with insolence, and is paid with flattery.

Samuel Johnson 1709–84: *A Dictionary of the English Language* (1755)

9 Born in a cellar . . . and living in a garret.

Samuel Foote 1720–77: *The Author* (1757)

10 No man but a blockhead ever wrote, except for money.

Samuel Johnson 1709–84: James Boswell *Life of Samuel Johnson* (1791) 5 April 1776

11 When men write for profit, they are not very delicate.

Horace Walpole 1717–97: letter to Revd William Cole, 1 September 1778

12 What affectionate parent would consent to see his son devote himself to his pen as his profession? . . . Most authors close their lives in apathy or despair, and too many of them live by means which few of them would not blush to describe.

Isaac D'Israeli 1766–1848: *Calamities of Authors* (1812)

13 You will be glad to hear that every copy of *Sense and Sensibility* is sold and that it has brought me £140 besides the copyright, if that should ever be of value.

Jane Austen 1775–1817: letter, 3 July 1813

14 Aristocratic prejudices are suitable for you but not for me . . . I look at a finished poem of mine as a cobbler looks at a pair of boots: I sell for profit.

Alexander Pushkin 1799–1837: letter to Prince Petr Vyazemsky, March 1823

15 They knew luxury; they knew beggary; but they never knew comfort.
    of writers struggling to make a living in Johnson's day

Lord Macaulay 1800–59: *Essays Contributed to the Edinburgh Review* (1843) 'Samuel Johnson'

16 Always waiting and what to do or to say in the meantime I don't know, and who wants poets at all in lean years?

Johann Christian Friedrich Hölderlin 1770–1843: 'Bread and Wine' (1800-01)

17 I need hardly tell you that poetry, even the best . . . is not a thing for a man to live upon while he is in the flesh, however immortal it may render him in spirit.

Leigh Hunt 1784–1859: letter to Rossetti, 31 March 1848

1 My object is remuneration.
   submitting her first short story for magazine publication

Frances Hodgson Burnett 1849–1924: letter, *c*.1867; Ann Thwaite *Waiting for the Party* (1994)

2 During the last twenty years I have made by literature something near £70,000. As I have said before in these pages, I look upon the result as comfortable, but not splendid.

Anthony Trollope 1815–82: *Autobiography* (1883)

3 Brains that are unbought will never serve the public much. Take away from English authors their copyrights, and you would very soon take away also from England her authors.

Anthony Trollope 1815–82: *Autobiography* (1883)

4 Medicine is my lawful wife and literature is my mistress. When I get tired of one I spend the night with the other.

Anton Chekhov 1860–1904: letter to A. S. Suvorin, 11 September 1888

5 I am the literary man of 1882 . . . I am learning my business. Literature nowadays is a trade. Putting aside men of genius, who may succeed by mere cosmic force, your successful man of letters is your successful tradesman. He thinks first and foremost of the markets; when one kind of goods begins to go off slackly, he is ready with something new and appetising.

George Gissing 1857–1903: 'Jasper Milvain' in *New Grub Street* (1891)

6 What an insane thing it is to make literature one's only means of support! When the most trivial accident may at any time prove fatal to one's power of work for weeks and months. No, that is the unpardonable sin! To make a trade of art!

George Gissing 1857–1903: 'Edwin Reardon' in *New Grub Street* (1891)

7 The profession of letters is, after all, the only one in which one can make no money without being ridiculous.

Jules Renard 1864–1910: diary, 1906

8 The tip's a good one, as for literature
   It gives no man a sinecure.

   And no one knows, at sight, a masterpiece.
   And give up verse, my boy,
   There's nothing in it.

Ezra Pound 1885–1972: *Hugh Selwyn Mauberley* (1920) 'Mr Nixon'

9 Poems are such very personal things. I can't get quite used to being paid for them at all.

Thomas Hardy 1840–1928: John Middleton Murry *Katherine Mansfield and Other Literary Portraits* (1949)

10 Poor Tom. He was a clever boy, but I never thought he would take to writing, and did not like it when he did. Writing, I think, is not a respectable way of earning a living.
   Hardy's spinster cousin, aged 84

Teresa Hardy : in 1928, James Gibson (ed.) *Thomas Hardy: Interviews and Recollections* (1999)

11 Go in for Celtic, lad; there's money in it.
   a philologist's advice to the young **Tolkien**

Joseph Wright 1855–1930: Humphrey Carpenter *J. R. R. Tolkien* (1977)

12 For me I never cared for fame
   Solvency was my only aim.

J. C. Squire 1884–1958: at a dinner given in his honour, 15 December 1932; Patrick Howarth *Squire: Most Generous of Men* (1963)

13 There is only one way to make money at writing, and that is to marry a publisher's daughter.

George Orwell 1903–50: *Down and Out in Paris and London* (1933)

14 I had to earn my own living and this is antipathetic to a purely aesthetic view of life.

Louis MacNeice 1907–63: *Modern Poetry* (1938)

1 High-priced commercial writing for the magazines is a very definite trick.

F. Scott Fitzgerald 1896–1940: letter 19 May 1940

2 However toplofty and idealistic a man may be, he can always rationalize his right to earn money.

Raymond Chandler 1888–1959: letter to Carl Brandt, his New York literary agent, 15 November 1951; *Raymond Chandler Speaking* (1962)

3 You don't write to support yourself; you work to support your writing.

Alfred Kazin 1915–98: Sylvia Plath, letter to her mother, 25 October 1954

4 If you want to write poetry you must earn a living some other way.

T. S. Eliot 1888–1965: attributed, 1958

5 The profession of book writing makes horse racing seem like a solid, stable business.

John Steinbeck 1902–68: in *Newsweek* 24 December 1962

6 It is a sad fact about our culture that a poet can earn much more money writing or talking about his art than he can by practising it.

W. H. Auden 1907–73: *The Dyer's Hand* (1962) foreword

7   Who would, for preference
be a bard in an oral culture,
obliged at drunken feasts to improvise a eulogy
of some beefy illiterate burner,
giver of rings, or depend for bread on the moods of a
     Baroque Prince, expected,
like his dwarf, to amuse?

W. H. Auden 1907–73: 'The Cave of Making' (1965)

8 Nowadays one's agent, and one's solicitor, and one's bank manager only do the irreducible minimum, but unfortunately it is the minimum one cannot do oneself.

Ivy Compton-Burnett 1884–1969: Hilary Spurling *Secrets of a Woman's Heart: the Later Life of Ivy Compton-Burnett* (1984)

9 [Feydeau] had the great traditional stimulant to the industry of an artist, laziness and debt.

John Mortimer 1923– : *Clinging to the Wreckage* (1982)

10 One of my great surprises when I was in America was about twenty-five years ago in Harvard, hearing Randall Jarrell deliver a bitter attack on the way poets were neglected. Yet there were about two thousand people present, and he was being paid five hundred dollars for delivering this attack.

Stephen Spender 1909–95: George Plimpton (ed.) *Writers at Work* (6th series, 1984)

11 Poetry? It's a hobby.
I run model trains.
Mr Shaw there breeds pigeons.

It's not work. You don't sweat.
Nobody pays for it.
You *could* advertise soap.

Basil Bunting 1900–85: 'What the Chairman Told Tom'; see **88:3**

12 Many books are written . . . for very mundane reasons. It tends to be forgotten, for example, that Johnson wrote *Rasselas* to defray the expenses of his mother's funeral, or that Dumas's terse, interrogative dialogue was the result of his being paid at so many centimes a line.

D. J. Taylor 1960– : *After the War* (1993)

13 Everyone involved with the production of a book—the editors and publishers, the manufacturers of paper, the binders, the van drivers, the accountants, the publicists, the booksellers, the office cleaners—makes a reasonable

Milton Shulman 1913– : Barry Turner *The Writer's Handbook 1996* (1995)

living except the majority of starry-eyed masochists who
actually provide the words without which all the others
would have to be doing something else.

1 Soon, like a chorus of cries from a sinking ship, the books
die away; they eddy into the back shelves of bookstores,
and then into the mountainous return piles, to reappear a
year or two later in the discount catalogues and in a
paperback version. The royalty statements, by the time
they appear, are like shreds of wreckage which float to the
surface of a cruel, inscrutable sea.

John Updike 1932– : 'Me and My
Books' in *New Yorker* 1997

2 I'm up to my neck in the real world, every day. Just you
try doing your VAT return with a head full of goblins.

Terry Pratchett 1948– : in *Sunday
Times* 27 February 2000 'Talking
Heads'

3 You just have to work with what God sends, and if God
doesn't seem to understand the concept of commercial
success, then that's your bad luck.

Michael Frayn 1933– : in *Sunday
Times* 3 February 2002

Editors and Editing see also Omission, Revision

4 They are now disfigured by all manner of crooked marks of
Papa's critical indignation, besides various abusive margin
notes.
   of the draft pages of her first book, Letters for Literary
   Ladies

Maria Edgeworth 1767–1849: letter
to Sophy Ruxton, February 1794

5 The poem will please if it is lively—if it is stupid it will
fail—but I will have none of your damned cutting and
slashing.

Lord Byron 1788–1824: letter to his
publisher John Murray, 6 April 1819

6 That passage is what I call the sublime dashed to pieces by
cutting too close with the fiery four-in-hand round the
corner of nonsense.
   on lines excluded from his own poem Limbo, *written 1817*

Samuel Taylor Coleridge
1772–1834: *Table Talk* (1835) 20
January 1834

7 Did you ever buy your own meat? That cutting down of
30 pages to 20, is what you proposed to the butcher when
you asked him to take off the bony bit at the end, and the
skinny bit at the other . . . the butcher told you that
nature had produced the joint bone and skin as you saw it.
   on being asked to make cuts in a short story

Anthony Trollope 1815–82: letter, 9
August 1860

8 Will you tell me my fault, frankly as to yourself, for I had
rather wince, than die. Men do not call the surgeon to
commend the bone, but to set it, Sir.

Emily Dickinson 1830–86: letter to
T. W. Higginson, July 1862

of the compilation of a dictionary of national biography:
9 The editor of such a work must, by the necessity of the
case, be autocratic. He will do his best to be a considerate
autocrat.

Leslie Stephen 1832–1904: in
Athenaeum 23 December 1882

10 After my marriage, she edited everything I wrote. And
what is more—she not only edited my works—she edited
me!
   of his wife, Livy

Mark Twain 1835–1910: Van Wyck
Brooks *The Ordeal of Mark Twain*
(1920)

11 I have done it . . . But it's a bloody trade.
   on cutting his Times Literary Supplement *review of*
   Balzac; *a similar response to being asked to cut an obituary,*
   'But yours is a butcher's trade', *is also attributed to James*

Henry James 1843–1916: letter to
Bruce Richmond, 4 June 1913

1 Whence came the intrusive comma on p. 4? It did not fall from the sky.

A. E. Housman 1859–1936: letter to the Richards Press, 3 July 1930

2 Everything seems now to be right with the book. And you will see, when we send you the page proof, what we have done about the words.
   letter to Ernest **Hemingway** *from his editor at Scribners*

Maxwell Perkins 1884–1947: letter to Hemingway, 22 July 1932

3 Again and again in my literary life I have encountered . . . editorial timidity. I think it was Edwin Godkin, then the masterly editor of the New York *Evening Post,* who said that the choice of articles published in American magazines was entirely determined by the fear of scandalizing a non-existent clergyman in the Mississippi Valley.

Edith Wharton 1862–1937: *A Backward Glance* (1934)

4 No passion in the world is equal to the passion to alter someone else's draft.

H. G. Wells 1866–1946: attributed

5 Editing is the same as quarrelling with writers—same thing exactly.

Harold Ross 1892–1951: in *Time* 6 March 1950

6 I shook with anger at their august editorial decisions, their fussy little changes and pipsqueak variations on my copy.

S. J. Perelman 1904–79: in 1957; attributed

7 [The editor] should say to himself, 'How can I help this writer to say it better in his own style?' and avoid 'How can I show him how I would write it, if it were my piece?'
   memo to New Yorker

James Thurber 1894–1961: in 1959; in *New York Times Book Review* 4 December 1988

8 If a poet has printed more than one version of his own poem, an editor . . . has the liberty of choice. Sometimes the first is preferable. Wordsworth, in old age, usually spoiled his earlier poems.

Robert Graves 1895–1985: 'Standards of Craftmanship' (Oxford Addresses on Poetry, 1964)

on being asked if he agreed with the view that 'most editors are failed writers':
9 Perhaps, but so are most writers.

T. S. Eliot 1888–1965: Robert Giroux in *Sewanee Review* Winter 1966 'A Personal Memoir'

10 It's just a matter of checking the facts and the spelling, crossing out the first sentence, and removing any attempts at jokes.
   defining the job of a sub-editor

Michael Frayn 1933– : *Towards the End of the Morning* (1967)

11 My definition of a good editor is a man I think charming, who sends me large cheques, praises my work, my physical beauty, and my sexual prowess, and who has a stranglehold on my publisher.

John Cheever 1912–82: George Plimpton (ed.) *The Writer's Chapbook* (1989)

12 What is an editor but a cross between a fall guy and a father figure?

Arthur Koestler 1905–83: George Greenfield *Scribblers for Bread* (1989)

13 Sometimes even sincerity should be edited.

Craig Raine 1944– : in *Literary Review* June 1985

14 I've had great fun doing some stories by phone with certain magazine editors . . . Bargaining goes on, horse-trading. 'You can have the dash if I get the semicolon.'

Margaret Atwood 1939– : in an interview, March 1986; in *Paris Review* Winter 1990

15 It's a little like going to the tailor or barber. I have never liked haircuts and I don't like being edited, even slightly.

John Updike 1932– : on *Blue Pencil* (BBC Radio 3) 6 August 1995

Effort

1   Give
Me leisure, all the time Maecenas found
For Horace and his Virgil, and I'll try
To build a masterpiece destined to live
And save my name from ashes. When the ground
Is poor, the ox works listlessly; rich soil
Tires, but there's satisfaction then in toil.

Martial AD c.40–c.104: *Epigrammata*
tr. James Michie

2 This manner of writing [prose] wherein knowing myself
inferior to myself . . . I have the use, as I may account it,
but of my left hand.

John Milton 1608–74: *The Reason of Church Government* (1642) bk. 2, introduction

3 While pensive poets painful vigils keep,
Sleepless themselves, to give their readers sleep.

Alexander Pope 1688–1744: *The Dunciad* (1742)

4 A man may write at any time, if he will set himself
doggedly to it.

Samuel Johnson 1709–84: James Boswell *Life of Samuel Johnson* (1791) March 1750

5 I often compare myself to a poor old woman, who having
no bellows, lays herself down on her hearth, and with her
mouth endeavours to blow up into a faint blaze a little
handful of sticks, half green, half dry, in order to warm a
mess of pottage, that, after all her pains, hardly keeps life
and soul together.

Samuel Richardson 1689–1761: letter 1751

6 You write with ease, to show your breeding,
But easy writing's vile hard reading.

Richard Brinsley Sheridan 1751–1816: 'Clio's Protest' (written 1771, published 1819)

7 What is written without effort is in general read without
pleasure.

Samuel Johnson 1709–84: William Seward *Biographia* (1799)

8 There is a pleasure in poetic pains
Which only poets know.

William Cowper 1731–1800: *The Task* (1785) 'The Timepiece'

9 'Tis hard indeed to toil, as we sometimes do, to our own
loss and disappointment; to sweat in the field of fame,
merely to reap a harvest of chaff, and pile up reams of
paper for the worm to dine upon. It is a cruel thing to rack
our brains for nothing, run our jaded fancies to a
standstill, and then lie down at the conclusion of our race,
a carcase for the critics.

Richard Cumberland 1732–1811: *Henry* (1795)

10 There was nothing spontaneous, no impulse or ease about
his genius: it was all forced, up-hill work, making a toil of
pleasure. And hence his overweening admiration of his
own works, from the effort they had cost him, and the
apprehension that they were not proportionately admired
by others.
    on Ben Jonson

William Hazlitt 1778–1830: *Lectures on the English Comic Writers* (1818)

11 Wrote six leaves today and am tired—that's all—

Sir Walter Scott 1771–1832: diary, 1827

12 I am a galley slave to pen and ink.

Honoré de Balzac 1799–1850: letter 1832

1 When Rogers produces a couplet, he goes to bed, and the knocker is tied—and straw is laid down—and caudle is made—and the answer to inquiries is that Mr Rogers is as well as can be expected.
   of the poet Samuel Rogers (1763-1855)

Sydney Smith 1771–1845: Harriet Martineau *Biographical Sketches* (1869)

2 What a heavy oar the pen is, and what a strong current ideas are to row in!

Gustave Flaubert 1821–80: letter, 23 October 1851

3 Look at such of my manuscripts as are in the library at Gad's, and think of the patient hours devoted year after year to single lines.

Charles Dickens 1812–70: letter to his son Harry, 11 February 1868

4 Inscribe all human effort with one word,
   Artistry's haunting curse, the Incomplete!

Robert Browning 1812–89: *The Ring and the Book* (1868-9)

5 Forethought is the elbow-grease which a novelist, or poet, or dramatist, requires.

Anthony Trollope 1815–82: *Thackeray* (1879)

6 It bored me hellishly to write the Emigrant; well, it's going to bore others to read it; that's only fair.

Robert Louis Stevenson 1850-94: letter to Sidney Colvin, January 1880

7 What a heavy thing is a pen!

Émile Zola 1840–1902: letter, 25 October 1882

8 Three hours a day will produce as much as a man ought to write.

Anthony Trollope 1815–82: *Autobiography* (1883)

9 After a man has done making love, there is no other thing on earth to make him happy except hard work.

Anthony Trollope 1815–82: *Autobiography* (1883)

10 Tom's most well, now . . . and so there ain't nothing more to write about, and I am rotten glad of it, because if I'd knowed what a trouble it was to make a book I wouldn't a tackled it and ain't agoing to no more.

Mark Twain 1835–1910: *The Adventures of Huckleberry Finn* (1884)

11 I find twenty-five years of practice only make *me* write slower and slower; so that I am rapidly reaching a fine maximum of twenty-five words a day.

Henry James 1843–1916: letter 30 March 1895

12 When I face that fatal manuscript it seems to me that I have forgotten how to think—worse! how to write. It is as if something in my head had given way to let in a cold grey mist. I knock about in it till I am positively, physically sick.

Joseph Conrad 1857–1924: letter, 5 August 1896

13 I can write only by thinking back; I have never written straight from nature. I need to let a subject strain through my memory until only what is important or typical remains as a filter.

Anton Chekhov 1860–1904: letter, 15 December 1897

14 My instinct is to multiply books and articles and plays. I constantly gloat over the number of words I have written in a given period.

Arnold Bennett 1867–1931: diary, 5 April 1908

15 The fascination of what's difficult
   Has dried the sap out of my veins, and rent
   Spontaneous joy and natural content
   Out of my heart.

W. B. Yeats 1865-1939: 'The Fascination of What's Difficult' (1910)

16 For twenty months . . . I had, like the prophet of old, 'wrestled with the Lord' for my creation . . . These are, perhaps, strong words, but it is difficult to characterize otherwise the intimacy and strain of a creative effort in which mind and will and conscience are engaged to the

Joseph Conrad 1857–1924: *A Personal Record* (1912)

full, hour after hour, day after day, away from the world, and to the exclusion of all that makes life really lovable and gentle—something for which a material parallel can only be found in the everlasting stress of the westward winter passage round Cape Horn.
on the writing of Nostromo

1 Determination not to give in, and the sense of an impending shape keep one at it more than anything.
on beginning a new book

Virginia Woolf 1882–1941: diary, 11 May 1920

2 The task I set myself technically in writing a book from eighteen different points of view and in as many styles, all apparently unknown or undiscovered by my fellow tradesmen, that and the nature of the legend chosen would be enough to upset anyone's mental balance.
of writing Ulysses

James Joyce 1882–1941: letter, 24 June 1921

3 A thousand things to be written had I time: had I power. A very little writing uses up my capacity for writing.

Virginia Woolf 1882–1941: *A Writer's Diary* (1953) 18 September 1927

4 Only amateurs say that they write for their own amusement. Writing is not an amusing occupation. It is a combination of ditch-digging, mountain-climbing, treadmill and childbirth. Writing may be interesting, absorbing, exhilarating, racking, relieving. But amusing? Never!

Edna Ferber 1887–1968: *A Peculiar Treasure* (1939)

5 You can't produce art by trying, by setting up exacting standards, by talking about critical minutiae, by the Flaubert method. It is produced with great ease, in an almost off-hand manner, and without self-consciousness.

Raymond Chandler 1888–1959: letter to Jamie Hamilton, 17 June 1949

6 Writing a book is a horrible, exhausting struggle, like a long bout of some painful illness.

George Orwell 1903–50: *Collected Essays* (1968) vol. 1 'Why I Write'

7 The art of writing, like the art of love, runs all the way from a kind of routine hard to distinguish from piling bricks to a kind of frenzy closely related to delirium tremens.

H. L. Mencken 1880–1956: *Minority Report* (1956)

8 Routine, in an intelligent man, is a sign of ambition.

W. H. Auden 1907–73: 'The Life of That-There Poet' (1958)

9 I am constantly meeting ladies who say 'how lovely it must be to write', as though one sat down at the *escritoire* after breakfast, and it poured out like a succession of bread and butter letters, instead of being dragged out, by tongs, a bloody mess, in the small hours.

Patrick White 1912–90: after finishing *The Solid Mandala* (1966); *Letters* (1996)

10 The conditions of writing change absolutely between the first novel and the second: the first is an adventure, the second is a duty.

Graham Greene 1904–91: *A Sort of Life* (1971)

11 I never knew anyone who had a passion for words who had as much difficulty in saying things as I do. I very seldom say them in a manner I like. If I do it's because I don't know I'm trying.

Marianne Moore 1887–1972: George Plimpton (ed.) *The Writer's Chapbook* (1989)

12 READER: Miss Moore, your poetry is very difficult to read.
MARIANNE MOORE: It is very difficult to write.

Marianne Moore 1887–1972: George Plimpton (ed.) *The Writer's Chapbook* (1989)

1 Novelists do not write as birds sing, by the push of nature. It is part of the job that there should be much routine and some daily stuff on the level of carpentry.

William Golding 1911–93: 'Rough Magic', lecture, 16 February 1977; *A Moving Target* (1982)

2 I love being a writer. What I can't stand is the paperwork.

Peter de Vries 1910–93: Laurence J. Peter (ed.) *Quotations for our Time* (1977)

3 For a writer, going back home means back to the pen, pencil, and typewriter—and the blank, implacable sheet of white paper.

Paul Scott 1920–78: Hilary Spurling *Paul Scott* (1990)

4 In my experience, after a few months, an author usually feels that his novel is taking control. There has been the drive at increasing speed of the plane along the runway, then the slow lift and you feel the wheels no longer touch the ground.

Graham Greene 1904–91: *Ways of Escape* (1980)

5 Ever tried. Ever failed. No matter. Try again. Fail again. Fail better.

Samuel Beckett 1906–89: *Worstward Ho* (1983)

6 89% work and worry over work, struggle against lunacy 10%, and friends 1%.
division of his life

Tennessee Williams 1911–83: John Lahr *Light Fantastic* (1996)

7 Many a poetic career begins and ends with poems which do no more than cry out in innocent primary glee, 'Listen, I can do it! Look how well it turned out! And I can do it again! See?'

Seamus Heaney 1939– : *The Government of the Tongue* (1988)

8 I doubt that an overwhelmingly jolly, optimistic person has ever been an artist of any sort. You are made melancholy, more than anything, by the struggle you have with words—the struggle you have with trying to express what sometimes resists expression.

William Trevor 1928– : in *Paris Review* 1989

9 Don't ask a writer what he's working on. It's like asking someone with cancer about the progress of his disease.

Jay McInerney 1955– : *Brightness Falls* (1992)

10 I had sticking power, which is just as important as literary talent. I just got on with the work. And I think there are such things as writing animals. I simply have to write.

Doris Lessing 1919– : in *Chicago Tribune* 3 January 1993

11 The hours spent writing are like giving a performance on the page, a prolonged one-man show which will grip the audience's attention . . . Writing fiction is exhausting; it's not the mechanical process that tires you out but the stage fright, the tension and the final collapse in the dressing room and the first drink of the evening.

John Mortimer 1923– : Clare Boylan (ed.) *The Agony and the Ego* (1993)

12 Trying to write with a bit more precision this morning and to come up with the right word, I remember a machine that used to be in every seaside amusement arcade. A big mirrored drum in a glass case slowly revolved and on it some (not very) desirable objects . . . One slid in a penny that activated a grab which one had to manoeuvre over one's chosen prize before at the critical moment releasing the grab to grip the object. Except that it never did. Either the grab moved or failed to grip or the drum revolved what one wanted out of reach. That was what happened this morning.

Alan Bennett 1934– : *Writing Home* (1994)

1 [I shelved the project] when I was told I had to track one butler down to a male brothel in Norway.
on her biography of friend L. P. Hartley

Penelope Fitzgerald 1916–2000: in *Daily Telegraph* 3 May 2000

2 I have made a strict point to take lavish periods away from writing, so much time that my writing life sometimes seems to involve not writing more than writing, a fact I warmly approve of.

Richard Ford 1944– : in *Writers on Writing: Collected Essays from The New York Times* (2001)

3 The act of writing is a kind of guerrilla warfare; there is no vacation, no leave, no relief. In actuality there is very little chance of victory. You are, you fear . . . likely to be defeated by your fondest dreams.

Walter Mosley 1952– : in *Writers on Writing: Collected Essays from The New York Times* (2001)

4 I can't write quickly. If I could write a book a year and maintain the same quality, I'd be happy. I'd love to write a book a year, but I don't think I'd have any fans.

Donna Tartt 1963– : in *Sunday Times* 2 June 2002

George Eliot 1819–80 see also **2:9**, **182:11**
English novelist

5 I *have* tried to be moral, and dislike her and dislike her books—but it won't do. There is not a wrong word, or a wrong thought in them, I do believe,—and though I should have been more 'comfortable' for some indefinable reason, if a *man* had written them instead of a *woman*, yet I think the author must be a noble creature; and I shut my eyes to the awkward blot in her life.

Elizabeth Gaskell 1810–65: letter, 1856

6 She is magnificently ugly—deliciously hideous. She has a low forehead, a dull grey eye, a vast pendulous nose . . . Now in this vast ugliness resides a most powerful beauty which, in a very few minutes steals forth and charms the mind, so that you end as I ended, in falling in love with her. Yes behold me literally in love with this great horse-faced blue-stocking.

Henry James 1843–1916: letter, 10 May 1869

7 I do not feel very confident that I can make anything satisfactory of Middlemarch.

George Eliot 1819–80: letter to John Blackwood, 11 September 1869

8 A marvellous mind *throbs* in every page of *Middlemarch*. It raises the standard of what is to be expected of women . . . We know all about the female heart; but apparently there is a female brain, too.

Henry James 1843–1916: letter, 5 March 1873

9 [She] is sometimes heavy—sometimes abstruse, sometimes almost dull, but always like an egg, full of meat.

Anthony Trollope 1815–82: letter, 18 September 1874

10 She was one whose private life should be left in privacy, as may be said of all who have achieved fame by literary merits.

Anthony Trollope 1815–82: letter, 17 January 1881

11 I found out in the first two pages that it was a woman's writing—she supposed that in making a door, you last of all put in the *panels*!

Thomas Carlyle 1795–1881: Gordon S. Haight *George Eliot* (1968)

1 She told me that, in all she considered her best writing there was a 'not herself' which took possession of her, and that she felt her own personality to be merely the instrument through which the spirit as it were was acting.
of his wife George Eliot

J . W. Cross 1840–1924: *Life of George Eliot* (1884)

2 What do I think of *Middlemarch*? What do I think of glory?

Emily Dickinson 1830–86: Gordon Haight *George Eliot* (1968)

T. S. Eliot 1888–1965
Anglo-American poet, critic, and dramatist

3 Many of my colleagues . . . think a banker has no business whatever to be a poet. They don't think the two things can combine. But I believe that anything a man does, whatever his *hobby* may be, it's all the better if he is really keen on it and does well. I think it helps him with his work . . . I don't see why—in time, of course, in time—he mightn't even become a Branch Manager.
view of a senior official of Lloyds Bank where Eliot was employed; see **80:11**

Anonymous: in conversation c.1920; I. A. Richards 'On T.S.E.' in *T. S. Eliot: the Man and His Work* (1967)

4 Mr Eliot . . . has arrived at the supreme Eminence among English critics largely through disguising himself as a corpse.

Ezra Pound 1885–1972: in *Front* November 1930

5 He is without pose and full of poise. he makes one feel that all cleverness is an excuse for thinking hard.

Harold Nicolson 1886–1968: *Diaries and Letters, 1930–1939* 2 March 1932

6 How unpleasant to meet Mr Eliot!
With his features of clerical cut,
And his brow so grim
And his mouth so prim
And his conversation, so nicely
Restricted to What Precisely
And If and Perhaps and But.

T. S. Eliot 1888–1965: 'Five-Finger Exercises' (1936); see **157:11**

7 Osbert was wonderful, as you would expect, and Edith, of course, but then we had this rather lugubrious man in a suit, and he read a poem . . . I think it was called The Desert. And first the girls got the giggles and then I did and then even the King.
of an evening at Windsor during the war, arranged by Osbert Sitwell, at which T. S. Eliot read from 'The Waste Land' to the King and Queen and the Princesses

Queen Elizabeth, the Queen Mother 1900–2002: private conversation, reported in *Spectator* 30 June 1990

8 [*The Waste Land*] was only the relief of a personal and wholly insignificant grouse against life; it is just a piece of rhythmical grumbling.

T. S. Eliot 1888–1965: *The Waste Land* (ed. Valerie Eliot, 1971) epigraph

9 'Mr Eliot' was a fictional character and Tom himself helped to create him. Among the roles the poet deftly played were The Anglican Clergyman, The Formidable Professor, Dr Johnson and the Genteel Bostonian.

Edmund Wilson 1895–1972: attributed

10 Self-contempt, well-grounded.
on the foundation of T. S. Eliot's work

F. R. Leavis 1895–1978: in *Times Literary Supplement* 21 October 1988

1 Even the greatest poets need something to cling to. Keats
had Beauty; Milton had God. T. S. Eliot's standby was
Worry.

John Carey 1934– : in *Sunday Times*
25 September 1988

Ralph Waldo Emerson 1803–82 see also **256:4**
American philosopher and poet

2 I think Emerson is more than a brilliant fellow. Be his stuff
begged, borrowed, or stolen, or of his own domestic
manufacture he is an uncommon man.

Herman Melville 1819–91: letter to
Evert Duychinck, 3 March 1849

Ending see also Beginning

3 Whoa, little book! Slow up! Easy there! Steady!
We've reached the finishing post, yet you're still ready
To gallop uncontrollably on, to run
Past the last page, as if your job weren't done.

Martial AD c.40–c.104: *Epigrammata*,
tr. James Michie

4 Be of good cheer, my weary readers, for I have espied land,
as Diogenes said to his weary scholars when he had read
to a waste leaf.
    waste *in the sense of* 'blank'

Thomas Nashe 1567–1601: *Nashes
Lenten Stuffe* (1599)

5 I would not give a groat for that man's knowledge in pen-
craft, who does not understand this—That the best plain
narrative in the world, tacked very close to the last spirited
apostrophe to my uncle Toby—would have felt both cold
and vapid upon the reader's palate;—therefore I forthwith
put an end to the chapter, though I was in the middle of
my story.

Laurence Sterne 1713–68: *Tristram
Shandy* (1759–67)

6 I think the book, in its present conclusion, somewhat
original, for the hero and heroine are neither plunged in
the depths of misery, nor exalted to unhuman
happiness,—Is not such a middle state more natural?
More according to real life, and less resembling every other
book of fiction?

Fanny Burney 1752–1840: letter to
Samuel Crisp, 6 April 1782

on his completion of The Decline and Fall of the Roman Empire:
7 I will not dissemble the first emotions of joy on the
recovery of my freedom, and, perhaps, the establishment
of my fame. But my pride was soon humbled, and a sober
melancholy was spread over my mind, by the idea that I
had taken an everlasting leave of an old and agreeable
companion.

Edward Gibbon 1737–94: *Memoirs
of My Life* (1796)

8 Readers . . . will see in the tell-tale compression of the
pages before them, that we are all hastening together to
perfect felicity.

Jane Austen 1775–1817: *Northanger
Abbey* (1818)

9 All tragedies are finished by a death,
All comedies are ended by a marriage;
The future states of both are left to faith.

Lord Byron 1788–1824: *Don Juan*
(1819–24)

10 I want to leave everybody dissatisfied and unhappy at the
end of the story—we ought all to be with our own and all
other stories.

William Makepeace Thackeray
1811–63: letter, 3 September 1848

1 It would concern the reader little, perhaps, to know, how sorrowfully the pen is laid down at the close of a two-years' imaginative task; or how an author feels as if he were dismissing some portion of himself into the shadowy world, when a crowd of the creatures of his brain are going from him for ever.

Charles Dickens 1812–70: preface to *David Copperfield* (1850)

2 Conclusions are the weak point of most authors, but some of the fault lies in the very nature of a conclusion, which is at best a negation.

George Eliot 1819–80: letter to John Blackwood, 1 May 1857

3 The end of a novel, like the end of a children's dinner-party, must be made up of sweetmeats and sugar-plums.

Anthony Trollope 1815–82: *Barchester Towers* (1857)

4 I *do* incline to melancholy endings.

Henry James 1843–1916: letter, 30 October 1878

5 Great is the art of beginning, but greater the art is of ending;
Many a poem is marred by a superfluous verse.

Henry Wadsworth Longfellow 1807–82: 'Elegiac Verse' (1880)

6 When I sit down to write a novel I do not at all know, and I do not very much care, how it is to end.

Anthony Trollope 1815–82: *Autobiography* (1883)

7 A 'happy ending' . . . a distribution at the last of prizes, pensions, husbands, wives, babies, millions, appended paragraphs, and cheerful remarks.

Henry James 1843–1916: 'The Art of Fiction' (1888)

8 It is just as well that it came to an end. The endless cohabitation with these imaginary people had begun to make me not a little nervous.
on finishing Hedda Gabler

Henrik Ibsen 1828–1906: letter, 1890

9 If you are going to make a book end badly, it must end badly from the beginning.

Robert Louis Stevenson 1850–94: letter to J. M. Barrie, November 1892

10 It's finished! A scratching of the pen writing the final word, and suddenly this entire company of people who have spoken into my ear, gesticulated before my eyes, lived with me for so many years, becomes a band of phantoms who retreat, fade, and dissolve—are made pallid and indistinct by the sunlight of this brilliant and sombre day.
on finishing Almayer's Folly

Joseph Conrad 1857–1924: letter, 24 April 1894

11 The time-honoured bread-sauce of the happy ending.

Henry James 1843–1916: *Theatricals* (1894) 2nd series

12 A poem is never finished; it's always an accident that puts a stop to it—that is to say, gives it to the public.

Paul Valéry 1871–1945: *Littérature* (1930)

13 My last page is always latent in my first; but the intervening windings of the way become clear only as I write.

Edith Wharton 1862–1937: *A Backward Glance* (1934)

14 I have three more chapters and an epilogue to do, and then I shall spend about two months putting on the twiddly bits.
of Keep the Aspidistra Flying

George Orwell 1903–50: letter to Rayner Heppenstall, September 1935

15 Ends always give me trouble. Characters run away with you, and so won't fit on to what is coming.

E. M. Forster 1879–1970: George Plimpton (ed.) *The Writer's Chapbook* (1989)

1 Not that the story seems all right, but that it seems
inevitable.
   on how she knows when a story is finished

Mavis Gallant 1922- : in *Canadian Fiction Magazine* November 1978

2 It's pure instinct. The curtain comes down when the
rhythm seems right—when the action calls for a finish.
I'm very fond of curtain lines, of doing them properly.

Harold Pinter 1930- : George Plimpton (ed.) *The Writer's Chapbook* (1989)

3 I'm always aware, when I've 'finished' a piece, of being
utterly defeated and excluded—as if I'd been shoved aside
by somebody I do not like one bit. Yet it seems to be the
only way I can do it.

Ted Hughes 1930-98: letter to William Scammell, 23 November 1990

4 You don't say, 'I've done it!' You come, with a kind of
horrible desperation, to realize that this will do.

Anthony Burgess 1917-93: Clare Boylan (ed.) *The Agony and the Ego* (1993)

5 For me, endings are never really endings. They're just
there for the sake of the book.

Carol Shields 1935- : interview in *Observer*, 28 April 2002

6 When you write happy endings you are not taken
seriously as a writer.

Carol Shields 1935- : interview in *Observer*, 28 April 2002

7 As soon as I put a full stop on a book, it's not my thing
any more. It ceases to be mine even more when the reader
picks it up.

Zadie Smith 1975- : in *Observer* 25 August 2002

Epitaphs

8 Good friend, for Jesu's sake forbear
To dig the dust enclosed here.
Blest be the man that spares these stones,
And curst be he that moves my bones.

William Shakespeare 1564-1616: inscription on his grave, Stratford upon Avon, probably composed by himself

9 O rare Ben Jonson.

Anonymous: inscription on the tomb of Ben Jonson in Westminster Abbey

10 Here lies my wife; here let her lie!
Now she's at peace and so am I.

John Dryden 1631-1700: epitaph; attributed but not traced in his works

11 The body of
Benjamin Franklin, printer,
(Like the cover of an old book,
Its contents worn out,
And stripped of its lettering and gilding)
Lies here, food for worms!
Yet the work itself shall not be lost,
For it will, as he believed, appear once more
In a new
And more beautiful edition,
Corrected and amended
By its Author!

Benjamin Franklin 1706-90: epitaph for himself (1728)

12 Where fierce indignation can no longer tear his heart.
   Swift's epitaph

Jonathan Swift 1667-1745: S. Leslie *The Skull of Swift* (1928)

13 To Oliver Goldsmith, A Poet, Naturalist, and Historian,
who left scarcely any style of writing untouched, and
touched none that he did not adorn.
   epitaph on **Goldsmith** (*1728-74*)

Samuel Johnson 1709-84: James Boswell *Life of Samuel Johnson* (1791) 22 June 1776

1 Here lies Sam Johnson:—Reader, have a care,
Tread lightly, lest you wake a sleeping bear:
Religious, moral, generous, and humane
He was: but self-sufficient, proud, and vain,
Fond of, and overbearing in, dispute,
A Christian and a scholar—but a brute.

Soame Jenyns 1704–87: suggested epitaph for Dr Johnson, 1784

2 Here lies one whose name was writ in water.
   epitaph for himself

John Keats 1795–1821: Richard Monckton Milnes *Life, Letters and Literary Remains of John Keats* (1848)

3 Beneath this stone does William Hazlitt lie,
Thankless of all that God or man could give.
He lived like one who never thought to die,
He died like one who dared not hope to live.

Samuel Taylor Coleridge 1772–1834: 'Epitaph on a Bad Man'

4 Beneath this Stone lies Walter Savage Landor,
Who half an Eagle was and half a Gander.

William Bodham Donne 1807–82: epigram; Henry Crabb Robinson's diary, 17 November 1864

5 This be the verse you grave for me:
'Here he lies where he longed to be;
Home is the sailor, home from sea,
And the hunter home from the hill.'

Robert Louis Stevenson 1850–94: 'Requiem' (1887)

6 Cast a cold eye
On life, on death.
Horseman pass by!

W. B. Yeats 1865–1939: 'Under Ben Bulben' (1939); used as Yeats's own epitaph

7 Poor G.K.C., his day is past—
Now God will know the truth at last.
   mock epitaph

E. V. Lucas 1868–1938: Dudley Barker *G. K. Chesterton* (1973)

8 God damn you all: I told you so.
   suggestion for his own epitaph, in conversation with Ernest Barker, 1939

H. G. Wells 1866–1946: Ernest Barker *Age and Youth* (1953)

9 So we beat on, boats against the current, borne back ceaselessly into the past.

F. Scott Fitzgerald 1896–1940: epitaph on Scott and Zelda Fitzgerald's tombstone; closing line of *The Great Gatsby* (1925)

10 And were an epitaph to be my story
I'd have a short one ready for my own.
I would have written of me on my stone:
I had a lover's quarrel with the world.

Robert Frost 1874–1963: 'The Lesson for Today' (1942)

11 Even amidst fierce flames the golden lotus can be planted.
   *on the gravestone of Sylvia **Plath***

Wu Cheng-en c.1500–82: *Monkey*

12 In the prison of his days
Teach the free man how to praise.

W. H. Auden 1907–73: 'In Memory of W. B. Yeats' (1940); Auden's epitaph in Westminster Abbey

Erotic Writing and Pornography see also Sex

13 Madam, I've warned you many times,
Skip when my book becomes obscene.

Martial AD c.40–c.104: *Epigrammata*, tr. James Michie

14 Up, and at my chamber all the morning and the office,
doing business and also reading a little of *L'escolle des Filles*, which is a mighty lewd book, but yet not amiss for a sober man once to read over to inform himself in the villainy of the world.

Samuel Pepys 1633–1703: diary, 1668

1 My English text is chaste, and all licentious passages are left in the obscurity of a learned language.
  parodied as 'decent obscurity' in the Anti-Jacobin, *1797–8*

Edward Gibbon 1737–94: *Memoirs of My Life* (1796)

2 It certainly is my wish, and it has been my study, to exclude from this publication whatever is unfit to be read aloud by a gentleman to a company of ladies.

Thomas Bowdler 1754–1825: preface to *The Family Shakespeare* (1818)

3 Juan was taught from out the best edition,
  Expurgated by learned men, who place
  Judiciously, from out the schoolboy's vision
  The grosser parts.

Lord Byron 1788–1824: *Don Juan* (1819–24)

4 Smut detected in it by moral men is theirs rather than mine. Scientific truth was my touchstone for every scene, even the most febrile.
  of his novel Thérèse Raquin

Émile Zola 1840–1902: preface to second edition, 1868

5 I was thinking the other day, while reading a very sensual love-scene in *Le Lys Rouge* [by Anatole France], that a novelist never describes the dishabille of the male in such scenes; I can't remember an instance where he even hints at it. This shows how incomplete 'realism' is. I see no reason why the appearance of the male should not be described in a manner to assist the charm of the scene. But tradition is decidedly against the practice.

Arnold Bennett 1867–1931: diary, 19 June 1904

6 It is not good enough to spend time and ink in describing the penultimate sensations and physical movements of people getting into a state of rut, we all know them too well.
  of D. H. Lawrence's Sons and Lovers

John Galsworthy 1867–1933: letter to Edward Garnett, 13 April 1914

7 We have long passed the Victorian Era when asterisks were followed after a certain interval by a baby.

W. Somerset Maugham 1874–1965: *The Constant Wife* (1926)

8 It is obvious that 'obscenity' is not a term capable of exact legal definition; in the practice of the Courts, it means 'anything that shocks the magistrate'.

Bertrand Russell 1872–1970: *Sceptical Essays* (1928) 'The Recrudescence of Puritanism'

9 At last an unprintable book that is readable.
  of Henry Miller's Tropic of Cancer

Ezra Pound 1885–1972: in 1934; attributed

10 Surely the sex business isn't worth all this damned fuss? I've met only a handful of people who cared a biscuit for it.
  on reading Lady Chatterley's Lover

T. E. Lawrence 1888–1935: Christopher Hassall *Edward Marsh* (1959)

11 You have left your hero and heroine tied up in a cavern under the Thames for a week, and they are not married.
  an editor's complaint to Chesterton's sister-in-law about a serial story

Anonymous: G. K. Chesterton *Autobiography* (1936)

12 Pornography is the attempt to insult sex, to do dirt on it.

D. H. Lawrence 1885–1930: *Phoenix* (1936) 'Pornography and Obscenity'

13 My poor Lolita is having a rough time. The pity is that if I had made her a boy, or a cow, or a bicycle, Philistines might never have flinched.

Vladimir Nabokov 1899–1977: letter to Graham Greene, 1956

14 Is it a book you would even wish your wife or your servants to read?
  of D. H. Lawrence's Lady Chatterley's Lover

Mervyn Griffith-Jones 1909–79: speech for the prosecution at the Central Criminal Court, Old Bailey, 20 October 1960

1 I think Lawrence tried to portray this [sex] relation as in a real sense an act of holy communion. For him flesh was sacramental of the spirit.
the Bishop of Woolwich as defence witness in the case against Penguin Books for publishing Lady Chatterley's Lover

John Robinson 1919–83: in *The Times* 28 October 1960

2 Pornography is rather like trying to find out about a Beethoven symphony by having somebody tell you about it and perhaps hum a few bars.

Robertson Davies 1913–95: in 1972; *The Enthusiasms of Robertson Davies* (1990)

3 Love-making is such a non-verbal thing. I hate the explicit 'he stuck it in her' kind of thing because it is so boring. You can only say 'he stuck it in her' so many ways.

Colleen McCullough 1937– : in *Guardian* 15 April 1977

4 Porn is altogether pragmatic. It exists to stimulate and satisfy an appetite just the way cookery books do, except the porn reader always has his ingredients to hand.

Irma Kurtz: *Malespeak* (1986)

5 With sex so much harder to write about maybe we'll have more novels about work from now on.
of the post-Aids era

David Lodge 1935– : in *Guardian* 7 March 1987

6 Reading about sex in yesterday's novels is like watching people smoke in old films.

Fay Weldon 1933– : in *Guardian* 1 December 1989

Essays

7 Mere essayists! A few loose sentences, and that's all.

Ben Jonson c.1573–1637: *Epicene* (1609)

8 Essays. The word is late but the thing is ancient.

Francis Bacon 1561–1626: *Essays* (1612) 'Dedication to Prince Henry'

9 The wildness of those compositions which go by the name of essays.

Joseph Addison 1672–1719: *The Spectator* no. 476 (5 September 1712)

10 *Essay.* A loose sally of the mind; an irregular indigested piece; not a regular and orderly composition.

Samuel Johnson 1709–84: *A Dictionary of the English Language* (1755)

11 A good essay must have this permanent quality about it; it must draw its curtains round us, but it must be a curtain that shuts us in, not out.

Virginia Woolf 1882–1941: *The Common Reader* (1925) 'The Modern Essay'

12 The essayist . . . can pull on any sort of shirt, be any sort of person, according to his mood or his subject matter—philosopher, scold, jester, raconteur, confidant, pundit, devil's advocate, enthusiast.

E. B. White 1899–1985: *Essays of E. B. White* (1977)

13 Essays come in all shapes and sizes. There are essays on Human Understanding, and essays on What I Did in the Holidays; essays on Truth, and essays on potato crisps . . . Essays that start out as book reviews, and essays that end up as sermons. Even more than most literary forms, the essay defies strict definition. It can shade into the character sketch, the travel sketch, the memoir, the *jeu d'esprit*.

John Gross 1935– : introduction to *The Oxford Book of Essays* (1991)

14 In a way, an essay is just a grown-up version of the tie-breakers in supermarket quizzes: Complete the line 'I think history is bunk because . . . ' in not more than 10,000 words. Essayists are preachers, but also the stand-up comedians of literature: there are no props to fall back on.

Robert Winder 1959– : in *Independent* 22 June 1996

Neither is there a plot. Novelists require their readers to sign an invisible contract promising to indulge their clever lies. But essayists tell the truth. They just say what they think, as nicely or as brutally as they can.

1 Bewitched by the example of his great precursor Montaigne, the habitual writer of non-fictional pieces goes on filling a long shelf in the belief that he will show the whole of his mind, but the reader he most fears—the one who will see through to his heart—should also be the one he most desires.

Clive James 1939– : *Reliable Essays* (2001)

Fables and Fairy Stories see also Fantasy

2 *Ich weiss nicht, was soll es bedeuten,*
Dass ich so traurig bin;
Ein Märchen aus alten Zeiten,
Das kommt mir nicht aus dem Sinn.

I know not why I am so sad; I cannot get out of my head a fairy-tale of olden times.

Heinrich Heine 1797–1856: 'Die Lorelei' (1826–31)

3 I left fairy stories lying on the floor of the nursery, and I have not found any books so sensible since.

G. K. Chesterton 1874–1936: *Orthodoxy* (1908) 'The Ethics of Elfland'

4 Our folk-tales prefigure our racial temperaments. Every race betrays itself thus in the tales it tells to its own children.

Rudyard Kipling 1865–1936: *A Book of Words* (1928) 'A Thesis'

5 I only tell fairytales for I would rather be seen in their sober vestments than in the prismatic unlikelihood of reality. Besides, every fairytale has a modern instance.

Christina Stead 1902–83: *The Salzburg Tales* (1934)

6 Fairy-tales are more than true: not because they tell us that dragons exist, but because they tell us that dragons can be beaten.

G. K. Chesterton 1874–1936: attributed

7 Yet the Myths will not fit us ready-made.
It is the meaning of the poet's trade
To re-create the fables and revive
In men the energies by which they live,
To reap the ancient harvests, plant again
And gather in the visionary grain.

A. D. Hope 1907–2000: 'An Epistle from Holofernes' (1960)

8 When I was ten, I read fairy tales in secret, and would have been ashamed of being found doing so. Now that I am fifty, I read them openly. When I became a man, I put away childish things, including the fear of childishness and the desire to be very grown up.

C. S. Lewis 1898–1963: 'On Three Ways of Writing for Children' (1952)

9 The value of fairy-stories is thus not, in my opinion, to be found by considering children in particular. Collections of fairy stories are, in fact, by nature attics and lumber-rooms, only by temporary and local custom playrooms. Their contents are disordered, and often battered, a jumble of different dates, purposes, and tastes; but among them may occasionally be found a thing of permanent value: an old work of art, not too much damaged, that only stupidity would ever have stuffed away.

J. R. R. Tolkien 1892–1973: *Tree and Leaf* (1964) 'On Fairy-Stories'

1 *Grimm's Fairy Tales* was the most influential book I ever read.

Margaret Atwood 1939– : in an interview, March/April 1976; Earl G. Ingersoll (ed.) *Margaret Atwood: Conversations* (1990)

2 Fairy tales, unlike any other sort of literature, direct the child to discover his identity and calling.

Bruno Bettelheim 1903–90: *The Uses of Enchantment* (1976)

3 Please God, make it stop, I used to say, when they read Hans Andersen's stories to me at bedtime. Is there no end to human suffering?

Angela Carter 1940–92: in *New Society* 1976

4 These stories are in a literal sense women's literature . . . For hundreds of years, while written literature was almost exclusively in the hands of men, these tales were being invented and passed on orally by women . . . it is women who most often are the central characters . . . and women who have the supernatural power.

Alison Lurie 1926– : *Don't Tell The Grown-Ups* (1990)

5 Myth does not mean something untrue, but a concentration of truth.

Doris Lessing 1919– : *African Laughter: Four Visits to Zimbabwe* (1992)

Fame see also **Reputation and Achievement**

6 I have erected a monument more lasting than bronze.

Horace 65–8 BC: *Odes*

7   Thank you, earnest fan
For having granted me the fame
Seldom enjoyed by a dead poet
While I'm alive and here to know it.

Martial AD c.40–c.104: *Epigrammata*, tr. James Michie

8 Even for learned men, love of fame is the last thing to be given up.

Tacitus AD c.56–after 117: *Histories*

9 He that cometh in print because he would be known, is like the fool that cometh into the market because he would be seen.

John Lyly c.1554–1606: *Euphues* (1580)

10 Not marble, nor the gilded monuments
Of princes, shall outlive this powerful rhyme;
But you shall shine more bright in these contents
Than unswept stone, besmeared with sluttish time.

William Shakespeare 1564–1616: sonnet 55

11 The universal object and idol of men of letters is reputation.

John Adams 1735–1826: *Discourses on Davila* (1791)

12 My great comfort is, that the temporary celebrity I have wrung from the world has been in the very teeth of all opinions and prejudices. I have flattered no ruling powers; I have never concealed a single thought that tempted me.

Lord Byron 1788–1824: letter to Thomas Moore, 9 April 1814

13 O the flummery of a birth place! Cant! Cant! Cant! It is enough to give a spirit the guts-ache.
   on visiting **Burns**'s *birthplace.*

John Keats 1795–1821: letter to John Hamilton Reynolds, 11 July 1818

14 I equally dislike the favour of the public with the love of a woman—they are both a cloying treacle to the wings of independence.

John Keats 1795–1821: letter to John Taylor, 23 August 1819

15 I awoke one morning and found myself famous.
   on the instantaneous success of Childe Harold

Lord Byron 1788–1824: Thomas Moore *Letters and Journals of Lord Byron* (1830)

1 Literary fame is the only fame of which a wise man ought to be ambitious, because it is the only lasting and living fame.

Robert Southey 1774–1843: John Forster *Life of Landor* (1876)

2 Ah, did you once see Shelley plain,
And did he stop and speak to you
And did you speak to him again?
How strange it seems, and new!

Robert Browning 1812–89: 'Memorabilia' (1855)

3 I was born in Düsseldorf on Rhine, and note this explicitly in case seven cities after my death—Schilda, Krähwinkel, Polkwitz, Bockum, Dülk, Göttingen and Schöppenstadt—compete for the honour of being my birthplace.

Heinrich Heine 1797–1856: attributed; see **125:11**, **125:12**

4 Whatever may be the success of my stories, I shall be resolute in preserving my incognito, having observed that a *nom de plume* secures all the advantages without the disagreeables of reputation.

George Eliot 1819–80: letter to William Blackwood, 4 February 1857

5 For several reasons I am very anxious to retain my incognito for some time to come, and to an author not already famous, anonymity is the highest *prestige*. Besides, if George Eliot turns out a dull dog and an ineffective writer—a mere flash in the pan—I, for one, am determined to cut him on the first intimation of that disagreeable fact.

George Eliot 1819–80: letter to John Blackwood, 14 March 1857

6 All this uproar around my first book seems so irrelevant to Art that it sickens me, it dazes me. How I miss the fish-like silence in which I had persisted until now.
on the publication of Madame Bovary, *1857*

Gustave Flaubert 1821–80: Geoffrey Wall *Flaubert: A Life* (2001)

7 Modern fame is too often a crown of thorns, and brings all the vulgarity of the world upon you. I sometimes wish I had never written a line.

Alfred, Lord Tennyson 1809–92: in conversation with Marie Corelli; Theresa Ransom *The Mysterious Miss Marie Corelli* (1999)

8 Enduring fame is promised only to those writers who can offer to successive generations a substance constantly renewed; for every generation arrives upon the scene with its own particular hunger.

André Gide 1869–1951: *Pretexts* (1903)

9 At Tennyson's funeral, Royalty was represented, but Royalty itself was conspicuously absent. The Prince of Wales was at Newmarket, where he personally congratulated a successful jockey.

George Gissing 1857–1903: *Commonplace Book* (1962)

10 I want no limelight, and celebrity is the last infirmity I desire.
Fame is the recognition of one's peers.

Wilfred Owen 1893–1918: letter to his mother, May 1918

11 The bower we shrined to Tennyson, Gentlemen,
Is roof-wrecked; damps there drip upon
Sagged seats, the creeper-nails are rust,
The spider is sole denizen;
Even she who voiced those rhymes is dust,
Gentlemen!

Thomas Hardy 1840–1928: 'An Ancient to Ancients' (1922)

12 A new shade for knickers and nightdresses has been named *Brighton Rock* . . . Is this fame?
his novel Brighton Rock *had been published in the previous year*

Graham Greene 1904–91: letter to his brother Hugh, 7 April 1939

1 I felt a very lonely, foreign midget orating up there, in a
huge hall, before all those faces.
   on giving poetry readings in the US

Dylan Thomas 1914–53: letter to
Caitlin Thomas, 25 February 1950

2 Fame often makes a writer vain, but seldom makes him
proud.

W. H. Auden 1907–73: *The Dyer's
Hand* (1962) 'Writing'

3 There's no such thing as bad publicity except your own
obituary.

Brendan Behan 1923–64: Dominic
Behan *My Brother Brendan* (1965)

4 The libraries of the East fight to own my verses,
The rulers seek me out to fill my mouth with gold,
The angels already know my last couplet by heart
The tools of my art are humiliation and anguish.
   from a twelfth-century Persian poem

Jorge Luis Borges 1899–1986:
Selected Poems, 1923–1967 (1972) 'The
Poet Tells of his Fame', tr. W. S.
Merwin

5 A poet's hope: to be,
like some valley cheese,
local, but prized elsewhere.

W. H. Auden 1907–73: 'Shorts II'
(1976)

6 Unfortunately many young writers are more concerned
with fame than with their own work . . . It's much more
important to write than to be written about.

Gabriel García Márquez 1928– : in
Writers at Work (6th series, 1984)

7 A famous writer who wants to continue writing has to be
constantly defending himself against fame.

Gabriel García Márquez 1928– : in
Writers at Work (6th series, 1984)

8 Celebrity is a mask that eats into the face.

John Updike 1932– : *Self-
Consciousness: Memoirs* (1989)

9 The shelf life of the modern hardback writer is somewhere
between the milk and the yoghurt.

Calvin Trillin 1935– : in *Sunday
Times* 9 June 1991; attributed

10 The best fame is a writer's fame: it's enough to get a table
at a good restaurant, but not enough that you get
interrupted when you eat.

Fran Lebowitz 1946– : in *Observer*
30 May 1993 'Sayings of the Week'

11 The trouble with fulfilling your ambitions is you think you
will be transformed into some sort of archangel and you're
not. You still have to wash your socks.

Louis de Bernières 1954– : in
Independent 14 February 1999

12 I go in and out of fashion like a double-breasted suit.

Alan Ayckbourn 1939– : in *Observer*
13 August 2000

Family and Friends

13 Rest in soft peace, and, asked, say here doth lie
Ben Jonson his best piece of poetry.

Ben Jonson c.1573–1637: 'On My
First Son' (1616)

14 I should, many a good day, have blown my brains out, but
for the recollection that it would have given pleasure to
my mother-in-law; and, even *then*, if I could have been
certain to haunt her . . .

Lord Byron 1788–1824: letter, 28
January 1817

15 The roaring of the wind is my wife and the stars through
the window pane are my children.

John Keats 1795–1821: letter to
George and Georgiana Keats, 24
October 1818

16 To one whose sweet voice has often encouraged, and
whose taste and judgement have ever guided, its pages;
the most severe of critics, but—a perfect wife!

Benjamin Disraeli 1804–81: *Sybil*
(1845); dedication

17 Reader, I married him.

Charlotte Brontë 1816–55: *Jane Eyre*
(1847)

1 My wish was that my husband should be distinguished for intellect, and my children too. I have had my wish,—and I now wish that there were a little less intellect in the family so as to allow for a little more common sense.
   a mother's view

Frances Rossetti 1800–86: William Rossetti (ed.) *Dante Gabriel Rossetti: His Family Letters with a Memoir* (1895)

2 Jack Sprat and his wife in the nursery rhyme, offer an ideal example of adaptation for co-existence.

Robert Louis Stevenson 1850–94: *Memories and Portraits* (1887) 'From his Notebooks'

3 Of all human struggles there is none so treacherous and remorseless as the struggle between the artist man and the mother woman.

George Bernard Shaw 1856–1950: *Man and Superman* (1903)

4 The true artist will let his wife starve, his children go barefoot, his mother drudge for his living at seventy, sooner than work at anything but his art.

George Bernard Shaw 1856–1950: *Man and Superman* (1903)

5 Wives can be an awful handicap. They are constantly telling their husbands to do this, fetch that, and ordering them from the house.
   to his mother, c.1926

Terence Rattigan 1911–77: John Lahr *Light Fantastic* (1996)

6 The public does not matter—only one's friends matter.

W. B. Yeats 1865–1939: letter to Edith Shackleton Heald, 18 May 1937

7 One's family . . . is marvellous material, and I'm inclined to think the *only* material . . . because it supplies enough tension to last several lifetimes.

Janet Frame 1924– : letter to Bill Brown, August 1972

8 I believe that all those painters and writers who leave their wives have an idea at the back of their minds that their painting or writing will be the better for it, whereas they only go from bad to worse.

Patrick White 1912–90: letter to Barry Humphries, 7 October 1973

9 Until I grew up I thought I hated everybody, but when I grew up I realized it was just children I didn't like.

Philip Larkin 1922–85: in *Observer* 16 December 1979

10 If you are a single father, it's lucky you're a writer, because you can stay at home all the time, you have the time for it.

J. G. Ballard 1930– : Alastair Reid *Whereabouts* (1987) 'Digging Up Scotland'

11 A novelist is a man who does not like his mother, or who never received mother-love.

Georges Simenon 1903–89: Patrick Marnham *The Man Who Wasn't Maigret* (1992)

12 Do not be disheartened if no one reads your book. It has already made me a happy woman because it has brought me closer to you.
   letter to her daughter Jung Chang, just before the publication of the best-selling Wild Swans

Xia Dehong 1931– : letter, 1991; in *Sunday Telegraph* 26 May 1996

13 With the birth of each child, you lose two novels.

Candia McWilliam 1955– : in *Guardian* 5 May 1993

14 One day I will write verses about him and see how he likes it.
   on his father, A. A. Milne

Christopher Milne 1920–96: attributed; in *The Times* 22 April 1996

15 I loved my parents (and I had more than the usual number to love).
   of Clive and Vanessa Bell, and Duncan Grant

Quentin Bell 1910–96: in *Daily Telegraph* 18 December 1996; obituary

1 I'm the only child in search of the imaginary brother or sister. That is probably why I like to invent characters.

Iris Murdoch 1919–99: in *The Times* 9 February 1999

2 At the heart of it all was friendship: that was the great thing. Bloomsbury was really a series of rings based on the Stephen and Strachey families and then the outer circles of their Cambridge friends.

Frances Partridge 1900– : in *The Times* 8 July 1999

3 They are self-evident abnormalities, like Fanny and Anthony Trollope. Writers are not like royal pastry chefs, handing down their talent and their badge of office from generation to generation.
  on 'the Amises, the Waughs' as cases of literary succession

Julian Barnes 1946– : in *Paris Review* Winter 2000

4 Most novelists, knowing that ongoing work is fed by ongoing life, prize their telephones, their correspondence, and their daily rubbing up against family and friends.

Carol Shields 1935– : *Jane Austen* (2001)

Fantasy see also Fables and Fairy Stories, Science Fiction

of the romance as distinct from the novel:
5 A fictitious narrative in prose or verse, the interest of which turns upon marvellous and uncommon incidents.

Sir Walter Scott 1771–1832: *Essay on Romance* (1824); see **194:11**

6 I find it difficult to take much interest in a man whose father was a dragon.
  *apologizing for his inability to appreciate William **Morris**'s epic poem* Sigurd the Volsung (1876)

Dante Gabriel Rossetti 1828–82: Osbert Sitwell *Noble Essences* (1950)

7 Fantasy deals with things that are not and cannot be. Science fiction deals with things that can be, that some day may be.

Frederic Brown 1906–72: *Angels and Spaceships* (1955)

8 [Fantasy] is the normal technique for fiction writers who do not believe in the permanence or continuity of the society they belong to.

Northrop Frye 1912–91: *The Secular Scripture: A Study of the Structure of Romance* (1976)

9 We like to think we live in daylight, but half the world is always dark; and fantasy, like poetry, speaks the language of the night.

Ursula Le Guin 1929– : in *World Magazine* 21 November 1979

10 We need metaphors of magic and monsters in order to understand the human condition.

Stephen Donaldson 1947– : Stan Nicholls (ed.) *Wordsmiths of Wonder* (1993)

11 Fantasy is the oldest form of literature and science fiction is just a new twist on it.

Katharine Kerr 1944– : Stan Nicholls (ed.) *Wordsmiths of Wonder* (1993)

12 The trouble is that many people think the boundaries of fantasy lie somewhere north of Camelot and south of Conan the Barbarian, which is like saying that *Star Trek* represents most of science fiction.

Terry Pratchett 1948– : in interview; Terry Pratchett and Stephen Briggs *The Discworld Companion* (1994)

13 Myths and fantastic legends, wonder-tales about the embroilment of the natural world with the supernatural, obviously held a quite special attraction for him [Ovid]—as they have done for most people throughout history.

Ted Hughes 1930–98: *Tales from Ovid* (1997)

William Faulkner 1897-1962
American novelist

1 Even those who call Mr Faulkner our greatest literary sadist do not fully appreciate him, for it is not merely his characters who have to run the gauntlet but also his readers.

Clifton Fadiman 1904-99: in *New Yorker* 21 April 1934

2 Without Faulkner and his contorted prose, how could we have imagined the South as it really is?

Philip Roth 1933- : in *Independent* 16 October 2002

Feeling

3 If writing did not exist, what terrible depressions we should suffer from.

Sei Shōnagon c.966-c.1013: *Pillow Book*

4 I write of melancholy, by being busy to avoid melancholy.

Robert Burton 1577-1640: *The Anatomy of Melancholy* (1621-51) 'Democritus to the Reader'

5 *Much more* lively and affecting . . . must be the style of those who write in the height of a present distress, the mind tortured by pangs of uncertainty (the events then hidden in the womb of fate); than the dry, narrative unanimated style of a person relating difficulties and danger surmounted, can be . . . The relater perfectly at ease; and if himself unmoved by his own story, not likely greatly to affect the reader.

Samuel Richardson 1689-1761: preface to *Clarissa* (1747-8)

6 But, spite of all the criticizing elves,
Those who would make us feel, must feel themselves.

Charles Churchill 1731-64: *The Rosciad* (1761)

7 The black dog I hope always to resist, and in time to drive, though I am deprived of almost all those that used to help me . . . When I rise my breakfast is solitary, the black dog waits to share it, from breakfast to dinner he continues barking, except that Dr Brocklesby for a little keeps him at a distance . . . Night comes at last, and some hours of restlessness and confusion bring me again to a day of solitude. What shall exclude the black dog from a habitation like this?
   on his attacks of melancholia; more recently associated with Winston Churchill, who used the phrase 'black dog' when alluding to his own periodic bouts of depression

Samuel Johnson 1709-84: letter to Mrs Thrale, 28 June 1783

8 Poetry is the spontaneous overflow of powerful feelings: it takes its origin from emotion recollected in tranquillity.

William Wordsworth 1770-1850: *Lyrical Ballads* (2nd ed., 1802)

9 I was sorely worried by the black dog this morning, that vile palpitation of the heart—that *tremor cordis*—that hysterical passion which forces unbidden sighs and tears and falls upon a contented life like a drop of ink on white paper which is not the less a stain because it conveys no meaning. I wrought three leaves however and the story goes on.

Sir Walter Scott 1771-1832: diary, 1828

1 To be *thoroughly* conversant with a man's heart, is to take our final lesson in the iron-clasped volume of despair.

Edgar Allan Poe 1809–49: 'Marginalia'; in *Southern Literary Messenger* (Richmond, Virginia) June 1849

on being found in tears by a friend, having received the last number of The Old Curiosity Shop:
2 Little Nelly, Boz's little Nelly, is dead.

Francis, Lord Jeffrey 1773–1850: Julian Charles Young *A Memoir of Charles Mayne Young* (1871) vol. 2; see **102:10**

on reading of the death of Little Nell:
3 I have never read printed words that gave me so much pain.

William Macready 1793–1873: diary, 1850; Edgar Johnson *Charles Dickens: His Tragedy and Triumph* (1952)

4 Only habit of persistent work can make one continually content; it produces an opium that numbs the soul.

Gustave Flaubert 1821–80: letter, 26 July 1851

5 The poisoning of Bovary made me throw up into my chamber pot; the assault on Carthage is giving me aches and pains in my arms.

Gustave Flaubert 1821–80: letter, 25 September 1861

6 Language has not the power to speak what love indites: The soul lies buried in the ink that writes.

John Clare 1793–1864: 'Language has not the power'

7 A man of letters should be as objective as a chemist; he has to renounce ordinary subjectivity and realize that manure plays a very respectable role in a landscape and that evil passions are as inherent in life as good ones.

Anton Chekhov 1860–1904: letter, 14 January 1887

8 I wrote such melancholy things when I was young that I am obliged to be unusually cheerful and robust in my old age.

Christina Rossetti 1830–94: Jan Marsh *Christina Rossetti* (1994)

9 Analysis is an abominable business. I am quite sure that people who work out subjects thoroughly are disagreeable wretches. One only feels as one should when one doesn't know much about the matter.
of the effect of the research done for his book The Stones of Venice (*1851–3*) *on his sense of* 'the charm of the place'

John Ruskin 1819–1900: in *Dictionary of National Biography* (1917–)

10 One must have a heart of stone to read the death of Little Nell without laughing.

Oscar Wilde 1854–1900: Ada Leverson *Letters to the Sphinx* (1930); see **102:2**

11 I tell you there is such a thing as creative hate!

Willa Cather 1873–1947: *The Song of the Lark* (1915)

12 I like to feel that a writer is perfectly cool and detached, regarding other people's feelings or his own, like a God who has got beyond them.

T. S. Eliot 1888–1965: letter 19 September 1917

13 Poetry is not a turning loose of emotion, but an escape from emotion; it is not the expression of personality but an escape from personality. But, of course, only those who have personality and emotions know what it means to want to escape from these things.

T. S. Eliot 1888–1965: *The Sacred Wood* (1920) 'Tradition and Individual Talent'

14 I may as well tell you, here and now, that if you are going about the place thinking things pretty, you will never make a modern poet. Be poignant, man, be poignant!

P. G. Wodehouse 1881–1975: *The Small Bachelor* (1927)

1 Only an aching heart
  Conceives a changeless work of art.

  W. B. Yeats 1865–1939: 'The Tower' (1928)

2 How one likes to suffer. Anyway writers do; it is their income.

  W. H. Auden 1907–73: Berlin diary, April 1929

3 Enthusiasm is taken through the prism of the intellect and spread on the screen in colour, all the way from hyperbole or overstatement at one end to understatement at the other end. It is a long strip of dark lines and many colours. I would be willing to throw away everything but that: enthusiasm tamed by metaphors.

  Robert Frost 1874–1963: 'Education by Poetry' in *Amherst Graduates' Quarterly* February 1931

4 Experience has taught me, when I am shaving of a morning, to keep watch over my thoughts, because, if a line of poetry strays into my memory, my skin bristles so that the razor ceases to act . . . The seat of this sensation is the pit of the stomach.

  A. E. Housman 1859–1936: lecture at Cambridge, 9 May 1933

5 No tears in the writer, no tears in the reader. No surprise for the writer, no surprise for the reader.

  Robert Frost 1874–1963: *Collected Poems* (1939) 'The Figure a Poem Makes'

6 Now that my ladder's gone
  I must lie down where all ladders start
  In the foul rag and bone shop of the heart.

  W. B. Yeats 1865–1939: 'The Circus Animals' Desertion' (1939)

7   Each venture
  Is a new beginning, a raid on the inarticulate
  With shabby equipment always deteriorating
  In the general mess of imprecision of feeling.

  T. S. Eliot 1888–1965: *Four Quartets* 'East Coker' (1940) pt. 5

8 I had to feel anything and everything that for me was existing so intensely that I could put it down in writing as a thing in itself without at all necessarily using its name.

  Gertrude Stein 1874–1946: *Look at me Now and Here I am: Writings and Lectures, 1909–45* (1971)

9 It is closing time in the gardens of the West and from now on an artist will be judged only by the resonance of his solitude or the quality of his despair.

  Cyril Connolly 1903–74: in *Horizon* December 1949—January 1950

10 Poetry should begin with emotion in the poet, and end with the same emotion in the reader. The poem is simply the instrument of transference.

  Philip Larkin 1922–85: BBC Third Programme, 13 April 1956

11 The more acute the experience, the less articulate its expression.

  Harold Pinter 1930– : in his 1960 programme notes to *The Room* and *The Dumb Waiter*; Malcolm Bradbury and James McFarlane (eds.) *Modernism* (1991)

12 Sentimentality is the emotional promiscuity of those who have no sentiment.

  Norman Mailer 1923– : *Cannibals and Christians* (1966)

13 Writing is not observation—it is feeling.

  Paul Scott 1920–78: Hilary Spurling *Paul Scott* (1990)

14 I think writing about unhappiness is probably the source of my popularity, if I have any—after all most people *are* unhappy, don't you think?

  Philip Larkin 1922–85: *Required Writing* (1983)

15 People always ask what do you teach in creative writing? People insist: there's nothing to teach. Well, of course, there is something you can teach; you teach people to find ways of tapping their own emotions.

  Edmund White 1940– : in interview in *Paris Review* 1988

1 There are many ways of educating our feelings, but I recommend reading as that which is most ready to hand.

Robertson Davies 1913–95: lecture, Yale, 20 February 1990

2 Sometimes poetry is emotion recollected in a highly emotional state.

Wendy Cope 1945– : 'An Argument with Wordsworth' (1992); see **101:8**

Fiction

3 Refuse profane and old wives' fables, and exercise thyself rather unto godliness.

Bible: I Timothy

4 Storys to rede ar delitabill,
Suppos that thai be nocht bot fabill.

John Barbour c.1320–95: *The Bruce* (1375)

5 If this were played upon a stage now, I could condemn it as an improbable fiction.

William Shakespeare 1564–1616: *Twelfth Night* (1601)

6 Poets . . . though liars by profession, always endeavour to give an air of truth to their fictions.

David Hume 1711–76: *A Treatise upon Human Nature* (1739)

7 I hate things all *fiction* . . . there should always be some foundation of fact for the most airy fabric and pure invention is but the talent of a liar.

Lord Byron 1788–1824: letter to John Murray, 2 April 1817

8 'Tis strange—but true; for truth is always strange; Stranger than fiction.

Lord Byron 1788–1824: *Don Juan* (1819–24)

9 It is with fiction as with religion; it should present another world, and yet one to which we feel the tie.

Herman Melville 1819–91: *The Confidence Man: His Masquerade* (1857)

10 Fiction is Truth in another shape, and gives as close embraces.

Leigh Hunt 1784–1859: *Autobiography* (rev. ed., 1860)

11 No author, without a trial, can conceive of the difficulty of writing a romance about a country where there is no shadow, no antiquity, no mystery, no picturesque and gloomy wrong, nor anything but a commonplace prosperity, in broad and simple daylight, as is happily the case with my dear native land.

Nathaniel Hawthorne 1804–64: preface to *The Marble Faun* (1860)

12 Fiction is to the grown man what play is to the child; it is there that he changes the atmosphere and tenor of his life.

Robert Louis Stevenson 1850–94: *Memories and Portraits* (1887) 'Gossip on Romance'

13 The good ended happily, and the bad unhappily. That is what fiction means.

Oscar Wilde 1854–1900: *The Importance of Being Earnest* (1895)

14 Literature is a luxury; fiction is a necessity.

G. K. Chesterton 1874–1936: *The Defendant* (1901) 'A Defence of Penny Dreadfuls'

15 Fiction, at the point of development at which it has arrived, demands from the writer a spirit of scrupulous abnegation. The only legitimate basis of creative work lies in the courageous recognition of all the irreconcilable antagonisms that make our life so enigmatic, so burdensome, so fascinating, so dangerous—so full of hope. They exist! And this is the only fundamental truth of fiction.

Joseph Conrad 1857–1924: letter 2 August 1901

16 The house of fiction has in short not one window, but a million . . . but they are, singly or together, as nothing without the posted presence of the watcher.

Henry James 1843–1916: *The Portrait of a Lady* (1908 ed.)

1 Reality, as usual, beats fiction out of sight.
commenting on 'this wartime atmosphere'

Joseph Conrad 1857–1924: letter 11 August 1915

2 Fiction is Truth's elder sister. Obviously. No one in the world knew what truth was till somebody had told a story.

Rudyard Kipling 1865–1936: *A Book of Words* (1928) 'Fiction'

3 Fiction, imaginative work that is, is not dropped like a pebble upon the ground, as science maybe; fiction is like a spider's web, attached ever so lightly perhaps, but still attached to life at all four corners. Often the attachment is scarcely perceptible.

Virginia Woolf 1882–1941: *A Room of One's Own* (1929)

4 For me a work of fiction exists only in so far as it affords me what I shall bluntly call aesthetic bliss, that is a sense of being somehow, somewhere, connected with other states of being where art (curiosity, tenderness, kindness, ecstasy) is the norm.

Vladimir Nabokov 1899–1977: *Lolita* (1955) 'On a book entitled *Lolita*'

5 Fiction to me is a kind of parable. You have got to make up your mind it's not true. Some kind of truth emerges from it, but it's not fact.

Muriel Spark 1918– : 'My Conversion' (1961)

6 I write fiction because it's a way of making statements I can disown, and I write plays because dialogue is the most respectable way of contradicting myself.

Tom Stoppard 1937– : in a television interview; in *Guardian* 21 March 1973

7 Writing fiction is of course the act of an impostor.

Paul Scott 1920–78: letter 1975; Hilary Spurling *Paul Scott* (1990)

8 There is no longer any such thing as fiction or non-fiction; there's only narrative.

E. L. Doctorow 1931– : in *New York Times Book Review* 27 January 1988

9 Good fiction often takes the banal around us and defamiliarizes it.

Edmund White 1940– : in interview in *Paris Review* 1988

10 Writers of fiction are collectors of useless information. They are the opposite of good, solid, wise citizens who collect good information and put it to good use. Fiction writers remember tiny little details, some of them almost malicious, but very telling.

William Trevor 1928– : in *Paris Review* 1989

11 The acceptance that all that is solid has melted into air, that reality and morality are not givens but imperfect human constructs, is the point from which fiction begins.

Salman Rushdie 1947– : 'Is Nothing Sacred?' (Herbert Read Memorial Lecture) 6 February 1990

12 Fiction is nothing less than the subtlest instrument for self-examination and self-display that mankind has invented yet.

John Updike 1932– : *Odd Jobs* (1991)

13 I still do not know what impels anyone sound of mind to leave dry land and spend a lifetime describing people who do not exist. If it is child's play, an extension of make believe—something one is frequently assured by people who write about writing—how to account for the overriding wish to do that, just that, only that, and consider it as rational an occupation as riding a bicycle over the Alps?

Mavis Gallant 1922– : *Selected Stories* (1996) preface

14 When you are writing journalism your task is to simplify the world and render it comprehensible in one reading; whereas when you are writing fiction your task is to reflect the fullest complications of the world.

Julian Barnes 1946– : in *Paris Review* Winter 2000–2001

1 Unfortunately for novelists, real life is getting way too funny and far-fetched. It's especially true in Miami, where the daily news seems to be scripted by David Lynch. Fact is routinely more fantastic than fiction.

Carl Hiaasen 1953– : in *Writers on Writing: Collected Essays from The New York Times* (2001)

2 The trial lawyer's job and the novelist's were, in some aspects, shockingly similar. Both involved the reconstruction of experience, usually through many voices, whether they were witnesses or characters.
on parallels between his life as a working lawyer and his attempts to write fiction

Scott Turow 1949– : in *Writers on Writing: Collected Essays from The New York Times* (2001)

Henry Fielding 1707–54
English novelist and dramatist

3 How charming, how wholesome, Fielding always is! To take him up after Richardson is like emerging from a sick room heated by stoves into an open lawn, on a breezy day in May.

Samuel Taylor Coleridge 1772–1834: *Table Talk* (1836)

4 The most singular genius which their island ever produced, whose works it has long been the fashion to abuse in public and to read in secret.

George Borrow 1803–81: *The Bible in Spain* (1843)

5 [Thackeray] resembles Fielding as an eagle does a vulture: Fielding could stoop on carrion, but Thackeray never does.

Charlotte Brontë 1816–55: *Jane Eyre* (2nd ed., 1848) preface; see **297:9**

Figures of Speech

6 By far the most important thing to master is the use of metaphor. This is one thing that cannot be learnt from anyone else, and it is the mark of great natural ability, for the ability to use metaphor implies a perception of resemblances.

Aristotle 384–322 BC: *Poetics*

7 The speaking in a perpetual hyperbole is comely in nothing but in love.

Francis Bacon 1561–1626: *Essays* (1625) 'Of Love'

8 For rhetoric he could not ope
His mouth, but out there flew a trope.

Samuel Butler 1612–80: *Hudibras* pt. 1 (1663)

9 What an image that is—*sea-shouldering whales*!
to his friend Charles Cowden-Clarke, while reading The Faerie Queene

John Keats 1795–1821: Charles Cowden-Clarke *Recollections of Writers* (1878)

10 All slang is metaphor, and all metaphor is poetry.

G. K. Chesterton 1874–1936: *Defendant* (1901) 'Defence of Slang'

11 I am a painstaking, conscientious, involved and devious craftsman in words . . . I use everything to make my poems work and move in the directions I want them to: old tricks, new tricks, puns, portmanteau-words, paradox, allusion, paranomasia, paragram, catachresis, slang, assonantal rhymes, vowel rhymes, sprung rhythm . . . Poets have got to enjoy themselves sometimes.

Dylan Thomas 1914–53: 'Poetic Manifesto' (1951)

12 It takes a sound realist to make a convincing symbolist.

D. J. Enright 1920– : *The Apothecary's Shop* (1957)

1 For twenty years I've stared my level best
To see if evening—any evening—would suggest
A patient etherized upon a table;
In vain. I simply wasn't able.
  *on contemporary poetry, as exemplified by T. S. **Eliot**'s
  'Prufrock'*

C. S. Lewis 1898–1963: 'A Confession' (1964)

2 It's a rare metaphor that doesn't become a bore after about three lines.

Philip Larkin 1922–85: letter, 1 November 1970

3 I was much tempted, perhaps because of my admiration for Metaphysical poets, by exaggerated similes.

Graham Greene 1904–91: *A Sort of Life* (1971)

4 You who with fierce joy celebrated swords hammered out of iron,
The Norseman's shame,
The banquet of raven and eagle,
Gathering in your military ode
The ritual metaphors of your kin.

Jorge Luis Borges 1899–1986: 'To a Saxon Poet' (1972), tr. Norman Thomas di Giovanni

5 The cure for mixed metaphors, I have always found, is for the patient to be obliged to draw a picture of the result.

Bernard Levin 1928– : *In These Times* (1986)

F. Scott Fitzgerald 1896–1940 see also **92:9**
American novelist

6 I have lived so long within the circle of this book [*Tender is the Night*] that often it seems to me that the real world does not exist but that only these characters exist.

F. Scott Fitzgerald 1896–1940: letter, 4 March 1934

7 He had one of the rarest qualities in all literature, and it's a great shame that the word for it has been thoroughly debased by the cosmetic racketeers, so that one is almost ashamed to use it to describe a real distinction. Nevertheless, the word is charm.

Raymond Chandler 1888–1959: letter to Dale Warren, 13 November 1950

8 I think he was more interested in capturing time and freezing it. I think very early on he decided that he'd been to a dance and danced with a girl, and even if he couldn't remember which dance or which girl, that it represented some glorious high point of his life, and everything he did was an attempt to recapture that moment. I don't think he was much interested in more general issues.

Jay McInerney 1955– : in *Guardian* 1 June 1996

Gustave Flaubert 1821–80 see also **15:9, 49:5, 291:15, 301:8**
French novelist

9 My deplorable mania for analysis exhausts me. I doubt everything, even my doubt.

Gustave Flaubert 1821–80: letter, 8–9 August 1846

10 Writing this book I am like a man playing the piano with lead balls attached to his knuckles.
  of Madame Bovary

Gustave Flaubert 1821–80: letter, 26 July 1856; see **17:3**

11 A great, stout, simple, kindly, elderly fellow, rather embarrassed at having a stranger presented to him, and bothering himself over what he can say or do . . . He looks like some weather-beaten old military man.

Henry James 1843–1916: letter 20 December 1875

1 *Madame Bovary, c'est moi.*
Madame Bovary is myself.

Gustave Flaubert 1821–80: attributed

2 A kind of opera in prose.
of Salammbô

Guy de Maupassant 1850–93: preface to *Lettres de Gustave Flaubert à George Sand* (1884)

3 It was in his nature to be more conscious of one broken spring in the couch of fate, more wounded by a pin-prick, more worried by an assonance, than he could ever be warmed or pacified from within. Literature and life were a single business to him, and the 'torment of style' that might occasionally intermit in one place was sufficiently sure to break out in another.

Henry James 1843–1916: 'Gustave Flaubert' (1893); see **17:3**

4 Flaubert was a perpetual adolescent. His distinction lay in never outgrowing the hatred and contempt that the normal teenager feels when confronted with adult human beings.

John Carey 1934– : in *Sunday Times* 2 April 1989

5 Flaubert, the writer's writer par excellence, the saint and martyr of literature, the perfector of realism, the creator of the modern novel with *Madame Bovary*, and then, a quarter of a century later, the assistant creator of the modernist novel with *Bouvard et Pécuchet*.

Julian Barnes 1946– : *Something to Declare* (2002)

Food

6   Though each dish
Is lavish and superb, the pleasure's nil
Since you recite your poems! To hell with brill,
Mushrooms and two-pound turbots! I don't need
Oysters: give me a host who doesn't read.

Martial AD c.40–c.104: *Epigrammata*, tr. James Michie

7 *Equi et poetae alendi, non saginandi.*
Horses and poets should be fed, not overfed.

Charles IX 1550–74: saying

8 When . . . [people] imagine that their food is only a cover for poison, and when they neither love nor trust the hand that serves it, it is not the name of the roast beef of old England that will persuade them to sit down to the table that is spread for them.

Edmund Burke 1729–97: *Thoughts on the Cause of the Present Discontents* (1770)

9 There is more reason for saying grace before a new book than before dinner.

Charles Lamb 1775–1834: *Elia* 'Grace before Meat'

10 HERBERT BEERBOHM TREE: Let us give Shaw a beefsteak and put some red blood into him.
MRS PATRICK CAMPBELL: For heaven's sake, don't. He is bad enough as it is; but if you give him meat no woman in London will be safe.
of the vegetarian G. B. **Shaw**

Mrs Patrick Campbell 1865–1940: Frank Harris *Contemporary Portraits* (1919)

11 Food comes first, then morals.

Bertolt Brecht 1898–1956: *Die Dreigroschenoper* (1928)

1 And now with some pleasure I find that it's seven; and must cook dinner. Haddock and sausage meat. I think it is true that one gains a certain hold on sausage and haddock by writing them down.

Virginia Woolf 1882–1941: diary, 8 March 1941

2 Take away that pudding—it has no theme.

Winston Churchill 1874–1965: Lord Home *The Way the Wind Blows* (1976)

E. M. Forster 1879–1970
English novelist

3 E. M. Forster never gets any further than warming the teapot. He's a rare fine hand at that. Feel this teapot. Is it not beautifully warm? Yes, but there ain't going to be no tea.

Katherine Mansfield 1888–1923: diary, May 1917

4 His style has not, like Henry James's or Meredith's or Hemingway's, spawned; it is not mannered enough for that, and the mind behind it is too rare to be successfully aped. His influence rather permeates, like a dye, than an outside model that can be copied.

Rose Macaulay 1881–1958: 'The Writings of E. M. Forster' (1938)

5 I don't belong to a world where E. M. Forster, a self-indulgent old liberal with hardly a brain in his head, could be taken as a national symbol of moral power.

Rebecca West 1892–1983: letter, 24 December 1973

6 The trouble began with Forster. After him it was considered ungentlemanly to write more than five or six novels.

Anthony Burgess 1917–93: in *Guardian* 24 February 1989

Friends see Family and Friends

Elizabeth Gaskell 1810–65
English novelist

7 A natural unassuming woman whom they have been doing their best to spoil by making a lioness of her.

Jane Welsh Carlyle 1801–66: letter, 17 May 1849

8 I wish to Heaven, her people would keep a little firmer on their legs!
on the constitutional lack of physical stamina shown by Mrs Gaskell's characters, in such stories as 'The Heart of John Middleton'

Charles Dickens 1812–70: letter to W. H. Wills, 12 December 1850

9 Mrs Gaskell herself is a woman of whose conversation and company I should not tire. She seems to me kind, clever, animated, and unaffected.

Charlotte Brontë 1816–55: letter, 1 July 1851

10 I have spent all my spare moments during the last week reading with avidity *Cranford*.
while serving on the Western Front

Charles Sorley 1895–1915: letter, August 1915

John Gay 1685–1732
English poet and dramatist

1 This play . . . was first offered to Cibber and his brethren at Drury-Lane, and rejected; it being then carried to Rich had the effect, as was ludicrously said, of making Gay *rich*, and Rich *gay*.
   of Gay's The Beggar's Opera

Samuel Johnson 1709–84: *Lives of the English Poets* (1779–81) 'John Gay'

2 A pastoral of an hundred lines may be endured, but who will hear of sheep and goats, and myrtle bowers and purling rivulets through five acts?
   of Gay's productions, other than The Beggar's Opera

Samuel Johnson 1709–84: *Lives of the English Poets* (1779–81) 'John Gay'

Genius see also Talent

3 When a true genius appears in the world, you may know him by this sign, that the dunces are all in confederacy against him.

Jonathan Swift 1667–1745: *Thoughts on Various Subjects* (1711)

4 There is more beauty in the works of a great genius who is ignorant of all the rules of art, than in the works of a little genius, who not only knows but scrupulously observes them.

Joseph Addison 1672–1719: in *The Spectator* 10 September 1714

5 Good God! what a genius I had when I wrote that book.
   of A Tale of a Tub

Jonathan Swift 1667–1745: Sir Walter Scott (ed.) *Works of Swift* (1814)

6 The true genius is a mind of large general powers, accidentally determined to some particular direction.

Samuel Johnson 1709–84: *Lives of the English Poets* (1779–81) 'Cowley'

7 It were hyper-criticism, it were pseudo-philosophy to expect from the soul of high-toned genius, the grovellings of a common mind.—The coruscations of talent, elicited by impassioned feeling in the breast of man, are perhaps incompatible with some of the prosaic decencies of life.

Jane Austen 1775–1817: 'Sir Edward Denham' in *Sanditon* (1925 ed.)

8 I really cannot know whether I am or am not the genius you are pleased to call me, but I am very willing to put up with the mistake, it if be one. It is a title dearly enough bought by most men, to render it endurable, even when not quite clearly made out, which it never *can* be till the posterity, whose decisions are merely dreams to ourselves, has sanctioned or denied it, while it can touch us no further.

Lord Byron 1788–1824: letter to Isaac D'Israeli, 10 June 1822; Leslie Marchand (ed.) *Byron's Letters and Journals* (1979) vol. 9

9 The works of genius are watered with its tears.

Honoré de Balzac 1799–1850: *Lost Illusions* (1837–43)

10 What is genius—but the power of expressing a new individuality?

Elizabeth Barrett Browning 1806–61: letter to Mary Russell Mitford, 14 January 1843

11 Since when was genius found respectable?

Elizabeth Barrett Browning 1806–61: *Aurora Leigh* (1857)

12 Does genius burn, Jo?
   her family's habitual enquiry to Jo March when engaged in writing

Louisa May Alcott 1832–88: *Good Wives* (1869)

1 Unless one is a genius, it is best to aim at being intelligible.

Anthony Hope 1863–1933: *The Dolly Dialogues* (1894)

2 I have nothing to declare except my genius.
at the New York Custom House

Oscar Wilde 1854–1900: Frank Harris *Oscar Wilde* (1918)

3 I have known no man of genius who had not to pay, in some affliction or defect either physical or spiritual, for what the gods had given him.

Max Beerbohm 1872–1956: *And Even Now* (1920)

4 A man of genius makes no mistakes. His errors are volitional and are the portals of discovery.

James Joyce 1882–1941: *Ulysses* (1922)

5 The Scots are incapable of considering their literary geniuses purely as writers or artists. They must be either an excuse for a glass or a text for the next sermon.

George Malcolm Thomson 1899– : *Caledonia* (1927)

6 Geniuses are the luckiest of mortals because what they must do is the same as what they most want to do.

W. H. Auden 1907–73: Dag Hammarskjöld *Markings* (1964)

7 I doubt that there is a writer over 40 who does not realize in his heart of hearts that literary genius, in prose, consists of proportions more on the order of 65 per cent material and 35 per cent the talent in the sacred crucible.

Tom Wolfe 1931– : 'Stalking the Billion-Footed Beast' (1989)

8 Greatness recognizes greatness and is shadowed by it.

Harold Bloom 1930– : *The Western Canon* (1995)

Ghost Stories

9 A sad tale's best for winter.
I have one of sprites and goblins.

William Shakespeare 1564–1616: *The Winter's Tale* (1610–11)

10 The only supernatural agents which can in any manner be allowed to us moderns, are ghosts; but of these I would advise an author to be extremely sparing. These are indeed like arsenic, and other dangerous drugs in physic, to be used with the utmost caution; nor would I advise the introduction of them at all in those works, or by those authors, to which or to whom a horse-laugh in the reader would be any great prejudice or mortification.

Henry Fielding 1707–54: *Tom Jones* (1749)

11 We can no longer get a good ghost story, either for love nor money. The materialists have it all their own way . . . That cold-blooded demon called Science has taken the place of all the other demons.

William Gilmore Simms 1806–70: *Murder Will Out* (1842)

12 The past, the more or less remote past, of which the prose is clean obliterated by distance—that is the place to get our ghosts from.

Vernon Lee 1856–1935: *Hauntings* (1890) preface

13 Whenever five or six English-speaking people meet round a fire on Christmas Eve, they start telling each other ghost stories.

Jerome K. Jerome 1859–1927: *Told After Supper* (1891) introduction

14 How are we to account for the strange human craving for the pleasure of feeling afraid which is so much involved in our love of ghost stories?

Virginia Woolf 1882–1941: in *Times Literary Supplement* 31 January 1918 'Across the Border'

15 We must admit that Henry James has conquered. That courtly, worldly, sentimental old gentleman can still make us afraid of the dark.

Virginia Woolf 1882–1941: in *Times Literary Supplement* 22 December 1921 'The Ghost Stories of Henry James'

1 Let us, then, be introduced to the actors in a placid way; let us see them going about their ordinary business, undisturbed by forebodings, pleased with their surroundings; and into this calm environment let the ominous thing put out its head, unobtrusively at first, and then more insistently, until it holds the stage.

M. R. James 1862–1936: *Ghosts and Marvels* (1924) introduction

2 The success of a ghost story may be judged by its thermometrical quality; if it sends a cold shiver down one's spine, it has done its job and done it well.

Edith Wharton 1862–1937: M. Cox and R. Gilbert (eds.) *Oxford Book of Ghost Stories* (1986) introduction

3 To be successful, a ghost story has to be terrifying, and it is much easier to be ingenious than to be terrifying. The writer of detective stories must present his readers with a crime and an ingenious solution for it. But the writer of ghost stories must freeze his reader's marrow, and that is anything but easy.

Robertson Davies 1913–95: in 1942; *The Enthusiasms of Robertson Davies* (1990)

4 The greatest of ghost-story writers have examined the terror and defined it—this is partly why we like to read them: round their circles of light, our fears gather.

Anne Ridler 1912– : *Best Ghost Stories* (1945) prefatory note

5 [The ghost story] is certainly the most exacting form of literary art, and perhaps the only one in which there is almost no intermediate step between success and failure. Either it comes off or it is a flop.

L. P. Hartley 1895–1972: Cynthia Asquith (ed.) *The Third Ghost Book* (1955) introduction

6 It gathers its strength through obliquity and operates most powerfully through a series of openings whose horror lies in their being just, just out of true.

Elizabeth Bowen 1899–1973: attributed

7 Ghost stories . . . tell us about things that lie hidden within all of us, and which lurk outside all around us.

Susan Hill 1942– : *Ghost Stories* (1983) introduction

Edward Gibbon 1737-94 see also **31:10**
English historian

8 He is an ugly, affected, disgusting fellow, and poisons our literary club to me.

James Boswell 1740–95: letter, May 1779

when his apparently flattering reference to Gibbon as the 'luminous' author of The Decline and Fall *was queried:*

9 Luminous! oh, I meant—voluminous.

Richard Brinsley Sheridan 1751–1816: during the trial of Warren Hastings in 1785; Samuel Rogers *Table Talk* (1903)

10 Johnson's style was grand and Gibbon's elegant; the stateliness of the former was sometimes pedantic, and the polish of the latter was occasionally finical. Johnson marched to kettle-drums and trumpets; Gibbon moved to flute and hautboys: Johnson hewed passages through the Alps, while Gibbon levelled walks through parks and gardens.

George Colman, the Younger 1762–1836: *Random Records* (1830)

1 When I read a chapter in Gibbon, I seem to be looking through a luminous haze or fog; figures come and go, I know not how or why, all larger than life, or distorted and discoloured; nothing is real, vivid, true; all is scenical, and, as it were, exhibited by candlelight.

Samuel Taylor Coleridge 1772–1834: *Table Talk* (1836)

André Gide 1869–1951
French novelist and critic

2 An elderly fallen angel travelling incognito.

Peter Quennell 1905–93: *The Sign of the Fish* (1960)

Johann Wolfgang von Goethe 1749–1832
German poet, novelist, and dramatist

3 If Goethe really died saying 'more light', it was very silly of him: what *he* wanted was more warmth.

Charles Sorley 1895–1915: letter, July 1914; see **156:7**

Oliver Goldsmith 1730–74 see also 91:13
Anglo-Irish writer, poet, and dramatist

4 Here lies Nolly Goldsmith, for shortness called Noll, Who wrote like an angel, but talked like poor Poll.

David Garrick 1717–79: 'Impromptu Epitaph' (written 1773/4)

Good and Bad Writing see also Style

5   *Namque tu solebas*
Meas esse aliquid putare nugas.
For you used to think my trifles were worth something.

Catullus c.84–c.54 BC: *Carmina* no. 1

6 Not gods, nor men, nor even booksellers have put up with poets being second-rate.

Horace 65–8 BC: *Ars Poetica*

7 There is scarcely any book so bad that nothing can be learnt from it.
   his father's customary remark

Pliny the Younger AD c.61–c.112: *Epistulae*

8 Pure and neat language I love, yet plain and customary. A barbarous phrase hath often made me out of love with a good sense, and doubtful writing hath wracked me beyond my patience.

Ben Jonson c.1573–1637: *Timber, or Discoveries made upon Men and Matter* (1641)

9 What woeful stuff this madrigal would be, In some starved hackney sonneteer, or me? But let a Lord once own the happy lines, How the wit brightens! how the style refines!

Alexander Pope 1688–1744: *An Essay on Criticism* (1711)

10 The harm done by bad poets in trivializing beautiful expressions and images, and associating disgust and indifference with the technical forms of poetry.

Samuel Taylor Coleridge 1772–1834: Notebook, 1798–1804

11 I am convinced more and more day by day that fine writing is next to fine doing the top thing in the world.

John Keats 1795–1821: letter to J. H. Reynolds, 24 August 1819

1 It is a wretched taste to be gratified with mediocrity when the excellent lies before us.

Isaac D'Israeli 1766–1848: *Curiosities of Literature. Second Series* (1823)

2 Too many flowers . . . too little fruit.
  describing the work of Felicia Hemans

Sir Walter Scott 1771–1832: letter to Joanna Baillie, 18 July 1823

3 Clear writers, like clear fountains, do not seem so deep as they are; the turbid look the most profound.

Walter Savage Landor 1775–1864: *Imaginary Conversations* (1824) 'Southey and Porson'

4 People don't deserve to have good writing, they are so pleased with bad.

Ralph Waldo Emerson 1803–82: *Journals* 1841

5 The amount of a certain sort of emasculate twaddle produced in the United States is not encouraging.

Henry James 1843–1916: letter, 14 September 1879

6 The best is the best, though a hundred judges have declared it so.

Arthur Quiller-Couch 1863–1944: *Oxford Book of English Verse* (1900) preface

7 The literary gift is a mere accident—is as often bestowed on idiots who have nothing to say worth hearing as it is denied to strenuous sages.

Max Beerbohm 1872–1956: letter to George Bernard Shaw, 21 September 1903

8 A good novel tells us the truth about its hero; but a bad novel tells us the truth about its author.

G. K. Chesterton 1874–1936: *Heretics* (1905)

9 This of course is not what he was trying to say, but the pen is mightier than the wrist.

A. E. Housman 1859–1936: in *Classical Review* 1920; see **227:6**

10 It is far easier to write ten passably effective sonnets, good enough to take in the not too inquiring critic, than one effective advertisement that will take in a few thousand of the uncritical buying public.

Aldous Huxley 1894–1963: *On the Margin* (1923) 'Advertisement'

11 Only two classes of books are of universal appeal. The very best and the very worst.

Ford Madox Ford 1873–1939: *Joseph Conrad* (1924)

12 We are nauseated by the sight of trivial personalities decomposing in the eternity of print.

Virginia Woolf 1882–1941: *The Common Reader* (1925) 'The Modern Essay'

13 It is with noble sentiments that bad literature gets written.

André Gide 1869–1951: letter to François Mauriac, 1928

14 A bad book is as much of a labour to write as a good one; it comes as sincerely from the author's soul.

Aldous Huxley 1894–1963: *Point Counter Point* (1928)

15 What I like in a good author is not what he says, but what he whispers.

Logan Pearsall Smith 1865–1946: *All Trivia* (1933) 'Afterthoughts'

16 A great writer creates a world of his own and his readers are proud to live in it. A lesser writer may entice them in for a moment, but soon he will watch them filing out.

Cyril Connolly 1903–74: *Enemies of Promise* (1938)

17 All good writing is *swimming under water* and holding your breath.

F. Scott Fitzgerald 1896–1940: letter (undated) to Frances Scott Fitzgerald

18 The more books we read, the sooner we perceive that the only function of a writer is to produce a masterpiece. No other task is of any consequence.

Cyril Connolly 1903–74: *The Unquiet Grave* (1944)

19 Good poets have a weakness for bad puns.

W. H. Auden 1907–73: 'The Shield of Achilles' (1955)

20 The world is over-stocked with people who are ready and eager to teach other people to write. It seems astonishing that so much bad writing should find its way into print when so much good advice is to be had.

Robertson Davies 1913–95: in 1959; *The Enthusiasms of Robertson Davies* (1990)

1 You know you're writing well when you're throwing good stuff into the wastebasket.

Ernest Hemingway 1899–1961: attributed

2 There's only one real sin, and that is to persuade oneself that the second-best is anything but the second-best.

Doris Lessing 1919– : *Golden Notebook* (1962)

3 Mediocrity is more dangerous in a critic than in a writer.

Eugène Ionesco 1912–94: attributed, 1966

4 This is not a novel to be tossed aside lightly. It should be thrown with great force.

Dorothy Parker 1893–1967: R. E. Drennan *Wit's End* (1973)

5 I suspect that the reason that the ability to write good prose and good dialogue go hand-in-hand is simply that a good writer knows how to listen.

John Braine 1922–86: *Writing a Novel* (1974)

6 For a writer, the bad elements stand out like a boil. It's all very well to recognize that a boil is only a part of the body, it's still disproportionately obtrusive.

Graham Greene 1904–91: Marie-Françoise Allain *The Other Man, Conversations with Graham Greene* (1983)

7 Nothing we write, if we hope to be any good, will ever turn out as we first thought.

Lillian Hellman 1905–84: attributed

Maxim Gorky 1868–1936
Russian writer and revolutionary

8 The question of what man *is* really meant, for Gorky, what man can become.

Eugene Lampert 1913– : Malcolm Bradbury and James McFarlane (eds.) *Modernism* (1991)

The Gothic see Horror and the Gothic

Graffiti

9 Popular education was bringing the graffito lower on the walls.

Oliver St John Gogarty 1878–1957: *As I was Going Down Sackville Street* (1937)

10 One reaches a time of life when limericks written on the walls of comfort stations are not just obscene, they are horribly dull.

Raymond Chandler 1888–1959: letter to Blanche Knopf, 27 March 1946

11 Italians . . . find sculpture irresistible to their biros.

James Lees-Milne 1908–97: *Midway on the Waves: Diaries 1948-49* (1985) 20 Feb 1949

12 In the dime stores and bus stations,
People talk of situations,
Read books, repeat quotations,
Draw conclusions on the wall.

Bob Dylan 1941– :'Love Minus Zero/ No Limit' (1965 song)

13 Mark my words, when a society has to resort to the lavatory for its humour, the writing is on the wall.

Alan Bennett 1934– : *Forty Years On* (1969)

14 If God had not meant us to write on walls he would never have set us an example.

Anonymous: Nigel Rees *Graffiti 2* (1980)

Grammar and Usage see also Spelling

1 *Multa renascentur quae iam cecidere, cadentque
Quae nunc sunt in honore vocabula, si volet usus,
Quem penes arbitrium est et ius et norma loquendi.*

Many terms which have now dropped out of favour will be
revived, and those that are at present respectable will drop
out, if usage so choose, with whom lies the decision, the
judgement, and the rule of speech.

Horace 65-8 BC: *Ars Poetica*

2 Grammer, the ground of al.

William Langland c.1330–c.1400:
The Vision of Piers Plowman

3 Syllables govern the world.

John Selden 1584–1654: *Table Talk*
(1689)

4 I have laboured to refine our language to grammatical
purity, and to clear it from colloquial barbarisms,
licentious idioms, and irregular combinations.

Samuel Johnson 1709–84: in *The
Rambler* 14 March 1752

5 An aspersion upon my parts of speech!

Richard Brinsley Sheridan
1751–1816: *The Rivals* (1775)

6 In language, the ignorant have prescribed laws to the
learned.

Richard Duppa 1770–1831: *Maxims*
(1830)

7 Correct English is the slang of prigs who write history and
essays. And the strongest slang of all is the slang of poets.

George Eliot 1819–80: *Middlemarch*
(1871–2)

8 For first you write a sentence,
And then you chop it small;
Then mix the bits, and sort them out
Just as they chance to fall:
The order of the phrases makes
No difference at all.

Lewis Carroll 1832–98:
'Phantasmagoria' (1876)

9 I will not go down to posterity talking bad grammar.
*while correcting proofs of his last Parliamentary speech, 31
March 1881*

Benjamin Disraeli 1804–81: Robert
Blake *Disraeli* (1966)

10 Good intentions are invariably ungrammatical.

Oscar Wilde 1854–1900: attributed

11 Prefer geniality to grammar.

H. W. Fowler 1858–1933 and **F. G.
Fowler** 1870–1918: *The King's English*
(1906)

12 Damn the subjunctive. It brings all our writers to shame.

Mark Twain 1835–1910: *Notebook*
(1935)

13 Only presidents, editors, and people with tapeworms have
the right to use the editorial 'we'.

Mark Twain 1835–1910: attributed

14 I'm glad you like adverbs—I adore them.

Henry James 1843–1916: letter to
Miss Edwards, 5 January 1912

15 I don't want to talk grammar, I want to talk like a lady.

George Bernard Shaw 1856–1950:
Pygmalion (1916)

16 Adjectives are the sugar of literature and adverbs the salt.

Henry James 1843–1916: Theodora
Bosanquet *Henry James at Work*
(1924)

17 The English-speaking world may be divided into (1) those
who neither know nor care what a split infinitive is; (2)
those who do not know, but care very much; (3) those
who know and condemn; (4) those who know and
distinguish. Those who neither know nor care are the vast

H. W. Fowler 1858–1933: *Modern
English Usage* (1926)

majority, and are a happy folk, to be envied by most of the minority classes.

1 The subjunctive mood is in its death throes, and the best thing to do is to put it out of its misery as soon as possible.

W. Somerset Maugham 1874–1965: *A Writer's Notebook* (1949) written in 1941

2 One can cure oneself of the *not un-* formation by memorizing this sentence: A not unblack dog was chasing a not unsmall rabbit across a not ungreen field.

George Orwell 1903–50: in *Horizon* April 1946

3 Would you convey my compliments to the purist who reads your proofs and tell him or her that I write in a sort of broken-down patois which is something like the way a Swiss waiter talks, and that when I split an infinitive, God damn it, I split it so it will stay split.

Raymond Chandler 1888–1959: letter to Edward Weeks, 18 January 1947

4 This is the sort of English up with which I will not put.

Winston Churchill 1874–1965: Ernest Gowers *Plain Words* (1948)

5 My mother . . . pointed out that one could not say 'a green great dragon', but had to say 'a great green dragon'. I wondered why, and still do.
of the first story he wrote, aged seven

J. R. R. Tolkien 1892–1973: letter to W. H. Auden, 7 June 1955

6 The notion 'grammatical' cannot be identified with 'meaningful' or 'significant' in any semantic sense. Sentences (1) and (2) are equally nonsensical, but . . . only the former is grammatical.
(1) Colourless green ideas sleep furiously.
(2) Furiously sleep ideas green colourless.

Noam Chomsky 1928– : *Syntactic Structures* (1957)

7 It takes a trained mind to relish a non sequitur.

N. F. Simpson 1919– : *A Resounding Tinkle* (1957)

8 Today the language of advertising enjoys an enormous circulation. With its deliberate infractions of grammatical rules and its crossbreeding of the parts of speech, it profoundly influences the tongues and pens of children and adults.

William Strunk 1869–1946 and **E. B. White** 1899–1985: *The Elements of Style* (1959 ed.)

9 You can be a little ungrammatical if you come from the right part of the country.

Robert Frost 1874–1963: in *Atlantic Monthly* January 1962

10 One has a few private rules: never split an adjective and its noun, for instance.

Philip Larkin 1922–85: in 1979; *Required Writing* (1983)

11 The beastly adverb—far more damaging to a writer than an adjective.

Graham Greene 1904–91: *Ways of Escape* (1980)

12 As far as I'm concerned, 'whom' is a word that was invented to make everyone sound like a butler.

Calvin Trillin 1935– : in *The Nation* 8 June 1985

13 I am quite capable of speaking, unprepared, a sentence containing anything up to forty subordinate clauses all embedded in their neighbours like those wooden Russian dolls, and many a native of these islands, speaking English as to the manner born, has followed me trustingly into the labyrinth only to perish miserably trying to find the way out.

Bernard Levin 1928– : *In These Times* (1986)

1 Women, fire, and dangerous things.
a grammatical classification in Dyirbal, an Australian
Aboriginal language, taken as an illustration of the tendency
of human beings to perceive categories generally

George Lakoff 1941– : title of book
(1987)

2 Save the gerund and screw the whale.

Tom Stoppard 1937– : *The Real*
Thing (1988 rev. ed.)

3 Language is more fashion than science, and matters of
usage, spelling and pronunciation tend to wander around
like hemlines.

Bill Bryson 1951– : in *Independent* 17
December 1994 (Quote Unquote)

4 The word *glamour* comes from the word *grammar*, and
since the Chomskyan revolution the etymology has been
fitting. Who could not be dazzled by the creative power of
the mental grammar, by its ability to convey an infinite
number of thoughts with a finite set of rules.

Steven Pinker 1954– : *The Language*
Instinct (1994)

5 The future perfect I have always regarded as an
oxymoron.

Tom Stoppard 1937– : *The Invention*
of Love (1997)

6 I'm deeply resistant to change; I can't bear what
happened to English sentence structure after the
eighteenth or nineteenth centuries.

Tom Stoppard 1937– : attributed,
1998

Robert Graves 1895–1985
English poet

7 Writing a poem for me is putting myself in a very odd state
indeed in which I am excessively sensitive to
interruption—I can hear, or think I can hear, people doing
disturbing things behind shut doors three houses off—and
really suffer very painfully, as though I were performing a
major operation on my own skull.

Robert Graves 1895–1985: letter, 31
July 1942

8 Robert Graves was unique. He followed no fads and set no
fashions. He had a mind like an alchemist's laboratory:
everything that got into it came out new, weird and
gleaming.

John Carey 1934– : in *Sunday Times*
8 December 1985

9 He was fond of declaring that 'he bred show dogs in order
to be able to afford a cat', the dogs being prose, the cat
poetry.

Alastair Reid 1926– : *Whereabouts*
(1987)

Thomas Gray 1716–71
English poet

10 The General . . . repeated nearly the whole of Gray's Elegy
. . . adding, as he concluded, that he would prefer being
the author of that poem to the glory of beating the French
to-morrow.

James Wolfe 1727–59: J. Playfair
Biographical Account of J. Robinson
(1815)

11 I shall be but a shrimp of an author.

Thomas Gray 1716–71: letter to
Horace Walpole, 25 February 1768

1 The *Church-yard* abounds with images which find a mirror in every mind, and with sentiments to which every bosom returns an echo.
on Gray's 'Elegy in a Country Churchyard'

Samuel Johnson 1709–84: *Lives of the English Poets* (1779–81) 'Gray'

2 Gray, a born poet, fell upon an age of reason.

Matthew Arnold 1822–88: *Essays in Criticism* (1865–88) 'Thomas Gray'

Graham Greene 1904–91
English novelist

3 Graham Greene, like a raddled Noel Coward with a bad colour.

James Lees-Milne 1908–97: *Midway on the Waves: Diaries 1948-49* (1985) 20 February 1949

4 I wouldn't give up writing about God at this stage, if I was you. It would be like P. G. Wodehouse dropping Jeeves half way through the Wooster series.

Evelyn Waugh 1903–66: to Graham Greene; Christopher Sykes *Evelyn Waugh* (1975)

5 *Brighton Rock* I began in 1937 as a detective story and continued, I am sometimes tempted to think, as an error of judgement.

Graham Greene 1904–91: *Ways of Escape* (1980)

6 It was typical of Graham that with the monthly cheques he often sent a few bottles of red wine to 'take the edge off cold charity'.
of the financial help he gave her as a struggling writer

Muriel Spark 1918– : Alec Guinness *My Name Escapes Me* (1996)

Thomas Hardy 1840–1928
English novelist and poet

7 Hardy went down to botanize in the swamp, while Meredith climbed towards the sun. Meredith became, at his best, a sort of daintily dressed Walt Whitman: Hardy became a sort of village atheist brooding and blaspheming over the village idiot.

G. K. Chesterton 1874–1936: *The Victorian Age in Literature* (1912)

8 In trotted a little puffy-cheeked cheerful old man, with an atmosphere cheerful and businesslike in addressing us, rather like an old doctor's or solicitor's, saying 'Well now—' or words like that as he shook hands. He was dressed in rough grey with a striped tie. His nose has a joint in it and the end curves down. A round whitish face, the eyes now faded and rather watery, but the whole aspect cheerful and vigorous.

Virginia Woolf 1882–1941: diary, 1926

9 If I had thought that story was going to be such a success I'd have made it a really good book.
on Tess of the D'Urbervilles

Thomas Hardy 1840–1928: Desmond McCarthy *Memories* (1953)

10 They are not harsh, only inevitable.
on his later poems

Thomas Hardy 1840–1928: Lillah McCarthy *Myself and My Friends* (1933)

1 I am quite sure he did not find all his queer characters hereabouts. He must have discovered a good many of them when he went to London.
 Hardy's spinster cousin, aged 84

Teresa Hardy: in 1928, James Gibson (ed.) *Thomas Hardy: Interviews and Recollections* (1999)

2 What a commonplace genius he has, or a genius for the commonplace, I don't know which. He doesn't rank so terribly high, really. But better than Bernard Shaw, even then.

D. H. Lawrence 1885–1930: letter to Martin Secker, 24 July 1928

3 No one has written worse English than Mr Hardy in some of his novels—cumbrous, stilted, ugly and inexpressive— yes, but at the same time so strangely expressive of something attractive to us in Mr Hardy himself that we would not change it for the perfection of Sterne at his best. It becomes coloured by its surroundings; it becomes literature.

Virginia Woolf 1882–1941: *The Moment and Other Essays* (1947) 'Personalities'

4 The nearest thing to Shakespeare I should ever go for a walk with.
 on Thomas Hardy

Siegfried Sassoon 1886–1967: *Siegfried's Journey* (1945)

Nathaniel Hawthorne 1804–64
American novelist

5 There is the grand truth about Nathaniel Hawthorne. He says NO! in thunder; but the Devil himself cannot make him say *yes*. For men who say *yes*, lie; and all men who say *no*,—why, they are in the happy condition of judicious, unincumbered travellers in Europe; they cross frontiers into Eternity with nothing but a carpet-bag.

Herman Melville 1819–91: letter to Nathaniel Hawthorne, c.16 April 1851

6 Hawthorne was silent with his lips; but he talked with his pen.

Henry James 1843–1916: *Hawthorne* (1879)

7 Out of the soil of New England he sprang—in a crevice of that immitigable granite he sprouted and bloomed.

Henry James 1843–1916: *Hawthorne* (1879)

8 My sensation throughout is of pity for the poor fellow, who had to feed his soul on such raw material.
 on reading Hawthorne's Notebooks

George Gissing 1857–1903: *Commonplace Book* (1962)

William Hazlitt 1778–1830 see also 92:3
English essayist

9 He is not a proper person to be admitted into respectable society, being the most perverse and malevolent creature that ill luck has ever thrown in my way.

William Wordsworth 1770–1850: letter to Haydon, 1817

receiving an apology from John Lamb, who had knocked him down:
10 I am a metaphysician, and do not mind a blow; nothing but an *idea* hurts me.

William Hazlitt 1778–1830: Thomas Moore diary, 9 September 1820

11 Though we are mighty fine fellows nowadays, we cannot write like Hazlitt.

Robert Louis Stevenson 1850–94: *Virginibus Puerisque* (1881)

Seamus Heaney 1939–
Irish poet

1 Heaney's dense and burnished rurality.

Philip Larkin 1922–85: *Further Requirements* (2001)

2 One of the fascinations of Heaney's work . . . is in observing how he shifts this way and that to find a genuinely comfortable *fit*, a non-fake, non-proud way of living in the sacred robes he knows he has the obligation and the right to wear.

Ian Hamilton 1938– : *Walking Possession* (1994) 'Seamus Heaney'

3 The laureate of ordinary things, he gives them back a reality that habit robs them of.

John Carey 1934– : in *Sunday Times* 28 April 1996

Ernest Hemingway 1899–1961 see also **50:4, 316:7**
American novelist

4 He writes very good verse and he's the finest prose stylist in the world.

Ezra Pound 1885–1972: introducing Hemingway to Ford Madox Ford, 1922; Kenneth S. Lynn *Hemingway* (1987)

5 Ernest's quality of a stick hardened in the fire.

F. Scott Fitzgerald 1896–1940: letter, 1 September 1930

6 [*The Sun Also Rises* is about] bullfighting, bullslinging, and bull—.

Zelda Fitzgerald 1900–47: Marion Meade *What Fresh Hell Is This?* (1988)

7 Did he have to attempt also the impossible task of proving he was more manly than she was?
  comparing Hemingway to Gertrude **Stein**

Brigid Brophy 1929–95: *Fifty Works of English and American Literature We Could Do Without* (1967) 'A Farewell to Arms'

8 What other culture could have produced someone like Hemingway and *not* seen the joke?

Gore Vidal 1925– : *Pink Triangle and Yellow Star* (1982)

George Herbert 1593–1633
English poet and clergyman

9 For three centuries and more, George Herbert exemplified the body heat of a healthy Anglican life.

Seamus Heaney 1939– : *The Redress of Poetry* (1995)

Robert Herrick 1591–1674
English poet and clergyman

10 The Ariel of poets, sucking 'Where the bee sucks' from the rose-heart of nature, and reproducing the fragrance idealized.

Elizabeth Barrett Browning 1806–61: *The Greek Christian Poets and the English Poets* (1842)

11 Of all our poets this man appears to have had the coarsest mind. Without being intentionally obscene, he is thoroughly filthy, and has not the slightest sense of decency.

Robert Southey 1774–1843: *Commonplace Book* (1849–51)

Historical Fiction

1 I am fully sensible that an historical romance, founded on the House of Saxe Coburg, might be much more to the purpose of profit or popularity than such pictures of domestic life in country villages as I deal in. But I could no more write a romance than an epic poem. I could not sit seriously down to write a serious romance under any other motive than to save my life; and if it were indispensable for me to keep it up and never relax into laughing at myself or other people, I am sure I should be hung before I had finished the first chapter.

Jane Austen 1775–1817: letter to James Stanier Clarke, 1 April 1816; see **66:1**

2 His is a mind brooding over antiquity . . . The old world is to him a crowded map; the new one a dull, hateful blank.
on Sir Walter Scott

William Hazlitt 1778–1830: *The Spirit of the Age* (1825)

3 It is said that Shakespeare depicted the Romans superbly. I don't see this. They are sheer, inveterate Englishmen, but they are truly human, fundamentally human, and so the Roman toga suits them well enough.

Johann Wolfgang von Goethe 1749–1832: 'Shakespeare without End' (1815)

4 All the time I was at work on the Two Cities, I read no books but such as had the air of time in them.
of writing A Tale of Two Cities

Charles Dickens 1812–70: letter to John Forster, 2 May 1860

5 Those who put the historical novel in a category apart are forgetting that what every novelist does is only to interpret, by means of the technique which his period affords, a certain number of past events; his memories, whether consciously or unconsciously recalled, whether personal or impersonal, are all woven of the same stuff as history itself.

Marguerite Yourcenar 1903–87: *Memoirs of Hadrian* (1955)

6 The journey of the imagination to a remote place is child's play compared to a journey into another time.

Thornton Wilder 1897–1975: in *Paris Review* 1956

7 There is no book which is not of its own time; the painstaking historical novel *Salammbô*, whose characters are mercenaries during the Punic Wars, is a typical nineteenth-century French novel. The one thing we know for sure about Carthaginian literature, which may have been very rich, is that it could not have had a book like Flaubert's.

Jorge Luis Borges 1899–1986: in 1969; James Woodall *The Man in the Mirror of the Book* (1996)

8 *Black Robe* is an historical novel, in a way, but it doesn't give you the heavy padding that historical novels do. They do a lot of research and then they must put the research in. I don't believe in that. Do a minimum of research, and then keep it out. Don't let it impede the story.

Brian Moore 1921–99: Rosemary Hartill *Writers Revealed* (1989)

9 It had never occurred to me that to shift the scene of a novel to another age . . . and to cast it in an English some degrees pleasanter than the current, put me in a disreputable genre. I met some very astonishing statements—such as that I was a writer of *adventure stories*.

Patrick O'Brian 1914–2000: interview in *Independent on Sunday* 15 March 1992

Historical Writing

1 The absence of romance in my history will, I fear, detract somewhat from its interest; but I shall be content if it is judged useful by those inquirers who desire an exact knowledge of the past as an aid to the interpretation of the future.

Thucydides c.460–400 BC: *The History of the Peloponnesian War*

2 History is philosophy from examples.

Dionysius of Halicarnassus fl. 30–7 BC: *Ars Rhetorica*

3 If history record good things of good men, the thoughtful hearer is encouraged to imitate what is good; or if it records evil of wicked men, the devout religious listener or reader is encouraged to avoid all that is sinful and perverse and to follow what he knows to be good and pleasing to God.

The Venerable Bede AD 673–735: *Ecclesiastical History of the English People* preface

4 Should the reader discover any inaccuracies in what I have written, I humbly beg that he will not impute them to me, because, as the laws of history require, I have laboured honestly to transmit whatever I could ascertain from common report for the instruction of posterity.

The Venerable Bede AD 673–735: *Ecclesiastical History of the English People* preface

5 In winter's tedious nights sit by the fire
With good old folks, and let them tell thee tales
Of woeful ages, long ago betid.

William Shakespeare 1564–1616: *Richard II* (1595)

6 Whosoever, in writing a modern history, shall follow truth too near the heels, it may happily strike out his teeth.

Walter Ralegh c.1552–1618: *The History of the World* (1614)

7 Historians desiring to write the actions of men, ought to set down the simple truth, and not say anything for love or hatred; also to choose such an opportunity for writing as it may be lawful to think what they will, and write what they think, which is a rare happiness of the time.

Walter Ralegh c.1552–1618: 'A Collection of Political Observations'; *The Works of Sir Walter Raleigh* (1751) vol. 1

8 Memoirs are true and useful stars, whilst studied histories are those stars joined in constellations, according to the fancy of the poet.

Samuel Pepys 1633–1703: J. R. Tanner (ed.) *Samuel Pepys's Naval Minutes* (1926)

9 They maintained the dignity of history.
of Thucydides and Xenophon

Henry St John, Lord Bolingbroke 1678–1751: *Letters on the Study and Use of History* (1752)

10 Great abilities are not requisite for an historian . . . imagination is not required in any high degree.

Samuel Johnson 1709–84: James Boswell *Life of Samuel Johnson* (1791) 6 July 1763

11 History . . . is, indeed, little more than the register of the crimes, follies, and misfortunes of mankind.

Edward Gibbon 1737–94: *The Decline and Fall of the Roman Empire* (1776–88)

12 The life of the historian must be short and precarious.

Edward Gibbon 1737–94: *Memoirs of My Life* (1796)

13 'I am fond of history.'
'I wish I were too. I read it a little as a duty, but it tells me nothing that does not vex or weary me. The quarrels of popes and kings, with wars and pestilences, in every page; the men all so good for nothing, and hardly any women at all.'

Jane Austen 1775–1817: *Northanger Abbey* (1818)

1 This province of literature is a debatable line. It lies on the confines of two distinct territories. It is under the jurisdiction of two hostile powers; and like other districts similarly situated it is ill-defined, ill-cultivated, and ill-regulated. Instead of being equally shared between its two rulers, the Reason and the Imagination, it falls alternately under the sole and absolute dominion of each. It is sometimes fiction. It is sometimes theory.

Lord Macaulay 1800–59: 'History' (1828)

2 Read no history: nothing but biography, for that is life without theory.

Benjamin Disraeli 1804–81: *Contarini Fleming* (1832); see **124:4**

3 History is the essence of innumerable biographies.

Thomas Carlyle 1795–1881: *Critical and Miscellaneous Essays* (1838) 'On History'

4 There is properly no history; only biography.

Ralph Waldo Emerson 1803–82: *Essays* (1841) 'History'; see **124:2**

5 History is a gallery of pictures in which there are few originals and many copies.

Alexis de Tocqueville 1805–59: *L'Ancien régime* (1856)

6 Anybody can make history. Only a great man can write it.

Oscar Wilde 1854–1900: *Intentions* (1891) 'The Critic as Artist'

7 It has been said that though God cannot alter the past, historians can; it is perhaps because they can be useful to Him in this respect that He tolerates their existence.

Samuel Butler 1835–1902: *Erewhon Revisited* (1901)

8 If I write nothing but fiction for some time I begin to get stupid, and to feel rather as if it had been a long meal of sweets; then history is a rest, for research or narration brings a different part of the mind into play.

Charlotte Yonge 1823–1901: Georgina Battiscombe *Charlotte Mary Yonge* (1943)

9 History repeats itself; historians repeat one another.

Rupert Brooke 1887–1915: letter to Geoffrey Keynes, 4 June 1906

10 The historian, essentially, wants more documents than he can really use; the dramatist only wants more liberties than he can really take.

Henry James 1843–1916: *The Aspern Papers* (1909 ed.) preface

11 Exiled Thucydides knew
All that a speech can say
About Democracy,
And what dictators do,
The elderly rubbish they talk
To an apathetic grave;
Analysed all in his book,
The enlightenment driven away,
The habit-forming pain,
Management and grief.

W. H. Auden 1907–73: 'September 1, 1939' (1940)

12 The highest history combines scholarship and art.

A. J. P. Taylor 1906–90: in *New Statesman and Nation* 13 November 1947

13 Historian—An unsuccessful novelist.

H. L. Mencken 1880–1956: *A Mencken Chrestomathy* (1949)

14 Man is a history-making creature who can neither repeat his past nor leave it behind.

W. H. Auden 1907–73: *The Dyer's Hand* (1962) 'D. H. Lawrence'

15 History gets thicker as it approaches recent times.

A. J. P. Taylor 1906–90: *English History 1914-45* (1965) bibliography

1 I have always felt that a clear choice existed between two states of mind, the writing of history and the making of history. He who is interested in the latter should only be detained by the former just long enough to absorb its lessons.

Oswald Mosley 1896–1980: *My Life* (1968)

2 History is the present. That's why every generation writes it anew. But what most people think of as history is its end product, myth.

E. L. Doctorow 1931– : George Plimpton (ed.) *Writers at Work* 8th series (1988)

3 History does not *invent*, it *discovers*. Through new situations, History reveals what man is, what has been in him 'for a long, long time,' what his possibilities are.

Milan Kundera 1929– : *The Art of the Novel* (1988)

4 History changes all the time. It is constantly being re-examined and re-evaluated, otherwise how would we be able to keep historians occupied? We can't possibly allow people with their sort of minds to walk around with time on their hands.

Terry Pratchett 1948– : *Jingo* (1997)

James Hogg 1770–1835
Scottish poet

5 The poor fellow has just talent enough to spoil him for his own trade without having enough to support him by literature.

Sir Walter Scott 1771–1832: letter, 14 August 1810

6 The said Hogg is a strange being, but of great, though uncouth, powers. I think very highly of him, as a poet; but he, and half of these Scotch and Lake troubadours, are spoilt by living in little circles and petty societies.

Lord Byron 1788–1824: letter to Thomas Moore, 3 August 1814

7 The honest grunter.

Sir Walter Scott 1771–1832: diary, 12 December 1825

Homer
Greek poet of the 8th century BC

8 *Indignor quandoque bonus dormitat Homerus.*
I'm aggrieved when sometimes even excellent Homer nods.

Horace 65–8 BC: *Ars Poetica*

9 In the Odyssey one may liken Homer to the setting sun, of which the grandeur remains without the intensity.

Longinus fl. 1st century AD: *On the Sublime* (supposedly by Longinus)

10 Homer, the sovereign poet.

Dante Alighieri 1265–1321: *Divina Commedia*

11 Seven cities warred for Homer, being dead,
Who, living, had no roof to shroud his head.

Thomas Heywood c.1574–1641: 'The Hierarchy of the Blessed Angels' (1635)

12 Seven wealthy towns contend for HOMER dead
Through which the living HOMER begged his bread.

Anonymous: epilogue to *Aesop at Tunbridge; or, a Few Selected Fables in Verse By No Person of Quality* (1698)

13 As learned commentators view
In Homer more than Homer knew.

Jonathan Swift 1667–1745: 'On Poetry' (1733)

1 Oft of one wide expanse had I been told
   That deep-browed Homer ruled as his demesne;
   Yet never did I breathe its pure serene
   Till I heard Chapman speak out loud and bold:
   Then felt I like some watcher of the skies
   When a new planet swims into his ken.

John Keats 1795–1821: 'On First Looking into Chapman's Homer' (1817)

2 Mr Gladstone read Homer for fun, which I thought served him right.

Winston Churchill 1874–1965: *My Early Life* (1930)

Gerard Manley Hopkins 1844–89
English poet and priest

3 One Hopkins is enough.

A. D. Hope 1907–2000: *A Book of Answers* (1978)

Horace 65–8 BC
Roman poet

4 *Horatii curiosa felicitas.*
   Horace's careful felicity.

Petronius d. AD 65: *Satyricon*

5 C—taught me to loathe Horace for two years; to forget him for twenty, and then to love him for the rest of my days and through many sleepless nights.
   of his school classics master, the model for 'King' in Stalky & Co

Rudyard Kipling 1865–1936: *Something of Myself*

Horror and the Gothic

6   But that I am forbid
   To tell the secrets of my prison-house,
   I could a tale unfold whose lightest word
   Would harrow up thy soul, freeze thy young blood,
   Make thy two eyes, like stars, start from their spheres,
   Thy knotted and combinèd locks to part,
   And each particular hair to stand on end,
   Like quills upon the fretful porpentine.

William Shakespeare 1564–1616: *Hamlet* (1601)

7 Every drop of ink in my pen ran cold.

Horace Walpole 1717–97: letter to George Montagu, 30 July 1752

8 I have heard that something very shocking indeed, will soon come out in London.

Jane Austen 1775–1817: *Northanger Abbey* (1818)

9 Charming as were all Mrs Radcliffe's works, and charming even as were the works of her imitators, it was not in them that human nature, at least in the midland counties of England, was to be looked for. Of the Alps and Pyrenees, with their pine forests and their vices, they might give a faithful delineation; and Italy, Switzerland, and the South of France, might be as fruitful in horrors as they were there represented. Catherine dared not doubt beyond her own country, and even of that, if hard pressed, would have yielded the northern and western extremities. But in

Jane Austen 1775–1817: *Northanger Abbey* (1818)

the central part of England there was surely some security
. . . in the laws of the land, and the manners of the age.

1 I wants to make your flesh creep.
   the Fat Boy's aspiration

Charles Dickens 1812–70: *Pickwick Papers* (1837)

2 I see you desire the blood to be curdled: be it so! . . . I have
. . . telegraphed for a draft story left elsewhere which is
ugly enough and ought to chill the blood of a grenadier.
   of his short story The Body Snatcher

Robert Louis Stevenson 1850–94: letter to Charles Morley, editor of *Pall Mall*, *c*.15 November 1884

3 The 'tale of terror', like pornography, with which it has
much in common, represents a carefree holiday from
ethics.

Angela Carter 1940–92: in *New Society* 1975

4 I'm interested in the Gothic novel because it's very much a
woman's form. Why is there such a wide readership for
books that essentially say, 'Your husband is trying to kill
you'?

Margaret Atwood 1939– : in an interview, July 1978; Earl G. Ingersoll (ed.) *Margaret Atwood: Conversations* (1990)

5 Terror . . . often arises from a pervasive sense of
disestablishment; that things are in the unmaking.

Stephen King 1947– : *Danse Macabre* (1981)

6 The site where the late-18th century buried its nuclear
waste of repression and neurosis.
   of Gothic literature

John Carey 1934– : in *Sunday Times* 1992

7 The great horror stories of the 19th century—starting
with Radcliffe, then entering the popular bloodstream with
Mary Shelley's *Frankenstein*, Robert Louis Stevenson's *The
Strange Case of Dr Jekyll and Mr Hyde* (1886), Bram
Stoker's *Dracula* (1897) and Sir Arthur Conan Doyle's *The
Hound of the Baskervilles* (1901)—represent the most
significant contribution by British writers of the past
century to the mass culture of this one.

Christopher Frayling 1946– : in *Sunday Times* 8 December 1996

A. E. Housman 1859–1936
English poet

8 Housman was Masefield with a dash of Theocritus.

George Orwell 1903–50: *Inside the Whale* (1940)

9 Housman was not taciturn because he had nothing to say
but because his first and last characteristic was
inscrutability—a buried life that he was determined to
keep buried.

Percy Wither: *A Buried Life* (1940)

10 To my generation, no other English poet seemed so
perfectly to express the sensibility of a male adolescent.

W. H. Auden 1907–73: Humphrey Carpenter *W. H. Auden* (1981)

11 Housman was a kind of human cactus. Hard and prickly
outside, and mushy in the middle, he flowered briefly and
surprisingly about twice a year. The poems he produced
on these rare occasions are among the most beautiful and
miserable in the language.

John Carey 1934– : in *Sunday Times* 1979

12 Housman is the poet of unhappiness; no one else has
reiterated his single message so plangently.

Philip Larkin 1922–85: in 1979; *Required Writing* (1983)

Ted Hughes 1930– see also **192:10**
English poet

1 We had the old crow over at Hull recently, looking like a Christmas present from Easter Island.

Philip Larkin 1922–85: letter, 1975

2 Hughes's art is one of clear outline and inner richness. His diction is consonantal, and it snicks through the air like an efficient blade, marking and carving out fast definite shapes; but within those shapes, mysteries and rituals are hinted at. They are circles within which he conjures up presences.

Seamus Heaney 1939– : Beckman lecture, 1976; in *Finders Keepers* (2002)

3 He makes language as physical as a bruise.

John Carey 1934– : in *Sunday Times* 9 December 1979

4 Hughes's voice, I think, is in rebellion against a certain kind of demeaned, mannerly voice . . . the Larkin voice, the Movement voice, even the Eliot voice, the Auden voice—the manners of that speech, the original voices behind that poetic voice, are those of literate English middle-class culture, and I think Hughes's great cry and call and bawl is that English language and English poetry is longer and deeper than that.

Seamus Heaney 1939– : John Haffenden (ed.) *Viewpoints* (1981)

5 As our leading nature poet, he might find some sort of inspiration from the wild life of Balmoral.
   greeting the appointment of Ted Hughes as Poet Laureate

David Holloway 1924– : in *Daily Telegraph* 1984

Victor Hugo 1802–85
French poet, novelist, and dramatist

6 *Victor Hugo était un fou qui se croyait Victor Hugo.*
   Victor Hugo was a madman who thought he was Victor Hugo.

Jean Cocteau 1889–1963: *Opium* (1930)

7 *Hugo—hélas!*
   Hugo—alas!
   when asked who was the greatest 19th-century poet

André Gide 1869–1951: Claude Martin *La Maturité d'André Gide* (1977)

The Human Race

8 *Quidquid agunt homines, votum timor ira voluptas Gaudia discursus nostri farrago libelli est.*
   Everything mankind does, their hope, fear, rage, pleasure, joys, business, are the hotch-potch of my little book.

Juvenal AD c.60–c.130: *Satires*

9 Man is man's A.B.C. There is none that can
   Read God aright, unless he first spell Man.

Francis Quarles 1592–1644: *Hieroglyphics of the Life of Man* (1638)

10 Mankind are the creatures of books.

Leigh Hunt 1784–1859: *A Book for a Corner* (1852)

11 Man is a creature who lives not upon bread alone, but principally by catchwords.

Robert Louis Stevenson 1850–94: *Virginibus Puerisque* (1881)

1 I am content to sympathize with common mortals . . . their hearts—like ours—must endure the load of the gifts from heaven: the curse of facts and the blessing of illusions, the bitterness of our wisdom and the deceptive consolation of our folly.

Joseph Conrad 1857–1924: *Almayer's Folly* (1895) author's note

2 The human race, to which so many of my readers belong.

G. K. Chesterton 1874–1936: *The Napoleon of Notting Hill* (1904)

3 The commonplaces of the Wasteland outlook, the cheap mental stimulants of Alienation, the cant and rant of pipsqueaks about inauthenticity and forlornness. I can't accept this foolish dreariness. We are talking about the whole life of mankind. The subject is too great, too deep for such weakness, cowardice—too deep, too great.

Saul Bellow 1915– : *Herzog* (1964)

4 If a writer writes truthfully out of individual experience then what is written inevitably speaks for other people. For thousands of years storytellers have taken for granted that their experiences must be general. It never occurred to them that it is possible to divorce oneself from life.

Doris Lessing 1919– : in *Partisan Review* fall, 1992 (special issue) 'Unexamined Mental Attitudes Left Behind by Communism'

Humour and Comedy see also **Irony, Wit and Satire**

5 Comedy represents the worse types of men; worse, however, not in the sense that it embraces any and every kind of badness, but in the sense that the ridiculous is a species of ugliness or badness. For the ridiculous consists in some form of error or ugliness that is not painful or injurious; the comic mask, for example, is distorted and ugly, but causes no pain.

Aristotle 384–322 BC: *Poetics*

6 Comedy is an imitation of the common errors of our life.

Philip Sidney 1554–86: *The Defence of Poetry* (1595)

7 A jest's prosperity lies in the ear
Of him that hears it, never in the tongue
Of him that makes it.

William Shakespeare 1564–1616: *Love's Labour's Lost* (1595)

8 As vinegar is not accounted good until the wine be corrupted, so jests that are true and natural seldom raise laughter with the beast, the multitude.

Ben Jonson c.1573–1637: *Timber, or Discoveries made upon Men and Matter* (1641)

9 It's an odd job, making decent people laugh.

Molière 1622–73: *La Critique de l'école des femmes* (1663)

10 It is the business of a comic poet to paint the vices and follies of human kind.

William Congreve 1670–1729: *The Double Dealer* (1694)

11 Among all kinds of writing, there is none in which authors are more apt to miscarry than in works of humour, as there is none in which they are more ambitious to excel.

Joseph Addison 1672–1719: *The Spectator* 10 April 1711

12 Comedy naturally wears itself out—destroys the very food on which it lives; and by constantly and successfully exposing the follies and weaknesses of mankind to ridicule, in the end leaves itself nothing worth laughing at.

William Hazlitt 1778–1830: 'On Modern Comedy'; *The Round Table* (1817)

13 Man is the only animal that laughs and weeps; for he is the only animal that is struck with the difference between what things are, and what they ought to be.

William Hazlitt 1778–1830: *Lectures on the English Comic Writers* (1818)

1 To read a good comedy is to keep the best company in the world, where the best things are said, and the most amusing happen. The wittiest remarks are always ready on the tongue, and the luckiest occasions are always at hand to give birth to the happiest conceptions.

William Hazlitt 1778–1830: *Lectures on the English Comic Writers* (1818)

2 My way of joking is to tell the truth. It's the funniest joke in the world.

George Bernard Shaw 1856–1950: *John Bull's Other Island* (1907)

3 Humorists of the 'mere' sort cannot survive. Humour must not professedly teach and it must not professedly preach, but it must do both if it would live forever. By forever, I mean thirty years.

Mark Twain 1835–1910: *The Autobiography of Mark Twain* (1924)

4 There are several kinds of stories, but only one difficult kind—the humorous.

Mark Twain 1835–1910: attributed

5 I did not intend to write a funny book, at first. I did not know I was a humorist. I have never been sure about it. In the middle ages, I should probably have gone about preaching and got myself burnt or hanged.

Jerome K. Jerome 1859–1927: *My Life and Times* (1926)

6 They lead, as a matter of fact, an existence of jumpiness and apprehension. They sit on the edge of the chair of Literature. In the house of Life they have the feeling that they have never taken off their overcoats.
of writers of humorous sketches

James Thurber 1894–1961: *My Life and Hard Times* (1937) preface

7 The funniest thing about comedy is that you never know why people laugh. I know *what* makes them laugh but trying to get your hands on the *why* of it is like trying to pick an eel out of a tub of water.

W. C. Fields 1880–1946: R. J. Anobile *A Flask of Fields* (1972)

8 Good taste and humour . . . are a contradiction in terms, like a chaste whore.

Malcolm Muggeridge 1903–90: in *Time* 14 September 1953

9 Comedy is the noblest form of Stoicism.

W. H. Auden 1907–73: 'Crying Spoils the Appearance' (1957)

10 Humour is the difference between man's aspiration and his achievement.
during his editorship of Punch

Malcolm Muggeridge 1903–90: attributed

11 Humour is emotional chaos remembered in tranquillity.

James Thurber 1894–1961: in *New York Post* 29 February 1960; see **101:8**

12 Comedy is felt to be artificial and escapist; tragedy, toughly real. The opposite view seems more accurate. Tragedy is tender to man's dignity and self-importance, and preserves the illusion that he is a noble creature.

John Carey 1934– : *The Violent Effigy* (1973)

13 [Comedy is] the kindly contemplation of the incongruous.

P. G. Wodehouse 1881–1975: attributed

14 Humour consists of the collision of two different frames of reference.

Arthur Koestler 1905–83: in 1982; attributed

15 Comedy is tragedy that happens to *other* people.

Angela Carter 1940–92: *Wise Children* (1991)

16 I have sat, at the moment of purest heartbreak, in mental agony, and put my thoughts on paper, and then I have taken those thoughts and allocated them to one of my characters, largely for comic effect.

Hilary Mantel 1952– : Clare Boylan (ed.) *The Agony and the Ego* (1993)

1 The world dwindles daily for the humorist . . . Jokes are fast running out, for a joke must transform real life in some perverse way, and real life has begun to perform the same operation perfectly professionally upon itself.

Craig Brown 1957– : *Craig Brown's Greatest Hits* (1993)

2 Anyone like myself who thinks making jokes is a serious matter must regret the eclipse of the Book of Common Prayer because it has diminished the common stock of shared reference on which jokes—and of course it's not only jokes—depend.

Alan Bennett 1934– : *Writing Home* (1994)

3 I think it's essential for comic writers to have a hate figure, a despot, a regime to react against, and I think Thatcher was perfect for me. I loathed everything she stood for.

Sue Townsend 1946– : attributed; in *Observer* 24 March 2002

Aldous Huxley 1894–1963
English novelist

4 People will call Mr Aldous Huxley a pessimist; in the sense of one who makes the worst of it. To me he is that far more gloomy character; the man who makes the best of it.

G. K. Chesterton 1874–1936: *The Common Man* (1950)

5 He is at once the truly clever person and the stupid person's idea of the clever person; he is expected to be relentless, to administer intellectual shocks.

Elizabeth Bowen 1899–1973: in *Spectator* 11 December 1936

6 You could always tell by his conversation which volume of the *Encyclopedia Britannica* he'd been reading. One day it would be Alps, Andes and Apennines, and the next it would be the Himalayas and the Hippocratic Oath.

Bertrand Russell 1872–1970: letter to R. W. Clark, July 1965

Henrik Ibsen 1828–1906
Norwegian dramatist

7 Ibsen strikes me as an extraordinary curiosity, and every time he sounds his note the miracle, to my perception, is renewed. I call it a miracle because it is the result of so dry a view of life . . . There is a positive odour of spiritual paraffin.

Henry James 1843–1916: in *Harper's Weekly* 15 January 1897

8 I resented being invited to admire dialogue so close to modern educated speech that music and style were impossible . . . As time passed Ibsen became in my eyes the chosen author of very clever young journalists who, condemned to their treadmill of abstraction, hated music and style.

W. B. Yeats 1865–1939: *Autobiographies* (1955)

9 Ibsen supplies the want left by Shakespeare. He gives us not only ourselves, but ourselves in our own situations. The things that happen to his stage figures are things that happen to us. One consequence is that his plays are much more important to us than Shakespeare's. Another is that they are capable both of hurting us cruelly and of filling us

George Bernard Shaw 1856–1950: 'Brand, 1866'

with excited hopes of escape from idealistic tyrannies, and with visions of intenser life in the future.

Illustrations

1 'What is the use of a book', thought Alice, 'without pictures or conversations?'

Lewis Carroll 1832–98: *Alice's Adventures in Wonderland* (1865)

2 I am afraid I can think of no suggestions for plates for my 'English Vignettes'—and to tell the truth the somewhat impracticable purpose of these few lines is to express my grief at my would-be-delicate and to-be-read-on-its-own-account prose being served up in that manner. The thought is painful to me.

Henry James 1843–1916: letter, 29 July 1878

3 It would have been a capital volume, if there had been no letterpress.
of Thomas Dibdin's lavishly illustrated account of his travels, Bibliographical, Antiquarian, and Picturesque Tour (*1821*)

Anonymous: in *Dictionary of National Biography* (1917–)

4 Why did you make the Lady of Shalott, in the illustration, with her hair wildly tossed about as if by tornado? . . . I didn't say that her hair was blown about like that . . . Why did you make the web wind round and round her like the threads of a cocoon? . . . I did not say it floated round and round her.
to the painter William Holman Hunt

Alfred, Lord Tennyson 1809–92: W. H. Hunt *Pre-Raphaelitism and the Pre-Raphaelite Brotherhood* (1905)

5 The illustrations, which are far more numerous and less apposite than comports with the dignity of history, may be imputed to the publishers, for publishers seek to attract readers whom authors would wish to repel.

A. E. Housman 1859–1936: in *Cambridge Review* 1923

6 One picture is worth ten thousand words.

Frederick R. Barnard: in *Printers' Ink* 10 March 1927

7 To illustrate any text is also to interpret it.

Alison Lurie 1926– : *Don't Tell The Grown-Ups* (1990)

8 Beatrix Potter portrayed the world from a mouse's- or rabbit's- or small child's-eye view. The vantage point in her exquisite watercolors varies from a few inches to a few feet from the ground, like that of a toddler.

Alison Lurie 1926– : *Don't Tell The Grown-Ups* (1990)

9 Can you imagine illustration in modern novels? . . . For instance, in Norman Mailer? They would have to be abstracts. Don't you think? Sort of barbed wire and blotches?

Alice Munro 1931– : *Open Secrets* (1994)

10 Illustration is a very old form, far older than the novel, balanced somewhere in between painting and literature but belonging to neither.

Shirley Hughes 1927– : *A Life Drawing* (2002)

11 I cannot imagine how it must feel for an author to see someone else's interpretation of their own inner vision. I am constantly amazed at how appreciative most of them manage to be.

Shirley Hughes 1927– : *A Life Drawing* (2002)

Imagination

1 The lunatic, the lover, and the poet,
Are of imagination all compact:
One sees more devils than vast hell can hold,
That is, the madman; the lover, all as frantic,
Sees Helen's beauty in a brow of Egypt:
The poet's eye, in a fine frenzy rolling,
Doth glance from heaven to earth, from earth to heaven.

William Shakespeare 1564–1616: *A Midsummer Night's Dream* (1595–6)

2 And, as imagination bodies forth
The forms of things unknown, the poet's pen
Turns them to shapes, and gives to airy nothing
A local habitation and a name.

William Shakespeare 1564–1616: *A Midsummer Night's Dream* (1595–6)

3 Tell me where is fancy bred.
Or in the heart or in the head?

William Shakespeare 1564–1616: *The Merchant of Venice* (1596–8)

4 That fairy kind of writing which depends only upon the force of imagination.

John Dryden 1631–1700: *King Arthur* (1691)

5 Imagination . . . is the mother of sentiment, the great distinction of our nature, the only purifier of the passions.—Animals have a portion of reason, and equal, if not more exquisite, senses; but no trace of imagination, or of her offspring taste, appears in any of their actions.

Mary Wollstonecraft 1759–97: letter *c.*1795

6 Fantasy abandoned by reason produces impossible monsters; united with her, she is the mother of the arts and the origin of their marvels.

Francisco Goya 1746–1828: *Los Caprichos* (1799) plate 43

7 But oh! each visitation
Suspends what nature gave me at my birth,
My shaping spirit of imagination.

Samuel Taylor Coleridge 1772–1834: 'Dejection: an Ode' (1802)

8 Whither is fled the visionary gleam?
Where is it now, the glory and the dream?

William Wordsworth 1770–1850: 'Ode. Intimations of Immortality' (1807)

9   The mind can make
Substance, and people planets of its own
With beings brighter than have been, and give
A breath to forms which can outlive all flesh.

Lord Byron 1788–1824: 'The Dream' (1816)

10 Heard melodies are sweet, but those unheard
Are sweeter.

John Keats 1795–1821: 'Ode on a Grecian Urn' (1820)

11 Such writing is a sort of mental masturbation—he is always f—gg—g his *imagination.*—I don't mean that he is indecent but viciously soliciting his own ideas into a state which is neither poetry nor any thing else but a Bedlam vision produced by raw pork and opium.
   of **Keats**

Lord Byron 1788–1824: letter to John Murray, 9 November 1820

12 The great instrument of moral good is the imagination; and poetry administers to the effect by acting on the cause.

Percy Bysshe Shelley 1792–1822: *A Defence of Poetry* (written 1821)

13 The longing to invent stories grew with violence; everything I heard or read became food for my distemper. The simplicity of truth was not enough for me; I must needs embroider imagination upon it . . . Even now, tho' watched, prayed and striven against, this is still the sin that most easily besets me.

Emily Gosse 1806–57: diary, *c.*1835; Edmund Gosse *Father and Son* (1907)

1 Imagination, which in truth,
Is but another name for absolute power
And clearest insight, amplitude of mind,
And Reason, in her most exalted mood.

William Wordsworth 1770–1850: *The Prelude* (1850)

2 His imagination resembled the wings of an ostrich. It enabled him to run, though not to soar.

Lord Macaulay 1800–59: 'John Dryden' (1828)

3 He said he should prefer not to know the sources of the Nile, and that there should be some unknown regions preserved as hunting-grounds for the poetic imagination.

George Eliot 1819–80: *Middlemarch* (1871–2)

4 Where there is no imagination there is no horror.

Arthur Conan Doyle 1859–1930: *A Study in Scarlet* (1888)

5 For art to exist, for any sort of aesthetic activity or perception to exist, a certain physiological precondition is indispensable: intoxication.

Friedrich Nietzsche 1844–1900: *Twilight of the Idols* (1889)

6 Poets do not go mad; but chess-players do. Mathematicians go mad, and cashiers; but creative artists very seldom. I am not, as will be seen, in any sense attacking logic: I only say that this danger does lie in logic, not in imagination.

G. K. Chesterton 1874–1936: *Orthodoxy* (1908)

7 The balloon of experience is in fact of course tied to the earth, and under that necessity we swing, thanks to a rope of remarkable length, in the more or less commodious car of the imagination; but it is by the rope we know where we are, and from the moment that cable is cut we are at large and unrelated.

Henry James 1843–1916: *The American* (1909 ed.) preface

8 Only in men's imagination does every truth find an effective and undeniable existence. Imagination, not invention, is the supreme master of art, as of life.

Joseph Conrad 1857–1924: *Some Reminiscences* (1912)

9 We had fed the heart on fantasies,
The heart's grown brutal from the fare.

W. B. Yeats 1865–1939: 'Meditations in Time of Civil War' no. 6 'The Stare's Nest by my Window' (1928)

10 Yet I am the necessary angel of earth,
Since, in my sight, you see the world again.

Wallace Stevens 1879–1955: 'Angel Surrounded By Paysans' (1950)

11 I've a kind of arrangement with a part of myself which is given the menial task of absorbing things . . . I don't know what these things are until I see them in an imaginative light—which is a bright light, without shade—a kind of inward sun.

Janet Frame 1924– : in *Listener* 27 July 1970

12 Imagination is not enough. Knowledge is necessary.

Paul Scott 1920–78: Hilary Spurling *Paul Scott* (1990)

13 The imagination is a kind of electronic machine that takes account of all possible combinations and chooses the ones that are appropriate to a particular purpose, or are simply the most interesting, pleasing, or amusing.

Italo Calvino 1923–85: *Six Memos for the Next Millennium* (1992)

14 A writer's visible life and the root of imagination do not connect above ground.

Mavis Gallant 1922– : *Paris Notebooks: Essays and Reviews* (1986)

1 To find the psychic energy to pursue a long career, it seems to me, a writer must juggle between a vigorous, recording curiosity about the world and how it works and the ongoing process of self-creation. It is the imagination, of course, that negotiates between reality and the ego.

Edmund White 1940– : *The Burning Library* (1994)

2 A true writer's imagination is always bigger than he is, it outreaches his personality. Sometimes this can be felt palpably and thrillingly in the very act of writing, and perhaps it is for this infrequent but soaring sensation that writers, truly, write.

Graham Swift 1949– : Clare Boylan (ed.) *The Agony and the Ego* (1993)

3 The imagination conjures gifts; what the ungrateful, unsentimental part of the mind has to do is to unwrap them, find fault with them, see them for what they are and then alter them.

Rose Tremain 1943– : Clare Boylan (ed.) *The Agony and the Ego* (1993)

4 Some novelists say they envy those of us who live in South Florida because our source material is so wondrously weird. True enough, but the toll on our imaginations is draining. On many days fiction seems like a futile mission.

Carl Hiaasen 1953– : in *Writers on Writing: Collected Essays from The New York Times* (2001)

5 For me, writing means having one foot in one world, and the other in the real one.

Carol Shields 1935– : interview in *Observer*, 28 April 2002

Inspiration and Creativity see also **Motivation, Writer's Block**

6 What is beauty saith my sufferings, then?
If all the pens that ever poets held
Had fed the feeling of their masters' thoughts,
And every sweetness that inspired their hearts,
Their minds, and muses on admired themes:
If all the heavenly quintessence they still
From their immortal flowers of Poesy,
Wherein as in a mirror we perceive
The highest reaches of a human wit;
If these had made one poem's period,
And all combined in beauty's worthiness,
Yet should there hover in their restless heads
One thought, one grace, one wonder at the least,
Which into words no virtue can digest.

Christopher Marlowe 1564–93: *Tamburlaine the Great* (1590)

7 Assist me some extemporal god of rime, for I am sure I shall turn sonneter. Devise, wit; write, pen; for I am for whole volumes in folio.

William Shakespeare 1564–1616: *Love's Labour's Lost* (1595)

8 O! for a Muse of fire, that would ascend
The brightest heaven of invention.

William Shakespeare 1564–1616: *Henry V* (1599)

9 Our poesy is as a gum, which oozes
From whence 'tis nourished: the fire i' the flint
Shows not till it be struck; our gentle flame
Provokes itself.

William Shakespeare 1564–1616: *Timon of Athens* (c.1607)

10 It came from mine own heart, so to my head,
And thence into my fingers tricklèd;
Then to my pen, from whence immediately
On paper I did dribble it daintily.

John Bunyan 1628–88: *The Holy War* (1682) 'Advice to the Reader'

1 What judgement I had increases rather than diminishes; and thoughts, such as they are, come crowding in so fast upon me, that my only difficulty is to choose or reject; to run them into verse or to give them the other harmony of prose.

John Dryden 1631–1700: *Fables Ancient and Modern* (1700)

2 Just now I've taen the fit o' rhyme,
My barmie noddle's working prime.

Robert Burns 1759–96: 'To J. S[mith]' (1786)

3 It was at Rome, on the fifteenth of October, 1764, as I sat musing amidst the ruins of the Capitol, while the barefoot friars were singing vespers in the Temple of Jupiter, that the idea of writing the decline and fall of the city first started to my mind.

Edward Gibbon 1737–94: *Memoirs of My Life* (1796)

4 I have come to this resolution—never to write for the sake of writing, or making a poem, but from running over with any little knowledge or experience which many years of reflection may perhaps give me—otherwise I shall be dumb.

John Keats 1795–1821: letter to B. R. Haydon, 8 March 1819

5 'We will each write a ghost story,' said Lord Byron; and his proposition was acceded to. There were four of us . . . *Have you thought of a story?* I was asked each morning, and each morning I was forced to reply with a mortifying negative . . . On the morrow I announced that I had *thought of a story* . . . At first I thought but of a few pages—of a short tale; but Shelley urged me to develop the idea at greater length.
    on beginning Frankenstein

Mary Shelley 1797–1851: introduction to *Frankenstein* (ed. 3, 1831)

6 Write while the heat is in you . . . The writer who postpones the recording of his thoughts uses an iron which has cooled to burn a hole with. He cannot inflame the minds of his audience.

Henry David Thoreau 1817–62: letter, 10 February 1852

7 From eight o'clock in the morning till half-past four in the evening, Pierre sits there in his room . . . Sometimes the intent ear of Isabel in the next room, overhears the alternate silence, and then the long lonely scratch of his pen. It is as if she heard the busy claw of some midnight mole in the ground . . . In the heart of such silence, surely something is at work? Is it creation, or destruction? Builds Pierre the noble world of a new book? or does the Pale Haggardness unbuild the lungs and the life in him?

Herman Melville 1819–91: *Pierre* (1852)

8 Romance and poetry, ivy, lichens, and wall-flowers need ruins to make them grow.

Nathaniel Hawthorne 1804–64: *The Marble Faun* 1860

9 Stung by the splendour of a sudden thought.

Robert Browning 1812–89: 'A Death in the Desert' (1864)

10 I kept a scorpion in an empty beer bottle on my table. Now and then the animal was sick; then I used to throw it a piece of soft fruit, which it hurled itself on with fury and into which it poured out its poison; then it became healthy again.
    Is there not something similar in us poets? The laws of Nature hold for the intellectual field as well.

Henrik Ibsen 1828–1906: letter, 1870

11 I have many irons on the fire, and am bursting with writableness.

Henry James 1843–1916: letter 29 May 1878

1 To me it would not be more absurd if the shoemaker were to wait for inspiration, or the tallow-chandler for the divine moment of melting.

Anthony Trollope 1815–82: *Autobiography* (1883)

2 Giving birth to a book is always an abominable torture for me, because it cannot answer my imperious need for universality and totality.

Émile Zola 1840–1902: letter, 26 January 1892

3 In Ireland, for a few years more, we have a popular imagination that is fiery and magnificent and tender, so that those of us who wish to write start with a chance that is not given to writers in places where the springtime of the local life has been forgotten and the harvest is a memory only, and the straw has been turned into bricks.

John Millington Synge 1871–1909: introduction to *The Playboy of the Western World* (1907)

4 And least of all can you condemn an artist pursuing, however humbly and imperfectly, a creative aim. In that interior world where his thought and his emotions go seeking for the experience of imagined adventures, there are no policemen, no law, no pressure of circumstance or dread of opinion to keep him within bounds.

Joseph Conrad 1857–1924: *A Personal Record* (1912)

5 A lady beside me made in the course of talk one of those allusions that I have always found myself recognizing on the spot as 'germs' . . . the stray suggestion, the wandering word, the vague echo, at touch of which the novelist's imagination winces as at the prick of some sharp point.
of the effect of a chance remark by a dinner companion

Henry James 1843–1916: preface to *The Spoils of Poynton* (New York edition, 1907–17)

6 We are only telephone wires . . . *You* didn't write *She*, you know. Something wrote it through you!

Rudyard Kipling 1865–1936: Rider Haggard's diary, 22 May 1918

7 Real books should be the offspring not of daylight and casual talk but of darkness and silence.

Marcel Proust 1871–1922: *Time Regained* (1926)

8 The old literature of Ireland . . . has been the chief illumination of my imagination all my life.

W. B. Yeats 1865–1939: speech in the Irish Senate on Irish manuscripts, 1923

9 As an experience, madness is terrific . . . and in its lava I still find most of the things I write about.

Virginia Woolf 1882–1941: letter to Ethel Smyth, 22 June 1930

10 This is the doom of the Makers—their Daemon lives in their pen.
If he be absent or sleeping, they are even as other men . . . My Daemon was with me in the *Jungle Books*, *Kim*, and both Puck books, and good care I took to walk delicately lest he should withdraw. I know that he did not, because when these books were finished they said so themselves with, almost, the water-hammer click of a tap turned off.

Rudyard Kipling 1865–1936: *Something of Myself* (1937)

11 Like a piece of ice on a hot stove the poem must ride on its own melting. A poem may be worked over once it is in being, but may not be worried into being.

Robert Frost 1874–1963: 'The Figure a Poem Makes' (1939)

12 I have that continuous uncomfortable feeling of 'things' in the head, like icebergs or rocks or awkwardly placed pieces of furniture. It's as if all the nouns were there but the verbs were lacking . . . And I can't help having the theory that if they are joggled around hard enough and long enough some kind of electricity will occur just by friction.

Elizabeth Bishop 1911–79: letter to Marianne Moore, 11 September 1940

1 I never consciously invented with a pen in my hand; I waited until the story had told itself and then wrote it down, and, since it was already a finished thing, I wrote it fast.

John Buchan 1875–1940: *Memory-Hold-the-Door* (1940)

2 From this the poem springs: that we live in a place
That is not our own and, much more, not ourselves
And hard it is in spite of blazoned days.

Wallace Stevens 1879–1955: 'Notes Towards a Supreme Fiction' (1942)

3 I had a poem in my head last night, flashing as only those unformed midnight poems can. It was all made up of unexpected burning words. I knew even in my half-sleep that it was nonsense, meaningless, but that forcing and hammering would clear its shape and form. Now not a word of it remains, not even a hint of its direction. What a pity one cannot sleepwrite on the ceiling with one's finger or lifted toe.

Denton Welch 1915–48: diary, 1946

4 I believe I've got a *book* coming. I feel so excited . . . I walked up Piccadilly and back and went into a Gent's in Brick Street, and suddenly in the Gent's, I saw the three chunks, the beginning, the middle and the end.
   on the genesis of The Third Man

Graham Greene 1904–91: letter to Catherine Walston, 30 September 1947

5 Every creative writer worth our consideration, every writer who can be called in the wide eighteenth century use of the term a poet, is a victim: a man given over to an obsession.

Graham Greene 1904–91: 'Walter De La Mare's Short Stories' (1948)

6 I don't know anything about inspiration because I don't know what inspiration is—I've heard about it, but I never saw it.

William Faulkner 1897–1962: interview in *Paris Review* Spring 1956

7 The literary world is not conducted according to Marquis of Queensberry rules; if you find someone's private papers, you immediately rootle through them, looking for raw material. This is something non-literary people never understand. They are apt to confuse it with a vulgar, prying nature. Moral: when you have authors in the house you needn't lock up your spoons or your daughters, but get your diaries into the Safe Deposit.

Robertson Davies 1913–95: in 1959; *The Enthusiasms of Robertson Davies* (1990)

8 The impulse to write a novel comes from a momentary unified vision of life.

Angus Wilson 1913–91: *The Wild Garden* (1963)

9 Why does my Muse only speak when she is unhappy?
She does not, I only listen when I am unhappy
When I am happy I live and despise writing
For my Muse this cannot but be dispiriting.

Stevie Smith 1902–71: 'My Muse' (1964)

10 I think I feel on the whole that something's there trying to get out . . . It's sort of trying to get out and wants help.

Ivy Compton-Burnett 1884–1969: Kay Dick *Ivy and Stevie* (1971)

describing the creation of The Lord of the Rings:
11 One writes such a story not out of the leaves of trees still to be observed, nor by means of botany and soil-science; but it grows like a seed in the dark out of the leaf-mould of the mind: out of all that has been seen or thought or read, that has long ago been forgotten, descending into the deeps. No doubt there is much selection, as with a gardener: what one throws on one's personal compost-

J. R. R. Tolkien 1892–1973: Humphrey Carpenter *J. R. R. Tolkien* (1977)

heap; and my mould is evidently made largely of linguistic matter.

1 Poets or artists are sometimes married happily to their muse; and sometimes they have a very difficult life with her.
   in conversation with Isaiah Berlin

W. H. Auden 1907–73: interview with Isaiah Berlin, *Daily Telegraph* 3 August 1996

2 The artist brings something into the world that didn't exist before, and . . . he does it without destroying something else.

John Updike 1932– : George Plimpton (ed.) *Writers at Work* (4th series, 1977)

3 I imagined the poet in him as an unborn twin, one that could be cruel to him as well as kind.

Paul Scott 1920–78: 'Barbie Batchelor' on her father; *The Towers of Silence* (1971)

4 Deprivation is for me what daffodils were for Wordsworth.

Philip Larkin 1922–85: *Required Writing* (1983)

5 One knows poetry can't be written to order. One waits for something to come through from The Management upstairs and The Management can be very capricious.
   responding to the lukewarm reception given to his celebratory poem on the wedding of Princess Anne

John Betjeman 1906–84: attributed

6 'The Wreck of the Deutschland' would have been markedly inferior if Hopkins had been a survivor from the passenger list.

Philip Larkin 1922–85: attributed

asked why he wrote The Name of the Rose*:*
7 I felt like poisoning a monk.

Umberto Eco 1932– : George Plimpton (ed.) *The Writer's Chapbook* (1989)

8 Childhood . . . the purest well from which the creative artist draws.

Patrick White 1912–90: *Patrick White Speaks* (1990)

9 It's inevitably the case that whatever idea impels you to write a novel turns out to appear in the book as an afterthought.

Douglas Adams 1952–2001: Stan Nicholls (ed.) *Wordsmiths of Wonder* (1993)

10 If I feel the need for inspiration I read the OED.

Anthony Burgess 1917–93: Clare Boylan (ed.) *The Agony and the Ego* (1993)

11 I came across a letter of Thackeray's in which he talked of a novel 'a-boilin' up in my interior' . . . But now, fifteen years later, I know they don't always boil up: sometimes the purpose can come before the inspiration.

Margaret Forster 1938– : Clare Boylan (ed.) *The Agony and the Ego* (1993)

12 The movement is from delight to wisdom and not vice versa. The felicity of a cadence, the chain reaction of a rhyme, the pleasuring of an etymology, such things can proceed happily and as it were autistically, in an area of mental operations cordoned off by and from the critical sense.

Seamus Heaney 1939– : *The Redress of Poetry* (1995)

13 I say a prayer and God gives me a plot immediately. I write almost as if it was dictated by him.

Barbara Cartland 1901–2000: in *Sunday Times* 10 March 1996

14 I wrote *Cider with Rosie* in an attic in London; I couldn't have written it here [in Gloucestershire] . . . You can't write about love while you're still in bed. You can't write a love story in a bedroom. I had to be in London, I had to get the atmospheres blowing through the distance of time.

Laurie Lee 1914–97: in *Guardian* 22 June 1996

1 A good spendthrift interval lasting a couple of seasons if not more, or at least until you can no longer stand to read the headlines of the newspaper, much less the articles that follow, can help to freshen the self, to reconfigure the new, while decommissioning worn-out preoccupations, habits, old stylistic tics.

Richard Ford 1944– : in *Writers on Writing: Collected Essays from The New York Times* (2001)

2 Literary criticism, which is bound to pursue meaning, can never really encompass the fact that some things are on the page because they gave the writer pleasure. A writer whose morning is going well, whose sentences are forming well, is experiencing a calm and private joy. This joy itself then liberates a richness of thought that can prompt new surprises. Writers crave these moments, these sessions.

Ian McEwan 1948– : in *Paris Review* Summer 2002

Intelligence see Knowledge and Intelligence

Interruption

3 When a writer's at work, someone talking aloud he cannot abide.
So, Chatterbox, there's no place for you here. Go on outside!
intended as an inscription to go over a library door

St Isidore c.560–636: 'To an Intruder'; Lionel Casson *Libraries in the Ancient World* (2001)

4 On awaking he . . . instantly and eagerly wrote down the lines that are here preserved. At this moment he was unfortunately called out by a person on business from Porlock.

Samuel Taylor Coleridge 1772–1834: 'Kubla Khan' (1816) preliminary note; see also **140:6**, **336:12**

5 I have only written books, it's a fact, when I had someone to do some of the housework.

Christina Stead 1902–83: letter to her sister Kate, 4 August 1961

6 I long for the Person from Porlock
To bring my thoughts to an end,
I am growing impatient to see him
I think of him as a friend.

Stevie Smith 1902–71: 'Thoughts about the "Person from Porlock" ' (1962); see **140:4**

7 When I wanted to finish a book I used to get myself admitted to the Salvator Mundi hospital in Rome. I had a doctor friend who used to sign me in. I would take a private room, quite a cheap one, and disappear from sight where nobody could get at me.
on writing her novels in Italy

Muriel Spark 1918– : in *Sunday Times* 1994

8 Weekends are a good working time because people think you've gone away and don't disturb you. So is Christmas. Everyone's out shopping and no one phones. I always work on Christmas morning—it's a ritual.

Julian Barnes 1946– : in *Paris Review* Winter 2000–2001

Irony see also Humour, Wit and Satire

9 By his needle he understands ironia,
That with one eye looks two ways at once.

Thomas Middleton c.1580–1627: *The World Tossed at Tennis* (with William Rowley, 1620)

10 An irony is a nipping jest, or a speech that hath the honey of pleasantness in its mouth, and a sting of rebuke in its tail.

Edward Reyner 1600–68: *Rules for the Government of the Tongue* (1656)

1 A mode of speech of which the meaning is contrary to the words.
   definition of irony

Samuel Johnson 1709–84: *A Dictionary of the English Language* (1755)

2 Irony is that little grain of salt which alone renders the dish palatable.

Johann Wolfgang von Goethe 1749–1832: attributed

3 A drayman, in a passion, calls out, 'You are a pretty fellow,' without suspecting that he is uttering irony.

Lord Macaulay 1800–59: 'Lord Bacon' (1843)

4 Remember . . . that women, children, and revolutionists hate irony, which is the negation of all faith, of all devotion, of all action.

Joseph Conrad 1857–1924: Sophia Antonovna in *Under Western Eyes* (1911)

5 Finding the inappropriate word—the device upon which irony depends.

John Carey 1934– : *The Violent Effigy* (1973)

6 The novel is, by definition, the ironic art: its 'truth' is concealed, undeclared, undeclarable.

Milan Kundera 1929– : *The Art of the Novel* (1988)

7 Irony . . . may be defined as what people miss.

Julian Barnes 1946– : *A History of the World in 10½ Chapters* (1989)

Henry James 1843–1916 see also 111:15, 185:2
American novelist

8 He chaws more than he bites off.

Mrs Henry Adams 1843–85: letter to her father, 4 December 1881

9 It is leviathan retrieving pebbles. It is a magnificent but painful hippopotamus resolved at any cost, even at the cost of its dignity, upon picking up a pea which has got into a corner of its den.

H. G. Wells 1866–1946: *Boon* (1915)

10 The work of Henry James has always seemed divisible by a simple dynastic arrangement into three reigns: James I, James II, and the Old Pretender.

Philip Guedalla 1889–1944: *Supers and Supermen* (1920)

11 The historian of fine consciences.
   on Henry James

Joseph Conrad 1857–1924: *Notes on Life and Letters* (1921)

12 He would close a book by Henry James, sigh deeply and say: 'I don't know how the Old Man does it. There's nothing he does not know; there's nothing he can't do. That's what it is when you have been privileged to go about with Turgenev.'

Joseph Conrad 1857–1924: Ford Madox Ford *Return to Yesterday* (1932)

13 James was a strange unnatural human being, a sensitive man lost in an immensely abundant brain, which had had neither a scientific nor a philosophical training, but which was by education and natural aptitude alike, formal, formally aesthetic, conscientiously fastidious and delicate. Wrapped about in elaborations of gesture and speech, James regarded his fellow creatures with a face of distress and a remote effort at intercourse, like some victim of enchantment placed in the centre of an immense bladder.

H. G. Wells 1866–1946: *Experiment in Autobiography* (1934)

14 It was worth losing a train (and sometimes you had to do that) while he rummaged for the right word.

J. M. Barrie 1860–1937: *The Greenwood Hat* (1937)

1 A curious talent. One has to respect him. But how one would like to give him a push.

Ivy Compton-Burnett 1884–1969: Hilary Spurling *Secrets of a Woman's Heart: the Later Life of Ivy Compton-Burnett* (1984)

2 James's late style achieves a kind of slow-motion representation of consciousness, enabling us to follow and relish every nuance in a complex interweaving of thought and feeling that occupies only a few fleeting seconds in real time.

David Lodge 1935– : *Consciousness and the Novel* (2002)

Samuel Johnson 1709–84 see also **112:10**
English poet, critic, and lexicographer

3 That great Cham of literature, Samuel Johnson.

Tobias Smollett 1721–71: letter to John Wilkes, 16 March 1759

4 I have seen some extracts from Johnson's Preface to his 'Shakespeare' . . . No feeling nor pathos in him! Altogether upon the high horse, and blustering about Imperial Tragedy!

John Brown 1715–66: letter to David Garrick, 27 October 1765

5 Dr Johnson's sayings would not appear so extraordinary, were it not for his bow-wow way.

Henry Herbert, 10th Earl of Pembroke 1734–94: James Boswell *Life of Samuel Johnson* (1791) 27 March 1775

6 This man . . . who has the most extensive knowledge, the clearest understanding, and the greatest abilities of any living author,—has a face the most ugly, a person the most awkward, and manners the most singular, that ever were, or ever can be seen. But all that is unfortunate in his *exterior*, is so greatly compensated for in his *interior*, that I can only, like Desdemona to Othello, '*see his visage in his mind*'.

Fanny Burney 1752–1840: letter to her sister Susan, August 1778

7 Oh! I could thresh his old jacket till I made his pension jingle in his pockets.
   on Johnson's inadequate treatment of Paradise Lost

William Cowper 1731–1800: letter to the Revd William Unwin, 31 October 1779

8 Ay, now that the old lion is dead, every ass thinks he may kick at him.

Samuel Parr 1747–1825: James Boswell *Life of Samuel Johnson* (1791) 20 December 1784

9 This man is just a hogshead of sense.

Alexander McLean: James Boswell *Life of Samuel Johnson* (1791)

10 Johnson writes like a teacher. He dictates to his readers as if from an academical chair. They attend with awe and admiration; and his precepts are impressed upon them by his commanding eloquence.

James Boswell 1740–95: *Life of Samuel Johnson* (1791)

11 The most melancholy and debilitating moral speculation that ever was put forth.
   on Johnson's Rasselas

William Hazlitt 1778–1830: *Lectures on the English Comic Writers* (1818)

12 Figure him there, with his scrofulous diseases, with his great greedy heart, and unspeakable chaos of thoughts; stalking mournful as a stranger in this earth; eagerly devouring what spiritual thing he could come at: school-languages and other merely grammatical stuff, if there

Thomas Carlyle 1795–1881: *On Heroes and Hero-Worship* (1841)

were nothing better! The largest soul that was in all England.

1 The gigantic body, the huge massy face, seamed with the scars of disease, the brown coat, the black worsted stockings, the grey wig with the scorched foretop, the dirty hands, the nails bitten and pared to the quick.

Lord Macaulay 1800–59: *Essays Contributed to the Edinburgh Review* (1843) vol. 1 'Samuel Johnson'

2 I have not wasted my life trifling with literary fools in taverns as Johnson did when he should have been shaking England with the thunder of his spirit.

George Bernard Shaw 1856–1950: preface to *Misalliance* (1914)

Ben Jonson c.1573–1637 see also **42:6**, **83:10**, **91:9**
English dramatist and poet

3 He invades authors like a monarch; and what would be theft in other poets, is only victory in him.

John Dryden 1631–1700: *Essay of Dramatic Poesy* (1668)

4 His genius . . . resembles the grub more than the butterfly, plods and grovels on, wants wings to wanton in the idle summer's air, and catch the golden light of poetry.

William Hazlitt 1778–1830: *Lectures on the English Comic Writers* (1818)

5 I can't read Ben Jonson, especially his comedies. To me he appears to move in a wide sea of glue.

Alfred, Lord Tennyson 1809–92: Hallam Tennyson *Alfred Lord Tennyson* (1897)

6 The comedies of Ben Jonson are clearly no laughing matter if we compare them with Shakespeare.

Nevill Coghill 1899–1980: *Collected Papers of Nevill Coghill* (1988) 'The Basis of Shakespearian Comedy'

7 Pioneer of the bizarre, racy, and often grotesque urban poetry of modern life.

Craig Raine 1944– : *Haydn and the Valve Trumpet* (1990)

Journalism see also Newpapers

8 The journalists have constructed for themselves a little wooden chapel, which they also call the Temple of Fame, in which they put up and take down portraits all day long and make such a hammering you can't hear yourself speak.

Georg Christoph Lichtenberg 1742–99: A. Leitzmann *Georg Christoph Lichtenberg Aphorismen* (1904)

9 The man must have a rare recipe for melancholy, who can be dull in Fleet Street.

Charles Lamb 1775–1834: letter to Thomas Manning, 15 February 1802

10 Newspaper writing is a thing *sui generis*; it is to literature what brandy is to beverage.

Thomas Barnes 1785–1841: P. Howard *We Thundered Out* (1985)

11 All newspaper and journalistic activity is an intellectual brothel from which there is no retreat.

Leo Tolstoy 1828–1910: letter to Prince V. P. Meshchersky, 22 August 1871

12 To any young writer who solicited my advice I would say: 'As you learn to swim by flinging yourself into water, so learn to write by flinging yourself into journalism.' It is the only virile school we have; it is there that one measures oneself against other men, and there . . . that one forges one's style on the terrible anvil of daily deadlines.

Émile Zola 1840–1902: *Le Figaro* 1881

1 I hate journalists. There is nothing in them but tittering, jeering emptiness. They have all made what Dante calls the Great Refusal. That is, they have ceased to be self-centred, have given up their individuality.

W. B. Yeats 1865–1939: letter to Katharine Tynan, 1888

2 Over a fortnight has passed since I joined the *Daily Express*. Now I am a journalist—in *reality*; and we Fleet Street men (!) have little time for private dreaming in diaries! What we write we give to the world!

Sydney Moseley 1888–1961: diary, 1910

3 Journalism largely consists in saying 'Lord Jones Dead' to people who never knew that Lord Jones was alive.

G. K. Chesterton 1874–1936: *The Wisdom of Father Brown* (1914)

4 Journalists say a thing that they know isn't true, in the hope that if they keep on saying it long enough it *will* be true.

Arnold Bennett 1867–1931: *The Title* (1918)

5 Comment is free, but facts are sacred.

C. P. Scott 1846–1932: in *Manchester Guardian* 5 May 1921; see **145:4**

6 The art of newspaper paragraphing is to stroke a platitude until it purrs like an epigram.

Don Marquis 1878–1937: E. Anthony *O Rare Don Marquis* (1962)

7 You cannot hope
to bribe or twist,
thank God! the
British journalist.
But, seeing what
the man will do
unbribed, there's
no occasion to.

Humbert Wolfe 1886–1940: 'Over the Fire' (1930)

8 Journalism's a shrew and scold; I like her.
She makes you sick, she makes you old; I like her.
She's daily trouble, storm and strife;
She's love and hate and death and life;
She ain't no lady—she's my wife; I like her.

Franklin P. Adams 1881–1960: in *The New York World* 27 February 1931 (final issue)

9 It is questionable whether anyone who has had long experience as a freelance journalist ought to become an editor. It is too like taking a convict out of his cell and making him governor of a prison.

George Orwell 1903–50: in *Tribune* 31 January 1947

10 The first aim of the journalist is to interest; of the historian it is to instruct—of course the good journalist and the good historian try to do both.

A. J. P. Taylor 1906–90: BBC broadcast 13 January 1948

11 Usually he confined himself to written comments. His later famed 'What mean?' 'Who he?' and the like began to appear on manuscripts and proofs.
   of Harold Ross (1892–1951) as editor of the New Yorker

Dale Kramer 1936– : *Ross and The New Yorker* (1952)

12 Journalist is to politician as dog is to lamppost.

H. L. Mencken 1880–1956: attributed

13 It is really more like manufacturing synthetic whipped cream out of the by-products of a plastic factory than anything remotely connected with writing—even journalistic writing.
   of writing under contract to Life *magazine*

Elizabeth Bishop 1911–79: letter to Pearl Kazin, 13 August 1961

14 In journalism one has to be so brash and glib with generalities and labels.

Philip Larkin 1922–85: letter, 8 April 1963

1 Journalism is still an underdeveloped profession and, accordingly, newspapermen are quite often regarded as were surgeons and musicians a century ago, as having the rank, roughly speaking, of barbers and riding masters.

Walter Lippmann 1889–1974: attributed, 1965

2 As a general rule television is better than words in newspapers at communicating wars, and words are better than television at communicating peace.

Nicholas Tomalin 1931–1973: in *Listener* 29 April 1971

3 A journalist is somebody who possesses himself of a fantasy and lures the truth towards it.

Arnold Wesker 1932– : *Journey into Journalism* (1977)

4 Comment is free but facts are on expenses.

Tom Stoppard 1937– : *Night and Day* (1978); see **144:5**

5 The media. It sounds like a convention of spiritualists.

Tom Stoppard 1937– : *Night and Day* (1978)

6 Rock journalism is people who can't write interviewing people who can't talk for people who can't read.

Frank Zappa 1940–93: Linda Botts *Loose Talk* (1980)

7 Every journalist should be a dissident.

John Pilger 1939– : in *Guardian* 16 October 1989

8 Journalists belong in the gutter because that is where the ruling classes throw their guilty secrets.

Gerald Priestland 1927–91: in *Observer* 22 May 1988 'Sayings of the Week'

9 It was always fun—like being in a rather badly-run girls' school: people getting hysterical on the stairs and falling down and not knowing what they were doing. St Trinian's basically.
   on working as a literary editor at the Spectator

Peter Ackroyd 1949– : in *Sunday Times* 1989

10 I used to tell young reporters that if they wanted to learn to write magnificent NEWSPAPER English they should learn to write like Daniel Defoe. None of them did.

Robertson Davies 1913–95: in *Paris Review* 1989

11 Journalists are a different breed. Their roots are air roots.

Patrick White 1912–90: *Patrick White Speaks* (1990)

12 Journalism could be described as turning one's enemies into money.

Craig Brown 1957– : in *Daily Telegraph* 28 September 1990

13 What the man in the street wants to read is not what he has said already but what he would like to have said if he had thought of it first.

Keith Waterhouse 1929– : in *Intercity* 26 October 1990

14 Fleet Street can scent the possibilities of sex like a tile-tripping tomcat.

Julian Barnes 1946– : *Letters from London* (1995)

15 Many people . . . would no more think of entering journalism than the sewage business, which at least does us all some good.

Stephen Fry 1957– : in *Independent* 25 February 1995 'Quote Unquote'

16 Journalism encourages haste . . . and haste is the enemy of art.

Jeanette Winterson 1959– : *Art Objects* (1995)

James Joyce 1882–1941 see also **49:9**
Irish novelist

1 It is not my fault that the odour of ashpits and old weeds and offal hangs round my stories. I seriously believe that you will retard the course of civilization in Ireland by preventing the Irish people from having one good look at themselves in my nicely polished looking-glass.

James Joyce 1882–1941: letter, 23 June 1906

2 I am inclined to think that Mr Joyce is riding his method to death.

Ford Madox Ford 1873–1939: *Thus to Revisit* (1921)

3 The scratching of pimples on the body of the bootboy at Claridges.
of Ulysses

Virginia Woolf 1882–1941: letter to Lytton Strachey, 24 April 1922

4 A cruel playful mind like a great soft tiger cat.

W. B. Yeats 1865–1939: letter to Olivia Shakespear, 8 March 1922

5 A dogged attempt to cover the universe with mud, an inverted Victorianism, an attempt to make crossness and dirt succeed where sweetness and light failed.
of Ulysses

E. M. Forster 1879–1970: *Aspects of the Novel* (1927)

6 I do not know whether Joyce's *Ulysses* is a great work of literature. I have puzzled a great deal over that question . . . All I will say is that it is the work of an heroic mind.

W. B. Yeats 1865–1939: speech in the Irish Senate on copyright protection, 1927

7 My God, what a clumsy *olla putrida* James Joyce is! Nothing but old fags and cabbage-stumps of quotations from the Bible and the rest, stewed in the juice of deliberate, journalistic dirty-mindedness.

D. H. Lawrence 1885–1930: letter to Aldous and Maria Huxley, 15 August 1928

8 His writing is not about something. It is the thing itself.

Samuel Beckett 1906–89: *Our Exagmination Round His Factification for Incamination of Work in Progress* (1929)

9 Joyce is a poet and also an elephantine pedant.

George Orwell 1903–50: *Inside the Whale and Other Essays* (1940)

10 When a young man came up to him in Zurich and said, 'May I kiss the hand that wrote *Ulysses?*' Joyce replied, somewhat like King Lear, 'No, it did lots of other things too.'

James Joyce 1882–1941: Richard Ellmann *James Joyce* (1959)

Franz Kafka 1883–1924 see also **8:13, 194:7**
Czech novelist

11 Kafka was a tough, neurasthenic unetiolated visionary who lived from the inside out, spinning his writing out of his guts.

D. J. Enright 1920– : in *Observer* 5 August 1984

12 Kafka could never have written as he did had he lived in a house. His writing is that of someone whose whole life was spent in apartments, with lifts, stairwells, muffled voices behind closed doors, and sounds through walls. Put him in a nice detached villa and he'd never have written a word.

Alan Bennett 1934– : *Writing Home* (1994)

1 For our century, it is he who gave legitimacy to the implausible in the art of the novel.

Milan Kundera 1929– : *Testaments Betrayed* (1995)

John Keats 1795–1821 see also **92:2, 248:6**
English poet

2 It is a better and a wiser thing to be a starved apothecary than a starved poet; so back to the shop Mr John, back to 'plasters, pills, and ointment boxes.'
  reviewing Endymion

John Gibson Lockhart 1794–1854: in *Blackwood's Edinburgh Magazine* August 1818

*on Keats's enthusiasm for **Spenser**'s The Faerie Queene:*
3 He went through it as a young horse would through a spring meadow—ramping!

Charles Cowden-Clarke 1787–1877: *Recollections of Writers* (1878)

4 In Endymion, I leaped headlong into the sea, and thereby have become better acquainted with the soundings, the quicksands, and the rocks, than if I had stayed upon the green shore, and piped a silly pipe, and took tea and comfortable advice.

John Keats 1795–1821: letter to James Hessey, 8 October 1818

5 It is true that in the height of enthusiasm I have been cheated into some fine passages but that is nothing.

John Keats 1795–1821: letter to B. R. Haydon, 8 March 1819

6 Johnny Keats's piss-a-bed poetry.

Lord Byron 1788–1824: letter to John Murray, 12 October 1820

7 Keats is a miserable creature, hungering after sweets which he can't get; going about saying, 'I am so hungry; I should so like something pleasant!'

Thomas Carlyle 1795–1881: Wemyss Reid *Life of Richard Monckton Milnes* (1891)

8 I see a schoolboy when I think of him
With face and nose pressed to a sweet-shop window,
For certainly he sank into his grave
His senses and his heart unsatisfied,
And made—being poor, ailing and ignorant,
Shut out from all the luxury of the world,
The ill-bred son of a livery stable-keeper—
Luxuriant song.

W. B. Yeats 1865–1939: 'Ego Dominus Tuus' (1917)

9 For awhile after you quit Keats all other poetry seems to be only whistling or humming.

F. Scott Fitzgerald 1896–1940: letter to his daughter Scottie (Frances Scott Fitzgerald), 3 August 1940

Rudyard Kipling 1865–1936
English writer and poet

10 Will there never come a season
Which shall rid us from the curse
Of a prose which knows no reason
And an unmelodious verse . . .
When there stands a muzzled stripling,
Mute, beside a muzzled bore:
When the Rudyards cease from kipling
And the Haggards ride no more.

J. K. Stephen 1859–92: 'To R.K.' (1891)

1 In his earliest times I thought he perhaps contained the seeds of an English Balzac, but . . . he has come down steadily from the simple in subject to the more simple— from the Anglo-Indian to the natives, from the natives to the Tommies, from the Tommies to the quadrupeds, from the quadrupeds to the fish, and from the fish to the engines and screws.

Henry James 1843–1916: letter to Grace Norton, 25 December 1897

2 He is a most remarkable man—and I am the other one. Between us we cover all knowledge; he knows all that can be known and I know the rest.

Mark Twain 1835–1910: *Autobiography* (1924)

3 I have always thought it was a sound impulse by which he [Kipling] was driven to put his 'Recessional' into the waste-paper basket, and a great pity that Mrs Kipling fished it out and made him send it to *The Times*.

Max Beerbohm 1872–1956: letter, 30 October 1913

4 His virtuosity with language is not unlike that of one of his drill sergeants with an awkward squad . . . The vulgarest words learn to wash behind their ears and to execute complicated movements at the word of command, but they can hardly be said to learn to think for themselves.

W. H. Auden 1907–73: in *New Republic* 24 October 1943

5 Kipling is intensely loved and hated. Hardly any reader likes him a little.

C. S. Lewis 1898–1963: in 1950; Roger Lancelyn Green *Kipling: the Critical Heritage* (1971)

Knowledge and Intelligence

6 The scribbling bookworms who are found
in Egypt's populous nation,
in endless debate as they flock around
the muses' feeding station.
on the literati in the Alexandria of the Ptolomies

Athenaeus fl. *c.*200 AD: *Deipnosophistae*

7 Whence is thy learning? Hath thy toil
O'er books consumed the midnight oil?

John Gay 1685–1732: *Fables* (1727)

8 There is a North-west passage to the intellectual World.

Laurence Sterne 1713–68: *Tristram Shandy* (1759–67)

9 If the doors of perception were cleansed everything would appear to man as it is, infinite.

William Blake 1757–1827: *The Marriage of Heaven and Hell* (1790–3)

10 The petrifactions of a plodding brain.

Lord Byron 1788–1824: *English Bards and Scotch Reviewers* (1809)

11 Negative Capability, that is when man is capable of being in uncertainties, mysteries, doubts, without any irritable reaching after fact and reason.

John Keats 1795–1821: letter to George and Thomas Keats, 21 December 1817

12 You, for example, clever to a fault,
The rough and ready man who write apace,
Read somewhat seldomer, think perhaps even less.

Robert Browning 1812–89: 'Bishop Blougram's Apology' (1855)

13 So complete was my father's reliance on the influence of reason over the mind of mankind, whenever it is allowed to reach them, that he felt as if all would be gained if the whole population were taught to read, if all sorts of opinions were allowed to be addressed to them by word and in writing, and if, by means of the suffrage, they could

John Stuart Mill 1806–73: *Autobiography* (1873)

nominate a legislation to give effect to the opinions they adopted.

1 The intellect is not a serious thing, and never has been. It is an instrument on which one plays, that is all.

Oscar Wilde 1854–1900: *A Woman of No Importance* (1893)

2 The nihilists, the intellectual, hopeless people—Ibsen, Flaubert, Hardy—represent the dream we are waking from.

D. H. Lawrence 1885–1930: in *Rhythm* March 1913 'Georgian Poetry'

3 Nothing leads so straight to futility as literary ambitions without systematic knowledge.

H. G. Wells 1866–1946: letter to Alan H. Jones, 21 May 1920

4 *La trahison des clercs.*
The treachery of the intellectuals.

Julien Benda 1867–1956: title of book (1927)

5 What is a highbrow? He is a man who has found something more interesting than women.

Edgar Wallace 1875–1932: in *New York Times* 24 January 1932

6 The test of a first-rate intelligence is the ability to hold two opposed ideas in the mind at the same time, and still retain the ability to function.

F. Scott Fitzgerald 1896–1940: in *Esquire* February 1936, 'The Crack-Up'

7 To the man-in-the-street, who, I'm sorry to say,
Is a keen observer of life,
The word 'Intellectual' suggests straight away
A man who's untrue to his wife.

W. H. Auden 1907–73: *New Year Letter* (1941)

8 There can be no two opinions as to what a highbrow is. He is the man or woman of thoroughbred intelligence who rides his mind at a gallop across country in pursuit of an idea.

Virginia Woolf 1882–1941: *The Death of the Moth* (1942) 'Middlebrow'

9 An intellectual is someone whose mind watches itself.

Albert Camus 1913–60: *Carnets, 1935–42* (1962)

10 Man is an intelligence, not served by, but in servitude to his organs.

Aldous Huxley 1894–1963: *Theme and Variations* (1950)

11 Knowledge is a polite word for dead but not buried imagination.

e. e. cummings 1894–1962: *Jottings* in *Wake* (1951)

12 Intellectuals are people who believe that ideas are of more importance than values. That is to say, their own ideas and other people's values.

Gerald Brenan 1894–1987: *Thoughts in a Dry Season* (1978) 'Life'

13 But I'm such a bad scholar, I feel like a man with a white cane knocking into knowledge.

Peter Carey 1943– : in *Sunday Times* 20 March 1988

14 Great novels are always a little more intelligent than their authors.

Milan Kundera 1929– : *The Art of the Novel* (1988)

15 We shed as we pick up, like travellers who must carry everything in their arms, and what we let fall will be picked up by those behind. The procession is very long and the life is very short. We die on the march. But there is nothing outside the march so nothing can be lost to it. The missing plays of Sophocles will turn up piece by piece, or be written again in another language.

Tom Stoppard 1937– : *Arcadia* (1993)

16 When an old man dies, a library burns down.

Anonymous: African proverb

Charles Lamb 1775–1834
English writer

1 His sayings are generally like women's letters; all the pith is in the postscript.

William Hazlitt 1778–1830: *Conversations of James Northcote* (1826–7)

Language see also Grammar, Languages

2 The chief merit of language is clearness, and we know that nothing detracts so much from this as do unfamiliar terms.

Galen AD 129–99: *On the Natural Faculties*

3 It has been well said, that heart speaks to heart, whereas language only speaks to the ears.

St Francis of Sales 1567–1622: letter to the Archbishop of Bourges, 5 October 1604, which John Henry Newman paraphrased for his motto as '*cor ad cor loquitur* [heart speaks to heart]'

4 Lovely enchanting language, sugar-cane,
Honey of roses!

George Herbert 1593–1633: 'The Forerunners' (1633)

5 Good heavens! For more than forty years I have been speaking prose without knowing it.

Molière 1622–73: *Le Bourgeois Gentilhomme* (1671)

6 Words may be false and full of art,
Sighs are the natural language of the heart.

Thomas Shadwell c.1642–92: *Psyche* (1675)

7 The true use of speech is not so much to express our wants as to conceal them.

Oliver Goldsmith 1728–74: in *The Bee* 20 October 1759 'On the Use of Language'

8 Language is the dress of thought.

Samuel Johnson 1709–84: *Lives of the English Poets* (1779–81); see **150:12**

9 He gave man speech, and speech created thought,
Which is the measure of the universe.

Percy Bysshe Shelley 1792–1822: *Prometheus Unbound* (1820)

10 He writes in a language of his own that darkens knowledge. His works have been translated into French— they ought to be translated into English.
   on Jeremy Bentham

William Hazlitt 1778–1830: *The Spirit of the Age* (1825)

11 Every age has a language of its own; and the difference in the words is often far greater than in the thoughts. The main employment of authors, in their collective capacity, is to translate the thoughts of other ages into the language of their own.

Augustus Hare 1834–1903: *Guesses at Truth* (1827)

12 Language is called the garment of thought: however, it should rather be, language is the flesh-garment, the body, of thought.

Thomas Carlyle 1795–1881: *Sartor Resartus* (1834); see **150:8**

13 Language is fossil poetry.

Ralph Waldo Emerson 1803–82: *Essays. Second Series* (1844) 'The Poet'

14 Human speech is like a cracked kettle on which we tap crude rhythms for bears to dance to, while we long to make music that will melt the stars.

Gustave Flaubert 1821–80: *Madame Bovary* (1857)

1 Take care of the sense, and the sounds will take care of themselves.

Lewis Carroll 1832–98: *Alice's Adventures in Wonderland* (1865)

2 The bond between the signifier and the signified is arbitrary.

Ferdinand de Saussure 1857–1913: *Course in General Linguistics* (1916)

3 Language is a system of interdependent terms in which the value of each term results solely from the simultaneous presence of the others.

Ferdinand de Saussure 1857–1913: *Course in General Linguistics* (1916)

4 In language there are only differences.

Ferdinand de Saussure 1857–1913: *Course in General Linguistics* (1916)

5 Language can . . . be compared with a sheet of paper: thought is the front and sound the back; one cannot cut the front without cutting the back at the same time.

Ferdinand de Saussure 1857–1913: *Course in General Linguistics* (1916)

6 The limits of my language mean the limits of my world.

Ludwig Wittgenstein 1889–1951: *Tractatus Logico-Philosophicus* (1922)

7 What can be said at all can be said clearly; and whereof one cannot speak thereof one must be silent.

Ludwig Wittgenstein 1889–1951: *Tractatus Logico-Philosophicus* (1922)

8 There's a cool web of language winds us in, Retreat from too much joy or too much fear.

Robert Graves 1895–1985: 'The Cool Web' (1927)

9 Since our concern was speech, and speech impelled us To purify the dialect of the tribe And urge the mind to aftersight and foresight.

T. S. Eliot 1888–1965: *Four Quartets* 'Little Gidding' (1942)

10 Don't you see that the whole aim of Newspeak is to narrow the range of thought? In the end we shall make thoughtcrime literally impossible, because there will be no words in which to express it.

George Orwell 1903–50: *Nineteen Eighty-Four* (1949)

11 The great enemy of clear language is insincerity. When there is a gap between one's real and one's declared aims, one turns as it were instinctively to long words and exhausted idioms, like a cuttlefish squirting out ink.

George Orwell 1903–50: *Shooting an Elephant* (1950) 'Politics and the English Language'

12 The linguistic philosophy, which cares only about language, and not about the world, is like the boy who preferred the clock without the pendulum because, although it no longer told the time, it went more easily than before and at a more exhilarating pace.

Bertrand Russell 1872–1970: foreword to Ernest Gellner *Words and Things* (1959)

13 Slang is a language that rolls up its sleeves, spits on its hands and goes to work.

Carl Sandburg 1878–1967: in *New York Times* 13 February 1959

14 Different persons growing up in the same language are like different bushes trimmed and trained to take the shape of identical elephants. The anatomical details of twigs and branches will fulfill the elephantine shape differently from bush to bush, but the overall outward results are alike.

W. V. Quine 1908– : *Word and Object* (1960)

15 Language is a form of human reason, and has its reasons which are unknown to man.

Claude Lévi-Strauss 1908– : *La Pensée sauvage* (1962)

16 It is language which speaks, not the author.

Roland Barthes 1915–80: *The Death of the Author* (1968)

17 A language is a dialect with an army and a navy.

Max Weinreich 1894–1969: Steven Pinker *The Language Instinct* (1994)

18 The unconscious is structured like a language.

Jacques Lacan 1901–81: *Escrits* (1966)

1 Linguistic analysis. A lot of chaps pointing out that we don't always mean what we say, even when we manage to say what we meant.

Tom Stoppard 1937– : *Professional Foul* (1978)

2 As long as our language is inadequate, our vision remains formless.

Adrienne Rich 1929– : *On Lies, Secrets, and Silence* (1980)

3 The polymorphic visions of the eyes and the spirit are contained in uniform lines of small or capital letters, periods, commas, parentheses—pages of signs, packed as closely together as grains of sand, representing the many-coloured spectacle of the world on a surface that is always the same and always different, like dunes shifted by the desert wind.

Italo Calvino 1923–85: *Six Memos for the Next Millennium* (1992)

4 Literature . . . is the Promised Land in which language becomes what it really ought to be.

Italo Calvino 1923–85: *Six Memos for the Next Millennium* (1992)

5 We want to create a sort of linguistic Lourdes, where evil and misfortune are dispelled by a dip in the waters of euphemism.

Robert Hughes 1938– : *Culture of Complaint* (1993)

6 Language is obviously as different from other animals' communication systems as the elephant's trunk is different from other animals' nostrils.

Steven Pinker 1954– : *The Language Instinct* (1994)

Languages see also **Language**

7 Ye knowe ek that in forme of speche is chaunge
Withinne a thousand yeer, and wordes tho
That hadden pris, now wonder nyce and straunge
Us thinketh hem, and yet thei spake hem so.

Geoffrey Chaucer c.1343–1400: *Troilus and Criseyde*

8 So now they have made our English tongue a gallimaufry or hodgepodge of all other speeches.

Edmund Spenser c.1552–99: *The Shepherd's Calendar* (1579)

9 Away with him! away with him! he speaks Latin.

William Shakespeare 1564–1616: *Henry VI, Part 2* (1592)

10 Poets that lasting marble seek
Must carve in Latin or in Greek.

Edmund Waller 1606–87: 'Of English Verse' (1645)

11 To speak English, one must place the tongue between the teeth, and I have lost my teeth
to James **Boswell**, *24 December 1764*

Voltaire 1694–1778: Frederick A Pottle (ed.) *Boswell on the Grand Tour* (1953)

12 I am not like a lady at the court of Versailles, who said: 'What a dreadful pity that the bother at the tower of Babel should have got language all mixed up; but for that, everyone would always have spoken French.'

Voltaire 1694–1778: letter to Catherine the Great, 26 May 1767

13 I am always sorry when any language is lost, because languages are the pedigree of nations.

Samuel Johnson 1709–84: James Boswell *Journal of a Tour to the Hebrides* (1785) 18 September 1773

14 Philologists, who chase
A panting syllable through time and space,
Start it at home, and hunt it in the dark,
To Gaul, to Greece, and into Noah's ark.

William Cowper 1731–1800: 'Retirement' (1782)

15 What is not clear is not French.

Antoine de Rivarol 1753–1801: *Discours sur l'Universalité de la Langue Française* (1784)

1 I like that ancient Saxon phrase, which calls
The burial-ground God's-Acre!

Henry Wadsworth Longfellow
1807–82: 'God's-Acre' (1841)

2 I must learn Spanish, one of these days,
Only for that slow sweet name's sake.

Robert Browning 1812–89: 'The
Flower's Name' (1845)

3 None of your live languages for Miss Blimber. They must
be dead—stone dead—and then Miss Blimber dug them up
like a Ghoul.

Charles Dickens 1812–70: *Dombey
and Son* (1848)

4 The great breeding people had gone out and multiplied;
colonies in every clime attest our success; French is the
patois of Europe; English is the language of the world.

Walter Bagehot 1826–77: in
National Review January 1856
'Edward Gibbon'

5 Life is short and art is long, indeed nearly impossible when
one is writing in a language that is worn to the point of
being threadbare, so worm-eaten that it frays at every
touch.

Gustave Flaubert 1821–80: letter, 18
February 1859; see **6:8**

6 Speak in French when you can't think of the English for a
thing.

Lewis Carroll 1832–98: *Through the
Looking-Glass* (1872)

7 I once heard a Californian student in Heidelberg say, in
one of his calmest moods, that he would rather decline
two drinks than one German adjective.

Mark Twain 1835–1910: *A Tramp
Abroad* (1880)

8 Daudet spoke of his envy and admiration of the 'serenity of
production' of Turgenev—working in a field and a
language where the white snow had as yet so few footprints. In French, he said, it is all one trampled slosh.

Henry James 1843–1916: letter to
Thomas Bailey Aldrich, 13 February
1884

9 The knowledge of the ancient languages is mainly a
luxury.

John Bright 1811–89: letter in *Pall
Mall Gazette* 30 November 1886

10 Among the many reasons which make me glad to have
been born in England, one of the first is that I read
Shakespeare in my native tongue.

George Gissing 1857–1903: *The
Private Papers of Henry Ryecroft* (1903)

11 Nobody can say a word against Greek: it stamps a man at
once as an educated gentleman.

George Bernard Shaw 1856–1950:
Major Barbara (1907)

12 There is no language like the Irish for soothing and
quieting.

John Millington Synge 1871–1909:
The Aran Islands (1907)

13 Remember that you are a human being with a soul and
the divine gift of articulate speech: that your native
language is the language of Shakespeare and Milton and
The Bible; and don't sit there crooning like a bilious
pigeon.

George Bernard Shaw 1856–1950:
Pygmalion (1916)

14 Written English is now inert and inorganic: not stem and
leaf and flower, not even trim and well-joined masonry,
but a daub of untempered mortar.

A. E. Housman 1859–1936: in
Cambridge Review 1917

15 By being so long in the lowest form [at Harrow] I gained
an immense advantage over the cleverer boys. They all
went on to learn Latin and Greek . . . . But I was taught
English. . . . Thus I got into my bones the essential
structure of the ordinary British sentence—which is a
noble thing. . . . Naturally I am biased in favour of boys
learning English. I would make them all learn English: and
then I would let the clever ones learn Latin as an honour,
and Greek as a treat.

Winston Churchill 1874–1965: *My
Early Life* (1930)

1 Learning French is some trouble, but after that you have a clear and beautiful language; in English the undergrowth is part of the language and listed in NED.

NED = the New (*later the* Oxford) English Dictionary

William Empson 1906–84: in *Spectator* 14 June 1935

2 Heinrich Heine so loosened the corsets of the German language that even little salesmen can fondle her breasts.

Karl Kraus 1874–1936: *Half-truths and One-and-a-half Truths* 'Riddles'

3 It is a difficulty in writing English that the sound of the living voice dominates the look of the printed word.

W. Somerset Maugham 1874–1965: *The Summing Up* (1938)

4 I'm an intellectual snob who happens to have a fondness for the American vernacular because I grew up on Latin and Greek. I had to learn American just like a foreign language.

Raymond Chandler 1888–1959: letter to Alex Barris, 18 March 1949

5 For sheer dirtiness of fighting, the feud between the inventors of the international languages would take a lot of beating.

George Orwell 1903–50: Robert Pearce (ed.) *The Sayings of George Orwell* (1994)

6 England and America are two countries divided by a common language.

George Bernard Shaw 1856–1950: attributed in this and other forms, but not found in Shaw's published writings

7 Greek the language they gave me;
poor the house on Homer's shores.
My only care my language on Homer's shores.

Odysseus Elytēs 1911–96: 'The Axion Esti' (1959)

8 I don't know why you waste your time with Anglo-Saxon, instead of studying something useful like Latin or Greek!

to her son, Jorge Luis **Borges**, *c.1964*

Leonor Acevedo Borges 1876–1975: Alberto Manguel *A History of Reading* (1996); see **154:11, 171:11**

9 Waiting for the German verb is surely the ultimate thrill.

Flann O'Brien 1911–66: *The Hair of the Dogma* (1977)

10 At various times I have asked myself what reasons
Moved me to study while my night came down,
Without particular hope of satisfaction,
The language of the blunt-tongued Anglo-Saxons.

Jorge Luis Borges 1899–1986: 'Poem Written in a Copy of Beowulf' (1972), tr. Alastair Reid

11 All praise to the inexhaustible
Labyrinth of cause and effect
Which, before unveiling to me the mirror
Where I shall see no one or shall see some other self,
Has granted me this perfect contemplation
Of a language at its dawn.

Jorge Luis Borges 1899–1986: 'Embarking on the Study of Anglo-Saxon Grammar' (1972), tr. Alastair Reid; see **154:8**

12 The fluidity of Greek, punctuated by hardness, and with its surface glitter captivated me. But part of the attraction was antiquity and alien remoteness (from me): it did not touch home.

J. R. R. Tolkien 1892–1973: Humphrey Carpenter *J. R. R. Tolkien* (1977)

of his discovery of Finnish:
13 It was like discovering a wine-cellar filled with bottles of amazing wine of a kind and flavour never tasted before. It quite intoxicated me.

J. R. R. Tolkien 1892–1973: Humphrey Carpenter *J. R. R. Tolkien* (1977)

14 [English] is an absolutely fabulous language. It's so misused, so underused. For writing there's no comparison between English and French. When Beckett chose French deliberately, it was because he wanted a tighter, smaller framework. I can't imagine anyone wanting that.

Mavis Gallant 1922– : in *Canadian Fiction Magazine* November 1978

1 Stylists used to revere 'pure' English, but in reality English is about as pure as factory effluent, and has displayed its mongrel toughness over the centuries by cannibalizing a picturesque array of foreign tongues from Greek to Polynesian.

John Carey 1934– : in *Sunday Times* 27 January 1985

2 Italian is the only language in which the word *vago* (vague) also means 'lovely, attractive'.

Italo Calvino 1923–85: *Six Memos for the Next Millennium* (1992)

3 We are walking lexicons. In a single sentence of idle chatter we preserve Latin, Anglo-Saxon, Norse; we carry a museum inside our heads, each day we commemorate peoples of whom we have never heard.

Penelope Lively 1933– : *Moon Tiger* (1987)

4 To deny a boy or girl the opportunity to read and write Latin is cruelty to children.

Enoch Powell 1912–98: in *Independent* 2 June 1990

5 Because the Welsh language has survived the oppression of the English language there are older words than Anglo-Saxon ones which are still heard on Welsh rugby touchlines.
   view of the author of 'the first erotic novel to be written in Welsh'

Andrew Bennett : in *Daily Telegraph* 8 October 1994 'They Said It'

6 There is no such thing as an ugly language. Today I hear every language as if it were the only one, and when I hear of one that is dying, it overwhelms me as though it were the death of the earth.

Elias Canetti 1905–94: *The Secret Heart of the Clock* (1994)

7 English is the great vacuum cleaner of languages: it sucks in anything it can get.

David Crystal 1941– : in *Daily Telegraph* 30 December 1995 'They Said It In 1995'

8 English is an all-devouring language that has moved across North America like the fabulous plagues of locusts that darkened the sky and devoured even the handles of rakes and hoes. Yet the omnivorous nature of a colonial language is a writer's gift. Raised in the English language, I partake of a mongrel feast.
   view of a Native American

Louise Erdrich: in *Writers on Writing: Collected Essays from The New York Times* (2001)

9 In my view, the greatest achievement of these islands was not arrived at by an individual, and not imagined by a single genius, but created, honed and sustained by millions over centuries: the English language.

Melvyn Bragg 1939– : in *Observer* 24 November 2002

Philip Larkin 1922–85
English poet

10 I very much feel the need to be on the periphery of things.

Philip Larkin 1922–85: in *Observer* 16 December 1979

11 His attitude to most accredited sources of pleasure would make Scrooge seem unduly frolicsome.

John Carey 1934– : in *Sunday Times* 1983

12 If poems can teach one anything, Larkin's teach that there is no desolation so bleak that it cannot be made habitable by style.

Jonathan Raban 1942– : *Coasting* (1986)

13 Larkin's readability seems so effortless that it tends to be thought of as something separate from his intelligence. But readability *is* intelligence.

Clive James 1939– : *Reliable Essays* (2001)

1 He is the poet of rational light, a light that has its own luminous beauty but which has also the effect of exposing clearly the truths which it touches.

Seamus Heaney 1939– : *Finder's Keepers: Selected prose 1971–2001* (2002)

Last Words see also Death

2 See in what peace a Christian can die.
dying words to his stepson Lord Warwick

Joseph Addison 1672–1719: Edward Young *Conjectures on Original Composition* (1759)

3 What Cato did, and Addison approved,
Cannot be wrong.
lines found on his desk after he, too, had taken his own life

Eustace Budgell 1686–1737: Colley Cibber *Lives of the Poets* (1753) vol. 5 'Life of Eustace Budgell'

4 This is no time for making new enemies.
on being asked to renounce the Devil on his deathbed

Voltaire 1694–1778: attributed

5 I can scarcely bid you goodbye even in a letter. I always made an awkward bow.
his last letter

John Keats 1795–1821: letter to Charles Brown, 30 November 1820

6 Well, I've had a happy life.

William Hazlitt 1778–1830: W. C. Hazlitt *Memoirs of William Hazlitt* (1867)

7 More light!

Johann Wolfgang von Goethe 1749–1832: attributed; actually 'Open the second shutter, so that more light can come in'

8 God will pardon me, it is His trade.

Heinrich Heine 1797–1856: Alfred Meissner *Heinrich Heine. Erinnerungen* (1856)

9 It's been so long since I've had champagne.
after which, he slowly drank the glass and died

Anton Chekhov 1860–1904: Henri Troyat *Chekhov* (1984)

10 On the contrary.
after a nurse had said that he 'seemed to be a little better'

Henrik Ibsen 1828–1906: Michael Meyer *Ibsen* (1967)

11 In this life there's nothing new in dying,
But nor, of course, is living any newer.
Yesenin's final poem, written in his own blood the day before he hanged himself in his Leningrad hotel room, 28 December 1925

Sergei Yesenin 1895–1925: 'Goodbye, my Friend, Goodbye', translated by Gordon McVay

12 If this is dying, then I don't think much of it.

Lytton Strachey 1880–1932: Michael Holroyd *Lytton Strachey* vol. 2 (1968)

13 Just before she [Stein] died she asked, 'What *is* the answer?' No answer came. She laughed and said, 'In that case what is the question?' Then she died.

Gertrude Stein 1874–1946: Donald Sutherland *Gertrude Stein, A Biography of her Work* (1951)

14 *Last words* . . . I do not see why one should try to pronounce them louder than the others. At least I do not feel the need of doing so.

André Gide 1869–1951: journal, 15 December 1948

15 The woman is perfected
Her dead
Body wears the smile of accomplishment.
opening lines of her last poem, written a week before her suicide

Sylvia Plath 1932–63: 'Edge'

1 Lord take my soul, but the struggle continues.
last words before he was hanged

Ken Saro-Wiwa 1941–95: in *Daily Telegraph* 13 November 1995

D. H. Lawrence 1885–1930 see also 93:14, 94:1, 249:8
English novelist and poet

2 I like to write when I feel spiteful; it's like having a good sneeze.

D. H. Lawrence 1885–1930: letter to Lady Cynthia Asquith, *c*.25 November 1913

3 Interesting, but a type I could not get on with. Obsessed with self. Dead eyes and a red beard, long narrow pale face. A strange bird.

John Galsworthy 1867–1933: diary 13 November 1917

4 He's like an express train running through a tunnel—one shriek, sparks, smoke and gone.

Virginia Woolf 1882–1941: letter, 25 June 1935

5 He was a bum poet, of course, being a bum person.

Robert Graves 1895–1985: letter to Liddell Hart, 21 December 1935

6 He had a glowing gift for nature, a real feeling for nature, and in this he was at his best. But through his landscapes cantered hallucinations.

Max Beerbohm 1872–1956: in June 1955; S. N. Behrman *Conversations with Max* (1960)

7 His descriptive powers were remarkable, but his ideas cannot too soon be forgotten.

Bertrand Russell 1872–1970: *Autobiography* (1967)

8 Gradually I discovered that he had no wish to make the world better but only to indulge in eloquent soliloquy about how bad it was.

Bertrand Russell 1872–1970: Noel Annan *Our Age* (1990)

9 One of the great denouncers, the great missionaries the English send to themselves to tell them that they are crass, gross, lost, dead, mad and addicted to unnatural vice.

Kingsley Amis 1922–95: *What Became of Jane Austen?* (1970)

10 Lawrence's passion for travel was only equalled by his dislike of the places he arrived at. He would have been a tour operator's nightmare.

John Carey 1934– : in *Sunday Times* 1987

Edward Lear 1812–88
English artist and writer of humorous verse

11 'How pleasant to know Mr Lear!'
Who has written such volumes of stuff!
Some think him ill-tempered and queer,
But a few think him pleasant enough.

Edward Lear 1812–88: *Nonsense Songs* (1871) preface

12 Children swarmed to him like settlers. He became a land.

W. H. Auden 1907–73: 'Edward Lear' (1939)

F. R. Leavis 1895–1978
English literary critic

13 He is liable to try to polish off an argument with a phrase rather as, in different circles it might be done by throwing a saucepan.

Alan Pryce-Jones 1908– : in *Times Literary Supplement* 29 February 1952

1 He cultivated to perfection the sneer which he used like an oyster-knife, inserting it into the shell of his victim, exposing him with a quick turn of the wrist, and finally flipping him over and inviting his audience to discard him as tainted and inedible.

Noel Annan 1916–2000: *Our Age* (1990)

Laurie Lee 1914–97
English writer

2 A Samuel Palmer, a maker of ravishing verbal woodcuts.
   on Laurie Lee

Cyril Connolly 1903–74: in *Sunday Times* 8 May 1955

Mikhail Lermontov 1814–41
Russian novelist and poet

3 No, I'm not Byron, it's my role
  To be an undiscovered wonder,
  Like him, a persecuted wand'rer,
  But furnished with a Russian soul.

Mikhail Lermontov 1814–41: 'No, I'm not Byron' (1832)

Letters

4 Ye see how large a letter I have written unto you with mine own hand.

Bible: Galatians

5 There is nothing to write about, you say. Well then, write and let me know just this—that there is nothing to write about; or tell me in the good old style if you are well.

Pliny the Younger AD c.61–c.112: *Letters*

6 . . . *Verbosa et grandis epistula venit*
  A Capreis.
  A huge wordy letter came from Capri.
  on the Emperor Tiberius's letter to the Senate, which caused the downfall of Sejanus in AD 31

Juvenal AD c.60–c.130: *Satires*

7 Sir, more than kisses, letters mingle souls.

John Donne 1572–1631: 'To Sir Henry Wotton' (1597–8)

8 I knew one that when he wrote a letter he would put that which was most material in the postscript, as if it had been a bymatter.

Francis Bacon 1561–1626: *Essays* (1625) 'Of Cunning'

9 All letters, methinks, should be free and easy as one's discourse, not studied as an oration, nor made up of hard words like a charm.

Dorothy Osborne 1627–95: letter to William Temple, September 1653

10 A woman seldom writes her mind but in her postscript.

Richard Steele 1672–1729: in *The Spectator* 31 May 1711

11 An odd thought strikes me:—we shall receive no letters in the grave.

Samuel Johnson 1709–84: James Boswell *Life of Samuel Johnson* (1791) December 1784

12 I have now attained the true art of letter-writing, which we are always told is to express on paper exactly what one would say to the same person by word of mouth.

Jane Austen 1775–1817: letter to her sister Cassandra, 3 January 1801

1 My dear Isa, I now sit down on my botom to answer all your kind and beloved letters which you was so good as to write to me.

Marjory Fleming 1803–11: letter to Isabella; *Journals, Letters and Verses* (ed. A. Esdaile, 1934)

2 She'll vish there wos more, and that's the great art o' letter writin'.

Charles Dickens 1812–70: *Pickwick Papers* (1837)

3 Correspondences are like small-clothes before the invention of suspenders; it is impossible to keep them up.

Sydney Smith 1771–1845: letter to Catherine Crowe, 31 January 1841

4 I would any day as soon kill a pig as write a letter.
   on his dislike of personal correspondence

Alfred, Lord Tennyson 1809–92: remark made in the 1850s; Ann Thwaite *Emily Tennyson* (1996)

5 The slowest and most intermittent talker must *seem* fluent in letter-writing. He may have taken half-an-hour to compose his second sentence; but there it is, close after the first!

Lewis Carroll 1832–98: *Sylvie and Bruno Concluded* (1893)

6 Letter writing is a terrible venture of a man's soul . . . You may have changed your mind, or seen reason to feel quite coldly towards your correspondent, long before your production finds its way into his hands.

Robert Louis Stevenson 1850–94: Roger C. Swearingen (ed.) *An Old Song and Edifying Letters of the Rutherford Family* (1982)

7 You don't know a woman until you have had a letter from her.

Ada Leverson 1865–1936: *Tenterhooks* (1912)

8 It is wonderful how much news there is when people write every other day; if they wait for a month, there is nothing that seems worth telling.

O. Douglas 1877–1948: *Penny Plain* (1920)

9 Ah, but when the post knocks and the letter comes always the miracle seems repeated—speech attempted.

Virginia Woolf 1882–1941: *Jacob's Room* (1922)

10 Letters of thanks, letters from banks,
   Letters of joy from girl and boy,
   Receipted bills and invitations
   To inspect new stock or to visit relations,
   And applications for situations,
   And timid lovers' declarations,
   And gossip, gossip from all the nations.

W. H. Auden 1907–73: 'Night Mail' (1936)

11 Try and look on correspondence as a conversation not a diary.

Evelyn Waugh 1903–66: letter to his second wife, 9 January 1945

12 It does me good to write a letter which is not a response to a demand, a gratuitous letter, so to speak, which has accumulated in me like the waters of a reservoir.

Henry Miller 1891–1980: *The Books in My Life* (1951)

13 I am sorry for people who can't write letters. But I suspect also that you and I . . . love to write them because it's kind of like working without really doing it.

Elizabeth Bishop 1911–79: letter to Kit and Ilse Barker, 5 September 1953

14 A man seldom puts his authentic self into a letter. He writes it to amuse a friend or to get rid of a social or business obligation, which is to say, a nuisance.

H. L. Mencken 1880–1956: *Minority Report* (1956)

15 Beware of writing to me. I always answer . . . My father spent the last 20 years of his life writing letters. If someone thanked him for a present, he thanked them for thanking him and there was no end to the exchange but death.

Evelyn Waugh 1903–66: letter to Lady Mosley, 30 March 1966

16 Don't think that this is a letter. It is only a small eruption of a disease called friendship.

Jean Renoir 1894–1979: letter to Janine Bazin, 12 June 1974

1 A man who publishes his letters becomes a nudist—
nothing shields him from the world's gaze except his bare
skin.

E. B. White 1899–1985: letter to
Corona Machemer, 11 June 1975

2 This is the advantage of letters over biography: letters exist
in real time. We read them at about the speed at which
they were written. Biography gives us the crane-shot, the
time-elision, the astute selectivity.

Julian Barnes 1946– : *Something to
Declare* (2002)

C. S. Lewis 1898–1963
British literary scholar

3 As a man, he combines the manner of Friar Tuck with the
mind of St Augustine.

Kenneth Tynan 1927–80: *Persona
Grata* (1953)

4 When it came to the Narnia books, I think he was actually
dangerous because those books celebrate death.

Philip Pullman 1946– : in *Sunday
Telegraph* 27 January 2002

Libraries and Librarians see also Borrowing Books

5 Clinic for the Soul.

Anonymous: inscription on the
library of Ramses II (*c.*1292–1225 BC);
Diodorus Siculus *Bibliotheca Historica*
60–30 BC

6 Clay tablet of Ashurbanipal, King of the World, King of
Assyria, who trusts in Ashur and Ninlil . . . Whoever
removes [it], writes his name in place of my name, may
Ashur and Ninlil, angered and grim, cast him down, erase
his name, his seed, in the land.

Anonymous: colophon on clay
tablet found at Nineveh in ruins of
palace of Ashurbanipal, King of
Assyria from 668 to 627 BC; Lionel
Casson *Libraries in the Ancient World*
(2001)

7 Let your bookcases and your shelves be your gardens and
your pleasure-grounds. Pluck the fruit that grows therein,
gather the roses, the spices and the myrrh.

Judah Ibn Tibbon 1120–90: Israel
Abrahams *Jewish Life in the Middle
Ages* (1932)

8 Come, and take choice of all my library,
And so beguile thy sorrow.

William Shakespeare 1564–1616:
Titus Andronicus (1590)

9   My library
Was dukedom large enough.

William Shakespeare 1564–1616:
The Tempest (1611)

10 Affect not as some do that bookish ambition to be stored
with books and have well-furnished libraries, yet keep
their heads empty of knowledge; to desire to have many
books, and never to use them, is like a child that will have
a candle burning by him all the while he is sleeping.

Henry Peacham *c.*1576–*c.*1643: *The
Compleat Gentleman* (1622)

11 No place affords a more striking conviction of the vanity of
human hopes, than a public library.

Samuel Johnson 1709–84: in *The
Rambler* 23 March 1751

12 Madam, a circulating library in a town is as an evergreen
tree of diabolical knowledge; it blossoms throughout the
year. And depend on it . . . that they who are so fond of
handling the leaves, will long for the fruit at last.

Richard Brinsley Sheridan
1751–1816: *The Rivals* (1775)

13 It is almost everywhere the case that soon after it is
begotten the greater part of human wisdom is laid to rest
in *repositories*.

Georg Christoph Lichtenberg
1742–99: A. Leitzmann (ed.) *Georg
Christoph Lichtenberg Aphorismen*
(1904)

1 Lo! all in silence, all in order stand,
And mighty folios first, a lordly band;
Then quartos their well-ordered ranks maintain,
And light octavos fill a spacious plain;
See yonder, ranged in more frequented rows,
A humbler band of duodecimos.

George Crabbe 1754–1832: 'The Library' (1808)

2 In his library he had been always sure of leisure and tranquillity; and though prepared . . . to meet with folly and conceit in every other room in the house, he was used to be free of them there.

Jane Austen 1775–1817: *Pride and Prejudice* (1813)

3 What a sad want I am in of libraries, of books to gather facts from! Why is there not a Majesty's library in every county town? There is a Majesty's jail and gallows in every one.

Thomas Carlyle 1795–1881: letter, 18 May 1832

4 We do not subscribe to a circulating library at Haworth, and consequently 'new novels' rarely indeed come in our way.

Charlotte Brontë 1816–55: letter to Ellen Nussey, 26 June 1848

5 We call ourselves a rich nation, and we are filthy and foolish enough to thumb each other's books out of circulating libraries!

John Ruskin 1819–1900: *Sesame and Lilies* (1865)

6 Here Greek and Roman find themselves
Alive along these crowded shelves;
And Shakespeare treads again his stage,
And Chaucer paints anew his age.

John Greenleaf Whittier 1807–92: 'The Library'

7 A great library contains the diary of the human race.

George Dawson 1821–76: speech on opening of Birmingham Free Library, 26 October 1866

8 Every library should try to be complete on something, if it were only the history of pinheads.

Oliver Wendell Holmes 1809–94: *The Poet at the Breakfast-Table* (1872)

9 Mr Quarmby laughed in a peculiar way, which was the result of long years of mirth-subdual in the Reading-room.

George Gissing 1857–1903: *New Grub Street* (1891)

10 The fog grew thicker; she looked up at the windows beneath the dome and saw that they were a dusky yellow. Then her eye discerned an official walking along the upper gallery, and in pursuance of her grotesque humour, her mocking misery, she likened him to a black, lost soul, doomed to wander in an eternity of vain research along endless shelves. Or again, the readers who sat here at these radiating lines of desks, what were they but hapless flies caught in a huge web, its nucleus the great circle of the Catalogue?
'Marian Yule' in the Reading Room of the British Museum

George Gissing 1857–1903: *New Grub Street* (1891)

11 A man should keep his little brain attic stocked with all the furniture that he is likely to use, and the rest he can put away in the lumber room of his library, where he can get it if he wants it.

Arthur Conan Doyle 1859–1930: *The Adventures of Sherlock Holmes* (1892)

12 We should burn all libraries and allow to remain only that which everyone knows by heart. A beautiful age of the legend would then begin.

Hugo Ball 1886–1927: *Flight out of Time: A Dada Diary* 9 January 1917

1 The London Library, for a private library, is surprisingly good; its terms are generous and its manners gracious.

T. S. Eliot 1888–1965: letter October 1919

2 Tuppenny dram-shops.
   the small suburban circulating libraries of the twenties and thirties

Q. D. Leavis 1906–81: *Fiction and the Reading Public* (1932)

3 A family library is a breeding-place of character.

Graham Greene 1904–91: 'Background for Heroes' (1937)

4 Even in houses commonly held to be 'booky' one finds, nine times out of ten, not a library but a book-dump.

Edith Wharton 1862–1937: attributed

5 I ransack public libraries, and find them full of sunk treasure.

Virginia Woolf 1882–1941: Hermione Lee *Virginia Woolf* (1996)

6 Some on commission, some for the love of learning,
   Some because they have nothing better to do
   Or because they hope these walls of books will deaden
   The drumming of the demon in their ears.

Louis MacNeice 1907–63: 'The British Museum Reading Room' (1941)

7 There can be few more unrewarding tasks for the educated man of curiosity than the routine duties of librarianship; while for the higher rungs of bibliography I soon realized that an avid taste for the contents of books was a hindrance.

Angus Wilson 1913–91: *The Wild Garden* (1963)

8 I'm a librarian, I never see a book from one year's end to another.

Philip Larkin 1922–85: in *Tracks* Summer 1967

9 What is more important in a library than anything else— than everything else—is the fact that it exists.

Archibald MacLeish 1892–1982: 'The Premise of Meaning' in *American Scholar* 5 June 1972

10 It's a librarian's duty to distinguish between poetry and a sort of belle-litter.

Tom Stoppard 1937– : *Travesties* (1975)

11 Being a librarian doesn't help. I've always found them close relatives of the walking dead.

Alan Bennett 1934– : Anthony Thwaite *Larkin at Sixty* (1982)

12 On the whole, as I am fond of saying, libraries are feminine: they respond, they do not initiate.

Philip Larkin 1922–85: *Required Writing* (1983)

13 Libraries are reservoirs of strength, grace and wit, reminders of order, calm, continuity, lakes of mental energy, neither warm nor cold, light nor dark. The pleasure they give is steady, unorgiastic, reliable, deep and long-lasting.

Germaine Greer 1939– : *Daddy, We Hardly Knew You* (1989)

14 He looked into the water and saw that it was made up of a thousand thousand thousand and one different currents, each one a different colour, weaving in and out of each other like a liquid tapestry of breathtaking complexity; and Iff explained that these were the Streams of Story, that each colour strand represented and contained a single tale. Different parts of the Ocean contained different sorts of stories, and as all the stories that had ever been told and many that were still in the process of being invented could be found here, the Ocean of the Streams of Story was in fact the biggest library in the world. And because the stories were held here in liquid form, they retained the ability to change, to become new versions of themselves, to join up with other stories and so become yet other

Salman Rushdie 1947– : *Haroun and the Sea of Stories* (1990)

stories; so that unlike a library of books, the Ocean of the Stream of Stories was much more than a storeroom of yarns. It was not dead but alive.

1 The Librarian was, of course, very much in favour of reading in general, but readers in particular got on his nerves . . . He liked people who loved and respected books, and the best way to do that, in the Librarian's opinion, was to leave them on the shelves where Nature intended them to be.

Terry Pratchett 1948– : *Men at Arms* (1993)

2 Whatever classifications have been chosen, every library tyrannizes the act of reading, and forces the reader—the curious reader, the alert reader—to *rescue* the book from the category to which it has been condemned.

Alberto Manguel 1948– : *A History of Reading* (1996)

3 I enjoy my library. It is a sort of large secretion of coral around a living organism. I can see chalky banks of books which reflect my interests.

Jonathan Miller 1934– : in *The Times* 13 November 2001

Life

4 My soul, sit thou a patient looker-on;
Judge not the play before the play is done:
Her plot hath many changes; every day
Speaks a new scene; the last act crowns the play.

Francis Quarles 1592–1644: *Emblems* (1635) 'Respice Finem'

5 No arts; no letters; no society; and which is worst of all, continual fear and danger of violent death; and the life of man, solitary, poor, nasty, brutish, and short.

Thomas Hobbes 1588–1679: *Leviathan* (1651)

6 When I consider how my light is spent,
E're half my days, in this dark world and wide,
And that one talent which is death to hide
Lodged with me useless . . .
Doth God exact day-labour, light denied,
I fondly ask; but patience to prevent
That murmur, soon replies, God doth not need
Either man's work or his own gifts, who best
Bear his mild yoke, they serve him best, his state
Is kingly. Thousands at his bidding speed
And post o'er land and ocean without rest:
They also serve who only stand and wait.

John Milton 1608–74: *Sonnet* 16 'When I consider how my light is spent' (1673)

7 This world is a comedy to those that think, a tragedy to those that feel.

Horace Walpole 1717–97: letter to Anne, Countess of Upper Ossory, 16 August 1776

8 I should have no objection to go over the same life from its beginning to the end: requesting only the advantage authors have, of correcting in a second edition the faults of the first.

Benjamin Franklin 1706–90: *Autobiography* (1868)

9 A man's life of any worth is a continual allegory.

John Keats 1795–1821: letter to George and Georgiana Keats, 19 February 1819

10 But, friends, I do not want to die,
I want to live, so as to think and suffer.

Alexander Pushkin 1799–1837: 'Elegy' (1830)

11 Life is infinitely more stubborn than theory, it goes its way independent of it and silently conquers it.

Alexander Herzen 1812–70: *From the Other Shore* (1847–50)

1 I strove with none; for none was worth my strife;
Nature I loved, and, next to Nature, Art.

Walter Savage Landor 1775–1864:
'Dying Speech of an Old Philosopher'
(1853)

2 Our life is frittered away by detail . . . Simplify, simplify.

Henry David Thoreau 1817–62:
Walden (1854)

3 Human life is a sad show, undoubtedly: ugly, heavy and
complex. Art has no other end, for people of feeling, than
to conjure away the burden and bitterness.

Gustave Flaubert 1821–80: letter to
Amelie Bosquet, July 1864

4 If we had a keen vision and feeling of all ordinary human
life, it would be like hearing the grass grow and the
squirrel's heart beat, and we should die of that roar which
lies on the other side of silence.

George Eliot 1819–80: *Middlemarch*
(1871–2)

5 Books are good enough in their own way, but they are a
mighty bloodless substitute for life.

Robert Louis Stevenson 1850–94:
Virginibus Puerisque (1881) 'An
Apology for Idlers'

6 And anyway no literature can outdo real life when it
comes to cynicism. You're not going to get a person drunk
with a jigger when he's just polished off a barrel.

Anton Chekhov 1860–1904: letter to
M. V. Kiseleva, 14 January 1887

7 One can read when one is middle-aged or old; but one can
mingle in the world with fresh perceptions only when one
is young. The great thing is to be *saturated*, with
something—that is, in one way or another, with life.

Henry James 1843–1916: letter 29
October 1888

8 My life has been in my poems . . . I have seen others
enjoying, while I stand alone with myself—commenting,
commenting—a mere dead mirror on which things reflect
themselves.

W. B. Yeats 1865–1939: letter to
Katharine Tynan, 1888

9 All that I desire to point out is the general principle that
Life imitates Art far more than Art imitates Life.

Oscar Wilde 1854–1900: *Intentions*
(1891)

10 The life of every man is a diary in which he means to write
one story, and writes another; and his humblest hour is
when he compares the volume as it is with what he vowed
to make it.

J. M. Barrie 1860–1937: *The Little
Minister* (1891)

11 It had taken too much of his life to produce too little of his
art.

Henry James 1843–1916: 'The Middle
Years' (1893)

12 Do you want to know the great drama of my life? It's that
I have put my genius into my life; all I've put into my
works is my talent.

Oscar Wilde 1854–1900: André Gide
Oscar Wilde (1910)

13 Life being all inclusion and confusion, and art being all
discrimination and selection.

Henry James 1843–1916: preface to
The Spoils of Poynton (1909 ed.)

14 The perfect delight of writing tales where so many lives
come and go at the cost of one which slips imperceptibly
away.

Joseph Conrad 1857–1924: *A
Personal Record* (1912)

15 Life deceives us so much that we come to believing that
literature has no relation with it and we are astonished to
observe that the wonderful ideas books have presented to
us are gratuitously exhibited in everyday life, without risk
of being spoilt by the writer.

Marcel Proust 1871–1922: *Time
Regained* (1926)

16 Most of life is so dull that there is nothing to be said about
it, and the books and talk that would describe it as
interesting are obliged to exaggerate, in the hope of
justifying their own existence.

E. M. Forster 1879–1970: *A Passage
to India* (1924)

1 Life is not a series of gig lamps symmetrically arranged; life is a luminous halo, a semi-transparent envelope surrounding us from the beginning of consciousness to the end.

Virginia Woolf 1882–1941: *The Common Reader* (1925) 'Modern Fiction'

2 I enjoy almost everything. Yet I have some restless searcher in me. Why is there not a discovery in life? Something one can lay one's hands on and say 'This is it'?

Virginia Woolf 1882–1941: diary, 27 February 1926

3 The intellect of man is forced to choose
Perfection of the life, or of the work.

W. B. Yeats 1865–1939: 'Coole Park and Ballylee, 1932' (1933)

4 For the majority of creative people, life is a pretty mean trick.

F. Scott Fitzgerald 1896–1940: Jeffrey Meyers *Scott Fitzgerald* (1994)

5 No art can completely reject reality. Real literary creation uses . . . reality and only reality with all its warmth and blood, its passion and its outcries. It simply adds something which transfigures reality.

Albert Camus 1913–60: *The Rebel* (1951)

6 An old teapot, used daily, can tell me more of my past than anything I recorded of it. Continuity . . . continuity . . . it is that which we cannot write down, it is that we cannot compass, record or control.

Sylvia Townsend Warner 1893–1978: letter to Alyse Gregory, 26 May 1953

7 Timeless fictional worlds
Of self-evident meaning
Would not delight
Were not our own
A temporal one, where nothing
Is what it seems.

W. H. Auden 1907–73: 'The Cave of Making' (1965)

8 Let no one demean to tears or reproach
This declaration of the skill of God
Who with such magnificent irony
Gave me at the same time darkness and the books.

Jorge Luis Borges 1899–1986: 'Poem of the Gifts' (1972) tr. Alastair Reid

9 Books say: she did this because. Life says: she did this. Books are where things are explained to you; life is where things aren't . . . Books make sense of life. The only problem is that the lives they make sense of are other people's lives, never your own.

Julian Barnes 1946– : *Flaubert's Parrot* (1984)

10 Life is a means of extracting fiction.

Robert Stone 1937– : George Plimpton (ed.) *Writers at Work* (8th series, 1988)

11 Though I liked reading (and showed off at it), it was soon borne in upon me that the world of books was only distantly related to the world in which I lived.

Alan Bennett 1934– : *Writing Home* (1994)

12 There is no point to life, though there is a point to art.
said the month before he died

Kingsley Amis 1922–95: attributed, 1995

13 Well there you are. This is life. What I've found as a writer is that you have to keep taming it down, making it less improbable in order to fit it into some sort of fictional context.

John Mortimer 1923– : in *Paris Review* 1995

14 What I had always loved was a kind of foursquareness about the utterance, a feeling of living inside a constantly indicative mood, in the presence of an understanding that assumes you share an awareness of the perilous nature of

Seamus Heaney 1939– : introduction to his translation of *Beowulf* (1999)

life and are yet capable of seeing it steadily and, when
necessary, sternly.

1 The writer's life seethes within but not without.
Nevertheless, it has to be recorded.

Anthony Burgess 1917–93: *You've Had Your Time* (1990)

2 Stories are like genes, they keep part of us alive after the
end of our story.

A. S. Byatt 1936– : *On Histories and Stories* (2000)

Literary Theory

3 *Il n'y a pas de hors-texte.*
There is nothing outside of the text.

Jacques Derrida 1930– : *Of Grammatology* (1967)

4 It attempts to make the not-seen accessible to sight.
 on deconstructive reading

Jacques Derrida 1930– : *Of Grammatology* (1967)

5 A text is not a line of words releasing a single 'theological'
meaning (the 'message' of the Author-God) but a multi-
dimensional space in which a variety of writings, none of
them original, blend and clash.

Roland Barthes 1915–80: *The Death of the Author* (1968)

6 Once the Author is removed, the claim to decipher a text
becomes quite futile.

Roland Barthes 1915–80: *The Death of the Author* (1968)

7 Interpretation is nothing but the possibility of error.

Paul de Man 1919–83: *Blindness and Insight* (1971)

8 The literary work has two poles, which we might call the
artistic and the aesthetic: the artistic refers to the text
created by the author, and the aesthetic to the realization
accomplished by the reader. From this polarity it follows
that the literary work cannot be completely identical with
the text, or with the realization of the text, but in fact
must lie half-way between the two.

Wolfgang Iser 1926– : 'The Reading Process' (1972)

9 Two people gazing at the night sky may both be looking at
the same collection of stars, but one will see the image of a
plough, and the other will make out a dipper. The 'stars'
in a literary text are fixed; the lines that join them are
variable.

Wolfgang Iser 1926– : 'The Reading Process' (1972)

10 All reading is misreading.

J. Hillis Miller 1928– : 'Walter Pater: a Partial Portrait' (1976)

11 The deconstructive critic seeks to find . . . the element in
the system studied which is alogical, the thread in the text
in question which will unravel it all, or the loose stone
which will pull down the whole building. The
deconstruction, rather, annihilates the ground on which
the building stands by showing that the text has already
annihilated that ground, knowingly or unknowingly.
Deconstruction is not a dismantling of the structure of a
text but a demonstration that it has dismantled itself.

J. Hillis Miller 1928– : 'Stevens' Rock and Criticism as Cure: II' (1976)

12 What we ask a theory for, is to give us back an old subject
illuminated by a new light in order to realize that only
from that point of view the object can be really
understood.

Umberto Eco 1932– : in *Drama Review* March 1977

1 Incredulity towards metanarratives.
  a definition of postmodernism

Jean-François Lyotard 1924–98: *The Postmodern Condition* (1979)

2 Structuralism is not a subject that grips the ordinary reader much. Its articles of faith are likely to strike him as a mixture of the self-evident and the impossible. Thus the proposition, solemnly repeated by structuralists, that language is a system of signs (or 'signifiers') seems to him too obvious to remark. Who ever imagined otherwise? On the other hand, the ideas floated by the wilder type of structuralist—that literary texts ought to mean anything we require them to, or that authors do not create their works but are created by them—pretty clearly call for a spell of sedation and devoted nursing.

John Carey 1934– : in *Sunday Times* 1981

3 Deconstruction is in one sense . . . a sort of patient, probing reformism of the text, which is not, so to speak, to be confronted over the barricades but cunningly waylaid in the corridors and suavely chivvied into revealing its ideological hand . . . But to say no more than this is to do deconstruction a severe injustice. For it ignores that other face of deconstruction which is its hair-raising *radicalism*—the nerve and daring with which it knocks the stuffing out of every smug concept and leaves the well-groomed text shamefully dishevelled. It ignores, in short, the *madness* and violence of deconstruction, its scandalous urge to think the unthinkable, the flamboyance with which it poses itself on the very brink of meaning and dances there, pounding away at the crumbling cliff-edge beneath its feet and prepared to fall with it into the sea of unlimited semiosis or schizophrenia.

Terry Eagleton 1943– : *Walter Benjamin or Towards a Revolutionary Criticism* (1981)

4 I tried for the longest time to find out what *deconstructionism* was. Nobody was able to explain it to me clearly. The best answer I got was from a writer, who said, 'Honey, it's bad news for you and me.'

Margaret Atwood 1939– : in an interview, December 1986; Earl G. Ingersoll (ed.) *Margaret Atwood: Conversations* (1990)

5 Theory on a dramatic scale happens when it is both possible and necessary for it to do so—when the traditional rationales which have silently underpinned our daily practices stand in danger of being discredited, and need either to be revised or discarded . . . Theory is just a practice forced into a new form of self-reflectiveness on account of certain grievous problems it has encountered. Like small lumps on the neck, it is a symptom that all is not well.

Terry Eagleton 1943– : *The Significance of Theory* (1990)

6 Though it often apes scientific language, critical theory would not be recognized as theory by any scientist, since it does not open itself to experimental verification. Composed purely of assertions, not testable hypotheses, it can have no bearing on reality, and no explanatory value.

John Carey 1934– : in *Sunday Times* 7 August 1994

7 Any desire to read that hasn't been destroyed by popular culture, television, films or computers, literature courses have taken care of! It's an intellectual tragedy. All these ideological methods represent is careerism and vanity.

Philip Roth 1933– : in *Independent* 16 October 2002

Literature see also Literatures

1 Your true lover of literature is never fastidious.

Robert Southey 1774–1843: *The Doctor* (1812)

2 A losing trade, I assure you, sir: literature is a drug.

George Borrow 1803–81: *Lavengro* (1851)

3 But literature, though the grandest occupation in the world for a man's leisure, is, I take it, a slavish profession.

Anthony Trollope 1815–82: *The Bertrams* (1859)

4 It takes a great deal of history to produce a little literature.

Henry James 1843–1916: *Hawthorne* (1879)

5 *Et tout le reste est littérature.*
All the rest is mere fine writing.

Paul Verlaine 1844–96: 'Art poétique' (1882)

6 *La pensée est à la littérature ce que la lumière est à la peinture.*
Ideas are to literature what light is to painting.

Paul Bourget 1852–1935: *La Physiologie de l'Amour Moderne* (1890)

7 Literature is a splendid mistress, but a bad wife.
advice to Edgar Wallace, c.1897

Rudyard Kipling 1865–1936: Margaret Lane *Edgar Wallace* (1964)

8 Oh literature, oh the glorious Art, how it preys upon the marrow of our bones. It scoops the stuffing out of us and chucks us aside. Alas!

D. H. Lawrence 1885–1930: letter to Walter de la Mare, 10 June 1912

9 Literature is a method of sudden arrangement of commonplaces. *The suddenness* makes us forget the commonplace.

T. E. Hulme 1883–1917: in *Criterion* 1925 vol. 3 'Notes on Language and Style'

10 The rest, called *literature*, is a dossier of human imbecility for the guidance of future professors.

Tristan Tzara 1896–1963: in *Dada* 4/5 Zurich May 1919

11 Literature flourishes best when it is half a trade and half an art.

William Ralph Inge 1860–1954: *Victorian Age* (1922)

12 All literature is, finally, autobiographical.

Jorge Luis Borges 1899–1986: in 1926; James Woodall *The Man in the Mirror of the Book* (1996)

13 Our American professors like their literature clear and cold and pure and very dead.

Sinclair Lewis 1885–1951: *The American Fear of Literature* (Nobel Prize Address, 12 December 1930)

14 Great literature is simply language charged with meaning to the utmost possible degree.

Ezra Pound 1885–1972: *How To Read* (1931)

15 Remarks are not literature.

Gertrude Stein 1874–1946: *Autobiography of Alice B. Toklas* (1933)

16 Literature is news that STAYS news.

Ezra Pound 1885–1972: *The ABC of Reading* (1934)

17 Literature is the art of writing something that will be read twice; journalism what will be read once.

Cyril Connolly 1903–74: *Enemies of Promise* (1938)

18 My theories and views of literature vary with the lateness of the hour, the quality of my companions, and the quantity of liquor.

James Thurber 1894–1961: Fred B. Millett *Contemporary American Authors* (1940)

19 *Longtemps, longtemps,* la voix humaine *fut base et condition de la* littérature . . .
Un jour vint où l'on sut lire des yeux sans épeler, sans entendre, et la littérature en fut tout altérée.
For a long, long time, *the human voice* was the foundation and condition of all *literature* . . .

Paul Valéry 1871–1945: *Tel Quel 1* (1941)

A day came when the reader could read with his eyes
alone without having to spell things out, or hear them,
and literature was completely transformed by this.

1 To turn events into ideas is the function of literature.

George Santayana 1863–1952:
attributed

2 Literature is the orchestration of platitudes.

Thornton Wilder 1897–1975: in
Time 12 January 1953

3 He knew everything about literature except how to enjoy
it.

Joseph Heller 1923–99: *Catch-22*
(1961)

4 Literature is mostly about having sex and not much about
having children. Life is the other way round.

David Lodge 1935– : *The British
Museum is Falling Down* (1965)

5 The image of literature to be found in ordinary culture is
tyrannically centred on the author, his person, his life, his
tastes, his passions.

Roland Barthes 1915–80: *The Death
of the Author* (1968)

6 The virtue of much literature is that it is dangerous and
may do you extreme harm.

John Mortimer 1923– : C. H. Rolph
Books in the Dock (1969)

7 Literature is the question minus the answer.

Roland Barthes 1915–80: in *New
York Times*, 1978

8 The central function of imaginative literature is to make
you realise that other people act on moral convictions
different from your own.

William Empson 1906–84: *Milton's
God* (1981)

9 In the . . . congested times that await us, literature must
aim at the maximum concentration of poetry and thought.

Italo Calvino 1923–85: *Six Memos for
the Next Millennium* (1992)

10 Among the values I would like passed on to the next
millennium, there is this above all: a literature that has
absorbed the taste for mental orderliness and exactitude,
the intelligence of poetry, but at the same time that of
science and of philosophy.

Italo Calvino 1923–85: *Six Memos for
the Next Millennium* (1992)

11 Literature is the one place in any society where, within the
secrecy of our own heads, we can hear *voices talking about
everything in every possible way.*

Salman Rushdie 1947– : lecture 'Is
Nothing Sacred' 6 February 1990

12 Literature . . . is the drudge, the unconsidered odd-job man
of the arts. Who among us can say that when he reads he
does not rush, and skip, does not stop in improbable
places, does not indeed commit the literary sin against the
Holy Ghost, which is to gobble a book in order to be able
to say that he has read it, without having given the book a
fair chance to declare to him why it should have been
read?

Robertson Davies 1913–95: lecture,
Yale, 20 February 1990

13 To me literature is forever blowing a horn, singing about
youth when youth is irretrievably gone, singing about
your homeland when in the schizophrenia of the times
you find yourself in a land that lies over the ocean, a
land—no matter how hospitable and friendly—where
your heart is not, because you landed on those shores too
late.

Josef Škvorecký 1924– : foreword
to *The Bass Saxophone* (1994)

14 Is there a greater privilege than to have a consciousness
expanded by, filled with, pointed to literature?

Susan Sontag 1933– : in *Writers on
Writing: Collected Essays from The
New York Times* (2001)

1 Literature is a competitive sport, but I'm the only one to admit it. When I read a good novel I read competitively.

Norman Mailer 1923– : in *Independent* 9 February 2002

Literatures see also Literature

2 *Satura quidem tota nostra est.*
Verse satire indeed is entirely our own.
 meaning Roman as opposed to Greek

Quintilian AD c.35–c.96: *Institutio Oratoria*

3 The language of the age is never the language of poetry, except among the French, whose verse, where the thought or image does not support it, differs in nothing from prose.

Thomas Gray 1716–71: letter to Richard West, 8 April 1742

4 But why should the Americans write books, when a six weeks passage brings them, in their own tongue, our sense, science, and genius, in bales and hogsheads? Prairies, steam-boats, grist-mills, are their natural objects for centuries to come.

Sydney Smith 1771–1845: in *Edinburgh Review* December 1818

5 The character of American literature is, generally speaking, pretty justly appreciated in Europe. The immense exhalation of periodical trash, which penetrates into every cot and corner of the country, and which is greedily sucked in by all ranks, is unquestionably one cause of its inferiority.

Frances Trollope 1780–1863: *Domestic Manners of the Americans* (1832)

6 Has Canada no poet to describe the glories of his parent land—no painter that can delineate her matchless scenery of land and wave? Are her children dumb and blind, that they leave to strangers the task of singing her praise? The standard literature of Canada must be looked for in the newspapers.

Susannah Moodie 1803–85: *Mark Hudlestone* (1853); introduction

7 Of these two literatures [French and German], as of the intellect of Europe in general, the main effort, for now many years, has been a *critical* effort; the endeavours, in all branches of knowledge—theology, philosophy, history, art, science—to see the object as in itself it really is.

Matthew Arnold 1822–88: *On Translating Homer* (1861)

8 The more I reflect on the destiny of Canadian literature, the less chance I find for its leaving a mark in history. Canada lacks its own language. If we spoke Iroquois or Huron, our literature would live.

Octave Crémazie 1827–79: letter to Abbé Henri-Raymond Casgrain, 29 January 1867

9 It would seem that in our great unendowed, unfurnished, unentertained and unentertaining continent [of North America], where we all sit sniffing, as it were, the very earth of our foundations, we ought to have leisure to turn out something handsome from the very heart of simple nature.

Henry James 1843–1916: letter, 14 January 1874

10 The floods of tepid soap and water which under the name of novels are being vomited forth in England, seem to me, by contrast [with French fiction], to do little honour to our race.

Henry James 1843–1916: letter, 21 February 1884

11 In France literature divides itself into schools, movements, and circles . . . In England . . . each man works by himself and for himself, for England is a land of literary Ishmaels.

W. B. Yeats 1865–1939: 'The Celt in London' (1892)

1 Alone, perhaps, among the nations of Europe we are in our ballad or epic age . . . Our poetry is still a poetry of the people in the main, for it still deals with the tales and thoughts of the people.

W. B. Yeats 1865–1939: 'Nationality and Literature', lecture 19 May 1893

2 Roman literature is Greek literature written in Latin.

Heinrich von Treitschke 1834–96: attributed

3 Sir Walter Scott gave Highland legends and Highland excitability so great a mastery over all romance that they seem romance itself.

W. B. Yeats 1865–1939: 'The Celtic Element in Literature' (1897)

4 What most offends an Englishman in the heroes of French fiction is the peculiar dastardliness to women they are capable of.

George Gissing 1857–1903: *Commonplace Book* (1962)

5 The more a man dreams, the less he believes. A great literature is thus chiefly the product of doubting and inquiring minds in revolt against the immovable certainties of the nation.

H. L. Mencken 1880–1956: *Prejudices* (2nd series, 1920) 'The National Letters'

6 God damn the continent of Europe. It is of merely antiquarian interest . . . France made me sick. Its silly pose as the thing the world has to save . . . They're through and done . . . Culture follows money and all the refinements of aestheticism can't stave off its change of seat . . . We will be the Romans in the next generation as the English are now.

F. Scott Fitzgerald 1896–1940: letter to Edmund Wilson, May 1921

7 That feeling you get in English books and so seldom in ours that the country with all its small details is a part of their lives and that they love it.

Raymond Chandler 1888–1959: letter to James Sandoe 28 December 1949

8 Many people now search for the epic in Western movies and in their hard riders. More than in the Greeks and Romans and in the Lay of the Nibelungs, I have found the epic in the prose and poetry of the North.

Jorge Luis Borges 1899–1986: *Seis poemas escandinavos* (1966) preface

9 It will take four or five hundred years for us to become indigenes; and to write poetry, unless you are an indigene, is very difficult.
on being an Australian writer

Judith Wright 1915–2000: W. N. Scott *Focus on Judith Wright* (1967)

10 The greatest of the nineteenth-century Russian novelists wrote out of the profundities of a silent country. In a real and literal sense Dostoyevsky wrote out of the nocturnal silence of St Petersburg, Tolstoy from the rural silence of Yasnaya Polyana and Turgenev from the summer quiet of Spasskoye.

Richard Freeborn: introduction to Ivan Turgenev *Home of the Gentry* (1970 ed.)

11 I had always thought of English literature as the richest in the world; the discovery now of a secret chamber at the very threshold of that literature came to me as an additional gift.

Jorge Luis Borges 1899–1986: *The Aleph and Other Stories* (1971) 'Autobiographical Essay'; see **154:8**

12 In [my] preference for short literary forms I am only following the true vocation of Italian literature, which is poor in novelists but rich in poets.

Italo Calvino 1923–85: *Six Memos for the Next Millennium* (1992)

13 I was determined to prove that the Australian novel is not necessarily the dreary, dun-coloured offspring of journalistic realism.

Patrick White 1912–90: *Patrick White Speaks* (1990)

1 The Channel is a slipper bath of irony through which we pass these serious Continentals in order not to be infected by their gloom.

Alan Bennett 1934– : *Writing Home* (1994)

2 The novels created below the thirty-fifth parallel, though a bit foreign to European taste, are the extension of the history of the European novel, of its form and of its spirit, and are even astonishingly close to its earliest beginnings. Nowhere else today does the old Rabelaisian sap run so joyfully as in the work of these non-European writers.

Milan Kundera 1929– : *Testaments Betrayed* (1995)

3 Obsessive denigration of English fiction is the dying chirrup of some sort of imperial misery.
    speech at the Booker awards, 29 October 1996

Carmen Callil 1938– : in *Daily Telegraph* 30 October 1996

4 The literary America in which I found myself . . . bore a strange resemblance to the St Louis I'd grown up in: a once-great city that had been gutted and drained by white flight and superhighways. Ringing the depressed urban core of serious fiction were prosperous new suburbs of mass entertainments. Much of the inner city's remaining vitality was concentrated in the black, Hispanic, Asian, gay and women's communities that had taken over the structures vacated by fleeing straight white males.

Jonathan Franzen 1959– : *How to be Alone* (2002) 'Why bother?'

Love

5 Dumb swans, not chattering pies, do lovers prove;
  They love indeed who quake to say they love.

Philip Sidney 1554–86: *Astrophel and Stella* (1591)

6 From women's eyes this doctrine I derive:
  They are the ground, the books, the academes,
  From whence doth spring the true Promethean fire.

William Shakespeare 1564–1616: *Love's Labour's Lost* (1595)

7 For these fellows of infinite tongue, that can rhyme themselves into ladies' favours, they do always reason themselves out again.

William Shakespeare 1564–1616: *Henry V* (1599)

8 If all the earth were paper white
  And all the sea were ink
  'Twere not enough for me to write
  As my poor heart doth think.

John Lyly c.1554–1606: 'If all the earth were paper white'

9 Love made me poet,
  And this I writ;
  My heart did do it,
  And not my wit.

Elizabeth, Lady Tanfield c.1565–1628: epitaph for her husband, in Burford Parish Church, Oxfordshire

10 I am two fools, I know,
   For loving, and for saying so
   In whining poetry.

John Donne 1572–1631: 'The Triple Fool'

11 She that with poetry is won,
   Is but a desk to write upon.

Samuel Butler 1612–80: *Hudibras* pt. 2 (1664)

12 No one would ever have fallen in love unless he had first read about it.

Duc de la Rochefoucauld 1613–80: Edmund White *The Burning Library* (1994); attributed

13 I court others in verse: but I love thee in prose:
   And they have my whimsies, but thou hast my heart.

Matthew Prior 1664–1721: 'A Better Answer' (1718)

1 Thro' all the drama—whether damned or not—
Love gilds the scene, and women guide the plot.

Richard Brinsley Sheridan 1751–1816: *The Rivals* (1775)

2 Lady Caroline Lamb stabbed herself at Lady Ilchester's Ball for the love of Lord Byron, as it is supposed. What a charming thing to be a Poet. I preached for many years in London and was rather popular, but never heard of a Lady doing herself the smallest mischief on my account.

Sydney Smith 1771–1845: letter to J. A. Murray, 12 July 1813

3 I have met with women whom I really think would like to be married to a poem and to be given away by a novel.

John Keats 1795–1821: letter to Fanny Brawne, 8 July 1819

4 Think you, if Laura had been Petrarch's wife,
He would have written sonnets all his life?

Lord Byron 1788–1824: *Don Juan* (1819–24)

5 When amatory poets sing their loves
In liquid lines mellifluously bland,
And pair their rhymes as Venus yokes her doves,
They little think what mischief is in hand.

Lord Byron 1788–1824: *Don Juan* (1819–24)

6 The ideal story is that of two people who go into love step for step, with a fluttered consciousness, like a pair of children venturing together into a dark room.

Robert Louis Stevenson 1850–94: *Virginibus Puerisque* (1881) 'El Dorado'

7 Only connect! . . . Only connect the prose and the passion, and both will be exalted, and human love will be seen at its height.

E. M. Forster 1879–1970: *Howards End* (1910)

8 Friendship is useless in the development of the artist. Only love (that is, jealousy) can train the writer's mind, since constant suspicious questioning of every motive, every movement, and the conversion of each innocent story into a guilty alibi—only this restless and piercing scrutiny can teach the writer to observe.

Marcel Proust 1871–1922: Edmund White *The Burning Library* (1994)

9 Should poets bicycle-pump the human heart
Or squash it flat?
Man's love is of man's life a thing apart;
Girls aren't like that.

Kingsley Amis 1922–95: 'A Bookshop Idyll' (1956)

10 Beware, madam, of the witty devil,
The arch intriguer who walks disguised
In a poet's cloak, his gay tongue oozing evil.

Robert Graves 1895–1985: 'Beware, Madam!'

11 In our culture, love needs a mixer before it qualifies as a subject for literature. Pour it out neat, and you get Mills & Boon.

John Carey 1934– : in *Sunday Times* 11 February 1996

12 Playwrights teach nothing about love, they make it pretty, they make it comical or they make it lust. They cannot make it true.

Tom Stoppard 1937– : *Shakespeare in Love* (1999 film, screenplay by Tom Stoppard and Mark Norman)

Lord Macaulay 1800–59 see also **17:5**
English politician and historian

13 Macaulay is well for a while, but one wouldn't *live* under Niagara.

Thomas Carlyle 1795–1881: R. M. Milnes *Notebook* (1838)

14 He is incomparably the first lion in the metropolis; that is, he writes, talks, and speaks better than any man in England.

Sydney Smith 1771–1845: letter to Mrs Meynell, April 1839

1 Nothing would do him more good than a course of the Waters of Lethe; if he could forget half of what he reads he would be less suffocating than he is.

Sydney Smith 1771–1845: letter to Lady Grey, 15 Nov 1841

2 I wish I was as cocksure of anything as Tom Macaulay is of everything.

Lord Melbourne 1779–1848: Lord Cowper's preface to *Lord Melbourne's Papers* (1889)

3 He [Macaulay] has occasional flashes of silence, that make his conversation perfectly delightful.

Sydney Smith 1771–1845: Lady Holland *Memoir* (1855) vol. 1

4 A sentence of Macaulay's . . . may have no more sense in it than a blot pinched between doubled paper.

John Ruskin 1819–1900: *Praeterita* (1887)

5 His conversation was a procession of one.

Florence Nightingale 1820–1910: Cecil Woodham Smith *Florence Nightingale* (1950)

Hugh MacDiarmid 1892–1978
Scottish poet and nationalist

6 My function in Scotland during the past twenty to thirty years has been that of the catfish that vitalises the other torpid denizens of the aquarium.

Hugh MacDiarmid 1892–1978: *Lucky Poet* (1943)

7 A symbol of all that's perfectly hideous about Scotland.

Irvine Welsh 1957– : in *Scotland on Sunday* 28 January 1996

Louis MacNeice 1907–63
British poet, born in Belfast

8 When we were young . . . his poetry was the poetry of our everyday life, of shop-windows, traffic policemen, ice-cream soda, lawn mowers, and an uneasy awareness of what the newsboys were shouting. In addition he displayed a sophisticated sentimentality about falling leaves and lipsticked cigarette stubs: he could have written the words of 'These Foolish Things'. We were grateful to him for having found a place in poetry for these properties.

Philip Larkin 1922–85: in *New Statesman* 1963

Magazines see Newspapers and Magazines

François Malherbe 1555–1628
French writer

9 *Ce que Malherbe escrit dure eternellement.*
What Malherbe writes will endure forever.

François Malherbe 1555–1628: 'Sonnet au Roy'

10 *Enfin Malherbe vint, et, le premier en France,*
Fit sentir dans les vers une juste cadence.
At last came Malherbe, and he was the first in France to give poetry a proper flow.

Nicolas Boileau 1636–1711: *L'Art poétique* (1674)

Katherine Mansfield 1888–1923 see also **256:6**
New Zealand-born short-story writer

1 Her mind is a very thin soil, laid an inch or two upon very barren rock.

Virginia Woolf 1882–1941: *A Writer's Diary* (1953) 7 August 1918

2 I have discovered that I cannot burn the candle at one end and write a book with the other.

Katherine Mansfield 1888–1923: diary, 1919

3 [She had] a quality I adored, and needed; I think her sharpness and reality.

Virginia Woolf 1882–1941: letter to Vita Sackville-West, 8 August 1931

Christopher Marlowe 1564–93
English dramatist and poet

4 Marlowe's mighty line.

Ben Jonson c.1573–1637: 'To the Memory of . . . Shakespeare' (1623)

5 There is a lust of power in his writings, a hunger and thirst after unrighteousness, a glow of the imagination unhallowed by any thing except its own energies. His thoughts burn within him like a furnace with flickering flames; or throwing out black smoke and mists, that hide the dawn of genius, or like a poisonous mineral, corrode the heart.

William Hazlitt 1778–1830: *Lectures chiefly on the dramatic literature of the age of Elizabeth* (1820)

6 The infernal tradition that Marlowe was a great dramatic poet instead of a xvi century Henley throws all the blame for his wretched half-achievement on the actor. Marlowe had words and a turn for their music, but nothing to say—a barren amateur with a great air.

George Bernard Shaw 1856–1950: letter, 2 September 1903

7 A kind of cross between Oscar Wilde and Jack the Ripper.

Seamus Heaney 1939– : *The Redress of Poetry* (1995)

W. Somerset Maugham 1874–1965
English novelist

8 It is this preoccupation with physical appetite, which he doesn't feel, that makes Maugham's work so intensely vulgar—rather like Balzac's to the rich, or Evelyn Waugh's to the highly born, or like Graham Greene's to the good.

Malcolm Muggeridge 1903–90: Noel Annan *Our Age* (1990)

Guy de Maupassant 1850–93
French novelist and short-story writer

9 No one but a Frenchman can write such pages as that— but no one but a Frenchman *would*, either.
  of de Maupassant's description of 'the love-making of poor Madame Walter' in Bel Ami

Henry James 1843–1916: letter, 29 May 1885

Meaning

1 And this is the writing that was written, MENE, MENE, TEKEL, UPHARSIN.
This is the interpretation of the thing: MENE; God hath numbered thy kingdom, and finished it.
TEKEL; Thou art weighed in the balances and art found wanting.
PERES; Thy kingdom is divided, and given to the Medes and Persians.

Bible: Daniel

2 I pray thee, understand a plain man in his plain meaning.

William Shakespeare 1564–1616: *The Merchant of Venice* (1596–8)

3 In all speech, words and sense are as the body and the soul. The sense is as the life and soul of language, without which all words are dead.

Ben Jonson c.1573–1637: *Timber, or Discoveries made upon Men and Matter* (1641)

4 Where more is meant than meets the ear.

John Milton 1608–74: 'Il Penseroso' (1645)

5 The rest to some faint meaning make pretence,
But Shadwell never deviates into sense.
Some beams of wit on other souls may fall,
Strike through and make a lucid interval;
But Shadwell's genuine night admits no ray,
His rising fogs prevail upon the day.

John Dryden 1631–1700: *MacFlecknoe* (1682)

6 Still follow sense, of ev'ry art the soul,
Parts answering parts shall slide into a whole.

Alexander Pope 1688–1744: *Epistles to Several Persons* 'To Lord Burlington' (1731)

7 God and I both knew what it meant once; now God alone knows.
also attributed to **Browning**, *apropos* Sordello, *in the form* 'When it was written, God and Robert Browning knew what it meant; now only God knows'

Friedrich Klopstock 1724–1803: C. Lombroso *The Man of Genius* (1891)

8 Until you understand a writer's ignorance, presume yourself ignorant of his understanding.

Samuel Taylor Coleridge 1772–1834: *Biographia Literaria* (1817)

9 Better the rudest work that tells a story or records a fact, than the richest without meaning.

John Ruskin 1819–1900: *Seven Lamps of Architecture* (1849)

10 'Then you should say what you mean,' the March Hare went on. 'I do,' Alice hastily replied; 'at least—at least I mean what I say—that's the same thing, you know.' 'Not the same thing a bit!' said the Hatter. 'Why, you might just as well say that "I see what I eat" is the same thing as "I eat what I see!" '

Lewis Carroll 1832–98: *Alice's Adventures in Wonderland* (1865)

11 Be sure that you go to the author to get at his meaning, not to find yours.

John Ruskin 1819–1900: *Sesame and Lilies* (1865)

12 'There's glory for you!' 'I don't know what you mean by "glory",' Alice said. 'I meant, "there's a nice knock-down argument for you!" ' 'But "glory" doesn't mean "a nice knock-down argument",' Alice objected. 'When I use a word,' Humpty Dumpty said in a rather scornful tone, 'it means just what I choose it to mean—neither more nor less.'

Lewis Carroll 1832–98: *Through the Looking-Glass* (1872)

1 You see it's like a portmanteau—there are two meanings packed up into one word.

Lewis Carroll 1832–98: *Through the Looking-Glass* (1872)

2 The meaning doesn't matter if it's only idle chatter of a transcendental kind.

W. S. Gilbert 1836–1911: *Patience* (1881)

3 Vereker's secret, my dear man—the general intention of his books: the string the pearls were strung on, the buried treasure, the figure in the carpet.

Henry James 1843–1916: *The Figure in the Carpet* (1896)

4 No one means all he says, and yet very few say all they mean, for words are slippery and thought is viscous.

Henry Brooks Adams 1838–1918: *The Education of Henry Adams* (1907)

5 I do not know which to prefer,
The beauty of inflections
Or the beauty of innuendoes,
The blackbird whistling
Or just after.

Wallace Stevens 1879–1955: 'Thirteen Ways of Looking at a Blackbird' (1923)

6 The little girl had the making of a poet in her who, being told to be sure of her meaning before she spoke, said, 'How can I know what I think till I see what I say?'

Graham Wallas 1858–1932: *The Art of Thought* (1926)

7 Even when poetry has a meaning, as it usually has, it may be inadvisable to draw it out . . . Perfect understanding will sometimes almost extinguish pleasure.

A. E. Housman 1859–1936: *The Name and Nature of Poetry* (1933)

8 Any general statement is like a cheque drawn on a bank. Its value depends on what is there to meet it.

Ezra Pound 1885–1972: *The ABC of Reading* (1934)

9 That was a way of putting it—not very satisfactory:
A periphrastic study in a worn-out poetical fashion,
Leaving one still with the intolerable wrestle
With words and meanings.

T. S. Eliot 1888–1965: *Four Quartets* 'East Coker' (1940)

10 I distrust the incommunicable: it is the source of all violence.

Jean-Paul Sartre 1905–80: 'Qu'est-ce que la littérature?' in *Les Temps Modernes* July 1947

11 Everywhere one seeks to produce meaning, to make the world signify, to render it visible. We are not, however, in danger of lacking meaning; quite the contrary, we are gorged with meaning and it is killing us.

Jean Baudrillard 1929– : *The Ecstasy of Communication* (1987)

12 She understood, as women often do more easily than men, that the declared meaning of a spoken sentence is only its overcoat, and the real meaning lies underneath its scarves and buttons.

Peter Carey 1943– : *Oscar and Lucinda* (1989)

13 Often what a poet does not say is as important as what he does.
at a reading in Prague of Seamus Heaney's poetry, April 1996

Miroslav Holub 1923– : in *Sunday Times* 28 April 1996

Herman Melville 1819–91
American novelist and poet

14 Melville has the strange, uncanny magic of sea-creatures, and some of their repulsiveness. He isn't quite a land animal. There is something slithery about him. Something always half-seas-over.

D. H. Lawrence 1885–1930: *Studies in Classic American Literature* (1924)

1 Herman Melville who split the atom of the traditional novel in the effort to make whaling a universal metaphor.

David Lodge 1935– : *Changing Places* (1975)

2 He was perhaps the first American writer of fiction to see England and Europe not as America's historic past but as its grim potential future, and not as a pastoral space but as an industrial realm.

Malcolm Bradbury 1932–2000: *Dangerous Pilgrimages* (1995)

George Meredith 1828–1909
English novelist and poet

3 Meredith! Who can define him? His style is chaos illuminated by flashes of lightning.

Oscar Wilde 1854–1900: 'The Decay of Lying' (1891); see **35:6**

4 Meredith became, at his best, a sort of daintily dressed Walt Whitman.

G. K. Chesterton 1874–1936: *The Victorian Age in Literature* (1912)

Henry Miller 1891–1980
American novelist

5 It is true I swim in a perpetual sea of sex but the actual excursions are fairly limited.

Henry Miller 1891–1980: letter, 1 Febuary 1932

John Milton 1608–74
English poet

6 Oval face. His eye a dark grey. He had auburn hair. His complexion exceeding fair—he was so fair that they called him *the lady of* Christ's College.

John Aubrey 1626–97: *Brief Lives* 'John Milton'

7 Our language sunk under him, and was unequal to that greatness of soul which furnished him with such glorious conceptions.

Joseph Addison 1672–1719: *The Spectator* no. 297, 1712

8 The living throne, the sapphire-blaze,
Where angels tremble, while they gaze,
He saw; but blasted with excess of light,
Closed his eyes in endless night.

Thomas Gray 1716–71: *The Progress of Poesy* (1757)

9 Its perusal is a duty rather than a pleasure.

Samuel Johnson 1709–84: *Lives of the English Poets* (1779–81) 'Milton'

10 Milton, Madam, was a genius that could cut a Colossus from a rock; but could not carve heads upon cherry-stones.
    to Hannah More, who had expressed a wonder that the poet who had written Paradise Lost *should write such poor sonnets*

Samuel Johnson 1709–84: James Boswell *Life of Samuel Johnson* (1791) 13 June 1784

11 The reason Milton wrote in fetters when he wrote of Angels and God, and at liberty when of Devils and Hell, is because he was a true Poet, and of the Devil's party without knowing it.

William Blake 1757–1827: *The Marriage of Heaven and Hell* (1790–3)

1 Milton! thou shouldst be living at this hour:
England hath need of thee: she is a fen
Of stagnant waters: altar, sword, and pen,
Fireside, the heroic wealth of hall and bower,
Have forfeited their ancient English dower
Of inward happiness.

William Wordsworth 1770–1850:
'Milton! thou shouldst be living at
this hour' (1807)

2 The *Paradise Lost* though so fine in itself is a corruption of
our language—it should be kept as it is unique—a
curiosity, a beautiful and grand curiosity. The most
remarkable production of the world—A northern dialect
accommodating itself to Greek and Latin inversions and
intonation.

John Keats 1795–1821: letter to J.A.
Hessey, 8 October 1818

3 I have but lately been on my guard against Milton. Life to
him would be death to me. Miltonic verse cannot be
written but in the vein of art—I wish to devote myself to
another sensation.

John Keats 1795–1821: letter to
George and Georgiana Keats, 17
September 1819

4 The words of Milton are true in all things, and were never
truer than in this: 'He who would write heroic poems
must make his whole life a heroic poem.'

Thomas Carlyle 1795–1881: *Critical
and Miscellaneous Essays* (1838)

5 O mighty-mouth'd inventor of harmonies,
O skilled to sing of Time or Eternity,
God-gifted organ-voice of England,
Milton, a name to resound for ages.

Alfred, Lord Tennyson 1809–92:
'Milton' (1847)

6 Formerly Milton's *Paradise Lost* had been my chief
favourite, and in my excursions during the voyage of the
Beagle, when I could take only a single volume, I always
chose Milton.

Charles Darwin 1809–82: Francis
Darwin (ed.) *The Life and Letters of
Charles Darwin* (1887)

7 No man can get the full flavour of Milton's poetry who is
not able, by knowledge of Latin, to derive the words as he
goes on.

George Gissing 1857–1903:
Commonplace Book (1962)

8 He was the first of the masculinists. He deals in horror and
immensity and squalor and sublimity but never in the
passions of the human heart. Has any great poem ever let
in so little light upon one's own joys and sorrows? I get no
help in judging life; I scarcely feel that Milton lived or
knew men and women.

Virginia Woolf 1882–1941: diary,
1918; *Diary of Virginia Woolf* (1977)
vol. 1

9 After the erection of the Chinese Wall of Milton, blank
verse has suffered not only arrest but retrogression.

T. S. Eliot 1888–1965: *Selected Essays*
(1932) 'Christopher Marlowe'

10 I should say that Milton's experience of propaganda is
what makes his later poetry so very dramatic; that is,
though he is a furious partisan, he can always imagine
with all its force exactly what the reply of the opponent
would be.

William Empson 1906–84: *Milton's
God* (1961)

Mishaps

11 O Diamond! Diamond! thou little knowest the mischief
done!
*to a dog, who knocked over a candle which set fire to some
papers and thereby 'destroyed the almost finished labours of
some years'*

Isaac Newton 1642–1727: Thomas
Maude *Wensley-Dale . . . a Poem*
(1773); probably apocryphal

1 The play-bill, which is said to have announced the tragedy of Hamlet, the character of the Prince of Denmark being left out.
commonly alluded to as 'Hamlet without the Prince'

Sir Walter Scott 1771–1832: *The Talisman* (1825)

2 I began *again* at the beginning. Early the day after tomorrow (after a hard and quite novel kind of battle) I count on having the First Chapter on paper a second time, no worse than it was, though considerably different.
*after John Stuart Mill's housemaid had accidentally burnt the manuscript of **Carlyle**'s* The French Revolution

Thomas Carlyle 1795–1881: letter to his brother John Carlyle, 23 March 1835

3 What do you think of this for a misprint: 'idle vistas and melancholy nooks'—'*idle sisters and melancholy monks*'!!

Henry James 1843–1916: letter, 13 June 1874

4 Last night the lamp exploded here and before I could run back into the room the whole round table was in a blaze, books, cigarettes, MS—alas. The whole second part of *End of the Tether* . . . This morning looking at the pile of charred paper—MS and typed copy—my head swam; it seemed to me the earth was turning backwards.

Joseph Conrad 1857–1924: letter to Ford Madox Ford, 24 June 1902; see **298:7**

5 It is nice, but in one of the chapters the author made a mistake. He describes the sun as rising twice on the same day.
*comment on **Dostoevsky**'s novel* Crime and Punishment

Paul Dirac 1902–84: G. Gamow *Thirty Years that Shook Physics* (1966)

6 I have always maintained that one of the lesser reasons for its success was a misprint. At one point Elizabeth wrote: 'Take 2/3 eggs . . . ' She did not however, notice when correcting the proofs that the compositor had printed: 'Take 23 eggs.' Visions of delicious plenty—for 1950!
on the popularity of Elizabeth David's Mediterranean Food

John Lehmann 1907–87: *The Ample Proposition* (1966)

7 I can only suppose that I was so intent on *misprints* I never saw staggering great absurdities; this is a kind of mistake I never thought to guard against. Nor do I well see how I could. *But how many more are there?* I can see myself joining Bowdler and Grainger: '*to larkinise*, v.t., to omit that part of poem printed on verso and subsequent pages, from a notorious anthology published in later half of 20th century'.
on his accidentally omitting sections of two poems from the Oxford Book of Twentieth-Century Verse

Philip Larkin 1922–85: letter, 11 April 1973

8 Everything went wrong with that poem: I got the hands wrong—it's right-hand gauntlet really—and anyway the hands were a nineteenth-century addition, not pre-Baroque at all. A friend of mine who visited the tomb in Chichester Cathedral told me that the guide said, 'A poem was written about this tomb by Philip Spender.' Muddle to the end.
on 'An Arundel Tomb'

Philip Larkin 1922–85: *Viewpoints: Poets in Conversation with John Haffenden* (1981)

9 On the books pages of the Saturday Review, page 10, May 1, we referred to 'the obtuse Elizabethan poet, Fulke Greville'. The writer of the piece meant to say abstruse, not obtuse.

Anonymous: 'Corrections and clarifications', in *Guardian* 6 May 1999

Molière 1622–73
French comic dramatist

1 *Il plaît à tout le monde, et ne saurait se plaire.*
He pleases all the world, but cannot please himself.

Nicolas Boileau 1636–1711: 'À M. de Molière'

Money see also Earning a Living

2 What! all this for a song?
 *to Queen Elizabeth, on being ordered to make a gratuity of £100 to **Spenser** in return for some poems*

William Cecil 1520–98: Edmund Spenser *The Faerie Queene* (1751 ed.) 'The Life of Mr Edmund Spenser' by Thomas Birch

3 It is much more easy to write on money than to obtain it, and those who gain it jest much at those who only write about it.

Voltaire 1694–1778: *Philosophical Dictionary* (1764)

4 I have imbibed such a love for money that I keep some sequins in a drawer to count, and cry over them once a week.

Lord Byron 1788–1824: letter, 27 January 1819

5 Money, which represents the prose of life, and which is hardly spoken of in parlours without an apology, is, in its effects and laws, as beautiful as roses.

Ralph Waldo Emerson 1803–82: *Essays. Second Series* (1844) 'Nominalist and Realist'

6 'And what dun they gi'e thee for that, lad?'
 'Fifty pounds, father.'
 'Fifty pounds!' He was dumbfounded, and looked at me with shrewd eyes, as if I were a swindler. 'Fifty pounds! An' tha's niver done a day's hard work in thy life.'
 *on hearing what his son, D. H. **Lawrence**, had received for* The White Peacock

John Arthur Lawrence d. 1924: c.1911; D. H. Lawrence *The Phoenix* (1936)

7 I'm tired of Love: I'm still more tired of Rhyme.
 But Money gives me pleasure all the time.

Hilaire Belloc 1870–1953: 'Fatigued' (1923)

8 We are having *two* water closets made, one paid for by Mrs Dalloway, the other by The Common Reader.

Virginia Woolf 1882–1941: letter to Vita Sackville-West, 17 February 1926

9 We were just in a financial position to afford Shakespeare at the moment when he presented himself!

John Maynard Keynes 1883–1946: *A Treatise on Money* (1930)

10 If you want to get rich from writing, write the sort of thing that's read by persons who move their lips when reading.

Don Marquis 1878–1937: attributed

11 I should like to see the custom introduced of readers who are pleased with a book sending the author some small cash token: anything between half-a-crown and a hundred pounds . . . Not more than a hundred pounds—that would be bad for my character—not less than half-a-crown—that would do no good to yours.

Cyril Connolly 1903–74: *Enemies of Promise* (1938)

12 If there's no money in poetry, neither is there poetry in money.

Robert Graves 1895–1985: speech at London School of Economics, 6 December 1963

13 Of all novelists in any country, Trollope best understands the role of money. Compared with him, even Balzac is too romantic.

W. H. Auden 1907–73: *Forewords and Afterwords* (1973)

14 It is well known that, when two authors meet, they at once start talking about money—like everyone else.

V. S. Pritchett 1900–97: in *The Author* Spring 1978

1 We all need money, but there are degrees of desperation.

Anthony Burgess 1917–93: in *Face* December 1984

2 Never make your publisher pay the postage is the first rule of literary life.

Julian Barnes 1946– : *Something to Declare* (2002)

3 There's never been much love lost between literature and the market. The consumer economy loves a product that sells at a premium, wears out quickly or is susceptible to regular improvement . . . A classic work of literature is inexpensive, infinitely re-usable, and, worst of all, unimprovable.

Jonathan Franzen 1959– : *How to be Alone* (2002) 'Why bother?'

Montaigne 1533–92 see also **95:1**
French essayist

4 The great merit of Montaigne . . . was, that he may be said to have been the first who had the courage to say as an author what he felt as a man.

William Hazlitt 1778–1830: *Lectures on the English Comic Writers* (1818)

Marianne Moore 1887–1972
American poet

5 If she speaks of a chair you can practically sit on it.

Elizabeth Bishop 1911–79: notebook, c.1934/5; D. Kalstone *Becoming a Poet* (1989)

Morality

6 He who would not be frustrate of his hope to write well hereafter in laudable things, ought himself to be a true poem.

John Milton 1608–74: *An Apology for Smectymnuus* (1642)

7 Upon the accuracy with which similitude in dissimilitude, and dissimilitude in similitude are perceived, depend our taste and moral feelings.

William Wordsworth 1770–1850: preface to *Lyrical Ballads* (1800)

8 The reading or non-reading a book—will never keep down a single petticoat.

Lord Byron 1788–1824: letter to Richard Hoppner, 29 October 1819

9 We know no spectacle so ridiculous as the British public in one of its periodical fits of morality.

Lord Macaulay 1800–59: *Essays Contributed to the Edinburgh Review* (1843) 'Moore's *Life of Lord Byron*'

10 Conventionality is not morality. Self-righteousness is not religion. To attack the first is not to assail the last. To pluck the mask from the face of the Pharisee, is not to lift an impious hand to the Crown of Thorns.

Charlotte Brontë 1816–55: *Jane Eyre* (2nd ed., 1848) preface

11 It is a noble grand book, whoever wrote it—but Miss Evans' life taken at the best construction, does so jar against the beautiful book that one cannot help hoping against hope.
   on first hearing of the true identity of '*George **Eliot**'*, author of* Adam Bede

Elizabeth Gaskell 1810–65: letter to George Smith, 4 August 1859

1 But a man or woman who publishes writings inevitably assumes the office of teacher or influences the public mind . . . He can no more escape influencing the moral taste, and with it the action of the intelligence, than a setter of fashion in furniture and dress can fill the shops with his designs and leave the garniture of persons and houses unaffected by his industry.

George Eliot 1819–80: attributed

2 A novel which does moral injury to a dozen imbeciles, and has bracing results upon a thousand intellects of normal vigour, can justify its existence; and probably a novel was never written by the purest minded author for which there could not be found some moral invalid or other whom it was capable of harming.

Thomas Hardy 1840–1928: in *The Forum* March 1888 'The Profitable Reading of Fiction'

3 There is no such thing as a moral or an immoral book. Books are well written, or badly written.

Oscar Wilde 1854–1900: *The Picture of Dorian Gray* (1891)

4 I believe that literature is the principal voice of the conscience, and it is its duty age after age to affirm its morality against the specific moralities of clergymen and churches; and of kings and parliaments and peoples.

W. B. Yeats 1865–1939: letter to the Editor of the *Freeman's Journal*, 14 November 1901

5 *No* novel worth anything can be anything but a novel 'with a purpose', and if anyone who cared for the moral issue did not see in my work that *I* care for it, I should have no-one to blame but myself—or at least my inadequate means of rendering my effects.

Edith Wharton 1862–1937: letter to Morgan Dix, 5 December 1905

6 As my poor father used to say
In 1863,
Once people start on all this Art
Goodbye, moralitee!

A. P. Herbert 1890–1971: 'Lines for a Worthy Person' (1930)

7 Morality in the novel is the trembling instability of the balance. When the novelist puts his thumb in the scale, to pull down the balance to his own predilection, that is immorality.

D. H. Lawrence 1885–1930: *Phoenix* (1936) 'Morality and the Novel'

8 Art may be served by morality: it can never be its servant. For the principles of art are eternal, while the principles of morality fluctuate with the spiritual ebb and flow of the ages.

Arthur Symons 1865–1945: Edmund White *The Burning Library* (1994); attributed

9 That a piece of writing is good doesn't override other considerations—moral considerations—when it comes to damaging others.

A. S. Byatt 1936– : *The Game* (1967)

10 The humanity of an artist's work is no guarantee that he is a decent human being.

Peter Hall 1930– : diary, 21 May 1978

11 Even fabulist fictions are moral. They are among the most moral of things. What's more moral than a fairy tale? Science fiction is dripping with message.

Margaret Atwood 1939– : in an interview, December 1986; Earl G. Ingersoll (ed.) *Margaret Atwood: Conversations* (1990)

12 As a form of moral insurance, at least, literature is much more dependable than a system of beliefs or a philosophical doctrine.

Joseph Brodsky 1940–96: 'Uncommon Visage', Nobel lecture 1987, in *On Grief and Reason* (1996)

1 There is an undeluded quality about the *Beowulf* poet's sense of the world that gives his lines immense emotional credibility and allows him to make general observations about life that are far too grounded in experience and reticence to be called 'moralizing'.

Seamus Heaney 1939– : introduction to his translation of *Beowulf* (1999)

William Morris 1834–96
English writer, artist, and designer

2 I can't understand how a man who, on the whole, enjoys dinner—and breakfast—and supper—to that extent of fat—can write such lovely poems about Misery.

John Ruskin 1819–1900: letter to Joan Agnew, 21 January 1870

3 He was quite aware of the greatness of this work, and used to recite passages from it, marking its swing by rocking from one foot to the other like an elephant.
   of Morris's Sigurd the Volsung

George Bernard Shaw 1856–1950: 'Morris as I Knew Him', introduction to May Morris *William Morris: Artist, Writer, Socialist* (1936) vol. 2

4 Of course he was a wonderful all-round man, but the act of walking round him has always tired me.

Max Beerbohm 1872–1956: letter to S. N. Behrman c.1953, in *Conversations with Max* (1960)

Motivation

5 Even if nature says no, indignation makes me write verse.

Juvenal AD c.60–c.130: *Satires*

6 The multitude of books is a great evil. There is no measure or limit to this fever of writing; everyone must be an author; some out of vanity to acquire celebrity; others for the sake of lucre or gain.

Martin Luther 1483–1546: *Table-Talk* (1569)

7 Shakespeare (whom you and every playhouse bill
Style the divine, the matchless, what you will)
For gain, not glory, wing'd his roving flight,
And grew immortal in his own despite.

Alexander Pope 1688–1744: *Imitations of Horace* (1737)

8 Instruction, Madam, is the pill; amusement is the gilding.

Samuel Richardson 1689–1761: lettter 22 September 1755

9 Some rhyme a neebor's name to lash;
Some rhyme (vain thought!) for needfu' cash;
Some rhyme to court the countra clash,
An' raise a din;
For me, an aim I never fash;
I rhyme for fun.

Robert Burns 1759–96: 'To J. S[mith]' (1786)

10 An old literary truth: What we write pleases us, otherwise we surely wouldn't have written it.

Johann Wolfgang von Goethe 1749–1832: *On Morphology* (1817) 'The Fate of the Manuscript'

11 I have no pleasure in writing myself—none, in the mere act,—though all pleasure in the sense of fulfilling a duty . . . My heart sinks whenever I open this desk, and rises when I shut it.

Robert Browning 1812–89: letter to Elizabeth Barrett, 11 March 1845

12 It needs a complex social machinery to set a writer into motion.

Henry James 1843–1916: *Hawthorne* 1879

13 One should write only those books from whose absence one suffers.

Marina Tsvetaeva 1892–1941: *Earthly Signs: Moscow Diaries, 1917–22* (2002)

1 God, what a hell of a profession to be a writer. One is one simply because one can't help it.

F. Scott Fitzgerald 1896–1940: letter, August 1935

2 The ruling fantasy which drove him to write: a sense of evil religious in its intensity.
*of Henry **James***

Graham Greene 1904–91: 'Henry James: the Private Universe' (1936)

3 I was driven into writing because I found it was the only way a lazy and ill-educated man could make a decent living. I am not complaining about the wages. They always seem to me disproportionately high. What I mind so much is the work.

Evelyn Waugh 1903–66: in *Nash's Pall Mall Magazine* March 1937

4 You don't write because you want to say something; you write because you've got something to say.

F. Scott Fitzgerald 1896–1940: Edmund Wilson (ed.) *The Crack-Up* (1945) 'Note-Books'

*the young Stephen **Spender** had told **Eliot** of his wish to become a poet:*
5 I can understand your wanting to write poems, but I don't quite know what you mean by 'being a poet' . . .

T. S. Eliot 1888–1965: Stephen Spender *World within World* (1951)

6 In the same way that a woman becomes a prostitute. First I did it to please myself, then I did it to please my friends, and finally I did it for money.
when asked how he became a writer

Ferenc Molnar 1878–1972: attributed

7 I write in order to discover on my shelf a new book which I would enjoy reading, or to see a new play that would engross me.

Thornton Wilder 1897–1975: in *Paris Review* 1956

8 The very impulse to write, I think, springs from an inner chaos crying for order, for meaning, and that meaning must be discovered in the process of writing or the work lies dead as it is finished. To speak, therefore, of a play as though it were the objective work of a propagandist is an almost biological kind of nonsense, provided, of course, that it is a play, which is to say, a work of art.

Arthur Miller 1915– : *The Collected Plays* (1958) introduction

9 There are three reasons for becoming a writer. The first is that you need the money; the second, that you have something to say that you think the world should know; and the third is that you can't think what to do with the long winter evenings.

Quentin Crisp 1908–99: *The Naked Civil Servant* (1968)

10 One needs a mentor, otherwise it's very lonely. You need someone to tell you to go on.

Paul Scott 1920–78: Hilary Spurling *Paul Scott* (1990)

11 What's writing? A way of escape, like travelling to a war, or to see the Mau Mau. Escaping what? Boredom. Death.

Graham Greene 1904–91: interview with John Mortimer, in *Sunday Times* 16 March 1980

12 That is why I write, and why I have to. When I feel swamped in my solitude and hidden by it, rendered invisible, in fact, writing is my way of piping up. Of reminding people that I am here.

Anita Brookner 1928– : *Look at Me* (1983)

13 It's probably a form of childish curiosity that keeps me going as a fiction writer. I . . . want to open everybody's bureau drawers and see what they keep in there. I'm nosy.

Margaret Atwood 1939– : in an interview, December 1986; Earl G. Ingersoll (ed.) *Margaret Atwood: Conversations* (1990)

1 Every writing career starts as a personal quest for sainthood, for self-betterment. Sooner or later, and as a rule quite soon, a man discovers that his pen accomplishes a lot more than his soul.

Joseph Brodsky 1940–96: *Less than One* (1986)

2 I sometimes get interested in stories because I notice a sort of blank—why hasn't anyone written about this? *Can* it be written about?

Margaret Atwood 1939– : in an interview, November 1989; Earl G. Ingersoll (ed.) *Margaret Atwood: Conversations'* (1990)

3 Helping to people a barely inhabited country with a race possessed of understanding.
his view of his purpose as a writer

Patrick White 1912–90: *Patrick White Speaks* (1990)

4 I think writing does come out of a deep well of loneliness and a desire to fill some gap. No one in his right mind would sit down to write a book if he were a well-adjusted, happy man.

Jay McInerney 1955– : in *Independent on Sunday* 19 April 1992

5 I write in order to replicate the information, the medicine, the balm we used to find in music.
on writing for an American black readership

Toni Morrison 1931– : in *Independent on Sunday* 26 April 1992

6 My fictional project has always been the invention or discovery of my own country.

Peter Carey 1943– : interview in *Boldtype* (online journal) March 1999

7 Reading, the love of reading, is what makes you dream of becoming a writer.

Susan Sontag 1933– : in *Writers on Writing: Collected Essays from The New York Times* (2001)

8 Wodehouse never burdened himself with the task of justifying the ways of God to Man, but only of making Man, for a few hours at a time, inextinguishably happy.

Douglas Adams 1952–2001: introduction to *Sunset at Blandings*; in *The Salmon of Doubt* (2002); see **245:1**

9 For me it's therapy. Anything that's going in my life, anything like that, I just give to Rebus as a plot. So I'm working through my worries through him.

Ian Rankin 1960– : in *Observer* 18 March 2001

10 I know, without sounding too masochistic, that I must not only write but keep writing, keep on the point of the sword.

Edna O'Brien 1932– : in *Observer* 28 April 2002

11 Perhaps we need to play out our fears within the safe confines of the imaginary, as a sort of hopeful exorcism.

Ian McEwan 1948– : in *Paris Review* Summer 2002

12 Slowly but surely the pen became mightier than the double-quick pick-up timestep with shuffle.
on switching her ambitions from a career as a dancer to one as an author

Zadie Smith 1975– : in *Independent* 7 September 2002

Movements and Trends

13 Come leave the loathsome stage,
And the more loathsome age
Where pride and impudence in faction knit,
Usurp the chair of wit . . .
Say that thou pour'st them wheat,
And they would acorns eat;
Twere simple fury, still thyself to waste
On such as have no taste.

Ben Jonson c.1573–1637: 'Ode to Himself'

1 The next Augustan age will dawn on the other side of the Atlantic. There will, perhaps, be a Thucydides at Boston, a Xenophon at New York, and, in time, a Virgil at Mexico, and a Newton at Peru. At last, some curious traveller from Lima will visit England and give a description of the ruins of St Paul's, like the editions of Balbec and Palmyra.

Horace Walpole 1717–97: letter to Horace Mann, 24 November 1774

2 About the beginning of the seventeenth century appeared a race of writers that may be termed the metaphysical poets . . . The metaphysical poets were men of learning, and to show their learning was their whole endeavour.

Samuel Johnson 1709–84: *Lives of the English Poets* (1779–81) 'Cowley'

3 It is proper that I should mention one other circumstance which disfigures these poems from the popular poetry of the day . . . The subject is indeed important! For the human mind is capable of excitement without the application of gross and violent stimulants.
   on the new popular literature

William Wordsworth 1770–1850: preface to *Lyrical Ballads* (1800)

4 The metaphysical school, which marred a good poet in Cowley and found its proper direction in Butler, expired in Norris of Bemerton.

Robert Southey 1774–1843: in *Quarterly Review* vol. 12 1814

5 The classical is health, the romantic sickness.

Johann Wolfgang von Goethe 1749–1832: *Sayings in Prose*

6 Wordsworth, Tennyson and Browning; or, pure, ornate, and grotesque art in English poetry.

Walter Bagehot 1826–77: in *National Review* November 1864, essay title

7 To say the word Romanticism is to say modern art–that is, intimacy, spirituality, colour, aspiration towards the infinite, expressed by every means available to the arts.

Charles Baudelaire 1821–67: *Curiosités Esthétiques* (1868)

8 Though the Philistines may jostle, you will rank as an
    apostle in the high aesthetic band,
If you walk down Piccadilly with a poppy or a lily in your
    medieval hand.

W. S. Gilbert 1836–1911: *Patience* (1881)

9 My choice is the old world—my choice, my need, my life.

Henry James 1843–1916: notebook, Boston, 25 November 1881

10 Consciousness, then, does not appear to itself chopped up in bits . . . It is nothing jointed; it flows. A 'river' or a 'stream' are the metaphors by which it is most naturally described. In talking of it hereafter, let us call it the stream of thought, of consciousness, or of *subjective life*.

William James 1842–1910: *Principles of Psychology* (1890) vol. 1

11 The nineteenth century dislike of Realism is the rage of Caliban seeing his own face in the glass.

Oscar Wilde 1854–1900: *The Picture of Dorian Gray* (1891)

12 It was only with the modern poets, with Goethe and Wordsworth and Browning, that poetry gave up the right to consider all things in the world as a dictionary of types and symbols and began to call itself a critic of life and an interpreter of things as they are.

W. B. Yeats 1865–1939: 'The Autumn of the Body' (1898)

13 Spliced cinematography in paintings and diarrhoea in writing.
    describing Futurism

Ezra Pound 1885–1972: letter to James Joyce, 6 September 1915

1 It is more than a technical accomplishment, or the vocabulary and syntax of an epoch; it is, what we have designated tentatively as wit, a tough reasonableness beneath the slight lyric grace.
  of the Cavalier poets

T. S. Eliot 1888–1965: 'Andrew Marvell' (1921)

2 In the seventeenth century a dissociation of sensibility set in, from which we have never recovered; and this dissociation, as is natural, was due to the influence of the two most powerful poets of the century, Milton and Dryden.

T. S. Eliot 1888–1965: 'The Metaphysical Poets' (1921)

3 A Movement in the Arts—*any* movement—leavens a whole Nation with astonishing rapidity: its ideas pour through the daily, the weekly and the monthly press with the rapidity of water pouring through interstices, until at last they reach the Quarterlies and disturb even the Academicians asleep over their paper baskets.

Ford Madox Ford 1873–1939: *Thus to Revisit* (1921)

4 The European moderns are all *trying* to be extreme. The great Americans just were it.

D. H. Lawrence 1885–1930: *Studies in Classic American Literature* (1923)

5 I am touched at your sending me a copy, for I feel that to your generation, which has taken such a flying leap into the future, I must represent the literary equivalent of tufted furniture and gas chandeliers.
  to F. Scott **Fitzgerald**, *who had sent her a copy of* The Great Gatsby

Edith Wharton 1862–1937: letter to F. Scott Fitzgerald, 8 June 1925

6 All our youth they hung about the houses of our minds like Uncles, the Big Four: H. G. Wells, George Bernard Shaw, John Galsworthy and Arnold Bennett.

Rebecca West 1892–1983: *The Strange Necessity* (1928)

7 Sodomhipped young men, with the inevitable sidewhiskers and cigarettes, the faulty livers and the stained teeth, reading Lawrence as an aphrodisiac and Marie Corelli in their infrequent baths, spew onto paper and canvas their ignorance and perversions, wetting the bed of their brains with discharges of fungoid verse. This is the art of today.

Dylan Thomas 1914–53: letter to Pamela Hansford Johnson, November 1933

8 The poets of the Romantic Movement gave an outlet to new ideas . . . beneath the crust of their age, just as the Metaphysicals had done for the new ideas of their time.

C. Day-Lewis 1904–72: *The Colloquial Element in English Poetry* (1947)

9 It is affectation that makes so many of today's writings, even the best among them, unbearable to me. The author takes on a tone that is not natural to him.

André Gide 1869–1951: *Ainsi Soit-il* (1952)

10 A group is always impressive to historians of literature.

Vladimir Nabokov 1899–1977: Alexander Pushkin *Eugene Onegin* (translated by Vladimir Nabokov, 1964)

11 The French fathered the Modern Movement, which slowly moved beyond the Channel and then across the Irish Sea until the Americans finally took it over, bringing to it their own demonic energy, extremism and taste for the colossal.

Cyril Connolly 1903–74: *The Modern Movement* (1965)

12 I think the emotional content of twentieth century English verse so far has been on the whole thinner than that of previous centuries.
  Larkin had edited the Oxford Book of Twentieth-Century Verse (*1954*)

Philip Larkin 1922–85: letter 20 January 1966

1 There certainly is a cult of the mad these days: think of all the boys who've been in the bin—I don't understand it. Chaucer, Shakespeare, Wordsworth, Hardy—it's the big, sane boys who get the medals.

Philip Larkin 1922–85: in *Guardian* 31 March 1973

2 Pinter, Wesker, Osborne and Arden suddenly showed up in the late fifties like the four horsemen—hoarse men—of the apocalypse.

Tom Stoppard 1937– : letter to Jon Bradshaw, 29 November 1976

3 This solemn pledge to abstain from truth was called socialist realism.

Alexander Solzhenitsyn 1918– : *The Oak and the Calf* (1980)

4 Post-modernism may be seen as the tendency to make ironic use of the stock images of the mass media, or to inject the taste for the marvellous inherited from the literary tradition into narrative mechanisms that accentuate its alienation.

Italo Calvino 1923–85: *Six Memos for the Next Millennium* (1992)

5 The morbid marriage of love and death which is the hallmark of the Romantic approach to life.

A. N. Wilson 1950– : *Penfriends from Porlock* (1988)

6 The introduction of realism into literature in the 18th century by Richardson, Fielding and Smollett was like the introduction of electricity into engineering.

Tom Wolfe 1931– : 'Stalking the Billion-Footed Beast' (1989)

7 For a serious young writer to stick with realism after 1960 required contrariness and courage.

Tom Wolfe 1931– : 'Stalking the Billion-Footed Beast' (1989)

8 [Roger Fry] gave us the term 'Post-Impressionist', without realising that the late twentieth century would soon be entirely fenced in with posts.

Jeanette Winterson 1959– : *Art Objects* (1995)

of the 'romanticism' of Rider Haggard, Robert Louis **Stevenson**, *and Rudyard* **Kipling**:

9 I think . . . they were the first British writers who woke up and said, My God, we've got an Empire and it stretches right round the world. We shouldn't still be writing parish pump novels.

Hammond Innes 1913–98: interview in *Daily Telegraph* 3 August 1996

10 From 1950 to 1999, the fictional genre of Ladlit provided British readers with a romantic, comic, popular male confessional literature . . . comic in the traditional sense that it had a happy ending . . . romantic in the modern sense that it confronted men's fear and final embrace of marriage, and adult responsibilities . . . confessional in the postmodern sense that the male protagonists and unreliable first-person narrators betrayed beneath their bravado the story of their insecurities, panic, cold sweats, performance anxieties, and phobias.

Elaine Showalter 1941– : Zachary Leader (ed.) *On Modern British Fiction* (2002) 'Ladlit'; see **199:2**

Iris Murdoch 1919–99
British novelist and philosopher

11 I liked the tousled, heel-less, ladder-stockinged little lady—crackling with intelligence but nothing at all of a prig.

George Lyttelton 1883–1962: letter, 10 June 1959

12 I do wish that she had not got involved in philosophy. If she had studied domestic science or trained to be a Norland nurse, I'm sure her books would have been much better.

Ivy Compton-Burnett 1884–1969: Francis King *Yesterday Came Suddenly* (1993)

1 My problem is not being great. I'm in the second league, not among the gods like Jane Austen and Henry James and Tolstoy.

Iris Murdoch 1919–99: attributed; in *The Times* 9 February 1999

Mystery see Crime and Mystery

Vladimir Nabokov 1899–1977
Russian novelist

2 I think like a genius, I write like a distinguished author, and I speak like a child.

Vladimir Nabokov 1899–1977: *Strong Opinions* (1973)

V. S. Naipaul 1932–
Trinidadian writer of Indian descent

3 I am the kind of writer that people think other people are reading.

V. S. Naipaul 1932– : in *Radio Times* 14 March 1979

4 My writing is like fine wine; the more you read, the more you get from it. Reading it once is like taking a dog to the theatre.

V. S. Naipaul 1932– : in *Sunday Times* 21 October 2001

Names

5 If you should have a boy do not christen him John . . . 'Tis a bad name and goes against a man. If my name had been Edmund I should have been more fortunate.

John Keats 1795–1821: letter to his sister-in-law, 13 January 1820

6 Call me Ishmael.

Herman Melville 1819–91: *Moby Dick* (1851)

7 Fiction-mongers collect proper names, surnames, etc.— make notes and lists of any odd or unusual, as handsome or ugly ones they see or hear—in newspapers (columns of births, deaths, marriages, etc.) or in directories and signs of shops or elsewhere fishing out of these memoranda in time of need the one that strikes them as good for a particular case.
    to a Mr Capadose, who had written to James about his use of the name in 'The Liar'

Henry James 1843–1916: letter 13 October 1896

8 I have fallen in love with American names,
The sharp, gaunt names that never get fat,
The snakeskin-titles of mining-claims,
The plumed war-bonnet of Medicine Hat,
Tucson and Deadwood and Lost Mule Flat.

Stephen Vincent Benét 1898–1943: 'American Names' (1927)

9 My characters always appear with their names. Sometimes these names seem to me affected, sometimes almost ridiculous; but I am obliged to own that they are never fundamentally unsuitable. And the proof that they are not, that they really belong to the people, is the difficulty I have in trying to substitute other names. For many years the attempt always ended fatally; any character I

Edith Wharton 1862–1937: *A Backward Glance* (1934)

unchristened instantly died on my hands, as if it were some kind of sensitive crustacean, and the name it brought with it were its shell.

1 Bingo Bolger-Baggins a bad name. Let Bingo = Frodo.
   on the first draft of The Lord of the Rings

J. R. R. Tolkien 1892–1973: note, c.1938; Humphrey Carpenter *J. R. R. Tolkien* (1977)

on being asked by William Carlos Williams how he had chosen the name 'West':
2 Horace Greeley said, 'Go West, young man. So I did.'

Nathanael West 1903–40: Jay Martin *Nathanael West* (1970)

3 He [James Joyce] liked to think how some day, way off in Tibet or Somaliland, some boy or girl reading that little book would be pleased to come upon the name of his or her home river.
   Joyce had worked 350 river names into the Anna Livia Plurabelle section of Finnegan's Wake

Richard Ellman 1918–87: *James Joyce* (1959)

4 If one uses an initial for one's principal character, people begin to talk about Kafka.

Graham Greene 1904–91: *In Search of a Character* (1961)

5 Proper names are poetry in the raw. Like all poetry they are untranslatable.

W. H. Auden 1907–73: *A Certain World* (1970)

6 There is a magical quality in names—to change the name is to change the character.

Graham Greene 1904–91: *Ways of Escape* (1980)

7 Why is it that her women have only Christian names and her men only surnames?
   on Simone de Beauvoir

Mavis Gallant 1922– : *Paris Notebooks: Essays and Reviews* (1986)

8 Names have to be appropriate. Therefore I spend a lot of time reading up on the meanings of names, in books like *Name Your Baby*.

Margaret Atwood 1939– : in an interview, December 1986; Earl G. Ingersoll (ed.) *Margaret Atwood: Conversations* (1990)

9 Names, once they are in common use, quickly become mere sounds, their etymology being buried, like so many of the earth's marvels, beneath the dust of habit.

Salman Rushdie 1947– : *The Satanic Verses* (1988)

pointing out that if she had kept her first husband's name she would still be 'Mrs Wisdom':
10 That would have been asking for trouble.

Doris Lessing 1919– : in *Times* 15 July 2000

Narrative see Plot and Narrative

Nature

11 Nature never set forth the earth in so rich tapestry as diverse poets have done . . . her world is brazen, the poets only deliver a golden.

Philip Sidney 1554–86: *The Defence of Poetry* (1595)

12 And this our life, exempt from public haunt,
Finds tongues in trees, books in the running brooks,
Sermons in stones, and good in everything.

William Shakespeare 1564–1616: *As You Like It* (1599)

13   I have learned
To look on nature, not as in the hour
Of thoughtless youth; but hearing oftentimes
The still, sad music of humanity.

William Wordsworth 1770–1850: 'Lines composed . . . above Tintern Abbey' (1798)

1 Wordsworth this evening related a pretty anecdote of his cook-maid. A stranger who was shown about the grounds, asked to see his study. The servant took him to the library and said: 'This is master's library, but he studies in the fields.'

Henry Crabb Robinson 1775–1867: diary, 7 January 1846

2 What a book a devil's chaplain might write on the clumsy, wasteful, blundering, low, and horridly cruel works of nature!

Charles Darwin 1809–82: letter to J. D. Hooker, 13 July 1856

3 No matter how often you knock at nature's door, she won't answer in words you can understand—for Nature is dumb. She'll vibrate and moan like a violin, but you mustn't expect a song.

Ivan Turgenev 1818–83: *On the Eve* (1860)

4 As a contribution to natural history the work is negligible.
  review of The Wind in the Willows

E. V. Lucas 1868–1938: in *Times Literary Supplement* 22 October 1908

5 Poems are made by fools like me,
But only God can make a tree.

Joyce Kilmer 1886–1918: 'Trees' (1914)

6 What happens when you idealize the soil, the mother-earth, and really go back to it? Then with overwhelming conviction it is borne in upon you, as it was upon Thomas Hardy, that the whole scheme of things is against you.

D. H. Lawrence 1885–1930: *Studies in Classic American Literature* (1923)

7 Nature and letters seem to have a natural antipathy . . . they tear each other to pieces.

Virginia Woolf 1882–1941: *Orlando* (1928)

8 After reading Thoreau I felt how much I have lost by leaving nature out of my life.

F. Scott Fitzgerald 1896–1940: letter 11 March 1939

9 Landscape is a passive creature which lends itself to an author's mood.

T. S. Eliot 1888–1965: *After Strange Gods* (1934) 'Thomas Hardy'

10 His poetry is as redolent of the lair as it is of the library . . . Its sensuous fetch, its redolence of blood and gland and grass and water, recalled English poetry in the fifties from a too suburban aversion of attention from the elemental.
  of Ted **Hughes**

Seamus Heaney 1939– : Beckman lecture, 1976; in *Finders Keepers* (2002)

11 I'm replacing some of the timber used up by my books. Books are just trees with squiggles on them.
  on growing trees

Hammond Innes 1913–98: interview in *Radio Times* 18 August 1984

12 Nature poetry is always a form of disguised social comment. It may face the campfire and the darkness of the cave, but its back is to the daylight.

Tom Paulin 1949– : *Minotaur: Poetry and the Nation State* (1992)

Newspapers and Magazines see also Journalism

13 It is to be noted that when any part of this paper appears dull there is a design in it.

Richard Steele 1672–1729: in *The Tatler* 7 July 1709

14 The liberty of the press is the *Palladium* of all the civil, political, and religious rights of an Englishman.

'Junius': *The Letters of Junius* (1772 ed.)

15 The newspapers! Sir, they are the most villainous—licentious—abominable—infernal—Not that I ever read them—No—I make it a rule never to look into a newspaper.

Richard Brinsley Sheridan 1751–1816: *The Critic* (1779)

16 Your newspaper people are the only traders that thrive upon convulsion. In quiet times who cares for the paper? In times of tumult, who does not?

Walter Bagehot 1826–77: in *Inquirer* 1852 'The French Newspaper Press'

1 The purchaser [of a newspaper] desires an article which he can appreciate at sight; which he can lay down and say, 'An excellent article, very excellent; exactly *my own* sentiments.'

Walter Bagehot 1826–77: in *National Review* July 1856 'The Character of Sir Robert Peel'

the founder of the New York Herald *justifying as legitimate hoaxes the paragraphs of fictitious news which appeared in his paper:*

2 I am always serious in my aims, but full of frolic in my means.

James Gordon Bennett 1800–72: in *Dictionary of National Biography* (1917–)

3 Newspaper editors sport daily with the names of men of whom they do not hesitate to publish almost the severest words that can be uttered; but let an editor be himself attacked, even without his name, and he thinks that the thunderbolt of heaven should fall upon the offender.

Anthony Trollope 1815–82: *Phineas Redux* (1874)

4 The screeching newspapers . . . for me, the danger that overtops all others.

Henry James 1843–1916: letter 20 April 1898

5 One of the many reasons why I should like to be a highly instructed Frenchman is, that I might have the luxury of appreciating as an exotic the peculiar blackguardism of an English sporting paper.

George Gissing 1857–1903: *Commonplace Book* (1962)

6 The Pope may launch his Interdict,
The Union its decree,
But the bubble is blown and the bubble is pricked
By Us and such as We.
Remember the battle and stand aside
While Thrones and Powers confess
That King over all the children of pride
Is the Press—the Press—the Press!

Rudyard Kipling 1865–1936: 'The Press' (1917)

7 We have in modern society a huge journalistic organism the 'critical' or review press which *must* be fed—there simply is not enough, nowhere near enough, good creative work to feed the 'critical' machine, and so reputations are manufactured to feed it, and works born perfectly dead enjoy an illusory life.

T. S. Eliot 1888–1965: letter 12 January 1920

8 It is the duty of newspapers to advocate a policy of optimism in the broadest sense and to declare almost daily their belief in the future of England.

Lord Beaverbrook 1879–1964: in 1922; Matthew Engel *Tickle the Public* (1996)

9 Of all the literary scenes
Saddest this sight to me:
The graves of little magazines
Who died to make verse free.

Keith Preston 1884–1927: 'The Liberators'

10 I do not know where the British and American papers get their scare headlines about me. I have never given an interview in my life and do not receive journalists. Nor do I understand why they should consider an unread writer as good copy.

James Joyce 1882–1941: letter, 10 November 1932

11 Small and obscure papers and reviews keep critical thought alive, and encourage authors of original talent.

T. S. Eliot 1888–1965: in *Criterion* January 1939

12 The *New Yorker* will be the magazine which is not edited for the old lady in Dubuque.

Harold Ross 1892–1951: James Thurber *The Years with Ross* (1959)

1 A good newspaper, I suppose, is a nation talking to itself.

Arthur Miller 1915– : in *Observer* 26 November 1961

2 News is whatever a good editor chooses to print.

Arthur MacEwen : Daniel J. Boorstin *The Image* (1961)

3 On the whole I would not say that our press is obscene. I would say that it trembles on the brink of obscenity.

Lord Longford 1905–2001: attributed, 1963

4 If you want to make mischief come and work on my papers.

Lord Beaverbrook 1879–1964: to Anthony Howard, in *Radio Times* 27 June (1981); attributed

5 A licence to steal money forever.
   of American newspapers

Rupert Murdoch 1931– : in *Washington Post* 24 July 1977

6 I'm with you on the free press. It's the newspapers I can't stand.

Tom Stoppard 1937– : *Night and Day* (1978)

7 It is unfair to confine *The New Yorker* to the theme of Angst, though at times the spirit of Franz Kafka and Sylvia Plath does seem to hang over its pages like a kitchen smell.

Robertson Davies 1913–95: speech, Toronto, 14 October 1993

The Novel see also Fiction

8 Sure no one will contend, that the epistolary style is in general the most proper to a novelist, or that it hath been used by the best writers of this kind.

Henry Fielding 1707–54: preface to Sarah Fielding *Familiar Letters* (1747)

9 'Oh! it is only a novel! . . . only Cecilia, or Camilla, or Belinda:' or, in short, only some work in which the most thorough knowledge of human nature, the happiest delineation of its varieties, the liveliest effusions of wit and humour are conveyed to the world in the best chosen language.

Jane Austen 1775–1817: *Northanger Abbey* (1818)

10 There are few works to which I am oftener tempted to turn for profit or delight, than to the standard productions in this species of composition. We find there a close imitation of men and manners; we see the very web and texture of society as it really exists, and as we meet it when we come into the world.
   on the novel

William Hazlitt 1778–1830: *Lectures on the English Comic Writers* (1818)

11 A fictitious narrative, differing from the romance, because the events are accommodated to the ordinary train of human events, and the modern state of society.

Sir Walter Scott 1771–1832: *Essay on Romance* (1824); see **100:5**

12 A novel is a mirror which passes over a highway. Sometimes it reflects to your eyes the blue of the skies, at others the churned-up mud of the road.

Stendhal 1783–1842: *Le Rouge et le noir* (1830)

13 The novel is a subjective epic in which the author requests permission to treat the world in his own way. So the only question is whether he has a way; the rest of it will follow of itself.

Johann Wolfgang von Goethe 1749–1832: *Art and Antiquity* (1816–32)

14 It is the test of a novel writer's art that he conceals his snake-in-the-grass; but the reader may be sure that it is always there. No man or woman with a conscience,—no man or woman with intellect sufficient to produce amusement, can go on from year to year without the desire of teaching.

Anthony Trollope 1815–82: *Ralph the Heir* (1871)

1 Fred's studies are not very deep . . . he is only reading a
novel.

George Eliot 1819–80: 'Rosamond Vincy' in *Middlemarch* (1871–2)

2 The regular resource of people who don't go enough into
the world to live a novel is to write one.

Thomas Hardy 1840–1928: *A Pair of Blue Eyes* (1873)

3 The advantages of the letter-system of telling a story
(passing over the disadvantages) are that, hearing what
one side has to say, you are led constantly to the
imagination of what the other side must be feeling, and at
last are anxious to know if the other side does really feel
what you imagine.

Thomas Hardy 1840–1928: notebook, April 1878

4 When I want to read a novel, I write one.

Benjamin Disraeli 1804–81: W. Monypenny and G. Buckle *Life of Benjamin Disraeli* (1920) vol. 6

5 I am of the opinion that the epistolary form is an
antiquated affair. It is all right when the gist of the matter
is in the letters themselves (e.g., in the case of a district
policeman who loves letter-writing), but as a literary form
it is no good in many respects: it puts the author into a
frame—that is its main weakness.

Anton Chekhov 1860–1904: letter 4 March 1886

6 One should not be too severe on English novels; they are
the only relaxation of the intellectually unemployed.

Oscar Wilde 1854–1900: in *Pall Mall Gazette* 4 August 1886

7 The only obligation to which in advance we may hold a
novel, without incurring the accusation of being arbitrary,
is that it be interesting.

Henry James 1843–1916: 'The Art of Fiction' (1888)

8 A novel is a living thing, all one and continuous, like any
other organism, and in proportion as it lives will it be
found, I think, that in each of the parts there is something
of each of the other parts.

Henry James 1843–1916: 'The Art of Fiction' (1888)

9 A triple-headed monster, sucking the blood of English
novelists.
   'Jasper Milvain' on the three-volume novel system

George Gissing 1857–1903: *New Grub Street* (1891)

10 A novel is an impression, not an argument.

Thomas Hardy 1840–1928: *Tess of the D'Urbervilles* (5th ed., 1892) preface

11 Essential characteristic of the really great novelist: a
Christ-like all-embracing compassion.

Arnold Bennett 1867–1931: diary, 15 October 1896

12 Fair held the breeze behind us—'twas warm with lovers'
   prayers.
We'd stolen wills for ballast and a crew of missing heirs.
They shipped as Able Bastards till the wicked nurse
   confessed,
And they worked the old three-decker to the Islands of the
   Blest.
   *responding to the statement that 'the three-volume novel is
   extinct'*

Rudyard Kipling 1865–1936: 'The Three-Decker' (1896)

13 What is a novel if not a conviction of our fellow-men's
existence strong enough to take upon itself a form of
imagined life clearer than reality and whose accumulated
verisimilitude of selected episodes puts to shame the pride
of documentary history?

Joseph Conrad 1857–1924: *A Personal Record* (1912)

1 I believe that all novels . . . deal with character, and that it is to express character—not to preach doctrines, sing songs, or celebrate the glories of the British Empire, that the form of the novel, so clumsy, verbose, and undramatic, so rich, elastic, and alive, has been evolved.

Virginia Woolf 1882–1941: 'Mr. Bennett and Mrs. Brown' (1924)

2 One consequence of the modern novel's shift away from realism and humanized representation is that art tends to become a game or a delightful fraud.

José Ortega y Gasset 1883–1955: *The Dehumanization of Art* (1925)

3 Yes—oh dear yes—the novel tells a story.

E. M. Forster 1879–1970: *Aspects of the Novel* (1927)

4 And here lies the vast importance of the novel, properly handled. It can inform and lead into new places the flow of our sympathetic consciousness and it can lead our sympathy away in recoil from things gone dead.

D. H. Lawrence 1885–1930: *Lady Chatterley's Lover* (1928)

5 A novelist must preserve a childlike belief in the importance of things which common sense considers of no great consequence.

W. Somerset Maugham 1874–1965: *A Writer's Notebook* (1949) written in 1933

6 What is writing a novel like?
The beginning: A ride through a spring wood.
The middle: The Gobi desert.
The end: Going down the Cresta run.

Edith Wharton 1862–1937: diary, 10 December 1934

7 Anyone could write a novel given six weeks, pen, paper, and no telephone or wife.

Evelyn Waugh 1903–66: Henry 'Chips' Channon diary, 16 December 1934

8   Novel writing is
A higher art than poetry altogether
In my opinion, and success implies
Both finer character and faculties
Perhaps that's why real novels are as rare
As winter thunder or a polar bear.

W. H. Auden 1907–73: *Letter to Lord Byron* (1936)

9 If you try to nail anything down in the novel, either it kills the novel, or the novel gets up and walks away with the nail.

D. H. Lawrence 1885–1930: *Phoenix* (1936) 'Morality and the Novel'

10 The novel is the one bright book of life.

D. H. Lawrence 1885–1930: *Phoenix* (1936) 'Why the novel matters'

11 I have written 349 novels, but all that amounts to nothing. I have not yet started the work I really want to do . . . When I am 40 I will publish my first real novel.

Georges Simenon 1903–89: in December 1937; Patrick Marnham *The Man Who Wasn't Maigret* (1992)

12 And in his own weak person, if he can,
Dully put up with all the wrongs of Man.

W. H. Auden 1907–73: 'The Novelist' (1938)

13 Just as the painter thinks with his brush and paints, the novelist thinks with his story.

W. Somerset Maugham 1874–1965: *The Summing Up* (1938)

14 Lady Peabury was in the morning room reading a novel; early training gave a guilty spice to this recreation, for she had been brought up to believe that to read a novel before luncheon was one of the gravest sins it was possible for a gentlewoman to commit.

Evelyn Waugh 1903–66: *Work Suspended* (1942) 'An Englishman's Home'

15 What, in fact, is a novel but a universe in which action is endowed with form, where final words are pronounced, where people possess one another completely and where life assumes the aspect of destiny?

Albert Camus 1913–60: *The Rebel* (1951) 'Rebellion and the Novel'

1 In our time the novel devours all other forms; one is almost forced to use it as the medium of expression.

Marguerite Yourcenar 1903–87: *Memoirs of Hadrian* (1955)

2 You can declare at the very start that it's impossible to write a novel nowadays, but then, behind your back, so to speak, give birth to a whopper, a novel to end all novels.

Günter Grass 1927– : *The Tin Drum* (1959)

3 I found that the novel enabled me to express the comic side of my mind and at the same time work out some serious theme.

Muriel Spark 1918– : 'How I Became a Novelist' (1960)

4 The economy of a novelist is a little like that of a careful housewife, who is unwilling to throw away anything that might perhaps serve its turn. Or perhaps the comparison is closer to the Chinese cook who leaves hardly any part of a duck unserved.

Graham Greene 1904–91: *In Search of a Character* (1961)

5 Too many people today who are writing novels are not novelists . . . A novelist enters the flesh of his characters, and has a need to live with other characters inside himself.

Georges Simenon 1903–89: TV interview with Roger Stephane, 1963

6 A great many novels nowadays are just travel books disguised, just travel books really.

Ivy Compton-Burnett 1884–1969: Hilary Spurling *Secrets of a Woman's Heart: the Later Life of Ivy Compton-Burnett* (1984)

7 A novel is balanced between a few true impressions and the multitude of false ones that make up most of what we call life. It tells us that for every human being there is a diversity of existences, that the single existence is itself an illusion in part . . . it promises us meaning, harmony, and even justice.

Saul Bellow 1915– : speech on receiving the Nobel Prize, 1976

8 The word 'novel', at root, means 'news', and no novelist, even though he explore no further than the closets and back stairs of his own home, can be without some news he wishes to bring.

John Updike 1932– : 'Melville's Withdrawal' (1981)

9 I still think novels are much more interesting than poems—a novel is so spreading, it can be so fascinating and so difficult.

Philip Larkin 1922–85: *Required Writing* (1983)

10 A novel that does not uncover a hitherto unknown segment of existence is immoral. Knowledge is the novel's only morality.

Milan Kundera 1929– : in *New York Review of Books* 19 July 1984

11 I do think that the novel, at its best, is a better picture of the human situation than the poem, because it has a broader impact; and the poem, or the lyric poem at any rate, is simply one emotion from one person.

Philip Larkin 1922–85: interview, BBC Radio 4, 29 March 1984

12 Writing novels preserves you in a state of innocence—a lot passes you by—simply because your attention is otherwise diverted.

Anita Brookner 1928– : John Haffenden (ed.) *Novelists in Interview* (1985)

13 I . . . see the novel as a vehicle for looking at society—an interface between language and what we choose to call reality.

Margaret Atwood 1939– : in an interview, March 1986; in *Paris Review* Winter 1990

14 I would say a novelist's proper job is to be sensitive to the way things look; I agree with Conrad that fiction is primarily a visual medium, and that there is something very concrete and valuable and eternal in any accurate description of the way things look.

Edmund White 1940– : interview in *Paris Review* 1988

1 Writing a novel is actually searching for victims. As I write I keep looking for casualties. The stories uncover the casualties.

John Irving 1942– : George Plimpton (ed.) *Writers at Work* 8th Series 1988

2 People assume that because a novel's invented it isn't true. In fact the reverse is the case. Biography and memoirs can never be wholly true, since they cannot include every conceivable circumstance of what happened. The novel can do that.

Anthony Powell 1905–2000: in *Independent* 25 November 1989

3 When you're a novelist, you're writing a play but you're acting all the parts, you're controlling the lights and the scenery and the whole business, and it's your show.

Robertson Davies 1913–95: in *Paris Review* 1989

4 All great novels, all true novels, are bisexual.

Milan Kundera 1929– : in *The Times* 16 May 1991

5 Put simply, the novel stands between us and the hardening concept of statistical man. There is no other medium in which we can live for so long and intimately with a character. That is the service a novel renders. It performs no less an act than the rescue and preservation of the individuality and dignity of the single being, be it man, woman or child.

William Golding 1911–93: attributed

6 Every novel is a story, but life isn't one, more of a sprawl of incidents.

Doris Lessing 1919– : *Under My Skin* (1994)

7 For me being a novelist was more than just working in one 'literary genre' rather than another; it was an outlook, a wisdom, a position; a position that would rule out identification with any politics, any religion, any ideology, any moral doctrine, any group.

Milan Kundera 1929– : *Testaments Betrayed* (1995)

8 A novelist must systematically desystematize his thought, kick at the barricade that he himself has erected around his ideas.

Milan Kundera 1929– : *Testaments Betrayed* (1995)

9 The word 'novel' itself now makes me feel ill.

V. S. Naipaul 1932– : in 1995; in *Observer* 18 August 1996

10 What novel can compete with the best of reportage?
to the centenary conference of the British Publishers' Association, 1996

George Steiner 1929– : in *Observer* 18 August 1996

11 The novel is not likely to die. There is no substitute, at least so far, that can handle psychological complexity and inwardness and reflection in the way that the novel can.

Julian Barnes 1946– : in *Paris Review* Winter 2000–2001

12 The novel, though a relatively late literary innovation, almost immediately crowded other forms aside. Its roots can be traced to travel writing, to essays, to narrative poetry, to lives of the saints, and to the French or Italian novella, but as a form it went off like a firecracker in the 1740s with the work of Richardson and Fielding.

Carol Shields 1935– : *Jane Austen* (2001)

13 Novels are never about what they are about . . . there is always deeper, or more general, significance.

Diane Johnson 1934– : in *Writers on Writing: Collected Essays from The New York Times* (2001)

1 Book of wisdom, exemplar of mental playfulness, dilator of sympathies, faithful recorder of a real world (not just the commotion inside one's head), servant of history, advocate of contrary and defiant emotions . . . a novel that feels necessary can be, should be, most of these things.

Susan Sontag 1933– : in *Writers on Writing: Collected Essays from The New York Times* (2001)

2 Lads don't write novels. They're down the pub. Being a writer means that you spend at least half your life by yourself; that's the defining thing. A lad is not a lad by himself, he's only a lad when he's with the lads.

Martin Amis 1949– : in *Guardian* 8 May 2002; see **189:10**

3 Novels help us to resist the temptation to think of the past as deficient of everything that informs the present.

Ian McEwan 1948– : in *Paris Review* Summer 2002

Omission see also **Editing**

4 Of every four words I write, I strike out three.

Nicolas Boileau 1636–1711: *Satire (2). A M. Molière* (1665)

5 Read over your compositions, and where ever you meet with a passage which you think is particularly fine, strike it out.

Samuel Johnson 1709–84: quoting a college tutor, James Boswell *Life of Samuel Johnson* (1791) 30 April 1773

6 Remove at least fifty superlatives in each chapter. Never say 'Oliver's burning passion for Helen'. The poor novelist has to make us believe in the burning passion without ever naming it: that would be immodest.

Stendhal 1783–1842: letter to Mme Gaulthier, 4 May 1834

7 When you read proof, take out adjectives and adverbs wherever you can.

Anton Chekhov 1860–1904: letter, 14 January 1887

8 There is but one art—to omit! O if I knew how to omit, I would ask no other knowledge. A man who knew how to omit would make an *Iliad* of a daily paper.

Robert Louis Stevenson 1850–94: letter to R. A. M. Stevenson, October 1883

9 As to the Adjective: when in doubt, strike it out.

Mark Twain 1835–1910: *Pudd'nhead Wilson* (1894)

10 A successful book is not made out of what is in it, but what is left out of it.

Mark Twain 1835–1910: letter to William Dean Howells, 23 February 1897

11 Omit needless words . . . A sentence should contain no unnecessary words, a paragraph no unnecessary sentences, for the same reason that a drawing should have no unnecessary lines and a machine no unnecessary parts.

William Strunk 1869–1946: *The Elements of Style* (1918)

12 I haven't quite reached the ruthless artistry which would let me cut out an exquisite bit that had no place in the context.

F. Scott Fitzgerald 1896–1940: letter, 9 August 1925

13 A tale from which pieces have been raked out is like a fire that has been poked. One does not know that the operation has been performed, but everyone feels the effect.

Rudyard Kipling 1865–1936: *Something of Myself* (1937)

14 The more you leave out, the more you highlight what you leave in.

Henry Green 1905–73: Jeremy Treglown *Romancing: The Life and Work of Henry Green* (2000)

15 There is a difference between a book of two hundred pages from the very beginning, and a book of two hundred pages which is the result of an original eight hundred pages. The six hundred are there. Only you don't see them.

Elie Wiesel 1928– : George Plimpton (ed.) *Writers at Work* (8th series, 1988)

1 The kind of theatre that interests me—the exercise of taking away, of finding the minimum means to express the maximum body of the content.

Harold Pinter 1930– : interview, in *Guardian* 12 October 2002

Eugene O'Neill 1888–1953
American dramatist

2 There's no finesse at all: he's the Dreiser of the stage. He writes with heavy pencils . . . But where he's wonderful, it's superb.

Arthur Miller 1915– : in *Paris Review* 1966

Opening Lines see also Closing Lines

3 In the beginning God created the heaven and the earth.

Bible: Genesis

4 Achilles' cursed anger sing, O goddess.

Homer: *The Iliad*

5 *Arma virumque cano.*
I sing of arms and the man.

Virgil 70–19 BC: *Aeneid*

6 *Nel mezzo del cammin di nostra vita.*
Midway along the path of our life.

Dante Alighieri 1265–1321: *Divina Commedia* 'Inferno'

7 Whan that Aprill with his shoures soote
The droghte of March hath perced to the roote.

Geoffrey Chaucer c.1343–1400: *The Canterbury Tales* 'The General Prologue'

8 Once upon a time . . .
traditional opening to a story, especially a fairy story

Anonymous: recorded from 1595

9 O! for a Muse of fire, that would ascend
The brightest heaven of invention.

William Shakespeare 1564–1616: *Henry V* (1599)

10 If music be the food of love, play on.

William Shakespeare 1564–1616: *Twelfth Night* (1601)

11 Yet once more, O ye laurels, and once more
Ye myrtles brown, with ivy never sere.

John Milton 1608–74: 'Lycidas' (1638)

12 Of man's first disobedience, and the fruit
Of that forbidden tree, whose mortal taste
Brought death into the world, and all our woe,
With loss of Eden.

John Milton 1608–74: *Paradise Lost* (1667)

13 As I walked through the wilderness of this world.

John Bunyan 1628–88: *The Pilgrim's Progress* (1678) pt. 1

14 I wish either my father or my mother, or indeed both of them, as they were in duty both equally bound to it, had minded what they were about when they begot me.

Laurence Sterne 1713–68: *Tristram Shandy* (1759–67)

15 It is a truth universally acknowledged, that a single man in possession of a good fortune, must be in want of a wife.

Jane Austen 1775–1817: *Pride and Prejudice* (1813)

16 Much have I travelled in the realms of gold,
And many goodly states and kingdoms seen.

John Keats 1795–1821: 'On First Looking into Chapman's Homer' (1817)

17 Oh, what can ail thee knight at arms
Alone and palely loitering?

John Keats 1795–1821: 'La belle dame sans merci' (1820)

18 Season of mists and mellow fruitfulness,
Close bosom-friend of the maturing sun.

John Keats 1795–1821: 'To Autumn' (1820)

1 I shall not say why and how I became, at the age of fifteen, the mistress of the Earl of Craven.

Harriette Wilson 1789–1846: *Memoirs* (1825); see **202:13**

2 It was a dark and stormy night.

Edward George Bulwer-Lytton 1803–73: *Paul Clifford* (1830)

3 There was no possibility of taking a walk that day.

Charlotte Brontë 1816–55: *Jane Eyre* (1847)

4 The boy stood on the burning deck
Whence all but he had fled.

Felicia Hemans 1793–1835: 'Casabianca' (1849)

5 Whether I shall turn out to be the hero of my own life, or whether that station will be held by anyone else, these pages must show. To begin my life with the beginning of my life, I record that I was born (as I have been informed and believe) on a Friday, at twelve o'clock at night. It was remarked that the clock began to strike, and I began to cry, simultaneously.

Charles Dickens 1812–70: *David Copperfield* (1850)

6 Call me Ishmael.

Herman Melville 1819–91: *Moby Dick* (1851); see **284:8**

7 It was the best of times, it was the worst of times.

Charles Dickens 1812–70: *A Tale of Two Cities* (1859)

8 This is the story of what a Woman's patience can endure, and what a Man's resolution can achieve.

Wilkie Collins 1824–89: *The Moonstone* (1868)

9 'Christmas won't be Christmas without any presents,' grumbled Jo, lying on the rug.

Louisa May Alcott 1832–88: *Little Women* (1868–9)

10 All happy families resemble one another, but each unhappy family is unhappy in its own way.

Leo Tolstoy 1828–1910: *Anna Karenina* (1875–7)

11 It is Christmas Day in the Workhouse.

George R. Sims 1847–1922: 'In the Workhouse—Christmas Day' (1879)

12 The opening was barred by a black bank of clouds, and the tranquil waterway leading to the uttermost ends of the earth flowed sombre under an overcast sky—seemed to lead into the heart of an immense darkness.

Joseph Conrad 1857–1924: *Heart of Darkness* (1902)

13 'Is there anybody there?' said the Traveller,
Knocking on the moonlit door.

Walter de la Mare 1873–1956: 'The Listeners' (1912)

14 If I should die, think only this of me:
That there's some corner of a foreign field
That is for ever England.

Rupert Brooke 1887–1915: 'The Soldier' (1914)

15 This is the saddest story I have ever heard.

Ford Madox Ford 1873–1939: *The Good Soldier* (1915)

16 When Gregor Samsa awoke one morning from uneasy dreams he found himself transformed in his bed into a gigantic insect.

Franz Kafka 1883–1924: *The Metamorphosis* (1915)

17 Once upon a time and a very good time it was there was a moocow coming down along the road and this moocow that was down along the road met a nicens little boy named baby tuckoo.

James Joyce 1882–1941: *A Portrait of the Artist as a Young Man* (1916)

18 Mr Salteena was an elderly man of 42.

Daisy Ashford 1881–1972: *The Young Visiters* (1919)

19 Stately, plump Buck Mulligan came from the stairhead, bearing a bowl of lather on which a mirror and a razor lay crossed.

James Joyce 1882–1941: *Ulysses* (1922)

1 In a hole in the ground there lived a hobbit.

J. R. R. Tolkien 1892–1973: *The Hobbit* (1937)

2 Last night I dreamt I went to Manderley again.

Daphne Du Maurier 1907–89: *Rebecca* (1938)

3 In my beginning is my end.

T. S. Eliot 1888–1965: *Four Quartets* 'East Coker' (1940)

4 *Aujourd'hui, maman est morte. Ou peut-être hier, je ne sais pas.*
Mother died today. Or perhaps it was yesterday, I don't know.

Albert Camus 1913–60: *L'Étranger* (1944)

5 It was a bright cold day in April, and the clocks were striking thirteen.

George Orwell 1903–50: *Nineteen Eighty-Four* (1949)

6 If you really want to hear about it, the first thing you'll probably want to know is where I was born, and what my lousy childhood was like, and how my parents were occupied and all before they had me, and all that David Copperfield kind of crap, but I don't feel like going into it.

J. D. Salinger 1919– : *Catcher in the Rye* (1951); see **201:5**

7 The past is a foreign country: they do things differently there.

L. P. Hartley 1895–1972: *The Go-Between* (1953)

8 To begin at the beginning: It is spring, moonless night in the small town, starless and bible-black.

Dylan Thomas 1914–53: *Under Milk Wood* (1954)

9 Lolita, light of my life, fire of my loins. My sin, my soul. Lo-lee-ta: the tip of the tongue taking a trip of three steps down the palate to tap, at three, on the teeth. Lo. Lee. Ta.

Vladimir Nabokov 1899–1977: *Lolita* (1955)

10 I was set down from the carrier's cart at the age of three; and there with a sense of bewilderment and terror my life in the village began.

Laurie Lee 1914–97: *Cider with Rosie* (1959)

11 If I am out of my mind, it's all right with me, thought Moses Herzog.

Saul Bellow 1915– : *Herzog* (1961)

12 It was the afternoon of my eighty-first birthday, and I was in bed with my catamite when Ali announced that the archbishop had come to see me.

Anthony Burgess 1917–93: *Earthly Powers* (1980)

13 At the age of fifteen my grandmother became the concubine of a warlord general.

Jung Chang 1952– : *Wild Swans* (1991); see **201:1**

14 Harry Potter was a highly unusual boy in many ways.

J. K. Rowling 1965– : *Harry Potter and the Prisoner of Azkaban* (1999)

Originality

15 The saying of the noble and glorious Aeschylus, who declared that his tragedies were large cuts taken from Homer's mighty dinners.

Aeschylus c.525–456 BC: Athenaeus *Deipnosophistae*

16 Nothing has yet been said that's not been said before.

Terence c.190–159 BC: *Eunuchus*

17 It is hard to utter common notions in an individual way.

Horace 65–8 BC: *Ars Poetica*

18 Not wrung from speculations and subtleties, but from common sense, and observation; not picked from the leaves of any author, but bred among the weeds and tares of mine own brain.

Thomas Browne 1605–82: *Religio Medici* (1643)

1 The original writer is not he who refrains from imitating others, but he who can be imitated by none.

François-René Chateaubriand 1768–1848: *Le Génie du Christianisme* (1802)

2 Never forget what I believe was observed to you by Coleridge, that every great and original writer, in proportion as he is great and original, must himself create the taste by which he is to be relished.

William Wordsworth 1770–1850: letter to Lady Beaumont, 21 May 1807

3 An original something, fair maid, you would win me To write—but how shall I begin? For I fear I have nothing original in me— Excepting Original Sin.

Thomas Campbell 1777–1844: 'To a Young Lady, Who Asked Me to Write Something Original for Her Album' (1843)

4 When Shakespeare is charged with debts to his originals, Landor replies, 'Yet he was more original than his originals. He breathed upon dead bodies and brought them life.'

Ralph Waldo Emerson 1803–82: *Letters and Social Aims* (1876)

5 Perhaps the hardest thing in all literature—at least *I* have found it so: by no voluntary effort can I accomplish it: I have to take it as it comes—is to write anything *original*. And perhaps the easiest is, when once an original line has been struck out, to follow it up, and to write any amount more of the same.

Lewis Carroll 1832–98: preface to *Sylvie and Bruno* (1889)

6 Blank cheques of intellectual bankruptcy.
   definition of catch-phrases

Oliver Wendell Holmes 1809–94: attributed

7 The history of art is the history of revivals.

Samuel Butler 1835–1902: *Notebooks* (1912)

8 It is not permitted to a man who takes up pen or chisel to seek originality, for passion is his only business, and he cannot but mould or sing after a new fashion because no disaster is like another.

W. B. Yeats 1865–1939: *Per Amica Silentia Lunae* (1918)

9 Another unsettling element in modern art is that common symptom of immaturity, the dread of doing what has been done before.

Edith Wharton 1862–1937: *The Writing of Fiction* (1925)

10 *Étonne-moi.*
   Astonish me.
     to Jean Cocteau

Sergei Diaghilev 1872–1929: Wallace Fowlie (ed.) *Journals of Jean Cocteau* (1956)

11 You merely loop the loop on a commonplace and come down between the lines.
     when asked how to make an epigram by a young man in the flying corps

W. Somerset Maugham 1874–1965: *A Writer's Notebook* (1949) written in 1933

12 Cliché hunting is a cruel and mischievous hobby—the badger digging of the literary blood sports.

Evelyn Waugh 1903–66: in *Tablet*, 3 December 1938

13 Where in this small-talking world can I find A longitude with no platitude?

Christopher Fry 1907– : *The Lady's not for Burning* (1949)

14 Tching prayed on the mountain and wrote MAKE IT NEW on his bath tub. Day by day make it new cut underbrush, pile the logs keep it growing.

Ezra Pound 1885–1972: *Cantos* (1954)

1 I've been influenced by Sophocles and Noël Coward.

Edward Albee 1928– : in *Paris Review* 1966

2 It is sometimes necessary to repeat what we all know. All mapmakers should place the Mississippi in the same location, and avoid originality.

Saul Bellow 1915– : *Mr Sammler's Planet* (1970)

3 Strong poets make . . . history by misreading one another, so as to clear imaginative space for themselves.

Harold Bloom 1930– : *The Anxiety of Influence* (1973)

4 Let's have some new clichés.

Sam Goldwyn 1882–1974: attributed, perhaps apocryphal

5 The slow discovery by a novelist of his individual method can be exciting, but a moment comes in middle age when he feels that he no longer controls his method, he has become its prisoner.

Graham Greene 1904–91: *Ways of Escape* (1980)

6 What obsesses a writer starting out on a lifetime's work is the panic-stricken search for a voice of his own.

John Mortimer 1923– : *Clinging to the Wreckage* (1982)

7 The task of the artist at any time is uncompromisingly simple—to discover what has not yet been done, and to do it.

Craig Raine 1944– : in *Observer* 21 August 1988 'Sayings of the Week'

George Orwell 1903–50
English novelist

8 He could not blow his nose without moralising on the state of the handkerchief industry.

Cyril Connolly 1903–74: in *Sunday Times* 29 September 1968

9 [Orwell] could recognize the putrescence seeping out of the pores of the time, and was unable to lift his nostrils clear . . . He never looked for the familiar deodorant of self-deception or sought out the sweetened balms of elegant literary evasion. He sniffed and wrote on the same quivering reflex.

Dennis Potter 1935–94: in *The Times* 5 October 1968

John Osborne 1929–94
English dramatist

10 Mr Osborne's reservoir of bile has swelled as his audience has dwindled.

Kenneth Tynan 1927–80: letter to *The Times*, 11 November 1973

11 I never deliberately set out to shock, but when people don't walk out of my plays I think there is something wrong.

John Osborne 1929–94: attributed, 1975

12 He had to be plied with extremely expensive champagne. He became more and more like the old Edwardian father he kept attacking in *Look Back in Anger*. That was what he always wanted to be. His fury in the 1950s was that he wasn't a rich squire.
   recording a 60th birthday TV interview, which was never used

Jonathan Miller 1934– : in *The Times* 27 December 1994

13 Lessons in feeling.
   his own description of his plays

John Osborne 1929–94: in *Guardian* 27 December 1994

Ovid 43 BC–AD c.17 see also **319:1**
Roman poet

1 Here are only numbers ratified; but, for the elegancy, facility, and golden cadence of poesy, *caret*. Ovidius Naso was the man: and why, indeed, Naso, but for smelling out the odoriferous flowers of fancy, the jerks of invention?

William Shakespeare 1564–1616: *Love's Labour's Lost* (1595)

2 Ovid, the soft philosopher of love.

John Dryden 1631–1700: *Love Triumphant* (1694)

3 As Ovid has sweetly in parable told,
We harden like trees, and like rivers grow cold.

Lady Mary Wortley Montagu 1689–1762: *Six Town Eclogues* (1747) 'The Lover'

4 Ovid remained classical even in exile: he looked for his suffering not in himself, but in his separation from the capital of the world.

Johann Wolfgang von Goethe 1749–1832: *Sayings in Prose*

5 Above all, Ovid was interested in passion. Or rather, in what a passion feels like to the one possessed by it. Not just ordinary passion either, but human passion *in extremis*— passion where it combusts, or levitates, or mutates into an experience of the supernatural.

Ted Hughes 1930–98: *Tales from Ovid* (1997)

Wilfred Owen 1893–1918
English poet

on his exclusion of Owen from The Oxford Book of Modern Verse:

6 I did not know I was excluding a revered sandwich-board man of the revolution and that somebody has put his worst and most famous poem in a glass-case at the British Museum—however if I had known it I would have excluded him just the same. He is all blood, dirt and sucked sugar stick.

W. B. Yeats 1865–1939: letter to Dorothy Wellesley, 21 December 1936

7 His verse, with its sumptuous epithets and large-scale imagery, its noble naturalness and the depth of meaning, had impressive affinities with Keats, whom he took as his supreme exemplar.

Siegfried Sassoon 1886–1967: *Siegried's Journey* (1945)

8 The only twentieth-century poet who can be read after Hardy without a sense of bathos.

Philip Larkin 1922–85: 'The War Poet' (1963), in *Required Writing* (1983)

Dorothy Parker 1893–1967
American critic and humorist

9 She is so odd a blend of Little Nell and Lady Macbeth. It is not so much the familiar phenomenon of a hand of steel in a velvet glove as a lacy sleeve with a bottle of vitriol concealed in its folds.

Alexander Woollcott 1887–1943: *While Rome Burns* (1934)

10 Four be the things I'd been better without:
Love, curiosity, freckles, and doubt.

Dorothy Parker 1893–1967: 'Inventory' (1937)

Boris Pasternak 1890–1960
Russian novelist and poet

1 A kind of masculine Emily Dickinson.

Vladimir Nabokov 1899–1977: Brian Boyd *Vladimir Nabokov: the American Years* (1991)

Walter Pater 1839–94
English essayist and critic

2 His prose has none of the freshness of life about it, resembling, in its elaborately cautious movements, a person in poor health making his way upstairs backwards on crutches.

John Carey 1934– : in *Sunday Times* 25 June 1978

Samuel Pepys 1633–1703
English diarist and naval administrator

3 He was a man known to his contemporaries in a halo of almost historical pomp, and to his remote descendants with an indecent familiarity, like a tap-room companion.

Robert Louis Stevenson 1850–94: *Familiar Studies of Men and Books* (1882)

4 Pepys lets us know that each of us inhabits a perpetually fluctuating environment, and that we are changed, moved and sometimes controlled by our inner tides and weather fronts even when we are most engaged in official functions.

Claire Tomalin 1933– : *Samuel Pepys: The Unequalled Self* (2002)

5 The greatest thing about Pepys, after the composition of the Diary, was his decision to preserve it.

Claire Tomalin 1933– : *Samuel Pepys: The Unequalled Self* (2002)

Harold Pinter 1930–
English dramatist

6 The weasel under the cocktail cabinet.
   on being asked what his plays were about

Harold Pinter 1930– : J. Russell Taylor *Anger and After* (1962)

7 A full house at the Aldwych for Pinter's *Old Times*. This elegant puzzle, as unaffecting and unhelpful as a crossword, held them rapt and respectful. At the end they clapped the solemn actors, whose demeanour implied that this was as *de trop* as whistling at Holy Communion.

Peter Nichols 1927– : diary, 12 July 1971

   on being telephoned by the Evening News *to ask if he had any comment to offer on the occasion of Harold Pinter's fiftieth birthday:*
8 I don't; it's only later I realize I could have suggested two minutes' silence.

Alan Bennett 1934– : *Writing Home* (1994) diary, 1 October 1980

9 Like Dickens, he can make one laugh in panic.

Simon Gray 1936– : Mel Gussow *Conversations with Pinter* (1994)

1 Oh, this dread word Pinteresque. It makes people reach for their guns. Or behave as if they were going to church. But when the audience is actually there, I am always gratified when I hear laughter. There is a great deal of humour in my plays.

Harold Pinter 1930– : in *Sunday Times* 9 July 1995

2 Harold has actually rung me up to say, 'I have a re-write. Page 37. Cut the pause'.

Peter Hall 1930– : in *The Times* 30 September 2000

Plagiarism

3 *Sic vos non vobis mellificatis apes.*
Sic vos non vobis nidificatis aves.
Sic vos non vobis vellera fertis oves.

Thus you bees make honey not for yourselves. Thus you birds build nests not for yourselves. Thus you sheep bear fleeces not for yourselves.
   on Bathyllus claiming authorship of certain lines by **Virgil**

Virgil 70–19 BC: attributed

4 *O imitatores, servum pecus.*

O imitators, you slavish herd.

Horace 65–8 BC: *Epistles*

5 Whatever is well said by another, is mine.

Seneca ('the Younger') c.4 BC–AD 65: *Epistulae ad Lucilium*

6 In comparing various authors with one another, I have discovered that some of the gravest and latest writers have transcribed, word for word, from former works, without making acknowledgement.

Pliny the Elder AD 23–79: dedication to *Natural History*

7 He buys up poems for recital
And then as 'author' reads.
Why not? the purchase proves the title.
Our words become his deeds.

Martial AD c.40–c.104: *Epigrammata*, tr. James Michie

8 It could be said of me that in this book I have only made up a bunch of other men's flowers, providing of my own only the string that ties them together.

Montaigne 1533–92: *Essais* (1580)

9 So all my best is dressing old words new,
Spending again what is already spent.

William Shakespeare 1564–1616: sonnet 76

10 They lard their lean books with the fat of others' works.

Robert Burton 1577–1640: *The Anatomy of Melancholy* (1621–51)

11 So, naturalists observe, a flea
Hath smaller fleas that on him prey;
And these have smaller fleas to bite 'em,
And so proceed *ad infinitum*.
Thus every poet, in his kind,
Is bit by him that comes behind.

Jonathan Swift 1667–1745: 'On Poetry' (1733)

12 Damn them! They will not let my play run, but they steal my thunder!
   on hearing his new thunder effects used at a performance of Macbeth, *following the withdrawal of one of his own plays after only a short run*

John Dennis 1657–1734: William S. Walsh *A Handy-Book of Literary Curiosities* (1893)

13 I hate like death the situation of the plagiarist; the glass I drink from is not large, but at least it is my own.

Alfred de Musset 1810–57: *La Coupe et les lèvres* (1832)

14 The truth is that the propensity of man to imitate what is before him is one of the strongest parts of his nature.

Walter Bagehot 1826–77: *Physics and Politics* (1872) 'Nation-Making'

1 When 'Omer smote 'is bloomin' lyre,
  He'd 'eard men sing by land an' sea;
  An' what he thought 'e might require,
  'E went an' took—the same as me!

Rudyard Kipling 1865–1936: 'When 'Omer smote 'is bloomin' lyre' (1896)

2 Great writers create; writers of smaller gifts copy.

W. Somerset Maugham 1874–1965: *A Writer's Notebook* (1949) written in 1917

3 Immature poets imitate; mature poets steal.

T. S. Eliot 1888–1965: *The Sacred Wood* (1920) 'Philip Massinger'

4 We writers all act and react on one another; and when I see a good thing in another man's book I react on it at once.

Stephen Leacock 1869–1944: *My Discovery of England* (1922) 'Impressions of London'

5 If you steal from one author, it's plagiarism; if you steal from many, it's research.

Wilson Mizner 1876–1933: Alva Johnston *The Legendary Mizners* (1953)

6 One must bear in mind that they can't steal your style, if you have one. They can only as a rule steal your faults.

Raymond Chandler 1888–1959: letter to Cleve Adams, 4 September 1948

7 Plagiarize! Let no one else's work evade your eyes, Remember why the good Lord made your eyes.

Tom Lehrer 1928– : 'Lobachevski' (1953 song)

8 My only excuse is that he [Shakespeare] is fair game, like the Bible, and may be made use of nowadays even for advertisements of soap and razors.

Ralph Vaughan Williams 1872–1958: programme note for his opera *Sir John in Love*; Simon Heffer *Vaughan Williams* (2000)

9 The history of literature is a history of appropriation . . . Literature, like property, is theft.
  in 1993, defending the writer David Leavitt against the charge of plagiarizing Stephen **Spender**'s World Within World

James Atlas 1949– : in *Daily Telegraph* 20 July 1996

10 All writers are thieves; theft is a necessary tool of the trade.

Nina Bawden 1924– : *Mothers: Reflections by Daughters* (1995)

11 It felt as if I had walked into my house and found a complete stranger in the kitchen helping himself to a beer from my fridge.
  on encountering what he believed to be a case of plagiarism

Ken Follett 1949– : in *Sunday Telegraph* 15 September 1996

12 It felt as if some woman had come out of nowhere saying she was my daughter's mother.
  on a false accusation of plagiarism

J. K. Rowling 1965– : in *The Times* 20 September 2002

Sylvia Plath 1932–63 see also **72:12**, **92:11**, **194:7**
American poet

13 Often, very often, Sylvia and I would talk at length about our first suicides, at length, in detail, in depth . . . Suicide is, after all, the opposite of the poem.

Anne Sexton 1928–74: *A Self-Portrait in Letters* (1978)

14 I see her as a kind of Hammer Films poet.

Philip Larkin 1922–85: letter, 15 November 1981

15 Her last poems . . . present themselves with all the pounce and irrefutability of a tiger lashing its tail.

Seamus Heaney 1939– : *The Government of the Tongue* (1988)

Plot and Narrative

1 Of plots and actions, the episodic are the worst. I call a plot 'episodic' in which the episodes or acts succeed one another without probable or necessary sequence.

Aristotle 384–322 BC: *Poetics*

2 With a tale forsooth he [the poet] cometh unto you, with a tale which holdeth children from play, and old men from the chimney corner.

Philip Sidney 1554–86: *The Defence of Poetry* (1595)

3 What a devil is the plot good for, but to bring in fine things?

George Villiers, 2nd Duke of Buckingham 1628–87: *The Rehearsal* (1672)

4 Ay, now the plot thickens very much upon us.

George Villiers, 2nd Duke of Buckingham 1628–87: *The Rehearsal* (1672)

5 The French writers do not burden themselves too much with plot, which has been reproached to them as a fault.

John Dryden 1631–1700: attributed

6 Digressions, incontestably, are the sunshine;—they are the life, the soul of reading;—take them out of this book for instance,—you might as well take the book along with them.

Laurence Sterne 1713–68: *Tristram Shandy* (1759–67)

7 Finished all of *Barnaby Rudge* yet published . . . I will read no more till the story is finished . . . I will not expose myself to further anxieties.

Henry Crabb Robinson 1775–1867: diary, 5 September 1841

8 I abhor a mystery. I would fain, were it possible, have my tale run through from its little prologue to the customary marriage in its last chapter, with all the smoothness incidental to ordinary life. I have no ambition to surprise my reader.

Anthony Trollope 1815–82: *The Bertrams* (1859)

9 In telling a tale it is, I think, always well to sink the personal pronoun. The old way, 'Once upon a time', with slight modifications is the best way of telling a story.

Anthony Trollope 1815–82: letter, 24 May 1868

10 We want incident, interest, action: to the devil with your philosophy.

Robert Louis Stevenson 1850–94: letter to John Meiklejohn, February 1880

11 Make-'em-laugh, make-'em-cry, make-'em-wait.
  formula for a successful novel

Charles Reade 1814–84: attributed

12 The whole secret of fiction and the drama—in the constructional part—lies in the adjustment of things unusual to things eternal and universal.

Thomas Hardy 1840–1928: notebook 23 February 1893

13 The Story is just the spoiled child of art.

Henry James 1843–1916: *The Ambassadors* (1909 ed.) preface

on being asked if novelists found plot-making their hardest task:
14 All ladies find it so except Miss Austen.

Charlotte Yonge 1823–1901: Christabel Coleridge *Charlotte Mary Yonge* (1903)

15 'The king died and then the queen died', is a story. 'The king died and then the queen died of grief' is a plot.

E. M. Forster 1879–1970: *Aspects of the Novel* (1927)

16 Intimacy is gained but at the expense of illusion and nobility. It is like standing a man a drink so that he may not criticize your opinions.
  on direct address to the reader

E. M. Forster 1879–1970: *Aspects of the Novel* (1927)

1 Stories tend to get out of hand, and this one has taken an unpremeditated turn.
   of the unplanned introduction of the 'Black Rider' into the story that was to become The Lord of the Rings

J. R. R. Tolkien 1892–1973: letter to his publisher, spring 1938; Humphrey Carpenter *J. R. R. Tolkien* (1977)

2 I suppose I was a natural story-teller, the kind of man who for the sake of his yarns would in prehistoric days have been given a seat by the fire and a special chunk of mammoth.

John Buchan 1875–1940: *Memory-Hold-the-Door* (1940)

3 A plot is like the bones of a person, not interesting like expression or signs of experience, but the support of the whole.

Ivy Compton-Burnett 1884–1969: 'A Conversation Between I. Compton-Burnett and M. Jourdain' (1945)

4 The structure of a play is always the story of how the birds came home to roost.

Arthur Miller 1915– : in *Harper's Magazine* August 1958

5 When in doubt have a man come through the door with a gun in his hand.

Raymond Chandler 1888–1959: attributed

6 No opera plot can be sensible, for in sensible situations people do not sing. An opera plot must be, in both senses of the word, a melodrama.

W. H. Auden 1907–73: in *Times Literary Supplement* 2 November 1967

7 The plot is not very important to me, though a novel must have one, of course. It's just a line to hang the washing on.

Ivy Compton-Burnett 1884–1969: Hilary Spurling *Secrets of a Woman's Heart: the Later Life of Ivy Compton-Burnett* (1984)

8 The Story has a magic necessary to our happiness.

Christina Stead 1902–83: *Ocean of Story* (1985)

9 With me it's story, story, story.

Bernard Malamud 1914–86: attributed

10 The narrative impulse is always with us; we couldn't imagine ourselves through a day without it.

Robert Coover 1932– : in *Time Out* 7 May 1986

11 If you're a writer, a real writer, you're a descendant of those medieval storytellers who used to go into the square of a town and spread a little mat on the ground and sit on it and beat on a bowl and say, 'If you give me a copper coin I will tell you a golden tale.'

Robertson Davies 1913–95: in *Paris Review* 1989

12 I don't have ugly ducklings turning into swans in my stories. I have ugly ducklings turning into confident ducks.

Maeve Binchy 1940– : in *Current Biography* November 1995

13 You do not think up a plot. You do not invent, you relate. The story is led by character. The character describes himself without knowing it.

V. S. Pritchett 1900–97: Clare Boylan (ed.) *The Agony and the Ego* (1993)

14 Story-telling is an instinct to come to terms with mystery, chaos, mess.

Graham Swift 1949– : Clare Boylan (ed.) *The Agony and the Ego* (1993); attributed

15 If I were asked what is the essence of storytelling I would say it is a simple thing: the relating of something strange.

Graham Swift 1949– : Clare Boylan (ed.) *The Agony and the Ego* (1993)

16 When I am thickening my plots, I like to think 'What if . . . What *if* . . . '

Patricia Highsmith 1921–95: Clare Boylan (ed.) *The Agony and the Ego* (1993)

17 Outlining is dangerous. I always describe a plot of a book as like footprints left in the snow after someone's run by. You must not put those footprints ahead of the person.

Michael Moorcock 1939– : Stan Nicholls (ed.) *Wordsmiths of Wonder* (1993)

1 In adult literary fiction, stories are there on sufferance. Other things are felt to be more important: technique, style, literary knowingness. The present day would-be George Eliots take up their stories as if with a pair of tongs. They're embarrassed by them. If they could write novels without stories in them, they would.

Philip Pullman 1946– : in *Independent* 18 July 1996

2 It is a ruse . . . which could not be achieved on film or television: long live the written word!
on a plot device employed by Ruth Rendell in The Keys to the Street *(1996)*

Antonia Fraser 1932– : in *Daily Telegraph* 7 September 1996

3 Narration is as much part of human nature as breath and the circulation of the blood.

A. S. Byatt 1936– : *On Histories and Stories* (2000)

4 The purpose of narrative is to present us with complexity and ambiguity. If life's lessons could be reduced to single sentences, there would be no need for fiction.

Scott Turow 1949– : in *Observer* 24 November 2002

Edgar Allan Poe 1809–49
American writer

5 Poe is a kind of Hawthorne and *delirium tremens*.

Leslie Stephen 1832–1904: *Hours in a Library* (1874)

6 There comes Poe, with his raven, like Barnaby Rudge, Three-fifths of him genius, and two-fifths sheer fudge.

James Russell Lowell 1819–91: *Poe and Longfellow* 'A Fable for Critics'

7 He was an adventurer into the vaults and cellars and horrible underground passages of the human soul. He sounded the horror and the warning of his own doom.

D. H. Lawrence 1885–1930: *Studies in Classic American Literature* (1924)

8 Poe . . . was perhaps the first great nonstop literary drinker of the American nineteenth century. He made the indulgences of Coleridge and De Quincey seem like a bit of mischief in the kitchen with the cooking sherry.

James Thurber 1894–1961: *Alarms and Diversions* (1957)

Poetry see also Rhyme and Rhythm

9 Painting is silent poetry, poetry is eloquent painting.

Simonides c.556–468 BC: Plutarch *Moralia*

10 So poetry is something more philosophical and more worthy of serious attention than history, for while poetry is concerned with universal truths, history treats of particular facts.

Aristotle 384–322 BC: *Poetics*

11 *At non effugies meos iambos.*
But you shall not escape my iambics.

Catullus c.84–c.54 BC: R. A. B. Mynors (ed.) *Catulli Carmina* (1958) Fragment 3

12 Skilled or unskilled, we all scribble poems.

Horace 65–8 BC: *Epistles*

13 Poetry is devil's wine.

St Augustine AD 354–430: *Contra Academicos*; see **212:3**

14 The poet ranks far below the painter in the representation of visible things, and far below the musician in that of invisible things.

Leonardo da Vinci 1452–1519: Irma A. Richter (ed.) *Selections from the Notebooks of Leonardo da Vinci* (1952)

1 Poetry therefore, is an art of *imitation* . . . that is to say, a representing, counterfeiting, or figuring forth to speak metaphorically. A speaking picture, with this end: to teach and delight.

Philip Sidney 1554–86: *The Defence of Poetry* (1595)

2 Poesy was ever thought to have some participation of divineness, because it doth raise and erect the mind, by submitting the shows of things to the desires of the mind; whereas reason doth buckle and bow the mind unto the nature of things.

Francis Bacon 1561–1626: *The Advancement of Learning* (1605)

3 Did not one of the fathers in great indignation call poesy *vinum daemonum?*

Francis Bacon 1561–1626: *The Advancement of Learning* (1605); *vinum daemonum* the wine of devils; see **211:13**

4 All poets are mad.

Robert Burton 1577–1640: *The Anatomy of Melancholy* (1621–51) 'Democritus to the Reader'

5 Blest pair of Sirens, pledges of heaven's joy, Sphere-born harmonious sisters, Voice, and Verse.

John Milton 1608–74: 'At a Solemn Music' (1645)

6 Things unattempted yet in prose or rhyme.

John Milton 1608–74: *Paradise Lost* (1667)

7 So poetry, which is in Oxford made An art, in London only is a trade.

John Dryden 1631–1700: 'Prologue to the University of Oxon . . . at the Acting of *The Silent Woman*' (1673)

8 Poetry's a mere drug, Sir.

George Farquhar 1678–1707: *Love and a Bottle* (1698)

9 He [the poet] must write as the interpreter of nature, and the legislator of mankind, and consider himself as presiding over the thoughts and manners of future generations; as a being superior to time and place.

Samuel Johnson 1709–84: *Rasselas* (1759)

10 BOSWELL: Sir, what is poetry? JOHNSON: Why Sir, it is much easier to say what it is not. We all *know* what light is; but it is not easy to *tell* what it is.

Samuel Johnson 1709–84: James Boswell *Life of Samuel Johnson* (1791) 12 April 1776

11 You will never be alone with a poet in your pocket.

John Adams 1735–1826: letter to John Quincy Adams, 14 May 1781

12 In common things that round us lie Some random truths he can impart,— The harvest of a quiet eye That broods and sleeps on his own heart.

William Wordsworth 1770–1850: 'A Poet's Epitaph' (1800)

requirement for a great poet:
13 The touch of a blind man feeling the face of a darling child.

Samuel Taylor Coleridge 1772–1834: letter, 13 July 1802

14 We poets in our youth begin in gladness; But thereof comes in the end despondency and madness.

William Wordsworth 1770–1850: 'Resolution and Independence' (1807)

15 I by no means rank poetry high in the scale of intelligence—this may look like affectation—but it is my real opinion—but it is the lava of the imagination whose eruption prevents an earthquake.

Lord Byron 1788–1824: letter to Annabella Milbanke, 29 November 1813

1 A long poem is a test of invention which I take to be the polar star of poetry, as fancy is the sails, and imagination the rudder.

John Keats 1795–1821: letter to Benjamin Bailey, 8 October 1817

2 She ventured to hope he did not always read only poetry; and to say, that she thought it was the misfortune of poetry, to be seldom safely enjoyed by those who enjoyed it completely; and that the strong feelings which alone could estimate it truly, were the very feelings which ought to taste it but sparingly.

Jane Austen 1775–1817: *Persuasion* (1818)

3 That willing suspension of disbelief for the moment, which constitutes poetic faith.

Samuel Taylor Coleridge 1772–1834: *Biographia Literaria* (1817)

4 The two cardinal points of poetry, the power of exciting the sympathy of the reader by a faithful adherence to the truth of nature, and the power of giving the interest of novelty by the modifying colours of imagination.

Samuel Taylor Coleridge 1772–1834: *Biographia Literaria* (1817)

5 Poetry should surprise by a fine excess, and not by singularity—it should strike the reader as a wording of his own highest thoughts, and appear almost a remembrance.

John Keats 1795–1821: letter to John Taylor, 27 February 1818

6 Most wretched men
Are cradled into poetry by wrong:
They learn in suffering what they teach in song.

Percy Bysshe Shelley 1792–1822: 'Julian and Maddalo' (1818)

7 We hate poetry that has a palpable design upon us—and if we do not agree, seems to put its hand in its breeches pocket. Poetry should be great and unobtrusive, a thing which enters into one's soul, and does not startle it or amaze it with itself, but with its subject.

John Keats 1795–1821: letter to J. H. Reynolds, 3 February 1818

8 If poetry comes not as naturally as the leaves to a tree it had better not come at all.

John Keats 1795–1821: letter to John Taylor, 27 February 1818

9 As to the poetical character itself, (I mean that sort of which, if I am any thing, I am a member; that sort distinguished from the Wordsworthian or egotistical sublime; which is a thing *per se* and stands alone) it is not itself—it has no self . . . It has as much delight in conceiving an Iago as an Imogen.

John Keats 1795–1821: letter to Richard Woodhouse, 27 October 1818

10 A poet is the most unpoetical of any thing in existence, because he has no identity; he is continually in for—and filling some other body.

John Keats 1795–1821: letter to Richard Woodhouse, 27 October 1818

11 The poet and the dreamer are distinct,
Diverse, sheer opposite, antipodes.
The one pours out a balm upon the world,
The other vexes it.

John Keats 1795–1821: 'The Fall of Hyperion' (written 1819)

12 Chameleons feed on light and air:
Poets' food is love and fame.

Percy Bysshe Shelley 1792–1822: 'An Exhortation' (1820)

13 Poetry is the record of the best and happiest moments of the happiest and best minds.

Percy Bysshe Shelley 1792–1822: *A Defence of Poetry* (written 1821)

14 Poets are the unacknowledged legislators of the world.

Percy Bysshe Shelley 1792–1822: *A Defence of Poetry* (written 1821)

15 It . . . purges from our inward sight the film of familiarity which obscures from us the wonder of our being. It compels us to feel that which we perceive, and to imagine that which we know.

Percy Bysshe Shelley 1792–1822: *A Defence of Poetry* (written 1821)

1 Perhaps no person can be a poet, or even enjoy poetry, without a certain unsoundness of mind.

Lord Macaulay 1800–59: 'Milton' (1825)

2 Scorn not the Sonnet; Critic, you have frowned, Mindless of its just honours; with this key Shakespeare unlocked his heart.

William Wordsworth 1770–1850: 'Scorn not the Sonnet' (1827)

3 Poetry is certainly something more than good sense, but it must be good sense at all events; just as a palace is more than a house, but it must be a house, at least.

Samuel Taylor Coleridge 1772–1834: *Table Talk* (1835) 9 May 1830

4 Vex not thou the poet's mind
With thy shallow wit:
Vex not thou the poet's mind;
For thou canst not fathom it.

Alfred, Lord Tennyson 1809–92: 'The Poet's Mind' (1830)

5 Poetry, in the most comprehensive application of the term, I take to be the flower of any kind of experience, rooted in truth, and issuing forth into beauty.

Leigh Hunt 1784–1859: *The Story of Rimini* (1832 ed.)

6 Poetry's unnat'ral; no man ever talked in poetry 'cept a beadle on boxin' day.
    spoken by 'Mr Weller'

Charles Dickens 1812–70: *Pickwick Papers* (1837)

7 The poets are full of false views: they make mankind believe that happiness consists in falling in love, and living in the country—I say: live in London; like many people, fall in love with nobody.

Sydney Smith 1771–1845: letter to Lady Dacre, 1837

8 What is a modern poet's fate?
To write his thoughts upon a slate;
The critic spits on what is done,
Gives it a wipe—and all is gone.

Thomas Hood 1799–1845: 'A Joke'; Hallam Tennyson *Alfred Lord Tennyson* (1897)

9 Not deep the Poet sees, but wide.

Matthew Arnold 1822–88: 'Resignation' (1849)

10 Everything you invent is true: you can be sure of that. Poetry is a subject as precise as geometry.

Gustave Flaubert 1821–80: letter to Louise Colet, 14 August 1853

11 We do not enjoy poetry unless we know it to be poetry.

Henry David Thoreau 1817–62: diary, 1 October 1856

12 What is poetry? . . . The suggestion, by the imagination, of noble grounds for the noble emotions.

John Ruskin 1819–1900: *Modern Painters* (1856)

13 Nay, if there's room for poets in this world
A little overgrown (I think there is)
Their sole work is to represent the age,
Their age, not Charlemagne's.

Elizabeth Barrett Browning 1806–61: *Aurora Leigh* (1857)

14 The poet is like the prince of the clouds, who rides out the tempest and laughs at the archer. But when he is exiled on the ground, amidst the clamour, his giant's wings prevent him from walking.

Charles Baudelaire 1821–67: *Les fleurs du mal* (1857) 'L'Albatross'—'Spleen et idéal'

15 The business of a poet is fundamentally to *see*, not to analyse.

Henrik Ibsen 1828–1906: letter, 1871

16 A sonnet is a moment's monument,—
Memorial from the Soul's eternity
To one dead deathless hour.

Dante Gabriel Rossetti 1828–82: *The House of Life* (1881)

17 Poetry is at bottom a criticism of life.

Matthew Arnold 1822–88: *Essays in Criticism* Second Series (1888) 'Wordsworth'

1 More and more mankind will discover that we have to turn to poetry to interpret life for us, to console us, to sustain us. Without poetry, our science will appear incomplete; and most of what now passes with us for religion and philosophy will be replaced by poetry.

Matthew Arnold 1822–88: *Essays in Criticism* Second Series (1888) 'The Study of Poetry'

2 The difference between genuine poetry and the poetry of Dryden, Pope, and all their school, is briefly this: their poetry is conceived and composed in their wits, genuine poetry is conceived and composed in the soul.

Matthew Arnold 1822–88: *Essays in Criticism* Second Series (1888) 'Thomas Gray'

3 You explain nothing, O poet, but thanks to you all things become explicable.

Paul Claudel 1868–1955: *La Ville* (1897)

4 We who with songs beguile your pilgrimage
And swear that beauty lives though lilies die,
We poets of the proud old lineage
Who sing to find your hearts, we know not why,—
What shall we tell you? Tales, marvellous tales
Of ships and stars and isles where good men rest.

James Elroy Flecker 1884–1915: *The Golden Journey to Samarkand* (1913) 'Prologue'

5 Poets in our civilization, as it exists at present, must be *difficult*.

T. S. Eliot 1888–1965: 'The Metaphysical Poets' (1921)

6 A poet's mind . . . is constantly amalgamating disparate experience; the ordinary man's experience is chaotic, irregular, fragmentary. The latter falls in love, or reads Spinoza, and these two experiences have nothing to do with each other, or with the noise of the typewriter or the smell of cooking; in the mind of the poet these experiences are always forming new wholes.

T. S. Eliot 1888–1965: 'The Metaphysical Poets' (1921)

7 Words in search of a meaning.

Roman Jakobson 1896–1982: 'The Newest Russian Poetry' (1919; revised 1921)

8 Poetry is a comforting piece of fiction set to more or less lascivious music.

H. L. Mencken 1880–1956: *Prejudices* (1922)

9 Poetry is the achievement of the synthesis of hyacinths and biscuits.

Carl Sandburg 1878–1967: in *Atlantic Monthly* March 1923

10 Poetry is the opening and closing of a door, leaving those who look through to guess about what is seen during a moment.

Carl Sandburg 1878–1967: in *Atlantic Monthly* March 1923

11 We make out of the quarrel with others, rhetoric, but of the quarrel with ourselves, poetry.

W. B. Yeats 1865–1939: *Essays* (1924) 'Anima Hominis'

12 Poetry has no role to play except beyond philosophy.

André Breton 1896–1966: *Les Pas Perdus* (1924)

13 A Poem should be palpable and mute
As a globed fruit
Dumb
As old medallions to the thumb
Silent as the sleeve-worn stone
Of casement ledges where the moss has grown—
A poem should be wordless
As the flight of birds.

Archibald MacLeish 1892–1982: 'Ars Poetica' (1926)

14 A poem should not mean
But be.

Archibald MacLeish 1892–1982: 'Ars Poetica' (1926)

1 It [poetry] is capable of saving us; it is a perfectly possible means of overcoming chaos.

I. A. Richards 1893–1979: *Science and Poetry* (1926)

2 The poet produces something beautiful by fixing his attention on something real.

Simone Weil 1909–43: *Gravity and Grace* (1927)

3 Genuine poetry can communicate before it is understood.

T. S. Eliot 1888–1965: *Dante* (1929)

4 Poetry is simply literature reduced to the essence of its active principle. It is purged of idols of every kind, of realistic illusions, or any conceivable equivocation between the language of 'truth' and the language of 'creation'.

Paul Valéry 1871–1945: *Literature* (1930)

5 The poet is a bird of strange moods. He descends from his lofty domain to tarry among us, singing; if we do not honour him he will unfold his wings and fly back to his dwelling place.

Khalil Gibran 1883–1931: *Thoughts and Meditations* (1960) 'The Poet from Baalbek'

6 The poet's business is not to describe things to us, or to tell us about things, but to create in our minds the very things themselves.

Lascelles Abercrombie 1881–1938: *Poetry: Its Music and Meaning* (1932)

7 A year or two ago . . . I received from America a request that I would define poetry. I replied that I could no more define poetry than a terrier can define a rat, but that I thought we both recognized the object by the symptoms which it provokes in us.

A. E. Housman 1859–1936: *The Name and Nature of Poetry* (1933)

8 I, too, dislike it: there are things that are important
   beyond all this fiddle.
   Reading it, however, with a perfect contempt for it, one
   discovers in it, after all, a place for the genuine.

Marianne Moore 1887–1972: 'Poetry' (1935)

9 Nor till the poets among us can be
'literalists of
the imagination'—above
insolence and triviality and can present
for inspection, imaginary gardens with real toads in them,
   shall we have
it.

Marianne Moore 1887–1972: 'Poetry' (1935)

10 And poems are all that matter. The utmost of ambition is to lodge a few poems where they will be hard to get rid of.

Robert Frost 1874–1963: letter to Louis Untermeyer 21 August 1935

11 Writing a book of poetry is like dropping a rose petal down the Grand Canyon and waiting for the echo.

Don Marquis 1878–1937: E. Anthony *O Rare Don Marquis* (1962)

12 I would have a poet able-bodied, fond of talking, a reader of the newspapers, capable of pity and laughter, informed in economics, appreciative of women, involved in personal relationships, actively interested in politics, susceptible to physical impressions.

Louis MacNeice 1907–63: *Modern Poetry* (1938)

13 Burdened with the complexity of the lives we lead, fretting over appearances, netted in with anxieties and apprehensions, half smothered in drifts of tepid thoughts and tepid feelings, we may refuse what poetry has to give; but under its influence serenity returns to the troubled mind, the world crumbles, loveliness shines like flowers after rain, and the further reality is once more charged with mystery.

Walter de la Mare 1873–1956: *Behold This Dreamer* (1939) 'Dream and Imagination'

1 A poem begins with a lump in the throat; a home sickness or a love sickness. It is a reaching-out toward expression; an effort to find fulfilment. A complete poem is one where an emotion has found its thought and the thought has found the words . . . My definition of poetry (if I were forced to give one) would be this: words that have become deeds.

Robert Frost 1874–1963: Lawrence Thompson *Fire and Ice* (1942)

2 Poetry is not the most important thing in life . . . I'd much rather lie in a hot bath reading Agatha Christie and sucking sweets.

Dylan Thomas 1914–53: Joan Wyndham *Love is Blue* (1986) 6 July 1943; see **297:2**

3 My method is simple: not to bother about poetry. It must come of its own accord. Merely whispering its name drives it away.

Jean Cocteau 1889–1963: on 26 August 1945; *Professional Secrets* (1972)

4 An age which is incapable of poetry is incapable of any kind of literature except the cleverness of a decadence.

Raymond Chandler 1888–1959: letter to Charles W. Morton, 5 January 1947

5 The function of poetry is religious invocation of the Muse; its use is the experience of mixed exultation and horror that her presence excites.

Robert Graves 1895–1985: *The White Goddess* (1948)

6 For God-sake don't call me a poet,
For I've never been guilty of that.

Robert Service 1874–1958: 'A Verseman's Apology' (1949)

7 He [the poet] may be used as the barometer, but let us not forget he is also part of the weather.

Lionel Trilling 1905–75: *The Sense of the Past* (1950)

8 The poet's voice need not merely be the record of man; it can be one of the props, the pillars, to help him endure and prevail.

William Faulkner 1897–1962: Nobel prize acceptance speech, Stockholm, 10 December 1950

9 [Poetry] is a violence from within that protects us from a violence without.

Wallace Stevens 1879–1955: 'The Noble Rider And The Sounds Of Words' (1951)

10 A verbal art like poetry is reflective. It stops to think. Music is immediate: it goes on to become.

W. H. Auden 1907–73: Aaron Copland *Music and Imagination* (1952)

11 Poetry is a religion with no hope.

Jean Cocteau 1889–1963: *Journal d'un inconnu* (1953) 'De l'invisibilité'

12 Peotry is sissy stuff that rhymes. Weedy people sa la and fie and swoon when they see a bunch of daffodils.

Geoffrey Willans 1911–58 and **Ronald Searle** 1920– : *Down with Skool!* (1953)

13 A true sonnet goes eight lines and then takes a turn for better or worse and goes six or eight lines more.

Robert Frost 1874–1963: remark made on TV, 29 March 1954

14 The poet is the priest of the invisible.

Wallace Stevens 1879–1955: 'Adagia' (1957)

15 QUESTIONNAIRE: As a poet what distinguishes you, do you think, from an ordinary man?
STEVENS: Inability to see much point to the life of an ordinary man.

Wallace Stevens 1879–1955: Ian Hamilton *Against Oblivion: Some Lives of the Twentieth-Century Poets* (2002)

16 Poetry must resist the intelligence almost successfully.

Wallace Stevens 1879–1955: 'Adagia' (1957)

17 You need not fear to be a poet.

Walter de la Mare 1873–1956: attributed

1 I like a man with poetry in him, but not a poet.

Marilyn Monroe 1926–62: attributed, 1956

2 Poetry is so emotional and very tiring.

Edith Sitwell 1887–1964: attributed, 1957

3   Doctors in verse
Being scarce now, most poets
Are their own patients, compelled to treat
Themselves first, their complaint being
Peculiar always.

R. S. Thomas 1913–2000: 'The Cure' (1958)

4 Poetry is a way of taking life by the throat.

Robert Frost 1874–1963: Elizabeth S. Sergeant *Robert Frost* (1960)

5 Poetry is the revelation of a feeling that the poet believes to be interior and personal but which the reader recognizes as his own.

Salvatore Quasimodo 1901–68: in *New York Times* 14 May 1960

6 Poetry is the only art people haven't yet learnt to consume like soup.

W. H. Auden 1907–73: in *New York Times* 1960

7 Even when the poet seems most himself . . . he is never the bundle of accident and incoherence that sits down to breakfast; he has been reborn as an idea, something intended, complete.

W. B. Yeats 1865–1939: *Essays and Introductions* (1961) 'A General Introduction for my Work'

8 Most people ignore most poetry
because
most poetry ignores most people.

Adrian Mitchell 1932– : *Poems* (1964)

9 Poetry before breakfast would be rather grisly.

Roy Fuller 1912–91: attributed, 1968

10 I don't think poetry expresses emotion. It evokes emotion from the reader, and that is a very different thing. As someone once said, 'If you want to express emotion, scream.'

Margaret Atwood 1939– : in an interview, 4 April 1972; Earl G. Ingersoll (ed.) *Margaret Atwood: Conversations* (1990)

11 Too many people in the modern world view poetry as a luxury, not a necessity like petrol. But to me it's the oil of life.

John Betjeman 1906–84: attributed, 1974

12 When all the living's done
it's poems that remain.

Judith Wright 1915–2000: 'For M. R.' (1976)

13 My favourite poem is the one that starts 'Thirty days hath September' because it actually tells you something.

Groucho Marx 1895–1977: Ned Sherrin *Cutting Edge* (1984); attributed

14 This passion for poetry readings has led to a kind of poetry that you *can* understand first go: easy rhythms, easy emotions, easy syntax. I don't think it stands up on the page.

Philip Larkin 1922–85: *Required Writing* (1983)

15 He reversed the traditional metaphor by making Poetry, as a dominant female, pursue the shrinking, womanish poet with masculine lustfulness.

Robert Graves 1895–1985: attributed

16 The fact that poetry is not of the slightest economic or political importance, that it has no attachment to any of the powers that control the modern world, may set it free to do the only thing that in this age it can do—to keep some neglected parts of the human experience alive until the weather changes; as in some unforeseeable way it may do.

Graham Hough 1908– : Malcolm Bradbury and James McFarlane (eds.) *Modernism* (1991)

1 In no other job have I ever had to deal with such utterly abnormal people. Yes, it is true, poetry does something to them.
   on working for the Poetry Society

Muriel Spark 1918- : *Curriculum Vitae* (1992)

2 I think people are born with a specific temperament . . . To become a poet you must, above all, be yourself.

Seamus Heaney 1939- : interviewed in *Athens News* 8 October 1995

3 Poetry cannot afford to lose its fundamentally self-delighting inventiveness, its joy in being a process of language as well as a representation of things in the world.

Seamus Heaney 1939- : *The Redress of Poetry* (1995)

4 What are poems for? They are to console us with their own gift, which is like perfect pitch. Let us commit that to our dust. What ought a poem be? Answer, *a sad and angry consolation.*

Geoffrey Hill 1932- : *The Triumph of Love* (1999)

Poetry versus Prose

5 All that is not prose is verse; and all that is not verse is prose.

Molière 1622-73: *Le Bourgeois Gentilhomme* (1671)

6 And this unpolished rugged verse I chose
   As fittest for discourse and nearest prose.

John Dryden 1631-1700: *Religio Laici* (1682)

7 WITWOUD: Madam, do you pin up your hair with all your letters?
   MILLAMANT: Only with those in verse, Mr Witwoud. I never pin up my hair with prose.

William Congreve 1670-1729: *The Way of the World* (1700)

8 And he, whose fustian's so sublimely bad,
   It is not poetry, but prose run mad.

Alexander Pope 1688-1744: 'An Epistle to Dr Arbuthnot' (1735)

9 Is there then, it will be asked, no essential difference between the language of prose and metrical composition? I answer that there neither is nor can be any essential difference.

William Wordsworth 1770-1850: preface to *Lyrical Ballads* (1800)

10 I've half a mind to tumble down to prose
   But verse is more in fashion—so here goes.

Lord Byron 1788-1824: *Beppo* (1818)

11 The habits of a poet's mind are not those of industry or research: his images come to him, he does not go to them; and in prose-subjects, and dry matters of fact and close reasoning, the natural stimulus that at other times warms and rouses, deserts him altogether . . . All is tame, literal, and barren, without the Nine.

William Hazlitt 1778-1830: *The Plain Speaker* (1826) vol. 1 'On the Prose Style of Poets'

12 Prose = words in their best order;—poetry = the *best* words in the best order.

Samuel Taylor Coleridge 1772-1834: *Table Talk* (1835) 12 July 1827

13 Prose is when all the lines except the last go on to the end. Poetry is when some of them fall short of it.

Jeremy Bentham 1748-1832: M. St. J. Packe *The Life of John Stuart Mill* (1954)

14 To write prose, one must have something to say; but he who has nothing to say can still make verses and rhymes, where one word suggests the other, and finally something comes out which in fact is nothing but looks as if it were something.

Johann Wolfgang von Goethe 1749-1832: Johann Peter Eckermann *Conversations with Goethe* (1836-48)

1 Prose was born yesterday—this is what we must tell ourselves. Poetry is pre-eminently the medium of past literatures. All the metrical combinations have been tried but nothing like this can be said of prose.

Gustave Flaubert 1821–80: letter to Louise Colet, 24 April 1852

2 Prose on certain occasions can bear a great deal of poetry: on the other hand, poetry sinks and swoons under a moderate weight of prose.

Walter Savage Landor 1775–1864: *Imaginary Conversations* 'Archdeacon Hare and Walter Landor' in *The Last Fruit off an Old Tree* (1853)

3 I shall be found by the fire, suppose,
O'er a great wise book as beseemeth age,
While the shutters flap as the cross-wind blows
And I turn the page, and I turn the page,
Not verse now, only prose!

Robert Browning 1812–89: 'By the Fireside' (1855)

4 They shut me up in prose—
As when a little girl
They put me in the closet—
Because they liked me 'still'.

Emily Dickinson 1830–86: 'They shut me up in prose' (c.1862)

5 Outside prose, no salvation.

Émile Zola 1840–1902: letter, 18 August 1864

6 Prose is for ideas, verse for visions.

Henrik Ibsen 1828–1906: 'Rhymed Letter for Fru Heiberg' (1871)

7 In the past 7–8 years, I have scarcely written a single verse, but exclusively cultivated the incomparably more difficult art of writing purely realistic everyday language.

Henrik Ibsen 1828–1906: letter, 1883

8 Mr Stone's hexameters are verses of no sort, but prose in ribands.

A. E. Housman 1859–1936: in *Classical Review* 1899

9 Prose wanders around with a lantern and laboriously schedules and verifies the details and particulars of a valley and its frame of crags and peaks, then Poetry comes, and lays bare the whole landscape with a single splendid flash.

Mark Twain 1835–1910: H. N. Smith and W. H. Gibson (eds.) *Mark Twain–Howells Letters* (1960) vol. 2

10 Poetry must be *as well written as prose*.

Ezra Pound 1885–1972: letter to Harriet Monroe, January 1915

11 It may be that civilization is dependent on good prose. The only thing that can prevent a nation from being a muddle of blindly conflicting creeds and classes, each shouting its war-cries at a top note, is the presence of some medium for a rational interchange of ideas. Not poetry. Poetry is related to the war-cry, coming as it does largely from the emotional side of man. Only good prose (of which drama may be considered a branch) can achieve the work of unity.

Vance Palmer 1885–1959: 'The Spirit of Prose' (1921)

12 In prose too much seems superfluous to me, in poetry (genuine) everything is necessary.

Marina Tsvetaeva 1892–1941: *Earthly Signs: Moscow Diaries, 1917–22* (2002)

13 I now tell the story of a novel in verse of twenty lines.

Thomas Hardy 1840–1928: Lillah McCarthy *Myself and My Friends* (1933)

14 ACQUAINTANCE: How are you?
YEATS: Not very well. I can only write prose today.

W. B. Yeats 1865–1939: attributed

1 I don't think anyone can write succinct prose unless they have at least tried and failed to write a good iambic pentameter sonnet, and read Browning's short dramatic poems.

F. Scott Fitzgerald 1896–1940: letter (undated) to Frances Scott Fitzgerald

2 Poetry is to prose as dancing is to walking.

John Wain 1925-94: BBC radio broadcast, 13 January 1976

3 If you tell a novelist, 'Life's not like that', he has to do something about it. The poet simply replies, 'No, but *I* am.'

Philip Larkin 1922-85: speech as Chairman of the Booker Prize judges, 1977; *Required Writing* (1983)

4 In poetry words are like notes from a flute, the tracery of a tune, whereas in fiction words are like notes of a symphony orchestra—compositional.

Edmund White 1940- : in (1981); Edmund White *The Burning Library* (1994)

5 I am convinced that writing prose should not be any different from writing poetry. In both cases it is a question of looking for the unique expression, one that is concise, concentrated, and memorable.

Italo Calvino 1923-85: *Six Memos for the Next Millennium* (1992)

6 Poets live by the ear much more than prose writers do.

Susan Sontag 1933- : in *Writers on Writing: Collected Essays from The New York Times* (2001)

Point of View

7 The only means of strengthening one's intellect is to make up one's mind about nothing—to let the mind be a thoroughfare for all thoughts. Not a select party.

John Keats 1795-1821: letter to George and Georgiana Keats, 24 September 1819

8 Do I contradict myself?
Very well then I contradict myself,
(I am large, I contain multitudes.)

Walt Whitman 1819-92: 'Song of Myself' (written 1855)

9 Subjectivity is a terrible thing. It is bad in this alone, that it reveals the author's hands and feet.

Anton Chekhov 1860-1904: letter to Alexander Chekhov, April 1883

10 A writer must be as objective as a chemist: he must abandon the subjective line; he must know that dung-heaps play a very reasonable part in a landscape, and that evil passions are as inherent in life as good ones.

Anton Chekhov 1860-1904: letter to M. V. Kiselev, 14 January 1887

11 We Cromwellian Directors laid down this principle twenty-five years ago, and have not departed from it: never accept or reject a play because of its opinions.

W. B. Yeats 1865-1939: in *Dublin Magazine* 1926

12 I am a camera with its shutter open, quite passive, recording, not thinking.

Christopher Isherwood 1904-86: *Goodbye to Berlin* (1939) 'Berlin Diary' Autumn 1930

13 A novelist must preserve a child-like belief in the importance of things which common-sense considers of no great consequence. He must never entirely grow up . . . The novelist is dead in the man who has become aware of the triviality of human affairs.

W. Somerset Maugham 1874-1965: *A Writer's Notebook* (1949) written in 1933

14 Time that with this strange excuse
Pardoned Kipling and his views,
And will pardon Paul Claudel,
Pardons him for writing well.

W. H. Auden 1907-73: *Another Time* (1940) 'In Memory of W. B. Yeats'

1 At bottom it is always a writer's tendency, his 'purpose', his 'message', that makes him liked or disliked. The proof of this is the extreme difficulty of seeing any literary merit in a book that seriously damages your deepest beliefs.

George Orwell 1903–50: *Inside the Whale* (1940)

2 A writer has to conform to two conflicting requirements: he must be involved in his novel and detached from himself.

Graham Greene 1904–91: Marie-Françoise Allain *The Other Man, Conversations with Graham Greene* (1983)

3 Beware the writer who puts forward his concern for you to embrace, who leaves you in no doubt of his worthiness, his usefulness, his altruism, who declares that his heart is in the right place and ensures that it can be seen in full view, a pulsating mass where his characters ought to be.

Harold Pinter 1930– : in *Observer* 16 October 1988

4 Journalism is about working yourself up into a lather over things you previously felt nothing about. It is diametrically opposed to what you do as a novelist, which is very slowly to discover what it is you really think about things.

Kazuo Ishiguro 1954– : in *Guardian* 15 May 1996

5 To write is to be self-conscious . . . What flows on to paper is more daring or more covert than a writer's own voice, or more exaggerated or effaced. This gap between consciousness and text is always ready to freeze the movement of the pen.

Carol Shields 1935– : *Jane Austen* (2001)

Politics

6 Politics in the middle of things that concern the imagination are like a pistol-shot in the middle of a concert.

Stendhal 1783–1842: *Scarlet and Black* (1830)

7 The English poet Thomson wrote a very good poem on the Seasons, but a very bad one on Liberty, and that not from want of poetry in the poet but from want of poetry in the subject. As soon as a poet exerts himself politically, he must give himself up to a party; and once he does that, he is lost as a poet; he must say farewell to his freedom of spirit, his impartial outlook, and pull over his ears the cap of bigotry and blind hatred.

Johann Wolfgang von Goethe 1749–1832: Johann Peter Eckermann *Conversations with Goethe* (1836–48)

8 God help the Minister that meddles with art!

Lord Melbourne 1779–1848: Lord David Cecil *Lord M* (1954)

9 True literature can exist only where it is created not by diligent and trustworthy officials, but by madmen, heretics, dreamers, rebels and sceptics. But when a writer must be sensible . . . there can be no bronze literature, there can only be a newspaper literature, which is read today, and used for wrapping soap tomorrow.

Yevgeny Zamyatin 1884–1937: 'I am Afraid' (1921)

10 The proletarian state must bring up thousands of excellent 'mechanics of culture', 'engineers of the soul'.

Maxim Gorky 1868–1936: speech at the Writers' Congress 1934; see **223:7**

11 I never dared be radical when young
For fear it would make me conservative when old.

Robert Frost 1874–1963: 'Precaution' (1936)

1 CONGRESSMAN STARNES: I believe Mr Euripides was guilty of teaching class consciousness also, wasn't he?
HALLIE FLANAGAN: I believe that was alleged against all the Greek dramatists.

Hallie Flanagan 1890–1969: in hearing on the Federal Theatre Project by the House Un-American Activities Committee, 6 December 1938

2 Political writing in our time consists almost entirely of prefabricated phrases bolted together like the pieces of a child's Meccano set.

George Orwell 1903–50: 'The Prevention of Literature' (1946)

3 Political language . . . is designed to make lies sound truthful and murder respectable, and to give an appearance of solidity to pure wind.

George Orwell 1903–50: *Shooting an Elephant* (1950) 'Politics and the English Language'

4 It is difficult
to get the news from poems
yet men die miserably every day
for lack
of what is found there.

William Carlos Williams 1883–1963: 'Asphodel, That Greeny Flower' (1955)

5 Letting a hundred flowers blossom and a hundred schools of thought contend is the policy for promoting progress in the arts and the sciences and a flourishing socialist culture in our land.

Mao Zedong 1893–1976: speech in Peking, 27 February 1957

6 Dictators are as scared of books as they are of cannon.

Harry Golden 1902–81: *Only in America* (1958)

7 In free society art is not a weapon . . . Artists are not engineers of the soul.

John F. Kennedy 1917–63: speech at Amherst College, Mass., 26 October 1963; see **222:10**

8 When power leads man toward arrogance, poetry reminds him of his limitations. When power narrows the areas of man's concern, poetry reminds him of the richness and diversity of his existence. When power corrupts, poetry cleanses. For art establishes the basic human truths which must serve as the touchstone of our judgement.

John F. Kennedy 1917–63: speech at Amherst College, Mass., 26 October 1963

9 And for a country to have a great writer is—don't be shocked, I'll whisper it—is like having another government. That's why no regime has ever loved great writers, only minor ones.

Alexander Solzhenitsyn 1918– : *The First Circle* (1964)

10 If ten or twelve Hungarian writers had been shot at the right moment, there would have been no revolution.

Nikita Khrushchev 1894–1971: attributed

11 A Roundhead? I'd have been Cromwell.
replying to a student who had asked him whether he would have been a Roundhead in the Civil War

F. R. Leavis 1895–1978: attributed

12 If writers leave the business of making pictures of the world to politicians, it will be one of history's greatest and most abject abdications.

Salman Rushdie 1947– : 'Outside the Whale' (1984)

13 The only thing politics and poetry have in common is the letter 'p' and the letter 'o'.

Joseph Brodsky 1940–96: in *Newsweek* 15 May 1986

14 It's very different from living in academia in Oxford. We called someone vicious in the *Times Literary Supplement*. We didn't know what vicious was.
on returning to Burma (Myanmar)

Aung San Suu Kyi 1945– : in *Observer* 25 September 1988 'Sayings of the Week'

15 Art is much older than democracy, and art is uncompromisingly elitist.

Robertson Davies 1913–95: lecture, Yale, February 1990

1 Not every fiction writer entering a relation with politics trades imagination for the hair shirt of the party hack.

Nadine Gordimer 1923– : Clare Boylan (ed.) *The Agony and the Ego* (1993)

2 If you want to find out what is happening in an age or in a nation, find out what is happening to the writers, the town criers.
on the death sentence passed on Ken Saro-Wiwa in Nigeria

Ben Okri 1959– : in *Observer* 5 November 1995

Alexander Pope 1688-1744
English poet

3 In Pope, I cannot read a line,
But with a sigh, I wish it mine;

When he can in one couplet fix
More sense than I can do in six:
It gives me such a jealous fit,
I cry, pox take him, and his wit.

Jonathan Swift 1667–1745: 'Verses on the Death of Dr Swift' (1731)

4 He hardly drank tea without a stratagem.

Samuel Johnson 1709–84: *Lives of the English Poets* (1779–81) 'Pope'

5 But he (his musical finesse was such,
So nice his ear, so delicate his touch)
Made poetry a mere mechanic art,
And ev'ry warbler has his tune by heart.

William Cowper 1731–1800: 'Table Talk' (1782)

6 Those miserable mountebanks of the day, the poets, disgrace themselves and deny God, in running down Pope, the most *faultless* of poets, and almost of men.

Lord Byron 1788–1824: letter, 4 November 1820

7 To escape from the grotesque tragedy which was his body, Pope perfected a series of immaculate masks and voices.

John Carey 1934– : in *Sunday Times* 1985

Popular Fiction see also Best-sellers

8 I thank God my taste still continues for the gay part of reading; wiser people may think it trifling, but it serves to sweeten life to me, and is, at worst, better than the generality of conversation.
on her liking for romances and novels

Lady Mary Wortley Montagu 1689–1762: letter to her daughter, Lady Bute, 24 December 1750

9 Quick, my dear Lucy, hide these books. Quick, quick! Fling 'Peregrine Pickle' under the toilette—throw 'Roderick Random' into the closet—put 'The Innocent Adultery' into 'The Whole Duty of Man'; thrust 'Lord Aimworth' under the sofa! cram 'Ovid' behind the bolster; there—put 'The Man of Feeling' into your pocket. Now for them.

Richard Brinsley Sheridan 1751–1816: *The Rivals* (1775)

10 A masquerade, a murdered peer,
His throat just cut from ear to ear—
A rake turned hermit—a fond maid
Run mad, by some false loon betrayed—
These stores supply the female pen,
Which writes them o'er and o'er again,
And readers likewise may be found
To circulate them round and round.

Mary Alcock c.1742–98: 'A Receipt for Writing a Novel'

1 I am no indiscriminate novel-reader. The mere trash of the common circulating library, I hold in the highest contempt. You will never hear of me advocating those puerile emanations which detail nothing but discordant principles incapable of amalgamation, or those vapid tissues of ordinary occurrences from which no useful deductions can be drawn.

Jane Austen 1775–1817: 'Sir Edward Denham' in *Sanditon* (1925 ed.)

2 It is a shame to women so to write; and it is a shame to the women who read and accept as a true representation of themselves and their ways the equivocal talk and fleshly inclinations herein attributed to them. Their patronage of such books is in reality an adoption and acceptance of them.
of the 'sensation novels' of the period

Margaret Oliphant 1828–97: in *Blackwood's Magazine* 1867 'Novels'

3 No *man* would have dared to write and publish such books . . . no *man could* have written such delineations of female passion . . . No! They are women, who by their writings have been doing the work of the enemy of souls . . . Women . . . who might have been bright and shining lights in their generation.

Francis E. Paget 1806–82: *Lucretia* (1868)

4 For I've read in many a novel that, unless they've souls that grovel,
Folks *prefer* in fact a hovel to your dreary marble halls.

C. S. Calverley 1831–84: 'In the Gloaming' (1872)

5 The amount of crime, treachery, murder, slow poisoning, and general infamy required by the halfpenny reader is something terrible.

Mary Elizabeth Braddon 1837–1915: to Bulwer Lytton; R. L. Woolf *Sensational Victorian* (1979)

6 Bad literature of the sort called amusing is spiritual gin.

George Eliot 1819–80: *Leaves from a Note-book: Authorship* (1879) 'The Impressions of Theophrastus Such'

7 My books are water; those of the great geniuses are wine. Everybody drinks water.

Mark Twain 1835–1910: notebook, 11 December 1885; *Mark Twain's Notebook* (1935)

8 It is only the fiction that lives that can hope for a triumph in this latter-day appeal at sixpence to the masses. Their knowledge extends to the books which cry from the heights, as it were, but it does not yet penetrate into the highways and byways of literature. In other words, the masses want what is of proved interest, the established story—that and that only.
on the commercial success of his sixpenny paperbacks and the new cheap fiction

Andrew Chatto: in *Author* 1 October 1900 'The Sixpenny Book'

9 Here is one of the fundamental defects of American fiction—perhaps the one character that sets it off sharply from all other known kinds of contemporary fiction. It habitually exhibits, not a man of delicate organization in revolt against the inexplicable tragedy of existence, but a man of low sensibilities and elemental desires yielding himself gladly to his environment, and so achieving what, under a third-rate civilization, passes for success.

H. L. Mencken 1880–1956: *Prejudices* (2nd series, 1920) 'The National Letters'

1 Don't read too much now: the dude
  Who lets the girl down before
  The hero arrives, the chap
  Who's yellow and keeps the store,
  Seem far too familiar. Get stewed:
  Books are a load of crap.

  Philip Larkin 1922–85: 'Study of Reading Habits' (1964)

2 He can't write fiction and he can't write non-fiction, so he's invented a bogus category in between.
  of Jeffrey Archer's new 'novelography'

  Ian Hislop 1960– : in *Observer* 14 April 1996 'Sayings of the Week'

3 It's a pity so many young women are trying to write that . . . It would be better perhaps if they wrote books about their lives as they saw them, and not these helpless girls, drunk and worrying about their weight.
  on the fashionable 'chick lit'

  Doris Lessing 1919– : in *BBC News* (online edition) 23 August 2001

4 I have no problem with chick lit, I love *Bridget Jones's Diary*, it's just great. It's all the muck in the middle I mind . . . Let's have art or let's have entertainment.

  Jeanette Winterson 1959– : in *BBC News* (online edition) 23 August 2001

Pornography see Erotic Writing and Pornography

Ezra Pound 1885–1972
American poet

5 Ezra was right half the time, and when he was wrong, he was so wrong you were never in any doubt about it.

  Ernest Hemingway 1899–1961: in *New Republic* 11 November 1936

6 He behaved like Baden-Powell getting everyone under canvas.
  on Pound's marshalling poets under the banner of 'Imagisme' c.1912

  Wyndham Lewis 1882–1957: Malcolm Bradbury and James McFarlane (eds.) *Modernism* (1991)

Anthony Powell 1905–2000
English novelist

7 I feel each volume of this series is like a great sustaining slice of Melton Pie. I can go on eating it with the recurring seasons until I drop.
  about A Dance to the Music of Time

  Evelyn Waugh 1903–66: letter to Anthony Powell, 25 April 1955

The Power of the Pen

8 Write the vision, and make it plain upon tables, that he may run that readeth it.

  Bible: Habakkuk; see **21:6**

9 And now I have finished the work, which neither the wrath of Jove, nor fire, nor the sword, nor devouring age shall be able to destroy.

  Ovid 43 BC–AD c.17: *Metamorphoses*

10 Let none presume to tell me that the pen is preferable to the sword.

  Cervantes 1547–1616: *Don Quixote* (1605)

11 Your tale, sir, would cure deafness.

  William Shakespeare 1564–1616: *The Tempest* (1611)

1 So long as men can breathe, or eyes can see,
So long lives this, and this gives life to thee.

William Shakespeare 1564–1616: sonnet 18

2 A good book is the precious life-blood of a master spirit, embalmed and treasured up on purpose to a life beyond life.

John Milton 1608–74: *Areopagitica* (1644)

3 To endeavour to work upon the vulgar with fine sense, is like attempting to hew blocks with a razor.

Alexander Pope 1688–1744: *Miscellanies* (1727) 'Thoughts on Various Subjects'

4 It is, however, with books as it is with men: a very small number play a great part; the rest are confounded with the multitude.

Voltaire 1694–1778: *A Philosophical Dictionary* (1764–70) 'Books'

5 Poetry is a sword of lightning, ever unsheathed, which consumes the scabbard that would contain it.

Percy Bysshe Shelley 1792–1822: *A Defence of Poetry* (written 1821)

6 Beneath the rule of men entirely great
The pen is mightier than the sword.

Edward George Bulwer-Lytton 1803–73: *Richelieu* (1839); see **114:9**

7 We need books of this tart cathartic virtue, more than books of political science or of private economy.
on Plutarch's Lives

Ralph Waldo Emerson 1803–82: *Essays* (1841) 'Heroism'

8 It is splendid to be a great writer, to put men into the frying pan of your words and make them pop like chestnuts.

Gustave Flaubert 1821–80: letter, 3 November 1851

9 There is first the literature of *knowledge*, and secondly, the literature of *power*.

Thomas De Quincey 1785–1859: review of the *Works of Pope* (1847 ed.) in *North British Review* August 1848

10 So you're the little woman who wrote the book that made this great war!
on meeting Harriet Beecher Stowe, author of Uncle Tom's Cabin (*1852*); see **227:14**

Abraham Lincoln 1809–65: Carl Sandburg *Abraham Lincoln: The War Years* (1936)

11 Dreamer of dreams, born out of my due time,
Why should I strive to set the crooked straight?
Let it suffice me that my murmuring rhyme
Beats with light wing against the ivory gate,
Telling a tale not too importunate
To those who in the sleepy region stay,
Lulled by the singer of an empty day.

William Morris 1834–96: *The Earthly Paradise* (1868–70) 'An Apology'

12 In our times, the task of every piece of literature is to move the frontier post.

Henrik Ibsen 1828–1906: attributed

13 All books are either dreams or swords,
You can cut, or you can drug, with words.

Amy Lowell 1874–1925: 'Sword Blades and Poppy Seed' (1914)

14 Harriet Beecher Stowe, whose *Uncle Tom's Cabin* was the first evidence to America that no hurricane can be so disastrous to a country as a ruthlessly humanitarian woman.

Sinclair Lewis 1885–1951: introduction to Paxton Hibben *Henry Ward Beecher: an American Portrait* (1927); see **227:10**

15 This is not the age of pamphleteers. It is the age of the engineers. The spark-gap is mightier than the pen.

Lancelot Hogben 1895–1975: *Science for the Citizen* (1938)

16 All that I have said and done,
Now that I am old and ill,
Turns into a question till
I lie awake night after night
And never get the answers right.

W. B. Yeats 1865–1939: 'The Man and the Echo' (1939)

Did that play of mine send out
Certain men the English shot?

1 Books can not be killed by fire. People die, but books never
die. No man and no force can abolish memory . . . In this
war, we know, books are weapons. And it is a part of your
dedication always to make them weapons for man's
freedom.

Franklin D. Roosevelt 1882–1945:
'Message to the Booksellers of
America' 6 May 1942

2 What makes the poet the potent figure that he is, or was,
or ought to be, is that he creates the world to which we
turn incessantly and without knowing it and that he gives
to life the supreme fictions without which we are unable to
conceive of it.

Wallace Stevens 1879–1955: *The
Noble Rider and the Sound of Words*
(1942)

3 Do not feel safe. The poet remembers.
You can kill one, but another is born.
The words are written down, the deed, the date.

Czeslaw Milosz 1911– : 'You Who
Wronged' (1950)

4 I suggest that the only books that influence us are those
for which we are ready, and which have gone a little
farther down our particular path than we have yet got
ourselves.

E. M. Forster 1879–1970: *Two Cheers
for Democracy* (1951) 'Books That
Influenced Me'

5 I discovered that writing was a mighty fine thing. You
could make people stand on their hind legs and cast a
shadow.

William Faulkner 1897–1962:
Malcolm Bradbury *The Modern
American Novel* (1992)

6 The book is alive and potent and fructifying and able to
promote thought and discussion *only* when its plan and
shape and intention are not understood, because that
moment of seeing the shape and plan and intention is also
the moment when there isn't anything more to be got out
of it.

Doris Lessing 1919– : *The Golden
Notebook* (1962) preface

7 I believe that Brecht did nothing for Communism, that the
revolution was not provoked by Beaumarchais's *The
Marriage of Figaro*. The closer a work of art is to perfection,
the more it turns in on itself. Still worse, it awakens a taste
for the past.

Jean Genet 1910–86: in the
periodical *Le Nouvel Observateur* 1971

8 To be arrested for the power of your writing is one of the
highest compliments an author can be paid, if an
unwelcome one.
   on being jailed without trial, in 1977

Ngugi wa Thiong'o 1938– :
attributed; in *Assistant Librarian*
September 1986

9 A writer is not so powerless as he usually feels, and a pen,
as well as a silver bullet, can draw blood.
   *in relation to President Duvalier's anger at the portrayal of
   Haiti in* **Greene**'s *The Comedians*

Graham Greene 1904–91: *Ways of
Escape* (1980)

10 Dead dictators are my speciality. I discovered to my horror
that all the political figures most featured in my writing—
Mrs G, Sanjay Gandhi, Bhutto, Zia—have now come to
sticky ends. It's the grand slam really. This is a service I
can perform, perhaps. A sort of literary contract.
   *Indira Gandhi, Prime Minister of India, was assassinated,
   Zulfikar Ali Bhutto was ousted as Prime Minister of
   Pakistan and subsequently hanged, and his successor Zia
   ul-Haq and Sanjay Gandhi both died in air crashes*

Salman Rushdie 1947– :interview in
Independent 10 September 1988

1 It would be absurd to think that a book can cause riots.

Salman Rushdie 1947– : to Indian interviewer in September 1988; in *Sunday Times* 23 July 1989; see **41:6**

2 I've never read a political poem that's accomplished anything. Poetry makes things happen, but rarely what the poet wants.

Howard Nemerov 1920–91: in *International Herald Tribune* 14 October 1988

3 I really do inhabit a system in which words are capable of shaking the entire structure of government, where words can prove mightier than ten military divisions.
   speech in Germany accepting a peace prize, October 1989

Václav Havel 1936– : in *Independent* 9 December 1989

4 The men who ordained and supervised this show of shame, this tragic charade, are frightened by the word, the power of ideas, the power of the pen . . . They are so scared of the word that they do not read. And that will be their funeral.
   shortly before his execution in 1995

Ken Saro-Wiwa 1941–95: in *London Review of Books* 4 April 1996

5 I've used my talents as a writer to enable the Ogoni people to confront their tormentors. I was not able to do it as a politician or a businessman. My writing did it . . . I think I have the moral victory.
   letter, shortly before his execution in 1995, to William Boyd

Ken Saro-Wiwa 1941–95: in *London Review of Books* 4 April 1996

6 In times of crisis it's interesting that people don't turn to the novel or say, 'We should all go out to a movie' or 'Ballet would help us.' It's always poetry. What we want to hear is a human voice speaking directly in our ear.
   in the aftermath of 11 September 2001

Billy Collins 1941– : in *New York Times* 1 October 2001

7 Writers are dangerous. They are also, frequently, not very nice. When they become famous, they can be not very nice in the manner of other famous people—vain, tyrannical, inflexible, and so on. But they can also be not very nice in a way specific to writers: by exploiting the one skill which sets them apart from others, by making clear that it is they who fix the official version of events. Those who live close to writers sooner or later inevitably strike against this discouraging truth:
Whatever happens,
They have got
The typewriter
And we have not.
   *referring to **Belloc**'s lines on the Maxim gun*

Julian Barnes 1946– : *Something to Declare* (2002)

Prizes

8 Were I my own man . . . I would refuse this offer (with all gratitude); but as I am situated, L.300 or L.400 a-year is not to be sneezed at.
   on being offered the Laureateship

Sir Walter Scott 1771–1832: letter to James Ballantyne, 24 August 1813

9 Just for a handful of silver he left us,
Just for a riband to stick in his coat.
   *of **Wordsworth**'s implied abandonment of radical principles by his acceptance of the Laureateship*

Robert Browning 1812–89: 'The Lost Leader' (1845)

1 Had they sent me ¼ lb of good tobacco, the addition to my happiness had probably been suitabler and greater!
on being awarded the Prussian Order of Merit

Thomas Carlyle 1795–1881: letter to his brother John Carlyle, 14 February 1874

2 In the end I accepted the honour, because during dinner Venables told me that, if I became Poet Laureate, I should always when I dined out be offered the liver-wing of a fowl.
on being made Poet Laureate in 1850

Alfred, Lord Tennyson 1809–92: in *Alfred Lord Tennyson: A Memoir by his Son* (1897) vol. 1

objecting to having been appointed a Companion of Honour without his consent:
3 How would you like it if you woke up and found yourself Archbishop of Canterbury?

Rudyard Kipling 1865–1936: letter to Bonar Law, 1917; Charles Carrington *Rudyard Kipling* (1978)

4 The award of a pure gold medal for poetry would flatter the recipient unduly: no poem ever attains such carat purity.

Robert Graves 1895–1985: *Address to the Oxford University Philological Society* January 1960

5 A writer must refuse, therefore, to allow himself to be transformed into an institution.

Jean-Paul Sartre 1905–80: refusing the Nobel Prize at Stockholm, 22 October 1964

6 I want to be read by people who feel like reading my books. Not by celebrity collectors.
on refusing the 1964 Nobel prize in literature

Jean-Paul Sartre 1905–80: interview in *Paris-Press-L'Intransigeant* 24 October 1964

7 The Nobel is a ticket to one's funeral. No one has ever done anything after he got it.

T. S. Eliot 1888–1965: attributed

8 After our work was over, the Secretary told me that I had been the weakest chairman they had ever had. He didn't put it quite like that, of course; what he said was that never before had members of the panel been encouraged to make so full a contribution.
of chairing the judges for the Booker Prize

Philip Larkin 1922–85: in 1977; *Required Writing* (1983)

9 It is extraordinary, an act of illiterates, to give prizes for literature.

Geoffrey Grigson 1905–85: *The Private Art* (1982)

10 It really means nothing in this country whatsoever—but then being a writer here means nothing either.

William Golding 1911–93: in *Observer* 31 May 1987

11 I don't think literature is ever finished in any country which has more writers than it has prizes.

Gore Vidal 1925– : in *Observer* 27 September 1987 'Sayings of the Week'

12 That one book is better than another is nothing more than a matter of taste. I find it difficult to accept that it's something that can be decided by a panel of judges.

Graham Swift 1949– : in *Observer* 24 June 1990 'Sayings of the Week'

13 I didn't think about the critics when I was writing. If I had, I would have been paralyzed.
on winning the Booker Prize 1995

Pat Barker 1943– : in *Athens News* 9 November 1995

14 The whole idea of an award just for women fills me with horror.
on the Orange prize for women's fiction

Anita Brookner 1928– : in *Sunday Times* 21 April 1996; see **325:8**

15 My father [Kingsley] always had doubts about the Booker prize although they evaporated on the announcement that he had won it.

Martin Amis 1949– : in *Independent on Sunday* 28 April 1996

1 With all those prizes the most interesting thing is getting on to the shortlist, because that tells you who people see as your peers.

David Malouf 1934– : in *Daily Telegraph* 7 September 1996

2 The Booker is murder. Absolutely nothing would be lost if it withered away and died.
view of the 1971 winner of the Booker Prize at the time of the 1996 awards

V. S. Naipaul 1932– : in *Guardian* 30 October 1996

3 On Booker night our table was always the most cheerful, because we didn't expect to win.
after being five times shortlisted for the prize

Beryl Bainbridge 1933– : in *Paris Review* Winter 2000

Marcel Proust 1871–1922
French novelist

4 The thing about Proust is his combination of the utmost sensibility with the utmost tenacity. He searches out these butterfly shades to the last grain. He is as tough as catgut and as evanescent as a butterfly's bloom.

Virginia Woolf 1882–1941: diary, 8 April 1925

5 The little lickspittle wasn't satirizing, he really thought his pimps, buggers and opulent idiots were *important*, instead of the last mould on the dying cheese.

Ezra Pound 1885–1972: letter, 23 November 1933

6 His greatness lay in his art, his incredible littleness in the quality of his social admirations.

Edith Wharton 1862–1937: *A Backward Glance* (1934)

7 I am reading Proust for the first time. Very poor stuff. I think he was mentally defective.

Evelyn Waugh 1903–66: letter to John Betjeman, c.February 1948

8 [Proust] is an exquisite writer but for pomposity and intricacy of style he makes Henry James and Osbert Sitwell look like Berta Ruck.

Noël Coward 1899–1973: diary, 25 July 1950

9 A garden in a concert hall and a picture gallery in a garden—this is one of my definitions of Proust's art.

Vladimir Nabokov 1899–1977: in c.1950; Brian Boyd *Vladimir Nabokov: the American Years* (1991)

10 After Proust, there are certain things that simply cannot be done again. He marks off for you the boundaries of your talent.

Françoise Sagan 1935– : Malcolm Cowley (ed.) *Writers at Work* (1958) 1st series

Publishers and Publishing

11 Frail book, although there's room for you to stay
Snug on my shelves, you'd rather fly away
To the bookshops and be published.

Martial AD c.40–c.104: *Epigrammata*, tr. James Michie

12 I, according to my copy, have done set it in imprint, to the intent that noble men may see and learn the noble acts of chivalry, the gentle and virtuous deeds that some knights used in those days.

William Caxton c.1421–91: Thomas Malory *Le Morte D'Arthur* (1485) prologue

13 I love a ballad in print, a-life, for then we are sure they are true.

William Shakespeare 1564–1616: *The Winter's Tale* (1610–11)

14 Some said, John, print it; other said, Not so:
Some said, It might do good; others said, No.

John Bunyan 1628–88: *The Pilgrim's Progress* (1678) pt. 1, 'Author's Apology'

1 I find all your trade are sharpers.
    to the publisher Jacob Tonson, c.1697

John Dryden 1631–1700: Ian Hamilton *Keepers of the Flame* (1992)

2 Never literary attempt was more unfortunate than my Treatise of Human Nature. It fell *dead-born from the press.*

David Hume 1711–76: *My Own Life* (1777)

3 You shall see them on a beautiful quarto page where a neat rivulet of text shall meander through a meadow of margin.

Richard Brinsley Sheridan 1751–1816: *The School for Scandal* (1777)

4 I have an exceedingly odd *sensation*, when I consider that . . . a work which was so lately lodged in all privacy, in my bureau may now be seen by every butcher and baker, cobbler and tinker, throughout the 3 kingdoms, for the small tribute of 3 pence.

Fanny Burney 1752–1840: diary, March 1778

5 Thou god of our idolatry, the press . . .
Thou fountain, at which drink the good and wise;
Thou ever-bubbling spring of endless lies;
Like Eden's dread probationary tree,
Knowledge of good and evil is from thee.

William Cowper 1731–1800: 'The Progress of Error' (1782)

6 EDMUND BURKE: You must remember that booksellers deal in commodities they are not supposed to understand.
ARTHUR MURPHY: True, some of 'em do deal in morality.

Arthur Murphy 1727–1805: in *Thraliana* (1942, ed. K. C. Balderston)

7   I'll publish, right or wrong:
Fools are my theme, let satire be my song.

Lord Byron 1788–1824: *English Bards and Scotch Reviewers* (1809)

8 Gentlemen, you must not mistake me. I admit that the French Emperor is a tyrant. I admit he is a monster. I admit that he is the sworn foe of our nation, and, if you will, of the whole human race. But, gentlemen, we must be just to our great enemy. We must not forget that he once shot a bookseller.
    proposing a toast to Napoleon at a literary dinner during the Napoleonic Wars

Thomas Campbell 1777–1844: G. O. Trevelyan *The Life of Lord Macaulay* (1876)

9 Publish and be damned.
    replying to Harriette Wilson's blackmail threat, c.1825

Duke of Wellington 1769–1852: attributed

10 Now Barabbas was a publisher.
    paraphrasing the biblical verse 'Now Barabbas was a robber'

Thomas Campbell 1777–1844: attributed, in Samuel Smiles *A Publisher and his Friends* (1891); also attributed, wrongly, to Byron

11 I suppose publishers are untrustworthy. They certainly always look it.

Oscar Wilde 1854–1900: letter, February 1898

12 I have seen enough of my publishers to know that they have no ideas of their own about literature save what they can clutch at as believing it to be a straight tip from a business point of view.

Samuel Butler 1835–1902: *Notebooks* (1912)

13 Only one thing, is impossible for God: to find any sense in any copyright law on the planet.

Mark Twain 1835–1910: notebook 23 May 1903

14 University printing presses exist, and are subsidised by the Government for the purpose of producing books which no one can read; and they are true to their high calling.

Francis M. Cornford 1874–1943: *Microcosmographia Academica* (1908)

15 All a publisher has to do is write cheques at intervals, while a lot of deserving and industrious chappies rally round and do the real work.

P. G. Wodehouse 1881–1975: *My Man Jeeves* (1919)

1 For several days after my first book was published I carried it about in my pocket, and took surreptitious peeps at it to make sure that the ink had not faded.

J. M. Barrie 1860–1937: speech at the Critics' Circle in London, 26 May 1922

2 Publishers and printers alike seemed to agree among themselves, no matter how divergent their points of view were in other matters, not to publish anything of mine as I wrote it.

James Joyce 1882–1941: letter, 2 April 1932

3 In my capacity as reader, I applaud the Penguin Books; in my capacity as writer I pronounce them anathema . . . The result may be a flood of cheap reprints which will cripple the lending libraries (the novelist's foster-mother) and check the output of new novels. This would be a fine thing for literature but a very bad thing for trade.

George Orwell 1903–50: in 1935; Hans Schmoller *The Paperback Revolution* (1974)

4 Publishers are always trying to fatten their literary fowls in egg-laying competitions.

Edward Garnett 1868–1936: Jeremy Treglown *Romancing: The Life and Work of Henry Green* (2000)

5 As repressed sadists are supposed to become policemen or butchers, so those with an irrational fear of life become publishers.

Cyril Connolly 1903–74: *Enemies of Promise* (1938)

6 Publishing is not ordinary trade: it is gambling. The publisher bets the cost of manufacturing, advertising and circulating a book, plus the overhead of his establishment, against every book he publishes exactly as a turf bookmaker bets against every horse in the race.

George Bernard Shaw 1856–1950: in *The Author* Summer 1945

7 You cannot or at least you should not try to argue with authors. Too many are like children whose tears can suddenly be changed to smiles if they are handled in the right way.
   a publisher's view

Michael Joseph 1897–1958: *The Adventure of Publishing* (1949)

8 I have always thought it one of the charms of dealing with publishers that if you start talking about money, they retire coldly to their professional eminence, and if you start talking about literature, they immediately yank the dollar sign before your eyes.

Raymond Chandler 1888–1959: letter to James Sandoe 20 September 1949

on the requirement as a publisher to compose blurbs for book jackets:
9 I don't know how to grow asparagus, or how to improve your lawn tennis, or the best diet for a 6-month old baby, but I have to write blurbs about them.

T. S. Eliot 1888–1965: reported by Milton Shulman in *Evening Standard* 8 August 1950

10 Publishing is merely a matter of saying Yes and No at the right time.

Michael Joseph 1897–1958: speaking at the Foyle's Jubilee Dinner, 1954

11 Being published by the Oxford University Press is rather like being married to a duchess: the honour is almost greater than the pleasure.

G. M. Young 1882–1959: Rupert Hart-Davis, letter to George Lyttelton, 29 April 1956

12 Very harsh things have been said about publishers, but there can be nothing but good in the heart of a man who regales an author with figgy pudding.
   after lunching with his publisher

Robertson Davies 1913–95: in 1959; *The Enthusiasms of Robertson Davies* (1990)

1 English publishers being what they are (i.e., chary about wasting stamps), I never get to find out what the press says about any book of mine until years later, and then only in red ink on the publisher's statement.

S. J. Perelman 1904–79: letter, 7 January 1960

2 I am told that printer's readers no longer exist because clergymen are no longer unfrocked for sodomy.

Evelyn Waugh 1903–66: letter to Tom Driberg, 11 June 1960

3 The lions looked like so many publishers satiated on a diet of mutual agreement over terms.
after a visit to Longleat

Paul Scott 1920–78: letter, 15 June 1968

4 A publisher who writes is like a cow in a milk bar.

Arthur Koestler 1905–83: attributed, 1982

5 Publishers should not have the Garter.
after declining the honour

Harold Macmillan 1894–1986: Alistair Horne *Harold Macmillan* (1991) vol. 2

6 I'd like the company to continue. I think it will, provided someone doesn't do anything silly. Someone might suddenly decide they want to *educate* the public. Bloody disaster. The public don't want to be educated by us. They want to be amused.
view of the chairman of Mills & Boon, publishers of romantic fiction

John Boon 1916–96: in 1989; in obituary, *Daily Telegraph* 16 July 1996

7 It is not wise to solicit the opinions of publishers—they become proud if you do.

Gore Vidal 1925– : George Greenfield *Scribblers for Bread* (1989)

8 All her life to labour and labour for Faber and Faber.
of a Faber's editor

Seamus Heaney 1939– : attributed; in *Sunday Telegraph* 24 September 1995

9 The whole world of publishing has changed. The accountants have moved in. It's now the bottom line, not is it a good book?

Hammond Innes 1913–98: interview in *Daily Telegraph* 3 August 1996

10 The bookmaking process—fussing with the type, the sample heads, the dust jacket, the flap copy, the cover cloth—has perhaps been dearer to me than the writing process. The latter has been endured as a process tributary to the former, whose envisioned final product, smelling of glue and freshly sliced paper, hangs as a shining mirage luring me through many a grey writing day.

John Updike 1932– : 'Me and My Books' in *New Yorker* 1997

11 The difference between a published and an unpublished author is enormous, and every novelist in the world would agree. *It is a truth universally acknowledged* that published authors, even those whose books have not yet appeared before the public, are filled with a new and reckless confidence in their own powers.

Carol Shields 1935– : *Jane Austen* (2001)

12 The great building of the university press, sometimes apparently mistaken for a rather distinguished college, not only by tourists (I have known editors who had the same impression).
of Oxford University Press

Philip Pullman 1946– : in *Guardian* 27 July 2002

13 Publishing a book is often very much like being put on trial, for some offence which is quite other than the one you know in your heart you've committed.

Margaret Atwood 1939– : *Negotiating with the Dead: A Writer on Writing* (2002)

Philip Pullman 1946–
British writer

1 The furniture is looted from the churches, even if the imagination that scatters and rearranges it is that of an intensely intelligent, moralising atheist.

Andrew Marr 1959– : in *Daily Telegraph* 24 January 2002

Punctuation

2 Another sport which wastes unlimited time is comma-hunting. Once start a comma and the whole pack will be off, full cry, especially if they have had a literary training.
on academic committees

Francis M. Cornford 1874–1943: *Microcosmographia Academica* (1908)

3 Cast iron rules will not answer . . . what is one man's colon is another man's comma.

Mark Twain 1835–1910: Charles Neider (ed.) *Life as I Find It* (1961)

4 Punctuation ought to be exact. Under ordinary circumstances, it is as hard for me to alter punctuation as to alter words, though I will admit that at times I am heady and irresponsible.

Marianne Moore 1887–1972: letter to Ezra **Pound**, 19 January 1919

5 No iron can stab the heart with such force as a full stop put just at the right place.

Isaac Babel 1894–1940: *Guy de Maupassant* (1932)

6 I have a certain system of punctuation which has no authority except in so far as it is founded on the Authorized Version of the Bible, which is not consistent . . . In the Bible there is not from beginning to end a single dash or inverted comma. If you met with either in it you would be shocked . . . I argue that if the Bible could do without dashes and inverted commas, both being disfigurements of the printer's work, any book can.

George Bernard Shaw 1856–1950: letter to May Morris, 13 April 1936

7 Cut out all these exclamation points. An exclamation point is like laughing at your own joke.
correcting a radio script by Sheilah Graham

F. Scott Fitzgerald 1896–1940: Sheilah Graham and Gerald Frank *Beloved Infidel* (1959)

8 The punctuation is pitiable but it never becomes unintelligible so I just shouldn't try. It is clearly not your subject—like theology.
of Love in a Cold Climate

Evelyn Waugh 1903–66: letter to Nancy Mitford, 24 October 1948

9 Do not be afraid of the semicolon; it can be most useful.

Ernest Gowers 1880–1966: *The Complete Plain Words* (1954)

10 The failure of English masters, at all the schools I attended, to give me any comprehension of the purpose of punctuation is splendidly evident in that story.
of his first short story, 'Raspberry Jam' (1946)

Angus Wilson 1913–91: *The Wild Garden* (1963)

11 I dictate everything to a secretary who is good at punctuation. Then a schoolmaster friend reads it all again, for grammar *and* punctuation.

Barbara Cartland 1901–2000: in *Bookseller* 21 January 1978

12 That's all we have, finally, the words, and they had better be the right ones, with the punctuation in the right places so that they can best say what they are meant to say.

Raymond Carver 1938–88: in *New York Times Book Review* 15 February 1981

1 There are things, of course, which the machines know, or think they know. They think they know how to punctuate, because a system of punctuation has been built into them. But they don't seem to know what a colon is, and as I use colons rather often, I conduct a running battle with machines and the people who own them, who assure me that the colon belongs to the past. This is nonsense. The colon is invaluable, and the machines will have to learn.
   on word processors

Robertson Davies 1913–95: speech, Ontario Science Centre, Toronto, 26 November 1989

2 If you take hyphens seriously you will surely go mad.

Anonymous: said to be from a style book in use with Oxford University Press, New York; perhaps apocryphal

3 Commas in *The New Yorker* fall with the precision of knives in a circus act, outlining the victim.

E. B. White 1899–1985: George Plimpton (ed.) *Writers at Work* 8th Series (1988)

4 Unconventional punctuation is, in fact, one of the most obvious and universal signs of Modernism in prose fiction.

David Lodge 1935– : Malcolm Bradbury and James McFarlane (eds.) *Modernism* (1991)

5 The only guide is: omit the hyphen whenever possible, so avoid not only *mechanically propelled vehicle users* (a beauty from *MEU*) but also a *man eating tiger*. And *no one* is right and *no-one* is wrong.

Kingsley Amis 1922–95: *The King's English* (1997)

6 To mark ordinary plurals (*carrot's*, *pickle's*), the so-called greengrocer's apostrophe, its use is illiterate.

Kingsley Amis 1922–95: *The King's English* (1997)

Alexander Pushkin 1799–1837 see also **309:1**
Russian poet

7 Little by little I discovered a whole buried treasure of sound reasoning and noble ideas, which he concealed under a soiled cloak of cynicism.

F. F. Vigel 1786–1856: on his friendship with Pushkin, 1823–4; Elaine Feinstein *Pushkin* (1998)

8 Perhaps I am elegant and dignified in my writing, but my heart is that of a completely common fellow.

Alexander Pushkin 1799–1837: Tatian Wolfe (ed.) *Pushkin on Literature* (1986)

9 A pair of boots is in every sense better than Pushkin, because . . . Pushkin is mere luxury and nonsense.
   frequently quoted in the form 'A pair of boots is worth more than Shakespeare', and for long wrongly associated with the Russian literary critic Dmitry Pisarev

Fedor Dostoevsky 1821–81: in *Epokha* 1864; see **7:1**

10 Russians know the conceptions of 'homeland' and 'Pushkin' are inseparable, and that to be Russian means to love Pushkin.

Vladimir Nabokov 1899–1977: Brian Boyd *Vladimir Nabokov: the American Years* (1991)

11 Pushkin shared with Shakespeare the same sense of character, of the freedom which a character can possess in a great work of art.

John Bayley 1925– : foreword to A. D. P. Briggs (ed.) *Alexander Pushkin: A Celebration of Russia's Best-loved Writer* (1999)

12 Pushkin's verse is taut, crystalline, of classical simplicity and purity, luminous, direct, passionate, sometimes ironical or gay, at other times sublime and magnificent,

Isaiah Berlin 1909–97: afterword to A. D. P. Briggs (ed.) *Alexander Pushkin: A Celebration of Russia's Best-loved Writer* (1999)

always of an indescribable freshness and beauty. It is as untranslatable as Sophocles or Racine. The only modern artist whom he resembles is Mozart; with Mozart and perhaps Goethe he can claim to be the greatest and most universal genius since the Renaissance.

Quotation and Allusion

1 Confound those who have said our remarks before us.

Aelius Donatus fl. 4th century AD: St Jerome *Commentary on Ecclesiastes*

2 He ranged his tropes, and preached up patience; Backed his opinion with quotations.

Matthew Prior 1664–1721: 'Paulo Purganti and his Wife' (1709)

3 Some for renown on scraps of learning dote, And think they grow immortal as they quote.

Edward Young 1683–1765: *The Love of Fame* (1725–8)

4 Classical quotation is the *parole* of literary men all over the world.

Samuel Johnson 1709–84: James Boswell *Life of Samuel Johnson* (1791) 8 May 1781

5 He liked those literary cooks Who skim the cream of others' books; And ruin half an author's graces By plucking bon-mots from their places.

Hannah More 1745–1833: *Florio* (1786)

6 No Greek; as much Latin as you like: never French in any circumstance: no English poet unless he has completed his century.
      advice for House of Commons quotations

Charles James Fox 1749–1806: J. A. Gere and John Sparrow (eds.) *Geoffrey Madan's Notebooks* (1981)

7 His works contain nothing worth quoting; and a book that furnishes no quotations is, *me judice*, no book—it's a plaything.

Thomas Love Peacock 1785–1866: *Crotchet Castle* (1831)

8 A proverb is one man's wit and all men's wisdom.

Lord John Russell 1792–1878: R. J. Mackintosh *Sir James Mackintosh* (1835)

9 To be occasionally quoted is the only fame I care for.

Alexander Smith 1830–67: *Dreamthorp* (1863) 'Men of Letters'

10 Next to the originator of a good sentence is the first quoter of it.

Ralph Waldo Emerson 1803–82: *Letters and Social Aims* (1876)

11 He wrapped himself in quotations—as a beggar would enfold himself in the purple of emperors.

Rudyard Kipling 1865–1936: *Many Inventions* (1893)

12 OSCAR WILDE: How I wish I had said that. WHISTLER: You will, Oscar, you will.

James McNeill Whistler 1834–1903: R. Ellman *Oscar Wilde* (1987)

13 Pretentious quotations being the surest road to tedium.

H. W. Fowler 1858–1933 and **F. G. Fowler** 1870–1918: *The King's English* (1906)

14 You must not treat my immortal works as quarries to be used at will by the various hacks whom you may employ to compile anthologies.

A. E. Housman 1859–1936: letter to his publisher Grant Richards, 29 June 1907

15 What a good thing Adam had. When he said a good thing he knew nobody had said it before.

Mark Twain 1835–1910: *Notebooks* (1935)

16 An anthology is like all the plums and orange peel picked out of a cake.

Walter Raleigh 1861–1922: letter to Mrs Robert Bridges, 15 January 1915

1 I know heaps of quotations, so I can always make quite a fair show of knowledge.

O. Douglas 1877–1948: *The Setons* (1917)

2 Quotations in my work are like wayside robbers who leap out armed and relieve the stroller of his conviction.

Walter Benjamin 1892–1940: *One-Way Street* (1928) 'Hardware'

3 It is a good thing for an uneducated man to read books of quotations.

Winston Churchill 1874–1965: *My Early Life* (1930)

4 I always have a quotation for everything—it saves original thinking.

Dorothy L. Sayers 1893–1957: *Have His Carcase* (1932)

5 Misquotation is, in fact, the pride and privilege of the learned. A widely-read man never quotes accurately, for the rather obvious reason that he has read too widely.

Hesketh Pearson 1887–1964: *Common Misquotations* (1934)

6 The surest way to make a monkey of a man is to quote him.

Robert Benchley 1889–1945: *My Ten Years in a Quandary* (1936)

7 In the dying world I come from quotation is a national vice. No one would think of making an after-dinner speech without the help of poetry. It used to be the classics, now it's lyric verse.

Evelyn Waugh 1903–66: *The Loved One* (1948)

8 I pray to God that I shall never be memorable like that again.
   on Lyndon B. Johnson's use of his line 'We must love one another or die' in a presidential campaign commercial

W. H. Auden 1907–73: in 1964; R. Davenport-Hines *Auden* (1995)

9 It seems pointless to be quoted if one isn't going to be quotable . . . It's better to be quotable than honest.

Tom Stoppard 1937– : in *Guardian* 21 March 1973

10 The nice thing about quotes is that they give us a nodding acquaintance with the originator which is often socially impressive.

Kenneth Williams 1926–88: *Acid Drops* (1980)

11 I am not against anthologies, as long as they are not attempts to enforce a poor idea of poetry, as long as they discover, and as long as they are born of excitement and generosity.

Geoffrey Grigson 1905–85: *The Private Art* (1982)

12 Life itself is a quotation.

Jorge Luis Borges 1899–1986: Jean Baudrillard *Cool Memories* (1987)

13 A quotation is what a speaker wants to say—unlike a soundbite which is all that an interviewer allows you to say.

Tony Benn 1925– : letter to Antony Jay, August 1996

14 In mobilizing support for a project or policy it is especially agreeable to be able to call upon the distinguished dead; their distinction adds intellectual weight and moral force to the argument, and their death makes it impossible for them to appear on television later and say that they meant something completely different.

Antony Jay 1930– : introduction to *Oxford Dictionary of Political Quotations* (1996)

15 The allusion is a private pleasure between you and those of your readers who happen to be able to share it.

James Whale 1951– : *Putting it in Writing* (1999)

Jean Racine 1639–99
French tragedian

16 Racine will go out of style like coffee.

Marie de Sévigné 1626–96: attributed

1 Collect all the facts that can be collected about the life of
Racine and you will never learn from them the art of his
verse.

Paul Valéry 1871–1945: *Introduction to the Method of Leonardo da Vinci* (1895)

Reading

2 When he was reading, he drew his eyes along over the
leaves, and his heart searched into the sense, but his voice
and tongue were silent.
  of St Ambrose

St Augustine AD 354–430: *Confessions* (AD 397–8)

3 Take up and read, take up and read.

St Augustine AD 354–430: *Confessions* (AD 397–8)

4 And as for me, though that I konne but lyte,
On bokes for to rede I me delyte,
And to hem yive I feyth and ful credence,
And in myn herte have hem in reverence
So hertely, that ther is game noon
That fro my bokes maketh me to goon.

Geoffrey Chaucer c.1343–1400: *The Legend of Good Women* 'The Prologue'

5 I have sought for happiness everywhere, but I have found
it nowhere except in a little corner with a little book.

Thomas à Kempis c.1380–1471: attributed; Gerald Donaldson *Books* (1981)

6 He hath not fed of the dainties that are bred in a book; he
hath not eat paper, as it were; he hath not drunk ink.

William Shakespeare 1564–1616: *Love's Labour's Lost* (1595)

7 POLONIUS: What do you read, my lord?
  HAMLET: Words, words, words.

William Shakespeare 1564–1616: *Hamlet* (1601)

8 Read not to contradict and confute, nor to believe and take
for granted, nor to find talk and discourse, but to weigh
and consider.

Francis Bacon 1561–1626: *Essays* (1625) 'Of Studies'

9 Reading maketh a full man.

Francis Bacon 1561–1626: *Essays* (1625) 'Of Studies'

10 Some books are to be tasted, others to be swallowed, and
some few to be chewed and digested; that is, some books
are to be read only in parts; others to be read but not
curiously; and some few to be read wholly, and with
diligence and attention. Some books also may be read by
deputy, and extracts made of them by others.

Francis Bacon 1561–1626: *Essays* (1625) 'Of Studies'

11 I wish thee as much pleasure in the reading, as I had in
the writing.

Francis Quarles 1592–1644: *Emblems* (1635) 'To the Reader'

12   Who reads
Incessantly, and to his reading brings not
A spirit and judgement equal or superior
(And what he brings, what needs he elsewhere seek?)
Uncertain and unsettled still remains,
Deep-versed in books and shallow in himself.

John Milton 1608–74: *Paradise Regained* (1671)

13 Choose an author as you choose a friend.

Wentworth Dillon, Lord Roscommon c.1633–1685: *Essay on Translated Verse* (1684)

14 He had read much, if one considers his long life; but his
contemplation was much more than his reading. He was
wont to say that if he had read as much as other men, he
should have known no more than other men.

John Aubrey 1626–97: *Brief Lives* 'Thomas Hobbes'

1 Reading is to the mind what exercise is to the body.

Richard Steele 1672–1729: in *The Tatler* 18 March 1710

2 The bookful blockhead, ignorantly read,
With loads of learned lumber in his head.

Alexander Pope 1688–1744: *An Essay on Criticism* (1711)

3 A reader seldom peruses a book with pleasure until he knows whether the writer of it be a black man or a fair man, of a mild or choleric disposition, married or a bachelor.

Joseph Addison 1672–1719: in *The Spectator* 1 March 1711

4 I have too much indulged my sedentary humour and have been a rake in reading.

Lady Mary Wortley Montagu 1689–1762: letter to her daughter, Lady Bute, 11 April 1759

5 A man ought to read just as inclination leads him; for what he reads as a task will do him little good.

Samuel Johnson 1709–84: James Boswell *Life of Samuel Johnson* (1791) 14 July 1763

6 ELPHINSTON: What, have you not read it through?
JOHNSON: No, Sir, do *you* read books *through*?

Samuel Johnson 1709–84: James Boswell *Life of Samuel Johnson* (1791) 19 April 1773

7 People in general do not willingly read, if they can have anything else to amuse them.

Samuel Johnson 1709–84: James Boswell *Life of Samuel Johnson* (1791)

8 There is an art of reading, as well as an art of thinking, and an art of writing.

Isaac D'Israeli 1766–1848: *The Literary Character* (1795)

9 But who shall be the master? The writer or the reader?

Denis Diderot 1713–84: *Jacques le Fataliste et son maître* (1796)

10 The time to read is any time: no apparatus, no appointment of time and place, is necessary.

John Aikin 1747–1822: *Letters from a Father to his Son* (1796)

11 4 Sorts of Readers. I. Sponges that suck up every thing and, when pressed give it out in the same state, only perhaps somewhat dirtier—. 2. Sand Glasses . . . whose reading is only a profitless measurement and dozing away of Time—. 3. Straining Bags, who get rid of whatever is good and pure, and retain the dregs. 4 and lastly, the Great-Moguls' Diamond Sieves . . . who assuredly retain the good, while the superfluous or impure passes away and leaves no trace.

Samuel Taylor Coleridge 1772–1834: Notebook, 1806–1810

12 Much have I travelled in the realms of gold,
And many goodly states and kingdoms seen.

John Keats 1795–1821: 'On First Looking into Chapman's Homer' (1817)

13 There are three kinds of readers: one, who enjoys without judging; a third, who judges without enjoying; another in the middle, who judges while enjoying and enjoys while judging. The last class truly reproduces a work of art anew; its members are not numerous.

Johann Wolfgang von Goethe 1749–1832: letter to Johann Friedrich Rochlitz, 13 June 1819

14 For those who have tasted the profound activity of writing, reading is no more than a secondary pleasure.

Stendhal 1783–1842: *De l'Amour* (1822)

15 I strive to amuse myself by reading novels, and have finished that of *The Black Dwarf* by Sir Walter Scott. I must be reduced to a sad state when I feel obliged to such nonsense for a pastime.

John Skinner 1788–1851: diary, 1830

16 One must be an inventor to read well.

Ralph Waldo Emerson 1803–82: *The American Scholar* (1837)

1 Books must be read as deliberately and reservedly as they are written.

Henry David Thoreau 1817–62: *Walden* (1854) 'Reading'

2 Read in order to live.

Gustave Flaubert 1821–80: letter to Mademoiselle de Chantepie, June 1857

on the books she was planning to read:
3 I have not had time yet. But I look at them as a child looks at a cake,—with glittering eyes and watering mouth, imagining the pleasure that awaits him!

Elizabeth Gaskell 1810–65: letter to George Smith, 4 August 1859

4 I do not know any reading more easy, more fascinating, more delightful than a catalogue.

Anatole France 1844–1924: *The Crime of Sylvestre Bonnard* (1881)

5 *La chair est triste, hélas! et j'ai lu tous les livres.*
The flesh, alas, is wearied; and I have read all the books there are.

Stéphane Mallarmé 1842–98: 'Brise Marin' (1887)

6 It is absurd to have a hard and fast rule about what one should read and what one shouldn't. More than half of modern culture depends on what one shouldn't read.

Oscar Wilde 1854–1900: *The Importance of Being Earnest* (1895)

7 The misery of having no time to read a thousand glorious books.

George Gissing 1857–1903: *Commonplace Book* (1962)

8 I would never read a book if it were possible to talk for half an hour with the man who wrote it.

Woodrow Wilson 1856–1924: speech to students at Princeton University in 1910

9 Only sheer ennui sometimes drives [the middle class] to seek distraction in the artist's work.

Arnold Bennett 1867–1931: *Books and Persons* (1917) 'Middle-Class'

10 Reading, that unpunished vice.

Logan Pearsall Smith 1865–1946: *Trivia* (1918)

11 Reading other people's books is better than having to read one's own: and it's much better doing something than nothing.

D. H. Lawrence 1885–1930: letter to Lady Cynthia Asquith, 1922

12 Every reader is, when he reads, reading only about himself.

Marcel Proust 1871–1922: Malcolm Bradbury and James McFarlane (eds.) *Modernism* (1991)

13 'She reads at such a pace,' she complained, 'and when I asked her *where* she had learnt to read so quickly, she replied "On the screens at cinemas."'

Ronald Firbank 1886–1926: *The Flower Beneath the Foot* (1923)

14 The desire to read, like all the other desires that distract our unhappy souls, is capable of analysis.

Virginia Woolf 1882–1941: 'Sir Thomas Browne' (1923)

15 The pain of living and the drug of dreams
Curl up the small soul in the window seat
Behind the *Encyclopedia Britannica*.

T. S. Eliot 1888–1965: 'Animula' (1929)

16 People say that life is the thing, but I prefer reading.

Logan Pearsall Smith 1865–1946: *Afterthoughts* (1931) 'Myself'

17 The reading habit is now often a form of the drug habit.

Q. D. Leavis 1906–81: *Fiction and the Reading Public* (1932)

18 I have sometimes dreamt that when the Day of Judgement dawns and the great conquerors and lawyers and statesmen come to receive their rewards—their crowns, their laurels, their names carved indelibly upon imperishable marble—the Almighty will turn to Peter and

Virginia Woolf 1882–1941: *The Common Reader* (2nd ser., 1932)

will say, not without a certain envy when He sees us coming with our books under our arms, 'Look, these need no reward. We have nothing to give them. They have loved reading.'

1 The mere brute pleasure of reading—the sort of pleasure a cow must have in grazing.

G. K. Chesterton 1874–1936: Dudley Barker *G. K. Chesterton* (1973)

2 I would sooner read a time-table or a catalogue than nothing at all . . . They are much more entertaining than half the novels that are written.

W. Somerset Maugham 1874–1965: *Summing Up* (1938)

3 I wish you read books (you know those things that look like blocks but come apart on one side).

F. Scott Fitzgerald 1896–1940: letter to his wife Zelda, 4 May 1940

4 Have you read any good books lately?

Richard Murdoch 1907–90 and **Kenneth Horne** 1900–69: catch-phrase used by Richard Murdoch in radio comedy series *Much-Binding-in-the-Marsh* (first broadcast 2 January 1947)

5 Imaginative readers rewrite books to suit their own taste, omitting and mentally altering what they read.

Robert Graves 1895–1985: *The Reader over your Shoulder* (1947)

6 What really knocks me out is a book that, when you're all done reading it, you wish the author that wrote it was a terrific friend of yours and you could call him up on the phone whenever you felt like it.

J. D. Salinger 1919– : *Catcher in the Rye* (1951)

7 Persons with manners do not read at table.

Anonymous: saying used by Dylan Thomas in *Under Milk Wood* (1954)

8 Starting a novel is opening a door on a misty landscape; you can still see very little but you can smell the earth and feel the wind blowing.
   on beginning to read a novel

Iris Murdoch 1919–99: *Under the Net* (1954)

9 I can turn from a classic to a thriller without any mental disruption.

Clement Attlee 1883–1967: attributed, 1964

10 Reading isn't an occupation we encourage among police officers. We try to keep the paper work down to a minimum.

Joe Orton 1933–67: *Loot* (1967)

11 The birth of the reader must be at the cost of the death of the Author.

Roland Barthes 1915–80: *The Death of the Author* (1968)

12 Curiously enough, one cannot *read* a book: one can only reread it. A good reader, a major reader, an active and creative reader is a rereader.

Vladimir Nabokov 1899–1977: *Lectures on Literature* (1980) 'Good Readers and Good Writers'

13 The allegory of reading narrates the impossibility of reading.

Paul de Man 1919–83: *The Allegory of Reading* (1979)

14 Reading a book is like rewriting it for yourself . . . You bring to . . . anything you read, all your experience of the world. You bring your history and you read it in your own terms.

Angela Carter 1940–92: in *Marxism Today* January 1985

15 I read for pleasure, and that is the moment at which I learn most. Subliminal learning.

Margaret Atwood 1939– : in an interview, December 1986; Earl G. Ingersoll (ed.) *Margaret Atwood: Conversations* (1990)

1 Many people go on reading now as the equivalent of turning on a television channel for white noise in the background.

Gardner Dozois 1947– : Stan Nicholls (ed.) *Wordsmiths of Wonder* (1993)

2 We may be the last generation, or the last few generations, that regard reading as anything more than a very specific, highly specialized entertainment interest. Like dressing up in cowboy clothes and going to Nashville.

Michael Moorcock 1939– : Stan Nicholls (ed.) *Wordsmiths of Wonder* (1993)

3 And, gentle reader, you as well,
The fountainhead of all remittance.
Buy me before good sense insists
You'll strain your purse and sprain your wrists.

Vikram Seth 1952– : 'A Word of Thanks', at the beginning of *A Suitable Boy* (1993)

4 I like to have exciting evenings on holiday, because after you've spent 8 hours reading on the beach you don't feel like turning in early with a good book.

Arthur Smith 1954– : *The Live Bed Show* (1995)

5 I too read in bed. In the long succession of beds in which I spent the nights of my childhood . . . the combination of bed and book granted me a sort of home which I knew I could go back to, night after night, under whichever skies.

Alberto Manguel 1948– : *A History of Reading* (1996)

6 I am sure everyone has had the experience of reading a book and finding it vibrating with aliveness, with colour and immediacy. And then, perhaps some weeks later, reading it again and finding it flat and empty. Well, the book hasn't changed: you have.

Doris Lessing 1919– : 'Writing Autobiography'; in David Fuller and Patricia Waugh (eds.) *The Arts and Sciences of Criticism* (1999)

7 The exhilaration of one imagination touching another.

William Trevor 1928– : acceptance speech on winning the David Cohen Award, 1999

8 A reader, like a pianist, is engaged in an intense creative operation. If you are used to it, you will notice the effort it takes only when you leave off. Put your book aside and switch on the television and the sense of relaxation is instant. This is because a large part of your brain has stopped working. The pictures beam straight into your brain.

John Carey 1934– : *Pure Pleasure* (2000)

9 Reading, real reading, is a strenuous and pleasurable contact sport.

Maureen Howard 1930– : in *Writers on Writing: Collected Essays from The New York Times* (2001)

10 Losing yourself in a book, the old phrase, is not an idle fantasy but an addictive, model reality.

Susan Sontag 1933– : in *Writers on Writing: Collected Essays from The New York Times* (2001)

11 The act of reading a text is like playing music and listening to it at the same time.

Margaret Atwood 1939– : *Negotiating with the Dead: A Writer on Writing* (2002)

12 After three days without reading, talk becomes flavourless.

Anonymous: Chinese proverb

13 If you believe everything you read, better not read.

Anonymous: Japanese proverb

Rejection

14 After being turned down by numerous publishers, he had decided to write for posterity.

George Ade 1866–1944: *Fables in Slang* (1900)

1 No less than twenty-two publishers and printers read the manuscript of *Dubliners* and when at last it was printed some very kind person bought out the entire edition and had it burnt in Dublin.

James Joyce 1882–1941: letter, 2 April 1932

2 My story 'The Sea and Its Shore' came back from *The Criterion* with *two* rejection slips enclosed, which seems unnecessarily cruel.

Elizabeth Bishop 1911–79: letter to Marianne Moore, 25 February 1937

3 It isn't easy for an author to remain a pleasant human being: both success and failure are usually of a crippling kind.

Graham Greene 1904–91: 'The Poker-Face' (1943)

4 It does not take weeks to tell a man (by pony express) that his piece is wrong when he can be told in a matter of days that it is right. Editors do not make enemies by rejecting manuscripts, but by the way they do it, by the change of atmosphere, the delay, the impersonal note that creeps in.

Raymond Chandler 1888–1959: letter to Charles Morton, 21 January 1945

5 To receive a bitter blow on an early Spring evening (such as that Cape don't want to publish *An Unsuitable Attachment*—but it might be that someone doesn't love you any more)—is it worse than on an Autumn or Winter evening?

Barbara Pym 1913–80: diary, 24 March 1963

a publisher's reader commenting on the manuscript of J. G. Ballard's novel Crash *(published 1973):*
6 This author is beyond psychiatric help . . . do not publish.

Anonymous: in *Independent on Sunday* 16 June 1996; perhaps apocryphal

7 The letter I wrote to *The Author* about not getting published was never published, which seems to be the final accolade of failure.

Barbara Pym 1913–80: letter to Philip Larkin, 19 July 1974

8 These little setbacks, amounting sometimes to thousands of dollars' worth of time wasted, writers must learn to take like Spartans.

Patricia Highsmith 1921–95: *Plotting and Writing Suspense Stories* (1983)

9 Writers and illustrators, involved in the unhinging business of working alone, dredging up ideas and fretting about whether they are any good or not, tend to combine fragile confidence with bottomless ego. They have difficulty in reacting with sanguine calm to their work being criticised or rejected.

Shirley Hughes 1927– : *A Life Drawing* (2002)

Religion

10 That is the Book [the Koran], wherein is no doubt,
a guidance to the godfearing
who believe in the Unseen.

The Koran: sura 2

11 If these writings of the Greeks agree with the book of God, they are useless and need not be preserved; if they disagree, they are pernicious and ought to be destroyed.
on burning the library of Alexandria, AD *c.641*

Caliph Omar AD c.581–644: Edward Gibbon *The Decline and Fall of the Roman Empire* (1776-88)

12 A verse may find him, who a sermon flies,
And turn delight into a sacrifice.

George Herbert 1593–1633: 'The Church Porch' (1633)

1   What in me is dark
Illumine, what is low raise and support;
That to the height of this great argument
I may assert eternal providence,
And justify the ways of God to men.

John Milton 1608–74: *Paradise Lost* (1667)

2   God is the perfect poet,
Who in his person acts his own creations.

Robert Browning 1812–89: *Paracelsus* (1835)

of the novels of Jane **Austen***:*
3 What vile creatures her parsons are.

John Henry Newman 1801–90: letter to Mrs John Morley, 10 January 1837

4 The word is the Verb, and the Verb is God.

Victor Hugo 1802–85: *Contemplations* (1856)

5 There are many who would laugh at the idea of a novelist teaching either virtue or nobility . . . I have regarded my art from so different a point of view that I have ever thought of myself as a preacher of sermons, and my pulpit as one which I could make both salutary and agreeable to my audience.

Anthony Trollope 1815–82: *Autobiography* (1883)

6 Our religion has materialized itself in the fact, in the supposed fact; it has attached its emotions to the fact, and now the fact is failing it. But for poetry the idea is everything; the rest is a world of illusion, of divine illusion. Poetry attaches its emotion to the idea; the idea *is* the fact. The strongest part of our religion today is its unconscious poetry.

Matthew Arnold 1822–88: *Essays in Criticism* Second Series (1888) 'The Study of Poetry'

7 Next to the Bible *In Memoriam* is my comfort.

Queen Victoria 1819–1901: Hallam Tennyson *Alfred Lord Tennyson: a Memoir by His Son* (1897)

8 There's no reason to bring religion into it. I think we ought to have as great a regard for religion as we can, so as to keep it out of as many things as possible.

Sean O'Casey 1880–1964: *The Plough and the Stars* (1926)

9 We know too much and are convinced of too little. Our literature is a substitute for religion, and so is our religion.

T. S. Eliot 1888–1965: *Selected Essays* (1932) 'A Dialogue on Dramatic Poetry' (1928)

10 If God exists, why write literature?
And if he doesn't, why write literature?

Eugène Ionesco 1912–94: *Non* (1934)

11 If God were a poet or took poetry seriously (or science for that matter), he would never have given man free will.

W. H. Auden 1907–73: *Poets at Work* (1948) 'Squares and Oblongs'

12 The poet is the priest of the invisible.

Wallace Stevens 1879–1955: 'Adagia' (1957)

13 Sin is the writer's element.

François Mauriac 1885–1970: *Second Thoughts* (1961) 'Literature and Sin'

14 Religion, oh, just another of those numerous failures resulting from an attempt to popularize art.

Ezra Pound 1885–1972: undated letter to Mary Moore; Humphrey Carpenter *A Serious Character* (1988)

15 Religion to me has always been the wound, not the bandage.

Dennis Potter 1935–94: interview with Melvyn Bragg on Channel 4, March 1994, in *Seeing the Blossom* (1994)

1 I'm sure there is a paper to be written on the evidence of the Prayer Book in the world of Bertie Wooster, and another on the influence of the Prayer Book on English detective fiction.

Alan Bennett 1934– : *Writing Home* (1994)

Reputation and Achievement see also Accolade and Admiration, Fame

2 In our neighbour country Ireland, where truly learning goeth very bare, yet are their poets held in a devout reverence.

Philip Sidney 1554–86: *Apologie for Poetrie* (1595)

3 It is harder to make one's name by a perfect work than it is for a mediocre one to win esteem through the name one already has.

Jean de la Bruyère 1645–96: *Les Caractères ou les moeurs de ce siècle* (1688)

4 One of our late great poets is sunk in his reputation, because he could never forgive any conceit which came in his way; but swept like a drag-net, great and small. There was plenty enough, but the dishes were ill-sorted; whole pyramids of sweetmeats, for boys and women; but little of solid meat for men.
   on Abraham **Cowley**

John Dryden 1631–1700: *Fables Ancient and Modern* (1700) preface; see **55:3**

5 I hold it as certain, that no man was ever written out of reputation but by himself.

Richard Bentley 1662–1742: William Warburton (ed.) *The Works of Alexander Pope* (1751)

6 I had done all that I could; and no man is well pleased to have his all neglected, be it ever so little.

Samuel Johnson 1709–84: letter to Lord Chesterfield, 7 February 1755

7 Fools admire everything in a respected author.

Voltaire 1694–1778: *Candide* (1759)

8 Oh, fond attempt to give a deathless lot
   To names ignoble, born to be forgot!

William Cowper 1731–1800: 'On Observing Some Names of Little Note Recorded in the Biographia Britannica' (1782)

9 Then my verse I dishonour, my pictures despise,
   My person degrade and my temper chastise;
   And the pen is my terror, the pencil my shame;
   And my talents I bury, and dead is my fame.

William Blake 1757–1827: letter to Thomas Butts, 16 August 1803

10 A great man's book in this country like a candle in Lapland, extinguished the moment after it was lit by insects, gnats, and buzzflies.

Samuel Taylor Coleridge 1772–1834: Notebook, 1798–1804

11 'If I should die,' said I to myself, 'I have left no immortal work behind me—nothing to make my friends proud of my memory—but I have loved the principle of beauty in all things, and if I had had time I would have made myself remembered.'

John Keats 1795–1821: letter to Fanny Brawne, c.February 1820

12 The poet's cemetery is the human mind, in which he sows the seeds of never-ending thought—his monument is to be found in his works.

William Hazlitt 1778–1830: *The Spirit of the Age* (1825)

13 If Mr. Coleridge had not been the most impressive talker of his age, he would probably have been the finest writer; but he lays down his pen to make sure of an auditor, and mortgages the admiration of posterity for the stare of an idler.

William Hazlitt 1778–1830: *The Spirit of the Age* (1825)

1 The effect of studying masterpieces is to make me admire and do otherwise.

Gerard Manley Hopkins 1844–89: letter to Robert Bridges, 25 September 1888

2 An artist should get his workmanship as good as he can, and make his work as perfect as possible. A small vessel, built on fine lines, is likely to float further down the stream of time than a big raft.

Alfred, Lord Tennyson 1809–92: Hallam Tennyson *Alfred Lord Tennyson: a Memoir By His Son* (1897)

3 I go out of this year a Poet, my dear Mother, as which I did not enter it. I am held peer by the Georgians; I am a poet's poet.

Wilfred Owen 1893–1918: letter to his mother, 31 December 1917

4 When I am dead, I hope it may be said:
'His sins were scarlet, but his books were read.'

Hilaire Belloc 1870–1953: 'On His Books' (1923)

5 There can be nothing so gratifying to an author as to arouse the respect and esteem of the reader. Make him laugh and he will think you a trivial fellow, but bore him in the right way and your reputation is assured.

W. Somerset Maugham 1874–1965: *Gentleman in the Parlour* (1930)

6 Parnassus after all is not a mountain,
Reserved for A.1. climbers such as you;
It's got a park, it's got a public fountain.
The most I ask is leave to share a pew
With Bradford or with Cottam, that will do.

W. H. Auden 1907–73: *Letter to Lord Byron* (1936)

7 Whom the gods wish to destroy they first call promising.

Cyril Connolly 1903–74: *Enemies of Promise* (1938)

8 God, what a fascinating document could be put together about Neglected Authors . . . There's Aaron Klopstein. Who ever heard of him? I don't suppose you have. He committed suicide at the age of 33 in Greenwich Village by shooting himself with an Amazonian blow gun, having published two novels entitled *Once More the Cicatrice* and *The Sea Gull has no Friends*, two volumes of poetry, *The Hydraulic Face Lift* and *Cat Hairs in the Custard*, one book of short stories called *Twenty Inches of Monkey*, and a book of critical essays entitled *Shakespeare in Baby Talk*.

Raymond Chandler 1888–1959: letter to Jamie Hamilton, 27 September 1954

9 Some books are undeservedly forgotten; none are undeservedly remembered.

W. H. Auden 1907–73: *The Dyer's Hand* (1962) 'Reading'

10 American writers want to be not good but great; and so are neither.

Gore Vidal 1925– : *Two Sisters* (1970)

11 If there is anything worse for a writer than missing the bus, it is being thought twenty years later, to have got on the wrong one.

Paul Scott 1920–78: 'Literature and the Social Conscience' (1972)

12 I don't want to go around pretending to be me.
   of being a 'great man of letters'

Philip Larkin 1922–85: interview in *Observer* 16 December 1979

13 I detest and despise success, yet I cannot do without it. I am like a drug addict—if nobody talks about me for a couple of months I have withdrawal symptoms.

Eugène Ionesco 1912–94: in *Paris Review* 1984

14 I've written more words than most people have spoken.

J. B. Priestley 1894–1984: attributed; in *The Author* autumn 1997

1 Were those real poems you read or did you write them
yourself?
    child's *question at a poetry reading, giving title to article*
    'Are Those Real Poems?'

Anonymous: in *New York Times Book Review* 12 February 1995 'Are Those Real Poems?'

2 Minor poets are lucky. Minor novelists are totally
forgotten, but if you get a poem into an anthology they
remember you.

Geoffrey Dearmer 1893–1996: in *The Times* 20 August 1996; obituary

3 When a writer says publicly that the novel is doomed, it's
a sure bet his new book isn't going well; in terms of his
reputation, it's like bleeding in shark-infested waters.

Jonathan Franzen 1959– : *How to be Alone* (2002) 'Why bother?'

Reviews see also Criticism

4 Reviewers are usually people who would have been poets,
historians, biographers, &c., if they could; they have tried
their talents at one or at the other, and have failed;
therefore they turn critics.

Samuel Taylor Coleridge 1772–1834: *Seven Lectures on Shakespeare and Milton* (delivered 1811–12)

5 Send me no more reviews of any kind.—I will read no
more of evil or good in that line.—Walter Scott has not
read a review of *himself* for *thirteen years*.

Lord Byron 1788–1824: letter to his publisher John Murray, 3 November 1821

6 'Tis strange the mind, that very fiery particle,
Should let itself be snuffed out by an article.
    on **Keats** *'who was killed off by one critique'; see* **58:10**

Lord Byron 1788–1824: *Don Juan* (1819–24)

7 He took the praise as a greedy boy takes apple pie, and the
criticism as a good dutiful boy takes senna-tea.
    of Bulwer Lytton, whose novels he had criticized

Lord Macaulay 1800–59: letter, 5 August 1831

8 We cannot sum up the merits of the stupendous mass of
paper which lies before us, better than by saying, that it
consists of about two thousand closely printed pages, that
it occupies fifteen hundred inches cubic measure, and that
it weighs sixty pounds avoirdupois.
    reviewing Edward Nares's three-volume Memoirs of
    William Cecil, Lord Burghley

Lord Macaulay 1800–59: in *Edinburgh Review* April 1832

9 I never read a book before reviewing it; it prejudices a man
so.

Sydney Smith 1771–1845: H. Pearson *The Smith of Smiths* (1934)

10 Puffing and plenty of tickets were . . . the system of the
day. It was an interchange of amenities over the dinner-
table; a flattery of power on the one side, and puns on the
other; and what the public took for a criticism on a play
was a draft upon the box-office, or reminiscences of last
Thursday's salmon and lobster sauce.
    on early 19th-century theatre reviewing

Leigh Hunt 1784–1859: *Autobiography* (rev. ed., 1860)

11 People who like this sort of thing will find this the sort of
thing they like.
    judgement of a book

Abraham Lincoln 1809–65: G. W. E. Russell *Collections and Recollections* (1898)

12 It is with utter indifference that I regard the critical
disturbance and all the insanity written about *Ghosts*. I
was prepared for this . . . There were screams about *Peer
Gynt*, and not less against *Pillars of Society* and *A Doll's
House*. The screams will die away on this occasion as they
did previously.

Henrik Ibsen 1828–1906: letter to Hegel, 1882

1 If this sort of thing continues no more novel-writing for me. A man must be a fool to deliberately stand up and be shot at.
of a hostile review of Tess of the D'Urbervilles, *1891*

Thomas Hardy 1840–1928: Florence Hardy *The Early Life of Thomas Hardy* (1928)

2 I am strongly of opinion that an author had far better not read any reviews of his books: the unfavourable ones are almost certain to make him cross, and the favourable ones conceited; and neither of these results is desirable.

Lewis Carroll 1832–98: *Sylvie and Bruno Concluded* (1893)

3 Browning made the verses
Your servant the critique
Browning couldn't sing at all
I fancy I could speak.
Although his book was clever
(To give the deil his due)
I wasn't pleased with Browning's verse
Nor he with my review.

Robert Louis Stevenson 1850–94: 'Light Verse'

4 A sound-headed costermonger who did not know the word *critic* would give better judgement.
on hack reviewers

George Gissing 1857–1903: *Commonplace Book* (1962)

5 I am sitting in the smallest room of my house. I have your review before me. In a moment it will be behind me.
responding to a savage review by Rudolph Louis in Münchener Neueste Nachrichten, *7 February 1906*

Max Reger 1873–1916: Nicolas Slonimsky *Lexicon of Musical Invective* (1953)

6 When I read reviews I crush the columns together to get at one or two sentences; is it a good book or a bad? And then I discount those two sentences according to what I know of the book and of the reviewer. But when I write a review I write every sentence as if it were going to be tried before three Chief Justices: I can't believe that I am crushed together and discounted.

Virginia Woolf 1882–1941: diary, 18 February 1922

7 From the moment I picked up your book until I laid it down, I was convulsed with laughter. Some day I intend reading it.
blurb written for S. J. Perelman's 1928 book Dawn Ginsberg's Revenge

Groucho Marx 1895–1977: Hector Arce *Groucho* (1979)

8 This fictional account of the day-by-day life of an English gamekeeper is still of considerable interest to outdoor-minded readers, as it contains many passages on pheasant raising, the apprehending of poachers, ways to control vermin, and other chores and duties of the professional gamekeeper. Unfortunately one is obliged to wade through many pages of extraneous material in order to discover and savour these sidelights on the management of a Midlands shooting estate, and in this reviewer's opinion this book cannot take the place of J. R. Miller's *Practical Gamekeeping*.

Anonymous: review of D. H. Lawrence *Lady Chatterley's Lover*, attributed to *Field and Stream*, c.1928

9 *House Beautiful* is play lousy.

Dorothy Parker 1893–1967: review of play in *New Yorker*, 1933; Phyllis Hartnoll *Plays and Players* (1984)

1 The professional reviewers: the light men who bubble at the mouth with enthusiasm because they see other bubbles floating around; the dumb men who regularly mistake your worst stuff for your best and your best for your worst, and, most of all, the cowards who straddle and the leeches who review your books in terms that they have cribbed out of the book itself, like scholars under some extraordinary dispensation which allows them to heckle the teacher.

F. Scott Fitzgerald 1896–1940: letter, 10 May 1934

2 Among the drudgeries by which the aesthetic professions have to save themselves from starvation, reviewing is not the worst.

George Bernard Shaw 1856–1950: in *The Author* Summer 1943

3 There is practically a stable of puff merchants back in your territory who will go on record over practically anything including the World Almanac, provided they get their names featured. A few names occur with such monotonous regularity that only the fact of their known success as writers keeps one from thinking this is the way they earn their groceries.
on over-generous English reviewers

Raymond Chandler 1888–1959: letter to Charles Morton, July 1951

4 One pleasure, come what may, is lying in bed with a beautiful young girl and hearing The Critics say nice things about one on the wireless.

Laurie Lee 1914–97: notebook, 1959; Valerie Grove *Laurie Lee* (1999)

5 One cannot review a bad book without showing off.

W. H. Auden 1907–73: *Dyer's Hand* (1962) 'Reading'

6 Writing reviews can be fun, but I don't think the practice is very good for the character.

W. H. Auden 1907–73: George Plimpton (ed.) *Writers at Work* 1977 4th series

7 The ones who get under my skin are the academic critics whose whole training is to detect faults. They call them 'flaws'. I call them 'flawyers'.
on reviewers

Robertson Davies 1913–95: in *Paris Review* 1989

8 Kingsley Amis said 'You should let a bad review ruin your breakfast but not your lunch'. I tend to move that forward a bit: let it ruin your lunch but not your dinner 'cause I probably get up later than him.

Arthur Smith 1954– : in *Independent on Sunday* 5 February 1995 'Overheard'

9 I have spent years as a professional writer and what I know now is that the only review that is no use to me is a review that lies.

Kazuo Ishiguro 1954– : in *Guardian* 15 May 1996

10 My own ideal review was exemplified when a former publicity director of my publishers reviewed one of my books under the headline, 'Literary Genius Writes Masterpiece.' Unfortunately it was published in an English-language Hong Kong newspaper of very small circulation.

David Lodge 1935– : *Consciousness and the Novel* (2002)

Revision see also **Choice of Words**, **Omission**, **Style**

11 Now, O king, establish the decree, and sign the writing, that it be not changed, according to the law of the Medes and Persians, which altereth not.

Bible: Daniel

1 In the mind, as in the body, there is the necessity of getting rid of waste, and a man of active literary habits will write for the fire as well as for the press.

Jerome Cardan 1501–76: William Osler *Aequanimites* (1904); epigraph

2 I had not time to lick it into form, as she [a bear] doth her young ones.

Robert Burton 1577–1640: *The Anatomy of Melancholy* (1621–51)

3 I have made this [letter] longer than usual, only because I have not had the time to make it shorter.

Blaise Pascal 1623–62: *Lettres Provinciales* (1657)

4 I write I neither know how nor why, and always make worse what I try to amend.

Horace Walpole 1717–97: letter to Rev. William Mason, 11 May 1769

5 Poetry, like schoolboys, by too frequent and severe correction, may be cowed into Dullness!

Samuel Taylor Coleridge 1772–1834: Notebook, 1794–1798

6 Not that the story need be long, but it will take a long while to make it short.

Henry David Thoreau 1817–62: letter to Harrison Blake, 16 November 1857

7 If I don't rewrite them it's because I don't see how to write them better, not because I don't think they should be.

Robert Louis Stevenson 1850–94: letter to W. E. Henley, April 1879

8 Sometimes the three hours' labour of a morning resulted in half a dozen lines, corrected into illegibility.

George Gissing 1857–1903: of 'Edwin Reardon' in *New Grub Street* (1891)

9 I generally go back and do over my yesterday's work, much like the snail in the arithmetical problem, who climbed four feet each day and slipped back three each night, besides sometimes going back to write whole masses again . . . I am happier rewriting than blocking out.

Charlotte Yonge 1823–1901: Georgina Battiscombe *Charlotte Mary Yonge* (1943)

10 I said 'a line will take us hours maybe,
Yet if it does not seem a moment's thought
Our stitching and unstitching has been naught.'

W. B. Yeats 1865–1939: 'Adam's Curse' (1904)

11 The friends that have it I do wrong
Whenever I remake a song,
Should know what issue is at stake:
It is myself that I remake.

W. B. Yeats 1865–1939: 'The friends that have it I do wrong' (1908)

12 The business of selection and revision is simply hell for me—my efforts to cut out 50,000 words may sometimes result in my adding 75,000.

Thomas Wolfe 1900–38: letter to Maxwell Perkins, his editor at Scribner's, 17 November 1928

13 I published it in the waste-paper basket.

Rudyard Kipling 1865–1936: Thomas Pinney in *Times Literary Supplement* 7 April 1995

14 I believe that any good writer has, in his early life, scrapped at least one book. It would not be a good sign if he started doing competent work at once, that way lies the mechanical prosperity of the higher journalists.

Evelyn Waugh 1903–66: letter, 29 June 1938

15 I often covered more than a hundred sheets of paper with drafts, revisions, rewritings, ravings, doodlings, and intensely concentrated work to construct a single verse.

Dylan Thomas 1914–53: letter, 25 May 1948

16 The manuscript was a delight to read . . . but isn't a book at all yet. No more 40 hour week. Blood, sweat and tears. That is to say if you want to produce a work of art. There is a work of art there, lurking in a hole, occasionally visible to the tip of its whiskers.
having read the manuscript of Nancy Mitford's Love in a Cold Climate

Evelyn Waugh 1903–66: letter to Nancy Mitford, 24 October 1948

1 Now none of this. No complaints about headaches. Revision is just as important as any other part of writing and must be done con amore.

Evelyn Waugh 1903–66: letter to Nancy Mitford, 31 March 1951

2 Tell them the author giveth and the author taketh away.
to a playwright afraid to tell the cast of cuts he had made

George S. Kaufman 1889–1961: Howard Teichmann *George S. Kaufman* (1973)

3 I constantly rewrite—an incinerator is a writer's best friend.

Thornton Wilder 1897–1975: in *New York Times* 6 November 1961

4 A writer is unfair to himself when he is unable to be hard on himself.

Marianne Moore 1887–1972: George Plimpton (ed.) *Writers at Work* (2nd series, 1963)

5 I do a lot of revising. Certain chapters six or seven times . . . I usually write to a point where the work is getting worse rather than better. That's the point to stop and the time to publish.

John Dos Passos 1896–1970: George Plimpton (ed.) *The Writer's Chapbook* (1989)

6 First drafts are for learning what your novel or story is about. Revision is working with that knowledge to enlarge and enhance an idea, to re-form it . . . Revision is one of the true pleasures of writing.

Bernard Malamud 1914–86: George Plimpton (ed.) *Writers at Work* (6th series, 1984)

7 If it sounds like writing, I rewrite it.

Elmore Leonard 1925– : interview in *Newsweek* 22 April 1985

8 The waste-paper basket is the writer's best friend.

Isaac Bashevis Singer 1904–91: George Plimpton (ed.) *The Writer's Chapbook* (1989)

9 I do a lot of rewriting. I find that the more versions you see of, say, the beginning of a chapter—blue paper, white paper, typed, longhand—the more you get it right in the end.

William Trevor 1928– : in *Paris Review* 1989

10 I correct or change words, but I can't rewrite a scene or make a major change because there's a sense then of someone looking over my shoulder.

Eudora Welty 1909–2001: George Plimpton (ed.) *The Writer's Chapbook* (1989)

11 I rewrite endlessly, sentence by sentence; it's more like oxywelding than writing.

Patrick White 1912–90: *Patrick White Speaks* (1990)

12 The pleasure of the first draft lies in deceiving yourself that it is quite close to the real thing. The pleasure of the subsequent drafts lies partly in realizing that you haven't been gulled by the first draft.

Julian Barnes 1946– : in *Paris Review* Winter 2000

Rhyme and Rhythm see also Poetry

13 Of its own accord my song would come in the right rhythms, and what I was trying to say was poetry.

Ovid 43 BC–AD c.17: *Tristia*

14 'By God,' quod he, 'for pleynly, at a word,
Thy drasty rymyng is nat worth a toord!'

Geoffrey Chaucer c.1343–1400: *The Canterbury Tales* 'Sir Thopas'

15 For rhyme the rudder is of verses,
With which like ships they steer their courses.

Samuel Butler 1612–80: *Hudibras* pt. 1 (1663)

16 Rhyme being no necessary adjunct or true ornament of poem or good verse, in longer works especially, but the invention of a barbarous age, to set off wretched matter and lame metre.

John Milton 1608–74: *Paradise Lost* (1667) 'The Verse' (preface, added 1668)

1 The troublesome and modern bondage of rhyming.

John Milton 1608–74: *Paradise Lost* (1667) 'The Verse' (preface, added 1668)

2 Rhyme is the rock on which thou art to wreck.

John Dryden 1631–1700: *Absalom and Achitophel* (1681)

3 But when loud surges lash the sounding shore,
The hoarse, rough verse should like the torrent roar.
When Ajax strives, some rock's vast weight to throw,
The line too labours, and the words move slow.

Alexander Pope 1688–1744: *An Essay on Criticism* (1711)

4 A needless Alexandrine ends the song,
That, like a wounded snake, drags its slow length along.

Alexander Pope 1688–1744: *An Essay on Criticism* (1711)

5 Let your little verses flow
Gently, sweetly, row by row;
Let the verse the subject fit,
Little subject, little wit.

Henry Carey c.1687–1743: 'Namby-Pamby: or, A Panegyric on the New Versification' (1725)

6 Iambics march from short to long;—
With a leap and a bound the swift Anapaests throng.

Samuel Taylor Coleridge 1772–1834: 'Metrical Feet' (1806)

7 Trochee trips from long to short.

Samuel Taylor Coleridge 1772–1834: 'Metrical Feet' (1806)

8 Spenserian vowels that elope with ease,
And float along like birds o'er summer seas.

John Keats 1795–1821: 'To Charles Cowden Clarke' (1817)

9 Prose poets like blank-verse. I'm fond of rhyme,
Good workmen never quarrel with their tools.

Lord Byron 1788–1824: *Don Juan* (1819–24)

10 There is something magical about rhythm; it even makes us believe we have taken possession of the sublime.

Johann Wolfgang von Goethe 1749–1832: *Art and Antiquity* (1816–32)

11 Mysterious and strong effects lie in different poetical forms. If the content of my *Roman Elegies* were transposed into the tone and metre of Byron's *Don Juan*, then what is said would sound quite infamous.

Johann Wolfgang von Goethe 1749–1832: Johann Peter Eckermann *Conversations with Goethe* (1836–48)

12 Keeping time, time, time,
In a sort of Runic rhyme,
To the tintinnabulation that so musically wells
From the bells, bells, bells.

Edgar Allan Poe 1809–49: 'The Bells' (1849)

13 In our language rhyme is a barrel. A barrel of dynamite. The line is a fuse. The line smoulders to the end and explodes; and the town is blown sky-high in a stanza.

Vladimir Mayakovsky 1893–1930: 'Conversation with an Inspector of Taxes about Poetry' (1926)

14 The author's conviction on this day of New Year is that music begins to atrophy when it departs too far from the dance; that poetry begins to atrophy when it gets too far from music.

Ezra Pound 1885–1972: *The ABC of Reading* (1934)

15 The useful trick of rhyming stressed with unstressed syllables, which I introduced into English poetry.

Robert Graves 1895–1985: letter, 1 September 1943

16 I'd as soon write free verse as play tennis with the net down.

Robert Frost 1874–1963: Edward Lathem *Interviews with Robert Frost* (1966)

17 One salient consequence of my blindness was my gradual abandonment of free verse in favour of classical metrics. In fact, blindness made me take up the writing of poetry again. Since rough drafts were denied me, I had to fall

Jorge Luis Borges 1899–1986: *The Aleph and Other Stories* (1971) 'Autobiographical Essay'

back on memory. It is obviously easier to remember verse than prose, and to remember regular verse forms rather than free ones. Regular verse is, so to speak, portable.

1 Don't let this aid to rhyming bitch your talent or your timing.
   in a rhyming dictionary given to Lionel Bart

Noël Coward 1899–1973: attributed

2 The notion of expressing sentiments in short lines having similar sounds at their ends seems as remote as mangoes on the moon.

Philip Larkin 1922–85: letter to Barbara Pym, 22 January 1975

3 Metrical poetry is ultimately allied to song, and I like the connection. Free verse is ultimately allied to conversation, and I like that connection too.

Thom Gunn 1929– : in *Paris Review* 1995

Samuel Richardson 1689–1761 see also **106:3**
English novelist

4 I love to write to the moment.

Samuel Richardson 1689–1761: *Clarissa* (1747–8)

5 I look upon this [*Clarissa*] and *Pamela* to be two books that will do more general mischief than the works of Lord Rochester.

Lady Mary Wortley Montagu 1689–1762: letter to Lady Bute, 1 March 1752

6 Why, Sir, if you were to read Richardson for the story, your impatience would be so much fretted that you would hang yourself.

Samuel Johnson 1709–84: James Boswell *Life of Samuel Johnson* (1791) 6 April 1772

7 Oh Richardson! thou singular genius.

Denis Diderot 1713–84: Isaac D'Israeli *Curiosities of Literature* (1849 ed.)

8 There is more knowledge of the heart in one letter of Richardson's than in all *Tom Jones*.

Samuel Johnson 1709–84: James Boswell *Life of Samuel Johnson* (1791)

9 Richardson was well qualified to be the discoverer of a new style of writing, for he was a cautious, deep, and minute examiner of the human heart, and . . . left neither head, bay nor inlet behind him, until he had traced its soundings, and laid it down in his chart, with all its minute sinuosities, its depths, and its shallows.

Sir Walter Scott 1771–1832: *Lives of the Poets* (1827) 'Samuel Richardson'

10 The censure which the Shakespeare of novelists has incurred for the tedious procrastination and the minute details of his fable; his slow unfolding characters, and the slightest gesture of his personages, is extremely unjust; for is it not evident that we could not have his peculiar excellences without these accompanying defects.

Isaac D'Israeli 1766–1848: *Curiosities of Literature* (1849 ed.)

Arthur Rimbaud 1854–91
French poet

11 The poet makes himself a visionary [*voyant*] through a long, immense and calculated *disordering of the senses*. Every form of love, suffering, madness; he searches for and consumes all the poisons, keeping only their quintessences.

Arthur Rimbaud 1854–91: letter to Paul Demeny, 15 May 1871

1 Mortal, angel AND demon, in other words Rimbaud.

Paul Verlaine 1844–96: *Dédicaces* (1894)

Rivalry see also Accolade and Admiration

2 My desire is . . . that mine adversary had written a book.

Bible: Job

3 *Multa fero, ut placem genus irritabile vatum.*
I have to put up with a lot, to please the touchy breed of poets.

Horace 65–8 BC: *Epistles*

4 Readers and listeners like my books,
Yet a certain poet calls them crude.
What do I care? I serve up food
To please my guests, not fellow cooks.

Martial AD c.40–c.104: *Epigrammata*, tr. James Michie

5 Sei Shōnagon . . . was dreadfully conceited. She thought herself so clever and littered her writings with Chinese characters; but if you examined them closely, they left a good deal to be desired . . . People who go out of their way to try and be sensitive in the most unpromising situations, trying to capture every moment of interest, however slight, are bound to look ridiculous and superficial.
one literary Japanese court lady's view of another

Murasaki Shikibu c.978–c.1031: diary, c.1010; see **292:7**

6 Envy's a sharper spur than pay,
No author ever spared a brother,
Wits are gamecocks to one another.

John Gay 1685–1732: *Fables* (1727) 'The Elephant and the Bookseller'

7 Hot, envious, noisy, proud, the scribbling fry
Burn, hiss and bounce, waste paper, stink, and die.

Edward Young 1683–1765: *The Love of Fame* (1725–8)

8 What poet would not grieve to see
His brother write as well as he?
But rather than they should excel,
Would wish his rivals all in Hell?

Jonathan Swift 1667–1745: 'Verses on the Death of Dr Swift' (1731)

9 Whaur's yer Wullie Shakespeare noo?
cry from a member of the audience at the first night of John Home's tragedy Douglas, Edinburgh, *14 December 1756*

Anonymous: traditional

10 The infamous trade of vilifying one's colleagues to earn a little money should be left to cheap journalists . . . It is those wretches who have made of literature an arena for gladiators.

Voltaire 1694–1778: letter to a friend, 20 February 1767

11 I think none but pikes and poets prey upon their kind.

William Warburton 1698–1779: to David Garrick, 22 April 1762

12 How odious all authors are, and how doubly so to each other!

Henry Fox, Lord Holland d. 1859: letter, 3 January 1821

13 In general I do not draw well with literary men—not that I dislike them but—I never know what to say to them after I have praised their last publication.

Lord Byron 1788–1824: 'Detached Thoughts' 15 October 1821

14 Authors are like cattle going to a fair: those of the same field can never move on without butting one another.

Walter Savage Landor 1775–1864: *Imaginary Conversations* (1824–9) 'Archdeacon Hare and Walter Landor'

1 Success in literature? What on earth does George Lewes know about success in literature?
on learning that Lewes had contributed articles on the theme of 'Success in Literature'

Charles Dickens 1812–70: Peter Ackroyd *Dickens* (1990)

2 The hateful spirit of literary rancour . . . enough to make all literature appear a morbid excrescence upon human life.

George Gissing 1857–1903: *New Grub Street* (1891)

3 Hateful as is the struggle for life in every form, this rough-and-tumble of the literary arena seems to me sordid and degrading beyond all others. Oh, your prices per thousand words! Oh, your paragraphs and your interviewings! and oh, the black despair that awaits those down-trodden in the fray.

George Gissing 1857–1903: *The Private Papers of Henry Ryecroft* (1903)

4 I called him a wrinkled and toothless baboon, who, first hoisted in notoriety on the shoulders of Carlyle, now spits and splutters on a filthier platform of his own finding and fouling.
*account of a letter, sent to **Emerson**, which did not receive a reply*

Algernon Charles Swinburne 1837–1909: in conversation with Edmund Gosse; Evan Charteris *Life and Letters of Sir Edmund Gosse* (1931)

5 But where's the wild dog that has praised his fleas?

W. B. Yeats 1865–1939: 'To a Poet, Who would have Me Praise certain bad Poets, Imitators of His and of Mine' (1910)

6 I was jealous of her writing—the only writing I have ever been jealous of.
*shortly after the death of Katherine **Mansfield***

Virginia Woolf 1882–1941: letter, 16 January 1923

7 Do we want laurels for ourselves most,
Or most that no one else shall have any?

Amy Lowell 1874–1925: *What's O'Clock* (1925) 'La Ronde du Diable'

8 Poets arguing about modern poetry: jackals snarling over a dried-up well.

Cyril Connolly 1903–74: *The Unquiet Grave* (1944)

9 My personal animosity against a writer never affects my opinion of what he writes. Nobody could be more anxious than myself, for instance, that Alan Alexander Milne should trip over a loose bootlace and break his bloody neck, yet I reread his early stuff at regular intervals with all the old enjoyment.
A. A. Milne had written a hostile letter to the Daily Telegraph *on the report of **Wodehouse**'s broadcasting from Germany*

P. G. Wodehouse 1881–1975: letter, 27 November 1945

10 I started out very quiet and I beat Mr Turgenev. Then I trained hard and I beat Mr de Maupassant. I've fought two draws with Mr Stendhal, and I think I had an edge in the last one. But nobody's going to get me in any ring with Mr Tolstoy unless I'm crazy or I keep getting better.

Ernest Hemingway 1899–1961: in *New Yorker* 13 May 1950

11 I had the freak of luck to start high on the mountain, and go down sharp while others were passing me.
of the period after the publication of his novel The Barbary Shore

Norman Mailer 1923– : Gore Vidal in *The Nation* 2 January 1960

of her time as editor of Poetry Review*:*

1 Their petty ambitions and their cut-throat behaviour was amazing, I had never seen anything like it. I could see how literature works up people's passions and ambitions for success—any little success, publication, anything.

Muriel Spark 1918– : on *Bookstand*, 1961 television programme; repeated on BBC2 *Bookmark* 9 March 1996

2 No poet or novelist wishes he were the only one who ever lived, but most of them wish they were the only one alive, and quite a number fondly believe their wish has been granted.

W. H. Auden 1907–73: *The Dyer's Hand* (1962) 'Writing'

3 I remember Charles Wood's response to hearing of O'Casey's death: 'One less to worry about'.

Peter Nichols 1927– : diary, 22 November 1970

4 Whenever a friend succeeds, a little something in me dies.

Gore Vidal 1925– : in *Sunday Times Magazine* 16 September 1973

5 Let Shakespeare do it his way, I'll do it mine. We'll see who comes out better.

Mae West 1892–1980: G. Eells and S. Musgrove *Mae West* (1989)

6 The book of my enemy has been remaindered
And I rejoice . . .
What avail him now his awards and prizes,
The praise expended upon his meticulous technique,
His individual new voice?

Clive James 1939– : 'The Book of My Enemy has been Remaindered' (1986)

7 Writers seldom wish other writers well.

Saul Bellow 1915– : attributed, 1989

of appreciations of other writers in Kingsley **Amis**'*s Memoirs:*

8 It is as if Amis is swimming slowly but surely under water, carefully slogging through the praise stroke by stroke, when all of a sudden he feels he can't go any further without rising to the surface and taking a quick slug of the air of misanthropy.

Craig Brown 1957– : *Craig Brown's Greatest Hits* (1993)

9 Being a minor poet is like being minor royalty. And no one, as a former lady-in-waiting to Princess Margaret once explained to me, is happy as that.

Stephen Spender 1909–95: in *Daily Telegraph* 18 July 1995; obituary

10 For a writer who has been quietly getting on with her work for over 30 years with malice towards none, it is shocking to discover how much ill-will and envy of the successful bubbles beneath the surface.

P. D. James 1920– : in *Daily Telegraph* 30 September 1995 'They Said It'

11 Good writing has always been attacked, notably by other good writers.

Salman Rushdie 1947– : interview in *Observer* 18 August 1996

12 Writers are always envious, mean-minded, filled with rage and envy at others' good fortune. There is nothing like the failure of a close friend to cheer us up.

Peter Carey 1943– : in *Observer* 18 August 2002

Romantic Fiction see also Popular Fiction

13 The novels which I approve are such as display human nature with grandeur—such as show her in the sublimities of intense feeling—such as exhibit the progress of strong passion from the first germ of incipient susceptibility to the utmost energies of reason half-dethroned,—where we see the strong spark of woman's captivations elicit such fire in the soul of man as lead him—(though at the risk of some aberration from the

Jane Austen 1775–1817: 'Sir Edward Denham' in *Sanditon* (1925 ed.)

strict line of primitive obligations)—to hazard all, dare all, achieve all, to obtain her.

1 Romantic novels have become a commercial enterprise in England much like tea and tobacco. Romances are read in much the same way as a cigar is smoked or a cup of tea is drunk. Hundreds of people, mostly women, are employed in the production of this reading matter.

Eça de Queiroz 1846–1900: letter,30 May 1877

2 And what's romance? Usually, a nice little tale where you have everything As You Like It, where rain never wets your jacket and gnats never bite your nose and it's always daisy-time.

D. H. Lawrence 1885–1930: *Studies in Classic American Literature* (1924)

3 It's our *own* story *exactly*! He bold as a hawk, she soft as the dawn.

James Thurber 1894–1961: cartoon caption in *New Yorker* 25 February 1939

4 As artists they're rot, but as providers they're oil wells; they gush.
   on lady novelists

Dorothy Parker 1893–1967: Malcolm Cowley *Writers at Work* 1st Series (1958)

5 We ought to be prescribed by the NHS. We're better than valium.
   view of the chairman of Mills & Boon, publishers of romantic fiction

John Boon 1916–96: in 1989; in obituary, *Daily Telegraph* 16 July 1996

6 You can't lose if you give them handsome highwaymen, duels, 3-foot fountains and whacking great horses and dogs all over the place.

Barbara Cartland 1901–2000: in *Attitude*; in *Guardian* 26 April 1996

Salman Rushdie 1947–
Indian-born British novelist

7 Frankly I wish I had written a more critical book.
   after The Satanic Verses *had provoked the fatwa invoked against him by Ayatollah Khomeini*

Salman Rushdie 1947– : in *Weekend Guardian* 18 February 1989; see **41:6**

8 There has always been something Olympian about Salman Rushdie. His belief in his own powers, however (unlike other kinds of belief), is not monolithic and therefore precarious. It is agile, capricious and droll.

Martin Amis 1949– : in *Vanity Fair* 1990

John Ruskin 1819–1900
English art and social critic

9 In face, in manner, in talk, in mind, he is weakness pure and simple. I use the word, not invidiously, but scientifically. He has the beauties of his defects; but to see him only confirms the impression given by his writing, that he has been scared back by the grim face of reality into the world of unreason and illusion, and that he wanders there without a compass and a guide—or any light save the fitful flashes of his beautiful genius.

Henry James 1843–1916: letter, 20 March 1869

10 He is a chartered libertine—he has possessed himself by prescription of the function of a general scold.

Henry James 1843–1916: in *Nation* 19 December 1878

1 I am, and my father was before me, a violent Tory of the old school; Walter Scott's school, that is to say, and Homer's.

John Ruskin 1819–1900: *Praeterita* (1885)

George Sand 1804–76
French novelist

2 Thou large-brained woman and large-hearted man.

Elizabeth Barrett Browning 1806–61: 'To George Sand—A Desire' (1844)

3 Now I can understand admiration of George Sand—for though I never saw any of her works which I admired throughout . . . yet she has a grasp of mind which, if I cannot fully comprehend, I can very deeply respect; she is sagacious and profound; Miss Austen is only shrewd and observant.

Charlotte Brontë 1816–55: letter, 12 January 1848

Sappho late 7th century BC
Greek lyric poet

4 Some say the muses are nine—how careless—behold Sappho of Lesbos is the tenth!

Plato 429–347 BC: attributed, *Anthologia Palatina* (c.1000)

5 Dark Sappho! could not verse immortal save That breast imbued with such immortal fire? Could she not live who life eternal gave?

Lord Byron 1788–1824: *Childe Harold's Pilgrimage* (1812–18)

6 The isles of Greece, the isles of Greece! Where burning Sappho loved and sung.

Lord Byron 1788–1824: *Don Juan* (1819–24)

Siegfried Sassoon 1886–1967 see also **1:9**
English poet

7 It is realism of the right, of the poetic kind.
reviewing Siegfried Sassoon's war poems 1917

Virginia Woolf 1882–1941: in *Times Literary Supplement* 31 May 1917

8 I have just been reading Siegried Sassoon, and am feeling at a very high pitch of emotion. Nothing like his trench life sketches has ever been written or ever will be written. Shakespeare reads vapid after these. Not of course because Sassoon is a greater artist, but because of the subjects, I mean.

Wilfred Owen 1893–1918: letter to his mother, 15 August 1917

9 A booby-trapped idealist.
on himself

Siegfried Sassoon 1886–1967: *Siegfried's Journey* (1945)

Satire see Wit and Satire

Scholarship

10 Of making many books there is no end; and much study is a weariness of the flesh.

Bible: Ecclesiastes

1 *Atque inter silvas Academi quaerere verum.*
And seek for truth in the groves of Academe.

Horace 65–8 BC: *Epistles*

2 In the usual course of study I had come to a book of a certain Cicero.

St Augustine AD 354–430: *Confessions* (AD 397–8)

3 And gladly wolde he lerne and gladly teche.

Geoffrey Chaucer c.1343–1400: *The Canterbury Tales* 'The General Prologue'

4 I would I had bestowed that time in the tongues that I have in fencing, dancing, and bear-baiting. O! had I but followed the arts!

William Shakespeare 1564–1616: *Twelfth Night* (1601)

5 Whilst others have been at the balloo, I have been at my book, and am now past the craggy paths of study, and come to the flowery plains of honour and reputation.

Ben Jonson c.1573–1637: *Volpone* (1606)

6 And let a scholar all Earth's volumes carry,
He will be but a walking dictionary.

George Chapman c.1559–1634: *The Tears of Peace* (1609)

7 Studies serve for delight, for ornament, and for ability.

Francis Bacon 1561–1626: *Essays* (1625) 'Of Studies'

8 I have not wished to enrich the edition with any references, as some have desired me to do, because the learned do not need such things, and the others do not bother about them.

St Francis of Sales 1567–1622: J. H. Adels *Wisdom of the Saints* (1987) frontispiece

9 Learning hath gained most by those books by which the printers have lost.

Thomas Fuller 1608–61: *The Holy State and the Profane State*

10 What song the Syrens sang, or what name Achilles assumed when he hid himself among women, though puzzling questions, are not beyond all conjecture.

Thomas Browne 1605–82: *Hydriotaphia* (Urn Burial, 1658)

11 But for the most part, women are not educated as they should be, I mean those of quality; oft their education is only to dance, sing, and fiddle, to write complimental letters, to read romances, to speak some languages that is not their native . . . their parents take more care of their feet than their head, more of their words than their reason.

Margaret Cavendish c.1624–74: *Sociable Letters* (1664)

12 I am not ambitious to appear a man of letters: I could be content the world should think I had scarce looked upon any other book than that of nature.

Robert Boyle 1627–91: *Philosophical Works* (1738) vol. 1

13 How science dwindles, and how volumes swell,
How commentators each dark passage shun,
And hold their farthing candle to the sun.

Edward Young 1683–1765: *The Love of Fame* (1725–8)

14 There mark what ills the scholar's life assail,
Toil, envy, want, the patron, and the jail.

Samuel Johnson 1709–84: *The Vanity of Human Wishes* (1749)

15 It is a great fault of commentators that they are apt to be silent or at most very concise where there is any difficulty, and to be very prolix and tedious where there is none.

Thomas Newton 1704–82: introduction to *Paradise Lost* (1749)

16 I have always suspected that the reading is right, which requires many words to prove it wrong; and the emendation wrong, that cannot without so much labour appear to be right.

Samuel Johnson 1709–84: *Plays of William Shakespeare* (1765)

1 Notes are often necessary, but they are necessary evils.

Samuel Johnson 1709–84: *Plays of William Shakespeare* (1765) preface

2 Take care not to understand editions and title-pages too well. It always smells of pedantry, and not always of learning . . . Beware of the *bibliomanie*.

Lord Chesterfield 1694–1773: *Letters to his Son* (1774)

3 Gie me ae spark o' Nature's fire,
That's a' the learning I desire.

Robert Burns 1759–96: 'Epistle to J. L[aprai]k' (1786)

4 Our meddling intellect
Mis-shapes the beauteous forms of things:—
We murder to dissect.

Enough of science and of art;
Close up these barren leaves;
Come forth, and bring with you a heart
That watches and receives.

William Wordsworth 1770–1850: 'The Tables Turned' (1798)

5 A votary of the desk—a notched and cropt scrivener—one that sucks his substance, as certain sick people are said to do, through a quill.

Charles Lamb 1775–1834: *Essays of Elia* (1823) 'Oxford in the Vacation'

6 The true University of these days is a collection of books.

Thomas Carlyle 1795–1881: *On Heroes, Hero-Worship, and the Heroic* (1841)

7 A classic lecture, rich in sentiment,
With scraps of thundrous epic lilted out
By violet-hooded Doctors, elegies
And quoted odes, and jewels five-words-long,
That on the stretched forefinger of all Time
Sparkle for ever.

Alfred, Lord Tennyson 1809–92: *The Princess* (1847)

8 A whaleship was my Yale College and my Harvard.

Herman Melville 1819–91: *Moby Dick* (1851)

9 You will find it a very good practice always to verify your references, sir!

Martin Joseph Routh 1755–1854: John William Burgon *Lives of Twelve Good Men* (1888 ed.)

10 Nor can I do better, in conclusion, than impress upon you the study of Greek literature, which not only elevates above the vulgar herd, but leads not infrequently to positions of considerable emolument.

Thomas Gaisford 1779–1855: Christmas Day Sermon in the Cathedral, Oxford; W. Tuckwell *Reminiscences of Oxford* (2nd ed., 1907)

11 I think aesthetic teaching is the highest of all teaching, because it deals with life in its highest complexity. But if it ceases to be purely aesthetic—if it lapses anywhere from the picture to the diagram—it becomes the most offensive of all teaching.

George Eliot 1819–80: letter, 15 August 1866

12 Bald heads forgetful of their sins,
Old, learned, respectable bald heads
Edit and annotate the lines
That young men, tossing on their beds,
Rhymed out in love's despair
To flatter beauty's ignorant ear.

W. B. Yeats 1865–1939: 'The Scholars' (1919)

13 They hunt a reference in dusty tomes; or wrestle wearily with cumbrous files of years-old newspapers, to earn the sorry pittance paid to those who gather long-forgotten facts from print.

Charles Inge 1868–1957: *Flashes of London* (1920) 'Sisters of Fear'

1 The proper study of mankind is books.

Aldous Huxley 1894–1963: *Crome Yellow* (1921)

2 I dreamt last night that Shakespeare's ghost
Sat for a Civil Service post;
The English paper for the year
Had several questions on *King Lear*
Which Shakespeare answered very badly
Because he hadn't read his Bradley.

Guy Boas b. 1896: in 1926; in *Spectator* 27 January 1990

3 I also like the absence of footnotes. I never see why one should put the jottings of one's laboratory at the bottom of the page.

John Buchan 1875–1940: to Liddell Hart, 26 October 1926

4 Pedantry is the dotage of knowledge.

Holbrook Jackson 1874–1948: *Anatomy of Bibliomania* (1930) vol. 1

5 One learns more from a good scholar in a rage than from a score of lucid and laborious drudges.

Rudyard Kipling 1865–1936: *Something of Myself* (1937)

6 I've put in so many enigmas and puzzles that it will keep the professors busy for centuries arguing over what I meant, and that's the only way of insuring one's immortality.
  of Ulysses

James Joyce 1882–1941: Richard Ellmann *James Joyce* (1982)

7 The primary object of a student of literature is to be delighted. His duty is to enjoy himself: his efforts should be directed to developing his faculty of appreciation.

Lord David Cecil 1902–86: *Reading as one of the Fine Arts* (1949)

8 Being a professor of poetry is rather like being a Kentucky colonel. It's not really a subject one can profess—unless one hires oneself out to write pieces of poetry for funerals or the marriages of dons.

W. H. Auden 1907–73: attributed, 1960

9 'What . . . is a text course?' 'One that uses books, of course . . . You remember books? They're what we used to read before we started discussing what we ought to read.'

Amanda Cross 1926– : *Poetic Justice* (1970)

10 A writer who lives long enough becomes an academic subject and almost qualified to teach it himself.

Harold Rosenberg 1906–78: *Discovering the Present* (1973)

11 I had measles at the age of four. I remember because I had to give up reading the *Encyclopedia Britannica* at the time.

Enoch Powell 1912–98: in *Observer* 7 October 1990 'Sayings of the Week'

12 Milton and Dante are the most pugnacious of the greatest Western writers. Scholars somehow manage to evade the ferocity of both poets and even dub them pious.

Harold Bloom 1930– : *The Western Canon* (1995)

13 At least one of my children did one of my plays at A-level. I think he got a 'B' with my help.
  on being a set text

Tom Stoppard 1937– : attributed, 1995

14 First time readers of *Beowulf* very quickly rediscover the meaning of the term 'the Dark Ages'.

Seamus Heaney 1939– : introduction to his translation of *Beowulf* (1999)

15 More sophisticated novelists pile up research like a compost heap, but then leave it alone, let it sink down, acquire heat and degrade usefully into fertilizing elements.

Julian Barnes 1946– : *Something to Declare* (2002)

Science and Literature

1 If the labours of the men of science should ever create any material revolution, direct or indirect, in our condition, and in the impressions which we habitually receive, the poet will sleep no more than at present, but he will be ready to follow the steps of the man of science, not only in those general indirect effects, but he will be at his side, carrying sensation into the midst of the objects of the science itself. The remotest discoveries of the chemist, the botanist, or mineralogist, will be as proper objects of the poet's art as any upon which it can be employed, if the time should ever come when these things shall be familiar to us, and the relations under which they are contemplated by the followers of these respective sciences shall be manifestly and palpably material to us as enjoying and suffering beings.

William Wordsworth 1770–1850: preface to *Lyrical Ballads* (1800)

2 In science, read, by preference, the newest works; in literature, the oldest.

Edward George Bulwer-Lytton 1803–73: *Caxtoniana* (1863) 'Hints on Mental Culture'

3 A contemporary poet has characterized this sense of the personality of art and of the impersonality of science in these words—'Art is myself; science is ourselves'.

Claude Bernard 1813–78: *Introduction à l'Étude de la Médecin Experiméntale* (1865)

4 Science is meaningless because it gives no answer to our question, the only question important for us: 'What shall we do and how shall we be?'

Leo Tolstoy 1828–1910: Lewis Wolpert *The Unnatural Nature of Science* (1993)

5 Why is it that the scholar is the only man of science of whom it is ever demanded that he should display taste and feeling?

A. E. Housman 1859–1936: 'Cambridge Inaugural Lecture' (1911)

6 Don't talk to me of your Archimedes' lever. He was an absent-minded person with a mathematical imagination. Mathematics commands all my respect, but I have no use for engines. Give me the right word and the right accent and I will move the world.

Joseph Conrad 1857–1924: *A Personal Record* (1919)

7 Even if I could be Shakespeare, I think I should still choose to be Faraday.

Aldous Huxley 1894–1963: in 1925; R. Weber *More Random Walks in Science* (1982)

8 When science arrives it expels literature.

Goldsworthy Lowes Dickinson 1862–1932: *Plato and his Dialogues* (1931)

9 Every good poem, in fact, is a bridge built from the known, familiar side of life over into the unknown. Science too, is always making expeditions into the unknown. But this does not mean that science can supersede poetry. For poetry enlightens us in a different way from science; it speaks directly to our feelings or imagination. The findings of poetry are no more and no less true than science.

C. Day-Lewis 1904–72: *Poetry for You* (1944)

10 Art is meant to disturb, science reassures.

Georges Braque 1882–1963: *Le Jour et la nuit: Cahiers* 1917–52

1 The intellectual life of the whole of western society is increasingly being split into two polar groups . . . Literary intellectuals at one pole—at the other scientists, and as the most representative, the physical scientists. Between the two a gulf of mutual incomprehension.

C. P. Snow 1905–80: *The Two Cultures and the Scientific Revolution* (1959 Rede Lecture)

2 The true men of action in our time, those who transform the world, are not the politicians and statesmen, but the scientists. Unfortunately poetry cannot celebrate them, because their deeds are concerned with things, not persons, and are, therefore, speechless. When I find myself in the company of scientists, I feel like a shabby curate who has strayed by mistake into a drawing room full of dukes.

W. H. Auden 1907–73: *The Dyer's Hand* (1962) 'The Poet and the City'

3 The precondition of any fruitful relationship between literature and science is knowledge.

Aldous Huxley 1894–1963: *Literature and Science* (1963)

4 People who write obscurely are either unskilled in writing or up to mischief.

Peter Medawar 1915–87: *Pluto's Republic* (1984) 'Science and Literature'

5 Shakespeare would have grasped wave functions, Donne would have understood complementarity and relative time. They would have been excited. What richness! They would have plundered this new science for their imagery. And they would have educated their audiences too. But you 'arts' people, you're not only ignorant of these magnificent things, you're rather proud of knowing nothing.

Ian McEwan 1948– : *The Child in Time* (1987)

6 If Watson and Crick had not discovered the nature of DNA, one can be virtually certain that other scientists would eventually have determined it. With art—whether painting, music or literature—it is quite different. If Shakespeare had not written *Hamlet*, no other playwright would have done so.

Lewis Wolpert 1929– : *The Unnatural Nature of Science* (1993)

7 Why have the sciences yielded great explainers like Richard Dawkins and Stephen Jay Gould, while the arts routinely produce some of the worst writing known to history?

Brian Eno 1948– : in *Daily Telegraph* 9 December 1995 'They Said It'

8 One of the disabling weaknesses of current Western literature is its unwillingness or inability to engage with the dance of the spirit in the sciences. Music and the arts are equipped to do better.

George Steiner 1929– : *A Festival Overture* (Edinburgh University Festival Lecture, August 1996)

9 I found in literature what in my romantic childish imagination I would have expected to find in science: a sense of risk, discovery, investigation.

Peter Carey 1943– : in *Sunday Telegraph* 21 October 2001

10 The boundaries of science have expanded in recent decades in a rather interesting way. Emotion, consciousness, human nature itself, have become legitimate topics for the biological sciences. And these subjects of course are of central interest to the novelist. This invasion of our territory ought to be fruitful.

Ian McEwan 1948– : in *Paris Review* Summer 2002

Science Fiction

1 Did you ever read what they call Science Fiction? It's a scream. It's written like this: 'I checked out with K19 on Adabaran III, and stepped out through the crummaliote hatch on my 22 Model Sirius Hardtop. I cocked the timejector in secondary and waded through the bright blue manda grass. My breath froze into pink pretzels. I flicked on the heat bars and the Bryllis ran swiftly on five legs using their other two to send out crylon vibrations . . . '

Raymond Chandler 1888–1959: letter to H.N. Swanson, 14 March 1953

2 Science fiction is a kind of archaeology of the future.

Clifton Fadiman 1904–99: *Selected Writings* (1955)

3 Science Fiction is no more written for scientists than ghost stories are written for ghosts.

Brian Aldiss 1925– : introduction to *Penguin Science Fiction* (1962)

4 If some fatal process of applied science enables us in fact to reach the moon, the real journey will not at all satisfy the impulse which we now seek to gratify by writing such stories.

C. S. Lewis 1898–1963: *Of Other Worlds* (1966)

5 Everything is becoming science fiction. From the margins of an almost invisible literature has sprung the intact reality of the 20th century.

J. G. Ballard 1930– : 'Fictions of Every Kind' in *Books and Bookmen* February 1971

6 I have been a soreheaded occupant of a file drawer labelled 'Science Fiction' . . . and I would like out, particularly since so many serious critics regularly mistake the drawer for a urinal.

Kurt Vonnegut Jr. 1922– : *Wampeters, Foma and Granfallons* (1974)

7 Science fiction writers foresee the inevitable, and although problems and catastrophes may be inevitable, solutions are not.

Isaac Asimov 1920–92: 'How Easy to See the Future' in *Natural History* April 1975

8 Don't read science fiction books. It'll look bad if you die in bed with one on the nightstand. Always read stuff that will make you look good if you die in the middle of the night.

P. J. O'Rourke 1947– : attributed, 1979

9 If science fiction is the myth of modern technology, then its myth is tragic.

Ursula Le Guin 1929– : 'The Carrier Bag Theory of Fiction' (written 1986); *Dancing at the Edge of the World* (1989)

10 Science fiction, like Brazil, is where the nuts come from.

Thomas M. Disch 1940– : in *Observer* 23 August 1987

11 Space or science fiction has become a dialect for our time.

Doris Lessing 1919– : in *Guardian* 7 November 1987

12 Science fiction is the literature of *might be*.

C. J. Cherryh 1942– : Stan Nicholls (ed.) *Wordsmiths of Wonder* (1993)

13 What you get in science fiction is what someone once called 'the view from a distant star'. It helps us to see our world from outside.

Frederik Pohl 1919– : Stan Nicholls (ed.) *Wordsmiths of Wonder* (1993)

14 The only genuine consciousness-expanding drug.
   on science fiction

Arthur C. Clarke 1917– : letter claiming coinage in *New Scientist* 2 April 1994

1 We live in a world where emissions from our refrigerators have caused the ozone layer to evaporate and we'll get skin cancer if we sunbathe. If that's not a science fiction scenario, I don't know what is.

William Gibson 1948– : 'Perspectives' in *Newsweek* 5 June 1995

2 Science fiction and fantasy are in a ghetto, with walls maintained from the outside and inside.

Terry Pratchett 1948– : in *The Times* 30 May 2001

Sir Walter Scott 1771–1832 see also 18:1, 122:2
Scottish poet and novelist

3 Walter Scott has no business to write novels, especially good ones—It is not fair.—He has fame and profit enough as a poet, and should not be taking the bread out of other people's mouths.—I do not like him, and do not mean to like *Waverley* if I can help it—but fear I must.

Jane Austen 1775–1817: letter to Anna Austen, 28 September 1814

4 Full many a gallant man lies slain
On Waterloo's ensanguined plain,
But none by bullet or by shot
Fell half so flat as Walter Scott.
   comment on Scott's poem 'The Field of Waterloo' (*1815*)

Anonymous: sometimes attributed to Thomas Erskine; Una Pope-Hennessy *The Laird of Abbotsford* (1932)

5 When I get hold of one of these novels, turnips, sermons, and justice-business are all forgotten.
   on the novels of Sir Walter Scott

Sydney Smith 1771–1845: letter to Archibald Constable 28 June 1819

6 Scott is the only very successful genius that could be cited as being as generally beloved as a man as he is admired as an author.

Lord Byron 1788–1824: Lady Blessington *Conversations with Lord Byron* (1834)

7 His works (taken together) are almost like a new edition of human nature. This is indeed to be an author!

William Hazlitt 1778–1830: *The Spirit of the Age* (1825)

Screenwriting see also Adaptation

8 Writers are the most important people in the business, and we must never let them find that out.

Irving Thalberg 1899–1936: attributed; Neill D. Hicks *Screenwriting 101* (1999)

9 The trouble, Mr Goldwyn, is that you are only interested in art and I am only interested in money.
   telegraphed version of the outcome of a conversation between **Shaw** *and Sam Goldwyn*

George Bernard Shaw 1856–1950: Alva Johnson *The Great Goldwyn* (1937)

10 The challenge of screenwriting is to say much in little and then take half of that little out and still preserve an effect of leisure and movement.

Raymond Chandler 1888–1959: in *Atlantic Monthly* November 1945

11 They don't want you until you have made a name, and by the time you have made a name, you have developed some kind of talent they can't use. All they will do is spoil it, if you let them.

Raymond Chandler 1888–1959: letter, to Dale Warren, 7 November 1951

12 Hollywood held this double lure for me, tremendous sums of money for work that required no more effort than a game of pinochle.

Ben Hecht 1894–1964: *A Child of the Century* (1954)

13 I went out there [Hollywood] for a thousand a week, and I worked Monday, and I got fired Wednesday. The guy that hired me was out of town Tuesday.

Nelson Algren 1909–81: Malcolm Cowley (ed.) *Writers at Work* 1st series (1958)

1 Radio and television . . . have succeeded in lifting the manufacture of banality out of the sphere of handicraft and placed it in that of a major industry.

Nathalie Sarraute 1902– : in *Times Literary Supplement* 10 June 1960

2 Take the money and run.

Ernest Hemingway 1899–1961: attributed; W. Goldman *Adventures in the Screen Trade* (1984)

3 Words are cheap. The biggest thing you can say is 'elephant'.
   on the universality of silent films

Charlie Chaplin 1889–1977: B. Norman *The Movie Greats* (1981)

4 Schmucks with Underwoods.
   describing writers

Jack Warner 1892–1978: attributed

5 For me it is impossible to write a film play without first writing a story.

Graham Greene 1904–91: *Ways of Escape* (1980)

6 The writer, in the eyes of many film producers, still seems to occupy a position of importance somewhere between the wardrobe lady and the tea boy, with this difference: it's often quite difficult to replace the wardrobe lady.

John Mortimer 1923– : *Clinging to the Wreckage* (1982)

7 A good film script should be able to do completely without dialogue.

David Mamet 1947– : in *Independent* 11 November 1988

8 It's not so much that I write well—I just don't write badly very often, and that passes for good on television.

Andy Rooney 1919– : in *Spectator* 3 March 1990

9 I don't think screenplay writing is the same as writing—I mean, I think it's blueprinting.

Robert Altman 1922– : in *Independent on Sunday* 10 July 1994

10 The difference between writing for stage and for television is almost an optical one. Language on the stage has to be slightly larger than life because it is being heard in a much larger space. Plot counts for less on the television screen because one is seeing the characters at closer quarters than in the theatre.

Alan Bennett 1934– : *Writing Home* (1994)

11 We don't need books to make films. It's the last thing we want—it turns cinema into the bastard art of illustration.

Peter Greenaway 1942– : in *Independent on Sunday* 10 July 1994

12 I've had great joy writing screenplays. Every single one has been a matter of joy . . . It's very fascinating work, and very difficult, but never-endingly stimulating.

Harold Pinter 1930– : interview, in *Guardian* 12 October 2002

Self-doubt and Self-esteem see also Fame, Reputation, Rivalry

13 I have never yet known a poet who did not think himself super-excellent.

Cicero 106–43 BC: *Tusculanae Disputationes*

14 *Quodsi me lyricis vatibus inseres,*
   Sublimi feriam sidera vertice.

   And if you include me among the lyric poets, I'll hold my head so high it'll strike the stars.

Horace 65–8 BC: *Odes*

15 *Odi profanum vulgus et arceo;*
   Favete linguis; carmina non prius
   Audita Musarum sacerdos
   Virginibus puerisque canto.

   I hate the common herd and keep them off. Hush your tongues; as a priest of the Muses, I sing songs never heard before to virgin girls and boys.

Horace 65–8 BC: *Odes*

1 May I present myself—the man
You read, admire, and long to meet,
Known the world over for his neat
And witty epigrams? The name
is Martial.

Martial AD c.40–c.104: *Epigrammata*, tr. James Michie

2   Oft-times nothing profits more
Than self esteem, grounded on just and right
Well managed.

John Milton 1608–74: *Paradise Lost* (1667)

3 Faith, that's as well said, as if I had said it myself.

Jonathan Swift 1667–1745: *Polite Conversation* (1738)

4 Poetry without egotism comparatively uninteresting.

Samuel Taylor Coleridge 1772–1834: Notebook, 1794–1798

5   For ne'er
Was flattery lost on poet's ear:
A simple race! they waste their toil
For the vain tribute of a smile.

Sir Walter Scott 1771–1832: *The Lay of the Last Minstrel* (1805)

6 As for conceit, what man will do any good who is not conceited? Nobody holds a good opinion of a man who has a low opinion of himself.

Anthony Trollope 1815–82: *Orley Farm* (1862)

7 I always have to pretend to forget when people talk to me about my own books. It looks modest . . . But the writer never forgets.

Anthony Trollope 1815–82: letter, 5 December 1881

8 It is the peculiar fate of literary hens to lay solid gold eggs at night, only to discover, in the cruel pallor of dawn, that the eggs have gilt shells and are as hollow as drums.

Ernest L. Meyer 1892–1952: 'The Columnist's Lot' in *Capital Times* 4 May 1928

9 Literature is strewn with the wreckage of men who have minded beyond reason the opinions of others.

Virginia Woolf 1882–1941: *A Room of One's Own* (1929)

10 What I have done is *excellent*. I don't think it could be better. Very gruesome. Rather like Webster in modern idiom.
    of his novel A Handful of Dust

Evelyn Waugh 1903–66: letter to Lady Diana Cooper, January 1934

11 How rare, how precious is frivolity! How few writers can prostitute all their powers! They are always implying, 'I am capable of higher things.'

E. M. Forster 1879–1970: *Abinger Harvest* (1936)

12 Every genius needs praise.

Gertrude Stein 1874–1946: Edmund White *The Burning Library* (1994)

13 A confessional passage has probably never been written that didn't stink a little bit of the writer's pride in having given up his pride.

J. D. Salinger 1919– : *Catcher in the Rye* (1951)

14 The state of simplicity and humility is the only desirable one for artist or for man. While to reach it may be impossible, to attempt to do so is imperative.

Patrick White 1912–90: 'The Prodigal Son' (1958)

15 What matters finally is not the world's judgement of oneself but one's judgement of the world. Any writer who lacks this final arrogance will not survive very long in America.

Gore Vidal 1925– : in *The Nation* 2 January 1960

16 However strong or egotistical your writing personality is, the *alter ego*—the reflection of you that looks at what you are writing and have written—must be a critic that is almost impossible to please, or get a good mark from.

Paul Scott 1920–78: Hilary Spurling *Paul Scott* (1990); advice to students of his writing class in Tulsa, Oklahoma

1 I don't lack confidence in what I can do, only in what is going to happen to it.

Paul Scott 1920–78: Hilary Spurling *Paul Scott* (1990)

2 I used to know several eminent writers who were given to boasting of the speed with which they created. It's not a lovable attribute, to put it mildly, and I'm afraid our acquaintanceship has languished.

S. J. Perelman 1904–79: George Plimpton (ed.) *The Writer's Chapbook* (1989)

3 Literature can do with any amount of egoism; but the merest pinch of narcissism spoils the broth.

John Updike 1932– : *Hugging the Shore* (1983)

4 When starting to think about any novel, part of the motive is: I'm going to show them, this time. Without that, a lot of what passes under the name of creative energy would be lost.

Kingsley Amis 1922–95: George Greenfield *Scribblers for Bread* (1989)

5 I tend to write in a fragile, edgy, doubtful sort of way, trying things out all the time, never confident that I've got something right.

William Trevor 1928– : in *Paris Review* 1989

6 My flawed self has only ever felt intensely alive in the fictions I create.

Patrick White 1912–90: *Patrick White Speaks* (1990)

7 When I read something saying I've not done anything as good as *Catch-22* I'm tempted to reply, 'Who has?'

Joseph Heller 1923–99: in *The Times* 9 June 1993

8 Most people are vain, so I try to ensure that any author who comes to stay will find at least one of their books in their room.

Duke of Devonshire 1920– : in *Spectator* 22 January 1994

9 No one working in the English language now comes close to my exuberance, my passion, my fidelity to words.
on being asked to name the best living author writing in English

Jeanette Winterson 1959– : in *Sunday Times* 13 March 1994

10 I need people's good opinion. This is something in myself I dislike because I even need the good opinion of people who I don't admire. I am afraid of them. I am afraid of what they will say to me. I am afraid of their tongues and their indifference.

Ruth Rendell 1930– : Anthony Clare *In the Psychiatrist's Chair II* (1995)

11 Novelists . . . tend to be solipsistic, especially in the fragile days immediately following publication.

Carol Shields 1935– : *Jane Austen* (2001)

12 I'm a very shy, private person and I camouflaged myself by display rather than by reticence. I became a repressed exhibitionist. I found emotional self-exposure embarrassing—and now I don't, or less so. The older I get, the less I care about self-concealment. Time is limited . . . You have to choose what matters.

Tom Stoppard 1937– : in *Guardian* 22 June 2002

Selling Books

13   No doubt you often go
Down Booksellers' Row.
Well, then, opposite Caesar's Forum there's a shop
With door-posts plastered with advertisements from
    bottom to top,
So that at a glance you can read
The list of available poets.

Martial AD c.40–c.104: *Epigrammata*, tr. James Michie

1 If I were to paint Sloth . . . I swear, I would draw it like a stationer that I know, with his thumb under his girdle, who if a man comes to his stall and asks him for a book, never stirs his head, or looks upon him, but stands stone still, and speaks not a word: only with his little finger points backwards to his boy, who must be his interpreter, and so all the day, gaping like a dumb image, he sits without motion.

Thomas Nashe 1567–1601: *Pierce Pennilesse* (1592)

2 Well! it is now public, and you will stand for your privileges we know: to read, and censure. Do so, but buy it first. That doth best commend a book, the stationer says.

John Heming 1556–1630 and **Henry Condell** d. 1627: First Folio Shakespeare (1623)

3 It is fair enough that a bookseller should guide the public to his own shop. And fair enough that a critic should tell the public they are going astray.

Sydney Smith 1771–1845: letter to Archibald Constable, 1803

4 Write what will sell! To this Golden rule every minor canon must be subordinate.

Edward Coplestone 1776–1849: *Advice to a Young Reviewer* (1807)

5 Our book is found to be a drug, no man needs it or heeds it. In the space of a year our publisher has disposed but of two copies.

Charlotte Brontë 1816–55: letter to De Quincey, 16 June 1847

6 Where is human nature so weak as in the bookstore?

Henry Ward Beecher 1813–87: *Star Papers* (1855) 'Subtleties of Book Buyers'

7 How long would most people look at the best book before they would give the price of a large turbot for it?

John Ruskin 1819–1900: *Sesame and Lilies* (1865)

8 Yon second-hand bookseller is second to none in the worth of the treasures which he dispenses.

Leigh Hunt 1784–1859: *On the Beneficence of Bookstalls* (1899)

9 What we want above all things is not more books, not more publishers, not more education, not more literary genius, but simply and prosaically more shops.

George Bernard Shaw 1856–1950: in *The Author* 1903

10 When I get hold of a first issue of *Last Poems* I insert the missing stops on p. 52. I believe that this destroys the value of the book for bibliophiles, so you can bring an action against me if you like.

A. E. Housman 1859–1936: letter, 13 June 1929

11 Between the GARDENING and the COOKERY
Comes the brief POETRY shelf.

Kingsley Amis 1922–95: *A Case of Samples* (1956) 'A Bookshop Idyll'

12 They praised the book in Leeds and Pimlico,
In Leicester Square and Paternoster Row,
Filling the town with tidings of its wit
Till even booksellers got wind of it,
And this unwelcome thought their slumbers shook,
That now at last they'd have to sell a book.

Gerald Bullett 1893–1958: attributed; George Greenfield *Scribblers for Bread* (1989)

Seneca ('the Younger') c.4 BC–AD 65
Roman philosopher and poet

13 Seneca writes as a boar does piss, *scilicet* by jerks.

Ralph Kettell 1563–1643: John Aubrey *Brief Lives* 'Ralph Kettell'

Sex see also **Erotic Writing and Pornography**

1 Everyone should study at least enough philosophy and *belles lettres* to make his sexual experience more delectable.

Georg Christoph Lichtenberg 1742–99: *The Lichtenberg Reader* (1959)

2 If people will stop at the first tense of the verb 'aimer' they must not be surprised if one finishes the conjugation with somebody else.

Lord Byron 1788–1824: letter, 13 January 1814

3 Is it not *life*, is it not *the thing?*—Could any man have written it—who has not lived in the world?—and tooled in a post-chaise? in a hackney coach? in a gondola? Against a wall? in a court carriage? in a *vis-à-vis?*—on a table?— and under it?
of Don Juan

Lord Byron 1788–1824: letter to Douglas Kinnaird, 26 October 1819

4 Not even the advocates of freedom [from censorship] seek to justify the free treatment of sexual matters in any other than a high moral-pointing vein. The notion that sexual themes might allowably be treated in the mere aim of amusement does not seem to have occurred to anybody at all.

Arnold Bennett 1867–1931: diary, 31 October 1907

5   While we think of it, and talk of it
Let us leave it alone, physically, keep apart.
For while we have sex in the mind, we truly have none in
     the body.

D. H. Lawrence 1885–1930: 'Leave Sex Alone' (1929)

6 It's not true the more sex that you have, the more it interferes with your work. I find that the more sex you have, the better work you do.
to Michael Foot, c.1938

H. G. Wells 1866–1946: Jill Craigie on *Bookmark* (BBC2) 24 August 1996; see **272:4**

7 I do object to one thing to do with sex: this scheme afoot on the part of many 'liberal-minded' persons to open up obscene language to general commerce. It should be the dark secret language of the underworld. There are very few words—you shouldn't kill them by overuse.

Harold Pinter 1930– : in *Paris Review* 1966

8 Sex can be indicated with asterisks. I've always felt that was as good a way as any.

John Dos Passos 1896–1970: George Plimpton (ed.) *The Writer's Chapbook* (1989)

9 Lord Longford is against us reading or seeing things that keep our minds below the navel.

William Hardcastle 1918–75: in *Punch* 1 December 1972

10 Sexual intercourse began
In nineteen sixty-three
(Which was rather late for me)—
Between the end of the *Chatterley* ban
And the Beatles' first LP.

Philip Larkin 1922–85: 'Annus Mirabilis' (1974)

11 Sex is more exciting on the screen and between the pages than between the sheets.

Andy Warhol 1927–87: *From A to B and Back Again* (1975)

12 There is no suggestion that either clubman or girl would recognize a double bed except as so much extra sweat to make an apple-pie bed of.
on the novels of P. G. Wodehouse

Richard Usborne 1910– : *Wodehouse at Work to the End* (1976)

13 I've led a good rich sexual life, and I don't see why it should be left out.

Henry Miller 1891–1980: George Plimpton (ed.) *The Writer's Chapbook* (1989)

1 It has been a lifelong, ceaseless quest. And how could I have created dozens, perhaps hundreds, of female characters in my novels if I had not experienced these adventures which lasted for two hours or ten minutes?
on his womanizing

Georges Simenon 1903–89: Patrick Marnham *The Man Who Wasn't Maigret* (1992)

2 There *is* sex in the Discworld books, but it usually takes place two pages after the ending.

Terry Pratchett 1948– : Terry Pratchett and Stephen Briggs *The Discworld Companion* (1994)

3 If you don't know about sex at my age, you never will. I am always asked questions about why I write about sex because I am so ancient.

Mary Wesley 1912–2002: attributed, 1995

4 H. G. Wells thought that the creative urge was the sexual urge . . . I was a bit scared that if it started to ease up, and one didn't think about sex, then maybe one couldn't write any more.

Beryl Bainbridge 1933– : interview in *Daily Telegraph* 10 September 1996; see **271:6**

5 I've mostly written about sex by means of the space break.

Barbara Kingsolver 1955– : in *Writers on Writing: Collected Essays from The New York Times* (2001)

Shakespeare 1564–1616 see also **91:8, 153:10, 184:7, 208:8, 255:9, 289:9**
English dramatist

6   Soul of the Age!
The applause, delight, the wonder of our stage!

Ben Jonson c.1573–1637: 'To the Memory of My Beloved, the Author, Mr William Shakespeare' (1623)

7 He was not of an age, but for all time!

Ben Jonson c.1573–1637: 'To the Memory of My Beloved, the Author, Mr William Shakespeare' (1623)

8 Sweet Swan of Avon!

Ben Jonson c.1573–1637: 'To the Memory of My Beloved, the Author, Mr William Shakespeare' (1623)

9 Thou hadst small Latin, and less Greek.

Ben Jonson c.1573–1637: 'To the Memory of My Beloved, the Author, Mr William Shakespeare' (1623)

10 Who, as he was a happy imitator of Nature, was a most gentle expresser of it. His mind and hand went together: And what he thought, he uttered with that easiness, that we have scarce received from him a blot.

John Heming 1556–1630 and **Henry Condell** d. 1627: First Folio Shakespeare (1623) preface

11 What needs my Shakespeare for his honoured bones,
The labour of an age in pilèd stones,
Or that his hallowed relics should be hid
Under a star-ypointing pyramid?

John Milton 1608–74: 'On Shakespeare' (1632)

12 The players have often mentioned it as an honour to Shakespeare that in his writing, whatsoever he penned, he never blotted out a line. My answer hath been 'Would he had blotted a thousand' . . . But he redeemed his vices with his virtues. There was ever more in him to be praised than to be pardoned.

Ben Jonson c.1573–1637: *Timber, or Discoveries made upon Men and Matter* (1641) 'De Shakespeare Nostrati'

1 He was the man who of all modern, and perhaps ancient poets, had the largest and most comprehensive soul . . . He was naturally learn'd; he needed not the spectacles of books to read Nature: he looked inwards, and found her there . . . He is many times flat, insipid; his comic wit degenerating into clenches, his serious swelling into bombast. But he is always great.

John Dryden 1631–1700: *An Essay of Dramatic Poesy* (1668)

2 [Shakespeare] is the very Janus of poets; he wears almost everywhere two faces; and you have scarce begun to admire the one, ere you despise the other.

John Dryden 1631–1700: *Essay on the Dramatic Poetry of the Last Age* (1672)

3 He was a handsome, well-shaped man: very good company, and of a very ready and pleasant smooth wit.

John Aubrey 1626–97: *Brief Lives* 'William Shakespeare'

4 One of the greatest geniuses that ever existed, Shakespeare, undoubtedly wanted taste.

Horace Walpole 1717–97: letter to Christopher Wren, 9 August 1764

5 Shakespeare has united the powers of exciting laughter and sorrow not only in one mind but in one composition . . . That this is a practice contrary to the rules of criticism will be readily allowed; but there is always an appeal open from criticism to nature.

Samuel Johnson 1709–84: *Plays of William Shakespeare . . .* (1765) preface

6 A quibble is to Shakespeare, what luminous vapours are to the traveller; he follows it at all adventures, it is sure to lead him out of his way and sure to engulf him in the mire.

Samuel Johnson 1709–84: *Plays of William Shakespeare . . .* (1765)

7 Was there ever such stuff as great part of Shakespeare? Only one must not say so! But what think you?—what?— Is there not sad stuff? what?—what?

George III 1738–1820: to Fanny Burney; Fanny Burney, diary, 19 December 1785

8 Shakespeare one gets acquainted with without knowing how. It is part of an Englishman's constitution. His thoughts and beauties are so spread abroad that one touches them everywhere, one is intimate with him by instinct.

Jane Austen 1775–1817: *Mansfield Park* (1814)

9 Our *myriad-minded* Shakespeare.

Samuel Taylor Coleridge 1772–1834: *Biographia Literaria* (1817)

10 He put his strength into his tragedies, and played with comedy. He was greatest in what was greatest.

William Hazlitt 1778–1830: *Lectures on the English Comic Writers* (1818)

11 Shakespeare . . . is of no age—nor of any religion, or party or profession. The body and substance of his works came out of the unfathomable depths of his own oceanic mind.

Samuel Taylor Coleridge 1772–1834: *Table Talk* (1835) 15 March 1834

12 Others abide our question. Thou art free.
We ask and ask: Thou smilest and art still,
Out-topping knowledge.

Matthew Arnold 1822–88: 'Shakespeare' (1849)

13 He was not a man, he was a continent; he contained whole crowds of great men, entire landscapes.

Gustave Flaubert 1821–80: letter, 19 September 1852

14   'With this same key
Shakespeare unlocked his heart,' once more!
Did Shakespeare? If so, the less Shakespeare he!

Robert Browning 1812–89: 'House' (1876); see **214:2**

15 One never sees Shakespeare played without being reminded at some new point of his greatness.

Henry James 1843–1916: review of production of *Romeo and Juliet*, 1876

1 With the single exception of Homer, there is no eminent
writer, not even Sir Walter Scott, whom I can despise so
entirely as I despise Shakespeare when I measure my mind
against his. The intensity of my impatience with him
occasionally reaches such a pitch, that it would positively
be a relief to me to dig him up and throw stones at him,
knowing as I do how incapable he and his worshippers are
of understanding any less obvious form of indignity.

George Bernard Shaw 1856–1950:
in *Saturday Review* 26 September
1896

2 When I read Shakespeare I am struck with wonder
That such trivial people should muse and thunder
In such lovely language.

D. H. Lawrence 1885–1930: 'When I
Read Shakespeare' (1929)

3 Brush up your Shakespeare,
Start quoting him now.
Brush up your Shakespeare
And the women you will wow . . .
If she says your behaviour is heinous
Kick her right in the 'Coriolanus'.
Brush up your Shakespeare
And they'll all kowtow.

Cole Porter 1891–1964: 'Brush Up
your Shakespeare' (1948 song)

4 Shakespeare is so tiring. You never get a chance to sit
down unless you're a king.

Josephine Hull ?1886–1957: in *Time*
16 November 1953

5 Shaw is like a train. One just speaks the words and sits in
one's place. But Shakespeare is like bathing in the sea—
one swims where one wants.

Vivien Leigh 1913–67: letter from
Harold Nicolson to Vita Sackville-
West, 1 February 1956

6 The remarkable thing about Shakespeare is that he is
really very good—in spite of all the people who say he is
very good.

Robert Graves 1895–1985:
attributed, 1964

7 Shakespeare—the nearest thing in incarnation to the eye
of God.

Laurence Olivier 1907–89: in
Kenneth Harris Talking To (1971) 'Sir
Laurence Olivier'

8 Fantastic! And it was all written with a feather!
on the works of Shakespeare

Sam Goldwyn 1882–1974:
attributed; John Gross *After
Shakespeare* (2002)

9 Shakespeare is the Canon. He sets the standards and the
limits of literature.

Harold Bloom 1930– : *The Western
Canon* (1995)

10 There is a sense in which every writer in English owes a
debt to Shakespeare. He is our theatrical DNA.

Richard Eyre 1943– : 'Changing
Stages', BBC2 TV, 5 November 2000

George Bernard Shaw 1856–1950 see also 108:10
Irish dramatist

11 He [Bernard Shaw] hasn't an enemy in the world, and
none of his friends like him.

Oscar Wilde 1854–1900: Bernard
Shaw *Sixteen Self Sketches* (1949)

12 Bernard Shaw is hopelessly wrong, as all these fellows are,
on fundamental things:—amongst others they punch
Xtianity and try to make it fit their civilization instead of
making their civilization fit it. He is an amusing liar, but
not much more.

Edward Elgar 1857–1934: letter, 14
July 1904

13 Mr Shaw is (I suspect) the only man on earth who has
never written any poetry.

G. K. Chesterton 1874–1936:
Orthodoxy (1908)

1 A good man fallen among Fabians.

Lenin 1870–1924: Arthur Ransome *Six Weeks in Russia in 1919* (1919) 'Notes of Conversations with Lenin'

2 Shaw's plays are the price we pay for Shaw's prefaces.

James Agate 1877–1947: diary, 10 March 1933

3 It seemed to me inorganic, logical straightness and not the crooked road of life.
of Arms and the Man

W. B. Yeats 1865–1939: *Autobiographies* (1955)

4 The basis of all Bernard Shaw's attacks on Shakespeare is really the charge—quite true, of course—that Shakespeare wasn't an enlightened member of the Fabian Society.

George Orwell 1903–50: in *Listener* 19 March 1942

5 I do not think that Shaw will be a great literary figure in 2000 AD. He is an amazingly brilliant contemporary; but not in the Hardy class.

Harold Nicolson 1886–1968: diary, 11 December 1950

6 Shaw's judgements were often scatterbrained, but at least he had brains to scatter.

Max Beerbohm 1872–1956: in 1954; S. N. Behrman *Conversations with Max* (1960)

7 As a demolition expert he has no rivals, and we are being grossly irrelevant if we ask a demolition expert, when his work is done: 'But what have you created?' . . . Shaw's genius was for intellectual slum-clearance, not for town planning.

Kenneth Tynan 1927–80: in *Observer* 22 July 1956

8 Although like many witty men he considered wit an adequate substitute for wisdom, he could defend any idea, however silly, so cleverly as to make those who did not accept it look like fools.

Bertrand Russell 1872–1970: Alistair Cooke *Memories of the Great and the Good* (1999)

Mary Shelley 1797–1851 see also **136:5**
English writer

9 Mrs Shelley is very clever, indeed it would be difficult for her not to be so; the daughter of Mary Wollstonecraft and Godwin, and the wife of Shelley, could be no common person.

Lord Byron 1788–1824: Lady Blessington *Conversations with Lord Byron* (1834)

10 [*Frankenstein* is] a book about what happens when a man tries to have a baby without a woman.

Anne K. Mellor 1941– : in *Sunday Correspondent* 8 April 1990

Percy Bysshe Shelley 1792–1822
English poet

11 You I am sure will forgive me for sincerely remarking that you might curb your magnanimity and be more of an artist, and 'load every rift' of your subject with ore.
echoing Edmund **Spenser** The Faerie Queen (*1596*): '*And with rich metal loaded every rift*'

John Keats 1795–1821: letter to Shelley, August 1820

12 Shelley is truth itself—and honour itself—notwithstanding his out-of-the-way notions about religion.

Lord Byron 1788–1824: letter to Douglas Kinnaird, 2 June 1821

1 The author of the *Prometheus Unbound* has a fire in his eye, a fever in his blood, a maggot in his brain, a hectic flutter in his speech, which mark out the philosophic fanatic.

William Hazlitt 1778–1830: *Table Talk* (1821–2) 'On Paradox and Common-Place'

2 In poetry, no less than in life, he is 'a beautiful and ineffectual angel, beating in the void his luminous wings in vain'.

Matthew Arnold 1822–88: *Essays in Criticism* Second Series (1888) 'Shelley' (quoting from his own essay on Byron in the same work)

3 I made my then famous declaration (among 100 people) 'I am a Socialist, an Atheist and a Vegetarian' (ergo, a true Shelleyan), whereupon two ladies who had been palpitating with enthusiasm for Shelley under the impression that he was a devout Anglican, resigned on the spot.

George Bernard Shaw 1856–1950: letter, 1 March 1908

Richard Brinsley Sheridan 1751–1816
Anglo-Irish dramatist

4 How should such a fellow as Sheridan, who has no diamonds to bestow, fascinate all the world?—yet witchcraft, no doubt there has been, for when did simple eloquence ever convince a majority?

Horace Walpole 1717–97: letter to Lady Ossory, 9 February 1787

5 The effect of the *School for Scandal* is something like reading a collection of epigrams, that of the *Rivals* is more like reading a novel.

William Hazlitt 1778–1830: *Lectures on the English Comic Writers* (1818)

6 Without means, without connection, without character . . . he beat them all, in all he ever attempted.

Lord Byron 1788–1824: letter to Thomas Moore, 1 June 1818

Short Stories

7 The dénouement of a long story is nothing; it is just a 'full close', which you may approach and accompany as you please—it is a coda, not an essential member in the rhythm; but the body and end of a short story is bone of the bone and blood of the blood of the beginning.

Robert Louis Stevenson 1850–94: letter to Sidney Colvin, September 1891

8 Chekhov made a mistake in thinking that if he had had more time he would have written more fully, described the rain, and the midwife and the doctor having tea. The truth is one can only get so *much* into a story; there is always a sacrifice. One has to leave out what one knows and longs to use.

Katherine Mansfield 1888–1923: diary, 1922

9 Poetic tautness and clarity are so essential to it that it may be said to stand on the edge of prose.

Elizabeth Bowen 1899–1973: introduction to *Faber Book of Modern Stories* (1937)

10 The first necessity for the short story, at the set out, is *necessariness*. The story, that is to say, must spring from an impression or perception pressing enough, acute enough, to have made the writer write.

Elizabeth Bowen 1899–1973: introduction to *Faber Book of Modern Stories* (1937)

11 Atmosphere and precision, however subtly concealed, are in fact two of the cardinal points in the art of the short-story writer.

H. E. Bates 1905–74: *The Modern Short Story* (1941)

1 The things I like to find in a story are punch and poetry.

Sean O'Faolain 1900–91: *The Short Story* (1948) foreword

2 From time to time there is an urge not to speed up and condense events and character development, which is what one does in a play, but to hold them frozen and to see things isolated in stillness, which I think is the great strength of a good short story.

Arthur Miller 1915– : *I Don't Need You Any More* (1967); foreword

3 I like it when there is some feeling of threat or sense of menace in short stories . . . There has to be tension, a sense that something is imminent, that certain things are in relentless motion.

Raymond Carver 1938–88: in *New York Times Book Review* 15 February 1981

4 I think it is the art of the glimpse. If the novel is like an intricate Renaissance painting, the short story is an Impressionist painting. It *should* be an explosion of truth.

William Trevor 1928– : in *Paris Review* 1989

5 The key to a short story is tension. At the end of a short story the reader's imagination should be able to take the story on in his mind, but at the end of a novel he is entitled to expect a rounding-off.

William Trevor 1928– : interview in *Sunday Telegraph* 21 January 1990

6 A short story is like a stripped-down racer; there's no room for anything extra in there.

Robert Asprin 1946– : Stan Nicholls (ed.) *Wordsmiths of Wonder* (1993)

7 The greatest masters of the form of the short story . . . have all tended to seek their material in the realm of the unremarkable—which turns out, under their patient illumination, to be remarkable after all.

John Wain 1925–94: attributed

8 Like full-rigged sailing ships in tight-necked bottles, or like the fabulous fairy palace which lies behind the tiny door in the wainscotting, they seem to contain infinite space within the nutshells of their neatly fitted narratives.
   on the work of Alice Munro

Lucy Hughes-Hallett 1951– : in *Sunday Times* 9 October 1994

9 The novel tends to tell us everything, whereas the short story tells us only one thing, and that intensely.

V. S. Pritchett 1900–97: attributed

Philip Sidney 1554–86
English poet

10 Will you have all in all for prose and verse? Take the miracle of our age, Sir Philip Sidney.

Richard Carew 1555–1620: William Camden *Remains concerning Britain* (1614) 'The Excellency of the English Tongue'

11 It is absurd; and yet there is a world of difference between writing like this with zest and wonder at the images that form upon one's pen and the writing of later ages when the dew was off the language.
   on Sidney's Arcadia

Virginia Woolf 1882–1941: *The Second Common Reader* (1932)

12 Often the realism and vigour of the verse comes with a shock after the drowsy languor of the prose.
   on Sidney's Arcadia

Virginia Woolf 1882–1941: *The Second Common Reader* (1932)

Georges Simenon 1903–89
Belgian novelist

1   It is a face so filled and alert with curiosity that even the pipe rocking constantly in a corner of his mouth is, one would swear, peering about and sizing things up.

Brendan Gill 1914–97: interview, in *New Yorker* 1952

2   Figures stud Simenon's life as pungently as cloves in an orange. The 400-plus books he wrote; the 55 cinema and 279 television films made from them; the 500 million copies sold in 55 languages; the 1,000,000 francs he took one Sunday morning in cash, in a suitcase, to buy back from Fayard the subsidiary rights on his first 19 Maigrets . . . Then there is his famous estimate of having bedded 10,000 women.

Julian Barnes 1946– : *Something to Declare* (2002)

3   Literature's pouncer, he wrote each novel in a swift, uninterruptible burst.

Julian Barnes 1946– : *Something to Declare* (2002)

Edith Sitwell 1887–1964
English poet

4   Edith Sitwell came to tea: transparent like some white bone one picks up on a moor, with sea water stones on her long frail hands which slide into yours much narrower than one expects like a folded fan.

Virginia Woolf 1882–1941: diary, 21 March 1927

5   A high altar on the move.

Elizabeth Bowen 1899–1973: V. Glendinning *Edith Sitwell* (1981)

Society and Social Responsibility see also The Power of the Pen

6   The only time a human being is free is when he or she makes a work of art.

Friedrich von Schiller 1759–1805: Edmund White *The Burning Library* (1994)

7   The more indignant I make the bourgeois, the happier I am.

Gustave Flaubert 1821–80: letter, 25 July 1842; see **278:10**

8   I regard him as the first social regenerator of the day—as the very master of that working corps who would restore to rectitude the warped system of things.
   of William Makepeace **Thackeray**

Charlotte Brontë 1816–55: *Jane Eyre* (2nd ed., 1848) preface

9   There are epochs when literature cannot *merely* be artistic, there are interests higher than poetry.

Ivan Turgenev 1818–83: letter to Vassili Botkin, 29 June 1855

10   *Il faut épater le bourgeois.*
   One must astonish the bourgeois.

Charles Baudelaire 1821–67: attributed; also attributed to Privat d'Anglemont (c.1820–59) in the form '*Je les ai épatés, les bourgeois* [I flabbergasted them, the bourgeois]'; see **278:7**

11   [Russian literature is] one uninterrupted indictment of Russian reality.

Alexander Herzen 1812–70: Isaiah Berlin *Personal Impressions* (1982); attributed

1 I am not in the habit of getting excited over novels that I
read, but there is one thing in fiction which always moves
me to an excess of rage—It is, Mrs Pendennis's treatment
of Fanny Bolton.
  in Thackeray's novel Pendennis, *the hero's mother fears
  that her son will marry the working-class Fanny*

George Gissing 1857–1903:
Commonplace Book (1962)

2 When the soul of a man is born in this country, there are
nets flung at it to hold it back from flight. You talk to me of
nationality, language, religion. I shall try to fly by those
nets.

James Joyce 1882–1941: *A Portrait of
the Artist as a Young Man* (1916)

3 Our duty is to blare like brazen-throated horns in the fog of
philistinism and in seething storms. The poet is always
indebted to the universe, paying interest and fines on
sorrow.

Vladimir Mayakovsky 1893–1930:
'Conversation with an Inspector of
Taxes about Poetry' (1926)

4 Now Ireland has her madness and her weather still,
For poetry makes nothing happen: it survives
In the valley of its saying where executives
Would never want to tamper, flows on south
From ranches of isolation and the busy griefs,
Raw towns that we believe and die in; it survives,
A way of happening, a mouth.

W. H. Auden 1907–73: 'In Memory
of W. B. Yeats' (1940)

5 There's nothing in the world for which a poet will give up
writing, not even when he is a Jew and the language of his
poems is German.

Paul Celan 1920–70: letter to
relatives, 2 August 1948

6 For a creative artist, someone who carries his factory
about with him, to have domicile in England is no longer
sensible.

Noël Coward 1899–1973: diary, 1955

7 It is barbarous to write a poem after Auschwitz.

Theodor Adorno 1903–69: I.
Buruma *Wages of Guilt* (1994)

8 Nothing I wrote in the thirties saved one Jew from
Auschwitz.

W. H. Auden 1907–73: attributed

9 I've often thought we'd have a utopia in this country if
every community adopted all the advice we offered from
time to time.
  *in 1972, at a reception at the White House for the 50th
  birthday of* Reader's Digest

DeWitt Wallace 1889–1981:
attributed

10 It cannot have escaped teachers of English literature that
much of their time is spent unfitting their pupils for the
lives they will eventually have to lead. Most twentieth-
century authors, and in particular the greats like Yeats,
Eliot and Lawrence, who regularly feature in A-level and
undergraduate syllabuses, inculcate an attitude of
contempt for ordinary, bread-earning citizens, which must
inevitably unsettle youngsters who are on the point of
choosing a career, unless they are mercifully too dense to
get the modernists' message at all.

John Carey 1934– : in *Listener* 1974

11 Art has its roots in social realities; when you see an Aztec
statue you don't doubt that it had an essential social
function. People believed in that god and made sacrifices to
it. I don't know why literature should be any different.

Margaret Atwood 1939– : in an
interview, March/April 1976; Earl G.
Ingersoll (ed.) *Margaret Atwood:
Conversations* (1990)

1 Russian literature saved my soul. When I was a young girl in school and I asked what is good and what is evil, no one in that corrupt system could show me.

Irina Ratushinskaya 1954– : in *Observer* 15 October 1989 'Sayings of the Week'

2 We shouldn't trust writers, but we should read them.

Ian McEwan 1948– : in *The Late Show* (BBC2) 7 February 1990

3 One glibly despises the photographer who zooms in on the starving child or the dying soldier without offering help. Writing is not different.

Alan Bennett 1934– : *Writing Home* (1994)

4 If we read the Western Canon in order to form our social, political, or personal moral values, I firmly believe we will become monsters of selfishness and exploitation.

Harold Bloom 1930– : *The Western Canon* (1995)

5 What literature can and should do is change the people who teach the people who don't read the books.

A. S. Byatt 1936– : interview in *Newsweek* 5 June 1995

6 It may seem footling to speculate about the effect of population explosion on reading habits. But it is clear that, whatever the external disasters, people's attitudes to privacy and solitude are going to change - and that, of course, is where books come in. Reading admits you to an inner space which, though virtually boundless, is inaccessible to the multitudes milling around. This is likely to make it more precious and sought after as ordinary terrestrial space gets used up.

John Carey 1934– : *Pure Pleasure* (2000)

7 Just as the camera drove a stake through the heart of serious portraiture, television has killed the novel of social reportage.

Jonathan Franzen 1959– : *How to be Alone* (2002) 'Why bother?'

Solitude

8 Conversation enriches the understanding, but solitude is the school of genius; and the uniformity of a work denotes the hand of a single artist.

Edward Gibbon 1737–94: *Memoirs of My Life and Writings* (1796)

9 Living in solitude till the fulness of time was come, I still kept the dew of my youth and the freshness of my heart.

Nathaniel Hawthorne 1804–64: *Note-Books* (1840)

10 When from our better selves we have too long
Been parted by the hurrying world, and droop,
Sick of its business, of its pleasures tired,
How gracious, how benign, is Solitude.

William Wordsworth 1770–1850: *The Prelude* (1850)

11 Great things of course have been done by solitary workers; but they have usually been done with double the pains they would have cost if they had been produced in more genial circumstances.

Henry James 1843–1916: *Hawthorne* (1879)

12 The port from which I set out was, I think, that of the *essential loneliness of my life.*

Henry James 1843–1916: letter, 2 October 1900

13 The poet *cannot* declaim: it's shameful and insulting. The poet—is solitary, the stage boards for him—are a pillory.

Marina Tsvetaeva 1892–1941: *Earthly Signs: Moscow Diaries, 1917-22* (2002)

14 Without my imprisonment, *Mein Kampf* would never have been written. That period gave me the chance of deepening various notions for which I then had only an instinctive feeling.

Adolf Hitler 1889–1945: *Hitler's Secret Conversations, 1941-44* (1953)

1 The writer's abiding problem is that he gets so sick of his own company but daren't take too long away from it.

Peter Nichols 1927– : diary, 2 January 1973

2 A writer is, on the whole, most alive when alone.

Martin Amis 1949– : in *Vanity Fair* 1990

3 I love solitude. I don't see how people can do without it. I love the self-pleasuring in writing. The sheer pleasure. The secrecy. The secret excitement. You don't tell anyone— you can't. If you tell, it might go.

Ian McEwan 1948– : in *Sunday Times* 6 May 1990

4 The ability to sustain long works of fiction is at least partially dependent on establishing a delicate balance between solitude and interaction. Too much human noise during the writing of a novel distracts from the cleanliness of its overarching plan. Too little social interruption, on the other hand, distorts a writer's sense of reality and allows feeling to 'prey' on the consciousness.

Carol Shields 1935– : *Jane Austen* (2001)

5 Writing fiction is a solitary occupation but not really a lonely one. The writer's head is mobbed with characters, images and language, making the creative process something like eavesdropping at a party for which you've had the fun of drawing up the guest list.

Hilma Wolitzer 1930– : in *Writers on Writing: Collected Essays from The New York Times* (2001)

6 The childhoods of writers are thought to have something to do with their vocation, but when you look at these childhoods they are in fact very different. What they often contain, however, are books and solitude.

Margaret Atwood 1939– : *Negotiating with the Dead: A Writer on Writing* (2002)

7 Readers and writers are united in their need for solitude . . . in their reach inward, via print, for a way out of loneliness.

Jonathan Franzen 1959– : *How to be Alone* (2002) 'Why bother?'

8 If week after week you do nothing but commune with ghosts, and move from your desk to your bed and back, you long for some sort of work that involves other people. But as I've grown older, I've become more reconciled to the ghosts, and slightly less interested in working with other people.

Ian McEwan 1948– : in *Paris Review* Summer 2002

Alexander Solzhenitsyn 1918–
Russian novelist

9 A bearer of light!
   on meeting Solzhenitsyn, summer 1962

Anna Akhmatova 1889–1966: Robert Reeder *Anna Akhmatova* (1995)

10 Here if anywhere outside *Parsifal* was a *heilge Tor*, a Prince Myshkin, a 'blessed fool' . . . One might not always agree with his tactics, but it is precisely because he is not a tactician that he is important in a world of degrees and accommodation. He is more than a writer. He is a cleansing personality, a prophet with a mission to his own country and to us all.

Yehudi Menuhin 1916–99: *Unfinished Journey* (1996)

Sophocles c.496–406 BC
Greek dramatist

1 But he was contented there, is contented here.
   there *on earth*; here *in Hades*

   Aristophanes c.450–c.385 BC: *The Frogs* (405 BC)

2 Who saw life steadily, and saw it whole:
   The mellow glory of the Attic stage;
   Singer of sweet Colonus, and its child.

   Matthew Arnold 1822–88: 'To a Friend' (1849)

Robert Southey 1774–1843
English poet

3 He had written much blank verse, and blanker prose,
   And more of both than anybody knows.

   Lord Byron 1788–1824: *The Vision of Judgement* (1822)

Muriel Spark 1918–
British novelist

4 Glimpses that seem like a microcosm of reality.
   of her own novels

   Muriel Spark 1918– : in *Sunday Times* 1962

5 I think I am still a poet. I think my novels are the novels of
   a poet. I think like a poet and react like one.

   Muriel Spark 1918– : in *Listener* 1970

6 Spark's oracular eye is, as always, on the skull of
   damnation behind society's grinning face.

   John Updike 1932– : *More Matter* (1999)

7 If a cat could write novels, they would be like Muriel
   Spark's . . . Cats are subtle, elegant, reserved and free from
   any foolish sentimentality about human beings. What
   makes them most Sparkish are the lethal talons they keep
   politely out of sight in their velvet pads. Behind Spark's
   purring ironies you sense something equally implacable.

   John Carey 1934– : *Pure Pleasure* (2000)

Speech

8 Then said they unto him, Say now Shibboleth: and he said
   Sibboleth: for he could not frame to pronounce it right.
   Then they took him, and slew him.

   Bible: Judges

9 Somwhat he lipsed, for his wantownesse,
   To make his Englissh sweete upon his tonge.

   Geoffrey Chaucer c.1343–1400: *The Canterbury Tales* 'The General Prologue'

10 He pronounced the letter R (*littera canina*) very hard—a
   certain sign of a satirical wit.

   John Aubrey 1626–97: *Brief Lives* 'John Milton'

11 And, when you stick on conversation's burrs,
   Don't strew your pathway with those dreadful *urs*.

   Oliver Wendell Holmes 1809–94: 'A Rhymed Lesson' (1848)

12 To Trinity Church, Dorchester. The rector in his sermon
   delivers himself of mean images in a very sublime voice,
   and the effect is that of a glowing landscape in which
   clothes are hung up to dry.

   Thomas Hardy 1840–1928: *Notebooks* 1 February 1874

1 Can the most accomplished pronouncer of English get through the foll. without a mistake of h's: 'It's he who owes you, not you who owe him.'

George Gissing 1857–1903: *Commonplace Book* (1962)

2 If, sir, I possessed, as you suggest, the power of conveying unlimited sexual attraction through the potency of my voice, I would not be reduced to accepting a miserable pittance from the BBC for interviewing a faded female in a damp basement.
reply to Mae West's manager who asked 'Can't you sound a bit more sexy when you interview her?'

Gilbert Harding 1907–60: S. Grenfell *Gilbert Harding by his Friends* (1961)

Speeches and Speech-making

3 . . . I, *demens, et saevas curre per Alpes*
Ut pueris placeas et declamatio fias.

Off you go, madman, and hurry across the horrible Alps, duly to delight schoolboys and become a subject for practising speech-making.
on Hannibal

Juvenal AD c.60–c.130: *Satires*

4 Speak the speech, I pray you, as I pronounced it to you, trippingly on the tongue; but if you mouth it, as many of your players do, I had as lief the town-crier spoke my lines.

William Shakespeare 1564–1616: *Hamlet* (1601)

5 Talking and eloquence are not the same: to speak, and to speak well, are two things.

Ben Jonson c.1573–1637: *Timber, or Discoveries made upon Men and Matter* (1641)

6 Continual eloquence is tedious.

Blaise Pascal 1623–62: *Pensées* (1670)

7   His tongue
Dropped manna, and could make the worse appear
The better reason.

John Milton 1608–74: *Paradise Lost* (1667)

8 His words came feebly, from a feeble chest,
Yet each in solemn order followed each,
With something of a lofty utterance drest;
Choice words, and measured phrase; above the reach
Of ordinary men; a stately speech!
Such as grave Livers do in Scotland use.

William Wordsworth 1770–1850: 'Resolution and Independence' (1807) st. 15

9 He is one of those orators of whom it was well said, 'Before they get up, they do not know what they are going to say; when they are speaking, they do not know what they are saying; and when they have sat down, they do not know what they have said.'
of Lord Charles Beresford

Winston Churchill 1874–1965: speech, House of Commons, 20 December 1912

10 If I am to speak for ten minutes, I need a week for preparation; if fifteen minutes, three days; if half an hour, two days; if an hour, I am ready now.

Woodrow Wilson 1856–1924: Josephus Daniels *The Wilson Era* (1946)

11 He mobilized the English language and sent it into battle to steady his fellow countrymen and hearten those Europeans upon whom the long dark night of tyranny had descended.
of Winston Churchill

Ed Murrow 1908–65: broadcast, 30 November 1954

1 Do you remember that in classical times when Cicero had finished speaking, the people said, 'How well he spoke', but when Demosthenes had finished speaking, they said, 'Let us march.'
   introducing John F. Kennedy in 1960

Adlai Stevenson 1900–65: Bert Cochran *Adlai Stevenson*

2 A speech is poetry: cadence, rhythm, imagery, sweep! A speech reminds us that words, like children, have the power to make dance the dullest beanbag of a heart.

Peggy Noonan 1950– : *What I Saw at the Revolution* (1999)

Spelling see also Grammar

3 Thou whoreson zed! thou unnecessary letter!

William Shakespeare 1564–1616: *King Lear* (1605–6)

4 'Do you spell it with a "V" or a "W"?' inquired the judge. 'That depends upon the taste and fancy of the speller, my Lord,' replied Sam [Weller].

Charles Dickens 1812–70: *Pickwick Papers* (1837)

5 They spell it Vinci and pronounce it Vinchy; foreigners always spell better than they pronounce.

Mark Twain 1835–1910: *The Innocents Abroad* (1869)

6 The impertinent compositors have taken it upon themselves to correct, as they suppose, my spelling and grammar: altering throughout *dwarves* to *dwarfs*; *elvish* to *elfish*; *further* to *farther*; and worst of all, *elven-* to *elfin*.
   of the galley proofs of The Lord of the Rings

J. R. R. Tolkien 1892–1973: letter to Christopher Tolkien, 4 August 1953

7 They [computers] will also have to learn that when I quote from some old author who spelled differently from the machine, the wishes of the long-dead author will have to be respected, and the machine will have to mind its manners.

Robertson Davies 1913–95: speech, Ontario Science Centre, Toronto, 26 November 1989

8 Sir, Perhaps the lack of literary inventiveness in modern opening lines is due to the effect of the word processor. When I ran the first line of *Moby Dick* through my spell-checker, it suggested changing this to 'Call me Fishmeal'.

Helen Grayson: letter to *The Times* 18 October 1997; see **201:6**

Stephen Spender 1909–95
English poet

9 To see him fumbling with our rich and delicate language is to experience all the horror of seeing a Sèvres vase in the hands of a chimpanzee.

Evelyn Waugh 1903–66: in *The Tablet* 5 May 1951

Edmund Spenser c.1552–99
English poet

10 Spenser more than once insinuates, that the soul of Chaucer was transfused into his body; and that he was begotten by him two hundred years after his decease.

John Dryden 1631–1700: *Fables Ancient and Modern* (1700)

1 Thee gentle Spenser fondly led;
But me he mostly sent to bed.

Walter Savage Landor 1775–1864: 'To Wordsworth: Those Who Have Laid the Harp Aside' (1846)

2 When Spenser wrote of Ireland he wrote as an official, and out of the thoughts and emotions that had been organized by the state. He was the first of many Englishmen to see nothing but what he was desired to see.

W. B. Yeats 1865–1939: 'Edmund Spenser' (1902)

3 The quotation of two or three lines of a stanza from Spenser's *Faerie Queene* is probably as good an all-round silencer as anything.

Stephen Potter 1900–69: *Lifemanship* (1950)

4 First I thought Troilus and Criseyde was the most *boring* poem in English. Then I thought Beowulf was. Then I thought Paradise Lost was. Now I *know* The Faerie Queene is the *dullest thing out. Blast* it.
   written in pencil in St John's College library copy of The Faerie Queene, *c.1941*

Philip Larkin 1922–85: Kingsley Amis *Memoirs* (1992)

Madame de Staël 1766–1817
French novelist and critic

5 She thinks like a man, but alas! she feels like a woman.

Lord Byron 1788–1824: J. Christopher Herold *Mistress to an Age* (1959)

6 Mme de Staël has succeeded in disguising us *both* as women.
   on her novel Delphine (*1802*)

Charles-Maurice de Talleyrand 1754–1838: Evangeline Bruce *Napoleon and Josephine* (1995)

Richard Steele 1672–1729
Irish-born essayist and dramatist

7 A rake among scholars, and a scholar among rakes.

Lord Macaulay 1800–59: *Essays Contributed to the Edinburgh Review* (1850) 'The Life and Writings of Addison'

8 I prefer open-hearted Steele with all his faults, to Addison with all his essays.

Leigh Hunt 1784–1859: *Autobiography* (rev. ed., 1860)

Gertrude Stein 1874–1946 see also **121:7**
American writer

9 Gertrude Stein's prose-song is a cold, black suet-pudding. We can represent it as a cold suet-roll of fabulously-reptilian length. Cut it at any point, it is the same thing; the same heavy, sticky, opaque mass all through, and all along. It is weighted, projected, with a sibylline urge. It is mournful and monstrous, composed of dead and inanimate material. It is all fat, without nerve. Or the evident vitality that informs it is vegetable rather than

Wyndham Lewis 1882–1957: *Time and Western Man* (1927)

animal. Its life is a low-grade, if tenacious one; of the sausage, by-the-yard, variety.

of Three Lives (*1909*)

1 Gertrude Stein and me are just like brothers.

Ernest Hemingway 1899–1961: John Malcolm Brinnin *The Third Rose* (1960)

2 The mama of dada.

Clifton Fadiman 1904–99: *Party of One* (1955)

Stendhal 1783–1842
French novelist

3 The great secret of Stendhal, his great shrewdness, consisted in writing *at once* . . . It would seem that his thought does not take time to put on its shoes before beginning to run.

André Gide 1869–1951: journal, 3 September 1937

Laurence Sterne 1713–68
English novelist

4 At present, nothing is talked of, nothing admired, but what I cannot help calling a very insipid and tedious performance: it is a kind of novel, called *The Life and Opinions of Tristram Shandy*; the great humour of which consists in the whole narration always going backwards.

Horace Walpole 1717–97: letter to David Dalrymple, 4 April 1760

Robert Louis Stevenson 1850–94 see also 92:5
Scottish novelist, poet, and travel writer

5 Valiant in velvet, light in ragged luck,
Most vain, most generous, sternly critical,
Buffoon and poet, lover and sensualist;
A deal of Ariel, just a streak of Puck,
Much Antony, of Hamlet most of all,
And something of the Shorter-Catechist.

W. E. Henley 1849–1903: 'In Hospital' (1888)

6 I am an Epick writer with a k to it, but without the necessary genius.

Robert Louis Stevenson 1850–94: letter to Henry James, 5 December 1892

7 What little reading I have been able to do during the last week has been in these gorgeous gold and red,—no, no, gules and or,—volumes. I feel younger also and heartened up; the man is so healthily good to one's soul and body.

Edward Elgar 1857–1934: letter, 26 December 1906

8 Stevenson seemed to pick the right word up on the point of his pen, like a man playing spillikins.

G. K. Chesterton 1874–1936: *The Victorian Age in Literature* (1912)

9 He worked at his style like a diamond-cutter, and responded to sensations with the delicacy of a poetical geiger counter.

John Carey 1934– : in *Sunday Times* 9 May 1993

Tom Stoppard 1937–
British dramatist, born in Czechoslovakia

1 Began working through a heap of mail, mostly brown envelopes with brochures from theatres telling me Tom Stoppard's plays are being done throughout the land.

Peter Nichols 1927– : diary, 3 September 1973

2 A dream interviewee, talking in eerily quotable sentences whose English has the faintly extraterritorial perfection of a Conrad or a Nabokov.

Clive James 1939– : Kenneth Tynan *Show People* (1980)

3 The subject matter may shift from moral philosophy to quantum physics, but the voice is that of the author caught in the act of badinage, arguing himself in and out of a quandary.

Mel Gussow 1933– : in *American Theatre* December 1995

Lytton Strachey 1880–1932
English biographer

4 My memory of his books tangles itself with my memory of Henry Lamb's marvellous portrait of an outraged wet mackerel of a man, dropped like an old cloak into a basket chair.

T. E. Lawrence 1888–1935: letter, 1 October 1927

5 He was, for all his brilliance, glitter, irony and wit, an unsound biographer: he was concerned with effect rather than truth.

Robert Blake 1916– : 'The Art of Biography' (1988)

Johan August Strindberg 1849–1912
Swedish dramatist and novelist

6 Strindberg was the precursor of all modernity in our present theatre . . . the most modern of moderns.

Eugene O'Neill 1888–1953: in 1924; Malcolm Bradbury and James McFarlane (eds.) *Modernism* (1991)

Structure

7 A whole is that which has a beginning, a middle, and an end. A beginning is that which does not itself follow anything by causal necessity, but after which something naturally is or comes to be. An end, on the contrary, is that which itself naturally follows some other thing, either by necessity, or as a rule, but has nothing following it. A middle is that which follows something as some other thing follows it. A well-constructed plot, therefore, must neither begin not end at haphazard, but conform to these principles.

Aristotle 384–322 BC: *Poetics*; see **288:9**

8 The famous rules, which the French call *Des Trois Unitez*, or, the Three Unities, which ought to be observed in every regular play; namely, of Time, Place, and Action.

John Dryden 1631–1700: *A Essay of Dramatic Poesy* (1668)

9 Homer to preserve the unity of his action hastens into the midst of things.

Joseph Addison 1672–1719: *The Spectator* no. 267 (1712)

1 It is fortunate for tale-tellers that they are not tied down like theatrical writers to the unities of time and place.

Sir Walter Scott 1771–1832: *Tales of My Landlord* (1st series, 1816) 'Old Mortality'

2 Two years . . . is a terrible gap in a story, but in these days the unities are not much considered.

Anthony Trollope 1815–82: *The Bertrams* (1859)

3 Don't let anyone persuade you . . . that Form *is* [not] substance to that degree that there is absolutely no substance without it. Form alone *takes*, and holds and preserves, substance.

Henry James 1843–1916: letter to Hugh Walpole, 19 May 1912

4 Form alone can indefinitely guard a work against the fluctuations in taste and culture, against the novelty and charm of works produced after it.

Paul Valéry 1871–1945: *The Art of Poetry*

5 You would do better, or at least no worse, to obliterate texts then to blacken margins, to fill in the holes of words till all is blank and flat and the whole ghastly business looks like what it is, senseless, speechless, issueless misery.

Samuel Beckett 1906–89: *Molloy* (1951)

6 To find a form that accommodates the mess, that is the task of the artist now.

Samuel Beckett 1906–89: *Proust* (1961)

7 I do think that poems are artificial in the sense that a play is artificial. There are strong second act curtains in poems as well as in plays.

Philip Larkin 1922–85: in *London Magazine* November 1964

8 Style and structure are the essence of a book; great ideas are hogwash.

Vladimir Nabokov 1899–1977: George Plimpton (ed.) *Writers at Work* (4th series, 1977)

9 A beginning, a muddle, and an end.
    on the 'classic formula' for a novel

Philip Larkin 1922–85: in *New Fiction* January 1978; see **287:7**

10 Sicilian storytellers use the formula '*lu cuntu nun metto tempo*' (time takes no time in a story) when they want to leave out links or indicate gaps of months or even years.

Italo Calvino 1923–85: *Six Memos for the Next Millennium* (1992)

11   We are driven
    By endings as by hunger. We *must know*
    How it comes out, the shape o' the whole, the thread
    Whose links are weak or solid, intricate
    Or boldly welded in great clumsy loops
    Of primitive workmanship. We feel our way
    Along the links and we cannot let go
    Of this bright chain of curiosity
    Which is become our fetter.

A. S. Byatt 1936– : poem by 'Randolph Ash' in *Possession* (1990)

12 Turning points are the inventions of story-tellers and dramatists, a necessary mechanism when life is reduced to, traduced by, a plot.

Ian McEwan 1948– : *Black Dogs* (1992)

13 It was sort of like reading a cafeteria tray before you've put anything on it.
    on Robbe-Grillet 'who declared that he was out to dispose of two obsolete concepts, character and plot'

Margaret Atwood 1939– : *Negotiating with the Dead: A Writer on Writing* (2002)

Style see also Choice of Words, Revision

14 Works of serious purpose and grand promises often have a purple patch or two stitched on, to shine far and wide.

Horace 65–8 BC: *Ars Poetica*; see **290:11**

1 An honest tale speeds best being plainly told.

William Shakespeare 1564–1616: *Richard III* (1591)

2 More matter with less art.

William Shakespeare 1564–1616: *Hamlet* (1601)

3 I do not much dislike the matter, but
The manner of his speech.

William Shakespeare 1564–1616: *Antony and Cleopatra* (1606–7)

4 When we see a natural style, we are quite surprised and delighted, for we expected to see an author and we find a man.

Blaise Pascal 1623–62: *Pensées* (1670)

5 A good writer, and one who writes with care, often finds that the expression he's spent a long time hunting for without finding it, and which he finds at last, turns out to be the simplest and most natural one, which looks as if it ought to have occurred to him at the beginning, without any effort.

Jean de la Bruyère 1645–96: *Les Caractères ou les moeurs de ce siècle* (1688)

6 Style is the dress of thought; a modest dress,
Neat, but not gaudy, will true critics please.

Samuel Wesley 1662–1735: 'An Epistle to a Friend concerning Poetry' (1700)

7 Proper words in proper places, make the true definition of a style.

Jonathan Swift 1667–1745: *Letter to a Young Gentleman lately entered into Holy Orders* 9 January 1720

8 These things [subject matter] are external to the man; style is the man.

Comte de Buffon 1707–88: *Discours sur le style*; address given to the Académie Française, 25 August 1753

9 In his plays you often find remarks doing a kitchen-hand's work in some remote corner of a sentence which would deserve pride of place in a disquisition by any other writer.
on Shakespeare

Georg Christoph Lichtenberg 1742–99: notebooks, 1765–99

10 I propose to myself to imitate, and as far as possible, to adopt the very language of men.

William Wordsworth 1770–1850: preface to *Lyrical Ballads* (1800)

11 Modern poetry characterized by the poets' *anxiety* to be always *striking* . . . Every line, nay, every word *stops*, looks full in your face, and asks and *begs* for praise.

Samuel Taylor Coleridge 1772–1834: Notebook, 1798–1804

12 One should only write when one has something important or profoundly beautiful to say, but then one must say it as simply as possible, as if one were trying one's best to prevent it being noticed.

Stendhal 1783–1842: letter to his sister Pauline, 20 August 1805

13 He read all the Essays, Letters, Tours and Criticisms of the day—and with the same ill-luck which made him derive only false principles from lessons of morality, and incentives to vice from the history of its overthrow, he gathered only hard words and involved sentences from the style of our most approved writers.

Jane Austen 1775–1817: 'Sir Edward Denham' in *Sanditon* (1926 ed.)

14 I know of only one rule: style cannot be too *clear*, too *simple*.

Stendhal 1783–1842: letter to Balzac, 30 October 1840

15 I would rather omit a touch of truth than fall into the abominable fault, now so common, of dropping into declamation.

Stendhal 1783–1842: *La Vie de Henri Brulard* (1890)

16 Style is life! It is the very life-blood of thought! Boileau was a little river, narrow, not very deep, but beautifully clear and well embanked. That's why its waters never run dry.

Gustave Flaubert 1821–80: letter to Louise Colet, 7 September 1853

1 Nothing has raised more questioning among my critics than these words—noble, the grand style . . . I think it will be found that the grand style arises in poetry, when a noble nature, poetically gifted, treats with simplicity or with severity a serious subject.

Matthew Arnold 1822–88: *On Translating Homer. Last Words* (1862)

2 Life has taught me not to believe in well-turned phrases.

Henrik Ibsen 1828–1906: *A Doll's House* (1879)

3 I have been asked whether anything in the way of 'literary style' is to be admitted. If style means superfluous ornament, I say emphatically, No. But style, and even high literary ability, is required for lucid and condensed narrative, and of such style I shall be anxious to get as much as I can.
   as editor of the Dictionary of National Biography

Leslie Stephen 1832–1904: in *Athenaeum* 23 December 1882

4 The web, then, or the pattern; a web at once sensuous and logical, an elegant and pregnant texture: that is style, that is the foundation of the art of literature.

Robert Louis Stevenson 1850–94: *The Art of Writing* (1905) 'On some technical Elements of Style in Literature' (written 1885)

5 People think that I can teach them style. What stuff it all is! Have something to say, and say it as clearly as you can. That is the only secret of style.

Matthew Arnold 1822–88: G. W. E. Russell *Collections and Recollections* (1898)

6 I don't wish to sign my name, though I am afraid everybody will know who the writer is: one's style is one's signature always.
   sending a letter for publication

Oscar Wilde 1854–1900: letter to the *Daily Telegraph*, 2 February 1891

7 No one in the world ever liked anything so much as Flaubert liked beauty of style.

Henry James 1843–1916: 'Gustave Flaubert' (1893)

8 You have so many modifiers that the reader has a hard time determining what deserves his attention, and it tires him out. If I write 'A man sat down on the grass,' it is understandable because it is clear and doesn't require a second reading. But it would be hard to follow and brain-taxing were I to write, 'A tall, narrow-chested, red-bearded man of medium height sat down noiselessly, looking around timidly and in fright, on a patch of green grass that had once been trampled by pedestrians.' The brain can't grasp all that at once, and the art of fiction ought to be immediately, instantly graspable.

Anton Chekhov 1860–1904: letter to Maxim Gorky, 2 September 1899

9 *Circumlocution*, n. A literary trick whereby the writer who has nothing to say breaks it gently to the reader.

Ambrose Bierce 1842–c.1914: *The Devil's Dictionary* (1911)

10 I hate the sort of licence that English people give themselves . . . to spread over and flop and roll about. I feel as fastidious as though I wrote with acid.

Katherine Mansfield 1888–1923: letter to John Middleton Murry, 19 May 1913

11 I know what you mean about purple patches. My new book is black with them but then I live by my pen as they say and you don't.

Evelyn Waugh 1903–66: letter to Henry Yorke, July 1929; see **288:14**

12 You praise the firm restraint with which they write—
   I'm with you there, of course:
   They use the snaffle and the curb all right,
   But where's the bloody horse?

Roy Campbell 1901–57: 'On Some South African Novelists' (1930)

1 Backward ran sentences until reeled the mind.
   satirizing the style of Time *magazine*

   Wolcott Gibbs 1902–58: in *New Yorker* 28 November 1936 'Time . . . Fortune . . . Life . . . Luce'

2 An author arrives at a good style when his language performs what is required of it without shyness.

   Cyril Connolly 1903–74: *Enemies of Promise* (1938)

3 The Mandarin style . . . is beloved by literary pundits, by those who would make the written word as unlike as possible to the spoken one. It is the style of those writers whose tendency is to make their language convey more than they mean or more than they feel, it is the style of most artists and all humbugs.

   Cyril Connolly 1903–74: *Enemies of Promise* (1938)

4 'Feather-footed through the plashy fen passes the questing vole' . . . 'Yes,' said the Managing Editor. 'That must be good style.'

   Evelyn Waugh 1903–66: *Scoop* (1938)

5 A good style doesn't form unless you absorb half a dozen top-flight authors every year. Or rather it *forms* but, instead of being a subconscious amalgam of all that you have admired, it is simply a reflection of the last writer you have read, a watered-down journalese.

   F. Scott Fitzgerald 1896–1940: letter, 18 July 1940

6 The test of good prose is that the reader does not notice it any more than a man looking through a window at a landscape notices the glass.

   W. H. Auden 1907–73: 'Who Shall Plan the Planners?' (1940); see **291:10**

7 For God's sake don't talk politics. I'm not interested in politics. The only thing that interests me is style.

   James Joyce 1882–1941: Richard Ellmann *James Joyce* (1982)

8 In literature the ambition of the novice is to acquire the literary language: the struggle of the adept is to get rid of it.

   George Bernard Shaw 1856–1950: Hesketh Pearson *Bernard Shaw* (1942)

9 The final elegance, not to console
   Nor sanctify, but plainly to propound.

   Wallace Stevens 1879–1955: 'Notes Towards a Supreme Fiction' (1942)

10 Good prose is like a window-pane.

   George Orwell 1903–50: *Collected Essays* (1968) vol. 1 'Why I Write'; see **291:6**

11 Be subtle, various, ornamental, clever,
   And do not listen to those critics ever
   Whose crude provincial gullets crave in books
   Plain cooking made still plainer by plain cooks.

   W. H. Auden 1907–73: 'The Shield of Achilles' (1955)

12 I am well aware that an addiction to silk underwear does not necessarily imply that one's feet are dirty. Nonetheless, style, like sheer silk, too often hides eczema.

   Albert Camus 1913–60: *The Fall* (1956)

13 Style is an increment in writing. When we speak of Fitzgerald's style, we don't mean his command of the relative pronoun, we mean the sound his words make on paper.

   William Strunk 1869–1946 and **E. B. White** 1899–1985: *The Elements of Style* (1959 ed.)

14 Style is the principle of decision in a work of art.

   Susan Sontag 1933– : *Against Interpretation and Other Essays* (1960)

15 Prose is architecture, not interior decoration, and the Baroque is over.

   Ernest Hemingway 1899–1961: Jeffrey Meyers *Hemingway* (1985)

16 In literature, vulgarity is preferable to nullity, just as grocer's port is preferable to distilled water.

   W. H. Auden 1907–73: 'Reading' (1964)

1 The day of the jewelled epigram is passed and, whether one likes it or not, one is moving into the stern puritanical era of the four-letter word.

Noel Annan 1916–2000: in the House of Lords, 1966; George Greenfield *Scribblers for Bread* (1989)

2 Every author of some value *transgresses* against 'good style', and in that transgression lies the originality (and hence the raison d'être) of his art.

Milan Kundera 1929– : *Testaments Betrayed* (1995)

Subject and Theme

3 Grasp the subject, the words will follow.

Cato the Elder 234–149 BC: Caius Julius Victor *Ars Rhetorica*

4 *Sicelides Musae, paulo maiora canamus!*
Non omnis arbusta iuvant humilesque myricae;
Si canimus silvas, silvae sint consule dignae.
Ultima Cumaei venit iam carminis aetas;
Magnus ab integro saeclorum nascitur ordo.
Iam redit et virgo, redeunt Saturnia regna,
Iam nova progenies caelo demittitur alto.

Virgil 70–19 BC: *Eclogues*

Sicilian Muses, let us sing of rather greater things. Bushes and low tamarisks do not please everyone; if we sing of the woods, let them be woods of consular dignity. Now has come the last age according to the oracle at Cumae; the great series of lifetimes starts anew. Now too the virgin goddess returns, the golden days of Saturn's reign return, now a new race is sent down from high heaven.

5 *Navita de ventis, de tauris narrat arator,*
Enumerat miles vulnera, pastor oves.

Propertius c.50–after 16 BC: *Elegies*

The seaman tells stories of winds, the ploughman of bulls; the soldier details his wounds, the shepherd his sheep.

6 *Quidquid agunt homines, votum timor ira voluptas*
Gaudia discursus nostri farrago libelli est.

Juvenal AD c.60–c.130: *Satires*

Everything mankind does, their hope, fear, rage, pleasure, joys, business, are the hotch-potch of my little book.

a list of poetic subjects:
7 The capital city. Arrowroot. Water-bur. Colts. Hail. Bamboo grass. The round-leaved violet. Club moss. Water oats. Flat river-boats. The mandarin duck. The scattered *chigaya* reed. Lawns. The green vine. The pear tree. The jujube tree. The althea.

Sei Shōnagon c.966–c.1013: *Pillow Book*; see **255:5**

8 Anything whatsoever may become the subject of a novel, provided only that it happens in this mundane life and not in some fairyland beyond our human ken.

Murasaki Shikibu c.978–c.1031: *The Tale of Genji*

9 A mere tale of a tub, my words are idle.

John Webster c.1580–c.1625: *The White Devil* (1612)

10 I describe not men, but manners; not an individual, but a species.

Henry Fielding 1707–54: *Joseph Andrews* (1742)

11 The moving accident is not my trade;
To freeze the blood I have no ready arts:
'Tis my delight, alone in summer shade,
To pipe a simple song for thinking hearts.

William Wordsworth 1770–1850: 'Hart-Leap Well' (1800)

1 Let other pens dwell on guilt and misery. I quit such odious subjects as soon as I can.

Jane Austen 1775–1817: *Mansfield Park* (1814)

2 3 or 4 families in a country village is the very thing to work on.

Jane Austen 1775–1817: letter to Anna Austen, 9 September 1814

3 I cannot write books handling the topics of the day; it is of no use trying. Nor can I write a book for its moral.

Charlotte Brontë 1816–55: letter to George Smith, 30 October 1852

4 The author has provided himself with a moral—the truth, namely, that the wrongdoing of one generation lives into the successive ones.

Nathaniel Hawthorne 1804–64: preface to *The House of the Seven Gables* (1851)

5 Shut not your doors to me proud libraries,
For that which was lacking on all your well-fill'd shelves,
    yet needed most, I bring
Forth from the war emerging, a book I have made,
The words of my book nothing, the drift of it everything,
A book separate, not link'd with the rest nor felt by the
    intellect,
But you ye untold latencies will thrill to every page.

Walt Whitman 1819–92: *Leaves of Grass* (1867) 'Shut Not Your Doors'

6 Everything that I have written is closely related to something that I have lived through.

Henrik Ibsen 1828–1906: letter, 1880

7 For one who takes it as I take it, London is on the whole the most possible form of life. I take it as an artist and as a bachelor; as one who has the passion of observation and whose business is the study of human life. It is the biggest aggregation of human life—the most complete compendium of the world.

Henry James 1843–1916: notebook, Boston, 25 November 1881

8 The business of the poet and novelist is to show the sorriness underlying the grandest things, and the grandeur underlying the sorriest things.

Thomas Hardy 1840–1928: notebook entry for 19 April 1885

9 NOTICE: Persons attempting to find a motive in this narrative will be prosecuted; persons attempting to find a moral in it will be banished; persons attempting to find a plot in it will be shot. BY ORDER OF THE AUTHOR.

Mark Twain 1835–1910: *The Adventures of Huckleberry Finn* (1884)

10 The life of man is not the subject of novels, but the inexhaustible magazine from which subjects are to be selected.

Robert Louis Stevenson 1850–94: *Memories and Portraits* (1887) 'A Humble Remonstrance'

11 Every good story is of course both a picture and an idea, and the more they are interfused the better the problem is solved.

Henry James 1843–1916: 'Guy de Maupassant' (1888)

12 Romance! Those first-class passengers they like it very
    well,
Printed, an' bound in little books; but why don't poets
    tell?
I'm sick of all their quirks an' turns—the loves an' doves
    they dream—
Lord, send a man like Robbie Burns to sing the Song o'
    Steam!

Rudyard Kipling 1865–1936: 'McAndrew's Hymn' (1896)

13 Am writing an essay on the life-history of insects and have abandoned the idea of writing on 'How Cats Spend their Time'.

W. N. P. Barbellion 1889–1919: *Journal of a Disappointed Man* (1919) 3 January 1903

14 This is an important book, the critic assumes, because it deals with war. This is an insignificant book because it deals with the feelings of women in a drawing-room.

Virginia Woolf 1882–1941: *A Room of One's Own* (1929)

1 Even to want to write about so-called artists who spend on sodomy what they have gained by sponging betrays a kind of spiritual inadequacy.
   reviewing Cyril Connolly's The Rock Pool

George Orwell 1903–50: in *New English Weekly* 23 July 1936

2 Irish poets, learn your trade,
Sing whatever is well made.

W. B. Yeats 1865–1939: 'Under Ben Bulben' (1939)

3 A writer should never write about the extraordinary. That is for the journalist.

James Joyce 1882–1941: letter to Djuna Barnes; Richard Ellman *James Joyce* (1959)

4 It was as if I had been supplied once and for all with a subject . . . Human nature is not black and white but black and grey. I read all that in *The Viper of Milan* and I looked round and I saw that it was so.
   of reading Marjorie Bowen's novel The Viper of Milan *at the age of fourteen*

Graham Greene 1904–91: 'The Lost Childhood' (1951)

5 The hardest part is having something to write about that succeeds in drawing words from your inner mind—that is very important, as one can always think of *subjects*, but they have to *matter* in that peculiar way that produces words and some kind of development of thought or theme, or else there's no poem in thought or words.

Philip Larkin 1922–85: letter, 10 April 1961

6 When I become interested in a subject, say old age, then the world is peopled for me—just peopled with them. And it's a narrow little small world, but it's full of old people, full of whatever I'm studying.

Muriel Spark 1918– : 'The House of Fiction' (1963)

7 The main concern of the fiction writer is with mystery as it is incarnated in real life.

Flannery O'Connor 1925–64: 'Catholic Novelists and their Readers' (1964)

8 The first twenty-five years, or even sixteen, provide a rich enough quarry to exploit for the rest of life.

Graham Greene 1904–91: Marie-Françoise Allain *The Other Man, Conversations with Graham Greene* (1983)

9 Novels are about other people and poems are about yourself.

Philip Larkin 1922–85: *Required Writing* (1983)

10 For a novelist, a given historic situation is an *anthropologic laboratory* in which he explores his basic question: *What is human existence?*

Milan Kundera 1929– : *Life is Elsewhere* (postscript, 1986 ed.)

11 Mostly in my stories I like to look at what people don't understand.

Alice Munro 1931– : Michelle Gadpaille *The Canadian Short Story* (1988)

12 One of the great challenges of living in a place like Australia is that so little of it has been analysed and mythologized. Whereas in any European country what you inherit is the interpretation of everything; of the past, of the present too, of buildings, of landscape, of light, of the structures of people's lives, rituals, habits. All of those things in Australia are still to be read.

David Malouf 1934– : in *Observer* 8 April 1990

on hearing that Watership Down *was a novel about rabbits written by a civil servant:*
13 I would rather read a novel about civil servants written by a rabbit.

Craig Brown 1957– : attributed; probably apocryphal

1 Bad behaviour is more interesting than good, isn't it? And that's why I'm afraid of middle age—it might not be good material! . . . I'm the kind of writer that almost has to make a laboratory out of himself to get the desired result. You don't want to keep, like, blowing up the test-tubes. But at the same time you do want an explosion.

Jay McInerney 1955– : in *Independent on Sunday* 19 April 1992

2 If, for the French, the United States frequently represented a futuristic fantasy, for the British, more or less since Dickens on, they had generally represented a comedy, a perfect example of extremity exotically developed under hothouse conditions.

Malcolm Bradbury 1932–2000: *Dangerous Pilgrimages* (1995)

replying to the question 'what is Rosencrantz and Guildenstern are Dead *about?' (after its first night in New York):*
3 It's about to make me rich.

Tom Stoppard 1937– : in *Independent* 2 December 1995

4 It's the moment when something deeply primitive breaks the surface of our supposedly grown-up lives—the crocodile's snout in the lily pond. Irresistible.
   on his taste for writing about jealousy

Julian Barnes 1946– : in *Paris Review* Winter 2000–2001

5 The basic tenet of the books is, it's impossible to escape history. Especially living in Edinburgh, and living in Scotland, you can never throw off the shackles of the past.
   on his Rebus crime novels

Ian Rankin 1960– : in *Guardian* 21 April 2001

Jonathan Swift 1667–1745 see also **91:12**
Anglo-Irish poet and satirist

6 Cousin Swift, you will never be a poet.

John Dryden 1631–1700: Samuel Johnson *Lives of the English Poets* (1779–81) 'Dryden'

7 From the highest to the lowest it is univerally read, from the cabinet-council to the nursery.
   of Gulliver's Travels

John Gay 1685–1732: letter to Swift, 17 November 1726

8 Yet malice never was his aim;
   He lashed the vice, but spared the name;
   No individual could resent,
   Where thousands equally were meant.

Jonathan Swift 1667–1745: 'Verses on the Death of Dr Swift' (1731)

9 His character seems to me a parallel with that of Caligula, and had he had the same power, would have made the same use of it.

Lady Mary Wortley Montagu 1689–1762: letter, 23 June 1754

10 Swift was *anima Rabelaisii habitans in sicco*—the soul of Rabelais dwelling in a dry place.

Samuel Taylor Coleridge 1772–1834: *Table Talk* (1835) 15 June 1830

11 Swift has sailed into his rest;
   Savage indignation there
   Cannot lacerate his breast.
   Imitate him if you dare,
   World-besotted traveller; he
   Served human liberty.

W. B. Yeats 1865–1939: 'Swift's Epitaph' (1933); see **91:12**

John Millington Synge 1871–1909
Irish dramatist

1 He loves all that has edge, all that is salt in the mouth, all that is rough to the hand, all that heightens the emotions by contest, all that strings into life the strength of tragedy.

W. B. Yeats 1865–1939: 'J. M. Synge and the Ireland of his Time' (1910)

Talent see also Genius

2 Genius does what it must, and Talent does what it can.

Owen Meredith 1831–91: 'Last Words of a Sensitive Second-Rate Poet' (1868)

3 Mediocrity knows nothing higher than itself, but talent instantly recognizes genius.

Arthur Conan Doyle 1859–1930: *The Valley of Fear* (1915)

4 Talent without genius comes to little. Genius without talent is *nothing*.

Paul Valéry 1871–1945: *At Moments* 'The Beautiful is Negative'

5 If I were shown a work written 'today' that could be placed only somewhere within the last fifty years, I should wonder if I were not in the presence of a considerable talent.

Philip Larkin 1922–85: in *London Magazine* May 1957

6 Nature is monstrously unjust. There is no substitute for talent. Industry and all the virtues are of no avail.

Aldous Huxley 1894–1963: George Greenfield *Scribblers for Bread* (1989)

7 What Romantic terminology called genius or talent or inspiration is nothing other than finding the right road empirically, following one's nose, taking shortcuts.

Italo Calvino 1923–85: 'Cybernetics and Ghosts', lecture in Turin, November 1969; *The Literature Machine* (1987)

8 What to do with all this talent, how to stay alive until I've gotten it down. I still feel that.

Saul Bellow 1915– : to his biographer on 30 August 1992; in *New Yorker* 26 June 1995

Alfred, Lord Tennyson 1809–92 see also 20:3, 245:7
English poet

9 Mr Tennyson belongs decidedly to the class we have already described as Poets of Sensation. He sees all forms of nature with the '*eruditus oculus*' and his ear has a fairy fineness.
  eruditus oculus = *erudite eye*

Arthur Hallam 1811–33: in *Englishman's Magazine* August 1831

10 Out-babying Wordsworth and out-glittering Keats.

Edward George Bulwer-Lytton 1803–73: *The New Timon* (1846)

11 It is beautiful; it is mournful; it is monotonous.
  of In Memoriam

Charlotte Brontë 1816–55: letter to Mrs Gaskell, 27 August 1850

12 I thought nothing could be grander than the first poem till I came to the third; but when I had read the last, it seemed to be absolutely unapproached and unapproachable.
  of Idylls of the King

Charles Dickens 1812–70: letter to John Forster, 25 August 1859

1 Whenever I feel disposed to reflect that Tennyson is not personally Tennysonian, I summon up the image of Browning, and this has the effect of making me check my complaints.

Henry James 1843–1916: letter, 17 November 1878

2 It is the height of luxury to sit in a hot bath and read about little birds.
  having had running hot water installed in his new house at Aldworth

Alfred, Lord Tennyson 1809–92: Hallam Tennyson *Tennyson and his Friends* (1911); see **217:2**

3 A Tennyson we may not see again for a century, or—in all his originality—ever again.

Queen Victoria 1819–1901: Philip Guedalla (ed.) *The Queen and Mr Gladstone* (1933)

4 Tennyson had the British Empire for God, and Queen Victoria for Virgin Mary.

Lady Gregory 1852–1932: W. B. Yeats diary, 17 March 1909

5 The great length of his mild fluency: the yards of linen-drapery for the delight of women.

George Meredith 1828–1909: Frank Harris *My Life and Loves* (1922–7)

6 He could not think up to the height of his own towering style.

G. K. Chesterton 1874–1936: *The Victorian Age in Literature* (1912)

7 There was little about melancholia that he didn't know; there was little else that he did.
  on Tennyson

W. H. Auden 1907–73: introduction to *A Selection From the Poems of Alfred, Lord Tennyson* (1947)

8 Until quite recently there was an academic fashion for looking down on Tennyson, who was said to be mellifluous but simple-minded. But *listen* to Tennyson, and his music will tell you something that the closest sort of mute analysis cannot do, and his stature as a poet is restored and perhaps increased thereby.

Robertson Davies 1913–95: lecture, Yale, 20 February 1990

William Makepeace Thackeray 1811–63 see also **139:11**
English novelist

9 They say he is like Fielding; they talk of his wit, humour, comic powers. He resembles Fielding as an eagle does a vulture: Fielding could stoop on carrion, but Thackeray never does.

Charlotte Brontë 1816–55: *Jane Eyre* (2nd ed., 1848) preface; see **106:5**

10 Thackeray is unique. I *can* say no more, I *will* say no less.

Charlotte Brontë 1816–55: letter to W. S. Williams, 29 March 1848

11 Papa, why do you not write books like Nicholas Nickleby?

Harriet Thackeray 1840–75: Anne Thackeray Ritchie *Records of Tennyson, Ruskin, and Robert and Elizabeth Browning* (1892)

12 Thackeray is like the edited and illustrated edition of a great dinner.

Walter Bagehot 1826–77: in *Spectator* 9 August 1862

13 Thackeray settled like a meat-fly on whatever one had got for dinner, and made one sick of it.

John Ruskin 1819–1900: *Fors Clavigera* (1871–84) Letter 31, 1 July 1873

Theme see Subject and Theme

Dylan Thomas 1914–53
Welsh poet

1 I am in the path of Blake, but so far behind him that only the wings of his heels are in sight.

Dylan Thomas 1914–53: letter to Pamela Hansford Johnson, undated, probably September 1933

2 I'm a freak user of words, not a poet. That's really the truth.

Dylan Thomas 1914–53: letter, 9 May 1934

3 A bulbous Taliessin, a spruce and small
   Bow-tied Silenus roistering his way
   Through lands of fruit and fable, well aware
   That even Dionysius has his day.

Louis MacNeice 1907–63: *Autumn Sequel* (1954)

4 He's exactly what I would have been if I had not been a Catholic.

Evelyn Waugh 1903–66: Noel Annan *Our Age* (1990); attributed

5 Thomas was more than ready to reclaim the poet's bardic robes. In doing so, he inaugurated that wave of fire-tongued pretentiousness which we now think of as typically 1940s.

Ian Hamilton 1938– : *Against Oblivion: Some Lives of the Twentieth-Century Poets* (2002)

Titles see also Borrowed Titles

6 *The Ancient Mariner* would not have taken so well if it had been called *The Old Sailor*.

Samuel Butler 1835–1902: attributed

7 A thing I am trying to write now called *The End of the Tether*—an inept title to heartbreaking bosh.

Joseph Conrad 1857–1924: letter, 10 June 1902; see **180:4**

8 The little importance of names of sterling books is shown by Charlotte Brontë's novels. Never had novel a worse title than 'Villette'.

George Gissing 1857–1903: *Commonplace Book* (1962)

9 *Author Hunting* is an excellent title. But I think there should be a hyphen between the two words. Otherwise people might think the book was an account of Anthony Trollope in his off-moments.

Max Beerbohm 1872–1956: letter, 16 July 1934

10 I have peculiar ideas about titles. They should never be obviously provocative, nor say anything about murder. They should be rather indirect and neutral, but the form of words should be a little unusual.

Raymond Chandler 1888–1959: letter to Dale Warren, 2 October 1946

11 There is no sale of cider in the States. The closest thing to your cider is applejack, and that has a rather low standing in the minds of American drinkers.
   *Laurie **Lee**'s American publishers, explaining the change of title from* Cider with Rosie *to* The Edge of Day *for the US market*

Anonymous: in 1960; Valerie Grove *Laurie Lee* (1999)

12 I always start with a title . . . and then work round different meanings. A novel is, for me, always an elaboration of a title.

Muriel Spark 1918– : in *Scotsman* 1962

1 Rereading Hardy, I was struck by his titles—just looking them over in the index—and thought what wonderful titles a lot of them would have made for Wallace Stevens, too—some even for Eliot—but with such differences in the poems.

Elizabeth Bishop 1911–79: letter, 21 December 1965

on being sent the manuscript of Travels with my Aunt, *Greene's American publishers had cabled, 'Terrific book, but we'll need to change the title':*

2 No need to change title. Easier to change publishers.

Graham Greene 1904–91: telegram to his American publishers in 1968; Giles Gordon *Aren't We Due a Royalty Statement?* (1993)

3 Thought of calling my Malayan play *Transvestites*, feeding off Tom's success and getting just in front of him in the alphabetical catalogues.
   referring to Privates on Parade *and Stoppard's* Travesties

Peter Nichols 1927– : diary, 15 July 1975

4 I think the title 'Four Point Turn' a little smart for so moving a book: it needs something sadder, more compassionate.
   on a possible title for Barbara **Pym***'s novel* Quartet in Autumn

Philip Larkin 1922–85: letter to Barbara Pym, 26 September 1976

5 Title: *Last Quartet* is better than *Four Point Turn*, but I still wish for something less literary, more striking, more . . . oh, I don't know. Titles are so very personal, one hesitates to plunge: *For the Dark, The Way into Winter, Doors into Dark*, something about *age*, something *poetic*.
   on a possible title for Quartet in Autumn

Philip Larkin 1922–85: letter to Barbara Pym, 26 September 1976

6 I thought of a splendid title for a novel *Blind Mouths at the Nipple*.
   watching a cat feeding her kittens

Barbara Pym 1913–80: letter to Philip Larkin, 1 May 1979

7 The most important part of the title is the comma. Because it seems to me that I am that comma.
   explaining the name of his forthcoming book East, West

Salman Rushdie 1947– : in *Daily Telegraph* 6 August 1994

8 I think they were rather shamefaced about altering the title, but they seemed to be quite serious when they explained that the *Henry V* film brought a number of enquiries about what had become of one to four.
   on changing The Madness of George III *to* The Madness of King George *for the American market*

Alan Bennett 1934– : in *The Times* 3 December 1994

9 The title is possibly a mistake: *Endure* would have been better, though hardly a crowd-puller.
   of his ill-fated play Enjoy

Alan Bennett 1934– : *Writing Home* (1994)

10 In my case the title comes either very early on, with no problem, or takes a long time and is found with difficulty.

P. D. James 1920– : in *Paris Review* 1995

J. R. R. Tolkien 1892–1973 see also **79:11**
British novelist and literary scholar

11 A real taste for fairy-stories was wakened by philology on the threshold of manhood, and quickened to full life by war.

J. R. R. Tolkien 1892–1973: *Tree and Leaf* (1964) 'On Fairy-Stories'

1 He could turn a lecture room into a mead hall in which he was the bard and we were the feasting, listening guests.

J. I. M. Stewart 1906–94: Humphrey Carpenter *J. R. R. Tolkien* (1977)

2 Most modern fantasy just rearranges the furniture in Tolkien's attic.

Terry Pratchett 1948– : Stan Nicholls (ed.) *Wordsmiths of Wonder* (1993)

Leo Tolstoy 1828–1910
Russian novelist

3 Tolstoy is a reflector as vast as a natural lake.

Henry James 1843–1916: 'Ivan Turgeneff' (1896)

4 When literature has a Tolstoy, it is easy and gratifying to be a writer.

Anton Chekhov 1860–1904: letter, 28 January 1900

5 Tolstoy's *Confessions*; terrifyingly sad and savagely flagellant; a fallacy in his very way of putting the question and in consequence a withering blight on all human achievement whether of the heart or the head.

Gustav Mahler 1860–1911: letter, 23 June 1904

6 It is hopeless to grapple with Tolstoy. The man is like yesterday's east wind, which brought tears when you faced it and numbed you meanwhile.

T. E. Lawrence 1888–1935: letter to E. M. Forster, 20 February 1924

7 He remains in many ways the foremost prophet of our time . . . There is no one today with Tolstoy's deep insight and moral force.

Albert Einstein 1879–1955: interview, in *Survey Graphic* August 1934

8 With God he maintains very suspicious relations. They are like two bears in one den.

Maxim Gorky 1868–1936: Conor Cruise O'Brien *The Great Melody* (1993)

9 I know as well as others that no man is more worthy than he of the name of genius; more complicated, contradictory, and great in everything—yes, yes, in everything. Great—in some curious sense, wide, indefinable by words—there is something in him which made me desire to cry aloud to everyone: 'Look what a wonderful man is living on earth.'

Maxim Gorky 1868–1936: *Reminiscences of Tolstoy* (1934)

10 As I reread *Hadji-Murad* again, I thought: this is the man one should learn from. Here the electric charge went from the earth, through the hands, straight to the paper, with no insulation at all, quite mercilessly stripping off all the outer layers with a sense of truth—a truth, furthermore, which was clothed in dress both transparent and beautiful.

Isaac Babel 1894–1940: interview, Union of Soviet Writers, 28 September 1937

Tools of the Trade see also Dictionaries

11 Is not this a lamentable thing, that of the skin of an innocent lamb should be made parchment? that parchment, being scribbled o'er, should undo a man?

William Shakespeare 1564–1616: *Henry VI, Part 2* (1592)

12 It is well to observe the force and virtue and consequence of discoveries, and these are to be seen nowhere more conspicuously than in those three which were unknown to the ancients, and of which the origins, though recent, are obscure and inglorious; namely, printing, gunpowder,

Francis Bacon 1561–1626: *Novum Organum* (1620); see **301:5**

and the mariner's needle [compass]. For these three have changed the whole face and state of things throughout the world.

1 I like writing with a peacock's quill; because its feathers are all eyes.

Thomas Fuller 1654—1734: *Gnomologia* (1732)

2 I was in a printing house in Hell, and saw the method in which knowledge is transmitted from generation to generation.

William Blake 1757-1827: *The Marriage of Heaven and Hell* (1790-3) 'A Memorable Fancy' plates 15-17

3 Oh! nature's noblest gift—my grey goose quill:
Slave of my thoughts, obedient to my will.
Torn from thy parent bird to form a pen.
That mighty instrument of little men!

Lord Byron 1788-1824: *English Bards and Scotch Reviewers* (1809)

4 For you know, dear—I may, without vanity, hint—
Though an angel should write, still 'tis *devils* must print.

Thomas Moore 1779-1852: *The Fudges in England* (1835)

5 The three great elements of modern civilization,
Gunpowder, Printing, and the Protestant Religion.

Thomas Carlyle 1795-1881: *Critical and Miscellaneous Essays* (1838) 'The State of German Literature'; see **300:12**

6 It came as a boon and a blessing to men,
The peaceful, the pure, the victorious PEN!
    almost certainly the inspiration for the advertisement by MacNiven and H. Cameron Ltd. (current by 1879), 'It came as a boon and a blessing to men, / The Pickwick, the Owl, and the Waverley pen'

J. C. Prince 1808-66: 'The Pen and the Press'

7 RIDDLE: *Je suis le capitaine de vingt-quatre soldats, et sans moi Paris serait pris?*
    ANSWER: *A.*

Anonymous: in Hugh Rowley *Puniana: or, Thoughts wise and otherwise* (1867)

RIDDLE: I am the captain of twenty-four soldiers, and without me Paris would be taken?
    ANSWER: A [i.e. 'Paris' minus 'a' = *pris* taken].
    the saying 'With twenty-six lead soldiers [the characters of the alphabet set up for printing] I can conquer the world' may derive from this riddle, but probably arose independently

8 When the doorbell announced the first visitor, he would throw a thin swatch of red silk over his worktable, hiding the paper mess and the tools of his trade, which were as sacred to him as liturgical objects to a priest.
    on **Flaubert**'*s reception of visitors to Sunday lunch*

Guy de Maupassant 1850-93: *Complete Works* (1910)

9 The sight of an inkwell and of a pen fills me with anger and horror.

Joseph Conrad 1857-1924: letter, 20 December 1896

10 The printing press is either the greatest blessing or the greatest curse of modern times, one sometimes forgets which.

J. M. Barrie 1860-1937: *Sentimental Tommy* (1896)

11 I am trying to make use of an accursed 'fountain' pen— but it's a vain struggle, it beats me.

Henry James 1843-1916: letter, 2 January 1908

12 *Ink,* n. A villainous compound of taumogallate of iron, gun-arabic and water, chiefly used to facilitate the infection of idiocy and promote intellectual crime.

Ambrose Bierce 1842-c.1914: *The Devil's Dictionary* (1911)

1 Henry James must altogether have spent several
thousands of the hours of his declining years in
apologizing for use of the typewriting machine.

Max Beerbohm 1872–1956: letter, 21
May 1921

2 Having found and bought, at a local paper-shop, a number
of copybooks similar to those I had used at school, I set to
work. The heavy grey-ruled pages, the vertical red line of
margins, the black cover and its inset medallion and the
ornamental title, *Le Calligraphe*, reawakened the urge, a
sort of itch in my fingers.
   on starting to write the 'Claudine' novels

Colette 1873–1954: *My
Apprenticeships* (1936)

3 The only thing that goes missing in Nature is a pencil.

Robert Benchley 1889–1945:
attributed, perhaps apocryphal

4 The [*or* A] quick brown fox jumps over the lazy dog.
   *used by keyboarders to ensure that all letters of the alphabet
   are functioning*

Anonymous: R. Hunter Middleton's
introduction to *The Quick Brown Fox*
(1945) by Richard H. Templeton Jr.

5 The biggest obstacle to professional writing is the necessity
for changing a typewriter ribbon.

Robert Benchley 1889–1945: *Chips
off the old Benchley* (1949) 'Learn to
Write'

6 I have known the inexorable sadness of pencils,
Neat in their boxes, dolour of pad and paper-weight,
All the misery of manilla folders and mucilage,
Desolation in immaculate public places.

Theodore Roethke 1908–63:
'Dolour' (1948)

7 I wrote all my formal communications to the press in
longhand. I have never had the secret knack of
typewriters. Typewriters can't spell, you know.

Max Beerbohm 1872–1956: S. N.
Behrman *Conversations with Max*
(1960)

8 My own experience has been that the tools I need for my
work are paper, tobacco, food and a little whiskey.

William Faulkner 1897–1962:
Malcolm Cowley (ed.) *Writers at
Work* (1st series, 1958)

9 Much as I loathe the typewriter, I must admit that it is a
help in self-criticism. Typescript is so impersonal and
hideous to look at, if I type out a poem, I immediately see
defects which I missed when I looked through it in
manuscript.

W. H. Auden 1907–73: *The Dyer's
Hand* (1962)

10 I never write except with a writing board. I've never had a
table in my life. And I use all sorts of things. Write on the
sole of my shoe.

Robert Frost 1874–1963: George
Plimpton (ed.) *The Writer's Chapbook*
(1989)

11 The medium is the message.

Marshall McLuhan 1911–80:
Understanding Media (1964)

12   From the Olivetti portable,
the dictionaries, (the very
best money can buy), the heaps of paper, it is evident
what must go on. Devoid of
flowers and family photographs, all is subordinate
here to a function.

W. H. Auden 1907–73: 'The Cave of
Making' (1965)

13 Between my finger and my thumb
The squat pen rests.
I'll dig with it.

Seamus Heaney 1939– : 'Digging'
(1966)

14 From the time I was nine or ten, it was a toss-up whether I
was going to be a writer or a painter, and I discovered by
the time I was sixteen or seventeen that paints cost too
much money, so I became a writer because you could be a
writer with a pencil and a penny notebook.

Frank O'Connor 1903–66: George
Plimpton (ed.) *The Writer's Chapbook*
(1989)

1 The typewriter holding up its dismembered black bits of words like some elaborate machine of torture.

Alison Lurie 1926- : *Real People* (1969)

2 My single-lined foolscap—a word which already had an ominous ring to it.

Graham Greene 1904-91: *A Sort of Life* (1971)

3 The typewriter separated me from a deeper intimacy with poetry, and my hand brought me closer to that intimacy again.

Pablo Neruda 1904-73: in *Writers at Work* (5th series, 1981)

4 I sat down before the blank sheets of foolscap . . . I had abandoned the single-lined variety where the lines seemed to me now like the bars on a prison window.

Graham Greene 1904-91: *Ways of Escape* (1980)

5 My memory is certainly in my hands. I can remember things only if I have a pencil and I can write with it and play with it. I think your hand concentrates for you.

Rebecca West 1892-1983: George Plimpton (ed.) *The Writer's Chapbook* (1989)

6 How very bold of you to buy an electric typewriter; the only time I tried one I was scared to death, as it seemed to be running away with me. I felt as if I had been put at the controls of Concorde after five minutes' tuition.

Philip Larkin 1922-85: letter to Anthony Powell, 7 August 1985

7 I think giving this computer to the last Luddite is ridiculous. It's like giving a Porsche to someone who just discovered the bicycle.

Michael Ondaatje 1943- : accepting a computer at the Wang International Festival of Authors, Toronto, 23 October 1988

8 I don't use a typewriter. It's too heavy, too much trouble. I use a notebook, and I write in bed. Ninety-five percent of everything I've written has been done in bed.

Paul Bowles 1910- : George Plimpton (ed.) *The Writer's Chapbook* (1989)

9 To scrutinise the trivial can be to discover the monumental.
  the principle behind his writing a history of the pencil

Henry Petroski 1942- : in *New Statesman* 9 November 1990

10 The PC is the LSD of the '90s.

Timothy Leary 1920-96: remark made in the early 1990s; in *Guardian* 1 June 1996

11 I use white paper in A4 size and I always use a black drawing pen with a very fine nib. The vital accessories to my work are my reference books, such as the complete Shakespeare and a prayer book, and a large black refuse bin.

Beryl Bainbridge 1933- : Clare Boylan (ed.) *The Agony and the Ego* (1993)

12 Electric typewriters keep going 'mmmmmmm—what are you waiting for?'

Anthony Burgess 1917-93: Clare Boylan (ed.) *The Agony and the Ego* (1993)

13 The dead-pan cloudiness of a word processor.

Seamus Heaney 1939- : *The Redress of Poetry* (1995)

14 The Internet is an elite organisation; most of the population of the world has never even made a phone call.

Noam Chomsky 1928- : in *Observer* 18 February 1996

15 This book was written with the world's finest word processor, a Waterman cartridge fountain pen.

Stephen King 1947- : *Dreamcatcher* (2001) Author's note

16 I talk about my pens and notebooks the way the master of a seraglio talked about his love slaves.

Mary Gordon 1949- : in *Writers on Writing: Collected Essays from The New York Times* (2001)

17 My pen . . . is a Waterman's, black enamel with a trim of gold. When I write with it, I feel as if I'm wearing a perfectly tailored suit, and my hair is pulled back into a chignon.

Mary Gordon 1949- : in *Writers on Writing: Collected Essays from The New York Times* (2001)

1 A whole set of metaphoric shovels is part of my tool collection, and for me the research that underlies the writing is the best part of the scribbling game.

Annie Proulx 1935– : in *Writers on Writing: Collected Essays from The New York Times* (2001)

2 In the mid-eighties I was a grateful convert to computers . . . I like the provisional nature of unprinted material held in the computer's memory—like an unspoken thought.

Ian McEwan 1948– : in *Paris Review* Summer 2002

Tradition see also **The Western Canon**

3 Turn the pages of your Greek models night and day.

Horace 65–8 BC: *Ars Poetica*

4 [A] requisite in our poet or maker is imitation, *imitatio*, to be able to convert the substance or riches of another poet to his own use. To make choice of one excellent man above the rest, and so to follow him . . . Not as a creature that swallows what it takes in, crude, raw and undigested; but that feeds with an appetite, and hath a stomach to concoct, divide, and turn all into nourishment.

Ben Jonson c.1573–1637: *Timber, or Discoveries made upon Men and Matter* (1641)

5 Nothing is more ridiculous than to make an author a dictator, as the schools have done with Aristotle.

Ben Jonson c.1573–1637: *Timber, or Discoveries made upon Men and Matter* (1641)

6 We feed on the ancients and the talented among the moderns, we squeeze them and extract all we can from them, we use them to blow up our works; and when finally we are authors and believe we can walk by ourselves, we turn against them, we mistreat them, like those children who have grown tough and strong from the milk they were given, and who attack their nurse.

Jean de la Bruyère 1645–96: *Les Caractères ou les moeurs de ce siècle* (1688)

7 Books, like proverbs, receive their chief value from the stamp and esteem of ages through which they have passed.

William Temple 1628–99: *Miscellanea. The Second Part* (1690) 'Ancient and Modern Learning'

8 Books are the legacies that a great genius leaves to mankind, which are delivered down from generation to generation, as presents to the posterity of those who are yet unborn.

Joseph Addison 1672–1719: *The Spectator* 10 September 1711

9 Speak of the moderns without contempt, and of the ancients without idolatry.

Lord Chesterfield 1694–1773: *Letters to his Son* (1774)

10 Meek young men grow up in libraries, believing it their duty to accept the views which Cicero, which Locke, which Bacon have given, forgetful that Cicero, Locke and Bacon were only young men in libraries when they wrote these books.

Ralph Waldo Emerson 1803–82: *The American Scholar* (1837)

11 Men grind and grind in the mill of a truism, and nothing comes out but what was put in. But the moment they desert the tradition for a spontaneous thought, then poetry, wit, hope, virtue, learning, anecdote, all flock to their aid.

Ralph Waldo Emerson 1803–82: *Literary Ethics* (1838)

12 The dust and smoke and noise of modern literature have nothing in common with the pure, silent air of immortality.

William Hazlitt 1778–1830: 'On Reading Old Books' (1852)

1 It takes an old civilization to set a novelist in motion—a proposition that seems to me so true as to be a truism. It is on manners, customs, usages, habits, forms, upon all these things matured and established, that a novelist lives—they are the very stuff his work is made of.

Henry James 1843–1916: letter, 31 January 1880

2 '*Classic*.' A book which people praise and don't read.

Mark Twain 1835–1910: *Following the Equator* (1897)

3 Someone said: 'The dead writers are remote from us because we *know* so much more than they did.' Precisely, and they are that which we know.

T. S. Eliot 1888–1965: *The Sacred Wood* (1920) 'Tradition and Individual Talent'

4 A classic . . . is a successful book that has survived the reaction of the next period or generation. Then it's safe, like a style in architecture or furniture. It's acquired a picturesque dignity to take the place of its fashion.

F. Scott Fitzgerald 1896–1940: *The Beautiful and the Damned* (1922)

5 I have, then, given my hostages. What I think and judge I have stated as responsibly and clearly as I can. Jane Austen, George Eliot, Henry James, Conrad, and D. H. Lawrence: the great tradition of the British novel is there.

F. R. Leavis 1895–1978: introduction to *The Great Tradition* (1948)

6 You're familiar with the tragedies of antiquity, are you? The great homicidal classics?

Tom Stoppard 1937– : *Rosencrantz and Guildenstern are Dead* (1967)

7 Thus when I started to verse,
I presently sat at the feet of
Hardy and *Thomas* and *Frost*.

Falling in love altered that,
now Someone, at least, was important:
Yeats was a help, so was *Graves* . . .

. . . Fondly I ponder You all:
Without you I couldn't have managed
even my weakest of lines.

W. H. Auden 1907–73: 'A Thanksgiving' (1974)

8 A classic is a book that has never finished saying what it has to say.

Italo Calvino 1923–85: *The Literature Machine* (1987)

9 Great literature cannot grow from a neglected soil. Only if we actually tend or care will it transpire that every hundred years or so we might get a *Middlemarch*.

P. D. James 1920– : in *Daily Telegraph* 14 April 1988

10 No story comes from nowhere; new stories are born from old—it is the new combinations that make them new.

Salman Rushdie 1947– : *Haroun and the Sea of Stories* (1990)

11 Every writer carries in his or her mind an invisible tribunal of dead writers, whose appointment is an imaginative act and not merely a browbeaten response to some notion of authority. This tribunal sits in judgement on our own work.

Robert Hughes 1938– : *Culture of Complaint* (1993)

12 Tradition is not only a handing-down or process of benign transmission; it is also a conflict between past genius and present aspiration, in which the prize is literary survival or canonical inclusion.

Harold Bloom 1930– : *The Western Canon* (1995)

13 Poems, stories, novels, plays come into being as a response to prior poems, stories, novels, and plays, and that response depends upon acts of reading and interpretation by the later writers, acts that are identical with the new works.

Harold Bloom 1930– : *The Western Canon* (1995)

1 Writers have to start out as readers, and before they put
pen to paper, even the most disaffected of them will have
internalized the norms and forms of the tradition from
which they wish to secede.

Seamus Heaney 1939– : *The Redress of Poetry* (1995)

2 It adds a new terror to the death of the novelist.
of the vogue for sequels

Peter Ackroyd 1949– : in *Independent on Sunday* 22 September 1996

3 Nowadays the real danger to dead authors isn't the
malicious biography but the avaricious sequel.

David Grylls 1947– : in *Sunday Times* 13 October 1996

4 Scheherazade's tales have lived on, like germ-cells, in
many literatures.

A. S. Byatt 1936– : *On Histories and Stories* (2000)

5 All writers learn from the dead. As long as you continue to
write, you continue to explore the work of writers who
have preceded you; you also feel judged and held to
account by them.

Margaret Atwood 1939– : *Negotiating with the Dead: A Writer on Writing* (2002)

Tragedy

6 Tragedy is thus a representation of an action that is worth
serious attention, complete in itself and of some amplitude
. . . by means of pity and fear bringing about the purgation
of such emotions.

Aristotle 384–322 BC: *Poetics*

7 The composition of a tragedy requires *testicles*.
*on being asked why no woman had ever written 'a tolerable
tragedy'*

Voltaire 1694–1778: letter from Byron to John Murray, 2 April 1817

8 One of Edward's Mistresses was Jane Shore, who has had a
play written about her, but it is a tragedy and therefore
not worth reading.

Jane Austen 1775–1817: *The History of England* (written 1791)

9 We do not expect people to be deeply moved by what is not
unusual. That element of tragedy which lies in the very
fact of frequency, has not yet wrought itself into the coarse
emotion of mankind.

George Eliot 1819–80: *Middlemarch* (1871–2)

10 Tragedy is like strong acid—it dissolves away all but the
very gold of truth.

D. H. Lawrence 1885–1930: letter, 1 April 1911

11 But the tragedy of modern life is that nothing happens,
and that the resultant dullness does not kill. Maupassant's
Une Vie is infinitely more tragic than the death of Juliet.

George Bernard Shaw 1856–1950: preface to *Three Plays by Brieux* (1911)

12 Tragedy is true guise, Comedy lies.

Thomas Hardy 1840–1928: *Winter Words* (1928)

13 None but a poet can write a tragedy. For tragedy is
nothing less than pain transmuted into exaltation by the
alchemy of poetry.

Edith Hamilton 1867–1963: *The Greek Way* (1930)

14 Show me a hero and I will write you a tragedy.

F. Scott Fitzgerald 1896–1940: Edmund Wilson (ed.) *The Crack-Up* (1945) 'Note-Books E'

15 The spring is wound up tight. It will uncoil of itself. That is
what is so convenient in tragedy. The least little turn of
the wrist will do the job. Anything will set it going.

Jean Anouilh 1910–87: *Antigone* (1944)

16 A tragic situation exists when virtue does not *triumph* but
when it is still felt that man is nobler than the forces that
destroy him.

George Orwell 1903–50: 'Lear, Tolstoy and the Fool' (1947)

1 The bad end unhappily, the good unluckily. That is what tragedy means.

Tom Stoppard 1937– : *Rosencrantz and Guildenstern are Dead* (1967)

Translation and Translators

2 When I recalled how knowledge of Latin had previously decayed throughout England, and yet many could still read things written in English, I then began, amidst the various and multifarious afflictions of this kingdom, to translate into English the book which in Latin is called *Pastoralis*, in English 'Shepherd-book', sometimes word for word, sometimes sense for sense.

Alfred the Great AD 849–99: preface to the Anglo-Saxon version of St Gregory's *Pastoral Care* (translated by S. Keynes and M. Lapidge, 1983)

3 Translation it is that openeth the window, to let in the light; that breaketh the shell, that we may eat the kernel; that putteth aside the curtain, that we may look into the most holy place; that removeth the cover of the well, that we may come by the water.

Bible: Authorized Version (1611) 'The Translators to the Reader'

4 Such is our pride, our folly, or our fate,
That few, but such as cannot write, translate.

John Denham 1615–69: 'To Richard Fanshaw' (1648)

5 He is translation's thief that addeth more,
As much as he that taketh from the store
Of the first author.

Andrew Marvell 1621–78: 'To His Worthy Friend Dr Witty' (1651)

6 Some hold translations not unlike to be
The wrong side of a Turkey tapestry.

James Howell 1594?–1666: *Familiar Letters* (1645–55)

7 It is a pretty poem, Mr Pope, but you must not call it Homer.
     when pressed by **Pope** *to comment on 'My Homer', i.e. his translation of* **Homer***'s* Iliad

Richard Bentley 1662–1742: John Hawkins (ed.) *The Works of Samuel Johnson* (1787)

8 Poetry, indeed, cannot be translated; and, therefore, it is poets that preserve languages; for we would not be at the trouble to learn a language, if we could have all that is written in it just as well in translation. But as the beauties of poetry cannot be preserved in any language except that in which it was originally written, we learn the language.

Samuel Johnson 1709–84: James Boswell *Life of Johnson* (1791)

9 It appears to me that men are hired to run down men of genius under the mask of translators.

William Blake 1757–1827: *Annotations to Boyd's Dante* (written c.1800)

10 The vanity of translation; it were as wise to cast a violet into a crucible that you might discover the formal principle of its colour and odour, as seek to transfuse from one language to another the creations of a poet. The plant must spring again from its seed, or it will bear no flower.

Percy Bysshe Shelley 1792–1822: *A Defence of Poetry* (written 1821)

11 Translators are like busy pimps extolling the surpassing charms of some half-veiled beauty. They excite an irresistible desire for the original.

Johann Wolfgang von Goethe 1749–1832: *Art and Antiquity* (1816–32)

12 Wordsworth says somewhere that wherever Virgil seems to have composed 'with his eye on the object', Dryden fails to render him. Homer invariably composes 'with his eye on the object', whether the object be a moral or a material one: Pope composes with his eye on his style, into which he translates his object, whatever it is.

Matthew Arnold 1822–88: *On Translating Homer* (1861)

1 I do not hesitate to read . . . all good books in translations. What is really best in any book is translatable—any real insight or broad human sentiment.

Ralph Waldo Emerson 1803–82: *Society and Solitude* (1870) 'Books'

2 I believe that a poem ought to be translated in the way the poet himself would have composed it, had he belonged to the nation for which he is being translated.

Henrik Ibsen 1828–1906: letter, 1872

3 These pearls of thought in Persian gulfs were bred,
Each softly lucent as a rounded moon;
The diver Omar plucked them from their bed,
Fitzgerald strung them on an English thread.

James Russell Lowell 1819–91: 'In a Copy of Omar Khayyám'

4 The only tribute a French translator can pay Shakespeare is not to translate him—even to please Sarah [Bernhardt].

Max Beerbohm 1872–1956: in *Saturday Review* 17 June 1899

5 A translation is no translation unless it will give you the music of a poem along with the words of it.

John Millington Synge 1871–1909: *The Aran Islands* (1907)

6 I have a prejudice against people who print things in a foreign language and add no translation. When I am the reader, and the author considers me able to do the translating myself, he pays me quite a nice compliment— but if he would do the translating for me I would try to get along without the compliment.

Mark Twain 1835–1910: A. B. Paine (ed.) *Moments with Mark Twain* (1920)

7 An idea does not pass from one language to another without change.

Miguel de Unamuno 1864–1936: *Tragic Sense of Life* (1913)

8 The original Greek is of great use in elucidating Browning's translation of the *Agamemnon*.

Robert Yelverton Tyrrell 1844–1914: Ulick O'Connor *Oliver St John Gogarty* (1964)

9 Translation is the purest procedure by which the poetic skill can be recognized.

Rainer Maria Rilke 1875–1926: in conversation in 1924; Albert Manguel *A History of Reading* (1996)

10 Humour is the first of the gifts to perish in a foreign tongue.

Virginia Woolf 1882–1941: *The Common Reader* (1st series, 1925) 'On Not Knowing Greek'

11 I understand that you are to translate *Ulysses*, and I have come from Paris to tell you not to alter a single word.
to a prospective translator

James Joyce 1882–1941: Richard Ellmann *James Joyce* (1982)

12 I do love translating it is the pure pleasure of writing without the misery of inventing.
while translating La Princesse de Clèves

Nancy Mitford 1904–73: letter to Evelyn Waugh, 11 January 1949

13 Translations (like wives) are seldom strictly faithful if they are in the least attractive.

Roy Campbell 1901–57: in *Poetry Review* June-July 1949

14 Pastiche and face-powder.
on T. E. Lawrence's translation of the Odyssey, *of which* **Beerbohm** *said that he 'would rather not have been that translator than have driven the Turks out of Arabia'*

Max Beerbohm 1872–1956: in June 1955; S. N. Behrman *Conversations with Max* (1960)

15 Almost all translations seem to me condemned to be poetic zombies, assemblages of properties walking round with no informing intelligence or soul, unless the original poem can be digested in the imagination of its translator and used to produce a new poem.

Philip Larkin 1922–85: in *Guardian* 25 March 1960

1 Pushkin has likened translators to horses changed at the
posthouses of civilization. The greatest reward I can think
of is that students may use my work as a pony.

Vladimir Nabokov 1899–1977:
Alexander Pushkin *Eugene Onegin*
(translated by Vladimir Nabokov,
1964)

2 The original is unfaithful to the translation.
  on Henley's translation of Beckford's Vathek

Jorge Luis Borges 1899–1986: *Sobre
el 'Vathek' de William Beckford*; in
Obras Completas (1974)

3 Poets belong to the language, not to the world.

Seamus Heaney 1939– :
interviewed in *Athens News* 8
October 1995

4 It can be as if you're writing a great play yourself. It's like
driving a Rolls Royce.
  on translating **Chekhov**

Michael Frayn 1933– : in *Guardian*
14 August 1999

5 It was labour-intensive work, scriptorium-slow.
  on translating Beowulf

Seamus Heaney 1939– :
introduction to his translation of
Beowulf (1999)

Travel Writing

6 Guide-books, Wellingborough, are the least reliable books
in all literature; and nearly all literature, in one sense, is
made up of guide-books . . . Every age makes its own
guide-books, and the old ones are used for waste paper.

Herman Melville 1819–91: *Redburn*
(1849)

7 The travel-book, if to be done at all, would cost me very
little trouble, and surely would go very far to pay charges,
whenever published.

Charles Dickens 1812–70: letter, 2
November 1843

8 Our instructed vagrancy, which has hardly time to linger
by the hedgerows, but runs away early to the tropics, and
is at home with palms and banyans—which is nourished
on books of travel, and stretches the theatre of its
imagination to the Zambesi.

George Eliot 1819–80: *The Mill on
the Floss* (1860)

9 Travel writing as a genre is *per se* almost impossible. To
eliminate all repetitions you would have had to refrain
from telling what you saw.

Gustave Flaubert 1821–80: letter,
November 1866

10 Of all possible subjects, travel is the most difficult for an
artist, as it is the easiest for a journalist.

W. H. Auden 1907–73: *The Dyer's
Hand* (1962)

11 Writing about travels is nearly always tedious, travelling
being, like war and fornication, exciting but not
interesting.

Malcolm Muggeridge 1903–90: in
Observer 5 September 1976

12 The travel writer seeks the world we have lost—the lost
valleys of the imagination.

Alexander Cockburn 1941– : in
Harper's August 1985

13 Life, as the most ancient of all metaphors insists, is a
journey; and the travel book, in its deceptive simulation of
the journey's fits and starts, rehearses life's own
fragmentation. More even than the novel, it embraces the
contingency of things.

Jonathan Raban 1942– : *For Love
and Money* (1987)

14 It is not travel that narrows the mind but travel writing.

James Buchan 1954– : in *Spectator*
11 August 1990

Trends see **Movements and Trends**

William Trevor 1928–
Anglo-Irish novelist and short story writer

1 I'm a short-story writer, really, who happens to write novels. Not the other way round.

> **William Trevor** 1928– : in *Paris Review* 1989

Anthony Trollope 1815–82
English novelist

2 He never leaves off . . . he always has two packages of manuscript in his desk, besides the one he's working on, and the one that's being published.
   on her husband

> **Rose Trollope** 1820–1917: Julian Hawthorne *Shapes that Pass: Memories of Old Days* (1928)

3 I have read Trollope's autobiography and regard it as one of the most curious and amazing books in all literature, for its density, blockishness and general thickness and soddenness.

> **Henry James** 1843–1916: letter, 25 November 1883

4 At the first glance, you would have taken him to be some civilized and modernized Squire Western, nourished with beef and ale, and roughly hewn out of the most robust and least refined variety of human clay. Looking at him more narrowly, however, you would have reconsidered this judgment. Though his general contour and aspect were massive and sturdy, the lines of his features were delicately cut; his complexion was remarkably pure and fine, and his face was susceptible of very subtle and sensitive changes of expression.

> **Julian Hawthorne** 1846–1934: *Confessions and Criticisms* (1887)

5 His first, his inestimable merit was a complete appreciation of the usual.

> **Henry James** 1843–1916: *Partial Portraits* (1888)

6 A big, red-faced, rather underbred Englishman of the bald with spectacles type. A good roaring positive fellow who deafened me (sitting on his right) till I thought of Dante's Cerberus.

> **James Russell Lowell** 1819–91: H. S. Scudder *James Russell Lowell* (1901)

7 Even the crowd seems to have been offended (consciously or not) by revelation of mechanism. Of course all artistic work is done, to a great extent, mechanically. Trollope merely talked about it in a wrong and vulgar tone.
   of public reaction to Trollope's Autobiograpy

> **George Gissing** 1857–1903: *Commonplace Book* (1962)

8 The whole of Barsetshire . . . seems to be mapped out in dear old Trollope's countenance.
   on Julia Cameron's photograph of Trollope

> **Max Beerbohm** 1872–1956: letter, 6 October 1954

Truth

9 A poem, whose subject is not truth, but things like truth.

> **George Chapman** c.1559–1634: *The Revenge of Bussy D'Ambois* (1613) dedication

1 Who says that fictions only and false hair
Become a verse? Is there in truth no beauty?
Is all good structure in a winding stair?

George Herbert 1593–1633: 'Jordan
(1)' (1633)

2 Beholding the bright countenance of truth in the quiet and
still air of delightful studies.

John Milton 1608–74: *The Reason of
Church Government* (1642)

3 Though all the winds of doctrine were let loose to play
upon the earth, so Truth be in the field, we do injuriously
by licensing and prohibiting to misdoubt her strength. Let
her and Falsehood grapple; who ever knew Truth put to
the worse, in a free and open encounter?

John Milton 1608–74: *Areopagitica*
(1644)

4 In lapidary inscriptions a man is not upon oath.

Samuel Johnson 1709–84: James
Boswell *Life of Samuel Johnson* (1791)
1775

5 I am certain of nothing but the holiness of the heart's
affections and the truth of imagination—what the
imagination seizes as beauty must be truth—whether it
existed before or not.

John Keats 1795–1821: letter to
Benjamin Bailey, 22 November 1817

6 'Tis strange—but true; for truth is always strange;
Stranger than fiction.

Lord Byron 1788–1824: *Don Juan*
(1819–24)

7 The hero of my tale—whom I love with all the power of
my soul, whom I have tried to portray in all his beauty,
who has been, is, and will be beautiful—is Truth.

Leo Tolstoy 1828–1910: *Sevastopol in
May* (1855)

8 You will say to me, perhaps, 'Are you sure that your tale
is a true one?' What do I care about the reality of the
world around me, if only it helps me to live, to feel I exist
and to know what I am.

Charles Baudelaire 1821–67: *The
Windows*

9 There was things which he stretched, but mainly he told
the truth.

Mark Twain 1835–1910: *The
Adventures of Huckleberry Finn* (1884)

10 There are two duties incumbent upon any man who
enters on the business of writing: truth to the fact and a
good spirit in the treatment.

Robert Louis Stevenson 1850–94:
Essays Literary and Critical (1923)
'Morality of the Profession of Letters'

11 The folly of mistaking a paradox for a discovery, a
metaphor for a proof, a torrent of verbiage for a spring of
capital truths, and oneself for an orator, is inborn in us.

Paul Valéry 1871–1945: *Introduction
to the Method of Leonardo da Vinci*
(1895)

12 The truth is rarely pure, and never simple.

Oscar Wilde 1854–1900: *The
Importance of Being Earnest* (1895)

13 There are no such things as facts, only interpretation.
found in Nietzsche's posthumous papers

Friedrich Nietzsche 1844–1900:
Malcolm Bradbury and James
McFarlane (eds.) *Modernism* (1991)

14 The art of fiction has this great ethical importance that it
enables one to tell the truth about human beings in a way
which is impossible in actual life.

George Gissing 1857–1903:
Commonplace Book (1962)

15 Though leaves are many, the root is one;
Through all the lying days of my youth
I swayed my leaves and flowers in the sun;
Now I may wither into the truth.

W. B. Yeats 1865–1939: 'The Coming
of Wisdom with Time' (1910)

16 Scepticism the tonic of minds, the tonic of life, the agent of
truth—the way of art and salvation.

Joseph Conrad 1857–1924: letter, 11
November 1911

1 Thought does not crush to stone.
  The great sledge drops in vain.
  Truth never is undone;
  Its shafts remain.

  Theodore Roethke 1908–63: 'The Adamant' (1941)

2 It doesn't have to be the truth, just your vision of it, written down.

  Virginia Woolf 1882–1941: attributed

3 At some time in the future, if the human mind becomes something totally different from what it now is, we may learn to separate literary creation from intellectual honesty. At present we know only that the imagination, like certain wild animals, will not breed in captivity.

  George Orwell 1903–50: 'The Prevention of Literature' in *Polemic* January 1946

4 A poem is a witness to man's knowledge of evil as well as good. It is not the duty of a witness to pass moral judgement on the evidence he has to give, but to give it clearly and accurately; the only crime of which a witness can be guilty is perjury.

  W. H. Auden 1907–73: *The Dyer's Hand* (1962)

5 All your life you live so close to truth, it becomes a permanent blur in the corner of your eye, and when something nudges it into outline it is like being ambushed by a grotesque.

  Tom Stoppard 1937– : *Rosencrantz and Guildenstern are Dead* (1967)

6 Every word she writes is a lie, including 'and' and 'the'.
  on Lilian Hellman

  Mary McCarthy 1912–89: in *New York Times* 16 February 1980

7 We don't go in for nondenominationalism and tolerance, we go in for strict truth and let the other guy be tolerant of us.

  Garrison Keillor 1942– : *Leaving Home* (1988)

8 I'm merely a reporter whose truth lies
  In diction clear as water.

  Georges Szirtes 1948– : *Bridge Passages* (1991) 'Street Entertainment'

9 The disturbing thing about false and erroneous statements is that well-meaning scholars tend to repeat one another. Lies are like fleas hopping from here to there, sucking the blood of the intellect.

  Muriel Spark 1918– : *Curriculum Vitae* (1992)

10 It's the best way of telling the truth; it's a process of producing grand, beautiful, well-ordered lies that tell more truth than any assemblage of facts.
  on literature

  Julian Barnes 1946– : in *Paris Review* Winter 2000

11 If you want to be brutal about it, a novel like, say, Updike's *Rabbit at Rest* is life, but *White Teeth* is TV.

  Zadie Smith 1975– : in *Observer* 25 August 2002

Ivan Turgenev 1818–83 see also **153:8**
Russian novelist

12 He is of a spirit so human that we almost wonder at his control of his matter; of a pity so deep and so general that we almost wonder at his curiosity. The element of poetry in him is constant, and yet reality stares through it without the loss of a wrinkle.

  Henry James 1843–1916: 'Ivan Turgeneff' (1896)

1 I am on my death-bed; there is no possibility of my recovery. I write you expressly to tell you how happy I have been to be your contemporary, and to utter my last, my urgent prayer. Come back, my friend, to your literary labours . . . My friend, great writer of our Russian land, respond to it, obey it!
   to Turgenev

Leo Tolstoy 1828–1910: Henry James 'Ivan Turgeneff' (1896)

2 Curiosity will never impel you to look at the last page of one of his books, and you reach it without regret. To read him is like travelling by river, a calm and steady transit without adventure or emotion.

W. Somerset Maugham 1874–1965: *A Writer's Notebook* (1949) written in 1917

Mark Twain 1835–1910
American writer

3 If Mr Clemens cannot think of something better to tell our pure-minded lads and lasses, he had best stop writing for them.

Louisa May Alcott 1832–88: *On Adventures of Huckleberry Finn* (1885)

4 Sole, incomparable, the Lincoln of our literature.

William Dean Howells 1837–1920: *My Mark Twain* (1910)

5 The true father of our national literature, the first genuinely American artist of the blood royal.

H. L. Mencken 1880–1956: in *Smart Set* February 1913

6 A hack writer who would not have been considered fourth rate in Europe, who tricked out a few of the old proven 'sure fire' literary skeletons with sufficient local colour to intrigue the superficial and the lazy.

William Faulkner 1897–1962: in *The Mississippian* 24 March 1922

7 All modern American literature comes from one book by Mark Twain called *Huckleberry Finn*.

Ernest Hemingway 1899–1961: *Green Hills of Africa* (1935)

8 Mark Twain and I are in very much the same position. We have to put things in such a way as to make people, who would otherwise hang us, believe that we are joking.

George Bernard Shaw 1856–1950: attributed

Usage see Grammar and Usage

Gore Vidal 1925–
American writer

9 Just the sight of Gore had the effect of instantly cleansing my palate—like some tart lemon sorbet.

Elaine Dundy 1947– : Gore Vidal *Palimpsest* (1995)

François Villon fl. c.1460
French poet

10 Villon, our sad bad glad mad brother's name.

Algernon Charles Swinburne 1837–1909: 'Ballad of François Villon' (1878)

Virgil 70–19 BC see also **64:2**
Roman poet

1 *Cedite Romani scriptores, cedite Grai!*
Nescioquid maius nascitur Iliade.

   Make way, you Roman writers, make way, Greeks!
   Something greater than the Iliad is born.
      of Virgil's Aeneid

Propertius c.50–after 16 BC: *Elegies*

2 *Animae dimidium meae.*

   Half my own soul.

Horace 65–8 BC: *Odes*

3 *Vergilium vidi tantum.*

   I have just seen Virgil.

Ovid 43 BC–AD c.17: *Tristia*

4 Thou art my master and my author. Thou art he from
   whom alone I took the style whose beauty has brought me
   honour.

Dante Alighieri 1265–1321: *Divina Commedia*

5 The shepherd in Virgil grew at last acquainted with Love,
   and found him a native of the rocks.

Samuel Johnson 1709–84: letter to Lord Chesterfield, 7 February 1755

6 Roman Virgil, thou that singest
   Ilion's lofty temples robed in fire,
   Ilion falling, Rome arising,
   wars, and filial faith, and Dido's pyre.

Alfred, Lord Tennyson 1809–92: 'To Virgil' (1882)

7 I salute thee, Mantovano,
   I that loved thee since my day began,
   Wielder of the stateliest measure
   ever moulded by the lips of man.

Alfred, Lord Tennyson 1809–92: 'To Virgil' (1882)

Voltaire 1694–1778
French writer, dramatist, and poet

8 Be the king of philosophers, while other princes are only
   the kings of men. I thank heaven every day that you exist.

Frederick the Great 1712–86: letter to Voltaire, 1737

9 I have a piece of news for you which you may have heard
   already, namely that that godless arch-rascal, Voltaire,
   has died like a dog, like a beast.

Wolfgang Amadeus Mozart 1756–91: letter, 3 July 1778

10 The most formidable antagonist of absurdities which the
   world had seen.

Leigh Hunt 1784–1859: *Autobiography* (rev. ed., 1860)

11 There's a Bible on that shelf there. But I keep it next to
   Voltaire—poison and antidote.

Bertrand Russell 1872–1970: in *Kenneth Harris Talking To* (1971) 'Bertrand Russell'

Horace Walpole 1717–97
English writer and Whig politician

12 He was a witty, sarcastic, ingenious, deeply-thinking,
   highly-cultivated, quaint, though evermore gallant and
   romantic, though very mundane, old bachelor of other
   days.

Fanny Burney 1752–1840: *Memoirs of Dr Burney* (1832)

War

1 Our swords shall play the orators for us.

Christopher Marlowe 1564–93: *Tamburlaine the Great* (1590)

2 Among the calamities of war may be jointly numbered the diminution of the love of truth, by the falsehoods which interest dictates and credulity encourages.

Samuel Johnson 1709–84: in *The Idler* 11 November 1758; possibly the source of 'When war is declared, Truth is the first casualty', epigraph to Arthur Ponsonby's *Falsehood in Wartime* (1928); attributed also to Hiram Johnson, speaking in the US Senate, 1918, but not recorded in his speech

3 The Minstrel Boy to the war is gone,
In the ranks of death you'll find him;
His father's sword he has girded on,
And his wild harp slung behind him.

Thomas Moore 1779–1852: *Irish Melodies* (1807) 'The Minstrel Boy'

4 It was not a propitious time for cultivating the Muse; when history herself is so hard at work, fiction has little left to say.
on the Civil War

Henry James 1843–1916: *Hawthorne* (1879)

5 The real war will never get in the books. And so goodbye to the war.
written after the American Civil war

Walt Whitman 1819–92: *Specimen Days* (1882) 'The Real War Will Never Get in the Books'

6 I am a soldier, convinced that I am acting on behalf of soldiers. I believe that this war, upon which I entered as a war of defence and liberation, has now become a war of aggression and conquest. I believe that the purposes for which I and my fellow-soldiers entered upon this war should have been so clearly stated as to have made it impossible to change them, and that, had this been done, the objects which actuated us would now be attainable by negotiation.

Siegfried Sassoon 1886–1967: 'A Soldier's Declaration' addressed to his commanding officer and sent to the *Bradford Pioneer* July 1917

7 For God's sake cheer up and write more optimistically— the war's not ended yet but a poet should have a spirit above wars.

Robert Graves 1895–1985: letter to Wilfred Owen, December 1917

8 How is the world ruled and led to war? Diplomats lie to journalists and believe these lies when they see them in print.

Karl Kraus 1874–1936: *Nachts* (1918)

9 All a poet can do today is warn.

Wilfred Owen 1893–1918: preface (written 1918) in *Poems* (1963)

10 My subject is War, and the pity of War.
The Poetry is in the pity.

Wilfred Owen 1893–1918: preface (written 1918) in *Poems* (1963)

11 If you could hear, at every jolt, the blood
Come gargling from the froth-corrupted lungs,
Obscene as cancer, bitter as the cud
Of vile, incurable sores on innocent tongues,—
My friend, you would not tell with such high zest
To children ardent for some desperate glory,
The old Lie: Dulce et decorum est
Pro patria mori.

Wilfred Owen 1893–1918: 'Dulce et Decorum Est'

1 I think it better that at times like these
We poets keep our mouths shut, for in truth
We have no gift to set a statesman right.

W. B. Yeats 1865–1939: 'On being asked for a War Poem' (1919)

2 Who live under the shadow of a war,
What can I do that matters?

Stephen Spender 1909–95: 'Who live under the shadow of a war' (1933)

3 As soon as war is declared it will be impossible to hold the poets back. Rhyme is still the most effective drum.

Jean Giraudoux 1882–1944: *La Guerre de Troie n'aura pas lieu* (1935)

4 Passive suffering is not the theme for poetry. If war is necessary in our time, best to forget its suffering as we forget the discomfort of fever.

W. B. Yeats 1865–1939: introduction to *Oxford Book of Modern Poetry* (1936)

*on being asked by Stephen **Spender** in the 1930s how best a poet could serve the Communist cause:*
5 Go to Spain and get killed. The movement needs a Byron.

Harry Pollitt 1890–1960: Frank Johnson *Out of Order* (1982); attributed, perhaps apocryphal

6 We only watch, and indicate and make our scribbled
   pencil notes.
We do not wish to moralize, only to ease our dusty
   throats.

Donald Bain 1922– : 'War Poet'; Brian Gardner *The Terrible Rain: The War Poets 1939–45* (1966)

7 I understand the hero keeps getting in bed with women, and the war wasn't fought that way.
   *of **Hemingway**'s* A Farewell to Arms

Harold Ross 1892–1951: James Thurber *The Years with Ross* (1959)

8 A 'war' poet is not one who chooses to commemorate or celebrate a war but one who reacts against having a war thrust upon him.

Philip Larkin 1922–85: *Required Writing* (1983)

9 War correspondents are surrealists. They follow war because throughout history it has shown itself to be the most generous provider of surreal spectacle, from Hannibal's African elephants floundering through Alpine snow, to the lavish fire-ceremony of London's blitz. To regard them as mere newsmongers is to miss the degree to which they are in the grip of an art form, prodigal beyond the wildest dreams of grand opera.

John Carey 1934– : in *Sunday Times* 30 April 1989

Evelyn Waugh 1903–66
English novelist

10 I regard writing not an as investigation of character but as an exercise in the use of language, and with this I am obsessed. I have no technical psychological interest; it is drama, speech and events that interest me.

Evelyn Waugh 1903–66: in *Paris Review* 1962

11 I know nobody who would hate Hollywood as intensely as you.
   his agent to Waugh, when MGM took up the film option on Brideshead Revisited *and invited Waugh to Hollywood*

A. D. Peters 1892–1973: Malcolm Bradbury *Dangerous Pilgrimages* (1995)

12 You have no idea how much nastier I would be if I was not a Catholic. Without supernatural aid I would hardly be a human being.
   replying to Nancy Mitford who rebuked him for cruelty

Evelyn Waugh 1903–66: Noel Annan *Our Age* (1990)

1 Despite all Waugh's efforts to appear to be an irascible, deaf old curmudgeon, a sort of inner saintliness kept breaking through.

Malcolm Muggeridge 1903–90: Miriam Gross *The World of George Orwell* (1971)

2 There was always in Evelyn a conflict between the satirist and the romantic.

Graham Greene 1904–91: *Ways of Escape* (1980)

3 Whereas most great writers are richer in imaginative resource than normal men or women, Waugh's distinction lay in being poorer. The acid refinement of his style required a certain part of his brain to remain dead. His blanket denunciations of fellow humans would have been impossible for a fully-formed intelligence.

John Carey 1934– : in *Sunday Times* 19 April 1992

John Webster c.1580—c.1625
English dramatist

4 A play of Webster's is full of the feverish and ghastly turmoil of a nest of maggots.

Rupert Brooke 1887–1915: *John Webster and the Elizabethan Drama* (1916)

5 Webster was much possessed by death
And saw the skull beneath the skin.

T. S. Eliot 1888–1965: 'Whispers of Immortality' (1919); see **64:7**

6 Webster is not concerned with humanity. He is the poet of bile and brainstorm, the sweet singer of apoplexy; ideally, one feels, he would have had all his characters drowned in a sea of cold sweat. His muse drew nourishment from Bedlam, and might, a few centuries later, have done the same from Belsen.

Kenneth Tynan 1927–80: in *Observer* 18 December 1960

Frank Wedekind 1864–1918
German dramatist

7 With Tolstoy and Strindberg one of the great educators of the new Europe.

Bertolt Brecht 1898–1956: in 1918; Malcolm Bradbury and James McFarlane (eds.) *Modernism* (1991)

H. G. Wells 1866–1946 see also **1:6**, **1:7**, **92:8**
English novelist

8 Whatever Wells writes is not only alive, but kicking.

Henry James 1843–1916: G. K. Chesterton *Autobiography* (1936)

9 What a little bourgeois! What a philistine!
after a 'barney' with H. G. Wells in the Kremlin

Lenin 1870–1924: Michael Foot *The History of Mr Wells* (1995)

10 It scarcely needs criticism to bring home to me that much of my work has been slovenly, haggard and irritated, most of it hurriedly and inadequately revised, and some of it as white and pasty in its texture as a starch-fed nun.

H. G. Wells 1866–1946: *Experiment in Autobiography* (1934)

11 Wells, in part of Europe and in the United States, will for some years have wielded an intellectual dominion comparable to that won and held by Voltaire in the eighteenth century.

André Maurois 1885–1967: *Poets and Prophets* (1936)

1 He's the Shakespeare of science fiction.

Brian Aldiss 1925– : on *Bookmark* (BBC2) 24 August 1996

The Western Canon

2 If you like poetry let it be first-rate; Milton, Shakespeare, Thomson, Goldsmith, Pope (if you will, though I don't admire him), Scott, Byron, Campbell, Wordsworth, and Southey.

Charlotte Brontë 1816–55: letter to Ellen Nussey, 4 July 1834

3 From time to time, every hundred years or so, it is desirable that some critic shall appear to review the past of our literature, and set the poets and the poems in a new order.

T. S. Eliot 1888–1965: 'The Use of Poetry and the Use of Criticism' (1933)

4 The great tradition.

F. R. Leavis 1895–1978: title of book (1948)

5 It is by lowering the transcendental pretensions of poetry that, strangely enough, its true greatness opens once more before us: we come out of the romantic-modernist labyrinth into the broad and high world of Virgil and Chaucer and Dante and Shakespeare where the true proportions of things are recognized, and the presumption of man is corrected by the measures of the gods.

James McAuley 1917–76: *The End of Modernity* (1959)

6 Dostoevsky the publicist is one of those megaphones of elephantine platitudes (still heard today), the roar of which so ridiculously demotes Shakespeare and Pushkin to the vague level of all the plaster idols of academic tradition, from Cervantes to George Eliot (not to speak of the crumbling Manns and Faulkners of our times).

Vladimir Nabokov 1899–1977: Alexander Pushkin *Eugene Onegin* (translated by Vladimir Nabokov, 1964)

7 Western culture . . . was a grand ancestral property that educated men had inherited from their intellectual forefathers, while their female relatives, like characters in a Jane Austen novel, were relegated to modest dower houses on the edge of the estate.

Sandra M. Gilbert 1936– : 'What Do Feminist Critics Want?' (1980)

8 I believe in the established canon of English and American literature and in the validity of the concept of privileged texts. I think it is more important to read Spenser, Shakespeare, or Milton than to read Borges in translation, or even, to say the truth, to read Virginia Woolf.

J. Hillis Miller 1928– : Sandra M. Gilbert 'What Do Feminist Critics Want?' (1980)

9 The only surviving Old English epic, thank God . . . the most shitty and boring part of one's heritage.
   on Beowulf

Kingsley Amis 1922–95: remark, 15 April 1993; in *Sunday Times* 17 March 1996

10 The western canon.

Harold Bloom 1930– : title of book, 1995

11 One breaks into the canon only by aesthetic strength, which is constituted primarily of an amalgam: mastery of figurative language, originality, cognitive power, knowledge, exuberance of diction.

Harold Bloom 1930– : *The Western Canon* (1995)

1 These stories are the seeds of European literature. Shakespeare and the other Elizabethans—virtually all western poets, in fact, until yesterday—read and memorised them as children. You cannot understand our culture without them.
   *on **Ovid**'s* Metamorphoses

John Carey 1934– : in *Sunday Times*

Edith Wharton 1862–1937
American novelist

2 The continued cry that I am an echo of Mr James (whose books of the last ten years I can't read, much as I delight in the man . . . makes me feel rather hopeless.

Edith Wharton 1862–1937: letter, 1904

3 Mrs Wharton at her best was an analyst of the paralysis that attends success. Hers was not a world where romance was apt to flourish.

Louis Auchincloss 1917– : Irving Howe (ed.) *Edith Wharton* (1962)

4 If there is a notable tradition of female social satire in modern American fiction, through to Mary McCarthy and Alison Lurie, Wharton is perhaps its essential source.

Malcolm Bradbury 1932–2000: *The Modern American Novel* (1992)

Patrick White 1912–90
Australian novelist

5 Patrick White is a dead loss to libraries, a great asset to English literature.

John Betjeman 1906–84: review of *The Aunt's Story* in 1948; attributed

6 If I am anything of a writer it is through my homosexuality, which has given me additional insights, and through a *very strong vein of vulgarity*.

Patrick White 1912–90: letter to Geoffrey Dutton, 17 September 1980

Walt Whitman 1819–92
American poet

7 The effort of an essentially prosaic mind to lift itself, by a prolonged muscular strain, into poetry.
   on Whitman's 'Drum-Taps'

Henry James 1843–1916: 'Mr Walt Whitman' (1865)

8 This awful Whitman. This post-mortem poet. This poet with the private soul leaking out of him all the time. All his privacy leaking out in a sort of dribble, oozing into the universe.

D. H. Lawrence 1885–1930: *Studies in Classic American Literature* (1924)

9 Whitman was like a prophet straying in a fog and shouting half-truths with a voice of great trumpets. He was seeking something, but he never knew quite what, and he never found it.

Amy Lowell 1874–1925: 'Walt Whitman and the New Poetry' (1926–7)

10 Walt Whitman who laid end to end words never seen in each other's company before outside of a dictionary.

David Lodge 1935– : *Changing Places* (1975)

Oscar Wilde 1854–1900
Anglo-Irish dramatist and poet

in his viva at Oxford Wilde was required to translate a passage from the Greek version of the New Testament. Having acquitted himself well, he was stopped:

1 Oh, do let me go on, I want to see how it ends.

Oscar Wilde 1854–1900: James Sutherland (ed.) *The Oxford Book of Literary Anecdotes* (1975)

2 That sovereign of insufferables.

Ambrose Bierce 1842–c.1914: in *Wasp*, San Francisco, 1882

3 What has Oscar in common with Art? except that he dines at our tables and picks from our platter the plums for the puddings he peddles in the provinces.

James McNeill Whistler 1834–1903: in *World* November 1886

4 To Oscar Wilde posing as a somdomite.
    misspelt message leading Wilde to sue for libel

Marquess of Queensberry 1844–1900: written on his card and left at the Albemarle Club, 18 February 1895

5 The doddering rococo and oh so flat 'fizz' . . . of *Lady Windermere's Fan*.

Henry James 1843–1916: letter, 25 October 1911

6 No, I've never cared for his work. Too scented.

Rudyard Kipling 1865–1936: Harry Ricketts *The Unforgiving Minute* (1999)

7 If, with the literate, I am
Impelled to try an epigram,
I never seek to take the credit;
We all assume that Oscar said it.

Dorothy Parker 1893–1967: 'A Pig's-Eye View of Literature' (1937)

8 An Assyrian wax statue, effeminate, but with the vitality of twenty men.

Max Beerbohm 1872–1956: Cecil Beaton's diary, September 1953

9 From the beginning Wilde performed his life and continued to do so even after fate had taken the plot out of his hands.

W. H. Auden 1907–73: in *New Yorker* 9 March 1963

Edmund Wilson 1895–1973
American writer

10 Hell with compensations.
    of life with her husband Edmund Wilson

Elena Wilson 1906–79: Jeffrey Meyers *Edmund Wilson* (1995)

11 Wilson is not like other critics; some critics are boring even when they are original; he fascinates even when he is wrong.

Alfred Kazin 1915–98: Max J. Herzberg (ed.) *The Reader's Encyclopedia of American Literature* (1963)

Wit and Satire see also Humour and Comedy

12 How easy it is to call rogue and villain, and that wittily! But how hard to make a man appear a fool, a blockhead, or a knave, without using any of those opprobrious terms! To spare the grossness of the names, and to do the thing yet more severely, is to draw a full face, and to make the

John Dryden 1631–1700: *Of Satire* (1693)

nose and cheeks stand out, and yet not to employ any depth of shadowing.

1 True wit is Nature to advantage dressed,
What oft was thought, but ne'er so well expressed.

Alexander Pope 1688–1744: *An Essay on Criticism* (1711)

2 Satire is a sort of glass, wherein beholders do generally discover everybody's face but their own; which is the chief reason for that kind of reception it meets in the world, and that so very few are offended with it.

Jonathan Swift 1667–1745: *The Battle of the Books* (1704), preface

3 A man who could make so vile a pun would not scruple to pick a pocket.

John Dennis 1657–1734: *The Gentleman's Magazine* (1781); editorial note

4 Parodies on new poems are a ridicule, on old ones a compliment.

Samuel Taylor Coleridge 1772–1834: Notebook, 1798–1804

5 What is an Epigram? a dwarfish whole,
Its body brevity, and wit its soul.

Samuel Taylor Coleridge 1772–1834: 'Epigram' (1809)

6 Wit is . . . the eloquence of indifference.

William Hazlitt 1778–1830: *Lectures on the English Comic Writers* (1818)

7 It is a common mistake . . . to suppose that parodies degrade, or imply a stigma on the subject: on the contrary, they in general imply something serious or sacred in the originals.

William Hazlitt 1778–1830: *Lectures on the English Comic Writers* (1818)

8 [A pun] is a pistol let off at the ear; not a feather to tickle the intellect.

Charles Lamb 1775–1834: *Last Essays of Elia* (1833) 'Popular Fallacies'

9 Flippancy, the most hopeless form of intellectual vice.

George Gissing 1857–1903: *New Grub Street* (1891)

10 Don't try to be witty in the writing, unless it's natural—just true and real.

F. Scott Fitzgerald 1896–1940: letter, 7 July 1938

11 Reality goes bounding past the satirist like a cheetah laughing as it lopes ahead of the greyhound.

Claud Cockburn 1904–81: *Crossing the Line* (1958)

12 Ridicule is the only honourable weapon we have left.

Muriel Spark 1918– : 'The Desegregation of Art' (1971)

13 Satire is a lesson, parody is a game.

Vladimir Nabokov 1899–1977: *Strong Opinions* (1974)

14 The English are very fond of humour, but they are afraid of wit. For wit is like a sword, but humour is like a jester's bladder.

J. B. Morton ('Beachcomber') 1893–1975: attributed

15 There is parody, when you make fun of people who are smarter than you; satire, when you make fun of people who are richer than you; and burlesque, when you make fun of both while taking off your clothes.

P. J. O'Rourke 1947– : in 1980; *Age and Guile* (1995)

16 I shouldn't call myself a satirist. To be a satirist, you have to know better than everyone else, and I've never done that.

Philip Larkin 1922–85: A. N. Wilson *Penfriends from Porlock* (1988)

17 Satire is dependent on strong beliefs, and on strong beliefs wounded.

Anita Brookner 1928– : in *Spectator* 23 March 1989

18 To hear some people talk, you would think humour was an aspect of satire, instead of the other way round. Satire is simply humour in uniform.

Paul Jennings 1918–89: in obituary in *Guardian* 1 January 1990

1 Only by parodying grown-ups does a child learn to speak, and every child below a certain age is an impersonator—often mercilessly embarrassing—of its parents. The parodist never relinquishes this oddly submissive form of power, ending up practising a toytown voodoo, constructing a doll that bears some sort of distorted resemblance to his intended victim, and then sticking in pins and bending limbs to his heart's content.

Craig Brown 1957– : in *Spectator* 27 November 1999

2 Parody is a knack and, like other knacks—the knack for juggling, say, or the hula-hoop—it is best performed in a trance-like state pitched somewhere between attention and instinct.

Craig Brown 1957– : in *Spectator* 27 November 1999

P. G. Wodehouse 1881–1975 see also **186:8**, **271:12**
English writer; an American citizen from 1955

3 Musical comedy without music.
on his own work

P. G. Wodehouse 1881–1975: attributed; in *Observer* 18 November 2001

4 It is nonsense to talk of 'Fascist tendencies' in his books. There are no post-1918 tendencies at all.

George Orwell 1903–50: in *Windmill* July 1945

5 English literature's performing flea.

Sean O'Casey 1880–1964: P. G. Wodehouse *Performing Flea* (1953)

6 One has to regard a man as a Master who can produce on average three uniquely brilliant and entirely original similes to every page.

Evelyn Waugh 1903–66: Frances Donaldson *Evelyn Waugh: Portrait of a Country Neighbour* (1967)

7 What Wodehouse writes is pure word music. It matters not one whit that he writes endless variations on a theme of pig kidnappings, lofty butlers, and ludicrous impostures. He is the greatest *musician* of the English language, and exploring variations of familiar material is what musicians do all day.

Douglas Adams 1952–2001: introduction to *Sunset at Blandings*; in *The Salmon of Doubt* (2002)

Women and Literature

8 Had I a husband or a house, and all that longs thereto
Myself could frame about to rouse as other women do,
But til some household cares me tie
My books and pen I will apply.

Isabella Whitney fl. 1573: *A Sweet Nosegay* (1573)

9 I am obnoxious to each carping tongue,
Who says my hand a needle better fits,
A poet's pen, all scorn, I should thus wrong;
For such despite they cast on female wits:
If what I do prove well, it won't advance,
They'll say it's stolne, or else, it was by chance.

Anne Bradstreet c.1612–72: 'The Prologue' (1650)

10 I'm hither come, but what d'ye think to say?
A woman's pen presents you with a play:
Who smiling told me I'd be sure to see
That once confirmed, the house would empty be.

Frances Boothby fl. 1670: *Marcelia* (1670) prologue

1 All I ask, is the privilege for my masculine part the poet in me . . . If I must not, because of my sex, have this freedom . . . I lay down my quill, and you shall hear no more of me.

Aphra Behn 1640–89: preface to *The Lucky Chance* (1686)

2 But of all plagues, the greatest is untold,
The book-learned wife in Greek and Latin bold,
The critic-dame, who at her table sits,
Homer and Virgil quotes, and wrights their wits.

John Dryden 1631–1700: translation of Juvenal *Satires*

3 The carping malice of the vulgar world; who think it a proof of sense to dislike every thing that is writ by Women.

Susannah Centlivre c.1669–1723: *The Platonic Lady* (1707)

4 Alas! a woman that attempts the pen
Such an intruder on the rights of men,
Such presumptuous creature is esteemed
The fault can by no virtue be redeemed.

Anne Finch, Lady Winchilsea 1661–1720: 'The Introduction' (1713)

5 Regularity and Decorum. 'Tis what we women-authors, in particular, have been thought greatly deficient in; and I should be concerned to find it an objection not to be removed.

Elizabeth Cooper fl. 1730: preface to *The Rival Widows* (1735)

6 Men have had every advantage of us in telling their own story. Education has been theirs in so much higher a degree; the pen has been in their hands.

Jane Austen 1775–1817: *Persuasion* (1818)

7 The difficulties in which she involves her heroines are too much 'Female Difficulties'; they are difficulties created out of nothing. The author appears to have no other idea of refinement than it is the reverse of vulgarity; but the reverse of vulgarity is fastidiousness and affectation.
    on Fanny **Burney**

William Hazlitt 1778–1830: *Lectures on the English Comic Writers* (1818)

8 Except some professional scholars, I have often observed that women in general read much more than men; but, for want of a plan, a method, a fixed object, their reading is of little benefit to themselves, or others.

Edward Gibbon 1737–94: *Autobiography* (1827)

9 Literature cannot be the business of a woman's life, and it ought not to be.

Robert Southey 1774–1843: letter to Charlotte Brontë, 1836

10 Oh! . . . that ladies would make puddings and mend stockings! That they would not meddle with religion, except to pray to God, to live quietly among their families.
    reviewing Fanny Trollope's novel The Vicar of Wrexhill

William Makepeace Thackeray 1811–63: in *Fraser's Magazine* (1837)

11 To such critics I would say, To you I am neither man nor woman—I come before you as an author only.

Charlotte Brontë 1816–55: letter to W. S. Williams, 16 August 1849

12 I wish critics would judge me as an *author*, not as a woman.

Charlotte Brontë 1816–55: letter to George Henry Lewes, 19 January 1850

13 *All* women, as authors, are feeble and tiresome. I wish they were forbidden to write, on pain of having their faces deeply scarified with an oyster shell.

Nathaniel Hawthorne 1804–64: letter to his publisher, 1852

14 America is now given over to a d—d mob of scribbling women, and I should have no chance of success while the public taste is occupied with their trash—and should be ashamed of myself if I did succeed.

Nathaniel Hawthorne 1804–64: letter, 1854

1 If those two volumes, or part of them, were not written by a woman, then should I begin to believe that I am a woman myself.
*of George **Eliot**'s Scenes of Clerical Life*

Charles Dickens 1812–70: letter to J. Langford, 18 January 1858

2 Women are capable only of a certain delicacy and sensitivity. Everything that is truly sublime, truly great, escapes them.

Gustave Flaubert 1821–80: letter, 11 January 1859

3 There is no good end attained by trying to persuade ourselves that women are all incorporeal, angelic, colourless, passionless, helpless creatures . . . Women have especial need, as the world goes, to be shrewd, self-reliant, and strong; and we do all we can in our literature to render them helpless, imbecile, and idiotic.

Justin McCarthy 1830–1912: in *Westminster Review* 1864

4 It is hard for a woman to define her feelings in language which is chiefly made by men to express theirs.

Thomas Hardy 1840–1928: *Far from the Madding Crowd* (1874)

5 To say in print what she thinks is the last thing the woman novelist or journalist is so rash as to attempt . . . Her publishers are not women.

Elizabeth Robins 1862–1952: in 1908, as first president of the Women Writers' Suffrage League

6 I have nothing to say to 'charming' women. I feel like a cat among tigers.
on her dislike of social occasions

Katherine Mansfield 1888–1923: John Middleton Murry *Between Two Worlds* (1935)

7 I struggle to keep the writing as much as possible in male hands, as I distrust the feminine in literature.
on editing The Egoist

T. S. Eliot 1888–1965: letter, 31 October 1917

8 A woman must have money and a room of her own if she is to write fiction.

Virginia Woolf 1882–1941: *A Room of One's Own* (1929)

9 Far from the vulgar haunts of men
Each sits in her 'successful room',
Housekeeping with her fountain pen
And writing novels with her broom.

Roy Campbell 1901–57: 'On Some South African Novelists'

10 The sniffs I get from the ink of the women are always fey, old-bat, Quaintsy, Gaysy, tiny, too dykily psychotic, crippled, creepish fashionable, frigid, outer-Baroque, maquille in mannequin's whimsey, or else bright and stillborn.

Norman Mailer 1923– : *Advertisements for Myself* (1959)

11 WHY 'Women in Literature'? No—It's *The Women Poets in English*, I see. But still, WHY? Why not *Men Poets in English*? . . . Literature is literature, no matter who produces it.
having been asked to contribute to an anthology of women poets

Elizabeth Bishop 1911–79: letter to May Swenson, 7 November 1971

12 Women must write through their bodies, they must invent the impregnable language that will wreck partitions, classes, and rhetorics, regulations and codes, they must submerge, cut through, get beyond the ultimate reserve-discourse, including the one that laughs at the very idea of pronouncing the word 'silence'.

Hélène Cixous 1937– :'The Laugh of the Medusa' (1975)

13 Before we can even begin to ask how the literature of women would be different and special, we need to reconstruct its past, to rediscover the scores of women novelists, poets and dramatists whose work has been obscured by time, and to establish the continuity of the

Elaine Showalter 1941– : 'Towards a Feminist Poetics' (1979)

female tradition from decade to decade, rather than from Great Woman to Great Woman.

1 Re-vision—the act of looking back, of seeing with fresh eyes, of entering an old text from a new critical direction— is for women more than a chapter in cultural history: it is an act of survival.

Adrienne Rich 1929– : *On Lies, Secrets, and Silence* (1980)

2 Men's novels are about men. Women's novels are about men too but from a different point of view. You can have a men's novel with no women in it except possibly the landlady or the horse, but you can't have a women's novel with no men in it. Sometimes men put women in men's novels but they leave out some of the parts: the heads, for instance, or the hands. Women's novels leave out parts of the men as well. Sometimes it's the stretch between the belly button and the knees, sometimes it's the sense of humour. It's hard to have a sense of humour in a cloak, in a high wind, on a moor.

Margaret Atwood 1939– : *Murder in the Dark* (1984) 'Women's Novels'

3 If you want your writing to be taken seriously, don't marry and have kids, and above all, don't die. But if you have to die, commit suicide. They approve of that.

Ursula Le Guin 1929– : 'Prospects for Women in Writing' (1986); *Dancing at the Edge of the World* (1989)

4 Men like women who write. Even though they don't say so. A writer is a foreign country.

Marguerite Duras 1914–96: *Practicalities* (1987)

5 I keep things up pretty well. But there's apt to be chaos underneath—in the backs of closets or cupboards—and it's the knowledge of this chaos which I use to keep myself from writing. I can get into housework very, very quickly, because I get a whole lot of virtuous feelings not from writing but from cleaning.

Alice Munro 1931– : in *New Yorker* 26 June 1995

6 One reason why women are good at writing detective stories may be our feminine eye for detail; clue-making demands attention to the detail of everyday life.

P. D. James 1920– : in *Paris Review* 1995

7 The solitary genius in the garret is a male myth, as he would undoubtedly have been supported by several unacknowledged women who cooked and ironed.

Michèle Roberts 1949– : in *Independent on Sunday* 4 February 1996

8 I am against sexism. I am against positive discrimination. I think literature is without gender.
refusing to enter for the Orange fiction award, reserved for women

Anita Brookner 1928– : in *Sunday Times* 18 February 1996; see **230:14**

9 I used to get very irritated being described as a women's author. But I don't any more. Why should I? Women read the most books!

Carol Shields 1935– : interview in *Observer*, 28 April 2002

Virginia Woolf 1882–1941
English novelist

10 Your novels beat me—black and blue. I retire howling, aching, sore; full, moreover, of an acute sense of disgrace. I return later, I re-submit myself to your discipline. No use: I am carried out half-dead. Of course I admire your

Max Beerbohm 1872–1956: letter to Virginia Woolf, 30 December 1927; see **326:1**

creative work immensely—but only in a bemused and miserable manner.

1 Can I put up any defence? . . . I'm afraid it's not a good one; it is simply that I can't write other than I do. I admit that when I spoke to the undergraduates I made up a plausible theory about the spirit of the age; but these theories are made after the art is done: I say to myself (as I might say about anybody's book) what made the poor woman write like that? And then I sit down and concoct something about life and literature, whereas the truth is I write these books which bruise you black and blue—you won't believe it, but so it is—simply to amuse myself.

Virginia Woolf 1882–1941: letter to Max Beerbohm, 29 January 1928; see **325:10**

2 It was like watching someone organize her own immortality. Every phrase and gesture was studied. Now and again, when she said something a little out of the ordinary, she wrote it down herself in a notebook.

Harold Laski 1893–1950: letter to Oliver Wendell Holmes, 30 November 1930

3 I enjoyed talking to her, but thought *nothing* of her writing. I considered her 'a beautiful little knitter'.

Edith Sitwell 1887–1964: letter to Geoffrey Singleton, 11 July 1955

4 She was a bit malicious, you know—she'd say the most dreadful things about people. Of course, one does oneself. But one doesn't expect it of Virginia Woolf.

Ivy Compton-Burnett 1884–1969: Hilary Spurling *Secrets of a Woman's Heart: the Later Life of Ivy Compton-Burnett* (1984)

Words

5 Winged words.

Homer: *The Iliad*

6 The words of his mouth were softer than butter, having war in his heart: his words were smoother than oil, and yet they be very swords.

Bible: Psalm 55

7 *Proicit ampullas et sesquipedalia verba.*
He throws aside his paint-pots and his words a foot and a half long.

Horace 65–8 BC: *Ars Poetica*

8 *Et semel emissum volat irrevocabile verbum.*
And once sent out a word takes wing beyond recall.

Horace 65–8 BC: *Epistles*

9 A gloton of wordes.

William Langland c.1330–c.1400: *The Vision of Piers Plowman*

10 Throughout the world, if it were sought,
Fair words enough a man shall find.
They be good cheap; they cost right naught;
Their substance is but only wind.
But well to say and so to mean—
That sweet accord is seldom seen.

Thomas Wyatt c.1503–42: 'Throughout the world, if it were sought' (1557)

11 The words of Mercury are harsh after the songs of Apollo.

William Shakespeare 1564–1616: *Love's Labour's Lost* (1595)

12 But words are words; I never yet did hear
That the bruised heart was piercèd through the ear.

William Shakespeare 1564–1616: *Othello* (1602–4)

13 Words are the tokens current and accepted for conceits, as moneys are for values.

Francis Bacon 1561–1626: *The Advancement of Learning* (1605)

14 Words are women, deeds are men.

George Herbert 1593–1633: *Outlandish Proverbs* (1640)

1 Words are wise men's counters, they do but reckon by them: but they are the money of fools, that value them by the authority of an Aristotle, a Cicero, or a Thomas, or any other doctor whatsoever, if but a man.

Thomas Hobbes 1588–1679: *Leviathan* (1651)

2 Oaths are but words, and words but wind.

Samuel Butler 1612–80: *Hudibras* pt. 2 (1664)

3 Thy genius calls thee not to purchase fame
In keen iambics, but mild anagram:
Leave writing plays, and choose for thy command
Some peaceful province in Acrostic Land.
There thou mayest wings display and altars raise,
And torture one poor word ten thousand ways.

John Dryden 1631–1700: *MacFlecknoe* (1682)

4 Th' artillery of words.

Jonathan Swift 1667–1745: 'Ode to Dr William Sancroft' (written 1692)

5 A barren superfluity of words.

Samuel Garth 1661–1719: *The Dispensary* (1699)

6 Grant me some wild expressions, Heavens, or I shall burst— . . . Words, words or I shall burst.

George Farquhar 1678–1707: *The Constant Couple* (1699)

7 Words are men's daughters, but God's sons are things.

Samuel Madden 1686–1765: *Boulter's Monument* (1745)

8 I am not yet so lost in lexicography as to forget that words are the daughters of earth, and that things are the sons of heaven. Language is only the instrument of science, and words are but the signs of ideas: I wish, however, that the instrument might be less apt to decay, and that signs might be permanent, like the things which they denote.

Samuel Johnson 1709–84: *A Dictionary of the English Language* (1755)

9 It's exactly where a thought is lacking
That, just in time, a word shows up instead.

Johann Wolfgang von Goethe 1749–1832: *Faust* (1808)

10 A single word even may be a spark of inextinguishable thought.

Percy Bysshe Shelley 1792–1822: *A Defence of Poetry* (written 1821)

11 For words, like Nature, half reveal
And half conceal the Soul within.

Alfred, Lord Tennyson 1809–92: *In Memoriam A. H. H.* (1850)

12 We talk about the tyranny of words, but we like to tyrannise over them too; we are fond of having a large superfluous establishment of words to wait upon us on great occasions; we think it looks important, and sounds well.

Charles Dickens 1812–70: *David Copperfield* (1850)

13 Oh, indelicate! How I do hate that word. If any word in the language reminds me of a whited sepulchre it is that:—all clean and polished outside with filth and rottenness within. Are your thoughts delicate? That's the thing.

Anthony Trollope 1815–82: 'Kate Vavasour' in *Can You Forgive Her?* (1864)

14 They've a temper, some of them—particularly verbs: they're the proudest—adjectives you can do anything with, but not verbs—however, I can manage the whole lot of them!

Lewis Carroll 1832–98: *Through the Looking-Glass* (1872)

15 All the charm of all the Muses
often flowering in a lonely word.

Alfred, Lord Tennyson 1809–92: 'To Virgil' (1882)

1 The vulgarity of the son of a Tory Duke having talked about 'pooh-poohing' something or other in the House of Commons: a vile new verb, unworthy of that high assembly.

Henry James 1843–1916: letter, 14 April 1884

2 Words alone are certain good.

W. B. Yeats 1865–1939: 'The Song of the Happy Shepherd' (1885)

3 Some word that teems with hidden meaning—like Basingstoke.

W. S. Gilbert 1836–1911: *Ruddigore* (1887)

4 Words are always getting conventionalized to some secondary meaning. It is one of the works of poetry to take the truants into custody and bring them back to their right senses. Poets are the policemen of language, they are always arresting those old reprobates the words.

W. B. Yeats 1865–1939: letter to Ellen O'Leary, 1889

5 All the words that I gather,
And all the words that I write,
Must spread out their wings untiring,
And never rest in their flight,
Till they come where your sad, sad heart is,
And sing to you in the night,
Beyond where the waters are moving
Storm-darkened or starry bright.

W. B. Yeats 1865–1939: 'Where My Books Go' (1892)

6 A definition is the enclosing a wilderness of idea within a wall of words.

Samuel Butler 1835–1902: *Notebooks* (1912)

7 I keep six honest serving-men
(They taught me all I knew);
Their names are What and Why and When
And How and Where and Who.

Rudyard Kipling 1865–1936: *Just So Stories* (1902) 'The Elephant's Child'

8 To illustrate calling a simple thing by a hard name, say that 'Baby, baby bunting' is written in Ithyphallics.

George Gissing 1857–1903: *Commonplace Book* (1962)

9 Words, as is well known, are the great foes of reality.

Joseph Conrad 1857–1924: *Under Western Eyes* (1911)

10 A swear-word in a rustic slum
A simple swear-word is to some,
To Masefield something more.

Max Beerbohm 1872–1956: *Fifty Caricatures* (1912)

11 The war has used up words; they have weakened, they have deteriorated like motor-car tyres; they have like millions of other things, been more overstrained and knocked about and voided of the happy semblance during the last six months than in all the long ages before, and we are now confronted with a depreciation of all our terms, or otherwise speaking, with a loss of expression through increase of limpness, that may well make us wonder what ghosts will be left to walk.

Henry James 1843–1916: in *New York Times* 21 March 1915

12 One of our defects as a nation is a tendency to use what have been called 'weasel words'. When a weasel sucks eggs the meat is sucked out of the egg. If you use a 'weasel word' after another, there is nothing left of the other.

Theodore Roosevelt 1858–1919: speech in St Louis, 31 May 1916

13 Summer afternoon—summer afternoon . . . the two most beautiful words in the English language.

Henry James 1843–1916: Edith Wharton *A Backward Glance* (1934)

14 I fear those big words, Stephen said, which make us so unhappy.

James Joyce 1882–1941: *Ulysses* (1922)

1 Words are, of course, the most powerful drug used by mankind.

Rudyard Kipling 1865–1936: speech, 14 February 1923

2 Slang is, at least, vigorous and apt. Probably most of our vital words were once slang.
presidential address to the English Association in 1924

John Galsworthy 1867–1933: *Castles in Spain and Other Screeds* (1927)

3 The Americans are doing what the Elizabethans did—they are coining new words . . . In England, save for the impetus given by war, the word-coining power has lapsed.

Virginia Woolf 1882–1941: 'American Fiction' (1925)

4 The Greeks had a word for it.

Zoë Akins 1886–1958: title of play (1930)

5 When I cannot see words curling like rings of smoke round me I am in darkness—I am nothing.

Virginia Woolf 1882–1941: *The Waves* (1931)

6 I gotta use words when I talk to you.

T. S. Eliot 1888–1965: *Sweeney Agonistes* (1932)

7   Words strain,
Crack and sometimes break, under the burden,
Under the tension, slip, slide, perish,
Decay with imprecision, will not stay in place,
Will not stay still.

T. S. Eliot 1888–1965: *Four Quartets* 'Burnt Norton' (1936)

8 I think that the deliberate invention of words is at least worth thinking over.

George Orwell 1903–50: 'New Words' (1940)

9 Do not become embittered by waiting and tears. Speak with calmness and serenity, and do as our holy sages have done—pour forth words and cast them into letters. Then the holy souls of your brothers and sisters will remain alive. These evil ones scheme to blot out their names from the face of the earth; but a man cannot destroy letters. For words have wings; they mount up to the heavenly heights and they endure for eternity.
a rabbi to his students in 1940, as the Germans were entering Kovno

Nachum Yanchiker: attributed

10 Words can be like tiny doses of arsenic: they are swallowed unnoticed, appear to have no effect, and then after a little time the toxic reaction sets in after all.

Victor Klemperer 1891–1960: *The Language of the Third Reich: LTI—Lingua Tertiii Imperii: A Philologist's Notebook* (1946)

11 There is no use indicting words, they are no shoddier than what they peddle.

Samuel Beckett 1906–89: *Malone Dies* (1958)

12 Man does not live by words alone, despite the fact that he sometimes has to eat them.

Adlai Stevenson 1900–65: *The Wit and Wisdom of Adlai Stevenson* (1965)

13 MIKE: There's no word in the Irish language for what you were doing.
WILSON: In Lapland they have no word for snow.

Joe Orton 1933–67: *The Ruffian on the Stair* (rev. ed. 1967)

14 Don't swear, boy. It shows a lack of vocabulary.

Alan Bennett 1934– : *Forty Years On* (1969)

15   Real poets never 'try
to use words', as you put it; your first blunder
Was treating them like slaves or tools.

A. D. Hope 1907–2000: 'Home Truths from Abroad' (1978); see **49:12**

16 If there's one word that sums up everything that's gone wrong since the War, it's Workshop.

Kingsley Amis 1922–95: *Jake's Thing* (1979)

1 Wordstruck is exactly what I was—and still am: crazy about the sound of words, the look of words, the taste of words, the feeling for words on the tongue and in the mind.

Robert MacNeil 1931– : *Wordstruck* (1989)

2 Words are undervalued as a means of expression. Pictures tend to trivialise experience.

Arthur Miller 1915– : attributed, 1990

3 A word, in a word, is complicated.

Steven Pinker 1954– : *The Language Instinct* (1994)

William Wordsworth 1770–1850 see also **82:8**
English poet

4 Who, both by precept and example, shows
That prose is verse, and verse is merely prose,
Convincing all by demonstration plain,
Poetic souls delight in prose insane;
And Christmas stories tortured into rhyme,
Contain the essence of the true sublime.

Lord Byron 1788–1824: *English Bards and Scotch Reviewers* (1809)

5 This will never do.
on The Excursion (*1814*)

Francis, Lord Jeffrey 1773–1850: in *Edinburgh Review* November 1814

6 Wordsworth—stupendous genius! damned fool! These poets run about their ponds though they cannot fish.

Lord Byron 1788–1824: fragment of a letter to James Hogg, recorded in the diary of Henry Crabb Robinson, 1 December 1816

7 For the sake of a few fine imaginative or domestic passages, are we to be bullied into a certain philosophy engendered in the whims of an egotist?
on the overbearing influence of Wordsworth upon his contemporaries

John Keats 1795–1821: letter to J. H. Reynolds, 3 February 1818

8 A drowsy frowzy poem, called the 'Excursion',
Writ in a manner which is my aversion.

Lord Byron 1788–1824: *Don Juan* (1819–24)

9 We learn from Horace, Homer sometimes sleeps;
We feel without him: Wordsworth sometimes wakes.

Lord Byron 1788–1824: *Don Juan* (1819–24); see **125:8**

10 As the lark ascends from its low bed on fluttering wing, and salutes the morning skies, so Mr. Wordsworth's unpretending muse in russet guise scales the summits of reflection, while it makes the round earth its footstool and its home!

William Hazlitt 1778–1830: *The Spirit of the Age* (1825)

11 Remote from the passions and events of the great world, he has communicated interest and dignity to the primal movements of the heart of man.
on Wordsworth

William Hazlitt 1778–1830: *The Spirit of the Age* (1825)

12 Just for a handful of silver he left us,
Just for a riband to stick in his coat.
of Wordsworth's implied abandonment of radical principles by his acceptance of the Laureateship

Robert Browning 1812–89: 'The Lost Leader' (1845)

13 He was . . . a man of an immense head and great jaws like a crocodile's, cast in a mould designed for prodigious work.

Thomas Carlyle 1795–1881: in conversation, *c*.1849; Charles Gavan Duffy *Conversations with Thomas Carlyle* (1892)

1 He spoke, and loosed our heart in tears.
  He laid us as we lay at birth
  On the cool flowery lap of earth.

Matthew Arnold 1822–88:
'Memorial Verses, April 1850' (1852)

2 I never beheld eyes that looked so inspired or supernatural.
  They were like fires half burning, half smouldering, with a
  sort of acrid fixture of regard, and seated at the further end
  of two caverns.
    on Wordsworth's eyes

Leigh Hunt 1784–1859:
Autobiography (rev. ed., 1860)

3 Wordsworth went to the lakes, but he was never a lake
  poet. He found in stones the sermons he had already
  hidden there.

Oscar Wilde 1854–1900: *Intentions*
(1891) 'The Decay of Lying'; see
191:12

4 How thankful we ought to be that Wordsworth was only a
  poet and not a musician. Fancy a symphony by
  Wordsworth! Fancy having to sit it out! And fancy what it
  would have been if he had written fugues!

Samuel Butler 1835–1902: *Notebooks*
(1912)

5 What a gross absurdity is the moral lesson of
  Wordsworth's 'Resolution and Independence'! How can a
  man strengthen himself by the example of another whose
  needs and capacities have nothing in common with his
  own? How can a fiery-hearted youth see an example to be
  imitated in a bloodless old fellow bent double with
  infirmities?
    on the example offered by the leech-gatherer of the poem

George Gissing 1857–1903:
Commonplace Book (1962)

6 Mr Wordsworth, a stupid man, with a decided gift for
  portraying nature in vignettes, never yet ruined anyone's
  morals, unless, perhaps, he has driven some susceptible
  persons to crime in a very fury of boredom.

Ezra Pound 1885–1972: in *Future*
September 1913

7 Snowdrifts of Wordsworth.
    a reviser's comment on the content of previous editions of
    ODQ

Anonymous: introduction to *Oxford
Dictionary of Quotations* (ed. 3, 1979)

8 Wordsworth was nearly the price of me once. I was
  driving down the M1 on a Saturday morning: they had
  this poetry slot on the radio . . . and someone suddenly
  started reading the Immortality ode, and I couldn't see for
  tears. And when you're driving down the middle lane at
  seventy miles an hour . . .

Philip Larkin 1922–85: *Required
Writing* (1983)

Writers see also Writing

9 He has gained every point who has mixed profit with
  pleasure, by delighting the reader at the same time as
  instructing him.

Horace 65–8 BC: *Ars Poetica*

10   *Tenet insanabile multos*
  Scribendi cacoethes et aegro in corde senescit.
  Many suffer from the incurable disease of writing, and it
  becomes chronic in their sick minds.

Juvenal AD c.60–c.130: *Satires*

11 Authors are judged by strange capricious rules
  The great ones are thought mad, the small ones fools.

Alexander Pope 1688–1744:
prologue to *Three Hours after
Marriage* (1717)

1 But those who cannot write, and those who can,
   All rhyme, and scrawl, and scribble, to a man.

Alexander Pope 1688–1744:
Imitations of Horace (1737)

2 Talk not with scorn of authors—it was the chattering of
   the geese that saved the Capitol.

Samuel Taylor Coleridge
1772–1834: Notebook, 1798–1804

3 I do think . . . the mighty stir made about scribbling and
   scribes, by themselves and others—a sign of effeminacy,
   degeneracy, and weakness. Who would write, who had
   any thing better to do?

Lord Byron 1788–1824: diary, 24
November 1813

4 Until you understand a writer's ignorance, presume
   yourself ignorant of his understanding.

Samuel Taylor Coleridge
1772–1834: *Biographia Literaria* (1817)

5 All clean and comfortable I sit down to write.

John Keats 1795–1821: letter to
George and Georgiana Keats, 17
September 1819

6 I know no person so perfectly disagreeable and even
   dangerous as an author.

William IV 1765–1837: Philip Ziegler
King William IV (1971)

7 When once the itch of literature comes over a man,
   nothing can cure it but the scratching of a pen.

Samuel Lover 1797–1868: *Handy
Andy* (1842)

8 An author in his book must be like God in his universe,
   present everywhere and visible nowhere.

Gustave Flaubert 1821–80: letter, 9
December 1852

9 Pray know that when a man begins writing a book he
   never gives over. The evil with which he is beset is as
   inveterate as drinking—as exciting as gambling.

Anthony Trollope 1815–82: letter to
an unknown correspondent, c.1855;
Letters (1983) vol. 1

10 Writers, like teeth, are divided into incisors and grinders.

Walter Bagehot 1826–77: *Estimates
of some Englishmen and Scotchmen*
(1858) 'The First Edinburgh
Reviewers'

11 We authors, Ma'am.
   to Queen Victoria after the publication of Leaves from the
   Journal of our Life in the Highlands *in 1868*

Benjamin Disraeli 1804–81:
Elizabeth Longford *Victoria R.I.* (1964)

12 One man is as good as another until he has written a
   book.

Benjamin Jowett 1817–93: Evelyn
Abbott and Lewis Campbell (eds.)
Life and Letters of Benjamin Jowett
(1897)

13 We work in the dark—we do what we can—we give what
   we have. Our doubt is our passion and our passion is our
   task. The rest is the madness of art.

Henry James 1843–1916: 'The Middle
Years' (short story, 1893)

14 The Llama is a woolly sort of fleecy hairy goat,
   With an indolent expression and an undulating throat
   Like an unsuccessful literary man.

Hilaire Belloc 1870–1953: *More
Beasts for Worse Children* (1897) 'The
Llama'

15 An artist is a dreamer consenting to dream of the actual
   world.

George Santayana 1863–1952: *The
Life of Reason* (1905)

16 Can anything be more bitter than to be doomed to a life of
   literature and hot-water bottles when one's a pirate at
   heart?

Lytton Strachey 1880–1932: to
George Mallory, 1913; Michael
Holroyd *Lytton Strachey* (1994 rev.
ed.)

17 I have often thought that the best mode of life for me
   would be to sit in the innermost room of a spacious locked
   cellar with my writing things and my lamp. Food would be
   brought and always put down far away from my room . . .
   For who am I?

Franz Kafka 1883–1924: attributed

1 In this
most Christian of worlds all poets
are Jews.

Marina Tsvetaeva 1892–1941: 'Poem of the End' (1924)

2 A serious writer is not to be confounded with a solemn writer. A serious writer may be a hawk or a buzzard or even a popinjay, but a solemn writer is always a bloody owl.

Ernest Hemingway 1899–1961: *Death in the Afternoon* (1932)

3 A writer wastes nothing.

F. Scott Fitzgerald 1896–1940: Sheilah Graham and Gerald Frank *Beloved Infidel* (1959)

4 It is the custom in the country, of course, but most writers are such horrible-looking people that their faces destroy something which perhaps wanted to like them . . . I have several times been so repelled by such faces that I have not been able to read the books without the face coming between.
on authors' book-jacket photographs

Raymond Chandler 1888–1959: letter to Alfred Knopf, 16 July 1942

5   Master of nuance and scruple
Pray for me and for all writers living or dead;
Because there are many whose works
Are in better taste than their lives; because there is no end
To the vanity of our calling: make intercession
For the treason of all clerks.

W. H. Auden 1907–73: 'At the Grave of Henry James' (1945); see **149:4**

6 An artist is his own fault.

John O'Hara 1905–70: *The Portable F. Scott Fitzgerald* (1945)

7 The great mass of human beings are not acutely selfish. After the age of about thirty they abandon individual ambition—in many cases, indeed, they almost abandon the sense of being individuals at all—and live chiefly for others, or are simply smothered under drudgery. But there is also the minority of gifted, wilful people who are determined to live their own lives to the end, and writers belong in this class.

George Orwell 1903–50: 'Why I Write' (1946)

8 Coleridge was a drug addict. Poe was an alcoholic. Marlowe was stabbed by a man whom he was treacherously trying to stab. Pope took money to keep a woman's name out of a satire then wrote a piece so that she could still be recognized anyhow. Chatterton killed himself. Byron was accused of incest. Do you still want to be a writer—and if so, why?

Bennett Cerf 1898–1971: *Shake Well Before Using* (1948)

9 Most writers have the egotism of actors with none of the good looks or charm.

Raymond Chandler 1888–1959: letter to Leonore Offord, December 1948

10 Talk about there being far too many writers. You can't of course prevent people writing any more than copulating, but there ought to be some sort of contraception to prevent publication.

James Lees-Milne 1908–97: *Midway on the Waves: Diaries 1948-49* (1985) 14 Feb 1949

11 There are things about the publishing business that I should like, but dealing with writers would not be one of them. Their egos require too much petting. They live over-strained lives in which far too much humanity is sacrificed to far too little art.

Raymond Chandler 1888–1959: letter to Jamie Hamilton 23 June 1950

1 He [the writer] must teach himself that the basest of all things is to be afraid and, teaching himself that, forget it forever, leaving no room in his workshop for anything but the old verities and truths of the heart, the old universal truths lacking which any story is ephemeral and doomed—love and honor and pity and pride and compassion and sacrifice.

William Faulkner 1897–1962: Nobel Prize speech, 1950

2 The greatest advantage of being a writer is that you can *spy* on people. You're there listening to every word, but part of you is observing. Everything is useful to a writer, you see—every scrap, even the longest and most boring of luncheon parties.
to Michael Korda on Alexander Korda's yacht, Antibes, 1950

Graham Greene 1904–91: in *New Yorker* 25 March 1996

3 There is only one position for an artist anywhere: and that is, upright.

Dylan Thomas 1914–53: *Quite Early One Morning* (1954) 'Wales and the Artist'

4 Artists are the antennae of the race, but the bullet-headed many will never learn to trust their great artists.

Ezra Pound 1885–1972: *Literary Essays* (1954)

5 The writer's only responsibility is to his art. He will be completely ruthless if he is a good one. He has a dream. It anguishes him so much he must get rid of it. He has no peace until then. Everything goes by the board . . . If a writer has to rob his mother, he will not hesitate; the *Ode on a Grecian Urn* is worth any number of old ladies.

William Faulkner 1897–1962: in *Paris Review* Spring 1956

6 The most essential gift for a good writer is a built-in, shock-proof shit detector. This is the writer's radar and all great writers have had it.

Ernest Hemingway 1899–1961: in *Paris Review* Spring 1958

7 The author is a modern figure, a product of our society insofar as, emerging from the Middle Ages with English empiricism, French rationalism and the personal faith of the Reformation, it discovered the prestige of the individual, or, as it is more nobly put, the 'human person'.

Roland Barthes 1915–80: *The Death of the Author* (1968)

8 Few if any of the great novelists are people one would like to know as friends. Hemingway the bully; Proust the snob; Waugh the snobbish bully; Fitzgerald the drunk; Dickens the exhibitionist—they are all great novelists because they like to exploit and manipulate people, to mock and devastate people, to torment and trample on people—and we are talking, remember, of people they have themselves created.

Kenneth Tynan 1927–80: diary, 7 January 1972

9 Feeling at odds is to be expected: no writer calls a truce. If he did, he would probably stop writing.

Mavis Gallant 1922– : *Home Truths* (1981)

10 Some writers take to drink, others take to audiences.

Gore Vidal 1925– : in *Paris Review* 1981

11 The writer must be universal in sympathy and an outcast by nature: only then can he see clearly.

Julian Barnes 1946– : *Flaubert's Parrot* (1984)

12 When I was a little boy, they called me a liar, but now that I am grown up, they call me a writer.

Isaac Bashevis Singer 1904–91: in *Bibliophile* July 1986

13 You should find that your writing overcomes the besetting feeling of vagueness and ennui which is characteristic of everyday life.

Edmund White 1940– : in interview in *Paris Review* 1988

1 All experience is good for writers—except for physical pain.

William Trevor 1928- : in *Paris Review* 1989

2 Writing is neither profession nor vocation, but an incurable illness. Those who give up are not writers and never were; those who persevere do so not from pluck or determination, but because they cannot help it: they are sick and advice is an impertinence.

Hugh Leonard 1926- : *Out After Dark* (1989)

3 One of the things a writer is for is to say the unsayable, speak the unspeakable and ask difficult questions.

Salman Rushdie 1947- : in *Independent on Sunday* 10 September 1995 'Quotes of the Week'

4 A high anxiety level is the novelist's normal condition.

Julian Barnes 1946- : in *Paris Review* Winter 2000-2001

5 Writers, those professionals of dissatisfaction.

Susan Sontag 1933- : in *Writers on Writing: Collected Essays from The New York Times* (2001)

6 If you were a Canadian writer you were assumed by your countryfolk to be not only inferior, but pitiable, pathetic, and pretentious.
on Canada in the 1950s when she started writing

Margaret Atwood 1939- : *Negotiating with the Dead: A Writer on Writing* (2002)

Writer's Block

7 It's almost a month now, and I've scarcely finished
A single page.

Martial AD c.40-c.104: *Epigrammata*, tr. James Michie

8 But words came halting forth, wanting Invention's stay;
Invention, Nature's child, fled step-dame Study's blows . . .
Biting my truant pen, beating myself for spite,
'Fool,' said my Muse to me; 'look in thy heart and write.'

Philip Sidney 1554-86: *Astrophil and Stella* (1591) sonnet 1

9 Invention flags, his brain goes muddy,
And black despair succeeds brown study.

William Congreve 1670-1729: *An Impossible Thing* (1720)

10 You beat your pate, and fancy wit will come:
Knock as you please, there's nobody at home.

Alexander Pope 1688-1744: 'Epigram: You beat your pate' (1732)

11 Tom Birch is as brisk as a bee in conversation; but no sooner does he take a pen in his hand, than it becomes a torpedo to him, and benumbs all his faculties.

Samuel Johnson 1709-84: James Boswell *Life of Samuel Johnson* (1791) 1743

12 I do not write—I have lived too long near Lord Byron and the sun has extinguished the glow-worm.

Percy Bysshe Shelley 1792-1822: letter to Horace Smith, 21 May 1822

13 Poetry is a distinct faculty—it won't come when called—you may as well whistle for a wind.

Lord Byron 1788-1824: E. J. Trelawny *Records of Shelley, Byron and the Author* (1878)

14 But I must say to the Muse of fiction, as the Earl of Pembroke said to the ejected nun of Wilton, 'Go spin, you jade, go spin!'

Sir Walter Scott 1771-1832: diary, 8 February 1826

15 Two or three years ago . . . he wouldn't sit at his desk after a night of conjugal effusion, knowing beforehand he couldn't construct a sentence, write a line. Now it's the opposite. After eight or ten days of mediocre work, coitus induces a slight fever that unblocks him.
of Zola

Edmond de Goncourt 1822-96: diary, 4 April 1875

1 If one waits for the right time to come before writing, the right time never comes.

James Russell Lowell 1819–91: letter to Charles Eliot Norton, 22 April 1883

2 Birds build—but not I build; no, but strain,
Time's eunuch, and not breed one work that wakes.
Mine, O thou lord of life, send my roots rain.

Gerard Manley Hopkins 1844–89: 'Thou art indeed just, Lord' (written 1889)

3 Reardon . . . walked in the darkness round the outer circle of Regent's Park, racking his fagged brain in a hopeless search for characters, situations, motives.

George Gissing 1857–1903: *New Grub Street* (1891)

4 I sit down for eight hours every day—and sitting down is all. In the course of that working day of eight hours I write three sentences which I erase before leaving the table in despair.

Joseph Conrad 1857–1924: letter to Edward Garnett, 29 March 1898

5 No pen, no ink, no table, no room, no time, no quiet, no inclination.

James Joyce 1882–1941: letter to his brother, 7 December 1906

6 All things can tempt me from this craft of verse.

W. B. Yeats 1865–1939: 'All Things Can Tempt Me' (1909)

7 In barrenness, at any rate, I hold a high place among English poets, excelling even Gray.

A. E. Housman 1859–1936: letter, 28 February 1910

8 Full 3 weeks—no two consecutive ideas, no six consecutive words to be found anywhere in the world. I would prefer a red hot gridiron to that cold blankness.

Joseph Conrad 1857–1924: letter to Galsworthy, May 1911

9 For the last two weeks I have written scarcely anything. I have been idle. I have *failed*.

Katherine Mansfield 1888–1923: diary, 13 November 1921

10 I am overcome by my own amazing sloth . . . Can you please forgive me and believe that it is really because I want to do something well that I don't do it at all?

Elizabeth Bishop 1911–79: letter to Marianne Moore, 25 February 1937

11 If you are in difficulties with a book, try the element of surprise: attack it at an hour when it isn't expecting it.

H. G. Wells 1866–1946: attributed

12 Coleridge received the Person from Porlock
And ever after called him a curse,
Then why did he hurry to let him in?
He could have hid in the house.
It was not right of Coleridge in fact it was wrong
(But often we all do wrong)
As the truth is I think he was already stuck
With Kubla Khan . . .

Stevie Smith 1902–71: 'Thoughts about the "Person from Porlock" ' (1962); see **140:4**

13 An hour at a poem without adding a single (sodding) *word* . . . One never gets any better at this lark.

Philip Larkin 1922–85: letter, 2 May 1974

14 Any memory of pain is deeply buried, and there is nothing more painful for a writer than an inability to work.

John Cheever 1912–82: in *Writers at Work* (5th series, 1981)

15 At the beginning of the 'block' one says to oneself, 'This time it's the *coup de grâce*; it's the end' . . . Only dreams enable me to fight these painful blocks.

Graham Greene 1904–91: Marie-Françoise Allain *The Other Man, Conversations with Graham Greene* (1983)

16 I am afraid the compulsion to write poems left me about seven years ago, since when I have written virtually nothing. Naturally this is a disappointment, but I would sooner write no poems than bad poems.

Philip Larkin 1922–85: letter, 11 August 1984

17 You can always write something. You write limericks. You write a love letter. You do something to get you into the habit of writing again, to bring back the desire.

Erskine Caldwell 1903–87: George Plimpton (ed.) *The Writer's Chapbook* (1989)

1 I often read, with amazement, of people who suffer from writer's block; I might enjoy a wee block, just to have time to catch my breath.

Robertson Davies 1913–95: in *Paris Review* 1989

2 Losing that gift to create is a terrible thing. It feels a bit like receiving a camera as a present but having nothing to photograph.

Bernard MacLaverty 1942– : in *The Times* 13 September 1997

3 I love deadlines. I love the whooshing noise they make as they go by.

Douglas Adams 1952–2001: in *Guardian* 14 May 2001

Writing see also Writers

4 Be a scribe! Engrave this in your heart!
So that your name might live on like theirs!
The scroll is better than the carved stone.
A man has died: his corpse is dust,
And his people have passed from the land.
It is a book which makes him be remembered
In the mouth of the speaker who reads him.
   composed by an Ancient Egyptian scribe, c.1300 BC

Anonymous: M. Lichtheim *Ancient Egyptian Literature* (1973) vol. 1

5 I and Pangur Bán, my cat,
'Tis a like task we are at;
Hunting mice is his delight,
Hunting words I sit all night.

Better far than praise of men
'Tis to sit with book and pen;
Pangur bears me no ill will,
He too plies his simple skill . . .

. . . So in peace our tasks we ply,
Pangur Bán, my cat, and I;
In our arts we find our bliss,
I have mine and he has his.

Anonymous: 'Pangur Bán', Latin poem found in the margins of an 8th-century *Epistles of St Paul* belonging to an Austrian monastery founded by Irish monks; translated 1931 by Robin Flower

6 He that will write well in any tongue, must follow this counsel of Aristotle, to speak as the common people do, to think as wise men do; and so should every man understand him, and the judgement of wise men allow him.

Roger Ascham 1515–68: *Toxophilus* (1545)

7 Making a book is a craft, as is making a clock; it takes more than wit to become an author.

Jean de la Bruyère 1645–96: *Les Caractères ou les moeurs de ce siècle* (1688) 'Des Ouvrages de l'esprit'

8 Eye Nature's walks, shoot Folly as it flies,
And catch the Manners living as they rise.
Laugh where we must, be candid where we can;
But vindicate the ways of God to man.

Alexander Pope 1688–1744: *An Essay on Man* Epistle 1 (1733)

9 To write well, lastingly well, immortally well, must one not leave Father and Mother and cleave unto the Muse?
. . . 'Tis such a task as scarce leaves a man time to be a good neighbour, an useful friend, nay to plant a tree, much less to save his soul.

Alexander Pope 1688–1744: letter to Viscount Bolingbroke

10 The only end of writing is to enable the readers better to enjoy life, or better to endure it.

Samuel Johnson 1709–84: *A Free Enquiry* (1757)

1 [I] will go through almost anything with a degree of satisfaction if I am to put an account of it in writing.

James Boswell 1740–95: diary, 1762–3; Frank Brady *James Boswell* (1984)

2 Writing, when properly managed (as you may be sure I think mine is) is but a different name for conversation.

Laurence Sterne 1713–68: *Tristram Shandy* (1759–67)

3 Any fool may write a most valuable book by chance, if he will only tell us what he heard and saw with veracity.

Thomas Gray 1716–71: letter to Horace Walpole, 25 February 1768

4 The greatest part of a writer's time is spent in reading, in order to write: a man will turn over half a library to make one book.

Samuel Johnson 1709–84: James Boswell *Life of Samuel Johnson* (1791) 6 April 1775

5 It is very difficult to depict from memory that which is *natural* in us; one too easily depicts that which is *factitious*, that which is *acted*, because the effort needed to *act* it imprints it on the memory. Training myself to recall my natural sentiments is a study which could give me the talent of Shakespeare.

Stendhal 1783–1842: diary, 1805

6 The candles are burnt down, and I am using the wax taper—which has a long snuff on it—the fire is at its last click—I am sitting with my back to it with one foot rather askew upon the rug and the other with the heel a little elevated from the carpet—I am writing this on the *Maid's Tragedy* which I have read since tea with great pleasure . . . These are trifles—but . . . could I see the same thing done of any great man long since dead it would be a great delight: as to know in what position Shakespeare sat when he began 'To be or not to be'—such things become interesting from distance of time or place.

John Keats 1795–1821: letter to George and Georgiana Keats, 12 March 1819

7 The artist must be in his work as God is in creation, invisible and all-powerful; one must sense him everywhere but never see him.

Gustave Flaubert 1821–80: letter to Mademoiselle Leroyer de Chantepie, 18 March 1857

8 My writing is simply a set of experiments in life—an endeavour to see what our thought and emotion may be capable of.

George Eliot 1819–80: letter, 25 January 1876

9 I finished on Thursday the novel I was writing, and on Friday I began another. Nothing really frightens me but the idea of enforced idleness. As long as I can write books even though they be not published, I think that I can be happy.

Anthony Trollope 1815–82: letter, 21 December 1880

10 The writer's problem is, how to strike the balance between the uncommon and the ordinary so as on the one hand to give interest, on the other to give reality.

Thomas Hardy 1840–1928: notebook July 1881

11 You are right in demanding that an artist should take a conscious attitude to his work, but you confuse two conceptions: *the solution of a question and the correct setting of a question*. The latter alone is obligatory for the artist. In *Anna Karenina* and *Onegin* not a single problem is solved, but they satisfy completely because all the problems are set correctly. The court is obliged to submit the case fairly, but let the jury do the deciding, each according to its own judgement.

Anton Chekhov 1860–1904: letter to Alexei Suvorin, 27 October 1888

1 My task which I am trying to achieve is by the power of the written word, to make you hear, to make you feel—it is, before all, to make you *see*. That—and no more, and it is everything.

Joseph Conrad 1857–1924: *The Nigger of the Narcissus* (1897) preface

2 When I was writing 'The Shadow of the Glen', some years ago, I got more aid than any learning could have given me from a chink in the floor of the old Wicklow house where I was staying, that let me hear what was being said by the servant girls in the kitchen.

John Millington Synge 1871–1909: *Playboy of the Western World* preface

3 Neither Christ nor Buddha nor Socrates wrote a book, for to do that is to exchange life for a logical process.

W. B. Yeats 1865–1939: *Estrangement* (1909)

4 The artist, like the God of the creation, remains within or behind or beyond or above his handiwork, invisible, refined out of existence, indifferent, paring his fingernails.

James Joyce 1882–1941: *A Portrait of the Artist as a Young Man* (1916)

5 My theory of writing I can sum up in one sentence. An author ought to write for the youth of his own generation, the critics of the next, and the schoolmasters of ever after.

F. Scott Fitzgerald 1896–1940: letter to the Booksellers' Convention, April 1920

6 Probably . . . the larger part of the labour of an author in composing his work is critical labour; the labour of sifting, combining, constructing, expunging, correcting, testing: this frightful toil is as much critical as creative.

T. S. Eliot 1888–1965: 'The Function of Criticism' (1923)

7 First I write one sentence: then I write another. That's how I write. But I have a feeling writing ought to be like running through a field.

Lytton Strachey 1880–1932: in conversation with Max Beerbohm; Virginia Woolf *A Writer's Diary* (1953) 1 November 1938

8 Often I think writing is a sheer paring away of oneself leaving always something thinner, barer, more meagre.

F. Scott Fitzgerald 1896–1940: letter to his daughter Scottie (Frances Scott Fitzgerald), 27 April 1940

9 By an epiphany he meant a sudden spiritual manifestation, whether in vulgarity of speech or of gesture or in a memorable phase of the mind itself. He believed that it was for the man of letters to recover these epiphanies with extreme care, seeing that they themselves are the most delicate and evanescent of moments.

James Joyce 1882–1941: *Stephen Hero* (1944); part of a first draft of *A Portrait of the Artist as a Young Man*

10 There should be a space of time, say four hours in a day at least, when a professional writer doesn't do anything else but write. He doesn't have to write, and if he doesn't feel like it, he shouldn't try. He can look out of the window or stand on his head or writhe on the floor. But he is not to do any other positive thing, not read, write letters, glance at magazines, or write checks. Write or nothing.

Raymond Chandler 1888–1959: letter to Alex Barris, 18 March 1949

11 Writing is not a profession but a vocation of unhappiness.

Georges Simenon 1903–89: interview in *Paris Review* Summer 1955

12 An author is like a horse pulling a coal-cart down an icy hill; he ought to stop, but when he reflects that it would probably kill him to try, he goes right on, neighing and rolling his eyes.

Robertson Davies 1913–95: in 1959; *The Enthusiasms of Robertson Davies* (1990)

1 Writing is the destruction of every voice, of every point of origin. Writing is that neutral, composite, oblique space where our subject slips away, the negative where all identity is lost, starting with the very identity of the body writing.

Roland Barthes 1915–80: *The Death of the Author* (1968)

2 The responsibility of a writer is to excavate the experience of the people who produced him.

James Baldwin 1924–87: *A Dialogue* (1973)

3 Writing is like getting married. One should never commit oneself until one is amazed at one's luck.

Iris Murdoch 1919–99: *The Black Prince* 'Bradley Pearson's Foreword' (1973)

4 Writing is turning one's worst moments into money.

J. P. Donleavy 1926– : in *Playboy* May 1979

5 The slow discovery by a novelist of his individual method can be exciting, but a moment comes in middle age when he feels he no longer controls his method; he has become its prisoner.

Graham Greene 1904–91: *Ways of Escape* (1980)

6 If you don't spend every morning of your life writing, it's awfully difficult to know what to do otherwise.

Anthony Powell 1905–2000: interview in *Observer* 3 April 1984

7 Writing a poem is like a short love affair, writing a short story like a long love affair, writing a novel like a marriage.

Amos Oz 1939– : in *Observer* 21 July 1985

8 Writing is very improvisational. It's like trying to fix a broken sewing machine with safety pins and rubber bands. A lot of tinkering.

Margaret Atwood 1939– : in an interview, December 1986; Earl G. Ingersoll (ed.) *Margaret Atwood: Conversations* (1990)

9 Writing is *play* in the same way that playing the piano is 'play', or putting on a theatrical 'play' is play. Just because something's fun doesn't mean it isn't serious.

Margaret Atwood 1939– : in an interview, November 1989; Earl G. Ingersoll (ed.) *Margaret Atwood: Conversations* (1990)

10 All novelists know their art proceeds by indirection. When tempted by didacticism, the writer should imagine a spruce sea-captain eyeing the storm ahead, bustling from instrument to instrument in a catherine wheel of gold braid, expelling crisp orders down the speaking tube. But there is nobody below decks; the engine-room was never installed, and the rudder broke off centuries ago.

Julian Barnes 1946– : *A History of the World in 10½ Chapters* (1989) 'Parenthesis'

11 I can't imagine not needing to write. I should be very unhappy if I couldn't write.

Iris Murdoch 1919–99: Rosemary Hartill *Writers Revealed* (1989)

12 Writing a novel was like driving to Edinburgh (from London). You knew the first 10 miles very well. You knew where you were heading. And you knew a few of the places along the way. The rest you filled in as you went along, or perhaps discovered.

Kingsley Amis 1922–95: remark, 11 December 1992, in *Sunday Times* 17 March 1996

13 You don't give up writing until writing gives you up.

Rumer Godden 1907–98: Michael Rosen and Jill Burridge *Treasure Islands 2* (1993)

14 My Catholic girlhood taught me two disciplines that are invaluable, I think, for writing: the daily examination of conscience and the meditation on holy pictures.

Marina Warner 1946– : Clare Boylan (ed.) *The Agony and the Ego* (1993)

on his discovery of writing:

1 It was sorta like being an athlete and using only the left side of your body, and then finding a game where you could use your whole body.

David Foster Wallace 1962– : interview in *Daily Telegraph* 29 June 1996

2 I've always thought people write because they are not living properly.

Beryl Bainbridge 1933– : interview in *Daily Telegraph* 10 September 1996

3 There is a moment in the movie *Lawrence of Arabia* when a tiny black dot on the shimmering desert horizon slowly enlarges into a galloping sheikh, played, if memory serves, by Omar Sharif. A book you write is like that—a small vibrant blur that gradually enlarges into a presence, preferably dashing and irresistible.

John Updike 1932– : 'Me and My Books' in *New Yorker* 1997

4 The process of writing . . . consists of sitting in one place for several hours every day and groaning immoderately while you make marks of one colour on a surface of another. Inspiration has precious little to do with it and brutal toil a great deal.

Philip Pullman 1946– : Barry Turner (ed.) *The Writer's Handbook 2000* (1999)

5 Yes, writing can be complicated, exhausting, isolating, abstracting, boring, dulling, briefly exhilarating; it can be made to be gruelling and demoralizing. And occasionally it can produce rewards. But it's never as hard as, say, piloting an L-1011 into O'Hare on a snowy night in January, or doing brain surgery when you have to stand up for ten hours straight, and once you start you can't just stop. If you're a writer, you can stop anywhere, any time, and no one will care or ever know. Plus, the results might be better if you do.

Richard Ford 1944– : in *Writers on Writing: Collected Essays from The New York Times* (2001)

6 John Cheever wrote some of his early stories in his underwear. Hemingway is said to have written some of his fiction while standing up. Thomas Wolfe reportedly wrote parts of his voluminous novels while leaning over the top of a refrigerator.

Kent Haruf 1943– : in *Writers on Writing: Collected Essays from The New York Times* (2001)

7 A story was a form of telepathy. By means of inking symbols onto a page, she was able to send thoughts and feelings from her mind to her reader's. It was a magical process, so commonplace that no one stopped to wonder at it.

Ian McEwan 1948– : *Atonement* (2001)

8 If you want to be a writer, you have to write every day. The consistency, the monotony, the certainty, all vagaries and passions are covered by this daily reoccurrence.

Walter Mosley 1952– : in *Writers on Writing: Collected Essays from The New York Times* (2001)

9 To write is to practice, with particular intensity and attentiveness, the art of reading. You write in order to read what you've written and see if it's OK and, since of course it never is, to rewrite it—once, twice, as many times as it takes to get it to be something you can bear to reread.

Susan Sontag 1933– : in *Writers on Writing: Collected Essays from The New York Times* (2001)

10 There's one characteristic that sets writing apart from most of the other arts—its apparent democracy, by which I mean its availability to almost everyone as a means of expression.

Margaret Atwood 1939– : *Negotiating with the Dead: A Writer on Writing* (2002)

W. B. Yeats 1865–1939
Irish poet

1 I, the poet William Yeats,
   With old mill boards and sea-green slates,
   And smithy work from the Gort forge,
   Restored this tower for my wife George;
   And may these characters remain
   When all is ruin once again.

W. B. Yeats 1865–1939: 'To be Carved on a Stone at Thoor Ballylee' (1918)

2 I declare this tower is my symbol; I declare
   This winding, gyring, spiring treadmill of a stair is my
      ancestral stair;
   That Goldsmith and the Dean, Berkeley and Burke have
      travelled there.

W. B. Yeats 1865–1939: 'Blood and the Moon' (1927)

3 Wherever one cut him, with a little question, he poured,
   spurted fountains of ideas.

Virginia Woolf 1882–1941: diary, 8 November 1930

4 Scoffed at fairies, but they made his living.

Anonymous: obituary of Yeats in *Daily Express* 30 January 1939; in *Quote Unquote Newsletter* October 1995 vol. 4 no. 4

5 You were silly like us; your gift survived it all:
   The parish of rich women, physical decay,
   Yourself. Mad Ireland hurt you into poetry.

W. H. Auden 1907–73: 'In Memory of W. B. Yeats' (1940)

6 He wrote like God. He could put words together with such
   certainty that they seem to have been graven on tablets of
   stone from the beginning of time.

John Carey 1934– : *Pure Pleasure* (2000)

Author Index

Abercrombie, Lascelles (1881–1938)
British poet and critic
216:6

Ackroyd, Peter (1949–)
British novelist and biographer
145:9, 306:2

Adams, Douglas (1952–2001)
British science fiction writer
2:8, 139:9, 186:8, 322:7, 337:3

Adams, Franklin P. (1881–1960)
American journalist and humorist
72:4, 72:5, 144:8

Adams, Henry Brooks (1838–1918)
American man of letters
177:4

Adams, John (1735–1826)
American statesman
39:9, 96:11, 212:11

Adams, Mrs Henry (1843–85)
141:8

Addison, Joseph (1672–1719)
English poet, dramatist, and essayist
9:12, 22:8, 55:3, 58:2, 94:9, 110:4, 129:11,
156:2, 178:7, 240:3, 287:9, 304:8

Ade, George (1866–1944)
American humorist and dramatist
243:14

Adorno, Theodor (1903–69)
German philosopher, sociologist, and musicologist
279:7

Aeschylus (c.525–456 BC)
Greek tragedian
202:15

Agate, James (1877–1947)
British drama critic and novelist
275:2

Aiken, Joan (1924–)
British novelist and children's writer
18:1, 47:12

Aikin, John (1747–1822)
English physician and writer
240:10

Akhmatova, Anna (1889–1966)
Russian poet
281:9

Akins, Zoë (1886–1958)
American poet and dramatist
329:4

Albee, Edward (1928–)
American dramatist
204:1

Alcock, Mary (c.1742–98)
English poet
224:10

Alcott, Louisa May (1832–88)
American novelist
110:12, 201:9, 313:3

Aldiss, Brian (1925–)
British science fiction writer
265:3, 318:1

Alfred the Great (AD 849–99)
King of Wessex from AD 871
307:2

Algren, Nelson (1909–81)
American novelist
266:13

Altman, Robert (1922–)
American film director
267:9

Amis, Kingsley (1922–95)
British novelist and poet
6:2, 65:5, 70:12, 157:9, 165:12, 173:9, 236:5,
236:6, 269:4, 270:11, 318:9, 329:16, 340:12

Amis, Martin (1949–)
British novelist
72:11, 199:2, 230:15, 258:8, 281:2

Annan, Noel (1916–2000)
British historian and writer
158:1, 292:1

Anonymous
9:9, 19:4, 25:10, 28:4, 28:5, 30:8, 39:2, 48:3,
51:1, 66:6, 88:3, 91:9, 93:11, 115:14, 125:12,
132:3, 149:16, 160:5, 160:6, 180:9, 200:8,
236:2, 242:7, 243:12, 243:13, 244:6, 248:1,
249:8, 255:9, 266:4, 298:11, 301:7, 302:4,
331:7, 337:4, 337:5, 342:4

Anouilh, Jean (1910–87)
French dramatist
306:15

Arbuthnot, John (1667–1735)
Scottish physician and pamphleteer
22:9

Aristophanes (c.450–c.385 BC)
Athenian comic dramatist
282:1

Aristotle (384–322 BC)
Greek philosopher
106:6, 129:5, 209:1, 211:10, 287:7, 306:6

Arnold, Matthew (1822–88)
English poet and essayist
3:9, 21:9, 33:6, 37:13, 38:6, 58:13, 119:2,
170:7, 214:9, 214:17, 215:1, 215:2, 245:6,
273:12, 276:2, 282:2, 290:1, 290:5, 307:12,
331:1

Ascham, Roger (1515–68)
English scholar, writer, and courtier
46:7, 337:6

Ashford, Daisy (1881–1972)
British child author
201:18

Asimov, Isaac (1920–92)
Russian-born biochemist and science fiction writer
265:7

Asprin, Robert (1946–)
277:6

Athenaeus (fl. c.200 AD)
Greek grammarian
148:6

Atlas, James (1949–)
American poet and short-story writer
208:9

Attlee, Clement (1883–1967)
British Labour statesman
242:9

Atwood, Margaret (1939–)
Canadian novelist and poet
8:15, 11:9, 14:3, 44:5, 60:4, 82:14, 96:1,
127:4, 167:4, 183:11, 185:13, 186:2, 191:8,
197:13, 218:10, 234:13, 242:15, 243:11,
279:11, 281:6, 288:13, 306:5, 325:2, 335:6,
340:8, 340:9, 341:10

Aubrey, John (1626–97)
English antiquary and biographer
178:6, 239:14, 273:3, 282:10

Auchincloss, Louis (1917–)
American novelist
319:3

Auden, W. H. (1907–73)
British poet
4:7, 8:5, 8:6, 8:9, 9:5, 12:12, 13:11, 24:6,
47:11, 77:1, 77:7, 78:5, 80:6, 80:7, 85:8,
92:12, 98:2, 98:5, 103:2, 111:6, 114:19,
124:11, 124:14, 127:10, 130:9, 139:1, 148:4,
149:7, 157:12, 159:10, 165:7, 181:13, 191:5,
196:8, 196:12, 210:6, 217:10, 218:6, 221:14,
238:8, 245:11, 247:6, 247:9, 250:5, 250:6,
257:2, 262:8, 264:2, 279:4, 279:8, 291:6,

291:11, 291:16, 297:7, 302:9, 302:12, 305:7,
309:10, 312:4, 320:9, 333:5, 342:5

Augustine, St (AD 354–430)
Early Christian theologian
211:13, 239:2, 239:3, 260:2

Aung San Suu Kyi (1945–)
Burmese political leader
223:14

Austen, Cassandra (1772–1845)
63:9

Austen, Jane (1775–1817)
English novelist
12:6, 12:8, 42:4, 42:5, 68:2, 78:13, 89:8,
110:7, 122:1, 123:13, 126:8, 126:9, 158:12,
161:2, 194:9, 200:15, 213:2, 225:1, 257:13,
266:3, 273:8, 289:13, 293:1, 293:2, 306:8,
323:6

Ayckbourn, Alan (1939–)
British dramatist
68:10, 75:8, 98:12

Babel, Isaac (1894–1940)
Russian short-story writer
49:11, 67:5, 235:5, 300:10

Bacon, Francis (1561–1626)
English lawyer, courtier, philosopher, and essayist
21:1, 63:4, 94:8, 106:7, 158:8, 212:2, 212:3,
239:8, 239:9, 239:10, 260:7, 300:12, 326:13

Bagehot, Walter (1826–77)
English economist and essayist
70:5, 70:6, 153:4, 187:6, 192:16, 193:1,
207:14, 297:12, 332:10

Bailey, Richard W. (1939–)
72:10

Bain, Donald (1922–)
British poet
316:6

Bainbridge, Beryl (1933–)
British novelist
231:3, 272:4, 303:11, 341:2

Baldwin, James (1924–87)
American novelist and essayist
340:2

Ball, Hugo (1886–1927)
German writer, actor, and dramatist
161:12

Ballard, J. G. (1930–)
British novelist and short-story writer
77:11, 99:10, 265:5

Balliett, Whitney (1926–)
American writer
62:2

Balzac, Honoré de (1799–1850)
French novelist
15:4, 15:5, 83:12, 110:9

Banks, Iain (1954–)
Scottish novelist
44:9

Barbellion, W. N. P. (1889–1919)
British diarist and biologist
293:13

Barbour, John (c.1320–95)
Scottish poet
104:4

Barker, Pat (1943–)
British novelist
230:13

Barnard, Frederick R.
132:6

Barnes, Julian (1946–)
British novelist and essayist
8:14, 25:4, 100:3, 105:14, 108:5, 140:8,
141:7, 145:14, 160:2, 165:9, 182:2, 198:11,
229:7, 252:12, 262:15, 278:2, 278:3, 295:4,
312:10, 334:11, 335:4, 340:10

Barnes, Thomas (1785–1841)
English journalist and editor
143:10

Barrie, J. M. (1860–1937)
Scottish writer and dramatist
64:10, 141:14, 164:10, 233:1, 301:10

Barstow, Stan (1928–)
British writer and dramatist
12:3

Barthes, Roland (1915–80)
French writer and critic
151:16, 166:5, 166:6, 169:5, 169:7, 242:11,
334:7, 340:1

Bates, H. E. (1905–74)
British novelist and short-story writer
29:2, 276:11

Baudelaire, Charles (1821–67)
French poet and critic
10:1, 76:9, 187:7, 214:14, 278:10, 311:8

Baudrillard, Jean (1929–)
French sociologist and cultural critic
177:11

Bawden, Nina (1924–)
British novelist
208:10

Bayley, John (1925–)
British literary scholar, critic, and writer
236:11

Beaumont, Francis (1584–1616)
English poet and dramatist
75:12

Beaverbrook, Lord (1879–1964)
Canadian-born British newspaper proprietor and Conservative politician
193:8, 194:4

Beckett, Samuel (1906–89)
Irish dramatist, novelist, and poet
2:7, 16:6, 86:5, 146:8, 288:5, 288:6, 329:11

Becon, Thomas (1512–67)
English clergyman
75:10

Bede, The Venerable (AD 673–735)
English historian and scholar
123:3, 123:4

Beecher, Henry Ward (1813–87)
American Congregational minister
270:6

Beerbohm, Max (1872–1956)
British critic, essayist, and caricaturist
1:5, 4:1, 8:3, 59:12, 111:3, 114:7, 148:3,
157:6, 184:4, 275:6, 298:9, 302:1, 302:7,
308:4, 308:14, 310:8, 320:8, 325:10, 328:10

Behan, Brendan (1923–64)
Irish dramatist
62:3, 98:3

Behn, Aphra (1640–89)
English dramatist, poet, and novelist
323:1

Bell, Clive (1881–1964)
British art critic
7:12, 59:4

Bell, Joseph (1837–1911)
Scottish physician
55:7

Bell, Quentin (1910–96)
British artist, critic, and writer
99:15

Belloc, Hilaire (1870–1953)
British writer and politician
4:3, 27:12, 181:7, 247:4, 332:14

Bellow, Saul (1915–)
American novelist
12:4, 26:2, 129:3, 197:7, 202:11, 204:2,
257:7, 296:8

Benchley, Robert (1889–1945)
American humorist
238:6, 302:3, 302:5

Benda, Julien (1867–1956)
French philosopher and novelist
149:4

Benét, Stephen Vincent (1898–1943)
American poet and novelist
24:12, 190:8

Benét, William Rose (1886–1950)
American poet
26:5

Benjamin, Walter (1892–1940)
German literary critic
238:2

Benn, Tony (1925–)
British Labour politician
238:13

Bennett, Alan (1934–)
British dramatist and diarist
8:16, 18:7, 18:9, 25:7, 40:15, 56:5, 86:12,
115:13, 131:2, 146:12, 162:11, 165:11,
172:1, 206:8, 246:1, 267:10, 280:3, 299:8,
299:9, 329:14

Bennett, Andrew (1935–)
British novelist
155:5

Bennett, Arnold (1867–1931)
British novelist
19:7, 59:3, 68:5, 84:14, 93:5, 144:4, 195:11,
241:9, 271:4

Bennett, James Gordon (1800–72)
Scottish-born American editor
193:2

Bentham, Jeremy (1748–1832)
English philosopher
219:13

Bentley, Richard (1662–1742)
English classical scholar
246:5, 307:7

Berlin, Isaiah (1909–97)
Latvian-born British philosopher
236:12

Bernard, Claude (1813–78)
French physiologist
263:3

Betjeman, John (1906–84)
British poet
139:5, 218:11, 319:5

Bettelheim, Bruno (1903–90)
Austrian-born American psychologist
96:2

Bible
31:4, 39:3, 48:8, 104:3, 158:4, 176:1, 200:3,
226:8, 250:11, 255:2, 259:10, 282:8, 307:3,
326:6

Bierce, Ambrose (1842–c.1914)
American writer
32:1, 290:9, 301:12, 320:2

Binchy, Maeve (1940–)
Irish novelist
210:12

Birtwistle, Sue (1945–)
British television producer
2:9

Bishop, Elizabeth (1911–79)
American poet
137:12, 144:13, 159:13, 182:5, 244:2, 299:1,
324:11, 336:10

Blake, Robert (1916–)
British historian
287:5

Blake, William (1757–1827)
English poet
148:9, 178:11, 246:9, 301:2, 307:9

Blishen, Edward (1920–)
British writer
2:5

Bloom, Harold (1930–)
American literary critic
111:8, 204:3, 262:12, 274:9, 280:4, 305:12,
305:13, 318:10, 318:11

Boas, Guy (b. 1896)
262:2

Boileau, Nicolas (1636–1711)
French critic and poet
74:7, 174:10, 181:1, 199:4

Bolingbroke, Henry St John, Lord (1678–1751)
English Tory politician
123:9

Book of Common Prayer, The (1662)
21:3

Boon, John (1916–96)
British publisher
234:6, 258:5

Boorstin, Daniel J. (1914–)
American historian
19:12

Boothby, Frances (fl. 1670)
English dramatist
322:10

Boreman, Thomas (fl. 1730–34)
British writer and publisher
46:9

Borges, Jorge Luis (1899–1986)
Argentinian writer
98:4, 107:4, 122:7, 154:10, 154:11, 165:8,
168:12, 171:8, 171:11, 238:12, 253:17, 309:2

Borges, Leonor Acevedo (1876–1975)
154:8

Borrow, George (1803–81)
English writer
106:4, 168:2

Boston, Lucy M. (1892–1990)
British children's writer
14:1

Buchan, John (1875–1940)
Scottish novelist
47:3, 55:9, 138:1, 210:2, 262:3

Buckingham, George Villiers, 2nd Duke of
(1628–87)
English courtier and writer
209:3, 209:4

Budgell, Eustace (1686–1737)
English writer
156:3

Buffon, Comte de (1707–88)
French naturalist
289:8

Bullett, Gerald (1893–1958)
British poet and novelist
270:12

Bulwer-Lytton, Edward George (1803–73)
British novelist and politician
201:2, 227:6, 263:2, 296:10

Bunting, Basil (1900–85)
British poet
80:11

Bunyan, John (1628–88)
English writer and Nonconformist preacher
21:4, 135:10, 200:13, 231:14

Burgess, Anthony (1917–93)
British novelist and critic
11:7, 54:10, 91:4, 109:6, 139:10, 166:1,
182:1, 202:12, 303:12

Burke, Edmund (1729–97)
Irish-born Whig politician and man of letters
108:8

Burnett, Frances Hodgson (1849–1924)
British-born American novelist
79:1

Burney, Fanny (1752–1840)
English novelist and diarist
89:6, 142:6, 232:4, 314:12

Burns, Robert (1759–96)
Scottish poet
14:12, 36:6, 76:2, 136:2, 184:9, 261:3

Burton, Robert (1577–1640)
English clergyman and scholar
48:11, 101:4, 207:10, 212:4, 251:2

Butler, Samuel (1612–80)
English poet
106:8, 172:11, 252:15, 327:2

Butler, Samuel (1835–1902)
English novelist
21:15, 38:7, 124:7, 203:7, 232:12, 298:6,
328:6, 331:4

Byatt, A. S. (1936–)
British novelist
6:1, 14:4, 65:9, 166:2, 183:9, 211:3, 280:5,
288:11, 306:4

Byron, Lord (1788–1824)
English poet
17:2, 36:7, 51:17, 66:10, 76:7, 81:5, 89:9,
93:3, 96:12, 96:15, 98:14, 104:7, 104:8,
110:8, 125:6, 133:9, 133:11, 147:6, 148:10,
173:4, 173:5, 181:4, 182:8, 212:15, 219:10,
224:6, 232:7, 248:5, 248:6, 253:9, 255:13,
259:5, 259:6, 266:6, 271:2, 271:3, 275:9,
275:12, 276:6, 282:3, 285:5, 301:3, 311:6,
330:4, 330:6, 330:8, 330:9, 332:3, 335:13

Caldwell, Erskine (1903–87)
American novelist and short-story writer
336:17

Callil, Carmen (1938–)
Australian-born publisher
172:3

Callimachus (c.305–c.240 BC)
Hellenistic poet and scholar
26:7

Calverley, C. S. (1831–84)
English writer of light verse
15:1, 225:4

Calvino, Italo (1923–85)
Italian novelist and short-story writer
134:13, 152:3, 152:4, 155:2, 169:9, 169:10,
171:12, 189:4, 221:5, 288:10, 296:7, 305:8

Campbell, Mrs Patrick (1865–1940)
English actress
15:11, 108:10

Campbell, Roy (1901–57)
South African poet
290:12, 308:13, 324:9

Campbell, Thomas (1777–1844)
Scottish poet
203:3, 232:8, 232:10

Camus, Albert (1913–60)
French novelist, dramatist, and essayist
149:9, 165:5, 196:15, 202:4, 291:12

Canetti, Elias (1905–94)
Bulgarian-born writer and novelist
43:14, 155:6

Cardan, Jerome (1501–76)
Italian physician and mathematician
251:1

Carew, Richard (1555–1620)
English poet
277:10

Carew, Thomas (c.1595–1640)
English poet and courtier
73:3

Carey, Henry (c.1687–1743)
English comic dramatist and songwriter
46:8, 253:5

Carey, John (1934–)
British literary scholar, critic, and writer
18:8, 20:6, 38:8, 46:2, 46:6, 89:1, 108:4,
118:8, 121:3, 127:6, 127:11, 128:3, 130:12,
141:5, 155:1, 155:11, 157:10, 167:2, 167:6,
173:11, 206:2, 224:7, 243:8, 279:10, 280:6,
282:7, 286:9, 316:9, 317:3, 319:1, 342:6

Carey, Peter (1943–)
Australian novelist
149:13, 177:12, 186:6, 257:12, 264:9

Carlyle, Jane Welsh (1801–66)
English wife of Thomas Carlyle
37:5, 109:7

Carlyle, Thomas (1795–1881)
Scottish historian and political philosopher
23:1, 23:2, 27:7, 36:9, 87:11, 124:3, 142:12,
147:7, 150:12, 161:3, 173:13, 179:4, 180:2,
230:1, 261:6, 301:5, 330:13

Carpenter, Humphrey (1946–)
British writer and biographer
25:11

Carroll, Lewis (1832–98)
English writer and logician
17:6, 40:3, 67:1, 71:12, 116:8, 132:1, 151:1,
153:6, 159:5, 176:10, 176:12, 177:1, 203:5,
249:2, 327:14

Carter, Angela (1940–92)
British novelist
96:3, 127:3, 130:15, 242:14

Cartland, Barbara (1901–2000)
British romantic novelist
139:13, 235:11, 258:6

Carver, Raymond (1938–88)
American short-story writer and poet
235:12, 277:3

Cather, Willa (1873–1947)
American novelist
102:11

Cato the Elder (234–149 BC)
Roman statesman, orator, and writer
292:3

Catullus (c.84–c.54 BC)
Roman poet
26:8, 38:11, 113:5, 211:11

Cavendish, Margaret (c.1624–74)
English woman of letters
260:11

Caxton, William (c.1421–91)
English printer
45:7, 231:12

Cecil, Lord David (1902–86)
British critic and man of letters
70:13, 262:7

Cecil, William (1520–98)
English courtier and politician
181:2

Celan, Paul (1920–70)
German poet
279:5

Centlivre, Susannah (c.1669–1723)
English actress and dramatist
323:3

Cerf, Bennett (1898–1971)
American humorist
333:8

Cervantes (1547–1616)
Spanish novelist
63:1, 226:10

Chandler, Raymond (1888–1959)
American writer of detective fiction
5:2, 11:4, 22:3, 42:2, 42:3, 55:10, 56:1, 56:2,
61:17, 66:7, 69:16, 77:4, 80:2, 85:5, 107:7,
115:10, 117:3, 154:4, 171:7, 208:6, 210:5,
217:4, 233:8, 244:4, 247:8, 250:3, 265:1,
266:10, 266:11, 298:10, 333:4, 333:9,
333:11, 339:10

Channon, Henry 'Chips' (1897–1958)
American-born British politician and diarist
13:7, 69:11

Chaplin, Charlie (1889–1977)
English film actor and director
267:3

Chapman, George (c.1559–1634)
English scholar, poet, and dramatist
260:6, 310:9

Chapman, John Jay (1862–1933)
American man of letters
21:13

Charles IX (1550–74)
King of France from 1560
108:7

Chateaubriand, François-René (1768–1848)
French writer and diplomat
203:1

Chatto, Andrew
British publisher
225:8

Chaucer, Geoffrey (c.1343–1400)
English poet
31:6, 65:11, 152:7, 200:7, 239:4, 252:14,
260:3, 282:9

Cheever, John (1912–82)
American novelist and short-story writer
82:11, 336:14

Chekhov, Anton (1860–1904)
Russian dramatist and short-story writer
31:13, 40:4, 43:7, 45:11, 67:4, 79:4, 84:13,
102:7, 156:9, 164:6, 195:5, 199:7, 221:9,
221:10, 290:8, 300:4, 338:11

Cherryh, C. J. (1942–)
American science fiction writer
265:12

Chesterfield, Lord (1694–1773)
English writer and politician
261:2, 304:9

Chesterton, G. K. (1874–1936)
British essayist, novelist, and poet
33:2, 41:11, 46:5, 95:3, 95:6, 104:14, 106:10,
114:8, 119:7, 129:2, 131:4, 134:6, 144:3,
178:4, 242:1, 274:13, 286:8, 297:6

Chomsky, Noam (1928–)
American linguistics scholar
117:6, 303:14

Christie, Agatha (1890–1976)
British writer of detective fiction
50:6

Churchill, Charles (1731–64)
English poet
49:1, 101:6

Churchill, Winston (1874–1965)
British Conservative statesman and historian
109:2, 117:4, 126:2, 153:15, 238:3, 283:9

Cicero (106–43 BC)
Roman orator and statesman
267:13

Cixous, Hélène (1937–)
Algerian-born feminist and writer
324:12

Clare, John (1793–1864)
English poet
102:6

Clarke, Arthur C. (1917–)
British science fiction writer
51:7, 265:14

Clarke, Charles Cowden- (1787–1877)
English writer and lecturer
147:3

Clarke, James Stanier (c.1765–1834)
English clergyman
66:1

Claudel, Paul (1868–1955)
French poet, dramatist, and essayist
215:3

Cockburn, Alexander (1941–)
309:12

Cockburn, Claud (1904–81)
British writer and journalist
321:11

Cocteau, Jean (1889–1963)
French dramatist and film director
1:10, 69:15, 72:8, 128:6, 217:3, 217:11

Coghill, Nevill (1899–1980)
British literary scholar
143:6

Coleridge, Samuel Taylor (1772–1834)
English poet, critic, and philosopher
58:8, 73:5, 78:2, 81:6, 92:3, 106:3, 113:1,
113:10, 133:7, 140:4, 176:8, 212:13, 213:3,
213:4, 214:3, 219:12, 240:11, 246:10, 248:4,
251:5, 253:6, 253:7, 268:4, 273:9, 273:11,
289:11, 295:10, 321:4, 321:5, 332:2, 332:4

Colette (1873–1954)
French novelist and writer
302:2

Collins, Billy (1941–)
American poet
229:6

Collins, Wilkie (1824–89)
English novelist
10:5, 201:8

Collins, William (1721–59)
English poet
21:5

Colman, George, the Younger (1762–1836)
English dramatist
112:10

Colvin, Sidney (1845–1927)
British critic and biographer
35:7

Compton-Burnett, Ivy (1884–1969)
British novelist
43:15, 46:1, 50:2, 53:5, 67:8, 80:8, 138:10,
142:1, 189:12, 197:6, 210:3, 210:7, 326:4

Condell, Henry (d. 1627)
see **Heming, John** and **Condell, Henry**

Congreve, William (1670–1729)
English dramatist
129:10, 219:7, 335:9

Connolly, Cyril (1903–74)
British critic and essayist
10:13, 103:9, 114:16, 114:18, 158:2, 168:17,
181:11, 188:11, 204:8, 233:5, 247:7, 256:8,
291:2, 291:3

Conrad, Jessie
British wife of Joseph Conrad
52:7

Farquhar, George (1678–1707)
Irish dramatist
212:8, 327:6

Faulkner, William (1897–1962)
American novelist
13:10, 30:1, 77:5, 138:6, 217:8, 228:5, 302:8,
313:6, 334:1, 334:5

Fenton, James (1949–)
British poet
32:5

Ferber, Edna (1887–1968)
American writer
85:4

Fielding, Henry (1707–54)
English novelist and dramatist
111:10, 194:8, 292:10

Fields, W. C. (1880–1946)
American humorist
130:7

Firbank, Ronald (1886–1926)
British novelist
241:13

Fitzgerald, Edward (1809–83)
English poet and translator
34:4

Fitzgerald, F. Scott (1896–1940)
American novelist
10:10, 24:10, 30:2, 77:2, 80:1, 92:9, 107:6,
114:17, 121:5, 147:9, 149:6, 165:4, 171:6,
185:1, 185:4, 192:8, 199:12, 221:1, 235:7,
242:3, 250:1, 291:5, 305:4, 306:14, 321:10,
333:3, 339:5, 339:8

Fitzgerald, Penelope (1916–2000)
British novelist and biographer
87:1

Fitzgerald, Zelda (1900–47)
American wife of F. Scott Fitzgerald
121:6

Flanagan, Hallie (1890–1969)
223:1

Flaubert, Gustave (1821–80)
French novelist
7:2, 15:6, 16:1, 17:3, 27:9, 42:10, 64:2, 84:2,
97:6, 102:4, 102:5, 107:9, 107:10, 108:1,
150:14, 153:5, 164:3, 214:10, 220:1, 227:8,
241:2, 273:13, 278:7, 289:16, 309:9, 324:2,
332:8, 338:7

Flecker, James Elroy (1884–1915)
British poet
215:4

Fleming, Marjory (1803–11)
English child writer
159:1

Follett, Ken (1949–)
British thriller writer
20:1, 208:11

Foote, Samuel (1720–77)
English actor and dramatist
78:9

Ford, Ford Madox (1873–1939)
British novelist and editor
54:7, 114:11, 146:2, 188:3, 201:15

Ford, Richard (1944–)
American novelist and short-story writer
87:2, 140:1, 341:5

Forster, E. M. (1879–1970)
British novelist and short-story writer
27:14, 30:3, 32:4, 43:11, 53:9, 54:5, 59:13,
65:4, 90:15, 146:5, 164:16, 173:7, 196:3,
209:15, 209:16, 228:4, 268:11

Forster, Margaret (1938–)
British novelist
139:11

Fowler, F. G. (1870–1918)
see **Fowler, H. W.** and **Fowler, F. G.**

Fowler, H. W. (1858–1933)
English lexicographer and grammarian
116:17

Fowler, H. W. (1858–1933) and **Fowler, F. G.**
(1870–1918)
English lexicographers and grammarians
116:11, 237:13

Fowles, John (1932–)
British novelist
70:2

Fox, Charles James (1749–1806)
English Whig politician
237:6

Frame, Janet (1924–)
New Zealand novelist
68:7, 99:7, 134:11

France, Anatole (1844–1924)
French novelist and man of letters
30:6, 61:9, 241:4

Francis, St of Sales (1567–1622)
French bishop of Geneva
150:3, 260:8

Frank, Anne (1929–45)
German-born Jewish diarist
64:13

Franklin, Benjamin (1706–90)
American politician, inventor, and scientist
91:11, 163:8

Franzen, Jonathan (1959-)
American novelist
172:4, 182:3, 248:3, 280:7, 281:7

Fraser, Antonia (1932-)
British biographer and novelist
211:2

Frayling, Christopher (1946-)
British academic and cultural critic
127:7

Frayn, Michael (1933-)
British dramatist and novelist
43:16, 81:3, 82:10, 309:4

Frazer, James George (1854-1941)
Scottish anthropologist
29:6

Frederick the Great (1712-86)
King of Prussia from 1740
314:8

Freeborn, Richard
171:10

Freud, Sigmund (1856-1939)
Austrian psychiatrist
24:9

Frost, Robert (1874-1963)
American poet
50:3, 59:15, 92:10, 103:3, 103:5, 117:9,
137:11, 216:10, 217:1, 217:13, 218:4,
222:11, 253:16, 302:10

Fry, Christopher (1907-)
British dramatist
203:13

Fry, Roger (1866-1934)
British art critic
8:4

Fry, Stephen (1957-)
British comedian, actor, and writer
145:15

Frye, Northrop (1912-91)
Canadian literary critic
56:4, 100:8

Fuentes, Carlos (1928-)
Mexican novelist and writer
65:7

Fuller, Roy (1912-91)
British poet and novelist
218:9

Fuller, Thomas (1608-61)
English preacher and historian
260:9

Fuller, Thomas (1654—1734)
English writer and physician
301:1

Gaisford, Thomas (1779-1855)
English classicist
261:10

Galen (AD 129-99)
Greek physician
150:2

Gallant, Mavis (1922-)
Canadian short-story writer and novelist
25:6, 60:6, 68:8, 91:1, 105:13, 134:14,
154:14, 191:7, 334:9

Galsworthy, John (1867-1933)
British novelist
93:6, 157:3, 329:2

Galton, Ray (1929-) and **Simpson, Alan** (1930-)
British scriptwriters
40:12

García Márquez, Gabriel (1928-)
Colombian novelist
18:3, 98:6, 98:7

Garfield, Leon (1921-96)
British writer for children
48:4

Garnett, Edward (1868-1936)
British writer and publisher's reader
233:4

Garrick, David (1717-79)
English actor-manager
113:4

Garth, Samuel (1661-1719)
English poet and physician
327:5

Gaskell, Elizabeth (1810-65)
English novelist
23:5, 87:5, 182:11, 241:3

Gautier, Théophile (1811-72)
French poet, novelist, and critic
7:1

Gay, John (1685-1732)
English poet and dramatist
75:13, 148:7, 255:6, 295:7

Genet, Jean (1910-86)
French novelist, poet, and dramatist
228:7

George III (1738-1820)
King from 1760
273:7

Gibbon, Edward (1737-94)
English historian
3:4, 89:7, 93:1, 123:11, 123:12, 136:3, 280:8,
323:8

Gibbs, Wolcott (1902-58)
American critic
291:1

Gibran, Khalil (1883–1931)
Syrian writer and painter
216:5

Gibson, William (1948–)
American science fiction writer
266:1

Gide, André (1869–1951)
French novelist and critic
1:14, 97:8, 114:13, 128:7, 156:14, 188:9,
286:3

Gilbert, Sandra M. (1936–)
American literary critic, feminist, and poet
318:7

Gilbert, W. S. (1836–1911)
English writer of comic and satirical verse
67:2, 177:2, 187:8, 328:3

Gill, Brendan (1914–97)
American writer and architect
278:1

Giraudoux, Jean (1882–1944)
French dramatist
316:3

Gissing, George (1857–1903)
English novelist
16:3, 40:5, 76:13, 79:5, 79:6, 97:9, 120:8,
153:10, 161:9, 161:10, 171:4, 179:7, 193:5,
195:9, 241:7, 249:4, 251:8, 256:2, 256:3,
279:1, 283:1, 298:8, 310:7, 311:14, 321:9,
328:8, 331:5, 336:3

Gladstone, W. E. (1809–98)
British Liberal statesman
23:10

Gloucester, William Henry, 1st Duke of
(1743–1805)
31:10

Godden, Rumer (1907–98)
British writer
340:13

Godwin, William (1756–1836)
English philosopher and novelist
46:12

Goethe, Johann Wolfgang von (1749–1832)
German poet, novelist, and dramatist
6:9, 17:1, 37:9, 37:11, 58:11, 122:3, 141:2,
156:7, 184:10, 187:5, 194:13, 205:4, 219:14,
222:7, 240:13, 253:10, 253:11, 307:11, 327:9

Gogarty, Oliver St John (1878–1957)
Irish writer and surgeon
115:9

Golden, Harry (1902–81)
223:6

Golding, William (1911–93)
British novelist
29:1, 86:1, 198:5, 230:10

Goldsmith, Oliver (1728–74)
Anglo-Irish writer, poet, and dramatist
75:14, 150:7

Goldwyn, Sam (1882–1974)
American film producer
204:4, 274:8

Goncourt, Edmond de (1822–96)
French novelist and critic
335:15

Gordimer, Nadine (1923–)
South African novelist and short-story writer
224:1

Gordon, Mary (1949–)
American writer
303:16, 303:17

Gorky, Maxim (1868–1936)
Russian writer and revolutionary
222:10, 300:8, 300:9

Gosse, Edmund (1849–1928)
British poet and man of letters
47:1

Gosse, Emily (1806–57)
English religious writer
133:13

Gowers, Ernest (1880–1966)
British public servant and grammarian
235:9

Goya, Francisco (1746–1828)
Spanish painter
133:6

Granville-Barker, Harley (1877–1946)
British dramatist, critic, theatre director, and actor
78:4

Grass, Günter (1927–)
German novelist, poet, and dramatist
197:2

Graves, Robert (1895–1985)
British poet
5:9, 50:5, 82:8, 118:7, 151:8, 157:5, 173:10,
181:12, 217:5, 218:15, 230:4, 242:5, 253:15,
274:6, 315:7

Gray, Simon (1936–)
British dramatist and diarist
5:8, 206:9

Gray, Thomas (1716–71)
English poet
63:6, 77:14, 118:11, 170:3, 178:8, 338:3

Grayson, Helen
284:8

Green, Henry (1905–73)
British novelist
199:14

Hecht, Ben (1894–1964)
American screenwriter
266:12

Heilbrun, Carolyn G. (1926–)
American academic and writer
60:8

Heine, Heinrich (1797–1856)
German poet
40:2, 61:6, 95:2, 97:3, 156:8

Heinemann, William (1863–1920)
British publisher
4:13

Heller, Joseph (1923–99)
American novelist
169:3, 269:7

Hellman, Lillian (1905–84)
American dramatist
115:7

Hemans, Felicia (1793–1835)
English poet
201:4

Heming, John (1556–1630) and **Condell, Henry**
(d. 1627)
editors of the First Folio
270:2, 272:10

Hemingway, Ernest (1899–1961)
American novelist and short-story writer
29:5, 32:3, 43:12, 72:7, 115:1, 226:5, 256:10,
267:2, 286:1, 291:15, 313:7, 333:2, 334:6

Henley, W. E. (1849–1903)
English poet and dramatist
286:5

Herbert, A. P. (1890–1971)
British writer and humorist
77:6, 183:6

Herbert, George (1593–1633)
English poet and clergyman
63:5, 150:4, 244:12, 311:1, 326:14

Herzen, Alexander (1812–70)
Russian political thinker and writer
7:6, 163:11, 278:11

Heywood, Thomas (c.1574–1641)
English dramatist
125:11

Hiaasen, Carl (1953–)
American crime writer and satirist
106:1, 135:4

Highsmith, Patricia (1921–95)
American writer of detective fiction
210:16, 244:8

Hill, Christopher (1912–)
British historian
35:10

Hill, Geoffrey (1932–)
British poet
219:4

Hill, Reginald (1936–)
British crime writer
2:11

Hill, Susan (1942–)
British novelist and dramatist
11:8, 112:7

Hippocrates (c.460–357 BC)
Greek physician
6:8

Hislop, Ian (1960–)
British satirical journalist
226:2

Hitchcock, Alfred (1899–1980)
British-born film director
75:3

Hitler, Adolf (1889–1945)
German dictator
280:14

Hoban, Russell (1925–)
American writer
48:2

Hobbes, Thomas (1588–1679)
English philosopher
1:2, 163:5, 327:1

Hogben, Lancelot (1895–1975)
British scientist
227:15

Hölderlin, Johann Christian Friedrich (1770–1843)
German lyric poet
78:16

Holland, Henry Fox, Lord (d. 1859)
255:12

Holloway, David (1924–)
128:5

Holmes, Oliver Wendell (1809–94)
American physician, poet, and essayist
71:10, 71:13, 161:8, 203:6, 282:11

Holmes, Oliver Wendell Jr. (1841–1935)
American lawyer
32:2, 49:8

Holub, Miroslav (1923–)
Czech poet
177:13

Homer
Greek poet
200:4, 326:5

Hood, Thomas (1799–1845)
English poet and humorist
214:8

Hope, A. D. (1907–2000)
Australian poet
55:5, 60:9, 95:7, 126:3, 329:15

Hope, Anthony (1863–1933)
British novelist
111:1

Hopkins, Gerard Manley (1844–89)
English poet and priest
78:3, 247:1, 336:2

Horace (65–8 BC)
Roman poet
16:11, 22:7, 31:5, 39:4, 48:9, 62:13, 74:1,
75:9, 78:6, 96:6, 113:6, 116:1, 125:8, 202:17,
207:4, 211:12, 255:3, 260:1, 267:14, 267:15,
288:14, 304:3, 314:2, 326:7, 326:8, 331:9

Horne, Kenneth (1900–69)
see **Murdoch, Richard** and **Horne, Kenneth**

Hough, Graham (1908–)
British literary critic
218:16

Housman, A. E. (1859–1936)
British poet
59:6, 76:11, 82:1, 103:4, 114:9, 132:5,
153:14, 177:7, 216:7, 220:8, 237:14, 263:5,
270:10, 336:7

Howard, Elizabeth Jane (1923–)
British novelist and short-story writer
14:8

Howard, Maureen (1930–)
American writer
243:9

Howell, James (1594?–1666)
Anglo-Welsh man of letters
307:6

Howells, William Dean (1837–1920)
American novelist and critic
74:13, 313:4

Hughes, Robert (1938–)
Australian art historian
152:5, 305:11

Hughes, Shirley (1927–)
British illustrator and writer
3:1, 48:6, 48:7, 132:10, 132:11, 244:9

Hughes, Ted (1930–98)
British poet
15:2, 51:9, 52:3, 72:12, 91:3, 100:13, 205:5

Hughes-Hallett, Lucy (1951–)
British writer and critic
277:8

Hugo, Victor (1802–85)
French poet, novelist, and dramatist
54:13, 245:4

Hull, Josephine (?1886–1957)
American actress
274:4

Hulme, T. E. (1883–1917)
British critic and poet
168:9

Hume, David (1711–76)
Scottish philosopher
63:8, 104:6, 232:2

Humphries, Barry (1934–)
Australian entertainer and writer
51:10, 62:8

Hunt, Leigh (1784–1859)
English poet and essayist
38:1, 52:2, 58:12, 78:17, 104:10, 128:10,
214:5, 248:10, 270:8, 285:8, 314:10, 331:2

Huxley, Aldous (1894–1963)
British novelist and writer
19:13, 28:6, 28:10, 59:8, 114:10, 114:14,
149:10, 262:1, 263:7, 264:3, 296:6

Ibsen, Henrik (1828–1906)
Norwegian dramatist
64:4, 66:4, 74:11, 90:8, 136:10, 156:10,
214:15, 220:6, 220:7, 227:12, 248:12, 290:2,
293:6, 308:2

Inge, Charles (1868–1957)
261:13

Inge, William Ralph (1860–1954)
British writer
168:11

Innes, Hammond (1913–98)
British novelist
189:9, 192:11, 234:9

Ionesco, Eugène (1912–94)
French dramatist
115:3, 245:10, 247:13

Irving, John (1942–)
American novelist
198:1

Iser, Wolfgang (1926–)
German literary theorist
166:8, 166:9

Isherwood, Christopher (1904–86)
British novelist
69:13, 221:12

Ishiguro, Kazuo (1954–)
Japanese-born British novelist
57:4, 222:4, 250:9

Isidore, St (c.560–636)
Spanish archbishop
140:3

Lermontov, Mikhail (1814–41)
Russian novelist and poet
158:3

Lessing, Doris (1919–)
British writer
14:7, 86:10, 96:5, 115:2, 129:4, 191:10,
198:6, 226:3, 228:6, 243:6, 265:11

Leverson, Ada (1865–1936)
British novelist
159:7

Levi, Primo (1919–87)
Italian novelist and poet
67:7

Levin, Bernard (1928–)
British journalist
107:5, 117:13

Levinson, Leonard Louis (1904–)
American writer
2:4

Lévi-Strauss, Claude (1908–)
French social anthropologist
151:15

Lewis, C. S. (1898–1963)
British literary scholar and writer
67:6, 95:8, 107:1, 148:5, 265:4

Lewis, Sinclair (1885–1951)
American novelist
168:13, 227:14

Lewis, Wyndham (1882–1957)
British novelist, painter, and critic
226:6, 285:9

Lichtenberg, Georg Christoph (1742–99)
German scientist and drama critic
9:14, 143:8, 160:13, 271:1, 289:9

Liebling, A. J. (1904–63)
American journalist and critic
40:13

Lincoln, Abraham (1809–65)
American statesman
227:10, 248:11

Lippmann, Walter (1889–1974)
American journalist
145:1

Lively, Penelope (1933–)
British novelist
155:3

Lockhart, John Gibson (1794–1854)
Scottish writer and critic
147:2

Lodge, David (1935–)
British novelist
94:5, 142:2, 169:4, 178:1, 236:4, 250:10,
319:10

Longfellow, Henry Wadsworth (1807–82)
American poet
22:16, 90:5, 153:1

Longford, Lord (1905–2001)
British Labour politician and philanthropist
194:3

Longinus (fl. 1st century AD)
Greek scholar
125:9

Lover, Samuel (1797–1868)
Irish writer
332:7

Lowell, Amy (1874–1925)
American poet
71:1, 227:13, 256:7, 319:9

Lowell, James Russell (1819–91)
American poet
211:6, 308:3, 310:6, 336:1

Lucas, E. V. (1868–1938)
British journalist, essayist, and critic
92:7, 192:4

Luce, Clare Booth (1903–87)
American diplomat, politician, and writer
41:3

Lurie, Alison (1926–)
American novelist and writer
47:14, 96:4, 132:7, 132:8, 303:1

Luther, Martin (1483–1546)
German Protestant theologian
184:6

Lyly, John (c.1554–1606)
English poet and dramatist
96:9, 172:8

Lynton, Michael
British publisher
28:2

Lyotard, Jean-François (1924–98)
French philosopher and literary critic
167:1

Lyttelton, George (1883–1962)
British writer
189:11

Macaulay, Lord (1800–59)
English politician and historian
1:4, 21:7, 22:15, 30:12, 36:5, 37:10, 37:12,
64:1, 78:1, 78:15, 124:1, 134:2, 141:3, 143:1,
182:9, 214:1, 248:7, 248:8, 285:7

Macaulay, Rose (1881–1958)
British novelist
109:4

Marr, Andrew (1959-)
British journalist and broadcaster
235:1

Mars-Jones, Adam (1954-)
British writer
6:3

Martial (AD c.40–c.104)
Spanish-born Latin epigrammatist
19:3, 26:9, 26:10, 39:5, 62:14, 83:1, 89:3,
92:13, 96:7, 108:6, 207:7, 231:11, 255:4,
268:1, 269:13, 335:7

Marvell, Andrew (1621–78)
English poet
307:5

Marx, Groucho (1895–1977)
American film comedian
218:13, 249:7

Maugham, W. Somerset (1874–1965)
British novelist and short-story writer
1:8, 5:7, 11:2, 28:11, 73:8, 93:7, 117:1,
154:3, 196:5, 196:13, 203:11, 208:2, 221:13,
242:2, 247:5, 313:2

Maupassant, Guy de (1850–93)
French novelist and short-story writer
43:4, 108:2, 301:8

Mauriac, François (1885–1970)
French novelist, dramatist, and critic
245:13

Maurois, André (1885–1967)
French biographer, novelist, and essayist
317:11

Mayakovsky, Vladimir (1893–1930)
Russian poet and dramatist
253:13, 279:3

Mayer, Louis B. (1885–1957)
Russian-born American film executive
22:4

Medawar, Peter (1915–87)
British immunologist and writer
264:4

Melbourne, Lord (1779–1848)
British Whig statesman
174:2, 222:8

Mellor, Anne K. (1941-)
275:10

Melville, Herman (1819–91)
American novelist and poet
89:2, 104:9, 120:5, 136:7, 190:6, 201:6,
261:8, 309:6

Mencken, H. L. (1880–1956)
American journalist and literary critic
13:9, 85:7, 124:13, 144:12, 159:14, 171:5,
215:8, 225:9, 313:5

Menuhin, Yehudi (1916–99)
American-born British violinist
281:10

Mercier, Vivian (1919–89)
Irish critic
16:4

Meredith, George (1828–1909)
British novelist and poet
6:5, 297:5

Meredith, Owen (1831–91)
English poet and statesman
296:2

Merrill, James (1926-)
American poet
72:9

Meyer, Ernest L. (1892–1952)
268:8

Middleton, Thomas (c.1580–1627)
English dramatist
140:9

Mill, John Stuart (1806–73)
English philosopher and economist
148:13

Miller, Arthur (1915-)
American dramatist
75:7, 185:8, 194:1, 200:2, 210:4, 277:2,
330:2

Miller, Henry (1891–1980)
American novelist
159:12, 178:5, 271:13

Miller, J. Hillis (1928-)
American literary critic
166:10, 166:11, 318:8

Miller, Jonathan (1934-)
British writer and director
4:12, 163:3, 204:12

Milne, A. A. (1882–1956)
British writer for children
47:2, 47:7

Milne, Christopher (1920–96)
British bookseller
99:14

Milosz, Czeslaw (1911-)
Polish-American poet
228:3

Milton, John (1608–74)
English poet
39:6, 39:7, 48:12, 50:9, 57:12, 74:5, 83:2,
163:6, 176:4, 182:6, 200:11, 200:12, 212:5,
212:6, 227:2, 239:12, 245:1, 252:16, 253:1,
268:2, 272:11, 283:7, 311:2, 311:3

Mitchell, Adrian (1932-)
British poet, novelist, and dramatist
218:8

Murrow, Ed (1908–65)
American broadcaster and journalist
283:11

Musset, Alfred de (1810–57)
French poet and dramatist
207:13

Nabokov, Vladimir (1899–1977)
Russian novelist
8:13, 11:6, 25:2, 41:12, 65:1, 93:13, 105:4,
188:10, 190:2, 202:9, 206:1, 231:9, 236:10,
242:12, 288:8, 309:1, 318:6, 321:13

Naipaul, V. S. (1932–)
Trinidadian writer of Indian descent
190:3, 190:4, 198:9, 231:2

Nashe, Thomas (1567–1601)
English pamphleteer and dramatist
89:4, 270:1

Nemerov, Howard (1920–91)
American poet and novelist
229:2

Neruda, Pablo (1904–73)
Chilean poet
303:3

Newman, John Henry (1801–90)
British theologian and writer
245:3

Newton, Isaac (1642–1727)
English mathematician and physicist
179:11

Newton, Thomas (1704–82)
English bishop of Bristol
260:15

Ngugi wa Thiong'o (1938–)
Kenyan novelist
228:8

Nichols, Peter (1927–)
British dramatist
62:6, 75:1, 206:7, 257:3, 281:1, 287:1, 299:3

Nicolson, Harold (1886–1968)
British diplomat, politician, and writer
88:5, 275:5

Nietzsche, Friedrich (1844–1900)
German philosopher and writer
134:5, 311:13

Nightingale, Florence (1820–1910)
English nurse
174:5

Noonan, Peggy (1950–)
American writer
284:2

O'Brian, Patrick (1914–2000)
British novelist
122:9

O'Brien, Edna (1932–)
Irish novelist and short-story writer
186:10

O'Brien, Flann (1911–66)
Irish novelist and journalist
10:16, 154:9

O'Casey, Sean (1880–1964)
Irish dramatist
245:8, 322:5

O'Connor, Flannery (1925–64)
American novelist and short-story writer
294:7

O'Connor, Frank (1903–66)
Irish novelist and short-story writer
302:14

O'Faolain, Sean (1900–91)
Irish novelist and short-story writer
277:1

Ogilvy, Eliza (1822–1912)
34:7

O'Hara, John (1905–70)
American writer
333:6

Okri, Ben (1959–)
Nigerian novelist and poet
42:1, 224:2

Oliphant, Margaret (1828–97)
Scottish novelist
225:2

Olivier, Laurence (1907–89)
British actor and director
274:7

Omar, Caliph (AD c.581–644)
Muslim caliph
244:11

Ondaatje, Michael (1943–)
Sri Lankan-born Canadian writer
303:7

O'Neill, Eugene (1888–1953)
American dramatist
287:6

O'Rourke, P. J. (1947–)
American humorous writer
265:8, 321:15

Ortega y Gasset, José (1883–1955)
Spanish writer and philosopher
196:2

Orton, Joe (1933–67)
British dramatist
242:10, 329:13

Orwell, George (1903–50)
British novelist, essayist, and social critic
9:2, 40:10, 40:11, 47:5, 51:5, 79:13, 85:6,
90:14, 117:2, 127:8, 144:9, 146:9, 151:10,
151:11, 154:5, 202:5, 222:1, 223:2, 223:3,
233:3, 275:4, 291:10, 294:1, 306:16, 312:3,
322:4, 329:8, 333:7
Osborne, Dorothy (1627–95)
English wife of William Temple
158:9
Osborne, John (1929–94)
British dramatist
5:4, 204:11, 204:13
Ovid (43 BC–AD c.17)
Roman poet
226:9, 252:13, 314:3
Owen, Wilfred (1893–1918)
British poet
1:9, 97:10, 247:3, 259:8, 315:9, 315:10,
315:11
Oz, Amos (1939–)
Israeli writer
28:1, 340:7

Paget, Francis E. (1806–82)
English divine and writer
225:3
Paget, Reginald (1908–90)
British Labour politician
22:5
Paine, Thomas (1737–1809)
English political theorist
36:1, 36:2
Palmer, Vance (1885–1959)
Australian writer and dramatist
220:11
Pargeter, Edith (1913–95)
British crime writer and historical novelist
56:9
Parker, Dorothy (1893–1967)
American critic and humorist
49:10, 115:4, 205:10, 249:9, 258:4, 320:7
Parr, Samuel (1747–1825)
English educator
142:8
Partridge, Frances (1900–)
British writer and diarist
100:2
Pascal, Blaise (1623–62)
French mathematician, physicist, and moralist
16:12, 251:3, 283:6, 289:4

Pater, Walter (1839–94)
English essayist and critic
61:8
Paulin, Tom (1949–)
Northern Irish poet and critic
192:12
Peacham, Henry (c.1576–c.1643)
English writer
160:10
Peacock, Thomas Love (1785–1866)
English novelist and poet
237:7
Pearson, Hesketh (1887–1964)
British actor and biographer
238:5
Pembroke, Henry Herbert, 10th Earl of (1734–94)
142:5
Pepys, Samuel (1633–1703)
English diarist
50:10, 69:1, 92:14, 123:8
Perelman, S. J. (1904–79)
American humorist
82:6, 234:1, 269:2
Perkins, Maxwell (1884–1947)
American editor
82:2
Peter, Laurence J. (1919–)
Canadian writer
41:4
Peters, A. D. (1892–1973)
German-born literary agent
316:11
Petronius (d. AD 65)
Roman writer
126:4
Petroski, Henry (1942–)
American writer and engineer
303:9
Pilger, John (1939–)
Australian journalist
145:7
Pinker, Steven (1954–)
Canadian-born experimental psychologist and writer
68:9, 118:4, 152:6, 330:3
Pinter, Harold (1930–)
British dramatist
91:2, 103:11, 200:1, 206:6, 207:1, 222:3,
267:12, 271:7
Pirandello, Luigi (1867–1936)
Italian dramatist and novelist
43:9, 43:10
Plath, Sylvia (1932–63)
American poet
65:2, 156:15

Plato (429–347 BC)
Greek philosopher
259:4

Pliny the Elder (AD 23–79)
Roman statesman and scholar
207:6

Pliny the Younger (AD c.61–c.112)
Roman senator and writer
113:7, 158:5

Poe, Edgar Allan (1809–49)
American short-story writer and poet
102:1, 253:12

Pohl, Frederik (1919–)
American science fiction writer
265:13

Pollitt, Harry (1890–1960)
British Communist politician
316:5

Pope, Alexander (1688–1744)
English poet
31:7, 48:14, 55:4, 58:1, 61:1, 74:8, 74:9,
77:13, 83:3, 113:9, 176:6, 184:7, 219:8,
227:3, 240:2, 253:3, 253:4, 321:1, 331:11,
332:1, 335:10, 337:8, 337:9

Porter, Cole (1891–1964)
American songwriter
52:8, 274:3

Potter, Dennis (1935–94)
British television dramatist
25:1, 28:9, 65:10, 204:9, 245:15

Potter, Stephen (1900–69)
British humorist and critic
61:15, 285:3

Pound, Ezra (1885–1972)
American poet
19:2, 46:3, 79:8, 88:4, 93:9, 121:4, 168:14,
168:16, 177:8, 187:13, 203:14, 220:10,
231:5, 245:14, 253:14, 331:6, 334:4

Powell, Anthony (1905–2000)
British novelist
27:15, 53:6, 198:2, 340:6

Powell, Enoch (1912–98)
British Conservative politician
38:2, 70:1, 155:4, 262:11

Pratchett, Terry (1948–)
British fantasy novelist
81:2, 100:12, 125:4, 163:1, 266:2, 272:2,
300:2

Preston, Keith (1884–1927)
American poet
193:9

Priestland, Gerald (1927–91)
British writer and journalist
145:8

Priestley, J. B. (1894–1984)
British novelist, dramatist, and critic
247:14

Prince, J. C. (1808–66)
English poet
301:6

Prior, Matthew (1664–1721)
English poet
172:13, 237:2

Pritchett, V. S. (1900–97)
British writer and critic
19:10, 181:14, 210:13, 277:9

Propertius (c.50–after 16 BC)
Roman poet
292:5, 314:1

Proulx, Annie (1935–)
American novelist and short-story writer
304:1

Proust, Marcel (1871–1922)
French novelist
29:11, 40:7, 137:7, 164:15, 173:8, 241:12

Pryce-Jones, Alan (1908–)
British literary critic
157:13

Pullman, Philip (1946–)
British children's writer
29:10, 48:5, 160:4, 211:1, 234:12, 341:4

Pushkin, Alexander (1799–1837)
Russian poet
66:2, 78:14, 163:10, 236:8

Puzo, Mario (1920–99)
American crime novelist
20:2

Pym, Barbara (1913–80)
British novelist
30:7, 76:14, 244:5, 244:7, 299:6

Quarles, Francis (1592–1644)
English poet
128:9, 163:4, 239:11

Quasimodo, Salvatore (1901–68)
Italian poet
218:5

Queensberry, Marquess of (1844–1900)
320:4

Queiroz, Eça de (1846–1900)
Portuguese novelist
258:1

Quennell, Peter (1905–93)
British writer
113:2

Quiller-Couch, Arthur (1863–1944)
English writer and critic
114:6

Quine, W. V. (1908–)
American philosopher
151:14

Quintilian (AD c.35–c.96)
Roman rhetorician
170:2

Raban, Jonathan (1942–)
British writer and critic
155:12, 309:13

Raine, Craig (1944–)
British poet and critic
82:13, 143:7, 204:7

Ralegh, Walter (c.1552–1618)
English explorer and courtier
123:6, 123:7

Raleigh, Walter (1861–1922)
British lecturer and critic
23:11, 237:16

Rankin, Ian (1960–)
Scottish novelist and short-story writer
186:9, 295:5

Ransome, Arthur (1884–1967)
British writer
47:10

Rattigan, Terence (1911–77)
British dramatist
11:5, 99:5

Ratushinskaya, Irina (1954–)
Russian poet and political dissident
280:1

Reade, Charles (1814–84)
English novelist and dramatist
209:11

Reger, Max (1873–1916)
German composer
249:5

Reid, Alastair (1926–)
Scottish writer and poet
118:9

Renard, Jules (1864–1910)
French novelist and dramatist
79:7

Rendell, Ruth (1930–)
British crime writer
56:12, 269:10

Renoir, Jean (1894–1979)
French film director
159:16

Reyner, Edward (1600–68)
English divine
140:10

Rich, Adrienne (1929–)
American poet and critic
152:2, 325:1

Richards, I. A. (1893–1979)
British literary critic
216:1

Richardson, Samuel (1689–1761)
English novelist
83:5, 101:5, 184:8, 254:4

Ridler, Anne (1912–)
British poet
112:4

Rilke, Rainer Maria (1875–1926)
German poet
59:2, 308:9

Rimbaud, Arthur (1854–91)
French poet
16:2, 254:11

Rivarol, Antoine de (1753–1801)
French man of letters
152:15

Roberts, Michèle (1949–)
British poet and dramatist
325:7

Robins, Elizabeth (1862–1952)
American writer
324:5

Robinson, Henry Crabb (1775–1867)
English diarist
17:4, 192:1, 209:7

Robinson, John (1919–83)
British theologian
94:1

Rodin, Auguste (1840–1917)
French sculptor
15:8

Roethke, Theodore (1908–63)
American poet
302:6, 312:1

Rogers, Samuel (1763–1855)
English poet
38:3, 68:3

Ronsard, Pierre de (1524–85)
French poet
3:6

Rooney, Andy (1919–)
American journalist and television writer-producer
267:8

Roosevelt, Franklin D. (1882–1945)
American Democratic statesman
228:1

Roosevelt, Theodore (1858–1919)
American statesman
328:12

Rosen, Michael (1946–)
British writer and performer
48:1

Rosenberg, Harold (1906–78)
62:5, 262:10

Ross, Harold (1892–1951)
American journalist and editor
82:5, 193:12, 316:7

Rossetti, Christina (1830–94)
English poet
102:8

Rossetti, Dante Gabriel (1828–82)
English poet and painter
100:6, 214:16

Rossetti, Frances (1800–86)
99:1

Rossetti, William Michael (1829–1919)
British man of letters
35:4

Roth, Philip (1933–)
American novelist and short-story writer
12:2, 51:8, 101:2, 167:7

Rousseau, Jean-Jacques (1712–78)
French philosopher and novelist
13:3, 27:2

Routh, Martin Joseph (1755–1854)
English classicist
261:9

Rowling, J. K. (1965–)
British writer for children
202:14, 208:12

Rowse, A. L. (1903–97)
British historian
6:7

Runcie, Robert (1921–99)
British Protestant clergyman
25:14

Rushdie, Salman (1947–)
Indian-born British novelist
12:1, 41:8, 41:9, 105:11, 162:14, 169:11,
191:9, 223:12, 228:10, 229:1, 257:11, 258:7,
299:7, 305:10, 335:3

Ruskin, John (1819–1900)
English art and social critic
21:14, 27:10, 49:6, 102:9, 161:5, 174:4,
176:9, 176:11, 184:2, 214:12, 259:1, 270:7,
297:13

Russell, Bertrand (1872–1970)
British philosopher and mathematician
54:9, 93:8, 131:6, 151:12, 157:7, 157:8,
275:8, 314:11

Russell, Lord John (1792–1878)
British Whig statesman
237:8

Sagan, Françoise (1935–)
French novelist
231:10

Salinger, J. D. (1919–)
American novelist and short-story writer
202:6, 242:6, 268:13

Sandburg, Carl (1878–1967)
American poet
151:13, 215:9, 215:10

Santayana, George (1863–1952)
Spanish-born philosopher and critic
169:1, 332:15

Saro-Wiwa, Ken (1941–95)
Nigerian writer
157:1, 229:4, 229:5

Sarraute, Nathalie (1902–)
French novelist
267:1

Sartre, Jean-Paul (1905–80)
French philosopher, novelist, dramatist, and critic
177:10, 230:5, 230:6

Sassoon, Siegfried (1886–1967)
British poet and autobiographer
120:4, 205:7, 259:9, 315:6

Saussure, Ferdinand de (1857–1913)
Swiss linguistics scholar
151:2, 151:3, 151:4, 151:5

Sayers, Dorothy L. (1893–1957)
British writer of detective fiction
55:8, 62:12, 238:4

Schiller, Friedrich von (1759–1805)
German dramatist and poet
6:10, 278:6

Scott, C. P. (1846–1932)
British journalist
144:5

Scott, Paul (1920–78)
British novelist
86:3, 103:13, 105:7, 134:12, 139:3, 185:10,
234:3, 247:11, 268:16, 269:1

Scott, Sir Walter (1771–1832)
Scottish novelist and poet
12:9, 30:5, 30:11, 36:8, 77:15, 83:11, 100:5,
101:9, 114:2, 125:5, 125:7, 180:1, 194:11,
229:8, 254:9, 268:5, 288:1, 335:14

Searle, Ronald (1920–)
see **Willans, Geoffrey** and **Searle, Ronald**

Sedgwick, Ellery (1872–1962)
13:8

Thoreau, Henry David (1817–62)
American writer
136:6, 164:2, 214:11, 241:1, 251:6

Thucydides (c.460–400 BC)
Greek historian
123:1

Thurber, James (1894–1961)
American humorist
4:6, 82:7, 130:6, 130:11, 168:18, 211:8,
258:3

Tibbon, Judah Ibn (1120–90)
Jewish physician and translator
160:7

Tocqueville, Alexis de (1805–59)
French historian and politician
124:5

Tolkien, J. R. R. (1892–1973)
British novelist and literary scholar
17:10, 47:8, 72:2, 95:9, 117:5, 138:11,
154:12, 154:13, 191:1, 202:1, 210:1, 284:6,
299:11

Tolstoy, Leo (1828–1910)
Russian novelist
7:10, 45:12, 143:11, 201:10, 263:4, 311:7,
313:1

Tomalin, Claire (1933–)
British literary critic and biographer
28:3, 206:4, 206:5

Tomalin, Nicholas (1931–1973)
British journalist and writer
145:2

Townsend, Sue (1946–)
British novelist
70:3, 131:3

Traherne, Thomas (c.1637–74)
English mystic
26:12

Treitschke, Heinrich von (1834–96)
German historian and political writer
171:2

Tremain, Rose (1943–)
British novelist and dramatist
135:3

Trevor, William (1928–)
Anglo-Irish novelist and short-story writer
53:4, 57:1, 86:8, 105:10, 243:7, 252:9, 269:5,
277:4, 277:5, 310:1, 335:1

Trillin, Calvin (1935–)
American journalist and writer
98:9, 117:12

Trilling, Lionel (1905–75)
American literary critic
217:7

Trollope, Anthony (1815–82)
English novelist
10:2, 13:5, 17:7, 43:1, 43:2, 79:2, 79:3, 81:7,
84:5, 84:8, 84:9, 87:9, 87:10, 90:3, 90:6,
137:1, 168:3, 193:3, 194:14, 209:8, 209:9,
245:5, 268:6, 268:7, 288:2, 327:13, 332:9,
338:9

Trollope, Frances (1780–1863)
English writer
42:8, 170:5

Trollope, Rose (1820–1917)
English wife of Anthony Trollope
310:2

Tsvetaeva, Marina (1892–1941)
Russian poet
184:13, 220:12, 280:13, 333:1

Tupper, Martin (1810–89)
English writer
27:6

Turgenev, Ivan (1818–83)
Russian novelist
192:3, 278:9

Turow, Scott (1949–)
American novelist and lawyer
57:7, 106:2, 211:4

Twain, Mark (1835–1910)
American novelist and humorist
12:11, 35:8, 49:7, 54:11, 61:13, 81:10, 84:10,
116:12, 116:13, 130:3, 130:4, 148:2, 153:7,
199:9, 199:10, 220:9, 225:7, 232:13, 235:3,
237:15, 284:5, 293:9, 305:2, 308:6, 311:9

Tynan, Kenneth (1927–80)
British theatre critic
8:10, 16:5, 53:8, 55:1, 59:14, 60:2, 62:4,
160:3, 204:10, 275:7, 317:6, 334:8

Tyrrell, Robert Yelverton (1844–1914)
Irish classical scolar
308:8

Tzara, Tristan (1896–1963)
Romanian-born French poet
168:10

Unamuno, Miguel de (1864–1936)
Spanish philosopher and writer
308:7

Updike, John (1932–)
American novelist and short-story writer
2:6, 4:11, 57:2, 60:5, 75:2, 81:1, 82:15, 98:8,
105:12, 139:2, 197:8, 234:10, 269:3, 282:6,
341:3

Usborne, Richard (1910–)
British literary critic
271:12

Valéry, Paul (1871–1945)
French poet, critic, and man of letters
90:12, 168:19, 216:4, 239:1, 288:4, 296:4,
311:11

Vaughan Williams, Ralph (1872–1958)
British composer
208:8

Verlaine, Paul (1844–96)
French poet
168:5, 255:1

Victoria, Queen (1819–1901)
Queen from 1837
70:9, 245:7, 297:3

Vidal, Gore (1925–)
American novelist and critic
44:1, 121:8, 230:11, 234:7, 247:10, 257:4,
268:15, 334:10

Vigel, F. F. (1786–1856)
236:7

Virgil (70–19 BC)
Roman poet
200:5, 207:3, 292:4

Voltaire (1694–1778)
French writer and philosopher
39:8, 71:7, 152:11, 152:12, 156:4, 181:3,
227:4, 246:7, 255:10, 306:7

Vonnegut, Kurt Jr. (1922–)
American novelist and short-story writer
12:5, 265:6

Wain, John (1925–94)
British writer and critic
221:2, 277:7

Wallace, David Foster (1962–)
American writer and academic
341:1

Wallace, DeWitt (1889–1981)
American publisher
279:9

Wallace, Edgar (1875–1932)
British thriller writer
149:5

Wallas, Graham (1858–1932)
British political scientist
177:6

Waller, Edmund (1606–87)
English poet
152:10

Walpole, Horace (1717–97)
English writer and connoisseur
30:10, 45:5, 78:11, 126:7, 163:7, 187:1,
251:4, 273:4, 276:4, 286:4

Walters, Minette (1949–)
British crime novelist
57:3

Walton, Izaak (1593–1683)
English writer
73:4

Warburton, William (1698–1779)
English theologian
255:11

Ward, Mrs Humphry (1851–1920)
English novelist
32:7

Warhol, Andy (1927–87)
American artist
271:11

Warner, Jack (1892–1978)
Canadian-born American film producer
267:4

Warner, Marina (1946–)
British writer and critic
340:14

Warner, Sylvia Townsend (1893–1978)
British writer
13:15, 69:8, 165:6

Waterfield, Edward
52:6

Waterhouse, Keith (1929–)
British novelist and dramatist
145:13

Watson, Colin (1920–83)
British writer of detective fiction
56:6

Waugh, Evelyn (1903–66)
British novelist
2:3, 8:12, 11:3, 13:12, 19:11, 40:9, 53:3,
119:4, 159:11, 159:15, 185:3, 196:7, 196:14,
203:12, 226:7, 231:7, 234:2, 235:8, 238:7,
251:14, 251:16, 252:1, 268:10, 284:9,
290:11, 291:4, 298:4, 316:10, 316:12, 322:6

Webster, John (c.1580–c.1625)
English dramatist
292:9

Weil, Simone (1909–43)
French essayist and philosopher
216:2

Weinreich, Max (1894–1969)
151:17

Welch, Denton (1915–48)
British writer and diarist
69:14, 138:3

Weldon, Fay (1933–)
British novelist and scriptwriter
94:6

Wilson, A. N. (1950–)
British novelist and biographer
189:5

Wilson, Angus (1913–91)
British novelist and short-story writer
138:8, 162:7, 235:10

Wilson, Edmund (1895–1972)
American critic and writer
61:14, 70:11, 88:9

Wilson, Elena (1906–79)
320:10

Wilson, Harriette (1789–1846)
English courtesan
201:1

Wilson, Woodrow (1856–1924)
American statesman
241:8, 283:10

Winchilsea, Anne Finch, Lady (1661–1720)
English poet
323:4

Winder, Robert (1959–)
British writer
94:14

Winterson, Jeanette (1959–)
British novelist and critic
14:6, 145:16, 189:8, 226:4, 269:9

Wither, Percy
127:9

Wittgenstein, Ludwig (1889–1951)
Austrian-born philosopher
151:6, 151:7

Wodehouse, P. G. (1881–1975)
British humorous writer
17:9, 66:5, 102:14, 130:13, 232:15, 256:9,
322:3

Wolfe, Humbert (1886–1940)
British poet
144:7

Wolfe, James (1727–59)
British general
118:10

Wolfe, Thomas (1900–38)
American novelist
251:12

Wolfe, Tom (1931–)
American novelist and cultural commentator
111:7, 189:6, 189:7

Wolitzer, Hilma (1930–)
American novelist and writer for children
281:5

Wollstonecraft, Mary (1759–97)
English feminist
133:5

Wolpert, Lewis (1929–)
British biologist
264:6

Woolf, Virginia (1882–1941)
British novelist, critic, and diarist
3:5, 4:4, 22:1, 24:4, 24:11, 33:3, 34:3, 69:7,
73:11, 85:1, 85:3, 94:11, 105:3, 109:1,
111:14, 111:15, 114:12, 119:8, 120:3, 137:9,
146:3, 149:8, 157:4, 159:9, 162:5, 165:1,
165:2, 175:1, 175:3, 179:8, 181:8, 192:7,
196:1, 231:4, 241:14, 241:18, 249:6, 256:6,
259:7, 268:9, 277:11, 277:12, 278:4, 293:14,
308:10, 312:2, 324:8, 326:1, 329:3, 329:5,
342:3

Woollcott, Alexander (1887–1943)
American writer
205:9

Wordsworth, Dorothy (1771–1855)
English diarist
51:12

Wordsworth, William (1770–1850)
English poet
26:4, 45:6, 101:8, 120:9, 133:8, 134:1, 179:1,
182:7, 187:3, 191:13, 203:2, 212:12, 212:14,
214:2, 219:9, 261:4, 263:1, 280:10, 283:8,
289:10, 292:11

Wotton, Henry (1568–1639)
English poet and diplomat
60:12

Wright, Joseph (1855–1930)
British philologist
79:11

Wright, Judith (1915–2000)
Australian poet
171:9, 218:12

Wu Cheng-en (c.1500–82)
Chinese poet
92:11

Wyatt, Thomas (c.1503–42)
English poet
326:10

Wycherley, William (c.1640–1716)
English dramatist
60:14

Xia Dehong (1931–)
99:12

Yanchiker, Nachum
329:9

Yeats, W. B. (1865–1939)
Irish poet
3:10, 4:2, 8:1, 15:9, 26:6, 40:8, 74:15, 84:15,
92:6, 99:6, 103:1, 103:6, 131:8, 134:9, 137:8,
144:1, 146:4, 146:6, 147:8, 164:8, 165:3,
170:11, 171:1, 171:3, 183:4, 187:12, 203:8,
205:6, 215:11, 218:7, 220:14, 221:11,
227:16, 251:10, 251:11, 256:5, 261:12,
275:3, 285:2, 294:2, 295:11, 296:1, 311:15,
316:1, 316:4, 328:2, 328:4, 328:5, 336:6,
339:3, 342:1, 342:2

Yesenin, Sergei (1895–1925)
Russian poet
156:11

Yonge, Charlotte (1823–1901)
English novelist
124:8, 209:14, 251:9

Young, Edward (1683–1765)
English poet and dramatist
237:3, 255:7, 260:13

Young, G. M. (1882–1959)
British scholar
233:11

Young, Judith (1940–)
22:6

Yourcenar, Marguerite (1903–87)
French novelist
122:5, 197:1

Zamyatin, Yevgeny (1884–1937)
Russian writer
222:9

Zappa, Frank (1940–93)
American rock musician and songwriter
145:6

Zedong, Mao (1893–1976)
Chinese statesman
223:5

Zhdanov, Andrei (1896–1948)
Soviet Politburo official
5:6

Zola, Émile (1840–1902)
French novelist
3:11, 7:5, 15:7, 84:7, 93:4, 137:2, 143:12,
220:5

Keyword Index

adorn touched none that he did not a.	91:13	**agent** author's a. fosters	4:13
adult confronted with a. human beings	108:4	dependent on an a.	5:4
adults too metaphysical for a.	48:2	much of a secret a.	20:4
very few a. take it seriously	48:1	one's a., and one's solicitor	80:8
adventure awfully big a.	64:10	wittily defined an a.	5:1
first is an a.	85:10	**ages** name to resound for a.	179:5
writer of *a.* stories	122:9	stamp and esteem of a.	304:7
adventures a. of his soul	61:9	**agglomerated** a. lucubrations	1:7
imagined a.	137:4	**aggression** war of a.	315:6
adverb beastly a.	117:11	**agree** a. with the book of God	244:11
adverbs a. the salt	116:16	**aid** Apt Alliteration's artful a.	49:1
glad you like a.	116:14	**ail** Oh, what can a. thee	200:17
take out adjectives and a.	199:7	**aimer** first tense of the verb 'a.'	271:2
adversary a. had written a book	255:2	**aims** always serious in my a.	193:2
advertisement one effective a.	114:10	**air** a. of time in them	122:4
advertisements plastered with a.	269:13	roots are a. roots	145:11
advertising language of a.	117:8	**Ajax** When A. strives	253:3
advice adopted all the a.	279:9	**alas** Hugo—a.	128:7
so much good a.	114:20	**alchemist** mind like an a.'s laboratory	118:8
took tea and comfortable a.	147:4	**alcohol** can write on a.	77:4
advocates of a. the best	38:11	replace a. in its power	77:10
aesthetic a. enjoyment is recognition	8:7	**ale** Cakes and a.	28:11
a. professions have to save	250:2	**A-level** A. and undergraduate syllabuses	279:10
a. teaching is the highest	261:11	one of my plays at A.	262:13
bluntly call a. bliss	105:4	**Alexandrine** needless A. ends	253:4
degree of my a. emotion	59:4	**alienation** stimulants of A.	129:3
high a. band	187:8	**alive** a. and here to know it	96:7
only by a. strength	318:11	a. in the fictions I create	269:6
purely a. view	79:14	book is a. and potent	228:6
affairs truth about love a.	24:13	how to stay a. until	296:8
affectation a. that makes so many	188:9	keep part of us a.	166:2
affliction some a. or defect	111:3	most a. when alone	281:2
afflictions a. of Job	21:1	not lifelike; it is a.	70:13
afford position to a. Shakespeare	181:9	not only a., but kicking	317:8
afraid a. of their tongues	269:10	only one a.	257:2
basest of all things is to be a.	334:1	When the characters are a.	43:10
make us a. of the dark	111:15	**aliveness** vibrating with a.	243:6
of whom everyone is a.	12:7	**all** a. in all for prose and verse	277:10
pleasure of feeling a.	111:14	have his a. neglected	246:6
really *a.* of her	36:4	**allegory** a. of reading narrates	242:13
after lived happily ever a.	51:1	any worth is a continual a.	163:9
afternoon summer a.	328:13	**alley** dropped it into the a.	56:1
afterthought as an a.	139:9	**alliteration** Apt A.'s artful aid	49:1
again I can do it a.	86:7	**all-round** wonderful a. man	184:4
Agamemnon lived before A.'s time	22:7	**allusion** a. is a private pleasure	238:15
age afraid of middle a.	295:1	**alone** A. and palely loitering	200:17
a. to write an autobiography	13:12	most alive when a.	281:2
He was not of an a.	272:7	never be a. with a poet	212:11
interested in a subject, say old a.	294:6	they never leave me a.	45:11
know about sex at my a.	272:3	**alphabetical** in the a. catalogues	299:3
language of the a.	170:3	**alps** passages through the A.	112:10
more loathsome a.	186:13	**altar** high a. on the move	278:5
nor devouring a.	226:9	**alter** a. someone else's draft	82:4
novel to another a.	122:9	hard for me to a. punctuation	235:4
Shakespeare . . . is of no a.	273:11	**amateur** it's a. work	31:12
Soul of the A.	272:6	**ambiguity** complexity and a.	211:4
Their a., not Charlemagne's	214:13	**ambition** a. is to lodge a few poems	216:10
You reach an a. when	4:11	sign of a.	85:8

approve men of sense a.   58:1
April bright cold day in A.   202:5
  Whan that A. with his shoures   200:7
apt A. Alliteration's artful aid   49:1
  vigorous and a.   329:2
Arabia movie *Lawrence of A.*   341:3
arcade every seaside amusement a.   86:12
archaeology a. and tomb-robbing   26:3
  a. of the future   265:2
archangel A. a little damaged   51:13
  some sort of a.   98:11
archbishop a. had come to see me   202:12
  A. of Canterbury   230:3
architecture Prose is a.   291:15
arch-rascal that godless a.   314:9
arena literary a.   256:3
argument height of this great a.   245:1
  impression, not an a.   195:10
  polish off an a.   157:13
Ariel A. of poets   121:10
  deal of A.   286:5
Aristotle follow this counsel of A.   337:6
  schools have done with A.   304:5
arithmetic believed that a. is important   32:3
arithmeticians friends are poor a.   30:5
arma *A. virumque cano*   200:5
armaments impression of a. catalogues   57:2
arms A. and the man   28:7
  sing of a. and the man   200:5
army dialect with an a.   151:17
arrangement skilful a. of your words   48:9
arrested To be a. for the power   228:8
ars *A. longa, vita brevis*   6:8
arsenic are indeed like a.   111:10
  tiny doses of a.   329:10
art A. and Religion   7:12
  A. and summer lightning   7:6
  A. a revolt against fate   8:8
  a. being all discrimination   164:13
  Art comes out of a.   8:16
  A. finds her own perfection   7:9
  a. has no importance   11:6
  A. has no other end   164:3
  A. is a human product   7:5
  a. is all life   7:7
  A. is born of humiliation   8:9
  a. is but a vision of reality   8:1
  a. is immoral   7:8
  A. is meant to disturb   263:10
  A. is much older   223:15
  A. is myself; science is ourselves   263:3
  A. is not a *brassière*   8:14
  a. is not a weapon   223:7
  A. is not life   8:5
  A. is parasitic on life   8:10
  A. is significant deformity   8:4
  A. is the imposing of a pattern   8:7
  A. is vice   8:2

A. may be served by morality   183:8
a. tends to become a game   196:2
a. that *makes* life   7:13
attempt to popularize a.   245:14
can't produce a. by trying   85:5
changeless work of a.   103:1
combines scholarship and a.   124:12
Dying Is an a.   65:2
element in modern a.   203:9
excellence of every a.   6:11
far too little a.   333:11
half a trade and half an a.   168:11
haste is the enemy of a.   145:16
he or she makes a work of a.   278:6
His greatness lay in his a.   231:6
history of a.   203:7
If a. does not enlarge   7:3
In a. the best   6:9
in Oxford made An a.   212:7
in the vein of a.   179:3
irrelevant to a.   97:6
last and greatest a.   77:13
Life imitates A.   164:9
Life is short, the a. long   6:8
make art out of a.   9:7
makes a work of a.   6:10
milieu in which a. is impossible   46:3
Minister that meddles with a.   222:8
More matter with less a.   289:2
next to Nature, A.   164:1
of the intellect upon a.   59:16
Once people start on all this A.   183:6
only a. and lies   14:6
only interested in a.   266:9
proper objects of the poet's a.   263:1
responsibility is to his a.   334:5
rest is the madness of a.   332:13
Romanticism is to say modern a.   187:7
sake of my a.   2:11
shut yourself up in A.   7:2
spoiled child of a.   209:13
supreme master of a.   134:8
technique of a.   7:14
there is a point to a.   165:12
This is the a. of today   188:7
To make a trade of a.   79:6
too little of his a.   164:11
want to produce a work of a.   251:16
way of a. and salvation   311:16
What has Oscar in common with A.   320:3
work of a. is to perfection   228:7
Works of a. are of an infinite   59:2
artful Apt alliteration's a. aid   49:1
article enjoyed your a.   60:7
  Excellent a., very excellent   193:1
  snuffed out by an a.   248:6
articulate less a. its expression   103:11
artificial poems are a.   288:7

banal takes the b. around us   105:9
banality manufacture of b.   267:1
bandage wound, not the b.   245:15
banker b. has no business whatever   88:3
bankruptcy intellectual b.   203:6
bar b. exercises are good   70:2
   When I have crossed the b.   64:5
Barabbas Now B. was a publisher   232:10
barbarism slow, funereal b.   24:2
barbarisms clear it from colloquial b.   116:4
barbarous b. phrase hath often   113:8
   invention of a b. age   252:16
barbarousness confess mine own b.   14:11
barber going to the tailor or b.   82:15
barbers b. and riding masters   145:1
bard b. in an oral culture   80:7
   Poor starving b.   78:7
bards worst of b. confessed   38:11
barkeeper feel like a b.   12:11
barmie b. noddle's working   136:2
barometer may be used as the b.   217:7
barrel just polished off a b.   164:6
   rhyme is a b.   253:13
barren b. superfluity of words   327:5
   Close up these b. leaves   261:4
   upon very b. rock   175:1
barrenness In b., at any rate   336:7
barricade kick at the b.   198:8
Barsetshire whole of B.   310:8
Basingstoke like B.   328:3
bath rather lie in a hot b.   217:2
   slipper b. of irony   172:1
   to sit in a hot b.   297:2
bathos without a sense of b.   205:8
battle sent it into b.   283:11
be poem should not mean But b.   215:14
beadle b. on boxin' day   214:6
beadroll On Fame's eternal b.   45:8
beanbag dullest b. of a heart   284:2
bear or a polar b.   196:8
   wake a sleeping b.   92:1
bearer b. of light   281:9
bears like two b. in one den   300:8
   tap crude rhythms for b.   150:14
beat he b. them all   276:6
Beatles B.' first LP   271:10
beauties concealed b. of a writer   58:2
beautiful b. and ineffectual angel   276:2
   important or profoundly b.   289:12
   It is b.   296:11
   poet produces something b.   216:2
   presence of b. objects   61:8
   two most b. words   328:13
beauty banner is b.   41:12
   b. of inflections   177:5
   B. plus pity   8:13
   Keats had B.   89:1
   liked b. of style   290:7

loved the principle of b.   246:11
more b. in the works   110:4
What is b.   135:6
Beckett Samuel B. one   44:1
become what man can b.   115:8
bed combination of b. and book   243:5
   hero keeps getting in b. with women   316:7
   in b. with a beautiful young girl   250:4
   I write in b.   303:8
   like the great b. of Ware   58:9
   me he mostly sent to b.   285:1
   no need to get out of b.   65:5
   recognize a double b.   271:12
bedevilled In conversation I am b.   68:7
Bedford tinker out of B.   35:9
bedlam B. vision   133:11
   drew nourishment from B.   317:6
bee brisk as a b. in conversation   335:11
beef roast b. of old England   108:8
beer helping himself to a b.   208:11
bees you b. make honey   207:3
Beethoven find out about a B. symphony   94:2
before not been said b.   202:16
begetter To the onlie b.   65:14
beggar b. would enfold himself   237:11
beggary they knew b.   78:15
begged living HOMER b. his bread   125:12
begin B. at the beginning   17:6
   b. with the beginning   17:2
   To b. at the beginning   202:8
beginning art of b.   90:5
   began *again* at the b.   180:2
   b., a middle, and an end   287:7
   b., a muddle, and an end   288:9
   b., the middle   138:4
   b. of a book   17:11
   Each venture Is a new b.   103:7
   end badly from the b.   90:9
   good b. means a good book   17:14
   In my b. is my end   202:3
   In the b.   200:3
   no difficulty in b.   17:8
beginnings B. are always troublesome   17:5
begot when they b. me   200:14
behave how my people would b.   55:9
behaviour Bad b. is more interesting   295:1
behind it will be b. me   249:5
being come into b. as a response   305:13
   worried into b.   137:11
belief b. in his own powers   258:8
beliefs damages your deepest b.   222:1
   dependent on strong b.   321:17
believe If you b. everything   243:13
   to b. and take for granted   239:8
bell For whom the b. tolls   29:5
   for whom the b. tolls   63:3
belle *j'étais b.*   3:6
belle-litter sort of b.   162:10

bruise you b. and blue 326:1
novels beat me—b. and blue 325:10
worried by the b. dog 101:9
blackbird b. whistling 177:5
bladder centre of an immense b. 141:13
humour is like a jester's b. 321:14
Blake in the path of B. 298:1
blame all the b. on the actor 175:6
Praise or b. 58:10
bland mellifluously b. 173:5
tend to be somewhat b. 48:7
blank awful and dreary b. 37:5
b., implacable sheet 86:3
B. cheques of intellectual 203:6
b. verse has suffered 179:9
dull hateful b. 122:2
face to face with a b. page 53:2
I notice a sort of b. 186:2
written much b. verse 282:3
blankness that cold b. 336:8
blank-verse Prose poets like b. 253:9
blasted b. with excess of light 178:8
Blazac even B. is too romantic 181:13
blaze blow up into a faint b. 83:5
orbit where you will b. 1:9
round table was in a b. 180:4
blazoned b. days 138:2
Bleak House first number of B. 17:4
bleaknesses there are superior b. 16:7
bleeding b. in shark-infested waters 248:3
pageant of his b. heart 37:13
blessed b. fool 281:10
blessing boon and a b. to men 301:6
either the greatest b. 301:10
blest B. pair of Sirens 212:5
blight b. on all human achievement 300:5
blind accompany my being b. 50:10
b. man feeling the face 212:13
blindness b. made me take up 253:17
bliss bluntly call aesthetic b. 105:4
blithe B. spirit 28:8
blitz fire-ceremony of London's b. 316:9
block suffer from writer's b. 337:1
blockhead bookful b. 240:2
No man but a b. ever wrote 78:10
blockishness b. and general thickness 310:3
blocks fight these painful b. 336:15
things that look like b. 242:3
to hew b. with a razor 227:3
blondes no innocent b. 45:3
blood artist of the b. royal 313:5
b. of the blood 276:7
b. to be curdled 127:2
can draw b. 228:9
He is all b., dirt 205:6
I know the colour of that b. 63:12
pay to make bad b. 5:1

To freeze the b. 292:11
trading on the b. 13:4
bloodless b. substitute for life 164:5
bloodstream didn't infect his b. 38:8
entered my literary b. 15:3
entering the popular b. 127:7
bloody It's a b. trade 81:11
bloom give B. a rest 43:13
bloomed sprouted and b. 120:7
Bloomsbury B. was really 100:2
blossom hundred flowers b. 223:5
blot art to b. 77:13
b. pinched between doubled paper 174:4
scarce received from him a b. 272:10
blots topography of its b. 27:4
blotted Would he had b. a thousand 272:12
blow do not mind a b. 120:10
To receive a bitter b. 244:5
blowing forever b. a horn 169:13
blue B. remembered hills 28:9
blueprinting it's b. 267:9
blue-stocking horse-faced b. 87:6
blunt b.-tongued Anglo-Saxons 154:10
blur becomes a permanent b. 312:5
small vibrant b. 341:3
blurbs have to write b. about them 233:9
boar writes as a b. does piss 270:13
boats b. against the current 92:9
bodies b. were being discovered 57:1
write through their b. 324:12
body as the b. and the soul 176:3
b., of thought 150:12
b. heat of a healthy Anglican 121:9
b. like a slag heap 46:6
b. of Benjamin Franklin 91:11
only the left side of your b. 341:1
tragedy which was his b. 224:7
we truly have none in the b. 271:5
what exercise is to the b. 240:1
body-bags responsible for 81 b. 57:8
boil stand out like a b. 115:6
Boileau B. was a little river 289:16
boiling novel 'a-b. up' 139:11
bold He b. as a hawk 258:3
bondage modern b. of rhyming 253:1
bone b. of the bone 276:7
b. stuck in your throat 40:4
transparent like some white b. 278:4
bones for his honoured b. 272:11
he that moves my b. 91:8
Plot is like the b. 210:3
preys upon the marrow of our b. 168:8
bon-mots plucking b. from their places 237:5
booby b.-trapped idealist 259:9
book after my first b. was published 233:1
as kill a good b. 39:6
b., who runs may read 21:6
b. a devil's chaplain 192:2

b. of the hour   27:10
b. remain forever   28:1
B. say: she did this because   165:9
B. that you may carry   27:3
B. think for me   27:5
b. which no one can read   232:14
borrowers of b.   30:4
but his b. were read   247:4
chalky banks of b.   163:3
collection of b.   261:6
creatures of b.   128:10
darkness and the b.   165:8
Deep-versed in b. and shallow   239:12
Dictators are as scared of b.   223:6
don't need b. to make films   267:11
do *you* read b. through   240:6
fate of b.   9:11
gained most by those b.   260:9
God has written all the b.   21:15
hide these b.   224:9
ideas b. have presented to us   164:15
If my b. had been any worse   42:2
I hate b.   27:2
I wish you read b.   242:3
made the b. and he died   13:10
multitude of b.   184:6
needed not the spectacles of b.   273:1
Never lend b.   30:6
Of making many b.   259:10
On b. for to rede I me delyte   239:4
one of their b. in their room   269:8
only b. that influence us   228:4
Only fools lend b.   30:8
parents buy the b.   46:11
people who loved and respected b.   163:1
proper study of mankind is b.   262:1
read all the b. there are   241:5
read any good b. lately   242:4
Read b., repeat quotations   115:12
read children's b.   46:12
Readers and listeners like my b.   255:4
reading of good b.   26:11
Reading other people's b.   241:11
Real b. should be   137:7
real war will never get in the b.   315:5
skim the cream of others' b.   237:5
Some b. are to be tasted   239:10
some very singular b.   4:4
spoke to me of my b.   1:11
Their b. like their clothes   47:8
They lard their lean b.   207:10
thumb each other's b.   161:5
walls of b. will deaden   162:6
Wherever b. will be burned   40:2
why should the Americans write b.   170:4
with b. as it is with men   227:4
world of b. was only distantly   165:11
write b. like Nicholas Nickleby   297:11

write only those b.   184:13
You remember b.   262:9
bookseller b. should guide the public   270:3
he once shot a b.   232:8
Your second-hand b.   270:8
booksellers b. deal in commodities   232:6
Down B.' Row   269:13
even b. got wind of it   270:12
nor even b. have put up   113:6
bookshops fly away To the b.   231:11
bookstore so weak as in the b.   270:6
bookstores back shelves of b.   81:1
bookworms scribbling b.   148:6
booky commonly held to be 'b.'   162:4
boon b. and a blessing to men   301:6
bootboy b. at Claridges   146:3
boot-licking helpless b.   25:1
boots cobbler looks at a pair of b.   78:14
novel is not a pair of b.   7:1
pair of b. is in every sense   236:9
booze shouldn't fool with b.   77:5
bore b. him in the right way   247:5
Description is always a b.   66:12
metaphor that doesn't become a b.   107:2
bored b. me hellishly to write   84:6
boredom Escaping what? B.   185:11
very fury of b.   331:6
Borges read B. in translation   318:8
boring most b. of luncheon parties   334:2
most *b.* poem   285:4
show you a b. book   44:5
born B. in a cellar   78:9
b. old and wise   4:10
b. out of my due time   227:11
where I was b.   202:6
borrowed begged, b., or stolen   89:2
borrowers *b. of books*   30:4
bosh inept title to heartbreaking b.   298:7
bosom every b. returns an echo   119:1
Boswell B. was one of the smallest   22:15
Boswelliana *Lues B.*   1:4
botanize b. in the swamp   119:7
bother not to b. about poetry   217:3
bottle cork out of the b.   77:11
bottles in tight-necked b.   277:8
bottom I now sit down on my b.   159:1
bough golden b.   29:6
boundaries b. of your talent   231:10
bourgeois b. climb up on them   27:9
Il faut épater le b.   278:10
more indignant I make the b.   278:7
What a little b.   317:9
bourne our b. of time and place   64:5
Bovary *Madame B., c'est moi*   108:1
My poor B. is suffering   42:10
poisoning of B.   102:5
bow always made an awkward b.   156:5
Bowdler B.'s is the most extraordinary   40:3

bower b. we shrined to Tennyson — 97:11
bow-wow Big B. strain — 12:9
  were it not for his b. way — 142:5
box play wasn't written for this b. — 2:7
boxes words and pictures in b. — 48:6
boxing beadle on b. day — 214:6
boy b. bushranger — 9:1
  b. stood on the burning deck — 201:4
  if I had made her a b. — 93:13
  wardrobe lady and the tea b. — 267:6
  When I was a little b. — 334:12
Boz B.'s little Nelly — 102:2
bracket last date slides into the b. — 65:8
Bradley he hadn't read his B. — 262:2
brain b. has been mulched — 4:12
  b. has stopped working — 243:8
  gleaned my teeming b. — 63:10
  immensely abundant b. — 141:13
  little b. attic stocked — 161:11
  petrifactions of a plodding b. — 148:10
  there is a female b. — 87:8
brained Thou large-b. woman — 259:2
brains he had b. to scatter — 275:6
brandy hero must drink b. — 76:1
  to literature what b. is — 143:10
brassière Art is not a b. — 8:14
brat perfectly stunning b. book — 47:10
brave B. new world — 28:10
  Many b. men lived before — 22:7
brazen her world is b. — 191:11
bread b.-sauce of the happy ending — 90:11
  depend for b. on the moods — 80:7
  lives not upon b. — 128:11
breakfast bad review ruin your b. — 250:8
  Poetry before b. — 218:9
  that sits down to b. — 218:7
breaks He who b. this tablet — 39:2
breath b. and the circulation — 211:3
  call the fleeting b. — 63:6
  last b. he drew in — 63:15
  time to catch my b. — 337:1
breathe So long as men can b. — 227:1
Brecht B. did nothing for Communism — 228:7
  collected works of B. — 31:3
breeding b.-place of character — 162:3
brevis *Ars longa, vita b.* — 6:8
brevity B. is the sister — 31:13
  conduces to b. — 32:2
  Its body b. — 321:5
bribe cannot hope to b. or twist — 144:7
Brideshead you liked *B.* — 19:11
bridge b. built from the known — 263:9
brief strive to be b. — 31:5
bright one b. book of life — 196:10
Brighton Rock *B.* I began — 119:5
brilliant shower of b. conceits — 53:7
  three uniquely b. — 322:6
brisk b. as a bee in conversation — 335:11

bristles my skin b. so — 103:4
British so ridiculous as the B. public — 182:9
brochures b. from theatres — 287:1
Brontë shown by Charlotte B.'s novels — 298:8
bronze more lasting than b. — 96:6
brooks books in the running b. — 191:12
broom writing novels with her b. — 324:9
brothel intellectual b. from which — 143:11
  male b. in Norway — 87:1
brother imaginary b. or sister — 100:1
  sad bad glad mad b.'s name — 313:10
brothers just like b. — 286:1
brown black despair succeeds b. study — 335:9
  brownest of b. studies — 72:2
Browning B. made the verses — 249:3
  elucidating B.'s translation — 308:8
  God and Robert B. knew — 176:7
  Meredith's a prose B. — 35:5
  Mrs B. guard a careful silence — 71:1
  summon up the image of B. — 297:1
  Wordsworth, Tennyson and B. — 187:6
bruise language as physical as a b. — 128:3
brush B. up your Shakespeare — 274:3
  so fine a b. — 12:8
brushers b. of noblemen's clothes — 60:12
brutal All Russians are b. — 46:1
  heart's grown b. — 134:9
brutality b. and sadistic conduct — 22:5
brute scholar—but a b. — 92:1
brutish most b. of all the arts — 25:1
bubble b. is blown — 193:6
  men who b. at the mouth — 250:1
Buddha Neither Christ nor B. — 339:3
buds darling b. of May — 29:2
build Birds b.—but not I build — 336:2
bull bullslinging, and b.— — 121:6
bullet pen, as well as a silver b. — 228:9
bullfighting b., bullslinging — 121:6
bullied b. into a certain philosophy — 330:7
bum He was a b. poet — 157:5
bunny just b. eat bunny — 48:3
bunting Baby, baby b. — 328:8
burden do not b. themselves too much — 209:5
burdened B. with the complexity — 216:13
burglar b. at the subject's keyhole — 25:9
buried all b. here — 32:9
  b. life — 127:9
burlesque b., when you make fun of — 321:15
burn Does genius b. — 110:12
  thoughts b. within him — 175:5
  We should b. all libraries — 161:12
burned what should be b. — 23:7
  Wherever books will be b. — 40:2
burning boy stood on the b. deck — 201:4
burns send a man like Robbie B. — 293:12
burnt b. the manuscript — 180:2
  got myself b. or hanged — 130:5
  had it b. in Dublin — 244:1

burst words, or I shall b.	327:6
bury my talents I b.	246:9
bus missing the b.	247:11
bushes B. and low tamarisks	292:4
like different b. trimmed	151:14
bushranger boy b.	9:1
businesslike cheerful and b.	119:8
but If and Perhaps and B.	88:6
butcher proposed to the b.	81:7
seen by every b.	232:4
yours is a b.'s trade	81:11
butler sound like a b.	117:12
track one b. down	87:1
butter B. and eggs	15:1
softer than b.	326:6
butterfly grub more than the b.	143:4
these b. shades	231:4
buy b. it first	270:2
B. me before good sense insists	243:3
parents b. the books	46:11
bymatter as if it had been a b.	158:8
Byron better educated than a B.	36:9
B.!—he would be all forgotten	4:1
B. was accused of incest	333:8
Daring, since B. died	33:6
for the love of Lord B.	173:2
metre of B.'s *Don Juan*	253:11
movement needs a B.	316:5
No, I'm not B.	158:3
too long near Lord B.	335:12
cabinet c.-council to the nursery	295:7
cactus kind of human c.	127:11
cadence *dans les vers une juste c.*	174:10
cake as a child looks at a c.	241:3
picked out of a c.	237:16
cakes C. and ale	28:11
Caliban C. seeing his own face	187:11
Caligula parallel with that of C.	295:9
call C. me Ishmael	201:6
calligrapher fine c. when he made	28:3
Camelot somewhere north of C.	100:12
camera c. as a present	337:2
I am a c.	221:12
camerado C., this is no book	10:4
cammin *Nel mezzo del c.*	200:6
camouflaged c. myself by display	269:12
Canada C. lacks its own language	170:8
standard literature of C.	170:6
Canadian If you were a C. writer	335:6
cancels Death c. everything	63:14
cancer asking someone with c.	86:9
candle burn the c. at one end	175:2
c. in Lapland	246:10
farthing c. to the sun	260:13
have a c. burning by him	160:10
candlelight exhibited by c.	113:1

cannibalism Higher C.	24:8
cannibalizing c. a picturesque array	155:1
canon believe in the established c.	318:8
If we read the Western C.	280:4
Shakespeare is the c.	274:9
western c.	318:10
canonical survival or c. inclusion	305:12
canonization sort of natural c.	63:14
cant C.! Cant! Cant	96:13
c. of criticism	58:5
canvas getting everyone under c.	226:6
capability Negative C.	148:11
capable c. of all things	26:12
capacity my c. for writing	85:3
Cape Horn passage round C.	84:16
Capitol ruins of the C.	136:3
captain c. of twenty-four soldiers	301:7
captivity will not breed in c.	312:3
car can't drive the c.	62:4
carcase c. for the critics	83:9
card like a literary c. trick	56:11
care neither know nor c.	116:17
career Every writing c. starts	186:1
point of choosing a c.	279:10
careerism c. and vanity	167:7
careful c. felicity	126:4
caricature *character* is a c.	43:12
caricatures Parodies and c.	59:8
Carlyle C. and Mrs Carlyle marry	38:7
on the shoulders of C.	256:4
carpenter You may scold a c.	58:4
carpet figure in the c.	177:3
unchanging pattern of the c.	2:1
carrier down from the c.'s cart	202:10
carrion Fielding could stoop on c.	297:9
Carthage assault on C.	102:5
Carthaginian about C. literature	122:7
cash level of c. takings	20:3
sending the author some small c.	181:11
(vain thought) for needfu' c.	184:9
casket secret c. of his genius	54:5
casting skilful at c. them	44:1
castles told of giants and c.	46:10
casualties stories uncover the c.	198:1
casualty Truth is the first c.	315:2
cat c. poetry	118:9
If a c. could write novels	282:7
like a c. among tigers	324:6
catalogue great circle of the C.	161:10
more delightful than a c.	241:4
read a time-table or a c.	242:2
catalogues in the alphabetical c.	299:3
catalyst became a c.	5:3
catamite in bed with my c.	202:12
cataract c. of drivel	55:7
Catch-22 as good as C.	269:7
catchwords principally by c.	128:11
catechist something of the Shorter-C.	286:5

Coleridge C. received the Person | 336:12
C. was a drug addict | 333:8
colleagues vilifying one's c. | 255:10
collectors c. of useless information | 105:10
college rather distinguished c. | 234:12
collision c. of two different frames | 130:14
colon know what a c. is | 236:1
one man's c. | 235:3
colonel like being a Kentucky c. | 262:8
colonial nature of a c. language | 155:8
Colonus Singer of sweet C. | 282:2
colossus genius that could cut a C. | 178:10
colour I know the c. of that blood | 63:12
spread on the screen in c. | 103:3
with a bad c. | 119:3
colourless C. green ideas | 117:6
combinations all possible c. | 134:13
comedies All c. are ended by | 89:9
c. of Ben Jonson | 143:6
Jonson, especially his c. | 143:5
comedy c. and drama to exist together | 75:8
C. is an imitation | 129:6
C. is felt to be artificial | 130:12
C. is the noblest form | 130:9
C. lies | 306:12
C. naturally wears itself | 129:12
C. represents the worse | 129:5
c. to those that think | 163:7
Musical c. without music | 322:3
played with c. | 273:10
represented a c. | 295:2
To read a good c. | 130:1
comet always a mad c. | 1:9
comfort c. a Dictionary is | 71:12
In Memoriam is my c. | 245:7
they never knew c. | 78:15
comfortable All clean and c. | 332:5
c., but not splendid | 79:2
find a c. fit | 121:2
comic business of a c. poet | 129:10
c. in the traditional sense | 189:10
c. side of my mind | 197:3
essential for c. writers | 131:3
largely for c. effect | 130:16
comma another man's c. | 235:3
intrusive c. on p. 4 | 82:1
part of the title is the c. | 299:7
unlimited time is c.-hunting | 235:2
commas C. in the New Yorker | 236:3
without dashes and inverted c. | 235:6
commemorate c. the dead | 24:2
commend call the surgeon to c. | 81:8
comment C. is free, but facts | 144:5
C. is free but facts | 145:4
commentators As learned c. view | 125:13
c. each dark passage shun | 260:13
great fault of c. | 260:15

commercial c. writing for the magazines | 80:1
concept of c. success | 81:3
committee written by a c. | 22:4
common c. notions in an individual way | 202:17
completely c. fellow | 236:8
concur with the c. reader | 58:7
I hate the c. herd | 267:15
no c. person | 275:9
speak as the c. people do | 337:6
commonplace his c. book be full | 69:2
loop on a c. | 203:11
ordinary c. things | 12:9
What a c. genius | 120:2
commonplaces sudden arrangement of c. | 168:9
Common Prayer eclipse of the Book of C. | 131:2
commons in the House of C. | 328:1
common sense c. and observation | 202:18
little more c. | 99:1
which c. considers | 196:5
commonsense make sense to c. people | 75:7
communicate birds were trying to c. | 77:7
c. before it is understood | 216:3
c. their ideas | 3:5
communication c. Of the dead | 64:12
communications best of the c. | 11:2
communion act of holy c. | 94:1
whistling at Holy C. | 206:7
communism Brecht did nothing for C. | 228:7
companion old and agreeable c. | 89:7
company best c. in the world | 130:1
entire c. of people | 90:10
never seen in each other's c. | 319:10
nice to have c. | 53:2
sick of his own c. | 281:1
That is not good c. | 68:2
very good c. | 273:3
compassion all-embracing c. | 195:11
compassionate more c. | 299:4
compendium c. of the world | 293:7
compensations Hell with c. | 320:10
competition c., and mutual envy | 1:2
competitive Literature is a c. sport | 170:1
complete library should try to be c. | 161:8
completed c. in six weeks | 77:8
completeness Amputated kind of c. | 52:3
complexity c. and ambiguity | 211:4
complicated word, in a word, is c. | 330:3
complications reflect the fullest c. | 105:14
compliment get along without the c. | 308:6
compliments one of the highest c. | 228:8
composed poet himself would have c. | 308:2
composition regular and orderly c. | 94:10
compositions wildness of those c. | 94:9
compost like a c. heap | 262:15
compulsion c. to write poems | 336:16
computer c. to the last Luddite | 303:7
convert to c. | 304:2

critic (*cont.*)
true c. ought to dwell	58:2
unconscious of the c.	60:1

critical composing his work is c. labour 339:6
'c.' or review press	193:7
c. sense	139:12
c. theory would not be recognized	167:6
low-rent precincts of c. esteem	57:7
marks of Papa's c. indignation	81:4
written a more c. book	258:7

critic-dame c., who at her table sits 323:2

criticism appeal from c. to nature 273:5
at bottom a c. of life	214:17
axiom of literary c.	33:8
cant of c.	58:5
c. as a dutiful boy	248:7
C. is a life without risk	60:10
c. is parasitic on art	8:10
C. makes its appearance	58:11
c.'s motto	59:13
Drama criticism . . . a self-knowing	60:2
French c. of English work	59:3
Literary c., which is bound	140:2
my own definition of c.	58:13
My own domestic c.	58:10
People ask you for c.	1:8
pleasure of c. destroys	57:13
public took for a c.	248:10

criticize ability to c. his own work 59:11

criticizes It c. you 21:13

critics academic c. whose whole training 250:7
become mass murderers or c.	62:8
carcase for the c.	83:9
C. are like brushers	60:12
C. are like eunuchs	62:3
c. move into your head	60:3
c. of the next	10:10
c. of the next	339:5
C. say nice things	250:4
c. should be thrown out	62:7
didn't think about the c.	230:13
great c., of whom there are	61:17
how he felt about c.	62:9
most severe of c.	98:16
read his favourable c.	2:1
sneer of c.	62:6
some c. are boring even when	320:11
supreme Eminence anong English c.	88:4
therefore they turn c.	248:4
Turn c. out of mere revenge	60:13
turned c. next	61:1
wish c. would judge me as an author	323:12

critique Your servant the c. 249:3

crocodile c.'s snout in the lily pond 295:4
jaws like a c.'s	330:13

Cromwell I'd have been C. 223:11
Just as Oliver C. aimed	35:10

Cromwellian We C. Directors 221:11

crooked c. road of life 275:3
strive to set the c. straight	227:11

crossbreeding c. of parts of speech 117:8

crossness make c. and dirt succeed 146:5

crow old c. over at Hull 128:1

crowd Far from the madding c. 29:4
hardly a c.-puller	299:9

crowding come c. in so fast 136:1

crown too often a c. of thorns 97:7

crucible cast a violet into a c. 307:10

cruel c. playful mind 146:4

cruelty attractions in its c. 59:1
c. to children	155:4

crush c. the columns together 249:6

crushes c. the entire century 15:7

crust beneath the c. of their age 188:8

crustacean kind of sensitive c. 190:9

crutches upstairs backwards on c. 206:2

cry Make-'em-laugh, make-'em-c. 209:11

cryptogram charm of a c. 13:9

cult c. of the mad 189:1

cultivate C. simplicity 51:11

cultivating c. the Muse 315:4

cultural chapter in c. history 325:1

culture cannot understand our c. 319:1
C. follows money	171:6
found in ordinary c.	169:5
half of modern c. depends	241:6
mass c. of this one	127:7
taste and c.	288:4
Western c. was a grand ancestral	318:7
What other c.	121:8

cultures Two C. 264:1

curate shabby c. who has strayed 264:2

curb use the snaffle and the c. 290:12

curdled blood to be c. 127:2

curds clot the c. a little 32:3

cure no known c. 5:9

curiosa *Horatii c. felicitas* 126:4

curiosity alert with c. 278:1
c. about the future	13:12
C. will never impel you	313:2
educated man of c.	162:7
form of childish c.	185:13
Love, c., freckles	205:10
read with hard c.	23:7

curious c. talent 142:1

curmudgeon irascible, deaf old c. 317:1

current boats against the c. 92:9
strong c. ideas are	84:2

curse Artistry's haunting c. 84:4
c. not less explicit than	23:12
c. of facts	129:1
c. which cannot be relieved	39:2
or the greatest c.	301:10

curst c. be he that moves my bones 91:8

curtain fond of c. lines 91:2
putteth aside the c.	307:3

death (cont.)

Fear of d.	64:17
finished by a d.	89:9
go on living even after d.	64:13
half in love with easeful D.	63:11
hearing of O'Casey's d.	257:3
I am on my d.-bed	313:1
If there wasn't d.	65:3
I had an interest in d.	56:10
Men fear d. as children fear	63:4
mood is in its d. throes	117:1
morbid marriage of love and d.	189:5
Mrs Browning's d.	34:4
much possessed by d.	64:7
much possessed by d.	317:5
new terrors of D.	22:9
new terror to d.	23:3
riding his method to d.	146:2
those books celebrate d.	160:4
wanted nothing but d.	63:9

deaths Most d. in novels	65:9
debatable d. line	124:1
debate in endless d.	148:6
debt laziness and d.	80:9
debts d. to his originals	203:4
decadence cleverness of a d.	217:4
decay D. with imprecision	329:7
decencies prosaic d. of life	110:7
decency slightest sense of d.	121:11
decent d. obscurity	93:1
he is a d. human being	183:10
decipher claim to d. a text	166:6
decision principle of d.	291:14
deck boy stood on the burning d.	201:4
declaim poet *cannot* d.	280:13
declamation dropping into d.	289:15
declare nothing to d. except	111:2
decline rather d. two drinks	153:7
writing the d. and fall	136:3
decomposing d. in the eternity of print	114:12
deconstruction D. is not a dismantling	166:11
other face of d.	167:3
deconstructionism find out what d. was	167:4
decoration architecture, not interior d.	291:15
I enjoy d.	67:10
decorum Regularity and d.	323:5
dedicate choose to d. your volumes	66:1
dedication delighted to accept the d.	66:8
dedications biography in the d.	66:6
deeds d. are men	326:14
words that have become d.	217:1
deedy I haven't been at all d.	53:5
deep D.-versed in books	239:12
I am not d.	15:5
Not d. the Poet sees, but wide	214:9
defamiliarizes d. it	105:9
defeated utterly d. and excluded	91:3
defective mentally d.	231:7

defend d. to the death your right	39:8
defending constantly d. himself	98:7
definite d. enough to appear in print	43:15
definition d. is the enclosing	328:6
essay defies strict d.	94:13
Defoe learn to write like Daniel D.	145:10
Salvation's first D.	35:9
deformity Art is significant d.	8:4
delay d., the impersonal note	244:4
deliberate d. invention of words	329:8
deliberately Books must be read as d.	241:1
delicacy certain d. and sensitivity	324:2
delicate they are not very d.	78:11
delight from d. to wisdom	139:12
joins instruction with d.	46:9
studies serve for d.	260:7
turn d. into a sacrifice	244:12
delighted to be d.	262:7
delightful as d. a creature as ever	42:4
thoroughly d. evenings	58:12
delighting by d. the reader	331:9
delirium Hawthorne and d. *tremens*	211:5
literary d. *tremens*	54:11
delitabill Storys to rede ar d.	104:4
democracy its apparent d.	341:10
older than d.	223:15
speech can say About D.	124:11
demolition As a d. expert	275:7
d. of a man	67:7
demon cold-blooded d. called Science	111:11
d. in their ears	162:6
Mortal, angel AND d.	255:1
Demosthenes D. had finished speaking	284:1
demotes d. Shakespeare and Pushkin	318:6
dénouement d. of a long story	276:7
denouncers One of the great d.	157:9
deodorant d. of self-deception	204:9
dependent d. on an agent	5:4
depressed d. unable-to-concentrate	77:1
depressions what terrible d.	101:3
deprivation D. is for me	139:4
deputy may be read by d.	239:10
derive d. the words as he goes on	179:7
describe not to d. things to us	216:6
describes He d. what he sees	37:3
description Damn d.	66:10
D. is always a bore	66:12
verbose d.	17:4
descriptions know if you care for d.	67:8
descriptive d. powers were remarkable	157:7
desert Gobi d.	196:6
deserve d. to have good writing	114:4
design there is a d. in it	192:13
desire bring back the d.	336:17
d. to read	241:14
desired You who d. so much	71:2
desires Devices and d.	29:3

desk but a d. to write upon 172:11
  manuscript in his d. 310:2
  resemble some deep old d. 69:7
  votary of the d. 261:5
  whenever I open this d. 184:11
desolation no d. so bleak 155:12
despair black d. succeeds brown study 335:9
  Disappointment, D., Doubt 4:3
  iron-clasped volume of d. 102:1
  quality of his d. 103:9
desperation kind of horrible d. 91:4
  there are degrees of d. 182:1
despise as I d. Shakespeare 274:1
destroy nobler than the forces that d. 306:16
  shall be able to d. 226:9
  Whom the gods wish to d. 247:7
destroyed ought to be d. 244:11
destroying without d. something 139:2
destruction acts of d. 25:11
  d. of every voice 340:1
destructive to say that is d. 1:15
desystematize d. his thought 198:8
detached d. from himself 222:2
detail feminine eye for d. 325:6
  frittered away by d. 164:2
  gluttons for d. 47:3
  interested in d. 67:10
  Leica-sharp in d. 20:5
  Merely corroborative d. 67:2
details I love to pile up d. 67:11
  remember tiny little d. 105:10
detection D. is an exact science 55:6
detective ardent readers of d. fiction 56:12
  began as a d. story 119:5
  D. stories—modern fairy tales 56:3
  good at writing d. stories 325:6
  Prayer Book on English d. fiction 246:1
  What the d. story is about 56:7
  writer of d. stories 112:3
detector shock-proof shit d. 334:6
determination d. of incident 43:5
devices D. and desires 29:3
devil apology for the D. 21:15
  Beware, madam, of the witty d. 173:10
  d. can cite Scripture 20:9
  d.'s chaplain might write 192:2
  d. that spoils my work 52:5
  of the D.'s party 178:11
  Poetry is d.'s wine 211:13
devils still 'tis d. must print 301:4
devours novel d. all other forms 197:1
dew d. was off the language 277:10
diabolical tree of d. knowledge 160:12
diagram from the picture to the d. 261:11
dialect d. with an army 151:17
  D. words 49:3
  purify the d. of the tribe 151:9
  science fiction has become a d. 265:11

dialogue as soon as the d. begins 68:6
  d. is the most respectable way 105:6
  d. so close to modern 131:8
  do completely without d. 267:7
  good d. creates 68:10
  good prose and good d. 115:5
  terse, interrogative d. 80:12
diamond D.! thou little knowest 179:11
  like a d.-cutter 286:9
diamonds into the five of d. 50:7
diaries d. into the Safe Deposit 138:7
  private dreaming in d. 144:2
diarrhoea d. in writing 187:13
diary composition of the D. 206:5
  conversation not a d. 159:11
  d. of the human race 161:7
  keep a d. and some day 69:12
  life of every man is a d. 164:10
  more dull than a discreet d. 69:11
  never travel without my d. 69:6
  One need not write in a d. 69:8
  To keep such a d. 69:13
  To write a d. every day 70:1
  What sort of d. should I like 69:7
Dickens Like D., he can make one laugh 206:9
Dickinson masculine Emily D. 206:1
dictator make an author a d. 304:5
dictators Dead d. are my speciality 228:10
  D. are as scared of books 223:6
diction d. clear as water 312:8
  His d. is consonantal 128:2
dictionaries All d. are made from 71:7
  d., (the very best) 302:12
  D. are like watches 71:8
  grammars and d. are excellent 71:9
  To make d. is dull work 71:4
  writer of d. 71:3
dictionary but a walking d. 260:6
  comfort a D. is 71:12
  d. a bad book to read 71:11
  d. of types and symbols 187:12
  d. out of order 72:8
  first time I ever made the d. 72:6
  How he loved that d. 72:11
  if a writer needs a d. 72:7
  outside of a d. 319:10
didacticism When tempted by d. 340:10
die Christian can d. 156:2
  d. before this book is published 25:14
  d. four pages too soon 65:10
  d. of that roar 164:4
  If I should d., think only 201:14
  if you d. in the middle of the night 265:8
  I shall not altogether d. 62:13
  men d. miserably every day 223:4
  never thought to d. 92:3
  People d., but books never die 228:1
  read before you d. 42:1

die (*cont.*)
seems it rich to d.	63:11
To d. will be an awfully big	64:10
Were you to die	30:9

died king d. and then the queen 209:15
| made the books and he d. | 13:10 |
| Mother d. today | 202:4 |

dies d. unsure of one's own value 64:2
matters not how a man d.	63:7
No one d. in the middle	64:4
something in me d.	257:4

difference d. between what things are 129:13
differences there are only d. 151:4
different moral convictions d. from your own
169:8

difficult fascination of what's d. 84:15
must be *d.*	215:5
only one d. kind	130:4
very d.	267:12
very d. to write	85:12

difficulties Female D. 323:7
| in d. with a book | 336:11 |

difficulty d. in saying things 85:11
| no d. in beginning | 17:8 |
| where there is any d. | 260:15 |

dig I'll d. with it 302:13
digest learn, and inwardly d. 21:3
dignified elegant and d. 236:8
dignify Dared d. the labour 71:2
dignity communicated interest and d. 330:11
| maintained the d. of history | 123:9 |
| tender to man's d. | 130:12 |

digressions D., incontestably 209:6
digs d. my grave at each remove 63:5
dinner illustrated edition of a great d. 297:12
| whatever one had got for d. | 297:13 |

dinners taken from Homer's mighty d. 202:15
Diogenes as D. said 89:4
diplomats D. lie to journalists 315:8
direction to some particular d. 110:6
dirt d. and sucked sugar-stick 205:6
| do d. on it | 93:12 |
| make crossness and d. succeed | 146:5 |

dirty d. hands 143:1
dirty-mindedness journalistic d. 146:7
disagree if they d., they are pernicious 244:11
disagreeable so perfectly d. 332:6
disagreeables all d. evaporate 6:11
disagreement strife and d. 52:7
disappointment D., Despair, Doubt 4:3
disapprove d. of what you say 39:8
disastrous no hurricane can be so d. 227:14
disbelief willing suspension of d. 213:3
disciples nowadays has his d. 23:9
discipline submit myself to your d. 325:10
discomforts all the d. that will 50:10
discovered d. the nature of DNA 264:6
discoveries consequence of d. 300:12

discovery invention or d. 186:6
| not a d. in life | 165:2 |
| portals of d. | 111:4 |

discreet more dull than a d. diary 69:11
discretion D. is not the better part 24:3
discrimination art being all d. 164:13
disease Biographers are generally a d. 23:8
d. called friendship	159:16
d. of admiration	1:4
incurable d. of writing	331:10
progress of his d.	86:9

disenchanting effect is d. 8:6
disestablishment sense of d. 127:5
disguising d. us *both* as women 285:6
disgust d. this refined age 74:6
disgusting it is always d. 66:10
dishabille d. of the male 93:5
disinterested d. endeavour to learn 58:13
dislike d. of the places 157:10
do not much d. the matter	289:3
I, too, d. it	216:8
proof of sense to d. every thing	323:3

dismantling Deconstruction is not a d. 166:11
disobedience Of man's first d. 200:12
disordering d. *of the senses* 254:11
disown making statements I can d. 105:6
dispiriting cannot but be d. 138:9
display camouflaged myself by d. 269:12
| self-examination and self-d. | 105:12 |

disreputable in a d. genre 122:9
dissatisfaction professionals of d. 335:5
dissatisfied d. and unhappy 89:10
dissect We murder to d. 261:4
dissecting d. for forty years 3:11
dissection biography should be a d. 24:5
dissident journalist should be a d. 145:7
dissociation d. of sensibility 188:2
distance d. of time 139:14
| d. of time or place | 338:6 |

distant view from a d. star 265:13
distinction great d. of our nature 133:5
distinguished call upon the d. dead 238:14
| d. thing | 64:6 |

distraction d. in the artist's work 241:9
| excellent for *d.* | 71:9 |

distress height of a present d. 101:5
distribution d. at the last 90:7
distrust all roads lead to a vast d. 57:2
| I d. the feminine | 324:7 |

disturb Art is meant to d. 263:10
| don't d. you | 140:8 |

divided d. by a common language 154:6
divineness participation of d. 212:2
DNA discovered the nature of D. 264:6
| our theatrical D. | 274:10 |

do confidence in what I can d. 269:1
| difficult to know what to d. | 340:6 |
| I can d. it | 86:7 |

I don't d. it at all	336:10	**dragon** father was a d.	100:6
realize that this will d.	91:4	green great d.	117:5
doctors D. in verse Being scarce	218:3	**dragons** tell us that d. exist	95:6
doctrine all the winds of d.	311:3	**dram** Tuppenny d.-shops	162:2
doctrines not to preach d.	196:1	**drama** comedy and d. to exist together	75:8
documents historian wants more d.	124:10	D. criticism . . . a self-knowing	60:2
plain truth of d.	25:2	D. criticism is essentially	59:14
dog as d. is to lamppost	144:12	secret of fiction and the d.	209:12
black d.	101:7	Thro' all the d.	173:1
blots, and d.'s ears	27:4	**dramatic** d. critic is a man	62:1
jumps over the lazy d.	302:4	d. work to be first made available	74:11
kettle to a d.'s tail	73:8	later poetry so very d.	179:10
not unblack d.	117:2	**dramatist** d. only wants more liberties	124:10
taking a d. to the theatre	190:4	would have been a d. indeed	78:4
wild d. that has praised his fleas	256:5	**dramatize** D. it, dramatize it	74:14
doggedly set himself d. to it	83:4	**draw** d. its curtains around us	94:11
dogs d. being prose	118:9	**drawer** occupant of a file d.	265:6
how it felt about d.	62:9	**drawers** open everybody's bureau d.	185:13
dolour d. of pad and paperweight	302:6	**drawing** no d. back	23:4
domestic studied d. science	189:12	**drayman** d., in a passion	141:3
dominant Poetry, as a d. female	218:15	**dream** d. we are waking from	149:2
dominion wielded an intellectual d.	317:11	glory and the d.	133:8
done doing what has been d. before	203:9	Let me d. a little	3:11
I have d. nothing yet	32:9	**dreamer** artist is a d. consenting	332:15
what has not yet been d.	204:7	D. of dreams	227:11
What I have d. is yours	65:13	poet and the d. are distinct	213:11
donnée his idea, his d.	58:14	**dreamers** madmen, heretics, d.	222:9
doom warning of his own d.	211:7	**dreaming** private d. in diaries	144:2
doomed novel is d.	248:3	**dreams** defeated by your fondest d.	87:3
door come through the d. with a gun	210:5	d. of a poet doomed	71:5
in making a d.	87:11	Only d. enable me to fight	336:15
knocking at the d.	16:8	pain of living and the drug of d.	241:15
opening a d.	242:8	**dreamt** Last night I d. I went	202:2
opening and closing of a d.	215:10	**dreariness** this foolish d.	129:3
doors d. of perception	148:9	**dress** Language is the d. of thought	150:8
set d. ajar and slam them	71:1	Style is the d. of thought	289:6
Shut not your d. to me	293:5	**dressing** d. old words new	207:9
dossier d. of human imbecility	168:10	**dribble** d. it daintily	135:10
dot tiny black d.	341:3	**drink** diary is like d.	69:10
dotage Pedantry is the d. of knowledge	262:4	D. heightens feeling	77:2
double done with d. the pains	280:11	Some writers take to d.	334:10
d.-breasted suit	98:12	terminate in d. or worse	77:6
double-cross every d. has another behind it		**drinker** great nonstop literary d.	211:8
	57:2	**drinkers** generation are d. and smokers	77:9
doubt Book wherein is no d.	244:10	**drinking** as inveterate as d.	332:9
curiosity, freckles, and d.	205:10	**drinks** d. as much as you do	77:3
I d. everything	107:9	**drive** can't d. the car	62:4
Our d. is our passion	332:13	**drivel** cataract of d.	55:7
When in d., strike it out	199:9	**driving** d. down the middle lane	331:8
doubtful d. sort of way	269:5	Writing a novel was like d.	340:12
doubting d. and inquiring minds	171:5	**dromedary** muse on d. trots	73:5
doubts d. about the Booker prize	230:15	**drought** d. of March hath perced	200:7
Doyle Conan D. is responsible	55:7	**drudge** d., the unconsidered	169:12
draft alter someone else's d.	82:4	harmless d.	71:3
pleasure of the first d.	252:12	**drudgeries** Among the d.	250:2
drafts d., revisions, rewritings	251:15	**drudges** lucid and laborious d.	262:5
First d. are for learning	252:6	**drug** can't imagine the d. scene	77:9
dragged d. out, by tongs	85:9	consciousness-expanding d.	265:14

drug (*cont.*)
literature is a d.	168:2
most powerful d.	329:1
often a form of the d. habit	241:17
Poetry's a mere d., Sir	212:8
You can cut, or you can d.	227:13
drum most effective d.	316:3
drunk d. and worrying	226:3
dry dwelling in a d. place	295:10
so d. a view of life	131:7
Dryden Milton and D.	188:2
poetry of D., Pope	215:2
Dubliners manuscript of *D.*	244:1
Dubuque old lady in D.	193:12
duchess like being married to a d.	233:11
ducklings ugly d. turning into	210:12
ducks turning into confident d.	210:12
duels handsome highwaymen, d.	258:6
dukedom library Was d. large enough	160:9
dukes drawing room full of d.	264:2
dulce D. et decorum est	315:11
dull can be d. in Fleet Street	143:9
life with the d. bits left out	75:3
Most of life is so d.	164:16
ought to be d. sometimes	9:12
part of this paper appears d.	192:13
they are horribly d.	115:10
To make dictionaries is d. work	71:4
dullness cowed into D.	251:5
No degree of d.	62:5
resultant d. does not kill	306:11
Dumas D.'s terse dialogue	80:12
dumb D. As old medallions	215:13
Nature is d.	192:3
dunces d. are all in confederacy	110:3
dung d.-heaps play a very reasonable	221:10
egg in someone else's d.	61:13
duodecimos humbler band of d.	161:1
dust d. and smoke and noise	304:12
forbear To dig the d.	91:8
duties two d. incumbent	311:10
duty d. rather than a pleasure	178:9
little as a d.	123:13
second is a d.	85:10
whole d. as a writer	10:11
dwarves d. to *dwarfs*	284:6
dye permeates, like a d.	109:4
dying act of d. is not of importance	63:7
D. Is an art	65:2
d. is more the survivors' affair	64:9
d. on active service	33:8
d. soldier without offering help	280:3
forgets the d. bird	36:1
hear of one that is d.	155:6
I am d. as fast	63:8
If this is d.	156:12

nothing new in d.	156:11
rage against the d.	64:14

eagle as an e. does a vulture	106:5
as an e. does a vulture	297:9
half an E. was	92:4
hooded e. among blinking owls	51:16
ear heart was piercèd through the e.	326:12
more is meant than meets the e.	176:4
Poets live by the e.	221:6
So nice his e.	224:5
early title comes either very e. on	299:10
earn e. a living some other way	80:4
had to e. my own living	79:14
earnestness preaching e. to a nation	38:6
earning not a respectable way of e.	79:10
ears language only speaks to the e.	150:3
earth cool flowery lap of e.	331:1
heaven and the e.	200:3
If all the e. were paper	172:8
round e. its footstool	330:10
sleepers in that quiet e.	50:12
soil, the mother-e.	192:6
words are the daughters of e.	327:8
earthly attached to anyone e.	73:7
ease produced with great e.	85:5
east like yesterday's e. wind	300:6
Easter Christmas present from E. Island	128:1
easy any reading more e.	241:14
e. rhythms, easy emotions	218:14
e. writing's vile hard reading	83:6
should be free and e.	158:9
eat e. and drunk and lived	22:11
I see what I e.	176:10
sometimes has to e. them	329:12
eavesdropping e. at a party	281:5
echo e. of Mr James	319:2
every bosom returns an e.	119:1
sound must seem an e. to the sense	48:14
waiting for the e.	216:11
economic e. or political importance	218:16
economy consumer e. loves	182:3
e. of a novelist	197:4
ecstasy from circumstance to e.	7:12
eczema too often hides e.	291:12
Eden Through E. took	50:9
edge e. of the chair of Literature	130:6
He loves all that has e.	296:1
edit E. and annotate the lines	261:12
edited even sincerity should be e.	82:13
I don't like being e.	82:15
she e. me	81:10
editing E. is the same as quarrelling	82:5
edition correcting in a second e.	163:8
illustrated e. of a great dinner	297:12
new And more beautiful e.	91:11
new e. of human nature	266:7

épater *Il faut é. le bourgeois* 278:10
epic found the e. in the prose 171:8
  novel is a subjective e. 194:13
  our ballad or e. age 171:1
  surviving Old English e. 318:9
  than an e. poem 122:1
epick E. writer with a k 286:6
epigram all existence in an e. 31:14
  day of the jewelled e. 292:1
  Impelled to try an e. 320:7
  purrs like an e. 144:6
  What is an E. 321:5
epigrams neat And witty e. 268:1
  reading a collection of e. 276:5
  tissue of e. 53:7
epilogue more chapters and an e. 90:14
epiphany By an e. he meant 339:9
episodic e. are the worst 209:1
epistolary e. form is an antiquated 195:5
  e. style is in general 194:8
epithets Such e., like pepper 67:1
erase e. his name 160:6
error e. of judgement 119:5
  possibility of e. 166:7
errors His e. are volitional 111:4
  imitation of the common e. 129:6
eruption small e. of a disease 159:16
escape e. from emotion 102:13
  excited hopes of e. 131:9
  not e. my iambics 211:11
  way of e. 185:11
escapes our real life e. 26:1
Esperanto poet writes in E. 59:6
essay Am writing an e. on 293:13
  e. defies strict definition 94:13
  e. is just a grown-up version 94:14
essayist e. . . . . can pull on 94:12
essayists Mere e. 94:7
essays Addison with all his e. 285:8
  E.. The word is late 94:8
  go by the name of e. 94:9
essence literature reduced to the e. 216:4
  purest e. of a human soul 27:7
essential e. part of all my education 21:14
esteem self e., grounded on just 268:2
eternities e. inside a manufacturer 33:2
eternity decomposing in the e. of print 114:12
etherealizes Flaubert e. all 15:9
etherized patient e. upon a table 107:1
ethical great e. importance 311:14
ethics carefree holiday from e. 127:3
  drew a system of e. 37:12
étonne É.-moi 203:10
etymology their e. being buried 191:9
Euclid fifth proposition of E. 55:6
eulogist foggy e. 59:12
eulogy improvise a e. 80:7
eunuch Time's e. 336:2

eunuchs like e. in a harem 62:3
euphemism waters of e. 152:5
Euripides Mr E. was guilty 223:1
Europe damn the continent of E. 171:6
  E. made his woe her own 37:13
European E. moderns are all *trying* to be 188:4
  E. view of a poet 59:6
  history of the E. novel 172:2
  seeds of E. literature 319:1
Evelina there is merit in E. 36:4
evening see if e.—any evening 107:1
evenings exciting e. 243:4
  long winter e. 185:9
event hurries to the main e. 16:11
events ordinary train of human e. 194:11
  turn e. into ideas 169:1
everyday poetry of our e. life 174:8
  realistic e. language 220:7
everything E. mankind does 292:6
  Macaulay is of e. 174:2
  novel tends to tell us e. 277:9
evil Inventing really e. people 44:12
  sense of e. 185:2
  witness to man's knowledge of e. 312:4
evils they are necessary e. 261:1
exaggerate obliged to e. 164:16
examination self-e. and self-display 105:12
example fiery-hearted youth see an e. 331:5
examples philosophy from e. 123:2
excavate e. the experience 340:2
excellence enlightening judge of e. 59:12
excellencies dwell rather upon e. 58:2
excellent e. lies before us 114:1
  think himself super-e. 267:13
excess blasted with e. of light 178:8
  surprise by a fine e. 213:5
excitement e. and the revelation 47:6
  secret e. 281:3
exclamation all these e. points 235:7
exclude e. from this publication 93:2
excluded utterly defeated and e. 91:3
excrescence appear a morbid e. 256:2
excursion called the 'E.' 330:8
excursions e. are fairly limited 178:5
excuse my only e. 208:8
execute Muslims to e. them quickly 41:6
exercise e. in the use of language 316:10
  what e. is to the body 240:1
exhausting Writing fiction is e. 86:11
exile classical even in e. 205:4
exist didn't e. before 139:1
  people who do not e. 105:13
existence single e. is itself 197:7
exists fact that it e. 162:9
exorcism sort of hopeful e. 186:11
expels it e. literature 263:8

field like running through a f.	339:7
fields f. of the Holy Scriptures	20:10
he studies in the f.	192:1
fifteen at the age of f.	201:1
At the age of f.	202:13
fifty F. pounds	181:6
with booze until he's f.	77:5
figgy regales an author with f. pudding	233:12
figurative mastery of f. language	318:11
figure f. in the carpet	177:3
figures F. stud Simenon's life	278:2
film good f. script	267:7
on f. or television	211:2
write a f. play	267:5
films don't need books to make f.	267:11
people smoke in old f.	94:6
financial f. position to afford	181:9
find never let them f. that out	266:8
finding day f. the *mot juste*	54:7
F. the inappropriate word	141:5
fine f. writing is next to fine doing	113:11
mighty f. fellows nowadays	120:11
think is particularly f.	199:5
to bring in f. things	209:3
fines interest and f. on sorrow	279:3
finesse no f. at all	200:2
finger Between my f. and my thumb	302:13
save from f. wet	27:1
fingernails paring his f.	339:4
fingers into my f. tricklèd	135:10
sort of itch in my f.	302:2
finish action calls for a f.	91:2
wanted to f. a book	140:7
finished f. in half the time	66:5
It's f.	90:10
may never be f.	17:11
Once I've f. a novel	11:8
scarcely f. A single page	335:7
till the story is f.	209:7
when I've 'f.' a piece	91:3
when these books were f.	137:10
finishing reached the f. post	89:3
Finnish his discovery of F.	154:13
fire carry to the f.	27:3
catches f. by its own motion	78:2
f. of my loins	202:9
f. that has been poked	199:13
f.-tongued pretentiousness	298:5
f. too much over	10:2
given a seat by the f.	210:2
O! for a Muse of f.	135:8
O! for a Muse of f.	200:9
round a f. on Christmas Eve	111:13
spark o' Nature's f.	261:3
stick hardened in the f.	121:5
tongued with f.	64:12
Women, f., and dangerous things	118:1
write for the f.	251:1

firecracker went off like a f.	198:12
fires like f. half burning	331:2
fireside glass of wine by his own f.	76:3
firmer little f. on their legs	109:8
first F. Chapter on paper	180:2
F. drafts are for learning	252:6
If you like poetry let it be f.-rate	318:2
latent in my f.	90:13
what to put f.	16:12
fish like the f. from the pool	71:13
though they cannot f.	330:6
fissures metallic f. of language	34:8
Fitzgerald F. strung them	308:3
five dies in the middle of Act F.	64:4
fixed 'stars' in a literary text are f.	166:9
fizz oh so flat 'f.'	320:5
flame so full of subtil f.	75:12
flames amid fierce f.	92:11
flash single splendid f.	220:9
flashes occasional f. of silence	174:3
flat divide characters into f. and round	43:11
Fell half so f. as Walter Scott	266:4
flattered f. by the censorship laws	41:5
flattery f. lost on poet's ear	268:5
f. of power	248:10
paid with f.	78:8
flavourless talk becomes f.	243:12
flawyers I call them 'f.'	250:7
flea English literature's performing f.	322:5
f. Hath smaller fleas	207:11
fleas Lies are like f.	312:9
wild dog that has praised his f.	256:5
Fleet Street can be dull in F.	143:9
F. can scent the possibilities	145:14
flesh f., alas, is wearied	241:5
f. was sacramental	94:1
make your f. creep	127:1
outlive all f.	133:9
flies hapless f. caught in a huge web	161:10
flippancy F., the most hopeless form	321:9
float f. along like birds	253:8
f. further down the stream	247:2
flocking F. together	68:8
floods f. of tepid soap and water	170:10
flopping not go f. along	8:12
flora Tasting of F.	76:6
Florida live in south F.	135:4
flower f. of any kind of experience	214:5
flowers bunch of other men's f.	207:8
hundred f. blossom	223:5
odiferous f. of fancy	205:1
Too many f.	114:2
too soon for f.	64:11
flowery cool f. lap of earth	331:1
f. plains of honour	260:5
fluency length of his mild f.	297:5
fluidity f. of Greek	154:12
flummery f. of a birth place	96:13

flush her beloved dog 'F.'   34:7
flute Gibbon moved to f.   112:10
fly try to f. by those nets   279:2
foes great f. of reality   328:9
fog as an English f.   16:1
  f. in my throat   64:3
  f. of philistinism   279:3
  London f. is disagreeable   17:4
  luminous haze or f.   113:1
  prophet straying in a f.   319:9
fogs rising f. prevail upon   176:5
folders misery of manilla f.   302:6
folios mighty f. first   161:1
folk Our f.-tales prefigure   95:4
follies crimes, f., and misfortunes   123:11
  vices and f. of human kind   129:10
folly meet with f. and conceit   161:2
  shoot F. as it flies   337:8
fond as f. of me as he could be   38:9
fondness single expression of f.   37:10
food F. comes first, then morals   108:11
  If music be the f. of love   200:10
fool f. may write a most valuable book   338:3
  make a man appear a f.   320:12
  shouldn't f. with booze   77:5
  stupendous genius! damned f.   330:6
foolish lean and f. knight   41:11
fools f. admire, but men of sense   58:1
  F. admire everything   246:7
  F. are my theme   232:7
  I am two f., I know   172:10
  Only f. lend books   30:8
  Poems are made by f. like me   192:5
  proved plain f. at last   61:1
  small ones f.   331:11
foolscap blank sheets of f.   303:4
  My single-lined f.   303:2
foot one f. already in the stirrup   63:1
  one f. in one world   135:5
footnotes like the absence of f.   262:3
footprints f. left in the snow   210:17
  F. on the sands of time   22:16
  so few f.   153:8
footstool round earth its f.   330:10
force intrusion of f.   41:1
forehead His f. was prodigious   52:2
foreign array of f. tongues   155:1
  corner of a f. field   201:14
  lonely f. midget   98:1
  past is a f. country   202:7
  perish in a f. tongue   308:10
  print things in a f. language   308:6
  school stories in f. languages   47:5
  writer is a f. country   325:4
foreigners f. always spell better   284:5
foresee writer did not f.   45:2
forest clipped hedge is to a f.   54:12
forethought F. is the elbow-grease   84:5

forever By f., I mean thirty years   130:3
forget if he could f. half   174:1
  to f. him for twenty   126:5
forgets writer never f.   268:7
forgot names ignoble, born to be f.   246:8
forgotten books are undeservedly f.   247:9
  f. how to think   84:12
  ideas cannot too soon be f.   157:7
  justice-business are all f.   266:5
form action is endowed with f.   196:15
  F. alone can indefinitely   288:4
  f. imposes a certain clarity   56:2
  f. of the novel   196:1
  f. that accommodates the mess   288:6
  persuade you . . . that F. *is*   288:3
  problems of F. and Content   4:7
  time to lick it into f.   251:2
forms breath to f.   133:9
  different poetical f.   253:11
  f. of things unknown   133:2
  novel devours all other f.   197:1
fornication like war and f.   309:11
fortunate should have been more f.   190:5
fortune in possession of a good f.   200:15
fossil Language is f. poetry   150:13
foul f. rag and bone shop   103:6
foundations very earth of our f.   170:9
fountain accursed 'f.' pen   301:11
four era of the f.-letter word   292:1
four-in-hand with the fiery f.   81:6
foursquareness kind of f.   165:14
fourteen those first f. years   47:6
fourth full of f.-rate writers   12:3
fowl liver-wing of a f.   230:4
fowls fatten their literary f.   233:4
fox quick brown f.   302:4
fragile combine f. confidence   244:9
fragment composed this glorious f.   14:12
fragments or rather, of f.   18:2
frame puts the author into a f.   195:5
framework tighter, smaller f.   154:14
France In F. literature divides itself   170:11
  vasty fields of F.   74:3
Frankenstein [F. is] a book about   275:10
freak f. user of words   298:2
freckles Love, curiosity, f.   205:10
free as soon write f. verse   253:16
  F. verse is ultimately   254:3
  human being is f.   6:10
  in favour of f. expression   40:15
  only time a human being is f.   278:6
  Teach the f. man   92:12
  Thou art f.   273:12
freedom destroy the f.   39:9
  documents in the history of f.   36:10
  F. and Whiskey gang thegither   76:2
  F. of the press   40:13
  What is f. of expression   41:8

freeze f. his reader's marrow	112:3
f. the movement of the pen	222:5
f. thy young blood	126:6
To f. the blood	292:11
freezing capturing time and f. it	107:8
French always have spoken F.	152:12
by contrast [with F. fiction]	170:10
comparison between English and F.	154:14
except among the F.	170:3
F. criticism of English work	59:3
F. fathered the Modern Movement	188:11
F. is the *patois* of Europe	153:4
F. writers do not burden themselves	209:5
glory of beating the F.	118:10
heroes of F. fiction	171:4
Learning F. is some trouble	154:1
never F. in any circumstance	237:6
not clear is not F.	152:15
only tribute a F. translator	308:4
reading a F. novel	61:15
Speak in F.	153:6
Frenchman highly instructed F.	193:5
No one but a F.	175:9
precise and slick as a F.	45:10
frenzy to a kind of f.	85:7
frequency very fact of f.	306:9
freshness f. of my heart	280:9
prose has none of the f.	206:2
Friar Tuck manner of F.	160:3
friction occur just by f.	137:12
friend as you choose a f.	239:13
How to be a f. to a reader	12:5
one damned goodnatured f.	58:6
terrific f. of yours	242:6
Whenever a f. succeeds	257:4
writer's best f.	252:8
friends as my best f. could desire	63:8
book is the best of f.	27:6
circular letter to the f.	10:3
did it to please my f.	185:6
none of his f. like him	274:11
only one's f. matter	99:6
Seek younger f.	4:5
friendship disease called f.	159:16
f. included in the price	11:3
F. is useless	173:8
heart of it was f.	100:2
frieze no striped f.	14:10
frigate no F. like a Book	27:11
frivolity how precious is f.	268:11
frivolous memoirs of the f.	13:7
Frodo Let Bingo = F.	191:1
frontier move the f. post	227:12
frost *Hardy* and *Thomas* and F.	305:7
frozen hold them f.	277:2
leaves it f.	67:9
fruit Too late for f.	64:11
too little f.	114:2

fruitfulness mists and mellow f.	200:18
fry scribbling f.	255:7
frying f. pan of your words	227:8
fudge two-fifths sheer f.	211:6
fugues if he had written f.	331:4
full his commonplace book be f.	69:2
Reading maketh a f. man	239:9
fun I rhyme for f.	184:9
Just because something's f.	340:9
read Homer for f.	126:2
funeral expenses of his mother's f.	80:12
f. oration rather than	22:13
Nobel is a ticket to one's f.	230:7
funereal slow, f. barbarism	24:2
funny both glum and f.	18:8
furnish Books do f. a room	27:15
furniture f. in Tolkien's attic	300:2
No f. so charming	27:8
fury sound and the f.	30:1
fuse line is a f.	253:13
fustian whose f.'s so sublimely bad	219:8
futility f. of all prefaces	17:1
so straight to f.	149:3
future archaeology of the f.	265:2
belief in the f. of England	193:8
curiosity about the f.	13:12
f. perfect I have always regarded	118:5
f. states of both	89:9
f. to your mother-in-law	5:4
grim potential f.	178:2
interpretation of the f.	123:1
futurism describing F.	187:13
fwowed Tonstant Weader f. up	49:10
gain For g., not glory	184:7
Galatians great text in G.	21:8
gallery picture g. in a garden	231:9
gallimaufry g. or hodgepodge	152:8
gallop g. uncontrollably on	89:3
rides his mind at a g.	149:8
Galsworthy G. and Arnold Bennett	188:6
gambling as exciting as g.	332:9
it is g.	233:6
gamekeeper life of an English g.	249:8
games enjoy playing g.	57:3
gander half a G.	92:4
gap desire to fill some g.	186:4
terrible g. in a story	288:2
gaps indicate g. of months	288:10
garden as a house does to a g.	25:6
g. carried in the pocket	28:5
g. in a concert hall	231:9
man and a woman in a g.	21:12
shadow in the g.	25:10
gardening delightful department of g.	52:4
G. and the COOKERY	270:11

grab penny that activated a g.   86:12
grace beneath the slight lyric g.   188:1
   saying g. before a new book   108:9
graces adorned by the female g.   3:4
graffito bringing the g. lower   115:9
grammar correct my spelling and g.   284:6
   don't want to talk g.   116:15
   for g. *and* punctuation   235:11
   G., the ground of al   116:2
   power of the mental g.   118:4
   Prefer geniality to g.   116:11
   talking bad g.   116:9
   With g., and nonsense   75:14
grammars g. and dictionaries are excellent
                                        71:9
grammatical g. purity   116:4
grand g. style arises   290:1
Grand Canyon rose petal down the G.   216:11
grandeur g. underlying the sorriest   293:8
granite that immitigable g.   120:7
grants about publishers and g.   68:8
grapes g. of wrath   29:8
graspable immediately, instantly g.   290:8
grass hearing the g. grow   164:4
gratuitous autobiography is the most g.   13:13
   g. letter   159:12
grave digs my g. at each remove   63:5
   g. of Christianity   22:2
   laid in the quiet g.   63:13
   no letters in the g.   158:11
   poem huger than the g.   64:16
   praise for poets in the g.   62:14
   see myself go into my g.   50:10
   see myself go into my g.   69:1
grave-digger wisdom of the g.   23:11
graven g. on tablets of stone   342:6
graves g. of little magazines   193:9
   so was G.   305:7
grazing cow must have in g.   242:1
great being a 'g. man of letters'   247:12
   ever loved g. writers   223:9
   Every g. man nowadays   23:9
   G. book, great evil   26:7
   g. in everything   300:9
   g. man's book   246:10
   g. theatre begins with great talkers 75:5
   G. things have of course   280:11
   g. tradition   318:4
   G. writers create   208:2
   green g. dragon   117:5
   not good but g.   247:10
   she cannot be g.   12:10
   whole crowds of g. men   273:13
greatest g. in what is greatest   273:10
   g. of superficial novelists   70:7
greatness g. of her two sisters   32:7
   G. recognizes greatness   111:8

His g. lay in his art   231:6
new point of his g.   273:15
Greece isles of G.   259:6
   to G., and into Noah's ark   152:14
greed g. for an immediate money return   4:13
Greek carve in Latin or in G.   152:10
   fluidity of G.   154:12
   G. and Latin inversions   179:2
   G. as a treat   153:15
   G. literature written in Latin   171:2
   G. the language they gave   154:7
   No G.   237:6
   original G. is of great use   308:8
   pages of your G. models   304:3
   say a word against G.   153:11
   small Latin, and less G.   272:9
   study of G. literature   261:10
   terms of a G. tragedy   53:6
   useful like Latin or G.   154:8
Greeks G. had a word for it   329:4
   make way, G.   314:1
green at the most, a pale g. man   24:1
   Colourless g. ideas   117:6
   g. great dragon   117:5
Greene G.'s to the good   175:8
greengrocer g.'s apostrophe   236:6
grenadier chill the blood of a g.   127:2
grey black and g.   294:4
   you are old and g.   3:10
gridiron prefer a hot g.   336:8
grief Passion, vehemence, g.   33:6
   queen died of g.   209:15
griefs busy g.   279:4
Grimm G.'s *Fairy Tales*   96:1
grinders into incisors and g.   332:10
groaning g. immoderately   341:4
grocer g.'s port is preferable   291:16
grotesque pure, ornate, and g.   187:6
group g. is always impressive   188:10
grovel mere gelatinous g.   1:6
groves g. of Academe   260:1
grown-ups they were meant for g.   47:4
growth should allow for g.   47:8
grub g. more than the butterfly   143:4
Grubstreet Our G. biographers   22:8
grumbling piece of rhythmical g.   88:8
grunter honest g.   125:7
guarantee no g. of what is written   14:1
guaranteed g. only to those   40:13
guerrilla kind of g. warfare   87:3
guide-books G. are the least reliable   309:6
guilt dwell on g. and misery   293:1
guilty I've never been g. of that   217:6
gulp g. the stuff down in gobbets   70:12
gum poesy is as a g.   135:9
gun come through the door with a g.   210:5
gunpowder G., Printing   301:5
gush they're oil wells, they g.   258:4

gutless sort of g. Kipling 9:2
guts right out of his own g. 14:5
  writing out of his g. 146:11
gutter Journalists belong in the g. 145:8

habit beneath the dust of h. 191:9
  h. of writing again 336:17
  reading h. is now often 241:17
hack h. writer who would not have 313:6
haddock hold on sausage and h. 109:1
Haggards H. ride no more 147:10
hair h. to stand on end 126:6
  her h. wildly tossed about 132:4
  never pin up my h. with prose 219:7
half h. is with the reader 10:7
  H. my soul 314:2
half-achievement wretched h. 175:6
halfpenny h. reader 225:5
hallucinations cantered h. 157:6
halo h. of almost historical pomp 206:3
  life is a luminous h. 165:1
halting words came h. forth 335:8
Hamlet H. without mentioning the ghost 76:10
  H. without the Prince 180:1
  If *H.* and *Oedipus* were published 19:6
  If Shakespeare had not written *H.* 264:6
  saw H. Prince of Denmark played 74:6
  To characterize H. 61:6
Hamletizes one h. 68:4
hammer kind of H. Films poet 208:14
hammering make such a h. 143:8
Hammett H. took murder out of 56:1
hand kiss the h. that wrote *Ulysses* 146:10
  with mine own h. 158:4
handicap Wives can be an awful h. 99:5
handkerchief state of the h. industry 204:8
hands got the h. wrong 180:8
  memory is certainly in my h. 303:5
  reveals the author's h. and feet 221:9
  spits on its h. 151:13
handsome as h. as his photographs 6:4
hang otherwise h. us 313:8
hanged got myself burnt or h. 130:5
hanging deserved h. 73:1
Hannibal H.'s African elephants 316:9
happen poetry makes nothing h. 279:4
  Poetry makes things h. 229:2
  what is going to h. to it 269:1
happening way of h., a mouth 279:4
happens It just h. 65:9
  nothing h., twice 16:4
  to see what h. 11:9
happiest best and h. moments 213:13
happily good ended h. 104:13
  lived h. ever after 51:1
happiness exalted to unhuman h. 89:6
  h. consists in falling 214:7

necessary to our h. 210:8
sought for h. everywhere 239:5
happy All h. families resemble 201:10
  already made me a h. woman 99:12
  bread-sauce of the h. ending 90:11
  h. ending 90:7
  inextinguishably h. 186:8
  I've had a h. life 156:6
  tragedy with a h. ending 74:13
  When you write h. endings 91:6
hard gathered only h. words 289:13
  unable to be h. on himself 252:4
hardback shelf life of the modern h. 98:9
hardening h. of the paragraphs 4:6
hardest h. thing in all literature 203:5
hardy as it was upon Thomas H. 192:6
  can be read after H. 205:8
  not in the H. class 275:5
  Rereading H., I was struck 299:1
  sat at the feet of *H.* 305:7
harem like eunuchs in a h. 62:3
harlot Half nun, half h. 5:6
harm may do you extreme h. 169:6
harmonies inventor of h. 179:5
harmony other h. of prose 136:1
harp wild h. slung behind him 315:3
Harrods as she moves out of H. 44:4
harrow h. up thy soul 126:6
harsh not h., only inevitable 119:10
Harvard my Yale College and my H. 261:8
harvest h. of a quiet eye 212:12
harvests reap the ancient h. 95:7
haste Journalism encourages h. 145:16
hastening all h. together 89:8
hate h. Hollywood as intensely 316:11
  h. your neighbour 37:12
  have a h. figure 131:3
  I h. the common herd 267:15
  I love, I h., I suffer 33:3
  such a thing as creative h. 102:11
hated intensely loved and h. 148:5
  loved well because he h. 62:11
  read them as if he h. them 35:2
  thought I h. everybody 99:9
hatred Regulated h. 13:1
haunt certain to h. her 98:14
haunted grimacing h. creature 73:10
Hawthorne H. and *delirium tremens* 211:5
hay Antic h. 28:6
haze luminous h. or fog 113:1
head critics move into your h. 60:3
  I'll hold my h. so high 267:14
  in the heart or in the h. 133:3
  their feet than of their h. 260:11
  What though his h. be empty 69:2
headlines their scare h. about me 193:10
heads over the h. of your readers 10:2
  secrecy of our own h. 169:11

health classical is h.	187:5
healthily so h. good	286:7
hear to make you h.	339:1
heart As my poor h. doth think	172:8
beat of my h.	66:7
bicycle-pump the human h.	173:9
bitter insights of the h.	66:2
but thou hast my h.	172:13
came from mine own h.	135:10
clutch at the h.	50:3
everyone knows by h.	161:12
examiner of the human h.	254:9
fed the h. on fantasies	134:9
found not my h. moved	14:11
freshness of my h.	280:9
great greedy h.	142:12
h. is a lonely hunter	29:9
h. is in the right place	222:3
h. of an immense darkness	201:12
h. of man	330:11
h. speaks to heart	150:3
h. was piercèd through the ear	326:12
holiness of the h.'s affections	311:5
hopeless h. of man	54:10
in the h. or in the head	133:3
language of the h.	150:6
look in thy h. and write	335:8
loosed our h. in tears	331:1
more knowledge of the h.	254:8
must have a h. of stone	102:10
My h. did do it	172:9
no longer tear his h.	91:12
Only an aching h.	103:1
passions of the human h.	179:8
rag and bone shop of the h.	103:6
sake of my h.	2:11
sealing up of a nation's h.	41:1
see through to his h.	95:1
Shakespeare unlocked his h.	214:2
Shakespeare unlocked his h.	273:14
squirrel's h. beat	164:4
tears the h. out of it	61:4
woman after his own h.	37:7
write straight from my own h.	19:5
heartbreak moment of purest h.	130:16
heartbreaking inept title to h. bosh	298:7
heartlessness H. masked by a style	70:10
Heart of Darkness H. prophetically	54:8
heat body h. of a healthy Anglican	121:9
while the h. is in you	136:6
heathen example in any h. author	21:2
heaven entering the kingdom of h.	12:11
h. and the earth	200:3
heavier seven stones h.	2:11
heavy h. thing is a pen	84:7
hedge clipped h. is to a forest	54:12
heels wings of his h. are in sight	298:1
Heine H. so loosened the corsets	154:2

heir first h. of my invention	65:12
heirs crew of missing h.	195:12
hell h. of a profession	185:1
H. with compensations	320:10
how deep is H.	26:5
printing house in H.	301:2
help get out and wants h.	138:10
How can I h. this writer	82:7
They look on and h.	64:8
helpless passionless, h. creatures	324:3
Hemingway admirable profile of H.	42:3
someone like H.	121:8
hens fate of literary h.	268:8
herbs goodly green h. of sentences	20:10
heritage boring part of one's h.	318:9
hero h. and heroine tied up	93:11
h. is the author	43:8
h. of my own life	201:5
h. of my tale	311:7
he who aspires to be a h.	76:1
Show me a h. and I will write	306:14
heroes h. and villains from fiction	47:11
h. of French fiction	171:4
heroic h. poem of its own sort	23:2
whole life a h. poem	179:4
work of an h. mind	146:6
heroine h. whom no-one but myself	42:5
she could not have been the h.	42:11
when a h. goes mad	74:10
herself there was a 'not h.'	88:1
hidden h. within all of us	112:7
hide h. these books	224:9
hideous perfectly h. about Scotland	174:7
high h.-water mark of Socialist literature	9:2
highbrow what a h. is	149:8
What is a h.	149:5
higher H. Cannibalism	24:8
I am capable of h. things	268:11
highland Scott gave H. legends	171:3
highlight h. what you leave in	199:14
highway passes over a h.	194:12
highwaymen handsome h., duels	258:6
hill coal-cart down an icy h.	339:12
half-way down a h.	60:4
hunter home from the h.	92:5
hills Blue remembered h.	28:9
hippopotamus h. resolved at any cost	141:9
hiss dismal universal h.	57:12
historian h. of fine consciences	141:11
h. wants more documents	124:10
life of the h.	123:12
not requisite for a h.	123:10
historians alter the past, h. can	124:7
H. desiring to write	123:7
h. repeat one another	124:12
impressive to h. of literature	188:10
keep h. occupied	125:4

no i. of their own	232:12
outlet to new i.	188:8
Prose is for i.	220:6
spoilt a number of jolly good i.	46:5
spurted fountains of i.	342:3
strong current i. are	84:2
turn events into i.	169:1
words are but the signs of i.	327:8
identity discover his i.	96:2
he has no i.	213:10
idiocy infection of i.	301:12
idioms licentious i.	116:4
idle I have been i.	336:9
idleness idea of enforced i.	338:9
i. keeps ignorant	61:2
idolatry ancients without i.	304:9
Thou god of our i.	232:5
idols plaster i. of academic tradition	318:6
ignoble names i., born to be forgot	246:8
ignorance understand a writer's i.	176:8
understand a writer's i.	332:4
ignorant idleness keeps i.	61:2
i. have prescribed laws	116:6
you're not only i.	264:5
ignore Most people i. most poetry	218:8
Iliad I. of a daily paper	199:8
Something greater than the I.	314:1
Ilion I.'s lofty temples	314:6
ill if I did not say i.-natured things	68:3
now makes me feel i.	198:9
illegibility corrected into i.	251:8
illiterates act of i.	230:9
illness bout of some painful i.	85:6
but an incurable i.	335:2
illusion expense of i. and nobility	209:16
world of unreason and i.	258:9
illusions blessing of i.	129:1
illustrate To i. any text	132:7
illustrated i. adult classic	3:1
i. edition of a great dinner	297:12
illustration bastard art of i.	267:11
i. in modern novels	132:9
illustrations i., which are far more	132:5
image i. of literature	169:5
man after his own i.	37:7
What an i. that is	106:9
imagery large-scale i.	205:7
science for their i.	264:5
images delivers himself of mean i.	282:12
i. that form upon one's pen	277:11
ironic use of the stock i.	189:4
imaginary characters in this story are i.	44:6
cohabitation with i. people	90:8
i. brother or sister	100:1
safe confines of the i.	186:11
imagination always f—gg—g his *i.*	133:11
car of the i.	134:7
dead but not buried i.	149:11
digested in the i.	308:15
force of i.	133:4
illumination of my i.	137:8
i., like certain wild animals	312:3
I., not invention	134:8
i. conjures gifts	135:3
i. is always bigger	135:2
I. is not enough	134:12
i. resembled the wings	134:2
i. the rudder	213:1
journey of the i.	122:6
lave of the i.	212:15
led constantly to the i.	195:3
literalists of the i.	216:9
lost valleys of the i.	309:12
modifying colours of i.	213:4
novelist's i. winces	137:5
of i. all compact	133:1
one i. touching another	243:7
reader's i. should be able	277:5
root of i.	134:14
shaping spirit of i.	133:7
stretches the theatre of its i.	309:8
trades i.	224:1
truth of i.	311:5
we have a popular i.	137:3
Where there is no i.	134:4
imaginative function of i. literature	169:8
I am too i.	13:15
I. readers rewrite books	242:5
richer in i. resource	317:3
imaginatively think more i.	4:12
imagine I describe what I i.	37:3
imagined form of i. life	195:13
i. adventures	137:4
i. the South	101:2
only i. that he has loved	73:7
imbeciles moral injury to a dozen i.	183:2
imbecility dossier of human i.	168:10
imitate I. him if you dare	295:11
i. what is good	123:3
Immature poets i.	208:3
to i. what is before him	207:14
imitated who can be i. by none	203:1
imitation art of i.	212:1
begins with i.	8:16
i. of men and manners	194:10
i. of the common errors	129:6
requisite is i.	304:4
imitator happy i. of Nature	272:10
never find an i.	13:3
imitators i., you slavish herd	207:4
immature I. poets imitate	208:3
immaturity common symptom of i.	203:9
immediateness (coin the word) i.	35:4
immoral art is i.	7:8
moral or an i. book	183:3

no word in the Irish l. 329:13
Our l. sunk under him 178:7
Poets belong to the l. 309:3
policemen of l. 328:4
Political l. . . . is designed 223:3
Pure and neat l. 113:8
realistic everyday l. 220:7
rich and delicate l. 284:9
structured like a l. 151:18
ugly l. 155:6
very l. of men 289:10
when his l. performs 291:2
writes in a l. of his own 150:10
languages inventors of international l. 154:5
knowledge of ancient l. 153:9
l. are the pedigree 152:13
None of your live l. 153:3
poets that preserve l. 307:8
wit in all l. 48:13
languor drowsy l. of the prose 277:12
lantern Prose wanders around with a l. 220:9
lapidary In l. inscriptions 311:4
Lapland In L. they have no word for 329:13
lard They l. their lean books 207:10
large how l. a letter 158:4
large-hearted l. man 259:2
larger l. the book must be 47:9
Larkin L. voice 128:4
larkinise to l., v.t. 180:7
La Rochefoucauld Maxims of L. 13:2
lascivious more or less l. music 215:8
last L. night I dreamt I went 202:2
l. page is always latent 90:13
l. thing one knows 16:12
L. words . . . I do not see 156:14
look at the l. page 313:2
Past the l. page 89:3
lateness vary with the l. of the hour 168:18
latent last page is always l. 90:13
Latin as much L. as you like 237:6
by knowledge of L. 179:7
carve in L. or in Greek 152:10
Greek and L. inversions 179:2
Greek literature written in L. 171:2
He speaks L. 152:9
learn L. as an honour 153:15
read and write L. 155:4
small L., and less Greek 272:9
useful like L. or Greek 154:8
laugh do not l. at him any longer 41:12
horse-l. in the reader 111:10
know why people l. 130:7
l. in panic 206:9
Make-'em-l., make-'em-cry 209:11
Make him l. and he will think 247:5
making decent people l. 129:9
those you l. at 9:6
went only to l. 58:12

laugh-at-with someone you could l. 9:6
laughing clearly no l. matter 143:6
Little Nell without l. 102:10
laughs animal that l. and weeps 129:13
laughter convulsed with l. 249:7
seldom raise l. 129:8
laureate if I became Poet L. 230:2
l. of ordinary things 121:3
laureateship acceptance of the L. 229:9
being offered the L. 229:8
laurels want l. for ourselves most 256:7
Yet once more, O ye l. 200:11
lava crust of barely cooled l. 54:9
in its l. I still find 137:9
l. of the imagination 212:15
lavatory l. for its humour 115:13
lawful l. to think what they will 123:7
lawn open l. on a breezy day 106:3
Lawrence Conrad, and D. H. L. 305:5
reading L. as an aphrodisiac 188:7
laws ignorant have prescribed l. 116:6
lawyer trial l.'s job 106:2
lax however l. my page 39:5
laziness l. and debt 80:9
lead with l. balls attached 107:10
leaf-mould l. of the mind 138:11
leaking private soul l. out 319:8
lean in l. years 78:16
Lear How pleasant to know Mr L. 157:11
learn All writers l. from the dead 306:5
gladly wolde he l. 260:3
had to l. American 154:4
moment at which I l. most 242:15
read, mark, l. 21:3
we l. the language 307:8
learned Even for l. men 96:8
l. do not need such things 260:8
loads of l. lumber 240:2
prescribed laws to the l. 116:6
learning a' the l. I desire 261:3
L. hath gained most 260:9
of human l. 22:14
on scraps of l. dote 237:3
truly l. goeth very bare 246:2
learnt nothing can be l. from it 113:7
leave more you l. out 199:14
leavens l. a whole Nation 188:3
leaves as the l. to a tree 213:8
Close up these barren l. 261:4
not out of the l. 138:11
Though l. are many 311:15
Words are like l. 31:7
lecture classic l. rich in sentiment 261:7
turn a l. room into 300:1
leech *offered by the l.-gatherer* 331:5
leeches l. who review your books 250:1
left of my l. hand 83:2
what is l. out of it 199:10

line (*cont.*)

Marlowe's mighty l.	175:4
so many centimes a l.	80:12

linen yards of l.-drapery · 297:5

lines all the l. except the last · 219:13

come down between the l.	203:11
consisted of l. like these	15:1
even my weakest of l.	305:7
In liquid l.	173:5
l. having similar sounds	254:2
l. seemed to me now like	303:4
l. that join them are variable	166:9
town-crier spoke my l.	283:4
verse of twenty l.	220:13
year after year to single l.	84:3

linguistic form of l. fascism · 41:10

L. analysis	152:1
l. philosophy	151:12
name for a l. predicament	65:6
sort of l. Lourdes	152:5

lion first l. in the metropolis · 173:14

now that the old l. is dead	142:8

lioness making a l. of her · 109:7

lions l. looked like so many publishers · 234:3

lips move their l. when reading · 181:10

Spitting from l. once	34:6

lipsed Somwhat he l. · 282:9

liquid In l. lines · 173:5

liquor Good l., I stoutly maintain · 75:14

quantity of l.	168:18

listen good writer knows how to l. · 115:5

great deal of l.	2:8
I only l. when	138:9
l. to Tennyson	297:8

literal intended as l. portraits · 42:9

literalists l. of the imagination · 216:9

literary achieved fame by l. merits · 87:10

acquire the l. language	291:8
axiom of l. criticism	33:8
connection with the l. world	18:7
do not draw well with l. men	255:13
Even more than most l. forms	94:13
fatten their l. fowls	233:4
great l. figure in 2000 AD	275:5
great nonstop l. drinker	211:8
He liked those l. cooks	237:5
In adult l. fiction	211:1
l. ambitions without	149:3
l. America	172:4
l. blood sports	203:12
L. fame is the only fame	97:1
L. Genius Writes Masterpiece	250:10
l. gift is a mere accident	114:7
Of all the l. scenes	193:9
parole of l. men	237:4
Real l. creation	165:5
represent the l. equivalent	188:5
sort of l. Cinderella	32:8

uncorrupted by l. prejudices	58:7
unsuccessful l. man	332:14
working in one 'l. genre'	198:7

literate semi-l. public · 11:4

literature All modern American l. · 313:7

American professors like their l.	168:13
as a subject for l.	173:11
as for l.	79:8
asset to English l.	319:5
bad l. gets written	114:13
Bad l. of the sort	225:6
between l. and science	264:3
can't stamp out l.	40:9
character of American l.	170:5
condition of all *l.*	168:19
disease of English l.	23:8
edge of the chair of L.	130:6
English l.'s performing flea	322:5
function of imaginative l.	169:8
great Cham of l.	142:3
greatest masterpiece in l.	72:8
Great l. cannot grow	305:9
Great l. is simply language	168:14
great l. is thus chiefly	171:5
great work of l.	146:6
Ideas are to l.	168:6
If God exists, why write l.	245:10
I have made by l.	79:2
impressive to historians of l.	188:10
in isolation as a piece of l.	74:11
in l., the oldest	263:2
it becomes l.	120:3
itch of l.	332:7
it expels l.	263:8
knew everything about l.	169:3
Lincoln of our l.	313:4
L., like property, is theft	208:9
l., oh the glorious Art	168:8
l., though the grandest occupation	168:3
l. and hot-water bottles	332:16
l. appear a morbid excrescence	256:2
l. can and should do	280:5
L. cannot be the business	323:9
l. cannot *merely* be artistic	278:9
L. flourishes best	168:11
l. has no relation with it	164:15
l. is, finally, autobiographical	168:12
L. is a competitive sport	170:1
l. is a drug	168:2
L. is a luxury	104:14
L. is a method of sudden	168:9
L. is a splendid mistress	168:7
l. is by writers	62:7
l. is cut short	41:1
l. is forever blowing a horn	169:13
Literature is l.	324:11
l. is more dependable	183:12
L. is mostly about having sex	169:4

l. is my mistress 79:4
L. is news that STAYS news 168:16
L. is strewn with the wreckage 268:9
L. is the orchestration 169:2
l. is the principal voice 183:4
L. is the question 169:7
l. is to move the frontier 227:12
l. is without gender 325:8
l. made up of guide-books 309:6
L. nowadays is a trade 79:5
l. of *knowledge* 227:9
l. of *might be* 265:12
l. of women would be different 324:13
l. one's only means of support 79:6
l. reduced to the essence 216:4
l. should be any different 279:11
L.'s pouncer 278:3
l. to render them helpless 324:3
looking down on l. 61:14
louse in the locks of l. 61:11
newspaper l. 222:9
noise of modern l. 304:12
no l. can outdo real life 164:6
object of a student of l. 262:7
our l. is a substitute 245:9
Remarks are not l. 168:15
Roman l. is Greek 171:2
Russian l. saved my soul 280:1
standard l. of Canada 170:6
standards and the limits of l. 274:9
start talking about l. 233:8
study of Greek l. 261:10
success in l. 256:1
teachers of English l. 279:10
theories and views of l. 168:18
think l. is ever finished 230:11
to give prizes for l. 230:9
to l. what brandy is 143:10
to produce a little l. 168:4
true lover of l. 168:1
When l. has a Tolstoy 300:4
littérature *tout le reste est l.* 168:5
little Go, l. bok 65:11
L. subject, little wit 253:5
say much in l. 266:10
littleness his incredible l. 231:6
long l. of life 33:7
live dared not hope to l. 92:3
I want to l. 163:10
l. too long 3:7
l. under Niagara 173:13
l. under the shadow of a war 316:2
not l. who life eternal gave 259:5
Read in order to l. 241:2
to l. a novel 195:2
lived l. in social intercourse 22:11
something that I have l. through 293:6
liver l.-wing of a fowl 230:2

livers grave L. do in Scotland use 283:8
lives determined to live their own l. 333:7
how he l. 63:7
novels as being the l. 44:8
so many l. come and go 164:14
living beyond the language of the l. 64:12
envy of the l. 1:2
go on l. even after death 64:13
l., had no roof 125:11
make a decent l. 185:3
makes a reasonable l. 80:13
novel is a l. thing 195:8
pain of l. and the drug of dreams 241:15
they made his l. 342:4
When all the l.'s done 218:12
write because they are not l. 341:2
load 'l. every rift' of your subject 275:11
loathe taught me to l. Horace 126:5
loathsome more l. age 186:13
local l., but prized elsewhere 98:5
l. habitation and a name 133:2
Locke Cicero, L. and Bacon 304:10
locked spacious l. cellar 332:17
locks louse in the l. of literature 61:11
locusts fabulous plagues of l. 155:8
logic danger does lie in l. 134:6
logical exchange life for a l. process 339:3
logo bears its manufacturer's l. 6:3
Lolita L., light of my life 202:9
poor L. is having a rough time 93:13
London He describes L. like 70:6
in L. only is a trade 212:7
L. is on the whole 293:7
L. Library, for a private 162:1
will soon come out in L. 126:8
loneliness deep well of l. 186:4
essential l. of my life 280:12
lonely heart is a l. hunter 29:9
l. life within 34:3
not really a l. one 281:5
otherwise it's very l. 185:10
long L. books, when read 32:4
l. poem is a test 213:1
Not that the story need be l. 251:6
So l. as men can breathe 227:1
to make a l. prologue 31:4
words a foot and a half l. 326:7
longa *Ars l., vita brevis* 6:8
longer wished l. by its readers 31:9
Longford Lord L. is against us 271:9
longhand interspersed with l. 28:3
to the press in l. 302:7
longitude l. with no platitude 203:13
look l. of words 330:1
sensitive to the way things l. 197:14
They l. on and help 64:8
looking glass my nicely polished l. 146:1
loop merely l. the loop 203:11

loosed l. our heart in tears	331:1	**lovely** how l. it must be to write	85:9
looted l. from the churches	235:1	**love-making** L. is such a non-verbal	94:3
lopped limb l. off	30:9	**lover** l.'s quarrel with the world	92:10
lord frown of a l.	58:9	**loves** in l.'s despair	261:12
let a L. once own	113:9	**love-story** l. or an elopement	55:6
saying 'L. Jones Dead'	144:3	**loving** For l., and for saying so	172:10
lose Winsome, l. some	18:9	**low** l. opinion of himself	268:6
losing l. yourself in a book	243:10	what is l. raise and support	245:1
loss dead l. to libraries	319:5	**LSD** L.? Nothing much happened	77:7
lost l. a whole day in reading	33:1	PC is the L. of the '90s	303:10
l. valleys of the imagination	309:12	**luck** freak of l. to start high	256:11
nothing can be l. to it	149:15	**luckiest** Geniuses are the l.	111:6
what is l. in translation	59:15	**Lucky Jim** L. is a remarkable novel	5:7
lotus l. can be planted	92:11	L. is Just William	5:8
louder try to pronounce them l.	156:14	**lucubrations** agglomerated l.	1:7
lounges l. with extravagance	37:6	**Luddite** computer to the last L.	303:7
Lourdes sort of linguistic L.	152:5	**lugubrious** l. man in a suit	88:7
louse l. in the locks of literature	61:11	**lumber** loads of learned l.	240:2
love After a man has done making l.	84:9	l. room of his library	161:11
as if they were l. objects	52:4	**luminous** L.! oh, I meant—voluminous	112:9
at last acquainted with L.	314:5	**lunch** ruin your l. but not your dinner	250:8
court of l.	60:9	**luncheon** to read a novel before l.	196:14
didn't l. God	9:9	**lures** l. the truth	145:3
falling in l.	214:7	**lurk** l. outside all around us	112:7
for the l. of Lord Byron	173:2	**lust** horrible that l. and rage	4:2
half in l. with easeful Death	63:11	**luxuriant** L. song	147:8
If music be the food of l.	200:10	**luxury** height of l. to sit	297:2
I l., I hate, I suffer	33:3	Literature is a l.	104:14
I'm tired of L.	181:7	mainly a l.	153:9
in nothing but in l.	106:7	They knew l.	78:15
into l. step for step	173:6	view poetry as a l.	218:11
L., curiosity, freckles	205:10	**lynching** self-righteousness of the l. mobs	56:4
L. gilds the scene	173:1	**lyre** When 'Omer smote 'is bloomin' l.	208:1
l. him for the rest	126:5	**lyric** beneath the slight l. grace	188:1
L. made me poet	172:9	include me among the l. poets	267:14
l. needs a mixer	173:11	now it's l. verse	238:7
l. of reading	186:7	**lyrical** remorseless and yet so l.	15:3
l. that moves the sun	50:8		
l. thee in prose	172:13		
l. your neighbour's wife	37:12	**Macaulay** Even M.'s few pages	17:5
morbid marriage of l. and death	189:5	**Macbeth** How many children had Lady M.	59:9
more than the usual number to l.	99:15	how many children had Lady M.	60:11
Only l. can apprehend	59:2	Little Nell and Lady M.	205:9
Playwrights teach nothing about l.	173:12	**machine** I'm a sausage m.	50:6
poem is like a short l. affair	340:7	remember a m.	86:12
Poets' food is l. and fame	213:12	spelled differently from the m.	284:7
soft philosopher of l.	205:2	**machinery** complex social m.	184:12
someone doesn't l. you any more	244:5	**machines** Jonson's are more like m.	42:6
They l. indeed who quake	172:5	m. will have to learn	236:1
to speal what l. indites	102:6	**mackerel** outraged wet m.	287:4
truth about l. affairs	24:13	**mad** All poets are m.	212:4
very sensual l.-scene	93:5	cult of the m.	189:1
would ever have fallen in l.	172:12	great ones are thought m.	331:11
loved I l. him too	44:13	M., bad, and dangerous	37:1
intensely l. and hated	148:5	m. about my book	19:3
l. well because he hated	62:11	Poets do not go m.	134:6
only imagined that he has l.	73:7	sad bad glad m. brother's name	313:10
They have l. reading	241:18	this poor man was m.	26:4

when a heroine goes m.	74:10
you will surely go m.	236:2
madding Far from the m. crowd	29:4
madman Victor Hugo was a m.	128:6
madmen m., heretics, dreamers	222:9
madness in the end despondency and m.	212:14
Ireland has her m.	279:4
m. is terrific	137:9
M. of George III	299:8
rest is the m. of art	332:13
Maecenas all the time M. found	83:1
Death is the great M.	65:7
magazine inexhaustable m. from which	293:10
magazines commercial writing for the m.	80:1
graves of little m.	193:9
maggots turmoil of a nest of m.	317:4
magic Art is not M.	8:6
metaphors of m. and monsters	100:10
Story has a m.	210:8
strange, uncanny m.	177:14
magical m. process	341:7
m. quality in names	191:6
something m. about rhythm	253:10
magisterial cannot help being m.	60:9
magistrate anything that shocks the m.	93:8
magnificence sluttish m.	78:1
magnifies Opium m. things	76:9
Mailer in Norman M.	132:9
main hurries to the m. event	16:11
majesty M.'s library in every county	161:3
make lest he should m. an end	14:9
M. IT NEW	203:14
makers doom of the M.	137:10
making m. of history	125:1
male as much as possible in m. hands	324:7
dishabille of the m.	93:5
genius in a garret is a m. myth	325:7
m. turkeycocking	6:1
sensibility of a m. adolescent	127:10
malevolent perverse and m. creature	120:9
malice m. never was his aim	295:8
with m. towards none	257:10
malicious She was a bit m.	326:4
malt m. does more than Milton can	76:11
mama m. of dada	286:2
mammoth special chunk of m.	210:2
man all the wrongs of M.	196:12
Arms and the m.	28:7
artist m. and the mother woman	99:3
As good almost kill a m.	39:6
demolition of a m.	67:7
first spell M.	128:9
hopeless heart of m.	54:10
if a m. had written them	87:5
large-hearted m.	259:2
looked from pig to m.	51:5
m. come through the door	210:5
M. does not live by words alone	329:12
m. eating tiger	236:5
m. tries to have a baby without	275:10
m. with poetry in him	218:1
neither m. nor woman	323:11
No m. would have dared to write	225:3
Of m.'s first disobedience	200:12
sing of arms and the m.	200:5
style is the m.	289:8
such fire in the soul of m.	257:13
what m. can become	115:8
management from The M. upstairs	139:5
Theatre business, m. of men	74:15
manager even become a Branch M.	88:3
mandarin M. style	291:3
Manderley went to M. again	202:2
mania deplorable m. for analysis	107:9
man in the street m. wants to read	145:13
To the m., who	149:7
manipulate exploit and m. people	334:8
mankind Everything m. does	128:8
general conscience of m.	40:8
legislator of m.	212:9
proper study of m. is books	262:1
manly more m. than she was	121:7
manna His tongue Dropt m.	283:7
manner m. of his speech	289:3
manners its m. gracious	162:1
not men, but m.	292:10
Persons with m. do not read	242:7
man of letters being a 'great m.'	247:12
mansion Back to its m. call	63:6
manufacturer bears its m.'s logo	6:3
manuscript face that fatal m.	84:12
looked through it in m.	302:9
m. was a delight to read	251:16
two packages of m.	310:2
manuscripts Look at such of my m.	84:3
map last incredible relief m.	9:8
mapmakers All m. should place	204:2
mapped seems to be m. out	310:8
marble Not m., nor the gilded monuments	96:10
piece of placid m.	52:2
Poets that lasting m. seek	152:10
unyielding as m.	16:1
your dreary m. halls	225:4
march droghte of M. hath perced	200:7
Let us m.	284:1
nothing outside the m.	149:15
margin meadow of m.	232:3
various abusive m. notes	81:4
mark get a good m. from	268:16
read, m., learn	21:3
market more mass-m. appeal	22:6
suit the mood of the m.	24:8
markets first and foremost of the m.	79:5

medicine m., the balm	186:5
M. is my lawful wife	79:4
mediocre than it is for a m. one	246:3
mediocrity gratified with m.	114:1
M. is more dangerous	115:3
M. knows nothing higher	296:3
meditation m. on holy pictures	340:14
medium greatest interactive m.	28:2
m. is the message	302:11
meet How unpleasant to m. Mr Eliot	88:6
meets more is meant than m. the ear	176:4
melancholia little about m.	297:7
melancholy incline to m. endings	90:4
I write of m.	101:4
most m. and debilitating	142:11
rare recipe for m.	143:9
wrote such m. things	102:8
mellifluous m. but simple-minded	297:8
melodies Heard m. are sweet	133:10
melodrama senses of the word, a m.	210:6
melting divine moment of m.	137:1
ride on its own m.	137:11
Melton Pie slice of M.	226:7
member m. of the Fabian Society	275:4
memoirs M. are true and useful stars	123:8
m. of the frivolous	13:7
memorable never be m. like that	238:8
memoranda fiching out of these m.	190:7
memories his m., whether consciously	122:5
memory m., a known cheat	14:1
m. is certainly in my hands	303:5
no force can abolish m.	228:1
subject strain through my m.	84:13
men deeds are m.	326:14
educated m. had inherited	318:7
language which is chiefly made by m.	324:4
little of solid meat for m.	246:4
M. have had every advantage	323:6
not m., but manners	292:10
Shakespeare's characters are m.	42:6
very language of m.	289:10
with books as it is with m.	227:4
women's novel with no m. in it	325:2
menace m. in short stories	277:3
mental area of m. operations	139:12
without any m. disruption	242:9
mentally m. defective	231:7
mentor One needs a m.	185:10
mercury words of M. are harsh	326:11
Meredith M. climbed towards the sun	119:7
M.'s a prose Browning	35:5
merit seeing any literary m.	222:1
merits achieved fame by literary m.	87:10
mermaid Choicer than the M. Tavern	76:4
Done at the M.	75:12
Which is the M.'s now	75:11
mesh Biography is the m.	26:1
mess form that accommodates the m.	288:6
message beaming its m.	11:8
dripping with m.	183:11
his 'purpose', his 'm.'	222:1
medium is the m.	302:11
metanarratives Incredulity towards m.	167:1
metaphor ability to use m.	106:6
all m. is poetry	106:10
m. for a proof	311:11
m. that doesn't become a bore	107:2
whaling a universal m.	178:1
metaphors cure for mixed m.	107:5
rhymes and m.	25:5
ritual m. of your kin	107:4
metaphysical admiration for M. poets	107:3
m. school, which marred	187:4
termed the m. poets	187:2
too deep or too m.	48:2
Metaphysicals just as the M. had done	188:8
metaphysician I am a m.	120:10
metaphysics Explaining m. to the nation	51:17
meteor cloud-encircled m.	51:16
method no longer controls his m.	204:5
no longer controls his m.	340:5
riding his m. to death	146:2
metre m. of Byron's *Don Juan*	253:11
wretched matter and lame m.	252:16
metrical All the m. combinations	220:1
m. composition	219:9
M. poetry is ultimately	254:3
metropolis first lion in the m.	173:14
write m. for seven cents	49:7
mezzo *Nel m. del cammin*	200:6
mice Hunting m. is his delight	337:5
microcosm m. of reality	282:4
middle beginning, a m., and an end	287:7
master of the m. style	78:5
m. of my story	89:5
middle age moment comes in m.	340:5
middle class English m. culture	128:4
Middlemarch adapting *M.*	2:9
anything satisfactory of M.	87:7
What do I think of *M.*	88:2
midget lonely foreign m.	98:1
midnight consumed the m. oil	148:7
To cease upon the m.	63:11
midway M. along the path	200:6
midwife m. to society	8:5
might literature of *m. be*	265:12
mightier pen is m. than the sword	227:6
pen is m. than the wrist	114:9
mighty Marlowe's m. line	1:1
Marlowe's m. line	175:4
migrated m. into the body	70:4
military mightier than ten m. divisions	229:3
weather-beaten old m. man	107:11
milk between the m. and the yoghurt	98:9
m. of human kindness	15:12
mill grind in the m. of a truism	304:11

millennium passed on to the next m.   169:10
  wanted the m.   35:10
millions m. of pounds changing hands   48:1
Mills & Boon you get M.   173:11
Milton language of Shakespeare and M.   153:13
  malt does more than M. can   76:11
  M. and Dante   262:12
  M. and Dryden   188:2
  M. had God   89:1
  M.! thou shouldst be living   179:1
  read Spenser, Shakespeare, or M.   318:8
  With M. it began to nod   55:5
Miltonic M. verse cannot be written   179:3
mind certain unsoundness of m.   214:1
  entertainment struck a unique m.   59:14
  Her m. is a very thin soil   175:1
  his own oceanic m.   273:11
  If I am out of my m.   202:11
  let the m. be a thoroughfare   221:7
  m., that very fiery particle   248:6
  m. like an alchemist's laboratory   118:8
  m. like the dawn sky   46:6
  m. of large general powers   110:6
  m.'s reflections coldly noted   66:2
  m. watches itself   149:9
  m. which keeps open house   52:1
  not travel that narrows the m.   309:14
  person with a Best-Seller m.   19:13
  praise and erect the m.   212:2
  Reading is to the m.   240:1
  see his visage in his m.   142:6
  until reeled the m.   291:1
  What an antithetical m.   36:7
  while we have sex in the m.   271:5
  wonder his m. didn't infect   38:8
  words from your inner m.   294:5
minded men who have m. beyond reason   268:9
minds She moves out of our m.   44:4
mine It ceases to be m.   91:7
  I wish it m.   224:3
minimum m. means to express   200:1
  only do the irreducible m.   80:8
mining snakeskin-titles of m.-claims   190:8
minister God help the M.   222:8
minor Being a m. poet   257:9
  M. poets are lucky   248:2
minority m. of gifted, wilful people   333:7
minstrel M. Boy to the war is gone   315:3
minute m. notices   22:14
minutes suggested two m.' silence   206:8
miracle always the m. seems repeated   159:9
  m. among human books   69:5
  m. of our age   277:10
mire engulf him in the m.   273:6
mirror as in a m. we perceive   135:6
  book is a m.   9:14
  mere dead m.   164:8
  m. in which they may   8:6

novel is a m. which passes   194:12
  veil, rather than a m.   7:9
mirrors looking at himself in m.   38:2
mirth m.-subdual in the Reading-room   161:9
misanthropy air of m.   257:8
miscarry more apt to m.   129:11
mischief If you want to make m.   194:4
  little knowest the m. done   179:11
  up to m.   264:4
  will do more general m.   254:5
miserable only two people m.   38:7
misery dwell on guilt and m.   293:1
  lovely poems about M.   184:2
  m. of having no time to read   241:7
  m. of manilla folders   302:6
  plunged in the depths of m.   89:6
  speechless, issueless m.   288:5
misfortunes crimes, follies, and m.   123:11
misleading generate m. thoughts   49:4
misprint its success was a m.   180:6
  think of this for a m.   180:3
misquotation M. is, in fact   238:5
misquotations gleeful m. of words   64:15
misreading All reading is m.   166:10
  by m. one another   204:3
miss defined as what people m.   141:7
missing m. the bus   247:11
  only thing that goes m.   302:3
missionaries great m. the English send   157:9
Mississippi clergyman in the M. Valley   82:3
  M. in the same location   204:2
mistake author made a m.   180:5
  put up with the m.   110:8
  title is possibly a m.   299:9
mistakes genius makes no m.   111:4
mistress Literature is a splendid m.   168:7
  literature is my m.   79:4
  m. of the Earl of Craven   201:1
mists Season of m. and mellow   200:18
misunderstood admired through being m.

    1:10
misused m. words generate misleading   49:4
mixer love needs a m.   173:11
models pages of your Greek m.   304:3
modern All m. American literature   313:7
  author is a m. figure   334:7
  creator of the m. novel   108:5
  element in m. art   203:9
  French fathered the M. Movement   188:11
  half of m. culture depends   241:6
  like Webster in m. idiom   268:10
  m. state of society   194:11
  never make a m. poet   102:14
  noise of m. literature   304:12
  Poets arguing about m. poetry   256:8
  Romanticism is to say m. art   187:7
  separates the ancient and the m.   62:10
  urban poetry of m. life   143:7

mountain after all is not a m. 247:6
  start high on the m. 256:11
mountebank m. and his zany 30:10
mournful it is m. 296:11
mouth pleasantness in its m. 140:10
  way of happening, a m. 279:4
mouthings fierce m. from prehistoric ages
   73:10
mouths We poets keep our m. shut 316:1
move m. the frontier post 227:12
moved m. by what is not unusual 306:9
  power of being deeply m. 61:8
movement M. in the Arts 188:3
movie make a m. out of 2:4
movies not to write for the m. 22:3
moving m. accident 292:11
  m. eye of the cine-camera 67:9
Mozart resembles is M. 236:12
much say m. in little 266:10
muck m. in the middle 226:4
mud cover the universe with m. 146:5
  pure clay out of time's m. 25:3
muddle beginning, a m., and an end 288:9
  M. to the end 180:8
muffins with buttered m. 27:4
Mulligan plump Buck M. 201:19
multitude m. of books 184:6
multitudes I contain m. 221:8
mundane romantic, though very m. 314:12
murder crime, treachery, m. 225:5
  m. in Mayfair 57:1
  M. itself is not interesting 56:12
  m. out of the Venetian vase 56:1
  m. respectable 223:3
  m. the thinker 41:7
  not m. but the restoration 56:7
  say anything about m. 298:10
  We m. to dissect 261:4
murderers become mass m. or critics 62:8
murders most hideous of m. 40:5
murmur ever-importunate m. 74:14
muscular by a prolonged m. strain 319:7
muse cultivating the M. 315:4
  married happily to their m. 139:1
  m. on dromedary trots 73:5
  my M. only speak 138:9
  O! for a M. of fire 135:8
  O! for a M. of fire 200:9
  religious invocation of the M. 217:5
  say to the M. of fiction 335:14
  splendid m. of fiction 70:8
  take my M. and me 75:11
  Tragic M. first trod the stage 74:8
  unpretending m. 330:10
muses charm of all the M. 327:15
  m.' feeding station 148:6
  Sicilian M., let us sing 292:4
  Some say the m. are nine 259:4

museum m. inside our heads 155:3
music give you the m. of a poem 308:5
  If m. be the food of love 200:10
  like playing m. and listening 243:11
  more or less lascivious m. 215:8
  m. and style were impossible 131:8
  m. heard faintly 66:7
  m. will tell you something 297:8
  pure word m. 322:7
  still, sad m. 191:13
  used to find in m. 186:5
  when it gets too far from m. 253:14
musical M. comedy without music 322:3
musician far below the m. 211:14
  poet and not a M. 331:4
myriad-minded Our *m.* Shakespeare 273:9
myself Art is m.; science is ourselves 263:3
  I've really lived inside m. 25:8
  Madame Bovary is m. 108:1
mystery come to terms with m. 210:14
  I abhor a m. 209:8
  m. as it is incarnated 294:7
  m. whose power 57:7
  penetralium of m. 51:14
myth its end product, the m. 125:2
  M. does not mean 96:5
  m. is endlessly adaptable 36:11
  m. of modern technology 265:9
mythologized analysed and m. 294:12
myths M. and fantastic legends 100:13
  M. will not fit us 95:7

nail walks away with the n. 196:9
nails n. bitten and pared 143:1
namby-pamby N.'s little rhymes 46:8
name but spared the n. 295:8
  harder to make one's n. 246:3
  If my n. had been Edmund 190:5
  local habitation and a n. 133:2
  Merely whispering its n. 217:3
  n. was writ in water 92:2
  neebor's n. to lash 184:9
  pleased to come upon the n. 191:3
  simple thing by a hard n. 328:8
  slow sweet n.'s sake 153:2
  until you have made a n. 266:11
  writes his n. 160:6
names always appear with their n. 190:9
  Fiction-mongers collect proper n. 190:7
  get their n. featured 250:3
  in love with American n. 190:8
  little importance of n. 298:8
  magical quality in n. 191:6
  meanings of n. 191:8
  n. clung to him 9:4
  n. ignoble, born to be forgot 246:8

only reading a n. 195:1
prove that the Australian n. 171:13
publish my first real n. 196:11
reading a French n. 61:15
sit down to write a n. 90:6
splendid title for a n. 299:6
split the atom of the traditional n. 178:1
starting to think about any n. 269:4
subject of a n. 292:8
teenage n. has a duty 47:12
tell the story of a n. 220:13
test of a n. writer's art 194:14
to live a n. 195:2
to read a n. before luncheon 196:14
to write a n. 139:9
vast importance of the n. 196:4
wanted millennium and got the n. 35:10
What is a n. but a universe 196:15
What n. can compete with the best 198:10
When I want to read a n. 195:4
word 'n.' itself now makes me feel 198:9
writing a n. like 196:6
writing a n. like a marriage 340:7
Writing a n. was like driving 340:12
novelist apprehensions for the n. 17:11
biography of a good N. 24:10
central interest to the n. 264:10
economy of a n. 197:4
For a n., a given historic 294:10
idea of a n. teaching 245:5
If you tell a n. 221:3
most proper to a n. 194:8
No poet or n. wishes 257:2
n. discovers his true bent 70:2
n. enters the flesh 197:5
n. has to make us believe 199:6
n. is a man who does not 99:11
n. must preserve a child-like 221:13
n. never describes the dishabille 93:5
n.'s foster-mother 233:3
n.'s imagination winces 137:5
n.'s normal condition 335:4
n.'s proper job is to be sensitive 197:14
n. was more than just working 198:7
really great n. 195:11
slow discovery by a n. 340:5
terror to the death of the n. 306:2
to set a n. in motion 305:1
unsuccessful n. 124:13
what every n. does 122:5
what you do as a n. 222:4
When you're a n. 198:3
novelists All n. know their art 340:10
any of the great n. 334:8
greatest of superficial n. 70:7
Minor n. are totally forgotten 248:2
n. pile up research 262:15
N. . . . tend to be solipsistic 269:11

n. treat sexual subjects 40:5
N. who write for 11:10
Of all n. in any country 181:13
Of all the Victorian n. 70:11
poor in n. 171:12
Shakespeare of n. 254:10
novels all true n., are bisexual 198:4
amuse myself by reading n. 240:15
female characters in my n. 272:1
getting excited over n. 279:1
Great n. are always 149:14
happens to write n. 310:1
ideal reader of my n. 11:7
illustration in modern n. 132:9
Lads don't write n. 199:2
more than five or six n. 109:6
Most deaths in n. 65:9
'new n.' rarely indeed come 161:4
no business to write n. 266:3
not the subject of n. 293:10
N. are about other people 294:9
n. are much more interesting 197:9
n. are the Maxims 13:2
n. as being the lives 44:8
n. beat me—black and blue 325:10
n. created below the 35th parallel 172:2
n. nowadays are just travel books 197:6
n. of a poet 282:5
n. which I approve 257:13
real n. are rare 196:8
reread one of his n. 25:4
under the name of n. 170:10
writing n. are not novelists 197:5
Writing n. preserves you 197:12
writing n. with her broom 324:9
writing parish pump n. 189:9
written 349 n. 196:11
you lose two n. 99:13
novelty giving the interest of n. 213:4
novice ambition of the n. 291:8
nuance Master of n. and scruple 333:5
nuclear n. waste of repression 127:6
nudist becomes a n. 160:1
nullity vulgarity is preferable to n. 291:16
number gloat over the n. of words 84:14
more than the usual n. to love 99:15
small n. play a great part 227:4
nun Half n., half harlot 5:6
starch-fed n. 317:10
nurse who attack their n. 304:6
nursery cabinet-council to the n. 295:7
lying on the floor of the n. 95:3
nuts where the n. come from 265:10

o Within this wooden O 74:3
oar heavy o. the pen is 84:2
oath man is not upon o. 311:4

pain (*cont.*)
upon the midnight with no p. 63:11
words that gave me so much p. 102:3
painful nothing more p. for a writer 336:14
pains pleasure in poetic p. 83:8
painter p. thinks with his brush 196:13
ranks far below the p. 211:14
painters P. and poets alike 39:4
painting between p. and literature 132:10
intricate Renaissance p. 277:4
P. is silent poetry 211:9
what light is to p. 168:6
palace p. is more than a house 214:3
palate instantly cleansing my p. 313:9
palladium *P.* of all the civil 192:14
palpable Poem should be p. 215:13
pamphleteers not the age of p. 227:15
panegyric to write *A P.* 22:12
Pangur I and P. Bán, my cat 337:5
panic laugh in p. 206:9
pantomime very amusing p. elephant 18:5
papa P., why do you not write 297:11
paper blot pinched between doubled p. 174:4
compared with a sheet of p. 151:5
English sporting p. 193:5
freshly sliced p. 234:10
heaps of p. 302:12
he hath not eat p. 239:6
If all the earth were p. 172:8
Iliad of a daily p. 199:8
implacable sheet of white p. 86:3
p., tobacco, food 302:8
part of this p. appears dull 192:13
pile of charred p. 180:4
pile up reams of p. 83:9
sets his thoughts down on p. 69:16
to express on p. exactly 158:12
try to keep the p. work down 242:10
who cares for the p. 192:16
papers come and work on my p. 194:4
obscure p. and reviews 193:11
paperwork can't stand is the p. 86:2
parable Fiction to me is a kind of p. 105:5
paradise Thou hast the keys of P. 76:8
paradox behind clumsy fun and p. 46:3
paraffin odour of spiritual p. 131:7
paragraph could have said in one p. 22:3
first p. 18:3
paragraphing art of newspaper p. 144:6
paragraphs appended p. 90:7
hardening of the p. 4:6
paralysis p. that attends success 319:3
paralyzed I would have been p. 230:13
parasitic Art is p. on life 8:10
parchment Homer on p. pages 26:10
should be made p. 300:11
tight into p. pages 26:9
pardon God will p. me 156:8

pardons P. him for writing well 221:14
parent affectionate p. would consent 78:12
parents I loved my p. 99:15
p. buy the books 46:11
p. take more care of 260:11
p. that choose them 46:12
paring writing is a sheer p. away 339:8
Paris without me P. would be taken 301:7
parish p. of rich women 342:5
writing p. pump novels 189:9
Parnassus P. after all is not 247:6
parochial p. in the beginning 7:11
parodies P. and caricatures 59:8
P. on new poems 321:4
suppose that p. degrade 321:7
parody often in the form of p. 8:16
p., when you make fun of 321:15
p. is a game 321:13
P. is a knack 322:2
parodying Only by p. grown-ups 322:1
parole p. of literary men 237:4
parsons vile creatures her p. are 245:3
part being p. in all I have 65:13
parts in each of the p. 195:8
P. answering parts 176:6
you're acting all the p. 198:3
party eavesdropping at a p. 281:5
hair shirt of the p. hack 224:1
passage North-west p. 148:8
p. round Cape Horn 84:16
p. which you think is fine 199:5
passages cheated into some fine p. 147:5
passion believe in the burning p. 199:6
delineations of female p. 225:3
drayman, in a p. 141:3
master in clenched p. 34:8
our p. is our task 332:13
Ovid was interested in p. 205:5
P., vehemence, grief 33:6
p. for words 85:11
p. is his only business 203:8
p. to alter 82:4
poet without p. 6:5
progress of strong p. 257:13
prose and the p. 173:7
passive Landscape is a p. creature 192:9
P. suffering is not the theme 316:4
past America's historic p. 178:2
borne back into the p. 92:9
can tell me more of my p. 165:6
exact knowledge of the p. 123:1
God cannot alter the p. 124:7
medium of p. literatures 220:1
more or less remote p. 111:12
neither repeat his p. 124:14
p. is a foreign country 202:7
Remembrance of things p. 29:11
review the p. of our literature 318:3

plot (*cont.*)

women guide the p.	173:1
You do not think up a p.	210:13

plots limited as to p.   48:7

Of p. and actions	209:1
When I am thickening my p.	210:16

plucking like p. a hummingbird   60:6
plumage pities the p.   36:1
plums all the p. and orange peel   237:16

    p. for the puddings he peddles   320:3

plunge just p. something down   69:14
pocket garden carried in the p.   28:5

hand in its breeches p.	213:7
not scruple to pick a p.	321:3
poet in your p.	212:11

pockets pension jingle in his p.   142:7
Poe P. was an alcoholic   333:8
poem author of that p.   118:10

drowsy frowzy p.	330:8
Every good p.	263:9
get a p. into an anthology	248:2
give you the music of a p.	308:5
grander than the first p.	296:12
Has any great p. ever let in	179:8
heroic p. of its own sort	23:2
hour at a p. without adding	336:13
It is a pretty p.	307:7
long p. is a test	213:1
look at a finished p.	78:14
made one p.'s period	135:6
married to a p.	173:3
most *boring* p.	285:4
never read a political p.	229:2
opposite of the p.	208:13
original p. can be digested	308:15
ought himself to be a true p.	182:6
p., whose subject is not truth	310:9
p. huger than the grave	64:16
p. in my head last night	138:3
p. is a witness	312:4
p. is like a short love affair	340:7
p. is never finished	90:12
p. is simply one emotion	197:11
p. must ride on	137:11
p. ought to be translated	308:2
P. should be palpable	215:13
p. should not mean But be	215:14
p. springs	138:2
version of his own p.	82:8
whole life a heroic p.	179:4
write a p. after Auschwitz	279:7
Writing a p. is for me	118:7

poems ambition is to lodge a few p.   216:10

Browning read his own p.	35:2
get the news from p.	223:4
He buys up p. for recital	207:7
If p. can teach one anything	155:12
it's p. that remain	218:12

lovely p. about Misery	184:2
much more interesting than p.	197:9
My life has been in my p.	164:8
p. about old age	4:9
p. are about yourself	294:9
p. are artificial	288:7
P. are made by fools like me	192:5
P. are such very personal things	79:9
Since you recite your p.	108:6
sooner write no p. than bad	336:16
take my p. wherever you go	26:9
wanting to write p.	185:5
we all scribble p.	211:12
Were those real p.	248:1
What are p. for	219:4

poesy call p. *vinum daemonum*   212:3

golden cadence of p.	205:1
Our p. is as a gum	135:9
P. was ever thought to have	212:2
viewless wings of P.	76:5

poet All a p. can do today is warn   315:9

Being a minor p.	257:9
business of the p.	66:9
can read about a p.	24:4
charming thing to be a P.	173:2
disguised In a p.'s cloak	173:10
dreams of a p. doomed	71:5
emotion in the p.	103:10
every p., in his kind	207:11
fame and profit enough as a p.	266:3
flattery lost on p.'s ear	268:5
For God-sake don't call me a p.	217:6
God is the perfect p.	245:2
good p. includes a critic	61:3
Gray, a born p.	119:2
great only as a p.	37:11
great p., in writing himself	10:14
habits of a p.'s mind	219:11
have a p. able-bodied	216:12
He was a bum p.	157:5
he was a true P.	178:11
Homer, the sovereign p.	125:10
I am a p.'s poet	247:3
If God were a p.	245:11
imagined the p. in him	139:3
kind of Hammer Films p.	208:14
lack their sacred p.	22:7
Love made me p.	172:9
lunatic, the lover, and the p.	133:1
makes the p. the potent figure	228:2
marred a good p. in Cowley	187:4
mean by 'being a p.'	185:5
need not fear to be a p.	217:17
never be alone with a p.	212:11
never make a modern p.	102:14
never yet known a p. who	267:13
no business whatever to be a p.	88:3
None but a p. can write a tragedy	306:13

poisons consumes all p.   254:11
  p. our literary club   112:8
poked fire that has been p.   199:13
poker she is still a p.   12:7
pokers wreathe iron p.   73:5
polar p. star of poetry   213:1
poles literary work has two p.   166:8
police encourage among p. officers   242:10
policemen p. of language   328:4
Polish P. nobleman   54:1
polite making p. conversation   2:10
political economic or p. importance   218:16
  never read a p. poem   229:2
  p. correctness can be a form   41:10
  P. language . . . is designed   223:3
politically poet exerts himself p.   222:7
politician Journalist is to p.   144:12
politics p. and poetry have in common   223:13
  P. in the middle of things   222:6
pome while I pen a p.   72:5
pomp halo of almost historical p.   206:3
pomposity p. and intricacy of style   231:8
pony use my work as a p.   309:1
pooh 'p.-poohing' something or other   328:1
  written Winnie the P.   31:3
poorer sympathy with the p. classes   70:9
pop make them p. like chestnuts   227:8
Pope poetry of Dryden, P.   215:2
  Pope composes with his eye on   307:12
  P. took money to keep   333:8
popes quarrels of p. and kings   123:13
popular loved to be p.   10:8
  we have a p. imagination   137:3
popularity blaze and dazzle of p.   12:4
  shaken by its p.   19:11
  source of my p.   103:14
popularize attempt to p. art   245:14
population effect of p. explosion   280:6
Porlock Person from P.   140:6
  person on business from P.   140:4
  received the Person from P.   336:12
porn p. reader always has his ingredients   94:4
pornography P. is rather like   94:2
  P. is the attempt to insult   93:12
  'tale of terror', like p.   127:3
port grocer's p. is preferable   291:16
  p., for men   76:1
  p. from which I set out   280:12
portable From the Olivetti p.   302:12
  p. pieces of thought   27:16
  Regular verse is p.   253:17
portmanteau it's like a p.   177:1
portraits put up and take down p.   143:8
pose without p.   88:5
position in what p. Shakespeare sat   338:6
  only one p. for an artist   334:3
  outlook, a wisdom, a p.   198:7
possibilities what his p. are   125:3

post p. it to somebody else   10:12
post-1918 no p. tendencies   322:4
postage patron who defrays the p.   10:3
  publisher pay the p.   182:2
posterity admiration of p.   246:13
  decided to write for p.   243:14
  He should write for p.   59:14
  instruction of p.   123:4
  not go down to p.   116:9
  special correspondent for p.   70:6
Post-Impressionist gave us the term 'P.'   189:8
post-modernism P. may be seen as   189:4
post-mortem frustrate the p. exploiter   23:12
  This p. poet   319:8
posts entirely fenced in with p.   189:8
postscript but in her p.   158:10
  most material in the p.   158:8
  pith is in the p.   150:1
Potter Beatrix P. portrayed the world   132:8
  Harry P. was an unusual boy   202:14
pounce p. and irrefutability   208:15
pouncer Literature's p.   278:3
pounds Fifty p.   181:6
poverty Barefaced p. drove me   78:6
powder Pastiche and face-p.   308:14
power jaws of p.   39:9
  literature of p.   227:9
  name for absolute p.   134:1
  p. of the pen   229:4
  raised to the p. of genius   46:2
  When p. corrupts, poetry cleanses   223:8
powers belief in his own p.   258:8
practice Theory is just a p.   167:5
  twenty-five years of p.   84:11
praise asks and begs for p.   289:11
  either to p. or blame   1:11
  Every genius needs p.   1:12
  Every genius needs p.   268:12
  how to p.   92:12
  people p. and don't read   305:2
  p. for poets in the grave   62:14
  p. of ancient authors   1:2
  P. or blame   58:10
  slogging through the p.   257:8
  they only want p.   1:8
  took the p. as a greedy boy   248:7
praised p. their last publication   255:13
praises p. one author by damning another   60:8
  singing someone's p.   1:15
  with faint p. one another damn   60:14
prancing p. Poetry   27:11
pray P. for me and for all writers   333:5
prayer complete Shakespeare and a p. book   303:11
  evidence of the P. Book   246:1
preach must not professedly p.   130:3
preacher myself as a p. of sermons   245:5

quotations Backed his opinion with q.	237:2
book that furnishes no q.	237:7
cabbage-stumps of q.	146:7
I know heaps of q.	238:1
Pretentious q.	237:13
Q. in my work are like	238:2
Read books, repeat q.	115:12
read books of q.	238:3
wrapped himself in q.	237:11
quote grow immortal as they q.	237:3
quoted To be occasionally q.	237:9
quoter first q. of it	237:10
quotes never q. accurately	238:5
nice thing about q.	238:10
r pronounced the letter R	282:10
rabbit not unsmall r.	117:2
r.'s or small child's-eye view	132:8
written by a r.	294:13
Rabelais soul of R.	295:10
Rabelaisian old R. sap run	172:2
racer like a stripped-down r.	277:6
racial prefigure our r. temperaments	95:4
Racine facts about the life of R.	239:1
R. has withered	54:13
racing writing makes horse r. seem	80:5
racking r. his fagged brain	336:3
radar This is the writer's r.	334:6
Radcliffe all Mrs R.'s works	126:9
raddled r. Noël Coward	119:3
radical dared be r. when young	222:11
radio poetry slot on the r.	331:8
R. and television	267:1
rag r. and bone shop of the heart	103:6
rage good scholar in a r.	262:5
horrible that lust and r.	4:2
moves me to an excess of r.	279:1
r. against the dying	64:14
r. of Caliban seeing	187:11
rain left out in the r.	9:5
r. never wets your jacket	258:2
rake r. among scholars	285:7
r. in reading	240:4
r. turned hermit	224:10
ramping spring meadow—r.	147:3
rancour hateful spirit of literary r.	256:2
rape procrastinated r.	19:10
you r. it	8:2
rapid train himself to r. writing	69:14
rare O r. Ben Jonson	91:9
rarest one of the r. qualities	107:7
rat like the r. that eat the malt	30:11
terrier can define a r.	216:7
rational poet of r. light	156:1
rationalize always r. his right	80:2
Rattigan Terence R. and myself	55:2
raven Poe, with his r.	211:6

raw poetry in the r.	191:5
razor mirror and a r.	201:19
to hew blocks with a r.	227:3
reached r. the finishing post	89:3
react I r. on it at once	208:4
reactionary artist must be a r.	8:12
read Always r. stuff that will	265:8
Any desire to r.	167:7
be an inventor to r. well	240:16
believe everything you r.	243:13
Books must be r. as deliberately	241:1
books which no one can r.	232:14
Browning r. his own poems	35:2
but his books were r.	247:4
can r. about a poet	24:4
depends on what one shouldn't r.	241:6
desire to r.	241:14
dictionary a bad book to r.	71:11
do not r. at table	242:7
do not willingly r.	240:7
Don't r. too much now	226:1
do *you* r. books through	240:6
he had first r. about it	172:12
he has r. too widely	238:5
if he had r. as much	239:14
In science, r.	263:2
I r. competitively	170:1
I would never r. a book if	241:8
learnt to r. so quickly	241:13
man in the street wants to r.	145:13
may be r. by deputy	239:10
misery of having no time to r.	241:7
never r. a book before reviewing	248:9
not been able to r. the books	333:4
On bokes for to r. I me delyte	239:4
one cannot *r.* a book	242:12
people praise and don't r.	305:2
people who can't r.	145:6
population were taught to r.	148:13
r., mark, learn	21:3
r. all the books there are	241:5
r. any good books lately	242:4
R. in order to live	241:2
r. just as inclination leads	240:5
R. not to contradict	239:8
r. Shakespeare in my native	153:10
R. somewhat seldomer	148:12
r. when one is middle-aged	164:7
r. without pleasure	83:7
something that will be r. twice	168:17
sooner r. a time-table	242:2
Take up and r.	239:3
They're what we used to r.	262:9
time to r. is any time	240:10
to r., and censure	270:2
to r. a novel before luncheon	196:14
to say that he has r. it	169:12
unfit to be r. aloud	93:2

read (*cont.*)
   want to be r. by people   230:6
   we should r. them   280:2
   What do you r., my lord   239:7
   When I want to r. a novel   195:4
   who runs may r.   21:6
   whose works are r. so generally   70:5
   women in general r. much more   323:8
   Women r. the most books   325:9
   write in order to r.   341:9
readability r. *is* intelligence   155:13
readable unprintable book that is r.   93:9
reader anti-Roth r.   12:2
   birth of the r. must be   242:11
   by delighting the r.   331:9
   concur with the common r.   58:7
   demand that I make of my r.   11:1
   emotion in the r.   103:10
   Every r. is reading only   241:12
   evokes emotion from the r.   218:10
   expect the r. to bring   12:1
   freeze his r.'s marrow   112:3
   gentle r., you as well   243:3
   half is with the r.   10:7
   halfpenny r.   225:5
   How to be a friend to a r.   12:5
   Hypocritical r.   10:1
   Ideal R. is the reader   11:9
   ideal r. of my novels   11:7
   ideal r. suffering   10:15
   In my capacity as r.   233:3
   no tears in the r.   103:5
   not likely greatly to affect the r.   101:5
   only the individual r.   11:6
   R., I married him   98:17
   r. could read with his eyes alone   168:19
   r. he most fears   95:1
   r. is made to think   17:7
   r. makes allowances   9:12
   r. recognizes as his own   218:5
   r. seldom peruses a book   240:3
   realization accomplished by the r.   166:8
   to r. my reader   209:8
   writer or the r.   240:9
readers ardent r. of detective fiction   56:12
   but also his r.   101:1
   enable the r. better to enjoy life   337:10
   full of fourth-rate r.   12:3
   Imaginative r. rewrite books   242:5
   my weary r.   89:4
   over the heads of your r.   10:2
   publishers seek to attract r.   132:5
   R. and listeners like my books   255:4
   R. and writers are united   281:7
   r. are proud to live in it   114:16
   r. in particular got on his nerves   163:1
   r. who sat here   161:10
   so many of my r. belong   129:2

three kinds of r.   240:13
to give their r. sleep   83:3
walking r.' digest   9:4
wished longer by its r.   31:9
Writers have to start out as r.   306:1
Reader's Digest *birthday of* R.   279:9
readeth he may run that r. it   226:8
reading act of r. a text   243:11
   After three days without r.   243:12
   All r. is misreading   166:10
   any r. more easy   241:4
   art of r.   240:8
   as much pleasure in the r.   239:11
   book which I would enjoy r.   185:7
   but I prefer r.   241:16
   daily r. of such a book   46:7
   easy writing's vile hard r.   83:6
   English r. public   10:9
   ever get nowadays from r.   47:6
   gay part of r.   224:8
   he was r.   239:2
   I had to give up r.   262:11
   impossibility of r.   242:13
   like r. a cafeteria tray   288:13
   Lord Longford is against us r.   271:9
   love of r.   186:7
   Many people go on r. now   243:1
   mere brute pleasure of r.   242:1
   mirth-subdual in the R.-room   161:9
   move their lips when r.   181:10
   murder novels are easy r.   56:2
   rake in r.   240:4
   r., in order to write   338:4
   R., that unpunished vice   241:10
   R. a book is like rewriting it   242:14
   r. a French novel   61:15
   r. and interpretation   305:13
   r. habit is now often a form   241:17
   r. is a secondary pleasure   240:14
   R. isn't an occupation we encourage   242:10
   R. is to the mind   240:1
   R. maketh a full man   239:9
   r. of good books   26:11
   r. on the beach   243:4
   r. or non-reading a book   182:8
   R. other people's books   241:11
   r. public of three millions   10:5
   r. with avidity *Cranford*   109:10
   regard r. as anything more   243:2
   Someday I intend r. it   249:7
   soul of r.   209:6
   suspected that the r. is right   260:16
   They have loved r.   241:18
   think other people are r.   190:3
   Though I liked r.   165:11
   tyrannizes the act of r.   163:2
reads if no one r. your book   99:12
ready those for which we are r.   228:4

R. is the rock	253:2
r. themselves into ladies' favours	172:7
r. the rudder is of verses	252:15
still more tired of R.	181:7
ta'en the fit o' r.	136:2
unattempted yet in prose or r.	212:6
rhymes pair their r.	173:5
Peotry is sissy stuff that r.	217:12
rhyming aid to r. bitch your talent	254:1
modern bondage of r.	253:1
Thy drasty r. is nat worth	252:14
rhythm something magical about r.	253:10
rhythmical piece of r. grumbling	88:8
riband r. to stick in his coat	229:9
r. to stick in his coat	330:12
ribands prose in r.	220:8
rich get r. from writing	181:10
It's about to make me r.	295:3
making Gay r.	110:1
parish of r. women	342:5
seems it r. to die	63:11
Richardson read R. for the story	254:6
richest r. without meaning	176:9
ride Haggards r. no more	147:10
ridicule R. is the only honourable weapon	321:12
ridiculous r. consists in some form	129:5
so r. as the British public	182:9
without being r.	79:7
riding r. his method to death	146:2
riff-raff associating with the r.	6:6
rift 'load every r.' of your subject	275:11
right get it r. in the end	252:9
r. half the time	226:5
r. part of the country	117:9
r. part wrote Liddell	52:6
waits for the r. time	336:1
your r. to say it	39:8
rights French R. of Man	36:10
intruder on the r. of men	323:4
ring in any r. with Mr Tolstoy	256:10
riots book can cause r.	229:1
ripper Oscar Wilde and Jack the R.	175:7
risk Criticism is a life without r.	60:10
sense of r.	264:9
rituals rules, regulation, and r.	56:8
rivalry With the dead there is no r.	64:1
rivals wish his r. all in Hell	255:8
river his or her home r.	191:3
like travelling by r.	313:2
rivers direct sentences, smooth r.	50:4
like r. grow cold	205:3
rivulet neat r. of text	232:3
road moocow coming down along the r.	201:17
rob has to r. his mother	334:5
robbers wayside r. who leap out	238:2
robes living in the sacred r.	121:2
robust most r. and least refined	310:4

Rochester than the works of Lord R.	254:5
rock Rhyme is the r.	253:2
R. journalism is people who can't	145:6
rocket rose like a r.	36:2
rocking r. from one foot	184:3
rocking-horse magnificent r.	38:1
rocks native of the r.	314:5
rococo doddering r.	320:5
rod wreathed the r. of criticism	61:5
Rogers When R. produces a couplet	84:1
rogue complete genius and a complete r.	45:5
role Poetry has no r. to play	215:12
roles r. the poet deftly played	88:9
Rolls Royce like driving a R.	309:4
Roman Make way, you R. writers	314:1
R. literature is Greek	171:2
R. Virgil, thou that singest	314:6
Tenderest of R. poets	39:1
romance absence of r.	123:1
And what's r.	258:2
Any historical r.	66:1
difficulty of writing a r.	104:11
mastery over all r.	171:3
no more write a r.	122:1
R. and poetry, ivy	136:8
r. as distinct from the novel	100:5
R.! Those first-class passengers	293:12
Romans R. in the next generation	171:6
Shakespeare depicted the R.	122:3
romantic hallmark of the R. approach	189:5
poets of the R. Movement	188:8
r., though very mundane	314:12
r. sickness	187:5
satirist and the r.	317:2
romanticism R. is to say modern art	187:7
Rome All R. is mad about	19:3
Ronsard R. me célébrait	3:6
roof living, had no r.	125:11
room r. of her own	324:8
sitting in the smallest r.	249:5
roost how the birds came home to r.	210:4
root r. is one	311:15
r. of imagination	134:14
roots roots are air r.	145:11
rope by the r. we know	134:7
rose immediately as the odour of a r.	73:6
like dropping a r. petal	216:11
roses Honey of r.	150:4
rod of criticism with r.	61:5
Roth anti-R. reader	12:2
rough all that is r. to the hand	296:1
r.-and-tumble of the literary arena	256:3
round act of walking r. him	184:4
divide characters into flat and r.	43:11
Roundhead R.? I'd have been	223:11
routine from a kind of r.	85:7
R., in an intelligent man	85:8
there should be much r.	86:1

royal artist of the blood r.	313:5
royalty like being minor r.	257:9
r. statements, by the time	81:1
R. was represented	97:9
rudder rhyme the r. is of verses	252:15
rudest r. work that tells a story	176:9
Rudyards R. cease from kipling	147:10
rugged R., mountainous, volcanic	38:5
unpolished r. verse	219:6
ruins need r. to make them grow	136:8
rule I know of only one r.	289:14
rulers r. seek me out	98:4
rules Cast iron r. will not answer	235:3
few private r.	117:10
finite set of r.	118:4
ignorant of all the r.	110:4
r., regulations, and rituals	56:8
r. how to pass judgement	58:8
r. were strict to a fault	5:5
ruling interests of the r. class	40:10
rummaged r. for the right word	141:14
run before beginning to r.	286:3
he may r. that readeth it	226:8
Take the money and r.	267:2
Runic In a sort of R. rhyme	253:12
running like r. through a field	339:7
runs book, who r. may read	21:6
rurality dense and burnished r.	121:1
ruse r. . . . which could not be achieved	211:2
rush days of r. and hurry	17:9
Russian furnished with a R. soul	158:3
great writer of our R. land	313:1
indictment of R. reality	278:11
nineteenth-century R. novelists	171:10
R. literature saved my soul	280:1
to be R. means to love Pushkin	236:10
Russians All R. are brutal	46:1
R. make us debate	15:9
rustic r. all through	33:4
rut getting into a state of r.	93:6

sacramental flesh was s.	94:1
sacred as s. to him	301:8
facts are s.	144:5
living in the s. robes	121:2
s. in the originals	321:7
sacrifice there is always a s.	276:8
turn delight into a s.	244:12
sacrificed accuracy must be s.	31:8
sacrifices made s. to it	279:11
sad know not why I am so s.	95:2
s. tale's best for winter	111:9
terrifyingly s.	300:5
saddest s. story I have ever heard	201:15
sadist greatest literary s.	101:1
sadistic brutality and s. conduct	22:5

safe diaries into the S. Deposit	138:7
Do not feel s.	228:3
no woman in London will be s.	108:10
safety with s. pins and rubber bands	340:8
sagacious s. and profound	259:3
said as if I had s. it myself	268:3
can be s. clearly	151:7
How I wish I had s. that	237:12
knew nobody had s. it before	237:15
not been s. before	202:16
s. by the servant girls	339:2
s. our remarks before us	237:1
Whatever is well s. by another	207:5
what he would like to have s.	145:13
sailor Home is the s.	92:5
If it had been called *The Old S.*	298:6
saintliness sort of inner s.	317:1
saints lives of the s.	198:12
Saintsbury thrill of reading S.	61:14
sake never to write for the s.	136:4
salesmen even little s. can fondle	154:2
sally loose s. of the mind	94:10
salt adverbs the s.	116:16
all that is s. in the mouth	296:1
little grain of s.	141:2
Salteena S. was an elderly man	201:18
salute I s. thee, Mantovano	314:7
salvation Outside prose, no s.	220:5
same s. to-day and for ever	27:6
sampler as a girl shows her s.	49:6
Sancho S. Panza, the Self	13:11
sand S. Glasses . . . whose reading	240:11
sands Footprints on the s. of time	22:16
sandstorms gyrating s.	73:11
sandwich-board s. man of the revolution	205:6
sane big, s. boys	189:1
sanity s. raised to the power	46:2
sap dried the s. out of my veins	84:15
Sappho burning S. loved and sang	259:6
S. would speak, I think	71:1
sat when they have s. down	283:9
Satanic Verses book entitled *The S.*	41:6
satin she always goes into white s.	74:10
satire female social s.	319:4
let s. be my song	232:7
s., when you make fun of	321:15
S. is a lesson	321:13
S. is a sort of glass	321:2
S. is dependent on strong beliefs	321:17
S. is simply humour in uniform	321:18
Verse s. indeed is entirely	170:2
satirical s. nomenclature	37:2
sign of a s. wit	282:10
satirist past the s. like a cheetah	321:11
s. and the romantic	317:2
shouldn't call myself a s.	321:16
satisfaction anything with a degree of s.	338:1
s. then in toil	83:1

satisfactory can make anything s. 87:7
saucepan throwing a s. 157:13
sausage hold on s. and haddock 109:1
I'm a s. machine 50:6
saving capable of s. us 216:1
Saxon ancient S. phrase 153:1
say courage to s. as an author 182:4
exactly what one would s. 158:12
had a great deal of s. 2:8
Have something to s. 290:5
manage to s. what we meant 152:1
must have something to s. 219:14
s. more than we ought 69:10
s. the most dreadful things 326:4
s. what they are meant to say 235:12
There's not much to s. 53:5
till I see what I s. 177:6
what a poet does not s. 177:13
what they are going to s. 283:9
writer who has nothing to s. 290:9
you have something to s. 185:9
you should s. what you mean 176:10
you've got something to s. 185:4
saying For loving, and for s. so 172:10
never finished s. 305:8
s. things they've said 75:2
says not what he s. 114:15
scabbard consumes the s. 227:5
scale puts his thumb in the s. 183:7
scarlet His sins were s. 247:4
scatterbrained judgements were often s. 275:6
scene can't rewrite a s. 252:10
scenery ever spoke of s. 67:3
scented Too s. 320:6
scepticism S. the tonic of minds 311:16
Scheherazade S.'s tales have lived on 306:4
schmucks S. with Underwoods 267:4
scholar good s. in a rage 262:5
ills the s.'s life assail 260:14
s. all Earth's volumes carry 260:6
s. among rakes 285:7
s.—but a brute 92:1
s. is the only man of science 263:5
such a bad s. 149:13
scholars S. somehow manage to evade 262:12
well-meaning s. tend to repeat 312:9
scholarship combines s. and art 124:12
school badly-run girls' s. 145:9
s. stories in foreign languages 47:5
schoolboy I see a s. when I think 147:8
schoolboys duly to delight s. 283:3
School for Scandal S. in its glory 3:8
schoolmaster s. friend reads it all 235:11
schoolmasters Let s. puzzle their brain 75:14
s. of ever after 339:5
schools at all the s. I attended 235:10
science Art is myself; s. is ourselves 263:3
boundaries of s. 264:10
cold-blooded demon called S. 111:11
expected to find in s. 264:9
fatal process of applied s. 265:4
If s. is the myth 265:9
In s., read 263:2
labours of the men of s. 263:1
more fashion than s. 118:3
plundered this new s. 264:5
scholar is the only man of s. 263:5
S. is meaningless 263:4
s. reassures 263:10
s. will appear incomplete 215:1
that of s. and of philosophy 169:10
When s. arrives it expels 263:8
science fiction becoming s. 265:5
If that's not a s. scenario 266:1
labelled 'S.' 265:6
read what they call S. 265:1
represents most of s. 100:12
S., like Brazil 265:10
S. deals with things 100:7
s. has become a dialect 265:11
S. is a kind of archaeology 265:2
S. is dripping with 183:11
s. is just a new twist 100:11
S. is no more written 265:3
S. is the literature 265:12
S. writers foresee 265:7
Shakespeare of s. 318:1
sciences dance of the spirit in the s. 264:8
s. yielded great explainers 264:7
scientific often apes s. language 167:6
scientists company of s. 264:2
no more written for s. 265:3
scissors working of a pair of s. 67:6
scoffed S. at fairies 342:4
scold function of a general s. 258:10
scorn S. not the Sonnet 214:2
sound Of public s. 57:12
scorpion I kept a s. 136:10
Scotch S. and Lake troubadours 125:6
Scotland grave Livers do in S. use 283:8
perfectly hideous about S. 174:7
Scots S. are incapable 111:5
Scott not even Sir Walter S. 274:1
S. gave Highland legends 171:3
S. has not read a review 248:5
Scottish years of S. craftsmanship 77:11
scrap s. with Virginia Woolf 68:5
scrapped s. at least one book 251:14
scratching s. of a pen 332:7
s. of pimples 146:3
scream want to express emotion, s. 218:10
screams s. will die away 248:12
screeching s. newspapers 193:4
screen more exciting on the s. 271:11
screenplays great joy writing s. 267:12
screenwriting challenge of s. 266:10

Shakespeare (*cont.*)

S. would have grasped wave functions — 264:5
sweetest S. fancy's child — 74:5
Whaur's yer Wullie S. — 255:9
worth more than S. — 236:9
shaking should have been s. England — 143:2
Shallott make the Lady of S. — 132:4
shallow s. in himself — 239:12
shame all our writers to s. — 116:12
s. to women so to write — 225:2
shape sense of an impending s. — 85:1
s. o' the whole — 288:11
s. that can't be changed — 43:13
shaping s. spirit of imagination — 133:7
shared stock of s. reference — 131:2
shark bleeding in s.-infested waters — 248:3
sharpers all your trade are s. — 232:1
sharpness her s. and reality — 175:3
shaving when I am s. — 103:4
Shaw S. is like a train — 274:5
S. talked practically — 68:5
Wells, George Bernard S. — 188:6
shed with Burke under a s. — 35:11
sheep you s. bear fleeces — 207:3
sheets into several little s. — 26:10
than between the s. — 271:11
shelf s. life of the modern hardback — 98:9
Shelley once see S. plain — 97:2
shells eggs have gilt s. — 268:8
shelves s. where Nature intended them — 163:1
Snug on my s. — 231:11
symmetry of s. — 30:4
your bookcases and your s. — 160:7
shepherd s. his sheep — 292:5
shibboleth Say now S. — 282:8
shilling s. life will give you — 24:6
shine you shall s. more bright — 96:10
ships Like full-rigged sailing s. — 277:8
shirt can pull on any sort of s. — 94:12
shit shock-proof s. detector — 334:6
shiver cold s. down one's spine — 112:2
shock deliberately set out to s. — 204:11
You could not s. her — 12:12
shocking something very s. indeed — 126:8
shocks anything that s. the magistrate — 93:8
shoddier no s. than what they peddle — 329:11
shoe Write on the sole of my s. — 302:10
shoemaker if the s. were to wait — 137:1
shoes time to put on its s. — 286:3
shop back to the s. — 147:2
rag and bone s. of the heart — 103:6
shops prosaically more s. — 270:9
s. stock it — 19:3
shore dark s. which separates — 62:10
hugging the s. is to sailing — 60:5
stayed upon the green s. — 147:4
shores house on Homer's s. — 154:7

short long while to make it s. — 251:6
nasty, brutish, and s. — 163:5
s. in the story itself — 31:4
shorter time to make it s. — 251:3
shortlist getting on to the s. — 231:1
short-story I'm a s. writer, really — 310:1
short story key to a s. is tension — 277:5
s. is an Impressionist — 277:4
s. like a long love affair — 340:7
s. tells us only one thing — 277:9
shot Certain men the English s. — 227:16
he once s. a bookseller — 232:8
Hungarian writers had been s. — 223:10
somebody s. one — 5:2
stand up and be s. at — 249:1
shoulder someone looking over my s. — 252:10
shovels set of metaphoric s. — 304:1
show I'm going to s. them, this time — 269:4
s. him how I would write it — 82:7
showers with his s. soote — 200:7
showing without s. off — 250:5
shrew Journalism's a s. — 144:8
shriek one s., sparks, smoke — 157:4
shrimp s. of an author — 118:11
shrined bower we s. to Tennyson — 97:11
shut just have to s. it — 41:9
sound of books slapping s. — 18:1
shyness required of it without s. — 291:2
Sicilian S. storytellers use — 288:10
sick emerging from a s. room — 106:3
sickens reader s. — 70:8
sickness romantic s. — 187:5
side only heard one s. — 21:15
sieves Great-Mogul's Diamond S. — 240:11
sighs S. are the natural language — 150:6
sight not-seen accessible to s. — 166:4
sign What a bad s. — 30:7
signature one's style is one's s. — 290:6
significance deeper, or more general, s. — 198:13
significant words that are, first, s. — 49:11
signifier bond between the s. — 151:2
signs pages of s. — 152:3
silence all in s., all in order — 161:1
darkness and s. — 137:7
miss the fish-like s. — 97:6
occasional flashes of s. — 174:3
on the other side of s. — 164:4
pronouncing the word 's.' — 324:12
s. all the airs — 39:7
stain upon the s. — 16:6
suggested two minutes' s. — 206:8
silencer all-round s. — 285:3
silent profundities of a s. country — 171:10
S., upon a peak in Darien — 50:11
S. as the sleeve-worn stone — 215:13
s. with his lips — 120:6
thereof one must be s. — 151:7
Silenus Bow-tied S. — 298:3

silk he was shot s. 14:10
style, like sheer s. 291:12
silliness snobbery and s. 20:7
silly any idea, however s. 275:8
You were s. like us 342:5
silver Just for a handful of s. 229:9
Just for a handful of s. 330:12
similes by exaggerated s. 107:3
entirely original s. 322:6
Wilstach's book of s. 72:4
similitude s. in dissimilitude 182:7
simple rarely pure, and never s. 311:12
s. in subject 148:1
too *clear*, too *s.* 289:14
simpler s. than a child 33:5
simplest s. and most natural one 289:5
simplicity Cultivate s. 51:11
holy s. 48:10
s. and humility 268:14
simplify s., simplify 164:2
task is to s. the world 105:14
simply as s. as possible 289:12
sin Excepting Original S. 203:3
My s., my soul 202:9
S. is the writer's element 245:13
sincerely s. from the author's soul 114:14
sincerity even s. should be edited 82:13
unintelligent—s. 69:5
sinecure gives no man a s. 79:8
sinew s. of the English language 78:3
sing S. whatever is well made 294:2
Who s. to find your hearts 215:4
singer s. of an empty day 227:11
S. of sweet Colonus 282:2
single If you are a s. father 99:10
s. completed action 74:7
s. man in possession of 200:15
year after year to s. lines 84:3
singular some very s. books 4:4
thou s. genius 254:7
singularity not by s. 213:5
sinkholes no s. 50:4
sins all s. had to be atoned for 5:5
His s. were scarlet 247:4
sirens Blest pair of S. 212:5
What song the S. sang 260:10
sissy Peotry is s. stuff that rhymes 217:12
sister Fiction is Truth's elder s. 105:2
sisters greatness of her two s. 32:7
sit I now s. down on my botom 159:1
I s. down for eight hours 336:4
never get a chance to s. down 274:4
sitting s. with my back to it 338:6
sixpence s. to the masses 225:8
skeletons 'sure-fire' literary s. 313:6
skies some watcher of the s. 126:1
skiing technique of s. 60:4
skilled S. or unskilled 211:12

skin locked within a piece of s. 26:10
my s. bristles so 103:4
saw the skull beneath the s. 317:5
s. came off with difficulty 2:5
s. of an innocent lamb 300:11
skull beneath the s. 64:7
skip does not rush, and s. 169:12
S. when my book becomes obscene 92:13
skull operation on my own s. 118:7
saw the s. beneath the skin 317:5
s. beneath the skin 64:7
s. of damnation 282:6
slam set doors ajar and s. them 71:1
slang All s. is metaphor 106:10
S. is, at least, vigorous 329:2
S. is a language 151:13
s. of prigs 116:7
slashing damned cutting and s. 81:5
slate write his thoughts upon a s. 214:8
slave galley s. to pen and ink 83:12
slavish imitators, you s. herd 207:4
sleep grey and full of s. 3:10
sleepers s. in that quiet earth 50:12
sleepless S. themselves 83:3
sleeps Homer sometimes s. 330:9
sleepwrite s. on the ceiling 138:3
sleeves rolls up its s. 151:13
slime deadly s. of his touch 37:4
slip s., slide, perish 329:7
slippers *OED* in carpet s. 9:10
slips *two* rejection s. enclosed 244:2
slip-slop s. of Henry James 54:6
slithery something s. about him 177:14
sloth If I were to paint S. 270:1
my own amazing s. 336:10
slovenly mind was of a s. character 78:1
slow scriptorium-s. 309:5
slower write s. and slower 84:11
slowly write its pages s. 69:14
slow-motion s. representation 142:2
slum swear-word in a rustic s. 328:10
sluttish s. magnificence 78:1
small s. Latin, and less Greek 272:9
s. men locked in a big space 2:7
small-clothes Correspondences are like s. 159:3
smaller flea Hath s. fleas 207:11
s. the child 47:9
smallest Boswell was one of the s. 22:15
sitting in the s. room 249:5
s. in the world 16:10
small-talking this s. world 203:13
smart little s. for so moving a book 299:4
smile but not as Sultans s. 41:11
sits with modest s. 78:5
s. of accomplishment 156:15
vain tribute of a s. 268:5

smoke black s. and mists	175:5
people s. in old films	94:6
words curling like rings of s.	329:5
smokers generation are drinkers and s.	77:9
smooth have to s. him out	9:3
smoother words were s. than oil	326:6
smut S. detected in it	93:4
snail s. in the arithmetical problem	251:9
snake conceals his s.-in-the-grass	194:14
like a wounded s.	253:4
snakeskin s.-titles of mining-claims	190:8
sneer s. of critics	62:6
s. which he used like	158:1
sneeze like having a good s.	157:2
sneezed not to be s. at	229:8
sniffed He s. and wrote	204:9
sniffs s. I get from the ink	324:10
snob intellectual s.	154:4
snobbery sadness and s.	20:7
S. with Violence	56:5
snobs bookish people are s.	19:7
snow footprints left in the s.	210:17
they have no word for s.	329:13
snowdrifts S. of Wordsworth	331:7
snuffed s. out by an article	248:6
sober too s. to be a champ	42:3
social complex s. machinery	184:12
disguised s. comment	192:12
female s. satire	319:4
first s. regenerator	278:8
novel of s. reportage	280:7
quality of his s. admirations	231:6
roots in s. realities	279:11
s., political, or personal	280:4
socialist called s. realism	189:3
high-water mark of S. literature	9:2
S., an Atheist	276:3
socially often s. impressive	238:10
society economic basis of s.	12:12
midwife to s.	8:5
no importance to s.	11:6
product of our s.	334:7
web and texture of s.	194:10
sock If Jonson's learnèd s. be on	74:5
socks You still have to wash your s.	98:11
Socrates nor Buddha nor S.	339:3
sodomite posing as a s.	320:4
sodomy artists who spend on s.	294:1
soft she s. as the dawn	258:3
s. philosopher of love	205:2
soil grow from a neglected s.	305:9
Her mind is a very thin s.	175:1
idealize the s.	192:6
s. of New England	120:7
sold book which somehow s. well	19:12
Sense and Sensibility is s.	78:13
soldier s. details his wounds	292:5

soldiers acting on behalf of s.	315:6
With twenty-six lead s.	301:7
solemn confounded with a s. writer	333:2
solicitor one's agent, and one's s.	80:8
solid all that is s. has melted	105:11
soliloquy indulge in eloquent s.	157:8
solipsistic tend to be s.	269:11
solitariness of an infinite s.	59:2
solitary poet—is s.	280:13
Their s. way	50:9
solitude balance between s.	281:4
books and s.	281:6
how benign, is S.	280:10
I love s.	281:3
resonance of his s.	103:9
swamped in my s.	185:12
Solomon felicities of S.	21:1
solutions S. are not	265:7
solved not a single problem is s.	338:11
solvency S. was my only aim	79:12
something writing is not about s.	146:8
you've got s. to say	185:4
song Alexandrine ends the s.	253:4
all this for a s.	181:2
Luxuriant s.	147:8
own accord my s. would come	252:13
spur me into s.	4:2
two men to write one s.	52:8
ultimately allied to s.	254:3
What s. the Syrens sang	260:10
what they teach in s.	213:6
Whenever I remake a s.	251:11
songs harsh after the s. of Apollo	326:11
I sing s. never heard before	267:15
We who with songs beguile	215:4
sonnet good iambic pentameter s.	221:1
Scorn not the S.	214:2
s. is a moment's monument	214:16
true s. goes eight lines	217:13
sonneteer I shall turn	135:7
sonnets ten passably effective s.	114:10
written s. all his life	173:4
sons God's s. are things	327:7
soothing for s. and quieting	153:12
sophisticated not a s. one	20:7
only s. playwright	53:8
Sophocles influenced by S.	204:1
missing plays of S.	149:15
sorbet like some tart lemon s.	313:9
sorriness s. underlying the grandest	293:8
sorrow interest and fines on s.	279:3
so beguile thy s.	160:8
sought Being, of all, least s. for	71:2
soul adventures of his s.	61:9
as the body and the s.	176:3
Clinic for the S.	160:5
composed in the s.	215:2

structured unconscious is s. like   151:18
struggle horrible, exhausting s.   85:6
  long uphill s.   17:13
  s. continues   157:1
  s. for life   256:3
  s. you have with words   86:8
St Trinian's S. basically   145:9
stubborn more s. than theory   163:11
stuck already s. With Kubla Khan   336:12
  he s. it in her   94:3
studies brownest of brown s.   72:2
  Fred's s. are not very deep   195:1
  he s. in the fields   192:1
  still air of delightful s.   311:2
  S. serve for delight   260:7
study asked to see his s.   192:1
  In the usual course of s.   260:2
  moved me to s.   154:10
  much s. is a weariness   259:10
  proper s. of mankind is books   262:1
stuff Was there ever such s.   273:7
stung S. by the splendour   136:9
stunt just a silly s.   2:2
stupid s. person's idea   131:5
style acid refinement of his s.   317:3
  attain an English s.   3:3
  author arrives at a good s.   291:2
  better in his own s.   82:7
  can't steal your s.   208:6
  good s. doesn't form   291:5
  go out of s. like coffee   238:16
  grand s. arises   290:1
  his own towering s.   297:6
  how the s. refines   113:9
  Hw worked at his s.   286:9
  If s. means superfluous ornament   290:3
  liked beauty of s.   290:7
  made habitable by s.   155:12
  master of the middle s.   78:5
  music and s. were impossible   131:8
  one forges one's s.   143:12
  one's s. is one's signature   290:6
  only secret of s.   290:5
  pomposity and intricacy of s.   231:8
  s., like sheer silk   291:12
  s., the tone   18:3
  S. and structure are the essence   288:3
  S. is life   289:16
  S. is the dress of thought   289:6
  s. is the man   289:8
  s. of our most approved writers   289:13
  s. overflowing with feeling   70:10
  torment of s.   108:3
  transgresses against 'good s.'   292:2
  true definition of a s.   289:7
  When we see a natural s.   289:4
  with his eye on his s.   307:12
styles All other s. seemed   36:3

stylist finest prose s.   121:4
stylistic s. abscesses   17:3
subject become interested in a s.   294:6
  becomes an academic s.   262:10
  grant the artist his s.   58:14
  Grasp the s.   292:3
  Little s., little wit   253:5
  My s. is war   315:10
  poem, whose s. is not truth   310:9
  simple in s.   148:1
  s. of a novel   292:8
  supplied with a s.   294:4
  want of poetry in the s.   222:7
subjective novel is a s. epic   194:13
subjectivity S. is a terrible thing   221:9
subjects because of the s.   259:8
  list of poetic s.   292:7
  one can always think of s.   294:5
  s. are to be selected   293:10
subjunctive Damn the s.   116:12
  s. mood is in its death   117:1
sublect old s. illuminated by a new light   166:12
sublime egotistical s.   213:9
  essence of the true s.   330:4
  s., truly great, escapes them   324:2
  s. dashed to pieces   81:6
subliminal S. learning   242:15
substance no s. without it   288:3
substitute bloodless s. for life   164:5
subtle Be s., various   291:11
suburban too s. aversion   192:10
succeeds generation that s. his   11:2
  Whenever a friend s.   257:4
success any little s.   257:1
  between s. and failure   112:5
  both s. and failure   244:3
  concept of commercial s.   81:3
  detest and despise s.   247:13
  going to be such a s.   119:9
  My literary s.   1:11
  paralysis that attends s.   319:3
  passes for s.   225:9
  s. in literature   256:1
  whatever s. I have attained   43:2
successful envy of the s.   257:10
  only very s. genius   266:6
  s. book is not made   199:10
sudden s. arrangement of commonplaces   168:9
suet-pudding cold, black s.   285:9
suffer How one likes to s.   103:2
  I love, I hate, I s.   33:3
  to think and s.   163:10
suffering learn in s.   213:6
  no end to human s.   96:3
  Passive s. is not the theme   316:4
  poor Bovary is s. and weeping   42:10
sufferings started a myriad s.   200:4
suffers from whose absence one s.   184:13

suffocated s. in its own wax 65:4
suffocating would be less s. 174:1
sugar Adjectives are the s. 116:16
 dirt and sucked s.-stick 205:6
 enchanting language, s.-cane 150:4
sugar-plums sweetmeats and s. 90:3
suggest suffer reality to s. 42:9
suicide if you have to die, commit s. 325:3
suicides about our first s. 208:13
suit double-breasted s. 98:12
 lugubrious man in a s. 88:7
suitcase elephant into a s. 2:9
summer Art and s. lightning 7:6
 s. afternoon 328:13
sumptuous its s. epithets 205:7
sun farthing candle to the s. 260:13
 inward s. 134:11
 liken Homer to the setting s. 125:9
 love that moves the sun 50:8
 new s. rose bringing 51:2
 s. has extinguished 335:12
sunbathe skin cancer if we s. 266:1
Sunday S. writers like myself 66:8
sunk Our language s. under him 178:7
sunshine Digressions are the s. 209:6
 opened in the s. 9:15
super think himself s.-excellent 267:13
superficial greatest of s. novelists 70:7
 intrigue the s. 313:6
superfluity barren s. of words 327:5
superfluous marred by a s. verse 90:5
 too much seems s. 220:12
superior pronounced her s. to Fielding 36:5
superlatives Remove at least fifty s. 199:6
superman S. wearing a fedora 57:5
supernatural natural world with the s. 100:13
 Without s. aid 316:12
support don't write to s. yourself 80:3
 one's only means of s. 79:6
 s. of the whole 210:3
supports s. with insolence 78:8
suppression s. of one's self 7:4
surface gold lies so near the s. 17:7
surgeon call the s. to commend 81:8
surgery doing brain s. 341:5
surges when loud s. lash 253:3
surnames her men only s. 191:7
surprise Life is a great s. 65:1
 no ambition to s. 209:8
 No s. for the writer 103:5
 try the element of s. 336:11
surprises can prompt new s. 140:2
surprising s. in a convincing way 43:11
surreal provider of s. spectacle 316:9
survival prize is literary s. 305:12
survivor if Hopkins had been a s. 139:6
survivors dying is more the s.' affair 64:9
suspenders before the invention of s. 159:3

suspension willing s. of disbelief 213:3
sustaining great s. slice 226:7
swan Sweet S. of Avon 272:8
swans ducklings turning into s. 210:12
 Dumb s., not chattering pies 172:5
swear Don't s., boy 329:14
swear-word s. in a rustic slum 328:10
sweat drowned in a sea of cold s. 317:6
sweeter those unheard Are s. 133:10
sweetmeats s. and sugar-plums 90:3
 whole pyramids of s. 246:4
sweets hungering after s. 147:7
 long meal of s. 124:8
sweet-shop pressed to a s. window 147:8
swimming good writing is s. under water 114:17
 s. in that sea 18:4
 s. slowly but surely 257:8
swine They're our herd of s. 43:16
swing marking its s. 184:3
sword keep on the point of the s. 186:10
 pen is mightier than the s. 227:6
 pen is preferable to the s. 226:10
 Poetry is a s. of lightning 227:5
 wit is like a s. 321:14
swords Our s. shall play the orators 315:1
 yet they be very s. 326:6
syllable chase A panting s. 152:14
syllables stressed with unstressed s. 253:15
 S. govern the world 116:3
symbol s. of civilization 27:17
symbolist to make a convincing s. 106:12
symbols dictionary of types and s. 187:12
 inking s. onto a page 341:7
sympathetic very 's.' easy creature 35:1
sympathies enlarge men's s. 7:3
sympathy exciting the s. of the reader 213:4
 lead our s. away 196:4
 never-failing s. and encouragement 66:5
 universal in s. 334:11
symphony Fancy a s. by Wordsworth 331:4
 find out about a Beethoven s. 94:2
 like notes of a s. orchestra 221:4
symptom s. that all is not well 167:5
synthesis s. of hyacinths and biscuits 215:9
synthetic s. whipped cream 144:13

table do not read at t. 242:7
 never had a t. in my life 302:10
 though you cannot make a t. 58:4
tablet He who breaks this t. 39:2
tabloid t. newspapers dig 26:3
tackled I wouldn't a t. it 84:10
tail rebuke in its t. 140:10
 tiger lashing its t. 208:15
tailor going to the t. or barber 82:15
tailored perfectly t. suit 303:17
taketh author t. away 252:2

think (*cont.*)

t. as wise men do	337:6
T. before you speak	59:13
t. only this of me	201:14
t. perhaps even less	148:12
to t. and suffer	163:10
What do I t. of *Middlemarch*	88:2
you really t. about things	222:4

thinker murder the t. 41:7

thinking art of t. 240:8

not t. accurately	49:8
saves original t.	238:4
simple song for t. hearts	292:11
write only by t. back	84:13

thinks novelist t. with his story 196:13

say in print what she t.	324:5
She t. like a man	285:5

thirteen clocks were striking t. 202:5

thirty below the t.-fifth parallel 172:2

I am past t.	3:9
T. days hath September	218:13

Thomas at the feet of *Hardy* and *T.* 305:7

Thomson T. wrote a very good poem 222:7

Thoreau After reading T. I felt 192:8

thorns too often a crown of t. 97:7

thoroughbred woman of t. intelligence 149:8

thoroughfare let the mind be a t. 221:7

thought carry all that t. 52:2

concentration of poetry and t.	169:9
desystematize his t.	198:8
for a spontaneous t.	304:11
garment of t.	150:12
Language is the dress of t.	150:8
One t., one grace	135:6
portable pieces of t.	27:16
seem a moment's t.	251:10
spark of inextinguishable t.	327:10
speech created t.	150:9
splendour of a sudden t.	136:9
stream of t.	187:10
Style is the dress of t.	289:6
t. and feeling	142:2
T. does not crush to stone	312:1
t. is the front	151:5
t. is viscous	177:4
t. to Donne was an experience	73:6
turn out as we first t.	115:7
very life-blood of t.	289:16
What oft was t.	321:1
what they t. *at that time*	14:7
where a t. is lacking	327:9

thoughtcrime t. literally impossible 151:10

thoughts generate misleading t. 49:4

infinite number of t.	118:4
offering of my t.	66:3
thoroughfare for all t.	221:7
To bring my t.	140:6

thousand worth ten t. words 132:6

Would he had blotted a t.	272:12

thread spider gets his t. 14:5

strung them on an English t.	308:3

threadbare point of being t. 153:5

threat feeling of t. or menace 277:3

three I strike out t. 199:4

three-decker they worked the old t. 195:12

thriller from a classic to a t. 242:9

melodrama of the brutal t.	56:4

throat bone stuck in your t. 40:4

fog in my t.	64:3
taking life by the t.	218:4

through do *you* read books t. 240:6

thrown t. with great force 115:4

Thucydides Exiled T. knew 124:11

T. and Xenophon	123:9

thumb puts his t. in the scale 183:7

t. each other's books	161:5

thunder As winter t. 196:8

He says NO! in t.	120:5
they steal my t.	207:12
t. of his spirit	143:2

ticket Nobel is a t. to one's funeral 230:7

tickle T. and entertain us 9:13

tides controlled by our inner t. 206:4

tie reader feels your t. is off 67:4

tie-breakers grown-up version of the t. 94:14

tied hero and heroine t. up 93:11

tiger great soft t. cat 146:4

man eating t.	236:5
t. lashing its tail	208:15
t.'s terrible heart	26:5

tigers like a cat among t. 324:6

time air of t. in them 122:4

books of all t.	27:10
but for all t.	272:7
distance of t.	139:14
dollars' worth of t. wasted	244:8
down the stream of t.	247:2
finished in half the t.	66:5
Footprints on the sands of t.	22:16
interested in capturing t.	107:8
journey into another t.	122:6
Keeping t., time, time	253:12
misery of having no t. to read	241:7
no longer told the t.	151:12
not of its own t.	122:7
Once upon a t.	200:8
pure clay out of t.'s mud	25:3
scarce leaves a man t.	337:9
stretched forefinger of all T.	261:7
T., Place, and Action	287:8
T.'s eunuch	336:2
time takes no t. in a story	288:10
t. to make it shorter	251:3
t. to read is any time	240:10
to spend t. and ink	93:6

weather also part of the w.	217:7	**Whitman** daintily dressed Walt W.	119:7
w.-beaten old military man	107:11	daintily dressed Walt W.	178:4
weathers face w. slowly	9:8	**who** For w. am I	332:17
web cool w. of language	151:8	W. he	144:11
fiction is like a spider's w.	105:3	**whole** slide into a w.	176:6
w., then, or the pattern	290:4	**wholes** always forming new w.	215:6
w. wind round and round	132:4	**wholesome** How charming, how w.	106:3
Webster like W. in modern idiom	268:10	**whom** 'w.' is a word	117:12
W. was much possessed	317:5	**whooshing** love the w. noise	337:3
wedding cake face looks like a w.	9:5	**whopper** give birth to a w.	197:2
wedding-clothes Miss Harriet Byron's w.		**whore** like a chaste w.	130:8
	66:11	theatrical w.	31:2
Wednesday I got fired W.	266:13	**why** know w. people laugh	130:7
weeds bred among the w. and tares	202:18	**wide** I am very w.	15:5
garden with pedantic w.	73:3	Not deep the Poet sees, but w.	214:9
week w. for preparation	283:10	**wide-angled** w. poet	9:4
weekends W. are a good working time	140:8	**wife** book-learned w.	323:2
weeps animal that laughs and w.	129:13	Here lies my w.	91:10
weighs w. sixty pounds avoirdupois	248:8	if Laura had been Petrarch's w.	173:4
weird so wondrously w.	135:4	let his w. starve	99:4
well as w. as can be expected	84:1	love your neighbour's w.	37:12
Childhood . . . the purest w.	139:8	Medicine is my lawful w.	79:4
I want to do something w.	336:10	must be in want of a w.	200:15
that's as w. said	268:3	no telephone or w.	196:7
wells Big Four: H. G. W.	188:6	perfect w.	98:16
W. thought that the creative	272:4	splendid mistress, but a bad w.	168:7
well-spent rare as a w. one	23:1	untrue to his w.	149:7
well-turned not to believe in w. phrases	290:2	w. or your servants to read	93:14
well-written w. Life is almost as rare	23:1	wind is my w.	98:15
Welsh W. language has survived	155:5	**Wilde** Oscar W. and Jack the Ripper	175:7
west Go W., young man	191:2	**wilderness** w. of idea	328:6
in the gardens of the W.	103:9	w. of this world	200:13
western If we read the W. Canon	280:4	**wildness** w. of those compositions	94:9
search for the epic in W. movies	171:8	**wilful** minority of gifted, w. people	333:7
w. canon	318:10	**will** You w., Oscar, you will	237:12
W. culture was a grand ancestral	318:7	**Williams** Tennessee W. has about five	44:1
wet save from finger w.	27:1	**willing** w. suspension of disbelief	213:3
whale screw the w.	118:2	**wills** stolen w. for breakfast	195:12
whales sea-shouldering w.	106:9	**win** didn't expect to w.	231:3
whaleship w. was my Yale College	261:8	**wince** rather w., than die	81:8
whaling w. a universal metaphor	178:1	**wind** Gone with the w.	29:7
what W. and Why and When	328:7	like yesterday's east w.	300:6
W. mean	144:11	substance is but only w.	326:10
where W.'s yer Wullie Shakespeare	255:9	w. is my wife	98:15
whimsies they have my w.	172:13	**windbags** W. can be right	32:5
whippersnapper Critic and w.	61:7	**winding** good structure in a w. stair	311:1
whirlpools seething w.	73:11	**windings** intervening w.	90:13
whiskers tip of its w.	251:16	**Wind in the Willows** review of The W.	192:4
whiskey food and a little w.	302:8	**window** deeply embrasured w. seat	47:13
Freedom and W. gang thegither	76:2	Good prose is like a w.-pane	291:10
whispering Merely w. its name	217:3	looking through a w.	291:6
whispers what he w.	114:15	not one w., but a million	104:16
whistle may as well w. for a wind	335:13	openeth the w.	307:3
whistling only w. or humming	147:9	**wine** cup of rich Canary w.	75:11
w. at Holy Communion	206:7	few bottles of red w.	119:6
white man with a w. cane knocking	149:13	glass of w. by his own fireside	76:3
whited reminds me of a w. sepulchre	327:13	great geniuses are w.	225:7
		left off w. and writing	75:13

write all the words that I w.	328:5	w. for the fire	251:1
As long as I can w. books	338:9	w. in order to read	341:9
as much as a man ought to w.	84:8	w. is to be self-conscious	222:5
Better to w. for yourself	10:13	w. it for himself first	47:2
bored me hellishly to w.	84:6	w. like a distinguished author	190:2
cannot w. like Hazlitt	120:11	W. or nothing	339:10
can't w. quickly	87:4	w. slower and slower	84:11
can w. on alcohol	77:4	w. straight from my own heart	19:5
compulsion to w. poems	336:16	w. the life of a man	22:11
do not w. as birds sing	86:1	w. to the moment	254:4
don't see how to w. them better	251:7	W. what will sell	270:4
don't w. badly very often	267:8	w. when I feel spiteful	157:2
don't w. to support yourself	80:3	**writer** animosity against a w.	256:9
His brother w. as well as he	255:8	anything worse for a w.	247:11
how lovely it must be to w.	85:9	being a w. here means nothing	230:10
if he had known how to w.	15:6	best answer I got was from a w.	167:4
imagine not needing to w.	340:11	best fame is a w.'s fame	98:10
I sit down to w.	332:5	Beware the w. who puts forward	222:3
I w. of melancholy	101:4	could be a w. with a pencil	302:14
look in thy heart and w.	335:8	Do you still want to be a w.	333:8
make me w. too much	3:7	dream of becoming a w.	186:7
man may w. at any time	83:4	good w. knows how to listen	115:5
maybe one couldn't w. any more	272:4	gratifying to be a w.	300:4
meant us to w. on walls	115:14	great and original w.	203:2
Men like women who w.	325:4	great w. creates a world	114:16
men w. in place lite	31:6	if a w. needs a dictionary	72:7
more easy to w. on money	181:3	If you're a w., a real writer	210:11
much more important to w.	98:6	in a critic than in a w.	115:3
never to w. for the sake	136:4	incinerator is a w.'s best friend	252:3
not enough for me to w.	172:8	in my capacity as w.	233:3
nothing to w. about	158:5	It's lucky if you're a w.	99:10
Nothing we w.	115:7	kind of w. that people think	190:3
One does not w. *for* children	48:4	modern hardback w.	98:9
One should only w. when	289:12	more damaging to a w.	117:11
Only a great man can w. it	124:6	most significant thing a w. does	25:13
people who can't w.	145:6	No tears in the w.	103:5
People who w. obscurely	264:4	only function of a w.	114:18
read a novel, I w. one	195:4	original w. is not he who refrains	203:1
reading, in order to w.	338:4	profession to be a w.	185:1
sex so much harder to w. about	94:5	reasons for becoming a w.	185:9
shame to women so to w.	225:2	serious w. is not to be confounded	333:2
such as cannot w., translate	307:4	Sin is the w.'s element	245:13
teach other people to w.	114:20	suffer from w.'s block	337:1
They who w. ill	60:13	they call me a w.	334:12
those who cannot w.	332:1	thirty pages by a w.	18:4
Though an angel should w.	301:4	Two women—one w.	53:4
To w.: that is to sit in judgement	66:4	understand a w.'s ignorance	176:8
To w. well, lastingly well	337:9	understand a w.'s ignorance	332:4
very difficult to w.	85:12	until he knows whether the w.	240:3
What we w. pleases us	184:10	When a w.'s at work	140:3
When men w. for profit	78:11	w., in the eyes of many	267:6
Who would w.	332:3	w. is unfair to himself	252:4
who w. apace	148:12	w. must be as objective	221:10
w. a book with the other	175:2	w. must refuse, therefore	230:5
w. because they are not living	341:2	w. never forgets	268:7
w. because you've got something	185:4	w. or the reader	240:9
w. every day	341:8	w.'s abiding problem	281:1
w. every other day	159:8	w.'s best friend	252:8

w.'s life seethes within	166:1	establish the principles of w.	58:8
w.'s only responsibility	334:5	every morning of your life w.	340:6
w.'s problem is	338:10	except with a w. board	302:10
w.'s writer par excellence	108:5	fairy kind of w.	133:4
w. who has nothing to say	290:9	fine w. is next to fine doing	113:11
w. who lives long enough	262:10	get rich from w.	181:10
writers All experience is good for w.	335:1	Good w. has always been attacked	257:11
all w. are thieves	208:10	good w. is *swimming under water*	114:17
All w. learn from the dead	306:5	habit of w. again	336:17
American w. want to be	247:10	If it sounds like w.	252:7
childhoods of w.	281:6	If w. did not exist	101:3
Clear w., like clear fountains	114:3	important as any other part of w.	252:1
dead w. are remote	305:3	incurable disease of w.	331:10
ever loved great w.	223:9	know you're w. well	115:1
full of fourth-rate w.	12:3	lavish periods away from w.	87:2
gravest and latest w.	207:6	left off wine and w.	75:13
Great w. create	208:2	more like oxywelding than w.	252:11
How few w. can prostitute	268:11	my capacity for w.	85:3
Hungarian w. had been shot	223:10	new style of w.	254:9
interpretation by later w.	305:13	no pleasure in w.	184:11
literary geniuses purely as w.	111:5	not from w. but from cleaning	325:5
literature is by w.	62:7	not only write but keep w.	186:10
more w. than it has prizes	230:11	only end of w.	337:10
Readers and w. are united	281:7	*only possible w.*	54:2
same as quarrelling with w.	82:5	pleasure of w. without the misery	308:12
seldom wish other w. well	257:7	profound activity of w.	240:14
so are most w.	82:9	put an account of it in w.	338:1
staff of 'w.'	2:3	rest is mere fine w.	168:5
Sunday w. like myself	66:8	same as w.	267:9
too many w.	333:10	sign the w.	250:11
We shouldn't trust w.	280:2	such things as w. animals	86:10
We w. all act and react	208:4	That a piece of w. is good	183:9
W., like teeth, are divided	332:10	this fever of w.	184:6
w., the town criers	224:2	This manner of w.	83:2
W. are always envious	257:12	wants to continue w.	98:7
W. are dangerous	229:7	when a man begins w. a book	332:9
W. are the most important	266:8	witty in the w.	321:10
w. do; it is their income	103:2	W., when properly managed	338:2
w. encounter their characters	43:14	w. a great play yourself	309:4
W. often achieve a power	40:7	W. a novel was like driving	340:12
w. who leave their wives	99:8	w. *at once*	286:3
writes one who w. with care	289:5	w. does come out of a deep well	186:4
publisher who w. is like a cow	234:4	w. I have ever been jealous of	256:6
w. as a boar does piss	270:13	w. is a sheer paring away	339:8
w. his time	10:14	W. is like getting married	340:3
w. like a teacher	142:10	W. is not an amusing occupation	85:4
writing And this is the w.	176:1	W. is not a profession	339:11
any style of w. untouched	91:13	W. is not a respectable way	79:10
art of w.	85:7	W. is not different	280:3
art of w.	240:8	w. is on the wall	115:13
as I had in the w.	239:11	W. is the destruction of every voice	340:1
Bad w., false sentiment	19:9	w. makes horse racing seem	80:5
Beware of w. to me	159:15	w. means having one foot in	135:5
by word and in w.	148:13	w. not as an investigation	316:10
by w. them down	109:1	W. novels preserves you	197:12
commercial w. for the magazines	80:1	w. of history	125:1
diarrhoea in w.	187:13	w. overcomes the besetting feeling	334:13
easy w.'s vile hard reading	83:6	You don't give up w.	340:13